Reinhold Ludwig

Schmuck–Design der Moderne — Modern Jewellery Design

Geschichte und Gegenwart
— Past and Present

ARNOLDSCHE

»Im Grunde aller gegenwärtigen künstlerischen Bemühungen
fühle ich ein Streben nach Harmonie und Heiterkeit.
Ich habe mein möglichstes getan, das Prinzip der Konstruktion
wieder zu seinem Recht zu bringen, wodurch wir einzig beides
erreichen können.«

Henry van de Velde, 1902

»At the bottom of all present-day artistic endeavours I sense
a striving for harmony and cheerfulness. I have done my
utmost to return to the construction principle what is owed to
it, which is the only way for us to attain both.«

Henry van de Velde, 1902

IMPRESSUM—IMPRINT

Verlag — Publisher
Arnoldsche Art Publishers,
Stuttgart

Herausgeber — Editor
Institut für Schmuckkultur, Ulm

Autor — Author
Reinhold Ludwig, Ulm

Co-Autor — Coauthor
Susanne Heuer, Pforzheim

Konzeptionelle Bearbeitung
— Conceptual development
Florian Ludwig, Berlin

Bildredaktion — Picture research
Christina Ludwig, Neu-Ulm

Übersetzung — Translation
Joan Clough, Penzance, Great
Britain

Grafische Gestaltung — Layout
Florian Ludwig, Berlin

Mitarbeit — With the help of
Christina Ludwig, Neu-Ulm

Druck — Printed by
OAN Offizin Anderson Nexö,
Zwenkau

Frontispiz — Frontispiece
Niessing Flechtreife – Braided
necklaces, Design Timo Küchler,
Photo H.P. Hoffmann, Düsseldorf

© 2008 Arnoldsche Art
Publishers,Stuttgart
und der Autor – and the author

www.arnoldsche.com
wwwwww.schmuckinstitut.de

Dieses Buch wurde gedruckt
auf 100% chlorfrei gebleichtem
Papier und entspricht damit dem
TCF-Standard.
— This book has been
printed on paper that is 100%
free of chlorine bleach
in conformity with TCF standards.

Bildnachweis — Photo credits
Seite — Page 398

© VG Bild-Kunst, Bonn
Marianne Brandt
René Lalique
Emmy van Leersum
Sigurd Persson

Für die Abdruckgenehmigung
wurden die jeweiligen Rechte-
inhaber kontaktiert, einige
konnten jedoch nicht ermittelt
werden. Der Verleger bittet in
solchen Fällen um Kontaktauf-
nahme.
— As far as possible each
copyright holder has been noti-
fied by the publishers. However,
since we have not been able to
contact all copyright holders,
we therefore request any and all
concerned to contact
us in this matter.

Bibliographische Information
Die Deutsche Bibliothek
verzeichnet diese Publikation in
der Deutschen Nationalbibliogra-
fie; detaillierte bibliografische
Daten sind im Internet über
http://dnb.ddb.de abrufbar.
— Bibliographical
information: Die Deutsche
Bibliothek lists this publication in
the Deutsche Nationalbibliogra-
fie; detailed bibliographical data
are available on the Internet at
http://dnb.ddb.de.

ISBN 978-3-89790-292-3

Made in Germany, 2008

ARNOLDSCHE art books are
available internationally at
selected bookstores and from the
following distribution partners:

USA
ACC/USA, Easthampton, MA
sales@antiquecc.com

CANADA
NBN Canada, Toronto
lpetriw@nbnbooks.com

UK
ACC/GB, Woodbridge, Suffolk
sales@antique-acc.com

FRANCE
Fischbacher International
Distribution, Paris,
libfisch@wanadoo.fr

BENELUX
Coen Sligting Bookimport,
Amsterdam, sligting@xs4all.nl

SWITZERLAND
OLF S.A., Fribourg,
Information@olf.ch

JAPAN
UPS United Publishers Services,
Tokyo, general@ups.co.jp

THAILAND
Paragon Asia Co., Ltd, Bangkok,
info@paragonasia.com

AUSTRALIA
/ NEW ZEALAND
Bookwise International,
Wingfield,
customer.service@bookwise.com

RUSSIA
MAGMA, Moscow,
magmabooks@mail.ru

CHINA
Book Art Trade Co., Shanghai,
alice.jin@bookart.com.cn

Besuchen Sie uns im Internet
— Please visit our homepage
www.arnoldsche.com

For general questions, please
contact ARNOLDSCHE Art
Publishers directly at
art@arnoldsche.com, or visit
our homepage at
www.arnoldsche.com for
further information.

Inhalt — Contents

Was ist modernes Schmuck-Design?
— What is Modern Jewellery Design?

Vorwort — Preface

Tradierte Juwelenpracht, billiger Massenschmuck, modische Beliebigkeiten, sie alle zehren von den verblassten Fragmenten einstiger Schmuckmythen, von vergangener Magie. Doch gibt es nach dem Impuls der Moderne ganz neue Themen im Schmuck: reduzierte Formen, meditative Klarheit, konzentrierte Kraftlinien, tragbare Skulpturen, scheinbar schwebende Diamanten, innovative Edelsteinschliffe, spannende Konstruktionen, neue Materialien, lustvoll kombiniert, erfrischende Spielfreude, humorvolle Anspielungen, poesievolle Alltagskultur, Erzählerisches in Metall und Stein, auch gefühlsbetonte Romantik und in jüngster Zeit, bei aller Klarheit, vermehrt luxuriöse Sinnlichkeit. Moderne Schmuckgestalter haben vielgestaltige Zeichen der Persönlichkeit hervorgebracht – für moderne Frauen und vermehrt auch für Männer. Sie haben den Glanz des Goldes und das Funkeln der Edelsteine im Schmuck um Aspekte ergänzt, die nicht im Aberglauben gründen, nicht in der Verehrung falscher Götter, nicht im Dominanz- und Machtstreben, nicht in dekorativen Peinlichkeiten und nicht im reinen Wertdenken. Sie widmen sich vielmehr dem Wunsch, stilvoll aufzutreten und zu gefallen, sich selbst und anderen. Der neue Schmuck verbindet Materie und Geist. Er ist eine Einladung zur Selbstinszenierung für Menschen mit Geschmack. Schmuck, der aus der immerwährenden Freude am Schöpferischen entsteht, mit einem sehr ernsten Anliegen.

Der Paradigmenwandel geschah in mehreren Anläufen gegen Traditionen und Konventionen, die im Schmuck stärker sind als in anderen Gestaltungsdisziplinen. Moderne Schmuckgestalter mussten seit Ende des 19. Jahrhunderts, seit der Belle Époque, gegen mächtige Beharrungskräfte ankämpfen: zunächst gegen den Historismus, dann gegen die Verführungskräfte reiner Luxusjuwelen in den 1920er Jahren, die durchaus ihre Faszination haben. Nach 1945 wendeten sich ambitionierte Goldschmiede gegen den wesenlosen Industrieschmuck und tradiertes Handwerk. In ihrer Renaissance, die zeitgleich mit dem Aufbegehren der Jugend gegen das Establishment, mit der sexuellen Befreiung und der Frauenbewegung in den 1960er und 1970er Jahren stattfand, haben es die Kreateure zunächst mit den Argumenten der freien Kunst versucht. Schmuck-Kunst ist für manche immer noch ein Thema, weltweit. Doch die Schmuck-Designer, die seit den 1970er Jahren deutsche und europäische Hochschulen und Fachakademien verließen, wollten nicht nur Unikate für einige Museen und Sammler machten. Sie wollten anspruchsvolle Schmuckserien gestalten für moderne Menschen. Ebenso wie einige innovative Manufakturen mussten sie auf die Käufer schauen und auf deren Bedürfnisse, sich zu schmücken. Den Besten ist es gelungen, dabei ihre authentische Handschrift zu bewahren und erfolgreich zu sein. Das Schmuck-Design der Moderne, das in den vergangenen drei Jahrzehnten zur Reife gelangte, ist die jüngste Bewegung, die das kreative Medium aus seiner selbstverschuldeten Unmündigkeit zu befreien sucht. Nach den beiden großen Epochen im Schmuck der Moderne, dem Jugendstil

und dem Art Déco, hat sich erneut eine kulturhistorisch relevante Schmuck-Kultur etabliert. Sie hat einen Reifeprozess vollzogen und bringt nicht mehr nur erotische Triebkräfte oder reine Maschinengläubigkeit zum Ausdruck wie vor dem Zweiten Weltkrieg. Sie schielt auch kaum mehr nach Anerkennung durch Kunstinstitutionen wie in den 1980er Jahren.

Das moderne Schmuck-Design ist bei all seinen Schwierigkeiten, die jede Gegenströmung hat, nicht mehr aufzuhalten. Es wird befruchtet von dem vitalen Wunsch junger Menschen, Schmuck immer wieder zeitgemäß zu erfinden. Den Nährboden bilden Fachschulen und Akademien in ganz Europa. Das Interesse wächst nicht nur im Land des Bauhauses und der HfG Ulm, das mittels neuer Gestaltungsvisionen auch seine Geschichte bewältigen wollte. Modernes Schmuck-Design findet heute auch Anhänger in Ländern mit anderen Schmucktraditionen, etwa in Spanien, Amerika und Asien. Die ausgeprägte deutsche Note in diesem Buch ist jedoch nicht zufällig, sondern entspricht dem weit überwiegenden Produktionsstandort. Damit sollen jedoch nicht die Verdienste der Schmuckgestalter Skandinaviens, Hollands, Englands, Italiens, der Schweiz und Österreichs für die Entwicklung des modernen Schmuck-Designs geschmälert werden.

Moderner Serienschmuck wird heute in kleinen Auflagen von hoch qualifizierten Ateliers und Manufakturen gefertigt. Viele Stücke wurden mit höchsten Designpreisen ausgezeichnet; manche finden sich in den Sammlungen von Museen. Die meisten der modernen Schmuck-Designer, darunter viele Frauen, haben nach einer Goldschmiedelehre an Fach- oder Kunstakademien studiert und anschließend eigene Unternehmen gegründet. Nur ganz wenige konnten auf Traditionsfirmen aufbauen. Doch alle Hersteller orientieren sich an der Ästhetik und den neuen Werten der Moderne sowie an einem selbst bestimmten, freien Menschenbild. Damit ist auch im Gegensatz zur traditionellen Schmuckindustrie eine ganz neue, gestalterisch geprägte, Unternehmenskultur entstanden, die interessante Parallelen zur Arts-and-Crafts-Bewegung des späten 19. Jahrhunderts aufweist.

Die Auswahl herausragender Protagonisten für dieses erste Werk, das die Entwicklung des seriellen Schmuck-Designs im historischen Kontext darstellt, hätte um weitere Beispiele ergänzt werden können. Das moderne Schmuck-Design weist noch mehr anspruchsvolle Gestalter auf. Doch hätte dies den Rahmen gesprengt, der für die Leser und den Verlag sinnvoll ist. Die Reihenfolge der Schmuck-Designer und Manufakturen in Kapitel 11 ist chronologisch. Jedoch nicht immer nach dem Gründungsdatum, sondern nach dem Zeitpunkt, in dem ein Hersteller mit modernem Schmuck begonnen hat.

E — Traditional magnificent jewels, cheap mass-produced jewellery, the passing whims of fashion: they all draw on the fading fragments of the old jewellery mystique, on enchantment long past. However, entirely new themes exist in jewellery, following the Modernist trend: meditative clarity, concentrated lines of force, wearable sculpture, innovative gemstone cutting, diamonds that seem to hover, constructions based on tension, new materials and symbols, combined with fun, refreshing playfulness, humorous allusions, poetic takes on the mundane, story-telling in metal and stone as well as romanticism with an emphasis on emotion and, most recently of all, increasingly luxurious sensuousness with the clarity retained.

Modern jewellery designers have brought forth polysemic signs – for modern women and, increasingly also, for men. They have complemented the gleam of gold and the sparkle of precious stones in jewellery with aspects that are grounded not in superstition, in idolatry, in striving for dominance and power, in embarrassing decorativeness or in naked materialism and mercenary values. On the contrary, they represent a commitment to the widespread desire to be stylish and pleasing, both to oneself and others. The new jewellery links matter and spirit. It invites people with discerning taste to showcase themselves. It springs from the eternal delight in what is creative, with a very serious purpose.

The paradigm shift has taken place in several stages of an onslaught against tradition and convention, which are stronger in jewellery than in other design disciplines. Since the late 19th century, since the Belle Époque, modern jewellery designers have had to contend with the powerful pull of inertia: at first against Historicism, then in the 1920s against the seductive powers of luxury jewels pure and simple, which certainly do have their fascinating sides. After 1945, ambitious goldsmiths turned against faceless industrial jewellery and the traditional crafts. In the »Renaissance« they sparked off, which took place synchronously with the movement for sexual liberation and the women's lib movement of the 1960s and 1970s, creators of jewellery at first tried out the fine arts argument. Jewellery as art is for some still a major concern, worldwide. However, the jewellery designers who have been graduating from German and other European institutes and specialist academies since the 1970s do not want to make only one-offs intended for a few museums and collectors. Instead, they want to produce ambitious edition jewellery, which reaches the public. Like the few innovative factories, they have to pay attention to buyers and their self-adornment needs. The best of these designers have managed to retain their distinctive signature and are successful just because they have done so.

Modern designer jewellery, which has matured in the past three decades, is the most recent movement to have sought to free this creative medium from the inchoate state it inflicted on itself. Following the two great eras in modern jewellery, Jugendstil/Art Nouveau and Art Déco, a jewellery culture with cultural and historical relevance has once again established itself. The designer jewellery that is shown today in upscale galleries and by modern jewellers has undergone a process of maturing and, unlike pre-war jewellery, no longer aims at expressing merely erotic urges or unalloyed faith in the machine. Recognition through art institutions and the scene is absolute but it no longer provides the standard by which designs and concepts are measured as they were in the 1980s.

With all its problems, modern designer jewellery can, despite all the countervailing movements, is by now unstoppable. It is fertilised by the crucial wish of young people to continue to invent jewellery that is cutting-edge. Fertile soil is provided by institutes and academies throughout Europe. Interest has grown not only in the land of the Bauhaus and the HfG Ulm, which has had to come to terms with its history by means of new, visionary design. Modern designer jewellery has its aficionados in countries, even continents, with different jewellery traditions, such as England and Spain, the Americas and Asia. The pronounced emphasis on Germany in this book is, however, not coincidental. Indeed it corresponds to the source of by far the most designer jewellery. However, this does not imply belittling what jewellery designers in Scandinavia, the Netherlands, England, Italy, Switzerland and Austria have accomplished in developing modern designer jewellery.

Today modern industrially produced jewellery is made in small editions by qualified studios and factories. Many such pieces have been awarded top design prizes; quite a few are in museum collections. Most modern jewellery designers, of whom many are women, studied at institutes or art academies after serving goldsmiths' apprenticeships before going on to found firms of their own. Only a few of them have been able to build on venerable family firms. All these jewellery-makers, however, are oriented towards the aesthetic and the new values of Modernism as well as an ideal of humanity as self-determined and free. Thus an entirely new, design-inspired entrepreneurial culture has, moreover, grown up, which reveals interesting parallels with the Arts and Crafts movement of the late 19th century.

The selection of outstanding exponents for this work, the first to represent the development of manufactured designer jewellery in its historical context, could have been enlarged by the addition of more examples. After all, there are plenty of other top-quality modern jewellery designers. However, that would have burst the bounds of what makes sense for readers and the publishers. The illustrated section with its historical survey of selected examples of modern jewellery culture is thematically arranged from Chapters 3 to 9. The histories of modern jewellery designers and makers in Chapter 10 are arranged in chronological order, albeit not always by foundation dates but rather from the time when each began to make modern jewellery. Young jewellery designers who have only recently finished their studies are not included with a portrait here. A small selection of their work is shown in Chapter 11 in the final picture section. If this book contributes to improving their prospects for self-determined, creative work, it will have already accomplished its purpose.

Dank — Acknowledgements

Mein herzlicher Dank gilt allen, die dieses Buch befürwortet und unterstützt haben. Besonders der Gold- und Silberscheideanstalt C. Hafner für ihren finanziellen Beitrag. Ebenso Susanne Heuer, die als Schmuck-Designerin und Autorin einige der Porträts geschrieben hat. Danke auch der Kunsthistorikerin Christianne Weber-Stöber, die eine profunde Beraterin für den historischen Rückblick war, und dem Schmuckmuseum Pforzheim, dass es seine Aufnahmen historischer Stücke zur Verfügung gestellt hat. Herzlichen Dank auch dem Fotografen H.P. Hoffmann, der mit seinen Aufnahmen und seinen Werbekonzepten vor allem für Niessing wesentlich zur Verbreitung modernen Schmuck-Designs beigetragen hat.

E — My sincere thanks are owed to all those who have approved and supported this book. Especially to the Gold- und Silberscheideanstalt C. Hafner for their financial support. Also to Susanne Heuer, who, as a jewellery designer and writer, contributed some of the portraits. Thanks also to the art historian Dr. Christianne Weber-Stöber, who has been an invaluable expert consultant for the historical survey, and to the Schmuckmuseum Pforzheim for making its photographs of historic pieces available. I also owe a huge debt of gratitude to the photographer H.P. Hoffmann. With his photos and advertising concepts for Niessing and other studios, he has contributed substantially to the spread of modern designer jewellery.

Reinhold Ludwig

Rückblick — Review

c. 1901

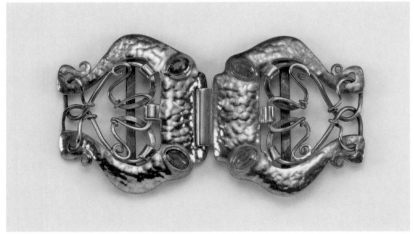

c. 1900

c. 1900

c. 1901 Gürtelschließe, Design Patriz Huber, Darmstadt, für Theodor Fahrner,
Pforzheim, Silber, gefärbte Achate — Belt clasp, design Patriz Huber,
Darmstadt, for Theodor Fahrner, Pforzheim, silver, coloured agates

c. 1900 Gürtelschließe, Design Otto Baker, Birmingham, für Liberty & Co., 1908,
Silber, Opale — Belt clasp, design Otto Baker, Birmingham, for Liberty & Co.,
1908, silver, opals

c. 1900 Gürtelschließe, Design Charles Robert Ashbee, London, Kupfer, Silber,
Citrine, Email — Belt clasp, design Charles Robert Ashbee, London, copper,
silver, citrines, enamel

Alle Stücke/all pieces Schmuckmuseum Pforzheim

Ursprünge modernen Schmuck-Designs — Origins of Modern Jewellery Design

Kapitel 1 — Chapter 1

Arts-and-Crafts-Bewegung und Werkbund

In der zweiten Hälfte des 19. Jahrhunderts propagierte die Arts-and-Crafts-Bewegung in England eine Rückkehr zu künstlerisch-handwerklichen Produktionsformen. Sie weist überraschende Parallelen nicht nur zum Schmuck-Design der Gegenwart auf. Wie vor über einem Jahrhundert entstehen seit den 1980er Jahren in Europa kleine Manufakturen und Ateliers mit anspruchsvollen Produktkonzepten. Kreative Gestaltung und sinnerfüllte Handarbeit, heute allerdings oft durch Hightech-Fertigung unterstützt, tritt wie vor 100 Jahren als Gegenkonzept zu niveauloser Massen- und Billigproduktion auf. Diese kommt im Zeitalter der Globalisierung heute zunehmend aus Billiglohnländern. Die von England ausgehende Arts-and-Crafts-Bewegung mit ihrer Blütezeit zwischen 1870 und 1920 war eine Reaktion auf die seelenlose Massenfertigung während der industriellen Revolution. Sie hatte zur Verelendung der Arbeiterschaft und zu extremen sozialen Problemen geführt. Die maschinelle Vervielfältigung historischer Ornamente in der Architektur und in anderen Bereichen bewirkte aber auch den Niedergang von Ateliers und Manufakturen, die noch im Biedermeier zwischen 1820 und 1848 beispielhafte Produkte hervorgebracht hatten.

Die wichtigsten Fürsprecher der Arts-and-Crafts-Bewegung waren William Morris, 1834–1896, und John Ruskin, 1819–1900. Auf der Suche nach einem authentischen Stil für das 19. Jahrhundert und als Antwort auf den Historismus der viktorianischen Ära idealisierten sie die Zeit vor dem italienischen Maler Raffael, die Gotik. Die gotische Dombauhütte, in der Handwerker und Künstler gemeinsam ein Gesamtkunstwerk schufen, diente später auch den Bauhaus-Gründern als Vorbild. Die Arts-and-Crafts-Bewegung verbreitete sich rasch in ganz Europa und in den USA. Sie betrieb eigene Werkstätten in England und Verkaufsniederlassungen in europäischen Großstädten wie London, Paris und Berlin. Eine besondere Bedeutung für die Erneuerung des Schmucks hatte das 1875 von Sir Arthur Lasenby Liberty, 1843–1917, gegründete Warenhaus in London. Nach ihm wurde der Liberty Style benannt, der mit dem späteren Jugendstil eng verknüpft ist. Für die Produktion gehobenen Gold- und Silberschmucks hatte sich Liberty an die großen Entwerfer der Zeit gewandt und arbeitete mit der Birmingham School of Art und mit Archibald Knox, 1864–1933, zusammen. Die Kooperation von Liberty mit Künstlern beeinflusste die Industrieproduktion positiv. Auch die Pforzheimer Firma Fahrner lieferte Schmuckkollektionen an das Liberty-Warenhaus.[1]

Die Arts-and-Crafts-Bewegung hatte starke programmatische Auswirkungen auf die Entstehung des Deutschen Werkbundes. Doch ging es diesem nicht mehr allein um die Ideale handwerklicher Fertigung. 1907 in München gegründet, bemühte sich der Werkbund, die Qualität handwerklicher Kultur und gute Formen in die unverzichtbare Industrieproduktion einzubringen. Als wesentliche Parameter der Gestaltung kristallisierten sich im Werkbund die Materialgerechtigkeit und eine schlichte, logische Formensprache heraus. Henry van de Velde, 1863–1957, einer der wichtigen Erneuerer der Angewandten Kunst, erklärte 1902 in seinen »Kunstgewerblichen Laienpredigten«: »Die Vernunft und ihre Schöpfung: die Logik sind die wenigen Prinzipien, aus denen die alten Stile entstanden sind, und darauf wollen auch wir den Stil unserer Zeit begründen.«[2] Der Belgier verehrte William Morris und war Mitbegründer eines linearen Jugendstils in Europa. Als Lehrer der Weimarer Kunstgewerbeschule, der späteren Keimzelle des Bauhauses, war Henry van de Velde maßgeblich an der Überwindung des Historismus und Eklektizismus des späten 19. Jahrhunderts beteiligt. Als Architekt und Designer propagierte er einen ganzheitlichen, alle Bereiche des Lebens durchdringenden neuen Stil.

Zur Schmuckgestaltung bemerkte Van de Velde in den Laienpredigten: »Unsere heutigen Schmuckgegenstände sind der minderwertigsten Erfindungskunst überlassen; und wenn der Vogel, der einen Brief im Schnabel trägt, ein etwas veraltetes und lächerliches Motiv ist, sehe ich nicht ein, warum man das Lächerliche nicht auch an den gegenwärtigen Schmuckgegenständen wahrnimmt; welche eine Libelle darstellen, die über eine Blume auf dem Wasser dahinschwebt, oder einen Frauenkopf, der Perlen aus dem üppigen Haupthaar streut.«[3] Hier findet sich eine Erklärung, warum die symbolistische, hauptsächlich in Frankreich und Belgien verbreitete Variante des Jugendstils, nur ein kurzes Zwischenspiel in der Moderne darstellte. Generell entstanden in der Wiener Werkstätte, im deutschen Jugendstil und vor allem in der Darmstädter Künstlerkolonie deutlich geometrischere Formen im Schmuck als in Frankreich.

The Arts and Crafts movement and the Werkbund

In the latter half of the 19th century, the Arts and Crafts movement in England called for a return to craftsmanly forms of production rather than manufacturing. This movement reveals astonishing parallels with contemporary designer jewellery. As was the case a century ago, small factories and studios have grown up in Europe with ambitious production concepts. Creative design and meaningful handiwork, albeit today often underpinned by high-tech means of production, have emerged as they did a hundred years ago as a concept countering substandard mass production on the cheap. In an age of globalisation, such products are being increasingly imported from low-wage countries. Originating in England, the Arts and Crafts movement was in its heyday between 1870 and 1920. It was a reaction to the soulless mass production that came with the Industrial Revolution, which had led to conditions of squalor prevailing in the working class and, therefore, to extreme social problems. Machine production of historic decoration in architecture and other fields, on the other hand, also led to the decline of studios and small factories, which had brought forth exemplary products in the Biedermeier era between 1820 and 1848.

The leading proponents of the Arts and Crafts movements were William Morris (1834–1896) and John Ruskin (1819–1900). Seeking an authentic 19th-century style that would represent a viable response to the historicism prevailing in the Victorian era, they idealised the Gothic style that reigned supreme before the time of the Italian painter Raphael. The Gothic stonemasons' guilds, in which craftsmen and artists together created total works of art in the form of cathedrals, would also later be the model for the founders of the Bauhaus.

The Arts and Crafts movement soon spread throughout Europe and the US. Its exponents operated workshops of their own in England with retail outlets in London and European capitals of fashion such as Paris and Berlin. Of particular importance to the renewal of jewellery was Liberty & Co., the department store founded in London in 1875 by Sir Arthur Lasenby Liberty (1843–1917). The Liberty Style, closely related to the later Jugendstil/Art Nouveau style, was named after him. Liberty had turned to the great designers of his day to make high-quality gold and silver jewellery and worked with both the Birmingham School of Art and Archibald Knox (1864–1933). The collaboration between Liberty and artists made a positive impact on industrial production. Fahrner, the Pforzheim jewellery manufactories, also delivered jewellery collections to the Liberty & Co. department store.[1]

The agenda espoused by the Arts and Crafts movement played a major role in the creation of the Deutscher Werkbund [German Work Federation] in Germany. However, the handiwork ideal was not all that the Werkbund was concerned with. Founded in Munich in 1907, it strove to introduce the quality and good form distinguishing craftsmanship to industrial manufacture, which it saw as the indispensable mode of production.

The essential design parameters advocated by the Werkbund were distilled into the ideal of doing justice to the materials used and a simple language of forms that was the logical consequence of using them in a rational manner. Henry van de Velde (1863–1957), one of the most important renewers of the decorative and applied arts, declared in 1902 in his Layman's Sermons devoted to the applied arts: »Reason and its creation, logic, are the few principles from which the old styles emerged and we, too, want to found the style of our time on them.«[2] The Belgian designer and architect revered William Morris and was a co-originator of the linear Art Nouveau/Jugendstil style in Europe. As an instructor at the Weimar Kunstgewerbeschule, from which the Bauhaus would later grow, van de Velde had a paramount share in overcoming the Historicism and the concomitant eclecticism of the late 19th century. In his capacity as an architect and designer, van de Velde propagated a holistic new style that would pervade all areas of life.

c. 1900

c. 1910

c. 1898

1900

c. 1900 Anhänger, Maison Vever, Paris, Gold, Rubin, Peridot, Amethyst, Smaragd, Topas, Kunzit, Perle, Email — Pendant, Maison Vever, Paris, gold, ruby, peridot, amethyst, emerald, topaz, kunzite, pearl, enamel

c. 1910 Brosche, Design Josef Hoffmann, Wien, Ausführung Wiener Werkstätte, Kupfer, Email — Brooch, design Josef Hoffmann, Vienna, executed by Wiener Werkstätte, copper, enamel

c. 1898 Anhänger-Brosche, René Lalique Paris, Gold, Email, Perle — Pendant-brooch, René Lalique, Paris, gold, enamel, pearl

1900 Brosche *Tintenfisch und Schmetterling*, Design Wilhelm Lukas von Cranach, Berlin, Ausführung Louis Werner, Gold, Perlen, Rubine, Amethyste, Topas, Email — Brooch *Cuttle and Butterfly*, design Wilhelm Lukas von Cranach, Berlin, executed by Louis Werner, gold, pearls, rubies, amethysts, topaz, enamel

Alle Stücke/all pieces Schmuckmuseum Pforzheim

On designing jewellery, van de Velde remarked in his Layman's Sermons: »The jewellery objects we have today have been abandoned to the most inferior artifice of invention; and if a bird carrying a letter in its bill is a rather outmoded and ridiculous motif, I do not at all see why the ridiculous should not also be perceived in the present jewellery objects, which represent a dragonfly hovering above a flower on the water or the head of a woman with pearls strewn from her luxuriant tresses.«[3] Here there is an explanation for why the Symbolist variant of Art Nouveau, which was widespread primarily in France and Belgium, only represented a brief interlude in Modernism. On the whole, more consistently geometric forms in jewellery were created at the Wiener Werkstätte, in German Jugendstil and especially at the Darmstadt Artists' Colony than they were in France.

Schmuckkunst als Beitrag zur Befreiung der Frau im Jugendstil

Art Nouveau, neue Kunst, wurde der Jugendstil in Frankreich genannt. Aber was war das Neue und Künstlerische? In der zweiten Hälfte des 19. Jahrhunderts waren die Goldschmiede ebenso wie andere Gestalter in Europa vielerorts auf der Suche nach einem bürgerlichen oder nationalen Stil. Dabei wurden zumeist die Formen der Romanik, der Gotik, der Antike oder der Natur nachgeahmt und nicht selten gedankenlos kombiniert. Der Schmuck des Jugendstils stellte nach langem wieder eine eigenständige schöpferische Leistung dar – frei von nationalistischem Gepränge.

Die Motive des Jugendstils, jungfräulich nackte Frauenkörper, Pfauen, Fabelwesen und Pflanzenornamente, erschöpften sich nicht im rein Dekorativen. Sie offenbarten Kraftlinien und Triebkräfte. Kunsthistoriker deuteten sie als Symbole für die im 19. Jahrhundert unterdrückten Gefühle des Organischen und Weiblichen. Zuerst erkannten Schaustellerinnen und Frauen der damaligen Halbwelt die kommunikative Wirkung dieser sinnlichen Motive. Sarah Bernhardt, die legendäre »femme fatale« ihrer Epoche, ließ sich erotische Arbeiten von den berühmten Pariser Künstlern René Lalique und Georges Fouquet fertigen. Wie andere weibliche Bühnenstars wollte sie damit ihre sexuelle Macht und Unabhängigkeit auch mit Schmuck demonstrieren. Und Tausende von Frauen in ganz Europa und den USA folgten ihrem Vorbild.

Zwar konnte sich nur eine kleine Schicht diesen Schmuck leisten. Doch wurde Schmuck im Jugendstil erstmals zu einem femininen, künstlerischen Ausdrucksmittel, das sich von ausschließlich dekorativen und prestigeträchtigen traditionellen Juwelen unterschied. Eva Neumeier bemerkt in ihrem Buch »Schmuck und Weiblichkeit in der Kaiserzeit« dazu: »Mit dem Tragen von kostbaren oder scheinbar kostbaren Schmuckstücken wähnte sich das Bürgertum im Einklang mit Verhaltensweisen des Adels und des Großbürgertums.«[4]

»Das Charakteristikum des modernen Lebens ist die Geschwindigkeit. Auch die Komposition eines Schmuckstücks muss rasch und leicht verständlich sein. Dafür bedarf es einfacher Linien, frei von Effekthascherei und überflüssigem Zierrat.«

George Fouquet, 1929

»The salient characteristic of modern life is speed. The composition of a piece of jewellery must also be easy to grasp rapidly. For that to happen, simple lines, devoid of effects that have been strained after and superfluous adornment, are needed.«

George Fouquet, 1929

Die maßgebenden Goldschmiede des Jugendstils wollten aber nicht nur dem prestigesüchtigen, neuen Geldadel dienen. Ihre Motivation basierte auch auf künstlerischen und gesellschaftlichen Werten, die zu Beginn der Moderne formuliert wurden: in der Hoffnung auf eine bessere Welt. Damit entstand ein vollkommen neues Paradigma, das bis heute moderne Schmuckgestaltung von konventionellem Juwelenschmuck unterscheidet.

Art jewellery as a contribution
to the emancipation of women in Jugendstil

Art Nouveau, the new art, was the name in France for what was known as Jugendstil in Germany. But what was so new or even arty about it? In the latter half of the 19th century, goldsmiths and other designers in many places in Europe were seeking to create a bourgeois or even national style. The most frequently imitated forms were taken from Romanesque, Gothic or ancient art or were even imitations of nature. All too frequently, those period styles were unthinkingly jumbled together. After such mindless eclecticism, Jugendstil jewellery represented the first independent creative achievement for a long time – free of nationalist posturing.

The Jugendstil/Art Nouveau motifs – virginal nude female bodies, peacocks, mythical beasts and vegetal decoration – were not all purely ornamental. Indeed they revealed forceful lines and powerful urges. Art historians have interpreted them as symbolising the feelings for the organic and the female that had been repressed in the 19th century. Actresses and demimondaine women of the time were the first to recognise the communicative potential of those sensuous motifs. Sarah Bernhardt, the legendary »femme fatale« of the era, commissioned pieces of jewellery steeped in erotic symbolism from the famed Paris artisans René Lalique and Georges Fouquet. Like other female stars of the stage, she wanted to demonstrate her sexual prowess and independence even through the jewellery she wore. And thousands of women throughout Europe and the US followed her example.

Of course, that was jewellery which only a small privileged class could afford. Nevertheless, jewellery first became a feminine means of artistic expression in Jugendstil, one that differed from traditional jewels that were merely decorative and nothing but status symbols. In her book Schmuck und Weiblichkeit in der Kaiserzeit, Eva Neumeier has made the following pertinent observation: »By wearing valuable or seemingly valuable pieces of jewellery, the bourgeoisie fancied itself in harmony with the behaviour patterns displayed by the aristocracy and gentry.«[4] The paramount Jugendstil goldsmiths, however, did not want to pander to the nouveaux riche addiction to status-seeking. They were motivated by aesthetic and social values that had been formulated at the outset of Modernism in hopes of a better world. Thus an entirely new paradigm was created that even today sets modern designer jewellery apart from conventional jewellery.

c. 1925

1938

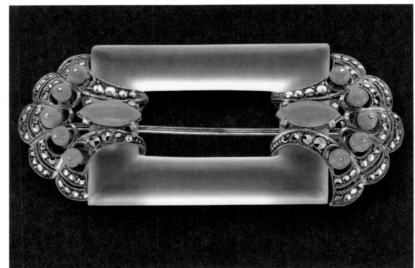

1926

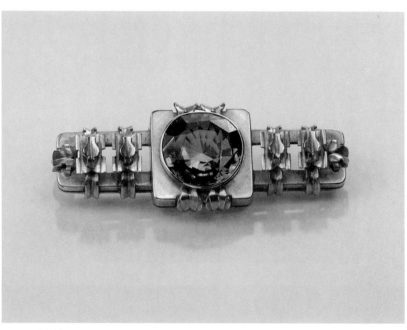

1936

c. 1925   Armreif, René Boivin, Paris, Bergkristall, Platin, Saphire, Diamanten
          — Bangle, René Boivin, Paris, rock crystal, platinum, sapphires, diamonds

1938   Anhänger, Wiwen Nilsson, Lund, Bergkristall, Onyx, Silber — Pendant,
          Wiwen Nilsson, Lund, rock crystal, onyx, silver

1926   Brosche, Gustav Braendle, Th. Fahrner Nachfolger, Pforzheim, Glas, Silber,
          Korallen, Markasite — Brooch, Gustav Braendle, Th. Fahrner Nachfolger,
          Pforzheim, glass, silver, coral, marcasite

1936   Brosche, Theodor Wende, Pforzheim, Gold, Citrin — Brooch,
          Theodor Wende, Pforzheim, gold, citrine

               Alle Stücke/all pieces Schmuckmuseum Pforzheim

Tradition contra Moderne im Art Déco

Die zweite wegweisende Epoche für den Schmuck der Moderne war der Art Déco zwischen 1920 und 1940. Im »Feuerwerk« der dekorativen Ideen und modernen Visionen spielte Schmuck im Gleichklang mit der Architektur, dem Design und der Mode eine bedeutende Rolle. In Paris, der damaligen Hochburg kreativer Schmuckkultur, traten jedoch strenge Gegensätze zwischen Traditionalisten und Avantgardisten zu Tage. Während traditionelle Juweliere wie Cartier, Van Cleef & Arpels oder Boucheron prächtigen dekorativen Juwelenschmuck kreierten, beriefen sich fortschrittliche Schmuckmacher auf die noch taufrische Formensprache und die Ideale der Moderne. Die Abspaltung der Avantgardisten von den Traditionalisten begann kurz nach der Pariser Exposition Internationale des Arts Décoratifs et Industriels Modernes im Jahr 1925, jener Ausstellung, von der später in den 1960er Jahren der Name Art Déco abgeleitet wurde.

Der Pariser Juwelier Georges Fouquet, Organisator der legendären Ausstellung, schrieb 1929: »Das Charakteristikum des modernen Lebens ist die Geschwindigkeit. Auch die Komposition eines Schmuckstücks muss rasch und leicht verständlich sein. Dafür bedarf es einfacher Linien, frei von Effekthascherei und überflüssigem Zierrat. Jedem Schmuckstück muss eine klare Komposition zugrunde liegen, bei der Proportionen und Farben harmonisch aufeinander abgestimmt sind.«[5] Die Orientierung an der Kunst der Moderne ist eindeutig.

1929 verließen die Schmuckgestalter Jean Fouquet, Gerard Sandoz, Jean Puiforcat und Raymond Templier die Société des Artistes Décorateurs und gründeten die Union des Artists Modernes (U.A.M.). Der Vereinigung gehörten auch Designer wie Charlotte Perriand und Architekten wie Le Corbusier an. Die »modernen Künstler« entwickelten den wirklich revolutionären Schmuck des Art Déco. Klare Formen in Platin, Gold, Silber bis hin zu verchromtem Metall, zum Teil kombiniert mit geometrisch geschliffenen Edelsteinen, waren vorherrschend. Die Avantgardisten experimentierten mit Edelstahl, Glas, Lack, Eierschalen, Elfenbein und anderen Materialien. In zahlreichen Arbeiten kam die Faszination für die Errungenschaften der Technik zum Ausdruck, die den Stücken manchmal einen technoiden Charakter verlieh. Dem Schmuck der Avantgardisten standen die üppigen Kreationen mit reichem Edelsteinbesatz der Juweliere gegenüber. Sie imitierten häufig ägyptische, chinesische und aztekische Motive und setzten starke Schwarz-Weiß- und Schwarz-Rot-Kontrasten ein. Nicht unerwähnt darf der Modeschmuck bleiben, der in den 1920er und 1930er Jahren sehr populär wurde. Wie der Juwelierschmuck lebte er von dekorativen Farbkontrasten, war jedoch in preiswerten Ersatzmaterialien gefertigt. »Viele deutsche Juweliere haben ausschließlich den französischen Stil übernommen«, sagt die Kunsthistorikerin Dr. Christianne Weber-Stöber. Typisch für deutsche

»herr slutzky ist nicht nur in technischer beziehung meisterlich durchgebildet, sondern geht auch neue erfindungsreiche wege in der formgebung und in der metalltechnik, die ich dahin charakterisieren möchte, dass er mit dem geringsten aufwand von mitteln technischer und materieller art starke wirkungen zu erzielen weiß.«

Walter Gropius, 1934 [B]

»herr slutzky is not just a consummate master of technique but also enters on new, inventive paths in design and in metalworking, which i should like to characterise as follows: that he is capable of achieving powerful effects effortlessly through technical and material means.«

Walter Gropius, 1934 [B]

Juweliere und Goldschmiede in den 1920er und 1930er Jahren waren Techniken wie Granulation, Filigran und Email. Doch auch erste konstruktivistische Schmuckstücke entstanden unter dem Einfluss des Bauhauses bzw. der Neuen Sachlichkeit.

Tradition versus
Modernism in Art Déco

The second ground-breaking era in Modern jewellery was Art Déco between 1920 and 1940. In a »blaze« of ideas for decoration and modern visions, jewellery played as important a role as architecture, design and fashion. However, a clash between traditionalists and avant-gardists in Paris, then the stronghold of creative jewellery culture, became apparent. Whereas traditional jewellers such as Cartier, Van Cleef & Arpels and Boucheron created pieces with magnificent decorative jewels, progressive jewellerymakers addressed the still fresh Modernist language of forms and ideals. The final rupture between the avant-garde and the traditionalists took place shortly after the 1925 Exposition Internationale des Arts Décoratifs et Industriels Modernes in Paris, the benchmark exposition from which the 1960s would derive the name »Art Déco«.

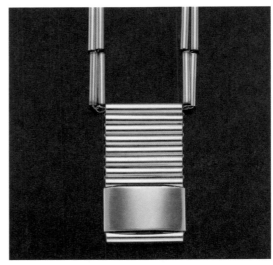

c. 1930

The Paris jeweller Georges Fouquet, the organiser of that legendary exposition, wrote in 1929: »The salient characteristic of modern life is speed. The composition of a piece of jewellery must also be easy to grasp rapidly. For that to happen, simple lines, devoid of effects that have been strained after and superfluous adornment, are needed. Every piece of jewellery must be based on a clear composition, with proportions and colour harmoniously attuned to each other.«[5] His bias towards Modernist art is unequivocal.

In 1929 the jewellery designers Jean Fouquet, Gerard Sandoz, Jean Puiforcat and Raymond Templier left the Société des Artistes Décorateurs to found the Union des Artists Modernes (U.A.M.). Designers such as Charlotte Perriand and architects, including Le Corbusier, also belonged to U.A.M. It was »modern artists« who developed the really revolutionary jewellery now known as Art Déco. Clear-cut forms in platinum, gold and silver and even chromium-plated base metals, in part combined with geometrically cut precious stones, predominated. Avant-gardists experimented with stainless steel, glass, eggshells, ivory and other unusual materials. Their fascination for the achievements of technology was expressed in many pieces, some of which even had a rather technoid look. The austere avant-garde jewellery, which often imitated Egyptian, Chinese and even Aztec motifs and adroitly exploited dramatic contrasts between black and white or black and red to great effect, contrasted sharply with the sumptuous creations so richly set with precious stones sold by jewellers. The costume jewellery which became so popular during the 1920s and 1930s is also relevant in this connection. Like the jewels purveyed by jewellers, costume jewellery was enlivened by deco-

1924–1926

1924

rative colour contrasts but they were realised in reasonably priced base materials. »Many German jewellers took over the French style wholesale,« says the art historian Dr. Christianne Weber-Stöber. Typical of 1920s and 1930s German jewellers and goldsmiths was the use of techniques such as granulation, filigree and enamelling. However, the first Constructivist pieces of jewellery emerged under the influence of the Bauhaus and New Objectivity.

Bauhaus und
Neue Sachlichkeit.

Das von Walter Gropius 1919 gegründete Bauhaus bestand nur 14 Jahre. Es wurde 1933 unter dem Druck der Nationalsozialisten geschlossen. Doch hat keine andere Institution die Moderne in Architektur, Design und Kunst stärker beeinflusst. Zwar spielte Schmuck am Bauhaus nur eine geringe Rolle. Die Metallwerkstatt diente in erster Linie der Gestaltung von Tischgerät, Leuchten und Möbeln. Dennoch war der Einfluss dieser Kunst- und Designschule für die Entwicklung einer modernen Schmuckauffassung wesentlich. Insbesondere das moderne Schmuck-Design in Deutschland ist ohne die formalen und geistigen Grundlagen des Bauhauses kaum denkbar. Sowohl die Goldschmiedekünstler der Nachkriegszeit ebenso wie Ateliers und Manufakturen seit den 1970er Jahren ließen sich von der ganzheitlichen, alle Lebensbereiche durchdringenden Kunstauffassung dazu anregen, mit traditionellen Schmuckvorstellungen zu brechen.

Am Anfang der Bauhausgründung stand die Idee, nach der Katastrophe des Ersten Weltkriegs mittels guter Gestaltung »einen neuen Menschen« erstehen zu lassen: »Ein Geschöpf, das mit allen Sinnen begabt, geschult durch die besten Künstler und Architekten der Zeit befähigt sei, Gegenwart und Zukunft eines modernen Jahrhunderts zu erfinden.«[6] Die gestalterischen Parameter des Bauhauses waren: Funktionalismus, sparsamer und durchdachter Einsatz passender Materialien sowie Reduktion auf geometrische Grundformen. Die Metallwerkstatt wurde von 1919 bis 1923 von Johannes Itten geleitet, ab 1921 gleichberechtigt mit Oskar Schlemmer. Das Thema Metall war für den modernen Funktionalismus wesentlich. Im Ausstellungskatalog zur Metallwerkstatt, herausgegeben vom Bauhaus-Archiv Berlin 1992, heißt es dazu: »Wenn das Bauhaus ein Ort war, von dem das Design des 20. Jahrhunderts entscheidende Impulse erhielt, so gibt es wohl kaum einen Bereich, der mit dieser Entwicklung unmittelbarer verknüpft ist als der des Metalls.«[7] Dies bezog sich natürlich vor allem auf den innovativen Einsatz von Metall in Möbeln, Leuchten bis hin zu Türgriffen. Entwürfe wie die Tischleuchte von Wilhelm Wagenfeld von 1924, der Türdrücker von Walter Gropius und Adolf Meyer, Entwurf 1922, oder die Kandem-Schreibtischleuchte von Marianne Brandt und Hin Bredendieck von 1928 wurden zu Klassikern der Moderne. Alle diese Gestalter haben jedoch auch beispielhaftes Tafelgerät, vom Milchkännchen bis zur Tee- und Kaffekanne,

> »Langsam wird man sich doch an diese zuerst fremd
> scheinenden Gegenstände gewöhnen können. Ja plötzlich
> wird ein Licht aufgehen: wie selbstverständlich klar und
> wunderschön das alles ist.«
>
> Kunst und Kunsthandwerk, 1926

> »One will probably be able to accustom oneself gradually to
> these objects that seem so strange at first. Behold, a light will
> shine: how matter-of-factly clear and beautiful it all is.«
>
> Kunst und Kunsthandwerk, 1926

in Silber und anderen Metallen gestaltet. Für den Schmuck, der direkt am Bauhaus entstand, war hauptsächlich Naum Slutzky zuständig. 1894 in Kiew in eine bekannte Goldschmiedefamilie geboren, hat er schon um 1912 in der Wiener Werkstätte Schmuckstücke nach den Entwürfen von berühmten Gestaltern wie Josef Hoffmann und Eduard Josef Wimmer ausgeführt. Walter Gropius berief Slutzky 1919 an das Bauhaus, wo er als »Hilfsmeister« für die Schmuckfertigung eine Sonderstellung einnahm. Eine seiner ersten Arbeiten war 1920 eine kugelförmige, getriebene Kupferdose. Ein Anhänger, gefertigt zwischen 1920 und 1922, zeigt noch reduzierte Ornamente. Danach verzichtete Slutzky bei seinen Schmuckstücken auf jegliches Dekor. Seine runden Anhänger, 1922–1924, sind aus verschiedenen Materialien wie Perlmutt, Opal, Horn mit einer Silberfassung konzentrisch aufgebaut und werden an einer Kordel getragen.

Naum Slutzky, der auch Tafelgerät, Leuchten und Möbel entwarf, verließ 1924 das Bauhaus. Im Zeugnis schreibt Walter Gropius, »dass er mit dem geringsten aufwand von mitteln technischer und materieller art starke wirkungen zu erzielen weiß.«[8] Dies bewies er auch mit seinen Arbeiten, die nach seiner Bauhauszeit entstanden. Konstruktivistisch erscheint ein Ring mit zwei übereinanderliegenden Schienen von Naum Slutzky um 1926. Hier wird eine Kugel aus Rosenquarz nur durch zwei Ösen gehalten. In einem Anhänger von 1929 tauchen erste kinetische Elemente auf. Hier wird bereits eine Auffassung sichtbar, wie sie nach dem Zweiten Weltkrieg der Düsseldorfer Schmuckkünstler und Lehrer Friedrich Becker zu großer Perfektion entwickelt hat. 1933 musste Slutzky nach England emigrieren, wo er als Designer, Künstler und Professor an verschiedenen Hochschulen lehrte. Bis zu seinem Tod 1965 entstanden noch zahlreiche Schmuckstücke, in denen er, dem Zeitgeist folgend, auch organische und skulpturale Formen umsetzte.

Die Bauhaus-Ideen verbreiteten sich rasch auch an den Ausbildungsstätten für Gold- und Silberschmiede in den deutschen Schmuckzentren Hanau, Pforzheim, Schwäbisch Gmünd und Burg Giebichenstein. Überzeugende Arbeiten im Stil der Neuen Sachlichkeit im Schmuck, Anfang der 1930er Jahre, stammen von Lotte Feickert, Hanau, Fritz Schwerdt, Pforzheim, Kurt Baer, u.a. Lehrer an der Kunstgewerbeschule in Pforzheim, sowie dessen Schülern Ernst Günter Odenwald und Julia Mayer. Von den Gold- und Silberschmieden, die am Bauhaus waren, machen auch die Schmuckstücke von Eveline Burchard und Wolfgang Tümpel die vollkommene Abwendung vom Ornament deutlich.[9]

The Bauhaus and New Objectivity

Founded by Walter Gropius in 1919, the Bauhaus existed for only fourteen years. Pressure brought to bear on it by the National Socialists forced it to close in 1933. For all its brief existence, no other institution exerted a comparably strong influence on Modernism in architecture, design and the arts. Jewellery, on the other hand, played only a minor role at the Bauhaus. The metalworking workshop there was used mainly for designing tableware, lighting and furniture. Still the influence exerted by this art and design school was crucial to the development of a Modernist concept of jewellery. The modern designer jewellery being made in Germany especially is inconceivable without the formal and intellectual principles promulgated by the Bauhaus. Both the post-war German goldsmiths and the studios and factories making jewellery since the 1970s were inspired by that holistic conception of art that pervades all areas of life to break with traditional notions of jewellery. At the beginning of the Bauhaus was the idea of allowing »a new person« to be created through good design after the catastrophe of the Great War: »A creature that is gifted in all senses, schooled by the best artists and architects who is capable of inventing the present and future of a modern century.«[6] The Bauhaus design paradigm consisted in functionalism, the economical and thought-out use of suitable materials and reduction to basic geometric forms.

Johannes Itten was director of the Bauhaus metalworking workshop from 1919 until 1923 and from 1921 the workshop was run by Itten and Oskar Schlemmer on an equal footing. Metal was crucial to modern Functionalism. In an exhibition catalogue from the metalworking workshop, re-issued by the Bauhaus Archives in Berlin in 1992, it says: »If the Bauhaus was a place from which 20th-century design received vital impulses, hardly any other field is more closely linked with this development than metalworking.«[7] That remark of course refers mainly to the innovative use of metal for furniture, lighting and even door handles. Designs such as the 1924 Wilhelm Wagenfeld table lamp, the door handle designed in 1922 by Walter Gropius and Adolf Meyer and the Kandem desk lamp designed by Marianne Brandt and Hin Bredendieck in 1928 all became Modern classics. Those designers, however, also designed superlative tableware, ranging from milk jugs to teapots and coffee pots in silver and other metals.

Naum Slutzky was the one mainly responsible for the jewellery made at the Bauhaus itself. Born in Kiev to a well-known goldsmithing family in 1894, he had executed jewellery designs by such luminaries as Josef Hoffmann and Eduard Josef Wimmer for the Wiener Werkstätte as early as 1912. Walter Gropius summoned Slutzky in 1919 to the Bauhaus, where he occupied a special position as an »assistant master« in jewellery-making. One of his first works, produced in 1920, was a spherical beaten copper jar. A pendant Slutzky made between 1920 and 1922, still sports decoration, albeit in a reduced form but after that Slutzky eschewed decoration entirely on his pieces of jewellery. The round pendants he produced between 1922 and 1924 are made of materials such as mother-of-pearl, opal and horn, concentrically arranged and set in silver to be worn on a cord.

Naum Slutzky, who also designed tableware, lighting and furniture, left the Bauhaus in 1924. In the testimonial he wrote for Slutzky, Walter Gropius says of him »that he is capable of achieving powerful effects with the slightest effort through technical and material means.«[8] Slutzky demonstrated the same qualities in the works he produced after his Bauhaus years. A Naum Slutzky ring with two overlaid shafts (ca 1926) looks Constructivist. Here a rose quartz sphere is held in place by just two lugs. His first kinetic elements surface on a 1929 pendant. Here a conception is already manifest that would be developed to the utmost perfection after the Second World War by the Düsseldorf artist in jewellery and teacher Friedrich Becker.

In 1933 Slutzky was forced to emigrate to England, where he taught at various institutes as a designer, artist and professor. Until his death in 1965, he continued to produce a great deal of jewellery, in which he followed the Zeitgeist and also made use of organic and sculptural forms.

The Bauhaus ideas spread rapidly even to institutes that trained goldsmiths and silversmiths in the German jewellery centres Hanau, Pforzheim, Schwäbisch Gmünd and Burg Giebichenstein. In the early 1930s, compelling works in the New Objectivity style came from Lotte Feickert, Hanau, Fritz Schwerdt, Pforzheim, Kurt Baer, who inter alia taught at the Kunstgewerbeschule in Pforzheim, and his pupils Ernst Günter Odenwald and Julia Mayer. The jewellery designed by Eveline Burchard and Wolfgang Tümpel is also notable for the uncompromising repudiation of ornament.[9]

1. Ulrike v. Hase-Schmundt: Jugendstilschmuck. Die europäischen Zentren. München/Munich, 1998, S./p. 249–255.
2. Henry van de Velde: Kunstgewerbliche Laienpredigten. Berlin, 1999, S./p. 142.
3. Henry van de Velde: Kunstgewerbliche Laienpredigten. Berlin, 1999, S./p. 180.
4. Eva Neumeier: Schmuck und Weiblichkeit in der Kaiserzeit. Bonn, 2000, S./p. 109.
5. Christianne Weber: Art Déco Schmuck. München/Munich, 2000.
6. Jeannine Fiedler: Bauhaus. Köln/Cologne, 1999, S./p. 8.
7. Die Metallwerkstatt am Bauhaus. Bauhaus-Archiv, Berlin, 1992, S./p. 7.
8. Monika Rudolph: Naum Slutzky, Meister am Bauhaus, Goldschmied und Designer. Stuttgart, 1990, S./p. 40.

9. In »Schmuck der 20er und 30er Jahre in Deutschland«, Stuttgart, 1990, zeigt Christianne Weber, dass der Schmuck in der Zwischenkriegszeit von einer Vielzahl unterschiedlicher Stilrichtungen durchzogen war. Vom Historismus über Nachklänge des Jugendstils, vom französischen Art Déco sowie dem Kubismus und Futurismus in der Malerei. – In »Schmuck der 20er und 30er Jahre in Deutschland«, Stuttgart, 1990, Christianne Weber shows that jewellery in the interwar period was informed by a great many different stylistic influences, ranging from Historicism through echoes of Jugendstil and French Art Déco to Cubism and Futurism in painting.

A. Aus/from: Eva Neumeier: Schmuck und Weiblichkeit in der Kaiserzeit. Bonn, 2000, S./p. 291.
B. Aus/from: Die Metallwerkstatt am Bauhaus, Bauhaus-Archiv, Berlin, 1992, S./p. 28.

c. 1955

c. 1955   Collier, Brosche und Ohrclips, Christian Dior/Henkel & Grosse,
          Rhodium, Glassteine — Necklace, brooch and earrings, Christian Dior
          /Henkel & Grosse, rhodium, glass

New Look und traditonelle Frauenrolle

Renaissance der Schmuckkunst nach 1945
— The Goldsmithing Renaissance after 1945

New Look und
traditionelle Frauenrolle

Warum spielte Paris, als Zentrum der Schmuckavantgarde im Jugendstil und im Art Déco, kaum mehr eine Rolle im modernen Schmuck nach 1945? Warum verstummten die französischen Avantgardisten in der Nachkriegszeit so völlig? Eine Erklärung findet sich in der Entwicklung der Mode, die bis Ende der 1950er Jahre von französischen Couturiers wie Christian Dior, Hubert de Givenchy oder Louis Féraud dominiert wurde. Sie gingen nicht nur mit den Modemagazinen, sondern auch mit der Filmindustrie Hollywoods eine mächtige Liaison ein. Audrey Hepburn zum Beispiel, die sich in »Frühstück bei Tiffany« in teure Juwelen verliebt zeigte, trug im Film und auf dem Laufsteg die Kleider von Givenchy. Brigitte Bardot, Ingrid Bergman und Liz Taylor waren Kundinnen von Féraud. Die holländische Modeexpertin José Teunissen kommt in einem Beitrag über das Frauenbild der 1950er Jahre zu dem Schluss: »In dieser Zeit fließen der Geschmack und die visuelle Sprache der Mode zusammen mit der Hollywoods und erreichen einen Höhepunkt.«[1]

Der so genannte New Look, den Christian Dior in den 1950er Jahren kreiert hatte, bedeutete in Wirklichkeit für die Frauen einen Rückschritt. Die englische Feministin Mabel Ridealgh schreibt dazu: »Der New Look erinnert an die Haltung eines Vogels im goldenen Käfig.«[2] Die neue Mode zwang das weibliche Geschlecht zu Wespentaillen, Miedern und Korsetts, die sie nach dem Barock schon einmal dankbar abgelegt hatten. Zahlreiche Modezaren setzten auf enge Roben. Auch der Kult um Busenstars und Idealmaße nahm den Frauen die bereits im Jugendstil und Art Déco demonstrierte Bewegungsfreiheit.

Schmuck aus Gold, Edelsteinen und Perlen zeigte sich in diesem Umfeld entweder sehr klassisch oder wurde Accessoire der Mode. In Frankreich spielt modernes Schmuckdesign seitdem so gut wie keine Rolle mehr. In Deutschland schickten sich die Frauen der 1950er Jahre zunächst in traditionelle Rollenmuster, nachdem sie zuvor in den zerbombten Städten die Trümmer männlichen Größenwahns beseitigt hatten.

The New Look and
woman's traditional role

Why did Paris, the centre of avant-garde jewellery in Art Nouveau and Art Déco, play hardly any role to speak of in modern jewellery after 1945? What made the French avant-garde fall utterly silent in the post-war years? One explanation is to be found in developments in fashion, which until the late 1950s was dominated by French couturiers such as Christian Dior, Hubert de Givenchy and Louis Féraud. They entered into a powerful alliance not only with the fashion magazines but also with the Hollywood movie industry. Audrey Hepburn, for instance, who revealed herself enamoured of expensive jewels in Breakfast at Tiffany's, wore dresses by Givenchy both in the film and on the catwalk. Brigitte Bardot, Ingrid Bergman and Liz Taylor were clients of Féraud. In an essay on how women were perceived in the 1950s, the Dutch fashion expert José Teunissen concludes: »At that time, taste and the visual imagery of fashion were at their zenith when they converged with those of Hollywood.«[1]

What was universally known as the New Look, which Christian Dior had created in the 1950s, meant in reality a step backwards for women. The English MP and feminist Mabel Ridealgh wrote that the New Look was reminiscent of the posture of a bird in a golden cage.[2] The new fashion forced women into wasp-waisted clothes, stiffened bodices and corsets, constraints they had already been only too happy to abandon after the Barock and late Victorian eras. Arbiters of fashion insisted on tight-fitting apparel. The cult of bosomy film stars and ideal proportions also deprived women of the freedom of movement they had demonstrated in the Jugendstil/Art Nouveau periods and on into Art Déco.

In the New Look environment, jewellery of gold, precious stones and pearls represented either timeless classics or fashion accessories. In France, modern designer jewellery has played virtually no role at all since then. In 1950s Germany, women at first clung to traditional role patterns once they had removed the ruins of male-driven megalomania from the bombed cities.

Jugendrevolte, die Gute Form und
Neuer Schmuck

In den 1960er Jahren rebellierten nicht nur die Studenten gegen das rückwärts gerichtete Frauenbild. Kunst, Musik und Mode provozierten mit radikalen neuen Ausdrucksformen. Die Pop-Art entdeckte die Schönheit der Alltagsästhetik, die Popmusik wurde zu einem Massenphänomen und der Minirock machte die neue Freizügigkeit auf der Straße sichtbar.

Unbeeindruckt davon brachte die Sehnsucht nach Glanz und Glamour der Schmuckindustrie in Europa einen kräftigen Boom. Moderne Designkonzepte wie in der Elektroindustrie bei Braun oder bei Möbelherstellern wie Knoll gab es in der deutschen Schmuckindustrie vor 1970 nicht. Pforzheimer Fabrikanten begnügten sich mit einer Reise nach Paris, um sich in den Auslagen der Nobeljuweliere über »die Trends« zu informieren.

An Bildungsinstitutionen wie der Hochschule für Gestaltung in Ulm, 1953–1968, wurde intensiv über den Einfluss der »Guten Form« auf ein humanes Menschenbild diskutiert; auch für die Professoren und Studenten an den Schmuckakademien war dies ein Thema. Vor allem war die Aufmerksamkeit, die moderne Kunst seit den 1960er Jahren erhielt, ein entscheidender Impuls, das künstlerische Potential auch in ihrem Medium auszuschöpfen. Zum wichtigen Fürsprecher des Neuen Schmucks wurde Karl Schollmayer. Er war 1956 als Rektor der Kunst- und Werkschule von Düsseldorf nach Pforzheim gewechselt. 1974 erschien sein Buch »Neuer Schmuck – ornamentum humanum«. Darin werden ausgewählte Goldschmiede der Nachkriegszeit vorgestellt. In ihren Aussagen und Arbeiten finden sich zahlreiche Beispiele für ein neues Schmuckverständnis, das sich an den Idealen der Moderne orientierte. Schollmayers Idealismus war im abendländischen Humanismus begründet. Akademisch gebildete Gold- und Silberschmiede erhielten durch ihn und andere Professoren fundierte Argumente, sich von rein materialistischen Wertvorstellungen im Schmuck zu distanzieren und die Gestaltung in den Vordergrund zu rücken.

  Nach Schollmayer wurde der Neue Schmuck durch Goldschmiede entwickelt, »die in der Zeit von Anfang des Jahrhunderts bis etwa 1940 geboren sind.«[3] Er verweist in seinem Buch auf die Umstände, unter denen der Neubeginn im künstlerischen Schmuck stattfand: »Sie beginnen bewusst zu gestalten in einer Zeit, die einen kulturellen Tiefstand darstellt, als der Kampf um die Lebenserhaltung heute kaum mehr vorstellbare Formen annahm. In Kunstschulen fehlten oft die primitivsten äußeren Voraussetzungen.«[4] Und doch entstand eine vitale Bewegung in der Schmuckgestaltung.

The youth rebellion, good form and New Jewellery

In the 1960s, it was not just students who rebelled against the retrogressive image of the ideal woman. Art, music and fashion emerged as provocative vehicles for radically new forms of expression. Pop Art discovered the aesthetic of the mundane, pop music became a mass phenomenon and the mini skirt displayed the new permissiveness on the streets.

  Unimpressed by all that, yearnings for brilliance and glamour ensured that the jewellery industry throughout Europe underwent a tremendous upturn. Before 1970 there were no modern design concepts in the German jewellery industry to compare with those launched by Braun in the electrical appliances industry and furniture makers such as Knoll. Pforzheim industrialists were content with trips to Paris to glean information on »the trends« from the shop window displays of elegant jewellers.

  At institutions of higher learning focusing on the applied arts and design, such as the Hochschule für Gestaltung in Ulm (1953–1968), the influence exerted by »good form« in humanising mankind was heatedly debated; this was a concern also shared by professors and students at jewellery-making academies. Above all, the attention attracted by modern art since the 1960s was a vital stimulus for exhausting the artistic potential in their medium as well. Karl Schollmayer was a major advocate of the New Jewellery. He had moved in 1956 to Pforzheim from Düsseldorf as director of the Kunst- und Werkschule. In 1974, his book Neuer Schmuck – ornamentum humanum was published, presenting a selection of post-war goldsmiths. The statements they make and their work provide numerous examples of a new idea of jewellery that is oriented towards Modernist ideals. Schollmayer's

1979

1970

1996

1979   Brosche, Mario Pinton, Padua, Gold, Saphir — Brooch, Mario Pinton, Padua, gold, sapphire

1970   Brosche, Reinhold Reiling, Pforzheim, Gold, Diamanten — Brooch, Reinhold Reiling, Pforzheim, gold, diamonds. Schmuckmuseum Pforzheim

1996   Brosche *il dio felice*, Bruno Martinazzi, Gold — Brooch *il dio felice*, Bruno Martinazzi, gold. Schmuckmuseum Pforzheim

idealism was grounded in Western humanism. He furnished academically trained goldsmiths and silversmiths with sound arguments for distancing themselves from purely materialistic notions of value with regard to jewellery and for giving priority to design instead.

After Schollmayer the new jewellery was developed by goldsmiths »who were born in the period extending from the beginning of the century to about 1940.«[3] In his book, Schollmayer points out the circumstances under which the new beginning in art jewellery took place: »They began to design deliberately at a time which was culturally at a low ebb, when the battle for survival assumed forms scarcely imaginable today. Art schools often lacked the barest external essentials.«[4] Yet nonetheless a vigorous movement in jewellery design emerged.

Unikat-Schmuck als Kunst und modernes Schmuck-Design

Die Entwicklung im Neuen Schmuck mündete Ende der 1970er Jahre in zwei Hauptrichtungen. In der einen, der Schmuckkunst, fand eine wahre Revolte gegen viele Konventionen der Tradition statt. Schmuckkünstler forschten und arbeiteten nach dem Vorbild freier bildender Künstler. Sie versuchten, mit Unikat-Schmuck künstlerische Aussagen zu machen. Dies bedeutete, Traditionen radikal zu hinterfragen, manchmal auch bewusst zu provozieren und zu schockieren.

Moderne Schmuck-Designer und Manufakturen hingegen machten seit den 1970er Jahren anspruchsvollen Serienschmuck im Einklang mit dem Formenrepertoire der Moderne. Die Akzeptanz durch die Schmuckträgerin war dabei eine Grundvoraussetzung. Einig waren sich bislang alle Gestalter des modernen Schmucks, Goldschmiedekünstler wie Designer. Sie wollten beweisen, dass Schmuck mehr sein kann als nur ein feudales Repräsentationsmittel. Und alle fühlten zu Beginn der Bewegung ein Unbehagen über die Beliebigkeit und inhaltliche Verarmung von industriellem wie handwerklichem Schmuck nach dem Zweiten Weltkrieg.

Der Neue Schmuck der Goldschmiedekünstler fand seit den 1960er Jahren in zahlreichen Ausstellungen und durch Museen Beachtung. Wegweisend waren die Ausstellungen Modern Jewellery, 1890–1961 in London sowie Gold + Silber, Schmuck + Gerät, von Albrecht Dürer bis zur Gegenwart 1971 in Nürnberg. An beiden Ausstellungen nahmen neben Gold- und Silberschmieden aus ganz Europa berühmte Maler und Bildhauer wie Hans Arp und Georges Braque teil. Alle Beteiligten waren überzeugt, an einer essentiellen Erneuerung der Goldschmiedekunst mitzuwirken.

Ende der 1980er Jahre erreichte die strenge künstlerische Ausrichtung mit Ausstellungen wie Schmuck – Zeichen am Körper in Linz und Ornamenta im Schmuckmuseum Pforzheim ihren Höhepunkt. Der englische Schmuckkenner Peter Dormer stellte 1987 in seinem Katalogbeitrag zur Ausstellung Joieria Europea Contemporània in Barcelona fest: »Die zeitgenössische Schmuckbewegung muss ihre augenblickliche Schwäche überwinden, den Konsumenten zu vergessen.« Dies zeigte in den 1990er Jahren Wirkung. Absolventen der Schmuckakademien produzierten verstärkt anspruchsvolles, aber tragbares serielles Schmuck-Design und stellten es auf Fachmessen vor.

Doch bereits zuvor gewann modernes Schmuck-Design speziell im deutschsprachigen Raum stetig an Bedeutung. Beide Entwicklungslinien, die des künstlerischen Unikat-Schmucks und die des modernen Schmuck-Designs, weisen Parallelen und Überschneidungen auf. Durch die Entwicklung des so genannten Autorenschmucks hat im letzten Jahrzehnt eine weitere Annäherung zwischen den Konzepten moderner Manufakturen und kleiner Schmuckateliers stattgefunden. Die »Verwandtschaft« wird auch in Schmuckgalerien deutlich, die beide Kategorien vertreten.

In den Arbeiten der frühen modernen Goldschmiede nach 1945 finden sich beide Möglichkeiten angelegt. Bei Gestaltern wie Sigurd Persson, Max Fröhlich und Friedrich Becker lassen sich bereits deutliche Elemente des späteren modernen Schmuck-Designs erkennen. Karl Schollmayer hat die prägenden Persönlichkeiten des Neuen Schmucks in seinem Buch von 1974 selbst zu Wort kommen lassen. Damit sind uns authentische Zeugnisse ihrer Gedanken gegenwärtig. Die folgende Auswahl ließe sich ergänzen. Doch von den vorgestellten Gold- und Silberschmieden, die als Lehrer an verschiedenen Schulen wirkten, lassen sich direkte Einflüsse bei vielen heutigen Schmuck-Designern nachweisen.

One-off jewellery as art and modern jewellery design

Developments in the New Jewellery split in the late 1970s into two main streams. On the one hand, there was art jewellery, where a real rebellion broke out against many traditional conventions. Artists in jewellery researched and worked along the same lines as exponents of the fine arts. They strove to make aesthetic statements with one-off pieces of jewellery. That meant radically questioning the assumptions underlying traditions, occasionally being deliberately provocative and even shocking.

Modern jewellery designers and factories, on the other hand, had been making ambitious mass-produced jewellery attuned to the repertory of forms launched by fashions. Their work was premised on acceptance of it by the women who were to wear it. Up to then, all designers of modern jewellery, goldsmiths and designers alike, were in agreement on wanting to prove that jewellery could be more than merely a feudal means of indulging in ostentation. And at the outset of the movement, they all felt qualms about the arbitrariness and impoverishment of content typical of both industrially manufactured and handmade jewellery following the Second World War.

»Ich schaffe mit Vorliebe einfache Dinge, einfach im Sinne
der Überschaubarkeit. Mich fasziniert das Plastische in
straffen Oberflächen, zum anderen die Struktur und Eigenart
des Materials.«

Max Fröhlich, 1974

»By preference I make simple things, simple in the sense
that they can be grasped at once. I am fascinated by the
sculptural in taut surfaces, on the other hand, by the texture
and properties of the material.«

Max Fröhlich, 1974

The New Jewellery by the artisan goldsmiths attracted attention from
the 1960s at numerous exhibitions and from museums. The exhibitions Modern Jewellery, 1890–1961 in London and Gold + Silber, Schmuck + Gerät, von
Albrecht Dürer bis zur Gegenwart (1971) in Nuremberg were groundbreaking events. Apart from goldsmiths and silversmiths from all over Europe,
celebrated painters and sculptors, including Hans Arp and Georges Braque
participated in both those seminal shows. Everyone involved was convinced
that they had been part and parcel of a vital renewal of goldsmithing as an
art. The late 1980s saw the strictly artistic trend in jewellery-making attain
its zenith in exhibitions such as Schmuck – Zeichen am Körper in Linz and
Ornamenta at the Pforzheim Jewellery Museum. In 1987 the English jewellery expert Peter Dormer concluded in his essay in the catalogue accompanying the exhibition Joieria Europea Contemporània in Barcelona that the
contemporary jewellery movement would have to overcome the momentary
weakness of ignoring the consumer. The comment took hold by the 1990s.
Graduates of jewellery-making academies were producing ambitious but
also wearable designer jewellery for mass production and exhibiting it at
specialist trade fairs.

However, even before that the importance of modern designer jewellery grew steadily, particularly in the German-speaking countries. The two
lines of development, one-off art jewellery and modern designer jewellery,
reveal parallels and overlapping tendencies. Through the development of
what is now known as auteur jewellery, a third approach to jewellery has
emerged midway between the concepts of modern manufactured jewellery
and small jewellery studios in the past decade. The »relationship« between
them also becomes apparent in jewellery galleries representing both cate-
gories.

Both possibilities are inherent in the work produced by early modern
goldsmiths after 1945. Designers such as Sigurd Persson, Max Fröhlich and
Friedrich Becker already clearly reveal elements which would later be integral to modern designer jewellery. In his 1947 book, Karl Schollmayer let the
designers who shaped the New Jewellery speak for themselves so that their
thinking is authentically before us. More names could be added to the following selection. However, influence on many current jewellery designers
can be traced directly to the goldsmiths and silversmiths who made an
impact by teaching at various schools.

Max Fröhlich,
ein Schweizer Vordenker

Geboren 1908 im Kanton Glarus besuchte der Schweizer von 1923 bis
1925 die École des Arts Industriels Genf und von 1925 bis 1928 die Kunstgewerbeschule Zürich. Bis Ende der 1930er Jahre war er vornehmlich als Silberschmied tätig. In dem traditionellen Handwerk erfüllte er bescheiden

1971

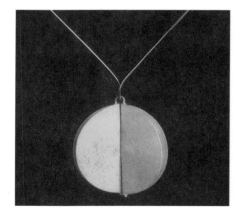

1970

1971   Halsschmuck, Armreif und Ringe, Max Fröhlich, Elektrodraht — Necklace,
       bracelet and rings, Max Fröhlich, electric wire

1970   Anhänger, Max Fröhlich, Gold, zweiteilig — Pendant, Max Fröhlich, gold,
       two parts

und idealistisch Forderungen, wie sie vor allem am Bauhaus erhoben wurden. Sein sakrales Gerät für kleine protestantische Gemeinden sollte möglichst preiswert sein. »Dies schien mir stets eine lohnende Aufgabe«, betonte der Gestalter. Gerne verpflichtete er sich zu »äußerster Reduktion in den anzuwendenden Mitteln und Materialien…«. Dabei erfüllte er die »implicite gegebene Forderung, ein Optimum an formalem und künstlerischem Gehalt mitzugeben.«[5]

1945 wurde Max Fröhlich Lehrer und stellvertretender Direktor an der Kunstgewerbeschule Zürich. Das Wesen seiner Schmuckstücke, die bis Mitte der 1970er Jahre entstanden, erschließt sich in folgender Aussage: »Ich schaffe mit Vorliebe einfache Dinge, einfach im Sinne der Überschaubarkeit. Mich fasziniert das Plastische in straffen Oberflächen, zum anderen die Struktur und Eigenart des Materials.«[6] Was seine Materialauswahl im Schmuck anbelangt, schreibt Fröhlich: »Zum Gold, wie ich es heute verwende, kam ich spät. Lange Jahre konnte ich mich nicht vom Silber mit seinem herrlichen schmiegsamen Weiß lösen, das viel vom Mondlicht in sich hat. Auch schien mir Silber als wenig teueres Material für unsere Jugend erschwinglicher zu sein – nur fand ich nie einen Fabrikanten, der meine als Prototypen gedachten Schmuckmodelle in Serie herzustellen bereit gewesen wäre.«[7] So folgerte er im Jahre 1974: »Anscheinend ist Silber und sind meine Dinge nicht im Speziellen verkaufsinteressant genug – oder waren es seinerzeit noch nicht.«[8] Der Schweizer war ein sensibler Lehrer und Protagonist des modernen Schmuckdesigns. Manche seiner Arbeiten, die häufig von plastischen »Bewegungen« durchdrungen sind, erscheinen noch im 21. Jahrhundert aktuell.

Max Fröhlich, a Swiss pioneer

Born in the canton of Glarus in 1908, Max Fröhlich attended the École des Arts Industriels in Geneva (1923–1925) and the Zurich Kunstgewerbeschule (1925–1928). Until the late 1930s, he worked chiefly as a silversmith. In that traditional craft, he modestly and idealistically met the requirements called for at the Bauhaus especially. His liturgical vessels for small Protestant congregations were intended to be as reasonably priced as possible. »That always seemed to me to be a rewarding task,« stresses the designer. He was only too pleased to commit himself to »extreme economy in the means and materials to be used …« In upholding that ideal, he met the »demand made implicitly for providing a maximum of formal and artistic content.«[5]

In 1945 Max Fröhlich became both an instructor and deputy director at the Zurich Kunstgewerbeschule. The essence of the pieces of jewellery he continued to produce until the mid-1970s is summed up in the following statement: »By preference I make simple things, simple in the sense that they can be grasped at once. I am fascinated by the sculptural in taut surfaces, on the other hand, by the texture and properties of the material.«[6] As far as his material of choice for making jewellery is concerned, Fröhlich has written: »I came late to gold as I use it today. For many long years I was unable to detach myself from silver with its wonderfully supple whiteness that has so much of the moonlight in it. Silver also seemed to me to be a material that was affordable for our young people because it wasn't all that expensive – but I never found a manufacturer who would have been willing to mass-produce my jewellery models, which were conceived as prototypes.«[7] Hence he concluded in 1974: »Apparently silver and my things in particular are not interesting enough from the marketing angle – or not yet at that time.«[8] The Swiss designer and silversmith was a sensitive teacher and an advocate of modern design in jewellery. Many of his works, which are often informed by sculptural »movements,« still look cutting-edge in the 21st century.

Sigurd Persson, der erste Schmuckdesigner

Über den Schweden schreibt Karl Schollmayer im Buch »Neuer Schmuck«: »Perssons Sonderstellung unter den Klassikern erweist sich auf den ersten Blick. Er ist nicht nur unter diesen, sondern wohl überhaupt – der erste Schmuck-Designer.«[9] 1914 in Hälsingborg geboren, studierte er nach der Gesellenprüfung 1937 an der Akademie der bildenden Künste in München bei den Professoren Schneider und Rickert. Danach besuchte er die Kunstfachschule in Stockholm und gründete 1942 sein Atelier in der schwedischen Hauptstadt. Auch von da pflegte er seine Beziehungen zur deutschen Schmuckszene. Perssons Schmuckarbeiten sind durch klare Formen gekennzeichnet, oft gemischt mit einer Prise Humor. Persson war, typisch für die Skandinavier jener Zeit, verliebt in Silber. Gold setzte er meist mit glatten, glänzenden Oberflächen ein. Wenn farbige Steine Anwendung fanden, dann in möglichst klaren Formen. Gerne arbeitete er auch mit Brillanten und Perlen.

Die durch Soziologen wie Georg Simmel im frühen 20. Jahrhundert formulierten Theorien über Schmuck boten ihm Anregungen »nicht bei ererbten Formen und Typen« haltzumachen.[10] Er entdeckte »die Freiheit und dass eigentlich alles möglich ist.«[11] Persson forderte jedoch, dass sich der Schmuckgestalter »demjenigen, der geschmückt werden soll oder geschmückt werden will, unterordnet.«[12] Er kritisiert und bedauert schon Anfang der 1970er Jahre die damals um sich greifende Tendenz, kleine Kunstwerke zu gestalten, die man sich als Bild um den Hals hängt oder auf dem Busen platziert und meinte: »Eine Blume hinter dem Ohr schmückt bedeutend besser als ein noch so intrikat gestaltetes Bild! Wir haben es ja mit dem Maßstab des menschlichen Körpers zu tun und mit den Abständen, die überbrückt werden sollen – rein konkret und auch geschlechtlich. Wenn Schmuck nicht dazu beiträgt, die körperlichen Vorzüge zu unterstreichen, nicht behilflich ist, schöner zu machen, dann ist er nur ein Ding – egal was, ein Miniaturgemälde, eine Miniaturplastik.« Sigurd Persson wollte Schmuck so gestalten, »dass er ein bereicherndes Moment im menschlichen Zusammensein« wird.[13]

Karl Schollmayer verglich die Formensprache Perssons mit Max Bill, die im Rationalen und Intellektuellen begründet sei, und fragte: »Ist das ein Negativum für Schmuck, für Neuen Schmuck, für Menschen des 20. Jahrhunderts, dem wissenschaftlichen Zeitalter der Industriegesellschaft?« Und seine Antwort lautete: »Sicher nicht! Dass Perssons Schmuck auch dann noch Schmuck bleibt, wo er sich anscheinend völlig konstruktiver Formen bedient, zeigt, dass er im Grunde den Zauber bejaht; nur verlegt er ihn nicht ins Transzendente, sucht ihn nicht im Spirituellen.«[14] Sigurd Persson entwickelte »überindividuelle« Ringreihen, bei denen eine Grundform variiert wurde. Damit bot er dem »Schmuckwilligen« eine breite Basis für die eigene Entscheidung. Ein Thema, das heute etwas schmunzeln lässt, waren Perssons Experimente, Schmuck am Körper als Signal, Blinkzeichen oder Blickpunkt anzubringen, ohne sich an »ererbte Formen und Typen« zu halten. Die Suche unter »Einbeziehen der psychologischen Hintergründe«[15] führte zu so originellen Objekten wie etwa einem Beinreif im Jahre 1966, der wie ein Außenspiegel für weibliche Fußgänger aussieht.

1963

Sigurd Persson, the first jewellery designer

In his book Neuer Schmuck, Karl Schollmayer wrote as follows on the Swedish designer: »Persson's special status among the classics is obvious at first glance. He is not just the first jewellery designer from among his peers – but probably the first one altogether.«[9] Born in Helsingborg in 1914, he studied at the Munich Fine Arts Academy under Professors Schneider and Rickert after taking his journeyman's certificate in 1937. He subsequently attended the Konstfackskolan in Stockholm and founded a studio of his own in the Swedish capital in 1942. Even from there he forged ties to the German jewellery scene of his day and maintained them. Persson's work in jewellery is distinguished by clarity of form, often leavened with a touch of humour. Typically of the Scandinavians of his day, Persson was in love with silver. His work in gold featured smooth, glossy surfaces. When he used coloured stones, he chose forms that were as clear as possible although he also enjoyed working with diamonds and pearls.

The theories on jewellery formulated in the early 20th century by sociologists such as Georg Simmel encouraged Persson »not to stop at inherited forms and types«.[10] He discovered »freedom and that everything was actually possible.«[11] However, Persson called for the jewellery designer »to subordinate himself to the person who is to be adorned or wants to be adorned.«[12] By the early 1970s, he criticised and deplored the tendency prevailing at the time to design little works of art, which could be hung as a picture about the

1962

1965

neck or placed on the bosom, saying: »A flower placed behind the ear adorns significantly better than a picture, no matter how intricately designed! After all, we are concerned with the proportions of the human body and with distances that have to be bridged – both specifically and sexually. If jewellery doesn't contribute to underscoring physical advantages, if it isn't beneficial in making more beautiful, then it's just a thing – no matter what, a miniature painting, a miniature sculpture.« Sigurd Persson wanted to design jewellery so »that it becomes an enriching aspect of human existence.«[13]

Karl Schollmayer compared Persson's language of forms with that of Max Bill because it was grounded in the rational and intellectual and asked: »Is that negative for jewellery, for the New Jewellery, for 20th-century people, the scientific age of industrial society?« And his answer reads: »Certainly not! That Persson's jewellery still remains jewellery even when he is apparently using entirely Constructivist forms shows that he is basically saying yes to enchantment; it's just that he doesn't move it to the transcendental plane, is not seeking it in the spiritual.«[14] Sigurd Persson developed »supra-individual« ring series, in which a basic form was varied. Thus he provided those »willing to adorn themselves« with a broad basis for taking their own decisions. Persson's experiments with putting jewellery on the body as a signal, a flashing light or eye-catcher without having to uphold »inherited forms and types« are a subject that today elicits a smile at best. His striving to »incorporate the psychological backgrounds«[15] led to original objects, such as a leg bangle he launched in 1966, which looks like a wing mirror for female pedestrians.

Mario Pinton,
Schmuckpoesie aus Italien

Mario Pinton, 1919 in Padua geboren, wurde als Gold- und Silberschmied sowie als Bildhauer an verschiedenen italienischen Kunstakademien ausgebildet. Ab 1944 war er Lehrer für Metallkunst und Schmuck am Istituto Statale »Pietro Selvatico« di Padova und von 1969 bis 1976 dessen Direktor. Seine neuen Ideen begründeten den internationalen Ruf und den lang anhaltenden Einfluss der »Schule von Padua« auf die Schmuckkunst der Nachkriegszeit. Pinton ist immer ein individueller Goldschmied und Künstler geblieben. Auch in Italien entwickelte sich nach 1945 ein strenger Gegensatz zwischen der Schmuckindustrie und künstlerisch gebildeten Goldschmieden. Doch wurde in Italien kaum serielles Schmuck-Design in der Tradition der Moderne wie in Skandinavien und später in Deutschland entwickelt.

Karl Schollmayer stellte 1974 Mario Pinton auf gleicher Stufe mit Sigurd Persson und Max Fröhlich als Klassiker des Neuen Schmucks vor. Wie andere große Schmuckgestalter jener Zeit, etwa seine Landsleute Bruno Martinazzi und Arnaldo Pomodoro, war Pinton gleichzeitig Goldschmied und Bildhauer. Doch verzichtete er weitgehend darauf, verkleinerte Skulpturen

1963   Armreif, Sigurd Persson, Stockholm, Gold, Rauchquarz — Bangle, Sigurd Persson, Stockholm, gold, smoky quartz. Schmuckmuseum Pforzheim

1962   Armschmuck, Sigurd Persson, Stockholm, Silber, Gold — Bangle, Sigurd Persson, Stockholm, silver, gold. Tillhör Nationalmuseum, Stockholm

1965   Halsschmuck, Sigurd Persson, Stockholm, Silber, Rosenquarz, Calcedon — Necklace, Sigurd Persson, Stockholm, silver, rose quartz, crysoprase

>»Es ist besser, nur zwei Steine von verschiedener Größe einander gegenüber zu stellen, um so eine Steigerung ihrer Wirkung durch Größe und Kostbarkeit zu erreichen.«
>
> Mario Pinton, 1974

>»It's better to confront just two stones of different size in order to thus enhance the impact they make through their size and exquisiteness.«
>
> Mario Pinton, 1974

zu machen. Schollmayer bemerkte zu Pintons Arbeiten: »Sein Schmuck ist immer zart, feingliedrig, von geringsten Ausmaßen und sensibelsten Proportionen.«[16] Mario Pinton achtete sorgsam auf das richtige Maß zwischen Mensch und Schmuck. Er schätzte den Wert der Proportion und das Maß des verwendeten Materials. Er war der Ansicht, dass so kostbare Werkstoffe wie Gold und Edelsteine auf die kleinstmögliche Menge beschränkt werden sollten, »um eben die Kostbarkeit zu unterstreichen.«[17] Zum Einsatz von Edelsteinen sagt der Klassiker der modernen Schmuckkunst aus Italien: »Es ist besser, nur zwei Steine von verschiedener Größe einander gegenüber zu stellen, um so eine Steigerung ihrer Wirkung durch Größe und Kostbarkeit zu erreichen.«[18] Pinton glaubte, dass je leichter und feiner ein Schmuckstück gearbeitet sei, die poetische Wirkung sich erhöhe. Dies war eine deutliche Absage an den üppigen Materialeinsatz und Besatz mit Edelsteinen, wie er bei den Juwelieren und Traditionalisten des Art Déco üblich war. Der sensible Umgang mit kostbarer Materie, die Handwerkskunst und das Kreative waren für ihn deutlich wichtiger als Karatzahlen.

Mario Pinton,
poetic jewellery from Italy

Born in Padua in 1919, Mario Pinton trained as a goldsmith and silversmith as well as a sculptor at various Italian art academies. From 1944 he taught metalworking and jewellery-making at the Istituto Statale Pietro Selvatico di Padova and was director of that institute from 1969 until 1976. His new ideas founded its international reputation and shored up the long-lasting influence exerted by the »Padua School« on post-war art jewellery. As a goldsmith, Pinton remained an individualist and artist. In Italy, too, a seemingly unbridgeable gulf yawned between the jewellery industry and goldsmiths trained as artists after 1945. However, designer jewellery for industrial production in the Modernist tradition hardly developed at all in Italy as it did in Scandinavia and later also in Germany.

In 1974, Karl Schollmayer ranked Mario Pinton on a level with Sigurd Persson and Max Fröhlich as a classic exponent of the New Jewellery. Like other great jewellery-designers of the time, including his compatriots Bruno Martinazzi and Arnaldo Pomodoro, Pinton was by training and inclination both a goldsmith and a sculptor. Yet he largely eschewed the production of sculpture on a miniature scale. Schollmayer remarked on Pinton's work: »His jewellery is always delicate, fine, on the smallest possible scale and most sensitively proportioned.«[16] Mario Pinton scrupulously kept the right proportion between the wearer and jewellery. He appreciated the value of proportion and the scale appropriate to the material he used. He was of the opinion that so costly materials as gold and precious stones should be limited to the smallest possible quantities »to underscore that very preciousness.«[17] On the use of gemstones, the classic exponent of modern art jew-

1982

c. 1962

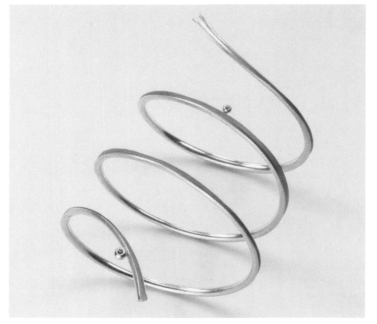

1976

1982   Ring, Mario Pinton, Padua, Gold — Ring, Mario Pinton, Padua, gold. Schmuckmuseum Pforzheim

c. 1962   Brosche, Mario Pinton, Padua, Gold — Brooch, Mario Pinton, Padua, gold

1976   Armschmuck, Mario Pinton, Padua, Gold, Rubine — Bangle, Mario Pinton, Padua, gold, rubies. Schmuckmuseum Pforzheim

ellery in Italy has said: »It's better to confront just two stones of different size in order to thus enhance the impact they make through their size and exquisiteness.«[18] Pinton believed that working a piece of jewellery to be as light and as fine as possible heightened the poetic effect achieved with it. This approach represented a clear rejection of the lavish use of materials and the heavy-handed approach to setting jewellery with precious stones which was the usual practice with jewellers and Art Déco traditionalists. Sensitive handling of exquisite materials, craftsmanship and creativity were far more important to Pinton than weight in carats.

Friedrich Becker,
Konstruktionen und Kinetik

Geboren wurde Friedrich Becker 1922 im Sauerland. Nach einer Lehre als Maschinenbauer studierte er Luftfahrttechnik und leistete seinen Militärdienst im Zweiten Weltkrieg bei der Luftwaffe. Verwundet und unter äußerst glücklichen Umständen heimgekehrt, lernte er das Goldschmiedehandwerk. Der Grund war seine Kriegsverletzung, die ihm einen sitzenden Beruf nahe legte. Friedrich Becker machte seine Meisterprüfung und studierte von 1949 bis 1951 bei Professor Karl Schollmayer, der zu dieser Zeit noch an der Werkkunstschule in Düsseldorf lehrte. 1973 wurde er dort selbst Professor. Er erntete nicht nur als Gold- und Silberschmied höchste Ehrungen, sondern auch für seine kinetischen Objekte und sein bildhauerisches Werk.

Aus seiner Begeisterung für technische Lösungen entstanden zahlreiche Schmuckformen, die auf dem Prinzip von Spannung beruhten. Friedrich Becker spannte auswechselbare Kugeln in Armreife ein oder Edelsteine in Ringe, Anhänger und Armschmuck. Der erste Armreif mit einem auswechselbaren Schmuckteil, einer Kugel, stammt aus dem Jahr 1952. So wurde Becker zum Erfinder für ganz neue Fassungen und einen neuen Umgang mit dem Edelmetall. Damit eröffnete er ein ganz neues Feld für Generationen von Schmuck-Designern. Er wies aber auch auf Möglichkeiten für variablen Schmuck hin. Gleichzeitig zeigte er Beziehungen von Schmuck zum Konstruktivismus in der Bildenden Kunst auf.

Ganz nebenbei erwies sich Friedrich Becker auch als Pionier für einen neuen Edelsteinschliff. Für seine Schmuckkonstruktionen ließ er in Idar-Oberstein Zylinder, Quader, Kugeln, Spindeln oder prismatische Rechtecke schleifen. Zwar waren einige dieser Formen schon im Art Déco aufgetaucht, doch diese waren nie so systematisch eingesetzt worden. Ganz bewusst verwendete Becker auch synthetische Edelsteine. Seine Auffassung, dem Funktionalismus der Moderne entsprechend, wird in folgender Aussage deutlich: »Kein Bogen, keine Kante soll Dekor sein, sondern einem sinnvollen Tun dienen. Nennen Sie diese Dinge ruhig Konstruktionen. Sie sollen nicht geschmückte Formen an sich sein, sondern dann schmücken, wenn sie getragen werden.«[19] Neben den vielen modernen Formen entwickelte Friedrich

Becker auch das Spielerische im Schmuck. Das sinnliche Spiel des Objekts am Körper befreit Schmuck von jeglicher Repräsentanz.

Selbst für die Erneuerung der modernen Schmuckmanufaktur erwies sich Friedrich Becker als Vordenker. In seiner Werkstatt in Düsseldorf-Oberkassel demonstrierte er den Einsatz von Maschinen wie Drehautomaten und Fräsen für die Schmuckfertigung. Maschinen, wie sie Becker benutzte, sind heute, CNC-gesteuert, in jeder modernen Schmuckmanufaktur ein Standard. Sie ergänzen das Handwerk da, wo es sinnvoll ist. Der Einsatz von moderner Technologie macht eine Qualität möglich, die mit traditionellen Werkzeugen und Goldschmiedetechniken nicht erreichbar wäre.

Eine ganze Reihe von Becker-Schülern wirkte an der Verbreitung von modernem Serienschmuck mit. Barbara Schulte-Hengesbach, Düsseldorf, begann sofort nach ihrem Studium Serien herzustellen, »weil man von künstlerischen Unikaten nicht leben konnte.« Mit einer Schmuckgalerie leistete sie in Düsseldorf Pionierarbeit für modernen Schmuck. Hans-Hermann Lingenbrink gründete 1983 die Firma Pur in Nettetal und entwickelt seitdem anspruchsvollen Serienschmuck. Günter Wermekes, der in der Werkstatt bei Friedrich Becker gelernt hat, überzeugt seit 1990 mit minimalistischem Schmuck aus Edelstahl mit Diamanten. Die Becker-Schülerin Sabine Brandenburg-Frank zählt zu den namhaften ersten deutschen Schmuck-Designerinnen.

Friedrich Becker,
Constructivism and Kinetics

Friedrich Becker was born in the Sauerland in 1922. After serving an apprenticeship in mechanical engineering, he studied aeronautics and served in the Luftwaffe during the Second World War. Wounded and extremely fortunate in being able to return home, he learned goldsmithing. The reason for this change was his war wound, which made it advisable for him to exercise a sedentary profession. Friedrich Becker took his master craftsman's certificate and studied from 1949 until 1951 under Professor Karl Schollmayer, who at that time was still teaching at the Werkkunstschule in Düsseldorf. In 1973 Friedrich Becker became a professor there himself. He was showered with top awards not just as a goldsmith and silversmith but also for his kinetic objects and his sculpture.

His enthusiasm for technical solutions led to numerous jewellery forms based on the tension principle. Friedrich Becker used tension to hold exchangeable balls in arm bangles and other arm jewellery as well as gemstones in rings and pendants. His first bangle with an exchangeable component, a ball, dates from 1952. Becker became the inventor of entirely new settings and a new way of dealing with noble metals. He also demonstrated the possibilities for variable jewellery. At the same time he pointed out the links between jewellery and Constructivism in fine art.

»Kein Bogen, keine Kante soll Dekor sein, sondern einem sinnvollen Tun dienen. Nennen Sie diese Dinge ruhig Konstruktionen. Sie sollen nicht geschmückte Formen an sich sein, sondern dann schmücken, wenn sie getragen werden.«

Friedrich Becker, 1974

»No arc, no edge is to be decorative but must serve a meaningful action. Go ahead and call these things construction. They are not meant to be adorned forms as such but to adorn when they are worn.«

Friedrich Becker, 1974

On the side, Friedrich Becker also showed himself to be a pioneering exponent of new cuts for gemstones. He had cylinders, cubes, spheres, spindles and prismatic rectangles cut in Idar-Oberstein for his jewellery constructions. Some of those forms had already surfaced in Art Déco but had never been used so systematically. Moreover, Becker made deliberate use of synthetic gemstones. His view of jewellery, in line with Modernist functionalism, is made clear in the following statement: »No arc, no edge is to be decorative but must serve a meaningful action. Go ahead and call these things construction. They are not meant to be adorned forms as such but to adorn when they are worn.«[19] Alongside the many modern forms he developed, Friedrich Becker also capitalised on the playful side of jewellery. The sensual play of the object on the body is what liberates jewellery from all ostentation. Friedrich Becker also turned out to be a pioneering renewer in modern jewellery manufacturing. At his workshop in Düsseldorf-Oberkassel, he demonstrated the use of machines such as automatic lathes and milling machines in jewellery-making. Machines of the kind Becker once used but now operated by computer numerical control (CNC) are now standard equipment in every modern jewellery factory. They supplement crafting by hand wherever it makes sense to do so. The use of modern technology makes possible a quality that could not have been attained with the tools and techniques traditional to goldsmithing.

Quite a few pupils of Becker have been active in ensuring the spread of modern mass-produced jewellery. Immediately after finishing her studies, Barbara Schulte-Hengesbach in Düsseldorf began to make jewellery for mass production »because you couldn't live on one-off pieces of art jewellery.« With her jewellery gallery in Düsseldorf, she is doing pioneering work for modern jewellery. In 1983, Hans-Hermann Lingenbrinck founded Pur, a firm in Nettetal, where he has been developing quality mass-produced jewellery ever since. Günter Wermekes, who trained in Friedrich Becker's workshop, has been producing stunning Minimalist stainless steel and diamond jewellery since 1990. Another pupil of Becker, Sabine Brandenburg-Frank, is one of the big names in the first wave of women jewellery designers in Germany.

Reinhold Reiling,
Erzählkunst und Minimalismus

Die Kunst- und Werkschule in Pforzheim war für den neuen Schmuck nach dem Zweiten Weltkrieg eine wichtige Institution. Mitten in der Goldstadt Pforzheim hätte man sich hier den Ort vorstellen können für einen regen Austausch zwischen der prosperierenden Schmuckindustrie und den künstlerisch ausgebildeten Schmuckgestaltern. Doch nirgends sonst zeigten sich die Widersprüche zwischen dem ambitionierten Neuen Schmuck und der traditionellen Industrie deutlicher als in der Schmuckstadt selbst. Dennoch hatten sowohl Reinhold Reiling wie auch Klaus Ullrich einen starken Einfluss

1959

1982

1962–1963

1997

auf das moderne Schmuckdesign. Über den 1922 in Ersingen bei Pforzheim geborenen Reiling schrieb Schollmayer: »Zu seinem Glück kam er nicht aus einer traditionsbelasteten Fabrikantenfamilie und musste sich selbst seinen Weg suchen. Er führte zunächst in die Badische Kunstgewerbeschule, wo er, wieder zu seinem Glück, auf Theodor Wende traf, der sein Lehrer wurde und ihm die Richtung wies: die Gestaltung eines Schmucks von Grunde auf aus einer Idee zu entwickeln. Das war etwas anderes als die Ideen anderer zu übernehmen, sie nach den Belangen eines auf bestimmte Kundschaft eingestellten Betriebs abzuwandeln und formal zu variieren, bis es keine Schwierigkeiten wegen der Urheberschaft mehr geben konnte.«[20]

Reilings Schmuckschaffen ist durch zwei Phasen bestimmt. Bis etwa 1970 gestaltete er phantasievolle Schmuckstücke mit figurativen Motiven. Er »formulierte in Metall«, wie es ein Maler mit Farbe auf der Leinwand macht. Auf seinen Stücken tauchten abstrahierte Köpfe, Bäumchen und organische Elemente auf. Eine Zeit lang integrierte Reiling Gesichter in Form von gerasterten Klischees in Broschen und Anhänger. Zudem komponierte der Pforzheimer Schmuckprofessor in dieser Schaffensphase auch mit Hilfe von Diamanten, Edelsteincabochons und »lebendigen« Goldelementen poesievolle Schmuckstücke. Ende der 1960er Jahre waren seine »Bildflächen«, die auch in Armreifen und Ringen auftauchten, häufig von geometrischen Linienrastern durchzogen.

Mit reduzierten klaren Formen wurde Reiling in der darauf folgenden Schaffensphase ab etwa 1977 zu einem der ersten Minimalisten im deutschen Schmuck. Wie kein anderer Hochschullehrer in Pforzheim hatte er eine Vorbildfunktion für das moderne Schmuck-Design in Deutschland. Reiling bekannte sich durch seine Entwürfe, vor allem für die Pforzheimer Schmuckmarke »art-design«, auch klar zum seriellen Schmuck.

Reinhold Reiling,
narrative art and Minimalism

The Kunst- und Werkschule in Pforzheim was an important institution for the New Jewellery after the Second World War. At the heart of Pforzheim, the golden city, this might conceivably have been just the place for a lively exchange of ideas between the prospering jewellery industry and artistically trained jewellery designers. However, nowhere else have the contradictions between the ambitious New Jewellery and the traditional industry shown up more clearly than in the city of jewellery itself. Still, both Reinhold Reiling (born in Ersingen near Pforzheim) and Klaus Ullrich exerted a strong influence on modern jewellery design. Schollmayer has written on Reiling: »Fortunately, he did not come from an industrial family burdened with tradition so he had to seek his own way. It led him first to the Badische Kunstgewerbeschule, where he was again fortunate in encountering Theodor Wende, who became his teacher and pointed him in the right direction: designing a

piece of jewellery on the basic principle of developing it out of an idea. That
was something different to taking over others' ideas, modifying them to
suit the needs of a business oriented to the concerns of a specific clientele
and varying them just enough formally so that there could be no copyright
difficulties.«[20]

Reiling's career as a jewellery-maker falls into two distinct phases.
Until about 1970 he designed imaginative pieces with figurative motifs. He
»formulated in metal« as a painter does with paint on canvas. Abstract but
still recognisable heads, trees and organic elements surfaced on his pieces.
For a while Reiling integrated faces in the form of raster clichés into brooches
and pendants. In addition, the Pforzheim professor for jewellery composed
poetic pieces in this phase of his œuvre using diamonds, cabochon-cut precious stones and »living« gold elements. By the late 1960s, his »picture surfaces,« which also featured in bangles and rings, were often criss-crossed by
geometric grids of lines.

In the phase that followed from about 1977, Reiling became one of
the first Minimalists in the German jewellery scene, drawing on clear, reductivist forms. More than any other teacher in Pforzheim, he was a paramount
role model for modern designer jewellery in Germany. Reiling also unequivocally demonstrated his commitment to industrially produced jewellery with
the designs he created, mainly for the Pforzheim jewellery label art-design.

Klaus Ullrich, Oberflächen und Strukturen

Klaus Ullrich, 1927 in Sensburg in Ostpreußen geboren, war prägend
für eine Richtung, die im Schmuck-Design der 1970er Jahren weit über die
Grenzen Deutschlands hinaus Bedeutung erlangte: die strukturierten Oberflächen. Ullrich war Gold- und Silberschmiedemeister. Zwischen 1952 und
1955 studierte er an der Werkkunstschule in Düsseldorf bei Professor
Schollmayer, bevor er 1957 an die Kunst- und Werkschule nach Pforzheim
berufen wurde. Durch eine Schweißtechnik gab er den Oberflächen seiner
Schmuckstücke eine raue, organische Oberfläche. »Ich schweiße viel, weil
ich die damit mögliche Spontaneität liebe«,[21] sagte Ullrich über diese Vorliebe. Strukturierte Goldoberflächen erreichte er auch durch feine Goldla-
mellen, die, hochkant gestellt, dem Gold Tiefe und Lebendigkeit verliehen.
Ullrich verwendete auch Perlen oder kleine Rohkristalle. Mitte der 1970er
Jahre wandte er sich verstärkt klaren Formen zu. Sein Schmuck sollte eine
Synthese aus »zeitgemäßer Gestaltung und Tragbarkeit« sein, sagte Ullrich.
Er erkannte, dass ohne das Verständnis der Träger moderner Schmuck provozierend wirkt. Für viele Goldschmiede und Schmuck-Designer, die in Pforz-
heim studiert haben, war Klaus Ullrich ein wichtiges Vorbild.

1967

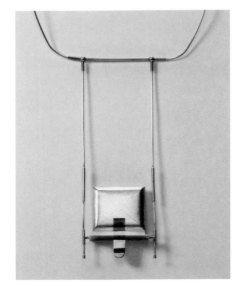

1977

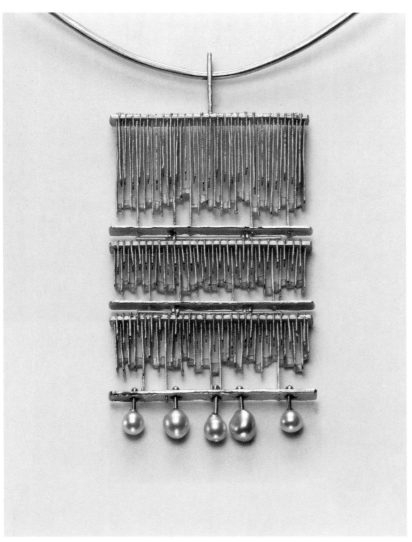

1963

Klaus Ullrich, surfaces and textures

Born in Sensburg, East Prussia, in 1927, Klaus Ullrich shaped a trend that would attain significance far beyond the borders of Germany in 1970s jewellery design: textured surfaces. Ullrich was a master goldsmith and silversmith. Between 1952 and 1955 he studied under Professor Schollmayer at the Werkkunstschule in Düsseldorf before taking up an appointment at the Kunst- und Werkschule in Pforzheim in 1957. Using welding techniques, he gave the surfaces of his pieces of jewellery a raw, organic surface texture. »I do a lot of welding because I love the spontaneity it makes possible,«[21] was Ullrich's explanation for his predilection for welding. He also created textured gold surfaces by using fine gold lamellae, which, placed at right angles to the surface, lent the gold depth and a lively finish. Ullrich also used pearls and small rough crystals. In the mid-1970s, he turned increasingly to clear-cut forms. His jewellery was to be a synthesis of »contemporary design and wearability,« declared Ullrich. He realised that, without the wearer's acceptance, modern jewellery was merely a provocation. Klaus Ullrich was an important role model for many goldsmiths and jewellery designers who studied in Pforzheim.

Hermann Jünger, Einheit von Kopf und Hand

Die verlorene Lebendigkeit von Goldschmiedearbeiten der Romanik wollte Hermann Jünger in der Moderne wieder gewinnen, das war sein kulturelles und künstlerisches Anliegen. 1928 in Hanau geboren, lernte er von 1947 bis 1949 an der dortigen Zeichenakademie das Silberschmieden. Von 1953 bis 1956 studierte er bei Professor Rickert an der Akademie der Bildenden Künste in München. Von 1972 bis 1992 war er hier als Professor für die Schmuckklasse zuständig. Hermann Jünger war ein sanfter Mahner, der den Verlust sah, der aus der Trennung von Kopf und Hand resultierte. Seine Versuche, jungen Leuten, die sich schmücken wollten, eine bessere Alternative als Modeschmuck anzubieten, waren allerdings erfolglos. Hermann Jünger war ein Goldschmied und Künstler, aber er war kein Designer.

Dennoch kamen neben zahlreichen Schmuckkünstlern der Gegenwart auch viele namhafte Schmuck-Designer aus seiner Klasse an der Münchner Kunstakademie. Zum Beispiel Peter Eiber, sieben Jahre lang Designchef in der Schmuckmanufaktur Niessing, Matthias Mönnich, der für Niessing den berühmten Ring Iris entwickelte, und Angela Hübel aus München. Die Bedeutung von Hermann Jünger für das moderne serielle Schmuckdesign in Deutschland liegt darin, dass er seinen Studenten Verantwortung, Freiheit und Intensität vorgelebt hat.

Alle Wegbereiter des modernen Schmucks nach 1945 haben den Traum vom guten Schmuck und von Schmuck als Kunst verfolgt. Dies war jedoch für die Mehrzahl ihrer Studenten schon in den 1970er Jahren nicht mehr möglich. Erstens waren es schlicht und einfach zu viele, als dass sie noch an Akademien wie ihre Lehrer Anstellungen finden konnten. In der Industrie gab es außer Niessing zu dieser Zeit so gut wie keine Firmen, die Schmuck-Designer aufnahmen. So entstand der moderne serielle Schmuck mit seiner Konzentration in Deutschland nicht zuletzt aus dem Zwang, wirtschaftlich zu überleben.

Hermann Jünger,
the unity of head and hand

Hermann Jünger wanted to restore the lost liveliness of Romanesque goldsmithing to Modernism. That was his chief cultural and aesthetic concern. Born in Hanau in 1928, he studied silversmithing at the Hanau Zeichenakademie (1947–1949). From 1953 until 1956 he studied under Professor Rickert at the Munich Fine Arts Academy, where he was the professor for the jewellery class from 1972 until 1992. Hermann Jünger uttered gentle warnings on what he saw as the loss that resulted from separating the head from the hand. His attempts to offer young people who wanted to wear jewellery a better alternative to costume jewellery, were, however, doomed to failure. Hermann Jünger was both a goldsmith and an artist but he was not a designer.

Nevertheless, many distinguished artists in contemporary jewellery came from Jünger's class at the Munich Art Academy. Their numbers included Peter Eiber, who for seven years was head of design at the Niessing jewellery factory; Matthias Mönnich, who designed the celebrated *Iris* ring for Niessing, and Angela Hübel from Munich. Hermann Jünger's importance for modern industrially manufactured designer jewellery in Germany lies in the circumstance that he consistently exemplified responsibility, freedom and intensity for his students.

All pioneers of modern jewellery after 1945 pursued the dream of good jewellery and jewellery as art. By the 1970s, however, that was no longer possible for most of their students. First of all, there were simply too many of them for the number of posts available at academies where their teachers had enjoyed academic tenure. In industry at that time there were hardly any firms except for Niessing that hired jewellery designers. Hence modern manufactured jewellery was concentrated in Germany, not least due to its designers' need to survive financially.

Emmy van Leersum und Gijs Bakker,
De Stijl und Popkultur

Emmy van Leersum, 1930–1984, und ihr Lebensgefährte Gijs Bakker, geboren 1942, waren ab Mitte der 1960er Jahre die führenden Gestalter der Schmuckerneuerung in Holland. Beide waren ausgebildete Goldschmiede und

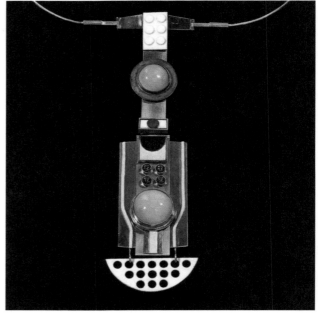

1970

1995

1970 Halsschmuck, Hermann Jünger, München, Edelstahl, Gold, Mondsteine, Blutsteine, Achat — Necklace, Hermann Jünger, Munich, stainless steel, gold, moonstones, ruddles, agate

1995 Brosche, Hermann Jünger, Gold — Brooch, Hermann Jünger, gold. Schmuckmuseum Pforzheim

studierten am Instituut voor Kunstnijverheidsonderwijs in Amsterdam, der heutigen Rietveld Academie. 1963 wechselten sie gemeinsam an die Konst-fack Skolan in Stockholm. Dazu bemerkt der holländische Kunstkritiker Gert Staal: »Verglichen mit den erstickenden Niederlanden gab es hier Raum und Atem, dennoch wurde das Versprechen von einer neuen Welt auch dort – jedenfalls im Design – nicht völlig erfüllt.« Gijs Bakker selbst erklärte zu dem Studienaufenthalt in Schweden: »Die skandinavische Klarheit, die wir so be-wunderten, der Schmuck von Koryphäen wie Sigurd Persson, mit denen sie ein ganzes Stockwerk des schwedischen Kaufhauses Enko füllten, das lockte einen nach Stockholm. Aber an Ort und Stelle zeigte sich das Design als Gan-zes viel weniger spektakulär. Im Grund blieb es bei den Vitrinen im Stadt-park, wo der Schmuck die typische Verschmelzung zwischen Kunstgewerbe und Design zeigte, die ihn berühmt gemacht hatte. Aber ich sah auf die Dauer vor allem die organischen Formen, gegen die wir uns in den Niederlanden bereits wehrten.«[22]

1966 präsentierten Emmy van Leersum und Gijs Bakker in der Galerie Swart und 1967 im Stedelijk Museum in Amsterdam ihren neuen Schmuck. Der englische Kenner der modernen Schmuckkunst, Ralph Turner, bemerk-te 1976 zu den strengen, großdimensionierten Schmuckobjekten in Alumi-nium: »Sie wählten dieses Material statt der traditionellen Metalle Silber und Gold hauptsächlich als Reaktion auf das Prahlerische im Schmuck.«[23] Dies ist aber nur die halbe Wahrheit. Gert Staal spricht in seinem Beitrag in »Art Aurea« 1989 von »unmenschlich steilen Halskragen« und von »visueller Agression«. Dies passte in die Zeit der späten 1960er Jahre, zur Pop-Kultur und dem Aufbegehren der Jugend gegen das Establishment. Es war die bis dahin radikalste Ablehnung des Dekorativen im traditionellen Schmuck. 1967 stellte Emmy van Leersum ihren berühmten Ofenrohr-Schmuck vor. In diesem wie in anderen Arbeiten war das Material Aluminium eher eine Not-lösung. Van Leersum und Bakker wollten jeden Eindruck von Handwerklich-keit vermeiden. Auch machten die großflächigen Stücke nur in einem sehr leichten Material als tragbare Schmuckobjekte Sinn. Die Arbeiten zeigten Parallelen zur Minimal Art. Ihr Ursprung lag jedoch weniger in der amerika-nischen Kunstbewegung als vielmehr in der Tradition der holländischen De Stijl-Gruppe, die 1917 von Malern wie Piet Mondrian und Architekten wie Gerrit Rietveld gegründet worden war. Dafür spricht allein die Farbigkeit, die van Leersum und Bakker einsetzten. Ihre frühen »Objects to wear« waren für die moderne Schmuck-Kunst wie für das Schmuck-Design so wichtig, weil sie nach dem Zweiten Weltkrieg eine grundsätzliche Diskussion über das Medium Schmuck auslösten. Das holländische Gestalterpaar setzte geome-trische Linien und Körper in Bezug zu der organischen Form des Körpers. Ihr Schmuck, für den sie auch die passenden Kleider entwarfen, war eine Ver-änderung der Körperkontur, ein formaler Kontrapunkt zum bewegten, sich permanent verändernden Ausdruck des Menschen.

Gijs Bakker, der in Holland 1993 mit »Droog Design« ein viel beach-tetes Designbüro gründete, blieb immer ein geistreicher Provokateur des traditionellen Schmucks. Seine strengen, reduzierten Formen gab er Ende der 1970er Jahr auf, als dieses Thema in der Schmuckindustrie aufgegrif-fen wurde. 1987 stellte er seine *Bouquet-Broschen* vor. Auf dem Bild eines Blumenstraußes, eingeschweißt in Kunststoff-Laminat, schwebt ein klas-sisch geschliffener Farbedelstein. Zur Rückkehr des Kostbaren im humorvol-len Kontext sagte der Holländer: »Die Steine sollten mit den unübertroffe-nen Farben das Gleichgewicht bewahren, nicht durch einen geschmackvollen Zusammenhang, sondern gerade durch den Kontrast.« Zahlreiche Museen, zuletzt 2007 die Pinakothek der Moderne in München, widmeten ihm Ein-zelausstellungen. Emmy van Leersum entwickelte in den 1970er Jahren ihre reduzierte Schmuckästhetik zu vollkommener Reife. Sie arbeitete mit Gold ebenso wie mit farbigem Nylon und lackiertem Edelstahl. Manchmal genügte ihr ein einfacher Knick, eine gekreuzte Linie, um eine starke zeichenhaf-te Wirkung zu erzielen. Den Minimalisten im deutschen Schmuck-Design ab 1980 lieferte Emmy van Leersum mit ihrem Werk die überzeugendsten Argumente.

Emmy van Leersum and Gijs Bakker, De Stijl and Pop Culture

Emmy van Leersum (1930–1984) and her partner of many years, Gijs Bakker (born in 1942), were in the vanguard of the revival of jewellery de-sign in the Netherlands from the mid-1960s. Both had trained as goldsmiths and had studied at the Instituut voor Kunstnijverheidsonderwijs in Amster-dam, now the Rietveld Academie. In 1963 they transferred to the Konstfack Skolan in Stockholm. The Dutch art critic Gert Staal commented on their move as follows: »Compared to the stuffy Netherlands, there was space to breathe there although even there the promise of a new world – in design at least – was not entirely fulfilled.« Gijs Bakker himself said about his studies in Sweden: »The Scandinavian clarity we admired so much, the jewellery by such celebrities as Sigurd Persson, with whom they filled an entire floor at Enko, the Swedish department store, was what lured us to Stockholm. But once we were there, the design turned out to be not quite so spectacular. Basically, it did not go beyond display cases in the municipal park, where the jewellery shown revealed the typical fusion of applied arts and design, which had made it so famous. But over the long term what I noticed above all were the organic forms which we had already resisted in the Netherlands.«[22]

In 1966 Emmy van Leersum and Gijs Bakker presented their new jew-ellery at Galerie Swart and in 1967 at the Stedelijk Museum in Amsterdam. Ralph Turner, an English expert on modern art jewellery, remarked on the austere, large-scale jewellery objects in aluminium in 1976: »they chose this metal in place of the traditional materials of silver and gold, largely as a reaction to the ostentation of jewellery.«[23] That is, however, only partly true. In an essay in »Art Aurea« (1989), Gert Staal speaks of »inhumanly tall neck ruffs« and »visual aggression«; all that was in tune with the times in the late 1960s, with Pop Culture and the youth rebellion against the establishment. It represented the most radical repudiation of the ornamental aspect of traditional jewellery voiced up to that time. In 1967 Emmy van Leersum launched her celebrated Stovepipe jewellery. In this, as in other works, aluminium as the choice of material represented a makeshift solution. Van Leersum and Bakker wanted to avoid any impression of craftsmanship. Moreover, the pieces with their large surfaces only made sense as wearable jewellery objects in a very light-weight material. These works revealed parallels with Minimal art. However, they owed more to the tradition of the Dutch De Stijl group founded in 1917 by painters such as Piet Mondrian and the architect Gerrit Rietveld than they did to any American art movement. This is immediately apparent in the colours van Leersum and Bakker used. Their early »objects to wear« were so important to modern art jewellery and designer jewellery because, after the Second World War, they triggered off a discussion of fundamentals in jewellery as a medium. The Dutch designer duo related geometric lines and figures to the organic form of the body. Their jewellery, for which they also designed clothes to match, altered the contours of the body in formal counterpoint to the expression of the human face and body, which is always in motion and constantly changing.

Gijs Bakker, who founded Droog Design, a highly respected design practice, in the Netherlands in 1993, never ceased his witty, tongue-in-cheek attacks on traditional jewellery. He abandoned his stringently reductive forms as soon as this concept was taken up by the jewellery industry. Bakker launched his *Bouquet brooches* in 1987: a classically cut coloured precious stone hovers over a picture of a nosegay sealed into laminated plastic. The Dutch designer comments as follows on the comeback of the precious in a parody context: »The stones are supposed to keep the balance with their unsurpassed colours, not through being in a tasteful context but just because of the contrast they create.« Numerous museums, most recently the Pinakothek der Moderne in Munich in 2007, have devoted solo shows to his work. Emmy van Leersum developed her reductionist jewellery aesthetic to full maturity in the 1970s. She worked with gold as well as coloured Nylon and lacquered stainless steel. Sometimes all that was needed was a simple bend or a crossed line to create an emphatically sign-like effect. With her work, Emmy van Leersum provided the Minimalist faction in German jewellery design from 1980 with the most compellingly cogent arguments for their approach.

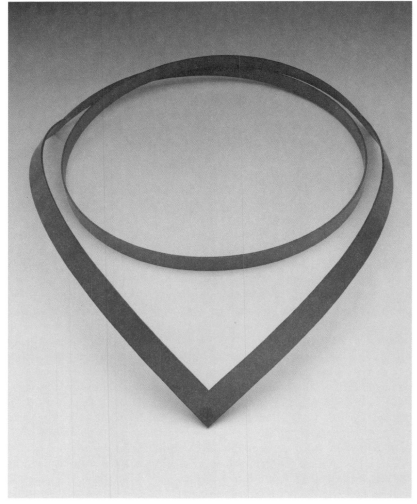

1982

1982   *Broken Lines* Halsschmuck, Emmy van Leersum, Nylon — *Broken Lines* Necklace, Emmy van Leersum, nylon

1968   Armreif, Emmy van Leersum, Stahl — Bangle, Emmy van Leersum, steel

1982   Armreif, Emmy van Leersum, Stahl lackiert — Bangle, Emmy van Leersum, lacquered steel

Emmy van Leersum und Gijs Bakker

1968

1. José Teunissen: Die Frau von ihrem Sockel stürzen. Aus/from Mode, Körper, Kult. Stuttgart, 2007, S./p. 181.
2. Charlotte Seeling: Mode – Das Jahrhundert der Designer, 1900–1999. Köln/Cologne, 1999, S./p. 235.
3–4. Karl Schollmayer: Neuer Schmuck. Tübingen, 1974, Einleitung/introduction.
5–8. Max Fröhlich in Neuer Schmuck. S./p. 18.
9–15. Karl Schollmayer in Neuer Schmuck. S./p. 28 ff.
16–18. Karl Schollmayer in Neuer Schmuck. S./p. 36 ff.
19. Aus/from Friedrich Becker, Schmuck. Kinetik.Objekte. Stuttgart, 1997, S./p. 20.
20. Karl Schollmayer in Neuer Schmuck. S./p. 42.
21. Klaus Ullrich in Neuer Schmuck. S./p. 76.
22. Gert Staal: Solo für einen Solisten. Art Aurea, Ausgabe/ed. 4. Ulm, 1989, S./p. 66.
23. Ralph Turner: Contemporary Jewellery. London, 1976, S./p. 56.

A. Aus/from Hermann Jünger, Schmuck nach 1945. Ausstellungskatalog/ Exhibition catalogue. Nürnberg/Nuremberg, S./p. 16
B. Aus/from Art Aurea, Ausgabe/ed. 4. Ulm, 1989, S./p. 67.

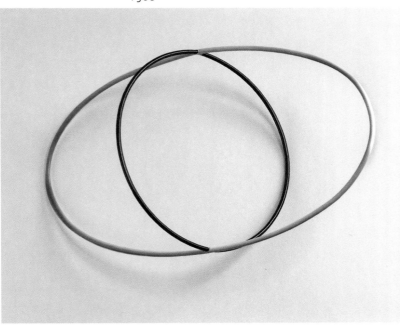

1982

Gegenwart — Present

Klare Form und Minimalismus — Clear Form and Minimalism

Klare Formen waren im Schmuck der 1980er Jahre gleichbedeutend mit modernem Design. Vorbildfunktion für diesen »deutschen Schmuckstil« hatte das Produkt-Design und die Architektur nach den Idealen des Bauhauses, der HfG Ulm sowie die De Stijl-Bewegung in Holland. Der reduzierten Formensprache im Schmuck-Design der deutschen Manufakturen und Ateliers waren Arbeiten von Schmuck-Künstlern wie Emmy van Leersum, Gijs Bakker, Reinhold Reiling oder Friedrich Becker vorausgegangen.

In the 1980s, clear forms were identical with modern design. The models for this »German jewellery style« were product design and architecture, following the ideals of the Bauhaus, HfG Ulm and the De Stijl movement in the Netherlands. The reductive language of forms in the designer jewellery made by German factories and studios was preceded by the work of artists in jewellery such as Emmy van Leersum, Gijs Bakker, Reinhold Reiling and Friedrich Becker.

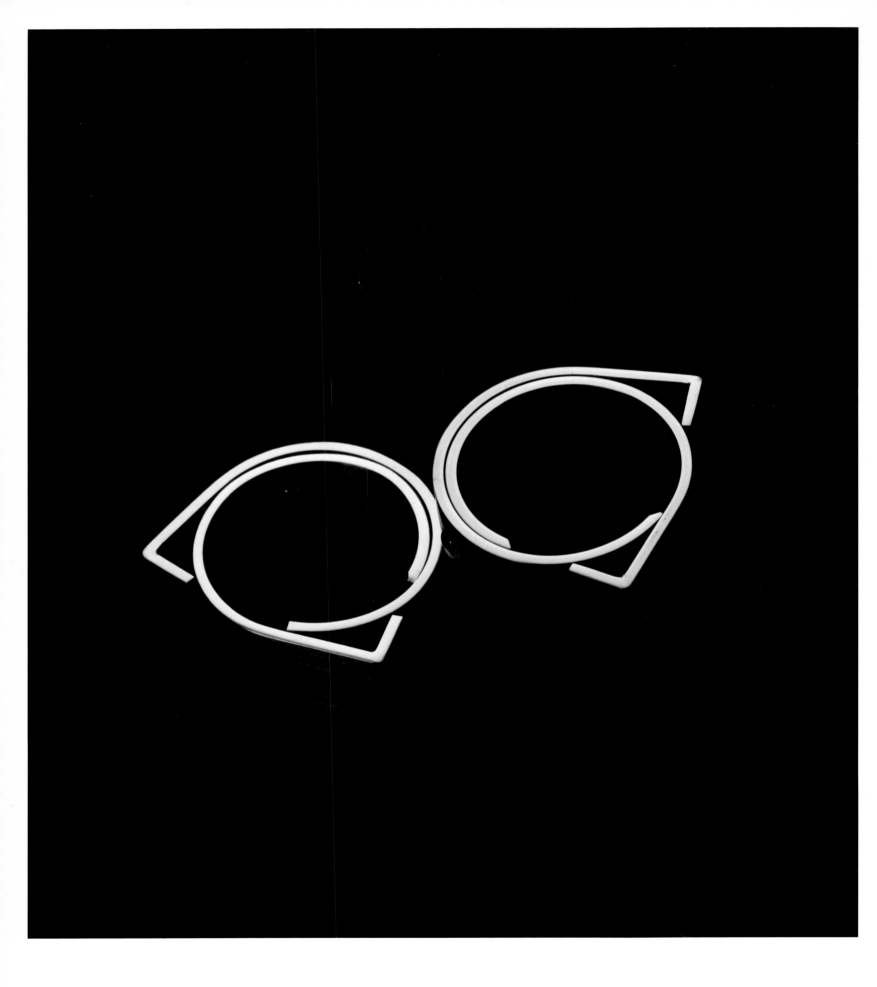

Seit Beginn der 1980er Jahre steht Carl Dau für klare
Formen bis hin zu konstruktivistischer Strenge.
— Since the early 1980s Carl Dau has stood for clarity
of form that can extend to constructivist astringency.

2006   Ringe, Edelstahl — Rings, stainless steel
2006   Armreif, Edelstahl — Bangle, stainless steel

Carl Dau

Farbigkeit und Diamanten sind ab 2004 neue
Elemente im Minimalismus des Berliner Designers.
— Since 2004 colour and diamonds have been new
elements of the Berlin designer's Minimalism.

2004   Ringe *Monochrom*, Gold, Lack, Diamanten — Rings *Monochrome*, gold,
        lacquer, diamonds

2004   Ohrschmuck *Monochrom*, Gold, Lack, Diamanten — Earrings *Monochrome*,
        gold, lacquer, diamonds

Hohe Funktionalität und sensibler Materialeinsatz:
puristische Ketten in der Tradition der Moderne.
—Highly functional and a sensitive use of materials:
purist chains in the Modernist tradition.

Kette *K97A*, Design Andrea Zarp und Hans-Hermann Lingenbrinck, Gold,
Platin — Chain *K97A,* design Andrea Zarp and Hans-Hermann Lingenbrinck,
gold, platinum

1984 Kette *K02C*, Design Cornelia Bürger und Hans-Hermann Lingenbrinck,
Gold, Platin — Chain *K02C,* design Cornelia Bürger and Hans-Hermann
Lingenbrinck, gold, platinum

Sichtbare Funktionselemente sind typisch für die
Schmuckästhetik von Herman Hermsen.
— Visible functional elements are typical of Herman
Hermsen's jewellery aesthetic.

1998   *Rohrkette*, Silber, Gold — *Tube chain*, silver, gold

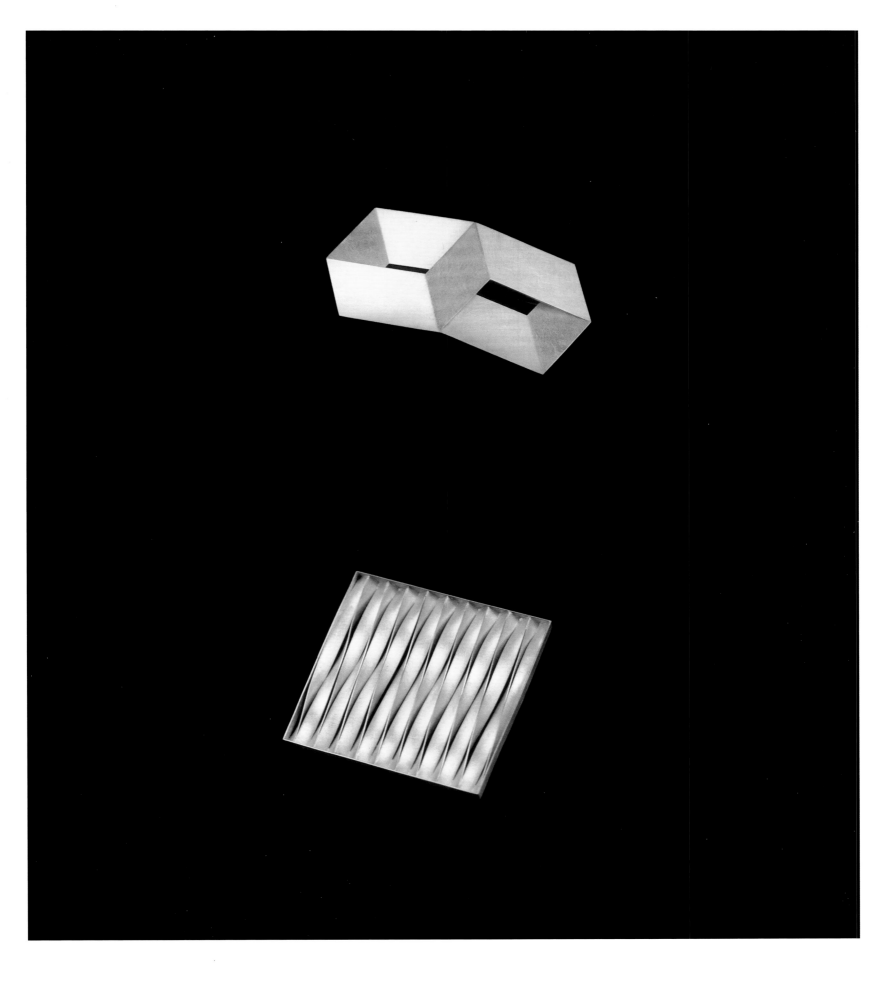

Moderne architektonische Einflüsse werden in
diesen Broschen von Batho Gündra sichtbar.
— Modern architectural influences are revealed
in these brooches by Batho Gündra.

1991   Brosche, Gold — Brooch, gold

1992   Brosche, Gold — Brooch, gold

Intelligenter Einsatz kostbarer Materialien. Üppiger
Reichtum liegt in den Variationen von Raum und Licht.
—Intelligent use of precious materials. Sumptuous
richness is induced by variations on space and light.

2001   Halsschmuck *Papyr*, Design Susanne Winckler, Gold — Necklace *Papyr*,
         design Susanne Winckler, gold

2006   Ring *Cirrus*, Design Iris Weyer, Platin — Ring *Cirrus*, design Iris Weyer,
         platinum

Innovative, preisgekrönte Entwicklungen und das Re-Design
bewährter Klassiker wie des *Spannrings*.
— Innovative, award-winning developments and redesigning
of tried and tested classics such as the *Tension ring*.

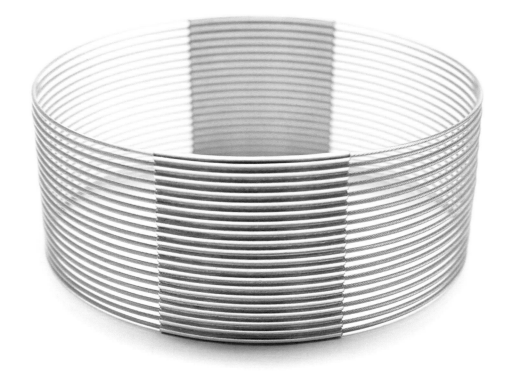

Birgitta Schulz, parsprototo, verbindet reduzierte
Formen mit anschmiegsamer Leichtigkeit.
— Birgitta Schulz, parsprototo, links reductive forms
with supple lightness.

1997   Armreif *Lilith No. 20*, Gold — Bangle *Lilith No. 20*, gold

parsprototo

Wiederholung von Strukturen und Typologien,
Spannung zwischen positiv und negativ.
— Repetition of structures and typologies, tension
between positive and negative.

2006   Brosche *Koralle*, Gold, Koralle — Brooch *Coral*, gold, coral

Präzise Proportionen intensivieren die Materialwirkung,
ihre Symbolik und ihre räumliche Präsenz.
— Precision of proportion intensifies the impact made
by the materials, their symbolism and spatial presence.

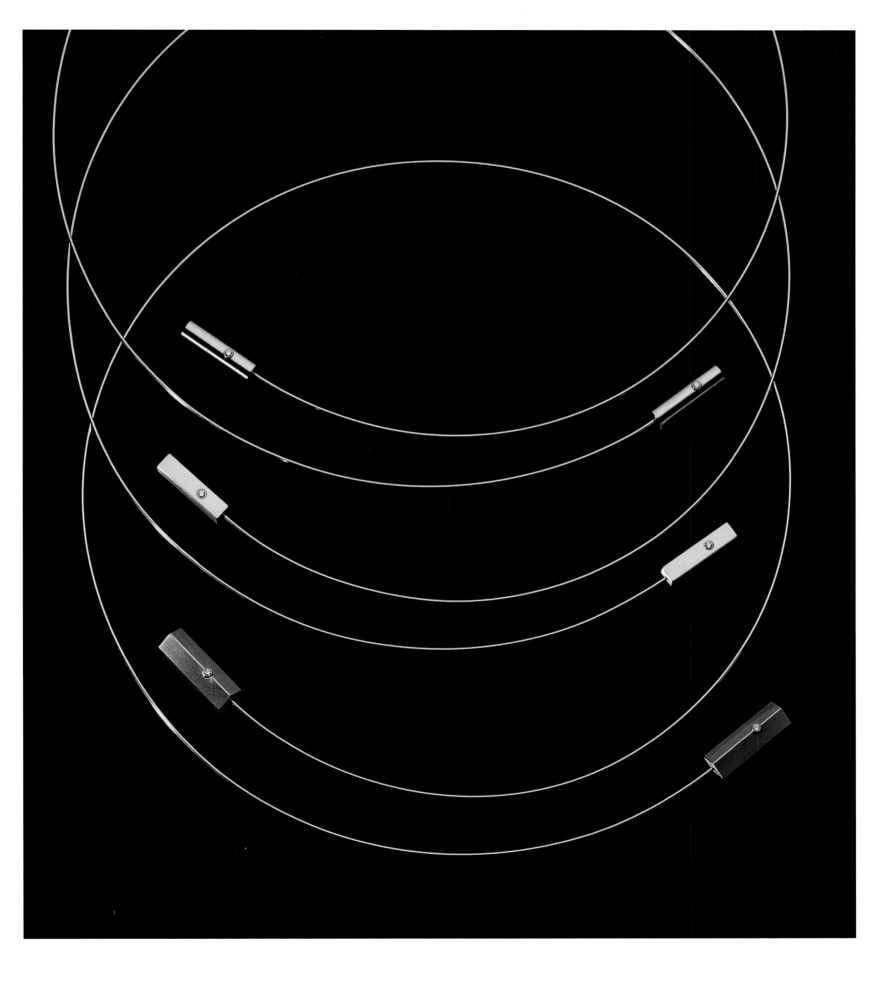

2000   Ring *Der Einkaräter,* Edelstahl, Brillant — Ring *The One carat piece,* stainless steel, diamond

1998   Ring *Der Halbkaräter,* Edelstahl, Brillant — Ring *The Half carat piece ,* stainless steel, diamond

1994   Halsreife, Edelstahl, Brillanten — Necklaces, stainless steel, diamonds

Günter Wermekes

Durch intensives Schmieden werden Goldbänder flexibel.
Räume, Spiegelungen und Zwischenräume entstehen.
— Intensive beating makes strips of gold flexible. Spaces,
reflections and interstices are created.

Mattschwarzer Kautschuk im extremen Kontrast
mit der Brillanz von echten Diamanten.
— Matt black hard rubber in an extreme contrast
with the brilliance of genuine diamonds.

1986   Armreife, Elastomer-Kautschuk, Brillanten, Gold — Bangles, hard rubber,
–1992   diamonds, gold

1999   Ringe, Elastomer-Kautschuk, Brillanten, Gold — Rings, hard rubber,
        diamonds, gold

André Ribeiro

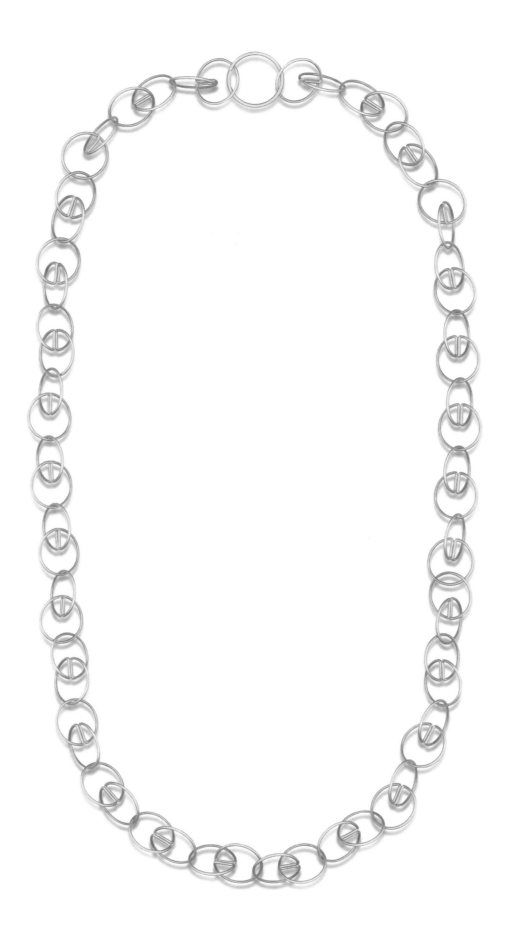

Elegante Bögen formen Schleifen aus dünnem Rohr
oder Draht. Klarheit in fließenden Bewegungen.
— Elegant arcs form loops of thin tubing or wire.
Clarity in fluid movement.

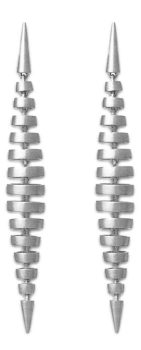

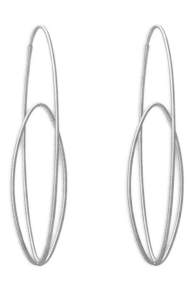

2004	Kette *Duplo Sentido*, Gold — Necklace *Duplo Sentido*, gold
2006	Ohrschmuck *Vivo*, Gold — Earring *Vivo*, gold
2004	Ohrschmuck *Impulso*, Gold — Earring *Impulso*, gold
2001	Ring *Ciclos*, Gold — Ring *Ciclos*, gold

Antonio Bernardo

Einladung zum Spiel und moderne Ornamente.
Konstruktivistische Ringe des brasilianischen Designers.
— An invitation to play and modern adornments.
Constructivist rings by the Brazilian designer.

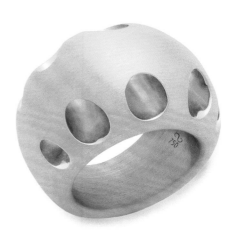

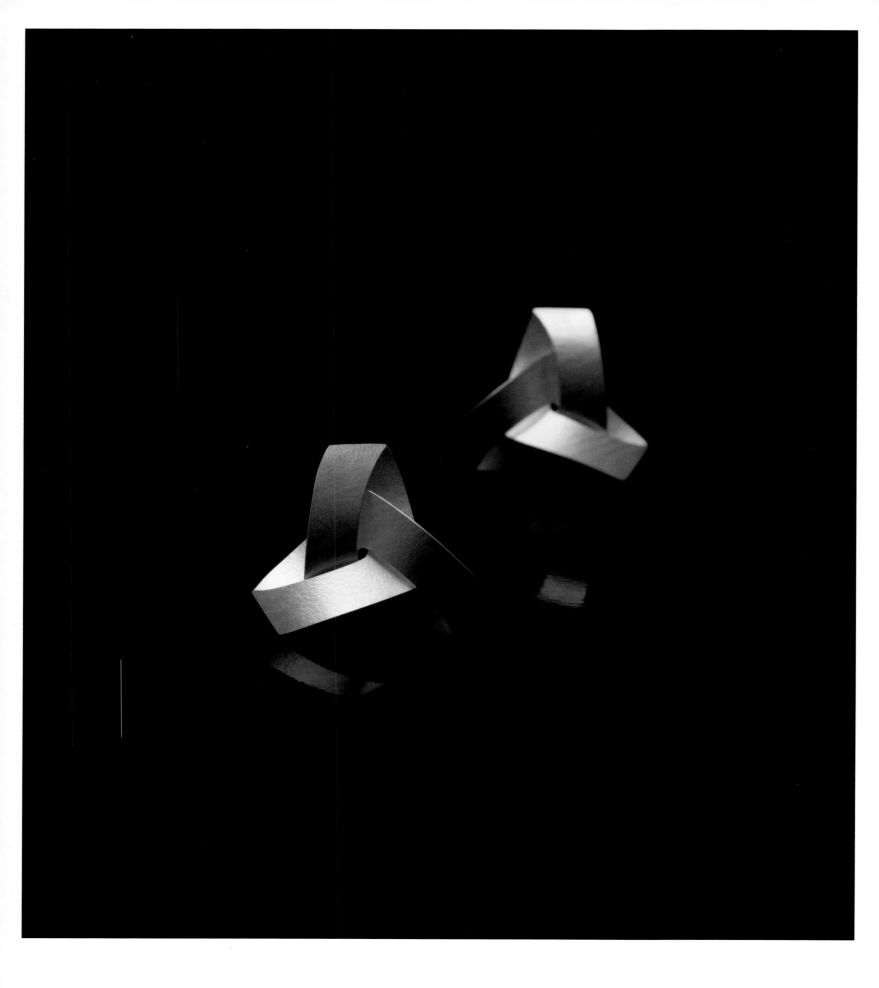

Schleifen, Knoten und Faltungen haben oft tiefe
Bedeutungen und begleiten das Alltagsleben in Japan.
— Loops, knots and folds often have profound
significance and accompany everyday living in Japan.

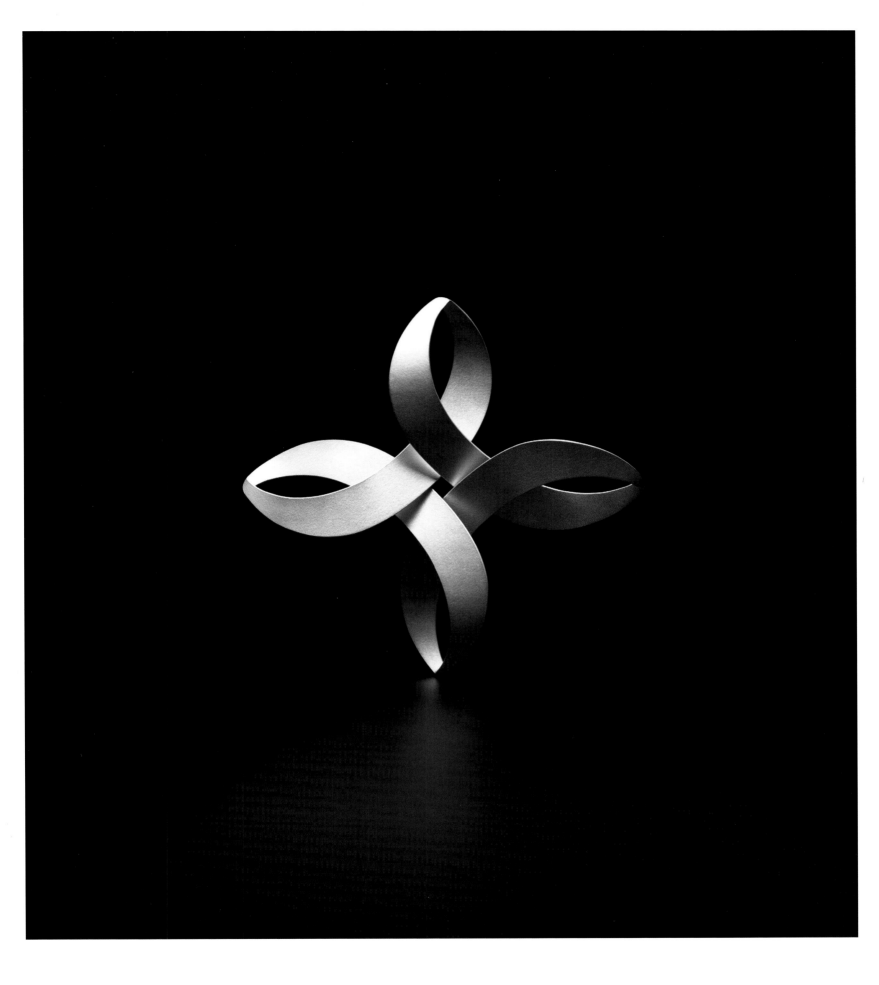

1998   Ohrschmuck *Kumi*, Gold — Earrings *Kumi*, gold

2000   Brosche *Musubi*, Silber — Brooch *Musubi*, silver

Kazuko Nishibayashi

So viel wie nötig, so wenig wie möglich!
Ausdrucksstarke Formen statt Dekor.
— As much as necessary, as little as possible!
Powerfully expressive forms instead of decoration.

2000   Ring *Trio*, Gold — Ring *Trio*, gold

2004   Ring *Schlossgarten*, Gold — Ring *Palace garden*, gold

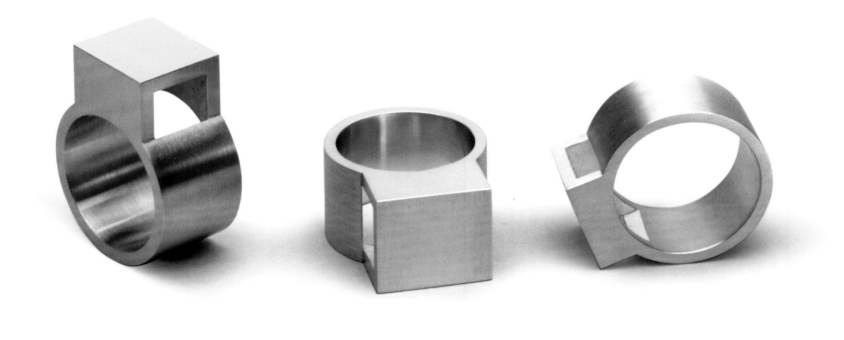

Monika Glöss ist fasziniert von technischen
Konstruktionen und äußerster Reduktion.
— Monika Glöss is fascinated with technical
constructs and reduction in the extreme

2005   Ringe *Cube*, Roségold, Silber — Rings *Cube*, rose gold, silver

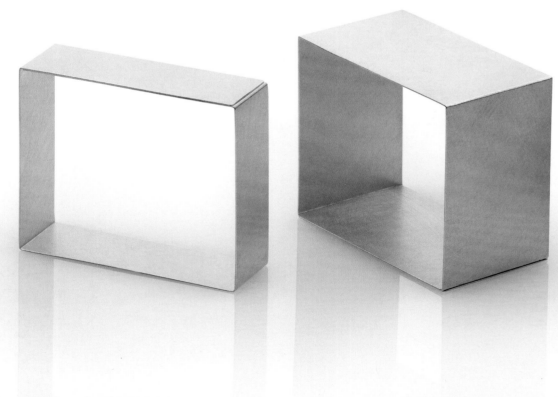

Musterbeispiele aus dem Repertoire der klassischen
Moderne, die Armreife von Claudia Hoppe.
— Prime examples from the classical Modern repertory:
Claudia Hoppe's bangles.

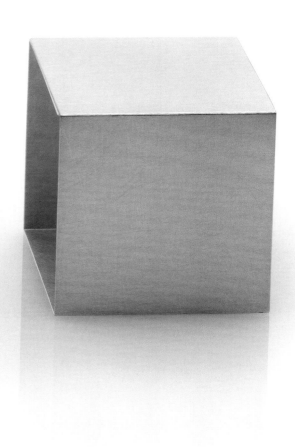

2003   Armreife *Blink*, Gold, Silber — Bangles *Blink*, gold, silver

2003   Armreife *Quader*, Silber. Schmuckidee als *Kubus* Armspange bei Niessing
       — Bangles *Quader*, silver. Design idea as *Kubus* bangle by Niessing

Claudia Hoppe

Jede Handbewegung bringt einen diamant-
besetzten Kubus in Rotation.
— Every movement of the wearer's hand causes
a small, diamond-set cube to rotate.

Barbara Schulte-Hengesbach

2005   Kinetischer Ring *Würfel im Würfel,* Gold, Brillanten — Kinetic ring
           Cube in the Cube, gold, diamonds

2006   Kette *Umrundet,* Gold — Necklace *Orbit,* gold

Barbara Schulte-Hengesbach

Wechselspiel von innen und außen, von Reflexion
und Schattenwurf, streng geometrisch.
— The interaction of inside and outside, reflection
and cast shadow, stringently geometric.

2005   Kette *29 in Folge*, Gold — Necklace *29 in a Row*, gold

Atelier Striffler & Krauß

Humorvolle Elemente brechen die handwerkliche
und formale Ernsthaftigkeit.
— Humorous elements break into the craftsmanly
and formal seriousness.

Die Form entspringt den Gesetzen der Geometrie
und dem Widerstand des Materials.
— The form emerges from the laws of geometry
and the resistance of the material.

Wie eine Faltschließe lässt sich das Armband öffnen und
kehrt sanft federnd zu seinem Ursprung zurück.
— Like a fastener with a folding clasp, the bracelet opens
and returns, gently springy, to its original position.

2000   Armreif, Anhänger und Ring *Leporello*, Gold, Brillanten — Bangle, pendant
        and ring *Leporello*, gold, diamonds

Elementare, der Natur entliehene Formen und
konstruktivistische Reihungen.
— Elemental forms borrowed from nature and
Constructivist parataxis.

2004   *Abschnittskette*, Feinsilber — *Segment chain*, fine silver

2007   *Wellenkette*, Feinsilber vergoldet, Gummiseil — *Wave chain*, fine silver-gilt, rubber cord

Armreife und Ketten, die an Schmuckstücke der
Antike und ursprüngliche Kulturen erinnern.
— Bangles and necklaces reminiscent of antiquity
and indigenous cultures.

2003   Armschmuck, Silber, Feingold — Bracelets, silver, fine gold

2006   Kette, Silber, Feingold — Necklace, silver, fine gold

Monika Killinger

Farbedelsteine in neuem Licht — Coloured Precious Stones in a New Light

Bereits im Art Déco der 1920er Jahre experimentierten avant-gardistische Gestalter mit neuartig geschliffenen Edelsteinen. Nach dem Zweiten Weltkrieg führten Goldschmiede und Künstler wie Friedrich Becker und Bernd Munsteiner diese Entwicklung fort und erweiterten das Spektrum ungewohnter Steinformen und Fassungen. Andere Schmuckgestalter verwenden weiterhin klassisch geschliffene Edelsteine – in Kombination mit innovativen Formen und Materialien erscheinen auch diese in einem neuen Licht.

As early as 1920s Art Déco, avant-garde designers were experimenting with gemstones cut in new ways. After the Second World War, goldsmiths and artists such as Friedrich Becker and Bernd Munsteiner developed this trend further and enlarged the range of unusual forms for stones and settings. Other jewellery designers continued to use gemstones in the classic cuts – in combination with innovative forms and materials, they, too, appear in a new light.

Der künstlerische Edelsteinschliff ist die Basis
aller Schmuckstücke von Bernd Munsteiner.
— Artistic gemstone cutting is the basis of all
Bernd Munsteiner jewellery.

Bernd Munsteiner

2002   Halsschmuck *Kristall-Reflexionen,* Turmalin, Gold — Neck jewellery
       Crystal reflections, tourmaline, gold

1994   Halsschmuck *Symbolon,* Bergkristall mit Rutil — Neck jewellery *Symbolon,*
       rock crystal with rutile

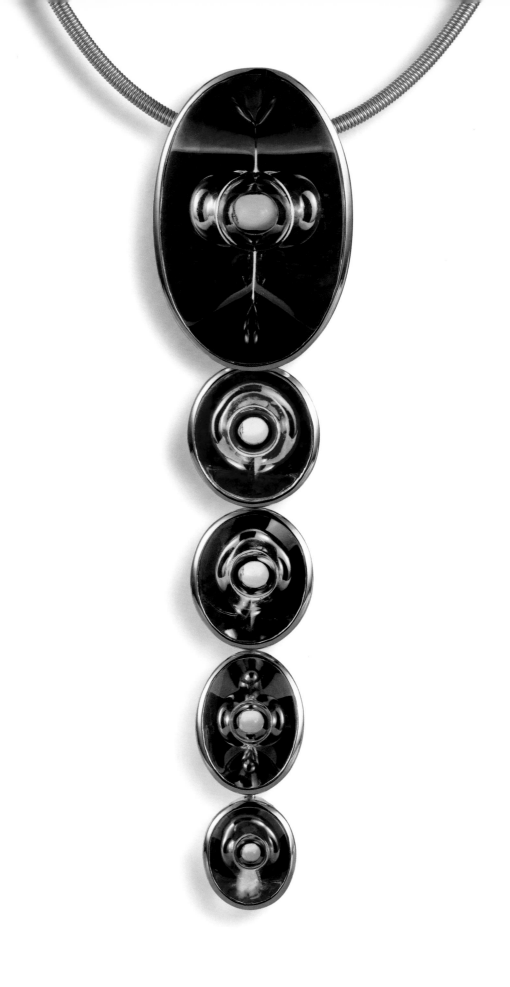

Edelstein-Cabochons erhalten durch Einschnitte
und kugelige Einschliffe ihren künstlerischen Ausdruck.
— Cabochon-cut precious stones are given artistic
expression through notches and spherical incision.

1994   Halsschmuck, fünf Turmaline, Gold — Neck jewellery, five tourmalines, gold

2003   Ring, Turmalinquarz, Gold — Ring, tourmaline quarz, gold

Wesensmerkmale im Schmuck des früheren Produkt-
designers sind prächtige Farben und humorvolle Namen.
— The salient features of the jewellery by this former
product designer are brilliant colours and funny names.

2005   Halsschmuck *Farbreigen,* Platin, Farbedelsteine — Neck jewellery
Coloured round dance, platinum, coloured precious stones

2004   Ringe *La Gondola, Blub,* Platin, Gold, Farbedelsteine — Rings *La Gondola,*
Blub, platinum, gold, coloured precious stones

Kosmische Harmonie: Seit 2007 tauchen verstärkt
weiche Cabochonschliffe und sanfte Farben auf.
— Cosmic harmony: since 2007 soft cabochon cuts and
delicate colours have been increasingly featured.

2004 Ringe *Blub, Orbit,* Platin, Aquamarin, Mondstein, Bergkristall, Diamant
–2008 — Rings *Blub, Orbit,* platinum, aquamarine, moonstone, rock crystal,
diamond

2007 Ringe *Ringelreihen,* Roségold, Rosenquarz, Rubellith, Diamant, Morganit
— Rings *Ring-a-ring-a-roses,* rose gold, rose quartz, rubellith, diamond,
morganite

Eine Lagune stand Pate. An der Hand
»schwimmt« ein farbiges Schiffchen.
— A lagoon was the inspiration. A coloured
boat »floats« on the wearer's hand.

2002   Ring *Magic Island*, Gold, Peridot — Ring *Magic Island,* gold, peridot
2005   Ring *Lagune Navette*, Gold, Granat — Ring *Lagune Navette,* gold, garnet

Angela Hübel

Prinzessinnen-Ringe als Persiflage auf den
Verlobungsring. Je größer, desto besser die Partie.
— *Princess rings* as a parody of engagement rings.
The bigger they are, the better the catch.

2003   *Prinzessinnen-Ring,* Platin, Aquamarin — *Princess ring*, platinum, aquamarine

2001   *Prinzessinnen-Ring,* Roségold, Lemon-Citrin — *Princess ring*, rose gold,
        lemon citrine

Sinnliche Formen und schmeichelnde Oberflächen.
Feinste Edelsteine bilden den Ausgangspunkt.
— Sensuous forms and flattering surfaces. They start
with the most exquisite precious stones.

Kostbarkeit als Symbiose aus Gestaltungsidee,
Materialwahl und bester Verarbeitung.
— Value as a synthesis of design idea, choice of
materials and consummate craftsmanship.

Corinna Heller

2007	Ring *Einsteiner*, Rotgold, Rosenquarz — Ring *Solitaire*, pink gold, rose quartz
2007	Ring *Einsteiner*, Gold, Peridot — Ring *Solitaire*, gold, peridot
2008	Ring *Einsteiner*, Gold, Citrin — Ring *Solitaire*, gold, citrine
2008	Ring *Einsteiner*, Weißgold, rosa Turmalin — Ring *Solitaire*, white gold, pink tourmaline
1988	Ring *Einsteiner*, Weißgold, Aquamarin, Brillanten — Ring *Solitaire*, white gold, aquamarine, diamonds

Ovale Ringformen in Platin, »gekrönt« mit klassischen
oder künstlerisch geschliffenen Edelsteinen.
— Ovoid ring forms in platinum, »crowned« by classic or
artistically cut precious stones.

2008	Ring *Flower Leaves*, Platin, grüner Turmalin, Brillanten — Rings *Flower Leaves*, platinum, green tourmaline, diamonds
2004	Ringe *Flower Leaves*, Weißgold, Aquamarin, Brillanten — Rings *Flower Leaves*, white gold, aquamarine, diamonds
2005	Ringe *Flower Leaves*, Weißgold, Palladium, Bergkristall, Rutilquarz — Rings *Flower Leaves*, white gold, palladium, rock crystal, rutile quartz

Vollkommen aus Edelstein. An der Hand wirken die
Ringobjekte überraschend leicht und warm.
— Completely made of gemstone. On the hand,
these ring objects feel astonishingly light and warm.

2008   Anhänger *Long,* Onyx, Citrin — Pendant *Long,* onyx, citrine

2008   Ring *Long,* Onyx, Citrin — Ring *Long,* onyx, citrine

1994   Ring *Herz,* Onyx — Ring *Heart,* onyx

2004   Ring *eggs,* Bergkristall, Citrin — Ring *eggs,* rock crystal, citrine

Innovative Schliffe, losgelöst von jeder Tradition,
mit optischen Effekten und Hintersinn.
— Innovative cutting, detached from tradition,
with visual effects and flashes of recondite wit.

2006 Anhänger *aeria,* Weißgold, Palladium, Rutilquarz — Pendant *aeria,*
   white gold, palladium, rutile quartz

2000 Ringe *acht,* Weißgold, Turmalin *Spirit Sun* Schliff — Rings *eight,* white gold,
   tourmaline *Spirit Sun* cut

2002 Anhänger *dish,* Turmalinquarz, Omegakette, Weißgold — Pendant *dish,*
   tourmaline quartz, Omega necklace, white gold

2008 Brosche *tube,* Naturachat, Weißgold, Edelstahl — Brooch *tube,* nature agate,
   white gold, stainless steel

Ein halber Edelstein wird im Spiegel vollkommen.
Ein Bergkristall ist ohne Fassung tragbar.
— Half a precious stone is made whole by being
reflected. A rock crystal can be worn without a setting.

2002   Ring *Upon Reflection,* Weißgold, Citrin, Amethyst — Ring, *Upon Reflection,*
white gold, citrine, amethyst

1989   Bergkristallring — Rock crystal ring

Herman Hermsen

Durch eingespannte Kugelgelenke sitzen die »Ringköpfe« beweglich in den Edelstahlschienen. — Ball joints held by tension allow »ring bezels« to be movable in stainless steel shanks.

2000 −2003	*Swivel* Ringe, Edelstahl, Farbsteine — *Swivel* rings, stainless steel, coloured stones
2004	*Swivel* Ringe, Edelstahl, Farbsteine — *Swivel* rings, stainless steel, coloured stones
2001 −2007	*Swivel* Ringe, Edelstahl, Farbsteine — *Swivel* rings, stainless steel, coloured stones

Farbig glänzender Kunststoff dient als »Ringschiene«
für kostbare Edelsteine, gefasst in Gold.
— Glossy coloured plastic serves as a »ring shank«
for valuable precious stones set in gold.

2006   Ringe *Athena,* Serie *Schmucklabor,* Gold, Farbedelsteine, Kunststoffspiralen
        — Rings *Athena,* series *Jewellery laboratory*, gold, coloured precious stones,
        plastic spirals

Sternförmige Platin- oder Goldfassungen, in denen farbige Edelsteine eingespannt sind.
— Star-shaped platinum or gold settings holding coloured precious stones by tension.

2006   Ring und Anhänger *Stars,* Platin, Gold, Aquamarine — Ring and pendant *Stars,* platinum, gold, aquamarines

Biegel

In symbolträchtiger Form berührt der Edelstein
die Hand der Schmuck-Trägerin.
— The precious stone touches the wearer's hand in
a form pregnant with symbolic meaning.

2008   Ringe *Unity,* Platin, Diamanten, Farbedelsteine — Rings *Unity,* platinum,
diamonds, coloured precious stones

Edelsteine spiegeln sich in den konkaven Flächen
des Hohlspiegels und steigern die Reflexionen.
— Precious stones are reflected in the concave
surfaces of a concave mirror to enhance reflections.

2006   Ringe *Helios*, Gold, Topas, Citrin — Rings *Helios*, gold, topaz, citrine

Gegenwart

Schmuck als Skulptur
— Jewellery as Sculpture

»Schmuck ist für mich Skulptur, Skulptur mit menschlichem Hintergrund. Auf dieser Linie spiegelt sich eine Natur, die man gewöhnlich nicht sieht.« Björn Weckströms Aussage aus dem Jahre 1974 gilt auch für die Arbeiten einer Reihe von jüngeren Gestaltern, deren Schmuck eine formale Nähe zu bildhauerischen Werken aufweist.

»To me, jewellery is sculpture, sculpture with a human background. Along these lines, nature is reflected as it is not usually seen.« This statement made by Björn Weckström in 1974 also applies to the work of a number of younger designers, whose jewellery reveals formal closeness to sculpture.

Expressive Oberflächen und skulpturale Formen: Damit hat
Björn Weckström in den 1970er Jahren einen Stil geprägt.
— Expressive surfaces and sculptural forms:
Björn Weckström shaped a style with them in the 1970s.

1999   Halsschmuck *Anastasia*, Design Björn Weckström, Gold, Aquamarin,
        Schliff Bernd Munsteiner — Necklace *Anastasia,* design Björn Weckström,
        gold, aquamarine, Bernd Munsteiner cut

1990   Armband *Goldfire,* Design Björn Weckström, Gold — Bracelet *Goldfire,*
        design Björn Weckström, gold

Die plastische Wirkung erreicht Claude Chavent allein durch
verschiedene Goldfarben und die Struktur der Oberfläche.
— Claude Chavent achieves the three-dimensional effect
solely with gold in different colours and surface texturing.

Eine geöffnete »Ring-Form« lässt den Finger durchscheinen.
Die Perle zwischen dem Symbol für die Unendlichkeit.
— An opened »ring form« lets the finger show through.
The pearl amid the symbol for infinity.

Angela Hübel

Ursula Gnädingers skulpturale Stücke sind raumgreifend,
emotional und zuweilen erfrischend provokativ.
— Ursula Gnädinger's sculptural pieces intervene in space,
are emotional and occasionally refreshingly provocative.

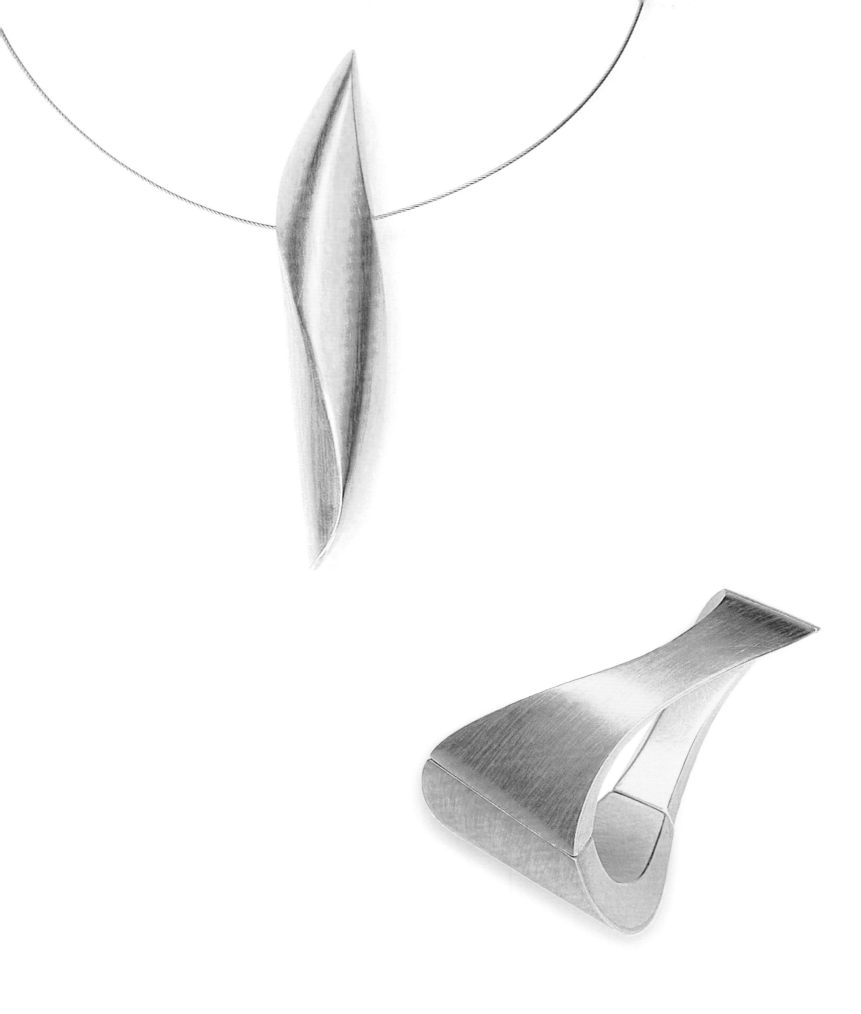

2003   Kette *K72*, Silber, Feingold — Necklace *K72*, silver, fine gold

2005   Anhänger *A43* Silber, Feingold — Pendant *A43,* silver, fine gold

2008   Armreif *S43*, Silber, Feingold— Bracelet *S43,* silver, fine gold

    Ursula Gnädinger

Der weiche *Faltenwurf* aus Platin und Gold entsteht
im Schmieden und Feilen von Hand.
— The soft *Fall of folds* in platinum and gold
is created by beating and filing by hand.

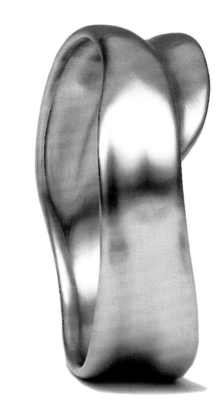

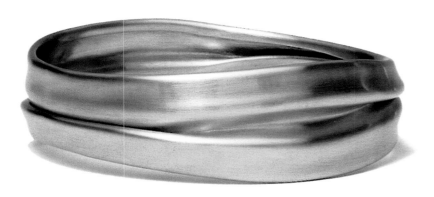

Mit präziser Silberschmiedetechnik wird Gold- oder
Platinblech zu Schoten oder Kokons geformt.
— Sheet gold or platinum is formed into pods or
cocoons by precisely applied silversmithing techniques.

1993   *Kokon* Armband, Gold — *Cocoon* bracelet, gold

1992   *Kokon* Collier, Gold — *Cocoon* necklace, gold

    Erich Zimmermann

Zeitgenössisches Perlendesign — Contemporary Pearl Design

Lange Zeit galten Perlen im modernen Schmuck-Design als zu konservativ. Unkonventionelle Gestaltungsideen verhalfen dem Klassiker in den 1990er Jahren zu neuem Ansehen. Originell konstruiert, im Einklang mit Platin- und Goldfarben oder im Kontrast mit Edelstahl und farbigem Acryl, erfüllen die Schöpfungen im 21. Jahrhundert das gewachsene Bedürfnis nach ästhetischer Harmonie im Einklang mit der Mode und naturnaher Sinnlichkeit.

For a long time, pearls were regarded as too conservative for modern designer jewellery. Unconventional design ideas helped classics to new popularity in the 1990s. Original in construction, attuned to the colours of platinum and gold or contrasting with stainless steel and colourless acrylic, the creations of the 21st century are meeting a growing need for aesthetic harmony in line with fashion and sensuousness that is close to nature.

Seit 1995 hat Gellner die Zusammenarbeit mit namhaften
freien Schmuck-Designern intensiviert.
— Since 1995 Gellner has collaborated more intensively
with distinguished freelance jewellery designers.

2007   Ringe, Design Angela Hübel, Gold, Südsee- und Tahiti-Zuchtperlen, Brillanten — Rings, design Angela Hübel, gold, South Sea and Tahitian cultured pearls, diamonds

2007   Colliers, Tahiti- Südsee- und Süßwasser-Zuchtperlen, Diamanten — Necklaces, Tahitian, South Sea and freshwater cultured pearls, diamonds

Fließende weiche, verspielte Formen im Dialog
mit schimmernden Tahiti- und Südsee-Zuchtperlen.
— Fluid, soft, playful forms in a dialogue with
iridescent Tahitian and South Sea cultured pearls.

2008   Ringe, Design Egon Frank, Südsee-und Tahiti-Zuchtperlen, Gold,
            Brillanten — Rings, design Egon Frank, South Sea and Tahitian cultured
            pearls, gold, diamonds

2008   Ohrschmuck und Collier, Design Dickson Yewn, Gold, Tahiti-Zuchtperlen
            — Earrings and necklace, design Dickson Yewn, gold, Tahitian cultured
            pearls

Tahiti-Perlen mit Diamantpavée, lustvoll kombiniert
mit Kunststoff in den Farben der jeweiligen Mode.
— Tahitian pearls with pavé diamonds,
lasciviously combined with plastic in colours made
trendy by fashion.

2006   *Ringe Orpheus,* Gold, Weißgold, Tahiti- und Südsee-Zuchtperlen, Diamanten,
        Kunststoff — Rings *Orpheus,* gold, white gold, Tahitian and South Sea
        cultured pearls, diamonds, plastic

Ideenreich inszenierte Perlen sind ein Thema von
Angela Hübel seit Ende der 1980er Jahre.
— Imaginatively staged pearls have been a motif
of Angela Hübel since the late 1980s.

2006   Ring *Lagune lang,* Gold, Akoya-Zuchtperle — Ring *Laguna long,* gold,
        Akoya cultured pearl

1995   Ring *Innenperlenreihe,* Gold, Akoya-Zuchtperlen — Ring *Internal row of pearls,*
        gold, Akoya cultured pearls

Angela Hübel

Die Perlen in den Ringen von Corinna Heller
scheinen wie von gefühlvollen Händen gefasst.
— The pearls in Corinna Heller's rings look as if
they were set by sensitive hands.

2007   Ringe *Einperler der Zweite,* Weißgold, Rotgold, Tahiti- und Südsee-
        Zuchtperlen, Brillanten, Rubine, Smaragde — Rings *One pearl the Second,*
        white gold, rose gold, Tahitian and South Sea cultured pearls, diamonds,
        rubies, emeralds

Corinna Heller

Alle Formen sind bei Heiko Schrem das Ergebnis
eines langjährigen Entwicklungsprozesses.
— In Heiko Schrem's work, all forms are the outcome
of a process entailing years of development.

2007   Perlenringe, Roségold, Südsee-Zuchtperle und Edelstahl, Tahiti-Zuchtperle
        — Pearl rings, rose gold, South Sea cultured pearl and stainless steel,
        Tahitian cultured pearl

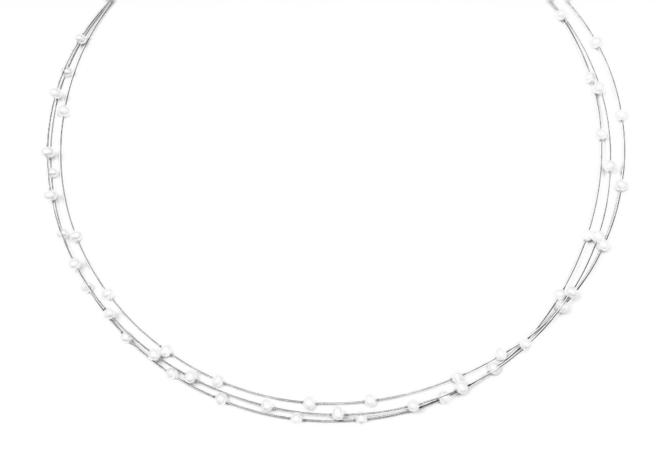

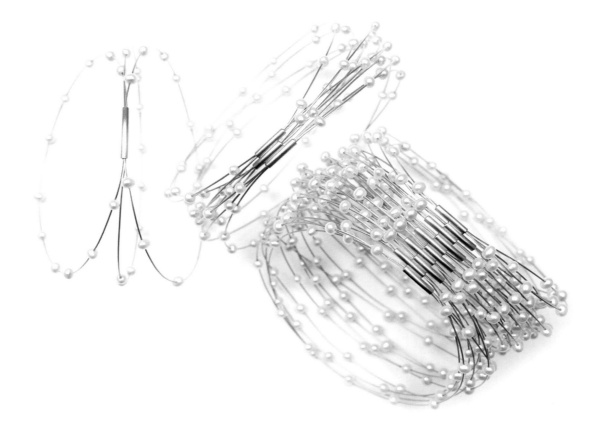

Birgitta Schulz entwickelte Mitte der 1990er Jahre
Perlschmuck von schwebender Leichtigkeit.
— In the mid-1990s Birgitta Schulz developed pearl
jewellery that is so light it seems to hover.

1997   Halsschmuck *Marie,* Gold, Zuchtperlen — Necklace *Marie,* gold, cultured pearls

1997   Armbänder *Galaxie,* Gold, Zuchtperlen — Bracelets *Galaxy,* gold, cultured pearls

2007   Halsschmuck *Ringcollier No. 3,* Gold, Zuchtperlen — Necklace *Ring necklet No. 3,* gold, cultured pearls

1999 entstanden die *Blätter* von Gudrun Jäger.
Inzwischen wurden sie durch Perlen ergänzt.
— Gudrun Jäger's *Leaves* were created in 1999.
In the meantime, they are complemented by pearls.

1999   Ringe, Kollektion *Blätter,* Gold, Akoya-Zuchtperlen — Rings, collection
Leaves, gold, Akoya cultured pearls

Eine Faltung nimmt die Perle im Schmuckset *Oyster* auf und hält sie durch die Materialspannung fest. — The pearl in the *Oyster* set is held by a fold and is clamped by the tensile strength of the material.

2007   Anhänger, Ohrschmuck und Ring *Oyster,* Design Saskia & Stefan Diez, Roségold, Zuchtperlen — Pendant, earrings and ring *Oyster,* design Saskia & Stefan Diez, rose gold, cultured pearls

Die *Wolkenkollektion* entspricht dem Wunsch nach mehr
Verspieltheit und Weichheit im modernen Schmuck-Design.
— The *Cloud Collection* represents a response to a desire for
more playfulness and softness in modern jewellery design.

2002	*Wolkenarmband,* Gold, Zuchtperlen — *Clouds bracelet,* gold, cultured pearls
2004	*Wolkencollier*, Gold, Zuchtperlen — *Clouds necklace*, gold, cultured pearls
1999	*Pickelring*, Gold, Zuchtperlen — *Pickle pearl ring*, gold, cultured pearls
2005	Ring *Chesterfield*, Gold, Zuchtperlen — Ring *Chesterfield*, gold, cultured pearls

Perlschmuck, der sinnliche Erlebnisse vermittelt.
schmuckwerk zählt zu den Erneuerern des Genres.
— Pearl jewellery that conveys sensual experiences.
schmuckwerk is a renewer of the genre.

1996   Perlschließe *Wechseln Sie Ihre Begleitung,* Gold, Zuchtperle — Pearl clasp
Change your Company, gold, cultured pearl

1996   *Perlspannring oval*, Gold, Zuchtperle — *Pearl tension oval ring*, gold,
cultured pearl

2006   Perlring, Gold, 3 Zuchtperlen — Pearl ring, gold, 3 cultured pearls

Variable Schmucksysteme — Variable Jewellery Systems

Schmuck als Spiel, beliebig kombinierbar, für unterschiedliche Gelegenheiten, für feminine »Rollenspiele« und die Launen der Mode. Variable Schmucksysteme entsprechen dem demokratischen Wesen modernen Schmucks. Die Trägerin wird zur aktiven Partnerin des Designers, indem sie seine Schmuckelemente nach eigenen Vorlieben und Ideen variiert.

Jewellery as a game, combinable as desired, for all sorts of occasions, for feminine »role play« and the whims of fashion. Variable jewellery systems match the democratic essence of modern jewellery. The woman wearing it becomes an active partner for the designer by varying his jewellery elements according to her own preferences and ideas.

Durch einen unsichtbaren Mechanismus wird
die Schmuckschließe von Jörg Heinz elegant als
Blickfang positioniert.
— An invisible mechanism ensures that Jörg Heinz's
jewellery clasps can be elegantly positioned to
catch the eye.

2004   *Brillantspirale*, Weißgold, Brillanten, Südsee-Zuchtperlenkette
       — *Diamond spiral*, white gold, diamonds, South Sea cultured pearl necklet

2003   Rahmenschließe *Ring*, Weißgold, Brillant, bunter Stahlstrang
       — Frame clasp *Ring*, white gold, diamond, coloured steel cords

Von klassischen Pavée-Kugeln bis zu innovativen Design-
objekten reicht das Spektrum der Schließen von Jörg Heinz.
— The gamut of Jörg Heinz's clasps ranges from pavé balls
to innovative design objects.

2006   Farbsteinpavée-Kugeln, Citrin, Peridot, Edeltopas, Gold
           — Coloured stone pavé balls, citrine, peridot, topaz, gold

2008   *Brillant-Solitär*, Roségold, Weißgold, Brillanten, Turmalin,
           Südsee-Zuchtperlenkette — *Diamond solitaire*, rose gold, white gold,
           diamonds, tourmaline, South Sea cultured pearl necklet

Der variable Schmuck *Charlotte 21* in reduzierten
Formen mit Farbedelsteinen.
— Variable *Charlotte 21* jewellery featuring
reductive forms with coloured precious stones.

2008   Drei Calcedonanhänger, Edelstahlscheiben, Edelstahlschnur
        — Three chalcedony pendants, stainless steel discs, stainless steel wire

2008   *Charlotte 21* Ringe, Bergkristall, Feueremail — *Charlotte 21* rings,
        rock crystal, enamel

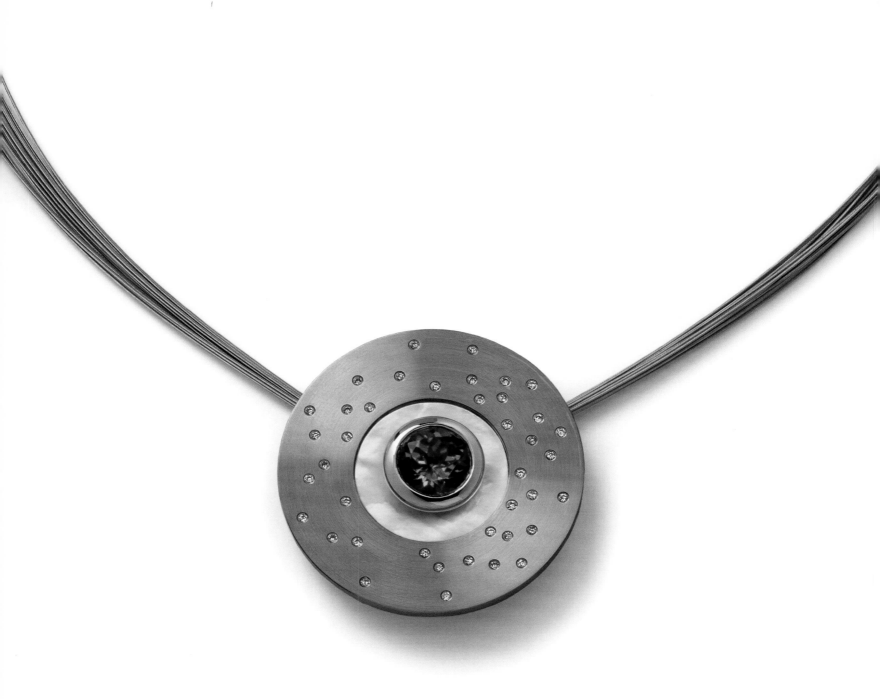

In der Antike war Schmuck ein Abbild des Kosmos.
Eine moderne Interpretation für unsere Zeit.
— In antiquity jewellery was a reflection of the cosmos.
A modern interpretation for our times.

Charlotte · Ehinger-Schwarz 1876

Japanischer Urushi-Lack bringt die Farbe in diesem
variabel kombinierbaren Ohrschmuck.
—Japanese urushi lacquer adds colour to this
variously combinable ear jewellery.

2006   Ohrschmuck *Lacknoten* klein, Silber, Gold, japanischer Lack, *Doppelhaken*,
          Edelstahl — Earrings *Lacquer notes* small, silver, gold, japanese lacquer,
          Double hook, stainless steel

1990   Ohrschmuck *Kreisstecker*, *Stäbe gebogen*, *Halbkugelstecker*, Gold, Diamanten,
–2006   japanischer Lack — Earrings *Circular clip*, *Curved bar*, *Half ball clip*, gold,
          diamonds, japanese lacquer

1992   *Scheibencreolen*, *Verschlusshalbkugeln*, Gold, Edelstahl, Silber,
          japanischer Lack — *Disc creoles*, *Half ball fastening*, gold, stainless steel,
          silver, japanese lacquer

Ende der 1990er Jahre wurden die ersten *Swivel*-Ringe
vorgestellt. Jedes Jahr entstehen seitdem neue Varianten.
— The first *Swivel* rings were launched in the late 1990s.
Since then new variants have appeared each year.

Traditionelle Werte mit modernen Einflüssen —Traditional Values with Modern Influences

Bis in die 1980er Jahre rebellierten Schmuckgestalter gegen das konventionelle Wertedenken im Goldschmiedehandwerk und in der Schmuck-Industrie. Mit intellektuellen Konzepten und unedlen Materialien wollten sie die Schmuckwelt verändern. Inzwischen hat eine Annäherung stattgefunden. Moderne Schmuck-Designer haben ihren Sinn für die Schönheit und Dauerhaftigkeit edler Metalle und Edelsteine wiederentdeckt. Ambitionierte Manufakturen schätzen kreative Gestaltung gepaart mit der Authentizität des Echten.

On into the 1980s, jewellery designers rebelled against the conventional notions of value associated with the goldsmith's craft and the jewellery industry. They wanted to shake up the jewellery establishment with intellectual concepts and base materials. In the meantime, a rapprochement has occurred. Modern jewellery designers have rediscovered a feeling for the beauty and permanence of precious metals and stones. Ambitious manufactories appreciate creative design coupled with the authenticity of what is genuine.

Platin kombiniert mit Diamanten ist ein zentrales Thema
vieler Schmuckentwicklungen der Manufaktur.
— Platinum combined with diamonds is pivotal to many
developments in the jewellery created by the manufactory.

2004   Trauringe, Platin, Diamanten — Wedding rings, platinum, diamonds

2006   Trauringe und Solitair, Platin, Gold, Diamanten — Wedding rings and solitaire, platinum, gold, diamonds

2007   Armreif, Platin, Diamanten — Bangle, platinum, diamonds

2006   Armreif, Platin, Diamanten — Bangle, platinum, diamonds

2004   Trauring und Solitair, Platin, Diamanten — Wedding ring and solitaire, platinum, diamonds

2007   Trauringe und Solitair, Platin, Diamanten — Wedding rings and solitaire, platinum, diamonds

Kostbares Platin mit Diamanten in dezenter, doch
im Detail spannungsvoller Schlichtheit.
— Precious platinum with diamonds in reticent
simplicity enlivened by exciting detail.

2008   Anhänger und Ohrstecker, Platin, Diamanten — Pendant and earrings,
        platinum, diamonds

2008   Armspange, Platin, Diamanten — Bangle, platinum, diamonds

Die typischen, großvolumigen Formen sind das Ergebnis
von jahrelangen Entwicklungsprozessen.
— These typically voluminous forms are the result of
developmental processes that have taken years.

2003   Hals- und Armreif, Navetteprofil, Roségold — Necklace and bangle,
        navette profile, rose gold

1987   Kette *Große Navette*, Roségold — Chain *Large Navette*, rose gold

Meisterhafte Handarbeit ist die Voraussetzung für
die Perfektion der Formen und Oberflächen.
— Masterly craftsmanship is the foundation on
which such perfection of form and surfaces rests.

2003   Armreife, Roségold, Diamanten — Bangles, rose gold, diamonds

1988   Kette, Armreif und Ringe, Roségold — Chain, bangle and rings, rose gold

Neben innovativem Perl-Design hat schmuckwerk auch Platin mit Diamanten zeitgemäß interpretiert. — Apart from innovative designs with pearls, schmuckwerk has also interpreted diamonds with contemporary verve.

1998	*Walzenring*, Platin, Diamanten — *Cylinder ring*, platinum, diamonds
2007	*Wellenring*, Platin, Diamanten — *Wave ring*, platinum, diamonds
1999	*Brillantrasselring*, Platin, Brillanten — *Diamond rattle ring*, platinum, diamonds
2008	*Rollenring*, Platin, Brillanten — *Rolling ring*, platinum, diamonds
2001	*Memoirering*, Platin, Brillanten — *Memoire ring*, platinum, diamonds
2008	*Rankenring*, Platin, Brillanten — *Tendrils ring*, platinum, diamonds

Ringe, deren Profil sich durch Drehung verändert.
Ringe aus zwei gleichen Segmenten.
— Rings with profiles that can be changed by rotating them. Rings consisting of two similar segments.

2004   *Drehringe Pavé,* Gold, Diamanten — *Rotation rings Pavé,* gold, diamonds

2003   *Mandarin* Ringe, Gold, Edelstahl, Edelstahl keramisch beschichtet,
        Diamanten — *Mandarin* rings, gold, stainless steel, stainless steel ceramic
        coated, diamonds

Die sanften Verformungen der *Spira*-Ringe
entstehen durch Biege- und Schmiedeprozesse.
— The gentle distortions that are the
distinctive feature of *Spira* rings are created
by bending and hammering.

2005   Ringe *Spira*, Roségold, Platin, Diamanten — Rings *Spira*, rose gold, platinum,
        diamonds

Ein schmaler Platinbügel überspannt den Brillanten,
der frei beweglich sein Feuer versprüht.
— A small platinum bow arches across a diamond,
leaving it free to move and flash its fire.

2002   Ringe *Liberté© Arcana*, Platin, Brillanten — Rings *Liberté© Arcana*, platinum, diamonds

2004   Collier *Symphonie*, Platin, *HR*-Cut Brillanten — Necklace *Symphony*, platinum, *HR*-cut diamonds

Winzige Kugellager erlauben die spielerische Drehung
und Veränderung der *Girello*-Ringe und -Anhänger.
— Minute ball-bearings allow for playful rotation and
changes to these *Girello* rings and pendants.

2007   Drehringe *Girello* Platin, Weiß- und Roségold, Diamanten — Rotation rings
        Girello, platinum, white and rose gold, diamonds

2008   Ringe *Sternenhimmel*, Rosé-, Weiß- und Gelbgold, Diamanten
        — Rings *Starry sky*, rose, white and yellow gold, diamonds

Neue Zeichen und Symbole — New Signs and Symbols

Schon immer hatte Schmuck symbolischen Charakter. Schmuck-Design der Gegenwart bringt neue Zeichen hervor – erinnert aber auch an vergangene Traditionen und Mythen. Themen aus der Märchenwelt stehen neben Religiösem, fremde Kulturen werden ebenso zitiert wie mittelalterliche Herrschaftsinsignien. Durch die Kombination moderner Formen mit historischen Motiven, nicht selten mit Humor und Selbstironie inszeniert, entstehen neue Aussagen.

Jewellery has always had a symbolic character. Cutting-edge designer jewellery generates new signs – but also recalls the traditions and myths of the past. Fairytale themes and motifs are juxtaposed with religious ones; exotic cultures are quoted along with the insignia of medieval power. New statements are being made through the combination of modern forms with historic motifs, quite often staged with humour and a tongue-in-cheek attitude to oneself.

In einem Acrylkörper leuchtet eine Sonnenscheibe aus
Blattgold. Zwei Ringe bilden ein beziehungsreiches Paar.
— A sun disc of gold foil gleams in an acrylic form.
Two rings form a pair in a multifaceted relationship.

2003   Halsschmuck *Atlantis*, Design Susanne Winckler, Gold, Acryl — Necklace
        Atlantis, design Susanne Winckler, gold, acrylic

2008   Trauringe *Impression*, Design Iris Weyer, Gold — Wedding rings *Impression*,
        design Iris Weyer, gold

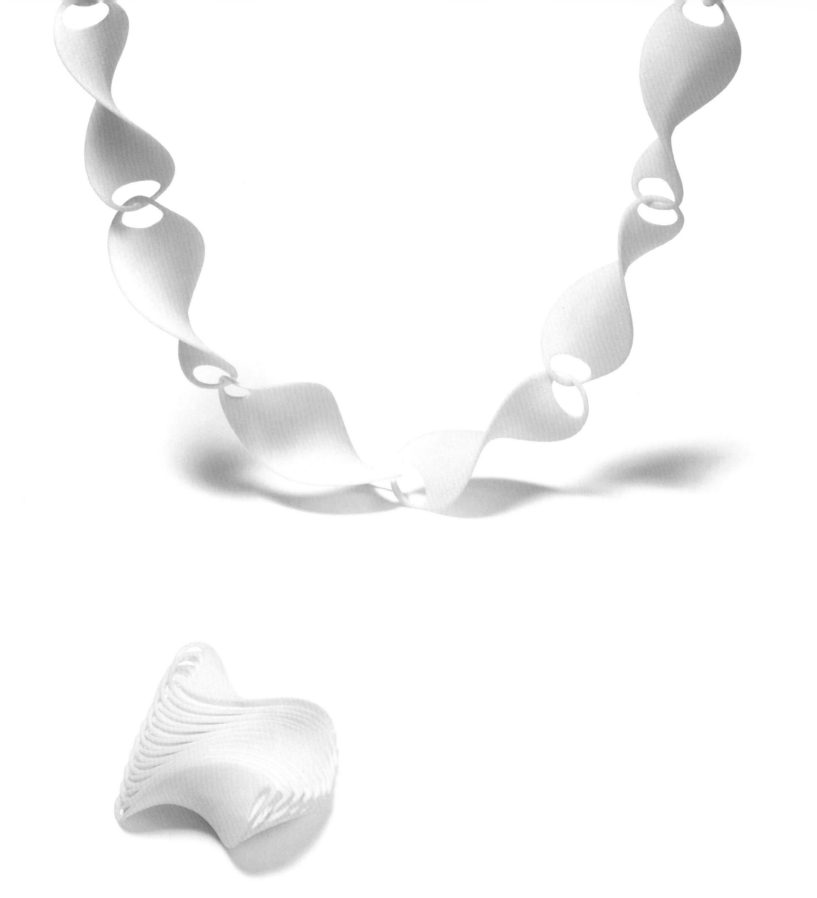

Beweglich fließender Halsschmuck aus 24 spiralförmigen Elementen, anschmiegsam und luftig.
— Fluidly mobile neck jewellery consisting of
24 spiral elements that make it supple and airy.

2008   Halsschmuck *Polymer*, Design Antje Bott, Polyamid — Necklace *Polymer*,
design Antje Bott, polyamide

Geometrische Formen mit spielerischen
Details und humorvoller Symbolik.
— Geometric forms with playful detailing
and humorous symbolism.

2003   Ring *Crown O*, Roségold, Brillant — Ring *Crown O*, rose gold, diamond

2002   Ring *Circle 2 A*, Roségold, Brillant — Ring *Circle 2 A*, rose gold, diamond

2007   Ring *Segment 6*, Roségold, Zirkonoxyd, Brillanten — Ring *Segment 6*,
        rose gold, zirconium dioxide, diamonds

Achim Gersmann

Der Porzellan-Schmuck mit historischen und neuen Motiven
entsteht in Zusammenarbeit mit KPM, Berlin.
— This porcelain jewellery featuring historical and new
motifs has been created in collaboration with KPM, Berlin.

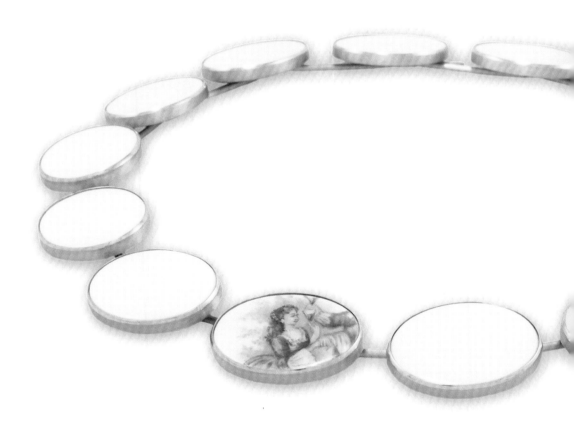

2004   Halsschmuck *Ameisenstrasse*, Gold, KPM-Porzellan — Necklace *Ant trail*,
        gold, KPM porcelain

2003   Ohrschmuck *Eisenrote Blumen*, Gold, KPM-Porzellan — Earrings
        Iron-red Flowers, gold, KPM porcelain

2005   Halsschmuck *Liebespaar*, Gold, KPM-Porzellan — Necklace *Lovers*,
        gold, KPM porcelain

Schmetterlinge und Blüten, ein zentrales Thema des
Jugendstils, in einer zeitgemäßen Interpretation.
— Butterflies and flowers, a central Jugendstil theme,
in a contemporary interpretation.

2008   Halsschmuck *Blütenweiß,* Platin, Diamanten — Necklace *Floral white*, platinum, diamonds

2005   Broschen *Schmetterling*, Platin, Edelsteine — Brooches *Butterfly*, platinum, precious stones

Harmonischer Einklang zwischen Edelsteinschliffen
und Ringformen. Meisterhaft gravierte Motive.
— Harmonious unity between gemstone cuts and ring
forms. Motifs engraved with consummate mastery.

2005   Ringe *Schwarzer Kristall*, Rotgold, Onyx — Rings *Black Crystal*, rose gold, onyx

2006   Ringe *Pistole*, Rotgold, Onyx handgraviert — Rings *Pistol*, rose gold, onyx engraved by hand

2005   Medaillons *Herzstück*, Roségold, Bergkristall, Perlmutt, schwarze Jade — Medallions *Core*, rose gold, rock crystal, nacre, black jade

Petra Giers

Prächtige Edelsteine, adelige und religiöse Herz-
und Kreuzmotive in zeitgemäßen Formen.
— Magnificent precious stones, aristocratic and devotional
heart and cross motifs in contemporary shapes.

Corinna Heller

1998	Anhänger *Herz im Kreuz*, Koralle, Rotgold, Rubin. Ring *Einperler*, Südsee-Zuchtperle, Rotgold, Brillanten — Pendant *Heart in the Cross*, coral, rose gold, ruby. Ring *One pearl*, South Sea cultured pearls, rose gold, diamonds. Model: Nele
2006	Anhänger *Großes Kreuz*, Silber schwarz rhodiniert, schwarze Brillanten, Rubine — Pendant *Large Cross*, silver black rhodanized, black diamonds, rubies
2002	*Kreuzring*, Rubelite, Rotgold — *Cross ring*, rubelite, rose gold
2004	Ring *Stein im Kreuz*, Weißgold, Bergkristall — Ring *Stone in the Cross*, white gold, rock crystal

Corinna Heller

Echte Diamanten in der sinnlich inspirierenden
Farbigkeit neuer synthetischer Materialien.
— Genuine diamonds in the lush colours of new
synthetic materials that are reminiscent of toys.

Monika Seitter

2008   *Marbles* Ringe *Sternhimmel*, Gold, mineralischer Kunststoff, Brillanten
         — *Marbles* rings *Starry sky*, gold, mineral plastic, diamonds

2008   *Marbles* Ringe *Solitair*, Gold, mineralischer Kunststoff, Brillanten
         — *Marbles* rings *Solitaire*, gold, mineral plastic, diamonds

Monika Seitter

Ursprüngliche Erfahrungen und alltägliche Handlungen
führen zu authentischen Schmuckstücken.
— Basic experiences and mundane actions lead to
authentic pieces of jewellery.

Kay Eppi Nölke

1998   Ringe *Vater, Mutter, Haus und Garten*, Filz, Waschanleitung, Polyester
bedruckt — Rings *Father, Mother, House and Garden*, felt,
washing instructions, printed on polyester

1995   *Grasringe,* Gras, Eisen, Edelstahl, Silber, Gold — *Grass rings,* grass, iron,
stainless steel, silver, gold

Kay Eppi Nölke

Verknotungen, Bänder und Schleifen in Schmuckstücken berühren ursprüngliche Gefühle.
— Knots, bands and loops stir primal emotions.

Oliver Schmidt, Juni

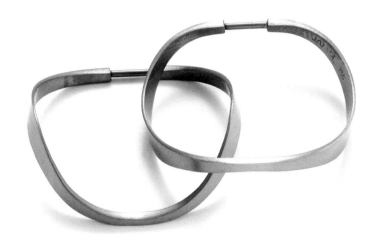

Durch Wiederholung und Kombination einfacher
Elemente entstehen komplexe Strukturen.
— The repetition and combination of simple
elements create complex structures.

Claudia Geiger, Juni

2005   *Mol-Band*, flexibler Halsschmuck, Granate, Gold, Edelstahlseil — *Mol ribbon*, flexible necklace, garnets, gold, stainless steel wire

2005   Halskette *Mol-Röschen*, Feingold, Edelstahl — Necklace *Mol roses,* fine gold, stainless steel

2006   Halsschmuck *Ling*, Kunststoff, Gold, Edelstahl — Necklace *Ling*, plastic, gold, stainless steel

Claudia Geiger, Juni

Puristische, technisch raffinierte Ringserien mit
feinsinniger, aussagestarker Symbolik.
— Purist, technically sophisticated ring collections with
discerning symbolism that makes a strong statement.

Patrick Malotki, Juni

2004   *Ur-Sprungsringe*, Gold, Edelstahl keramisch beschichtet, Diamanten
         — *Crackle rings*, gold, stainless steel ceramic coated, diamonds

2006   Ringe *Gemini*, Edelstahl, Diamanten — Rings *Gemini*, stainless steel,
         diamonds

Patrick Malotki, Juni

Gold in textilen Strukturen. Die Symbole erscheinen
als geometrische Gestaltungselemente.
— Gold in textile structures. The symbols function
as configuring geometric elements.

Dorothea Brill, Juni

2004   Halsschmuck *meter-weise*, Gold, Brillanten — Necklace *metre wise*, gold, diamonds

2001   *Näh-Ringe*, Gold, Edelstahl keramisch beschichtet — *Sew rings*, gold, stainless steel ceramic coated

Miniaturformen, der Natur entlehnt, bergen Geheimnisse
und erhalten im Schmuck neue Bedeutung.
Miniature forms, borrowed from nature, conceal secrets
and attain new significance in jewellery.

Gitta Pielcke

2000   Blumenkette *Klatschmohn*, echte Blumen, laminiert
              — Flower necklace *Corn poppy*, real flowers, laminated

1998   Ringserie *nature*, Gold, Silber. Ringe *Bambus*, *Schilf*, *Linsen*, *Rosen*, *Wildreis*,
              Blütenkelche, *Rosen* — Ring series *nature*, gold, silver. Rings *Bamboo*, *Reed*,
              Lenses, *Roses*, *Wild rice*, *Calyx*, *Roses*

2006   Anhänger *Schildkröte*, Silber — Pendant *Turtle*, silver

                                 Gitta Pielcke

Schmuckstücke, die beweisen, dass die Sehnsucht
nach Romantik in der Moderne nicht verschwunden ist.
— Pieces of jewellery that prove that yearnings
for romanticism have not vanished in Modernism.

1992   Serie *Froschkönig*, Silber und Silber feingoldplattiert, Süßwasser-Zuchtperle
          — Series *Frog prince*, silver, fine gold plated silver, freshwater cultured pearl

1992   *Heartbreaker*, Silber feingoldplattiert — *Heartbreaker*, fine gold plated silver

Themen aus der Welt der Märchen und Sagen übersetzt in
Schmuckstücke, die Gefühlswelten offenbaren.
— Themes from the realm of fairy tales and sagas translated
into pieces of jewellery that reveal emotional worlds.

2003   *Flammeninferno*, Anhänger, Ringe, Ohrschmuck, Silber feingoldplattiert, Lack
        — *Flame inferno*, pendant, rings, earrings, fine gold plated silver, lacquer

2005   Anhänger und Ohrschmuck *Dragonfly*, Granat, Tahiti Perle, Silber
        feingoldplattiert — Pendant and earrings *Dragonfly*, garnet, Tahitian pearl,
        fine gold plated silver

Konzepte junger Schmuck-Designer — Concepts of Young Jewellery Designers

Er ist nicht schwächer geworden, der Wunsch, einen anderen Schmuck zu machen: kreativer, künstlerischer, näher an der Zeit und am Menschen von heute und morgen. Die jungen Schmuck-Designer, die Mehrzahl davon Frauen, die heute die Akademien und Fachschulen verlassen, sind pragmatischer als viele ihrer VorgängerInnen, aber nicht illusionslos. Sie wissen, dass es nicht einfach ist, sich mit ihren Konzepten zu etablieren. Dies ändert aber nichts an ihrer Experimentierfreude und beflügelt ihre Intensität.

The urge to make jewellery that is different has not slackened: more creative, more artistic, closer to the times and the people of today and tomorrow. The young jewellery designers, the majority of them women, who today graduate from the academies and institutes, are more pragmatic than many of their predecessors but are not without illusions. They know that it is not easy to become established with the concepts they advocate. Nevertheless, this does not alter their delight in experimentation. Indeed, it gives wings to their intensity.

Industriematerialien in sanften Formen,
schwingend und reflektierend oder unregelmäßig
gebrochen, spontan und streng.
— Industrial materials in gentle forms, swinging
and reflecting or irregularly refracted, spontaneous
and stringent.

2006 Brosche *Jiggle*, Siliziumcarbid-Keramik, reflektierend, Stahlfeder, Magnet
       — Brooch *Jiggle*, reflective silicium carbide ceramics, steel spring, magnet

2007 Kette *SchwarzWeiß*, Melaminharz, Perlfaden — Necklace *Black white*,
       melamine resin, pearl thread

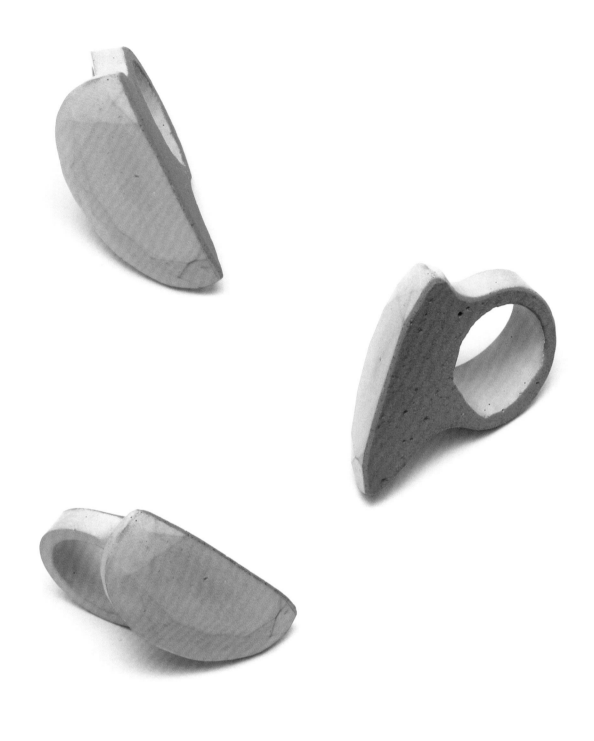

Farbige Grenzflächen und Kanten markieren
zweidimensionale, monochrome Bilder in den
dreidimensionalen Ringen.
— Coloured adjacent surfaces and edges
mark two-dimensional, monochrome images in
the three-dimensional rings.

2007   Ringe *Gemstone*, wasserundurchlässiger Vergussmörtel, Polypropylenspähne
        — Rings *Gemstone*, water-resistant cement, polypropylene swarf (filings)

Claudia Schmedding

Mit Magneten fixierte Plättchen lassen sich
frei variieren. Schmetterlinge verkörpern die
Wandlung ins Unerwartete.
— Scales fixed in place by magnets can be freely
varied. Butterflies embody transformation into
something unexpected.

2006   Variable Kette und Broschen *Die Raupe nennt es das Ende, der Rest der Welt Schmetterling*, Gold, Silber, Edelstahl brüniert, Mandaringranat, Magnete
— Variable necklace and brooches *The caterpillar calls it the end, the rest of the world a butterfly*, gold, silver, bronzed stainless steel, mandarin garnet, magnets

Svetlana Milosevic

Der Zauber, der jedem Anfang innewohnt,
ist nicht auf den ersten Blick zu erkennen, so wie
der Diamant im Schnittpunkt.
— The enchantment inherent in all beginnings
is not apparent at first glance, like the diamond at
the point of intersection.

2005   *Hesse* Ring, Gold oder Silber, geschwärzt, Diamant — *Hesse* ring,
blackened gold or silver, diamond

Annette Janecke

»Etikette« bewahren und »Steinreichtum« zeigen.
Humorvoll und vieldeutig wird hier Neuland betreten.
— Stick to »etiquette« and show »the riches of
stones«. Uncharted territory is entered into here with
wit and polysemy.

2004   Halsschmuck *etikette*, Papier (Kettenetiketten), Silber
       — Necklace *etikette*, paper (necklace tags), rubber band, silver

2006   Halsschmuck *kette no. 14*, Aktenhülle, getrommelte Edelsteine,
       Polyestergarn — Necklace *kette no. 14*, transparent file folder, tumbled
       gemstones, polyester thread

Janine Eisenhauer

Gold und Silber in »stofflich« erscheinender Form.
Erinnerung an die Tradition handgearbeiteter Spitze.
— Gold and silver in forms like »textiles«. Recalls
the tradition of hand-worked lace.

2007   Brosche *Flowercloud*, Gold — Brooch *Flower cloud*, gold

2007   Ringe *Bordure*, Gold, Weißgold, Brillanten — Rings *Bordure*, gold, white gold, diamonds

Brigitte Adolph

Pralinen sind wie Schmuckstücke Luxus und
werden verschenkt, um Freude zu bereiten.
— Sweets are luxury like pieces of jewellery and
are given as presents to joy delight.

2005   Ringe *Trüffel und Kaffee*, Halsband *Pistazie*, Silber, Hartgummi
        — Rings *Truffle and Coffee*, necklace *Pistachio*, silver, rubber

Aus dünnen Steinelementen zusammengefügt
überraschen die Ringe mit der Leichtigkeit frei
beweglicher Einschlüsse.
— Fitted together of thin stone elements,
these rings possess the surprising lightness of
mobile inclusions.

2007   Ring *Shirkan*, Tigerauge, Bergkristall, Zuchtperlen — Ring *Shirkan*, tiger's-eye, rock crystal, cultured pearls

2006   Steinringe *Aschenputtel* und *Schneewittchen*, Onyx, Bergkristall, Gold — Stone rings *Cinderella* and *Snow White*, onyx, rock crystal, gold

Eigenständige Schmuckstücke aus Perldraht von
eleganter Sachlichkeit und sinnlicher Haptik.
— Autonomous pieces of jewellery of gallery wire,
elegant in their stringency and sensuously tactile.

2005   Ringkollektion *Reine Zierde*, Modell *La*, »Eine schlafende Blume wird
        am Finger zur Form«, Perldraht — Ring collection *Pure Decoration*, model *La*,
        »A sleeping flower becomes a form on the wearer's finger,« gallery wire

2005   Ringkollektion *Reine Zierde*, Modell *Loope*, Perldraht — Ring collection
        Pure Decoration, model *Loope*, gallery wire

Spanlose Verformungstechniken bestimmen
die Stücke. Die geometrischen Ursprungsformen
begründen ihren Charakter.
— Unsprung forming techniques shape
these pieces. Their elegance is grounded in the
geometric original forms.

2001   *Würfelringe*, Gold, Silber, Eisen — *Cube rings*, gold, silver, iron

2004   *Würfelohrringe*, Gold, Silber, Eisen, Zuchtperlen — *Cube earrings*, gold, silver,
        iron, cultured pearls

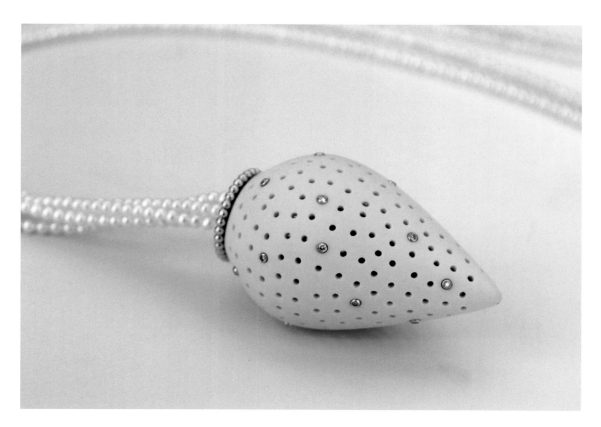

In der Zusammenarbeit mit Meissen entsteht aus »weißem Gold« echter Schmuck. Tradition und Moderne vereint.
— Real jewellery of »white gold« emerges from the collaboration with Meissen. Tradition and modernity united.

2007   Halsschmuck, Meissener Porzellan®, Gold, Brillanten, Süßwasser Zuchtperlen — Necklace, Meissener Porzellan®, gold, diamonds, freshwater cultured pearls

2006   Halschmuck, Meissener Porzellan®, Gold, Onyx — Necklace, Meissener Porzellan®, gold, onyx

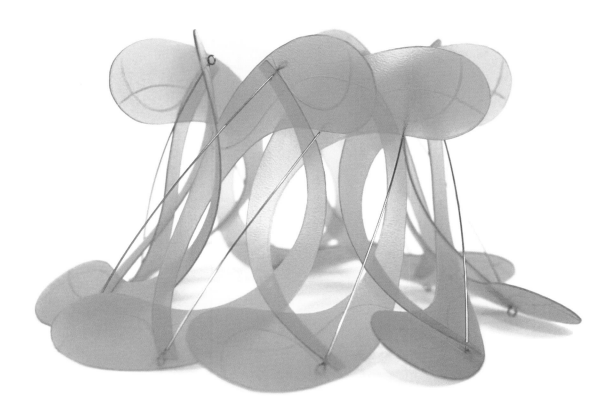

Wenn ein Schmuckstück entsteht, fragt
die Designerin nach der Korrespondenz zwischen
Rhythmus, Klang und innerer Gestalt.
— When a piece of jewellery is being created,
the designer inquires about the correspondence
between rhythm, sound and inner form.

2007   Armschmuck, Kunststoff, Stahl — Bracelet, plastic, steel

Durch rapid prototyping und traditionelle
Gusstechnik entstehen skulpturale Stücke von
architektonischer Wirkung.
— Sculptural pieces with a tectonic effect are
created by rapid prototyping and traditional
casting techniques.

2006   *Kanten-Armreif*, Gold — *Edge Lace bangle*, gold

2007   Broschen *small random* (kleiner Zufall), Aluminium, Stahl. *Medium random*
        (mittlerer Zufall), Silber, Stahl. *Medium lace* (mittlere Borte), Aluminium, Stahl
        — Brooches *small random*, aluminium, steel. *Medium random*, silver, steel.
        Medium lace, aluminium, steel

Zweidimensionale Strukturen in dreidimensionalen Objekten. Florale Formen erhalten neues Leben. — Two-dimensional structures in three-dimensional objects. Floral forms are given new life.

2007   *Schmuck-Postkarte*, Sperrholz — *Postable jewellery*, plywood

2007   *Blüten* Brosche, Silber, goldplattiert, Sperrholz, Zuchtperle — *Flourish* brooch, gold plated silver, plywood, cultured pearl

2007   Halsschmuck *Blütenkranz*, Silber goldplattiert, Sperrholz, Blattgold — Necklace *Petal wreath*, gold plated silver, plywood, goldleaf

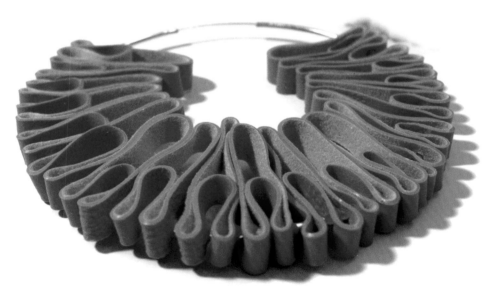

Schmuck, der auch ungetragen seine Ästhetik entfaltet. Die »Kostbarkeit« äußert sich in den Extremen von wertvoll und wertlos.
— Jewellery that unfolds its aesthetic even when not worn. »Value« is expressed in the extremes of valuable and worthless.

2007   Brosche *The Gloves' Dream* (Der Traum des Handschuhs), Gummi, Zuchtperlen, Silber — Brooch *The Gloves' Dream*, rubber, cultured pearls, silver

2007   Ohrring *The Gloves' Dream*, Gummi, Silber — Earring *The Gloves' Dream*, rubber, silver

Hinter der Reduziertheit verbergen sich
komplexe Formen. Schmuck als Einladung zur
Interaktion und zum Spiel.
— Complex forms are hidden behind reduction.
Jewellery as an invitation to interaction and play.

2006 Hals- oder Armschmuck *Garland*, Silber, vergoldet — Necklace or bracelet
Garland, silver-gilt

Neuinterpretation von Trachten und Trachtenschmuck
als individuelle Inszenierung am Körper. Diplomarbeit an
der Fachhochschule Düsseldorf.
— A new interpretation of livery and livery jewellery as
an individual staging on the body. A degree dissertation
at the University of Applied Science in Düsseldorf.

2008   Trachtenschmuck *EINTR8,* Kunststoff, Silikon, Textilien, Latex, Edelsteine, Silber, Glas, Gummi, Federn, etc. — Livery jewellery *EINTR8,* plastic, silicone, textiles, latex, gemstones, silver, glass, rubber, plumes, etc.

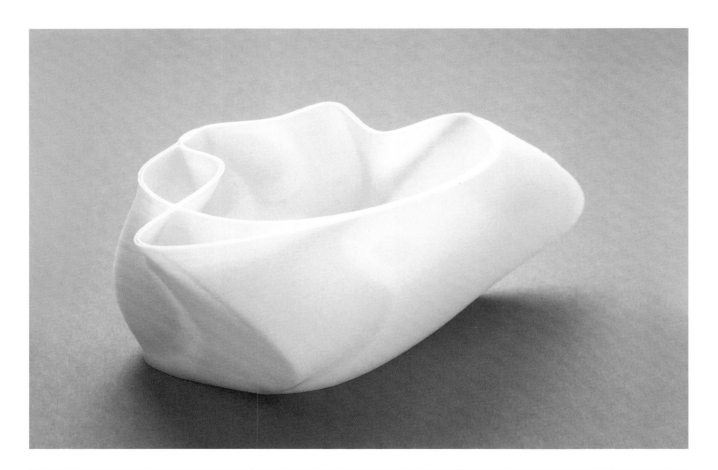

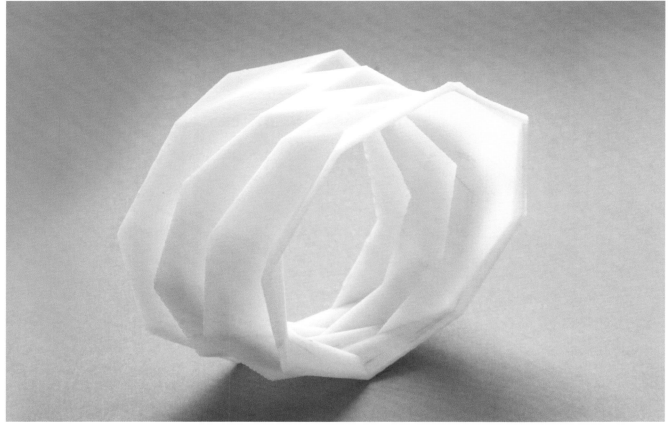

»Faltungen der Seele« des französischen
Philosophen Gilles Deleuze, übersetzt in Schmuck.
— »Folds of the soul« of the French philosopher
Gilles Deleuze translated into jewellery.

2006   Armreife, ABS-Kunststoff — Bangles, ABS plastic

Christina Karababa

Entwicklung
— Development

Schmuck-Designer und Manufakturen der Moderne — Jewellery Designers and Modern Manufactories

Kapitel 11 — Chapter 11

Die folgende Auswahl herausragender Protagonisten des modernen Schmuck-Designs ist chronologisch aufsteigend. Maßgebend ist das jeweilige Jahr, in dem die moderne Schmuckentwicklung begann. Nicht immer ist es das Gründungsjahr. Am Anfang steht die dänische Firma Georg Jensen, die bereits in den 1940er und 1950er Jahren gemeinsam mit namhaften Designern moderne Schmuck-Serien fertigte. Die Mehrzahl der modernen Schmuckateliers und Manufakturen entstand erst in den 1980er und 1990er Jahren.

The following selection of outstanding exponents of modern designer jewellery is arranged in chronological order, beginning with the earliest. The paramount aspect is the year in which the development towards modern jewellery began. That does not always mean the year a firm was founded. At the beginning is Georg Jensen, the Danish firm that was already making modern jewellery collections in collaboration with distinguished designers in the 1940s and 1950s. Most of the modern jewellery studios and makers only go back as far as the 1980s and 1990s.

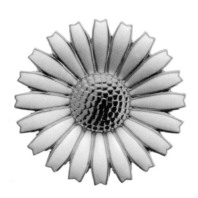

1941   1946

Georg Jensen

Georg Jensen war überzeugt, dass ein Schmuckstück oder eine Schale ebenso eine Skulptur sein kann wie die Plastik der Aphrodite. Der dänische Idealist und Romantiker, geboren in Raavad bei Kopenhagen, fühlte sich zum Künstler berufen. Deshalb studierte er nach der Lehre als Gold- und Silberschmied Bildhauerei. Dass er 1904 ein Unternehmen für Tafelsilber und für Schmuck gründete, hatte wirtschaftliche Gründe, doch seine gestalterischen Ambitionen bewahrte er sich. Entschieden lehnte er es ab, historische Formen industriell zu kopieren. Mit seiner handwerklichen Fertigung wurde er zum Begründer der Skornvirke-Bewegung in Dänemark, ein Äquivalent zur englischen Arts- and Crafts-Bewegung. Mit ihrer floralen Ornamentik gehören die Skornvirke-Schmuckstücke stilistisch zum Jugendstil.

Georg Jensen liebte das Silber, über das er 1926 poesievoll schrieb: »Silber ist das beste Material, das wir haben. Der Charakter des Silbers ist angenehm hartnäckig, er muss besiegt werden. Und das Silber hat diesen wundervollen Glanz des Mondlichts, etwas vom Licht einer dänischen Sommernacht.« Nach dem Tode Jensens 1935 wurde Harald Nielsen (1892–1977) künstlerischer Leiter der inzwischen auf mehrere hundert Mitarbeiter angewachsenen Firma. Nielsen war ein Anhänger der Neuen Sachlichkeit und schlichter Formen, wie folgendes Zitat belegt: »Das Dekor soll die Harmonie des Ganzen hervorheben, es existiert nicht um seiner selbst willen und darf nie dominieren.«

Unmittelbar nach dem Zweiten Weltkrieg wurden die Silberserien von Georg Jensen zum ersten großen Designthema im Schmuck, nicht nur in Dänemark, sondern auch in den USA, Japan und Deutschland. Der Sohn des Firmengründers, Søren Georg Jensen (1917–1982), hatte inzwischen die künstlerische Leitung übernommen. Er traf die weitsichtige Entscheidung, sofort nach Kriegsende die besten Designer Skandinaviens zu engagieren, darunter Henning Koppel (1918–1981), der vor den Nazis nach Schweden geflohen war und im Alter von 27 Jahren nach Kopenhagen zurückkehrte. Koppel entwarf Tafelsilber, Bestecke und Schmuck für Georg Jensen. Seine Stücke weisen in den 1940er Jahren reduzierte, jedoch organisch fließende Formen auf. Bezüge zu den Arbeiten des finnischen Designers Alvar Aalto und des Künstlers Alexander Calder sind erkennbar.

Nanna Ditzel (1923–2005) war die erste Designerin, die für Georg Jensen arbeitete. Die große Entwerferin des dänischen Möbeldesigns, für das sie mit höchsten Preisen ausgezeichnet wurde, entwarf von 1954 bis kurz vor ihrem Tod im Jahre 2005 für Georg Jensen Schmuck und Uhren in schlichten, doch immer raffinierten Formen. Als wichtigste Schmuck-Designerin für Georg Jensen entwickelte sich schließlich Vivianna Bülow-Hübe. 1927 im schwedischen Malmö geboren, lebte sie in den 1950er Jahren in Paris und gab sich den Künstlernamen Torun. Zu ihren Kunden zählten Brigitte Bardot, Ingrid Bergman und Billie Holiday. Alle liebten ihre weichen, fließenden Schmuckformen in Silber, die Torun gerne mit organisch

geschliffenen, preiswerten Edelsteinen und sogar mit Kieselsteinen ergänzte. Unkonventionell und selbstsicher bewegte sich die attraktive Persönlichkeit in der Kunst- und Modeszene in Paris, pflegte Umgang mit Picasso, Miró, Braque, Edith Piaf und Juliette Greco. Torun errang als Silberschmiedin Weltruhm und war bislang die einzige Schmuckdesignerin, die dank ihrer klassischen Schönheit auf die Titelseite einer »Vogue« kam.

Die Zusammenarbeit von Torun Bülow-Hübe mit Georg Jensen begann 1967. Ihre silberne Spangenuhr war wegweisend für die Schmuckuhren der 1960er und 1970er Jahre und zählt inzwischen zu den Archetypen des Uhrendesigns. In den 1970er Jahren rief die Idee von silbernen oder versilberten Spangenuhren viele Nachahmer auf den Plan. Mit ihrer *Ewigkeitsbrosche*, die auf dem Prinzip des Möbiusbandes basiert, schuf Torun eine Form, die geometrische Klarheit mit sinnlich erfahrbarer Transzendenz verbindet. Das Möbiusband, benannt nach dem deutschen Mathematiker und Astronomen August Ferdinand Möbius (1790–1868), hat nur eine Kante und eine Fläche. Die Form, die zum Nachdenken über die Unendlichkeit anregt, wurde im Schmuckdesign der Gegenwart von verschiedenen Designern aufgegriffen. Nach einem Aufenthalt von 1968 bis 1978 in Wolfsburg ging Torun im Auftrag ihrer Regierung 25 Jahre nach Jakarta in Indonesien, um ein soziales Pilotprojekt für Kinder durchzuführen. Für das moderne Schmuckdesign in Deutschland und vor allem für die Zusammenarbeit einer Manufaktur mit herausragenden Designern hatte Georg Jensen nach 1945 bis in die 1970er Jahre eine Vorbildfunktion.

E — Georg Jensen was convinced that a piece of jewellery or a bowl could be just as much a piece of sculpture as any Aphrodite statue. Born in Raavad near Copenhagen, the Danish idealist and romantic felt a vocation for art. He therefore served an apprenticeship as a goldsmith and silversmith, followed by academic training in sculpture. That he founded a business that sold table silver and jewellery in 1904 was primarily for economic reasons yet he never abandoned his ambitions in design. He emphatically refused to manufacture industrial copies of antique forms. His insistence on crafts over industry led him to found the Skornvirke movement in Denmark, the Danish equivalent of the English Arts and Crafts movement. Its floral decoration places Skornvirke jewellery close to Jugendstil/Art Nouveau.

Georg Jensen loved silver, about which he wrote the following poetically tinged comments in 1926: »Silver is the best material we have. The character of silver is agreeably intractable, it must be conquered. And silver has that marvellous gleam of moonlight, something of the light of a Danish summer night.« After Jensen's death in 1935, Harald Nielsen (1892–1977) became artistic director of the firm, which had by then grown large enough to employ a workforce of hundreds. Nielsen was an adherent of New Objectivity and simplicity of form, as the following quote proves: »Decora-

1957   2004   2005

tion should enhance the harmony of the whole; it does not exist for its own sake and must never be dominant.« The Georg Jensen lines in silver became the first big design hit immediately following the Second World War, not just in Denmark but also in the US, Japan and Germany. Søren Georg Jensen (1917–1982), son of the founder, had by then become artistic director. He took the far-sighted decision of hiring the best designers in Scandinavia as soon as the war was over. Among them was Henning Koppel (1918–1981), who had fled to Sweden to escape the National Socialists but returned to Copenhagen at the age of twenty-seven. Koppel designed table silver, cutlery and jewellery for Georg Jensen. His 1940s pieces are notable for reductive yet organically fluid forms. There are obvious links to the work of the Finnish designer Alvar Aalto and the American sculptor Alexander Calder.

Nanna Ditzel (1923–2005) was the first woman to work as a designer for Georg Jensen. The great innovator in Danish furniture design, for which she was awarded top prizes, designed jewellery and watches in simple yet invariably sophisticated forms for Georg Jensen from 1945 until shortly before she died in 2005. Vivianna Bülow-Hübe ultimately became the most important jewellery designer at Georg Jensen, second only to the founder himself. Born in Malmö, Sweden, in 1927, she lived in Paris in the 1950s and worked under the nom d'artiste Torun. Her distinguished clientele included such big names as Brigitte Bardot, Ingrid Bergman and Billie Holiday. They were all enamoured of the soft, fluid forms of the silver jewellery that Torun liked to set with organically cut, reasonably priced semiprecious stones and even with pebbles. Unconventional yet poised, Torun was a key member of the Paris art and fashion scene and kept company with the likes of Picasso, Miró, Braque, Edith Piaf and Juliette Greco. World-famous as a silversmith and a classic beauty, Torun remains the only jewellery designer ever to have made the cover of »Vogue«.

Torun Bülow-Hübe began working for Georg Jensen in 1967. Her silver bangle watch was groundbreaking in 1960s and 1970s watch design and is regarded as archetypal. In the 1970s the idea of silver or silvered bangle watches attracted a great many imitators. In the *Infinity brooch*, based on the principle of the Möbius strip, Torun launched a form that combines geometric astringency with sensuous experiential transcendency. The Möbius band, named after the German mathematician and astronomer August Ferdinand Möbius (1790–1868), has only one edge and a single surface. The form, that inspires contemplation of infinity, was taken up by various exponents of contemporary designer jewellery. After a ten-year stint at Wolfsburg, Germany (1968–1978), Torun was sent by the Swedish government to Jakarta, Indonesia, where she set up and managed a social pilot project for children. After 1945 and on into the 1970s, Georg Jensen's was the paramount influence on modern jewellery design in Germany, notably also for the practice of collaboration between jewellery factories and designers.

1941	Brosche *Daisy*, Design A. Michelsen, Silber, Email, Gold — Brooch *Daisy*, design A. Michelsen, silver, enamel, gold
1946	Brosche *Splash*, Design Henning Koppel, Silber — Brooch *Splash*, design Henning Koppel, silver
1957	Armreif *Möbius*, Design Vivianna Torun Bülow-Hübe, Silber — Bangle *Möbius*, design Vivianna Torun Bülow-Hübe, silver
2004	Ring *Cave*, Design Jacqueline Rabun, Silber — Ring *Cave*, design Jacqueline Rabun, silver
2005	Armreif *Infinity*, Design Regitze Overgaard, Silber — Bangle *Infinity*, design Regitze Overgaard, silver

Georg Jensen
1866–1935, geboren in Raavad bei Kopenhagen. Firmengründung 1904. Designer u.a. Henning Koppel, Torun Bülow-Hübe, Nana Ditzel.

Georg Jensen
1866–1935, born in Raavad near Copenhagen, founded firm in 1904. Designers Henning Koppel, Torun Bülow-Hübe, Nana Ditzel etc.

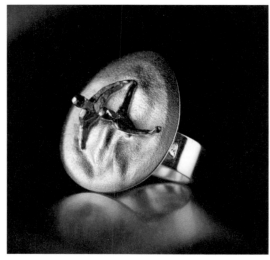

1969

1969

1969

1986

1995

1969	Ring *Dance in the galaxy*, Design Björn Weckström, Silber — Ring *Dance in the galaxy*, design Björn Weckström, silver
1969	Halsschmuck *Planetentäler*, Design Björn Weckström, Silber — Necklace *Planetoid valleys*, design Björn Weckström, silver
1970	Ring *Turmalinsteg*, Design Björn Weckström, Gold, Turmalin — Ring *Tourmaline river*, design Björn Weckström, gold, tourmaline
1971	Ring *Petrified lake*, Design Björn Weckström, Silber und Acryl — Ring *Petrified lake*, design Björn Weckström, silver and acrylic
1982	Ring *Spitzbergen*, Design Björn Weckström, Gold, Diamanten — Ring *Spitsbergen*, design Björn Weckström, gold, diamonds
1969	Werbemotiv: Ringe *Diamantstadt, Diamanttürme, Diamantbrücke*, Design Björn Weckström — Motive for advertising: Rings *Diamond city*, *Diamond turret, Diamond bridge*, design Björn Weckström
1986	Werbemotiv: Halsschmuck und Armband *Tenochtitlan*, Armband *Faro*, Design Björn Weckström — Motive for advertising: Necklace and bracelet *Tenochtitlan*, bracelet *Faro*, design Björn Weckström
1995	Werbemotiv: Halsschmuck *Poema*, Ohrschmuck *Nastassia*, Design Björn Weckström — Motive for advertising: Necklace *Poema*, earrings *Nastassia*, design Björn Weckström

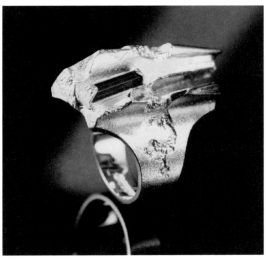

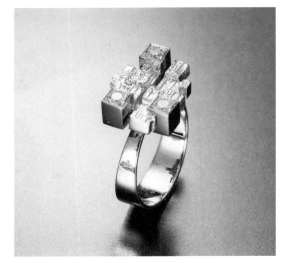

1970   1971   1982

Lapponia

Der Gründer von Lapponia, Pekka Valdemar Anttila, 1931–1985, und der Schmuckgestalter und Bildhauer Björn Weckström, geboren 1935, lernten sich auf der Goldschmiedeschule in Helsinki kennen, die sie beide von 1949 bis 1953 besuchten. Weckström nahm 1961 an der legendären ersten Ausstellung für Schmuckkunst in der Goldsmiths' Hall in London teil. Zu Beginn der 1960er Jahre entwickelte er eine Formensprache, die der finnischen Natur und der Kunst des Informel verbunden ist. Sie stand deutlich im Widerspruch zum reduzierten skandinavischen Design der 1950er Jahre.

In der Bildenden Kunst hatten ab etwa 1940 der abstrakte Expressionismus in den USA und das Informel in Europa den Konstruktivismus und den Surrealismus abgelöst oder in den Hintergrund gedrängt. Die Spontaneität war Malern wie Willem de Kooning und Jackson Pollock wichtiger als Perfektion und Reglementierung. Über die Motivation schreibt der finnische Kunstkritiker Kaj Kalin: »Weckströms Lapponia-Ästhetik, die sich auf den Informalismus stützt, widerspricht den Formmodellen, die von den Modernisten bewundert werden. Wir treffen auf eine Welt, die voller Fragmente, voller Aufhebung von Rangordnungen und Unvollkommenheiten ist und es auch immer sein wird. Wir bewegen uns in einem Raum, in dem die Möglichkeit, Zerbrechlichkeit und Zartheit, Bruchstückhaftes und Unfertiges zu suchen, nicht endet.«

Deutlicher als bei den mitteleuropäischen Goldschmieden resultierten die expressiven Schmuckformen bei Weckström aus einem Gefühl für die Großartigkeit der Natur. Seine Inspirationsquellen waren stürzende Wasserfälle, die »Ornamente« von Baumrinden, Faltungen und Brüche von Felsen. Auch die Oberflächen von Schnee und Eis übersetzte er gefühlvoll in Gold und Silber. Schließlich fand auch die nordische Mythologie und Naturromantik Eingang in seinen Schmuck. Zum Gründungsmythos von Lapponia gehört die Geschichte, dass Frau Aho, eine Kundin Björn Weckströms, 1961 eine »interessante und anspruchsvolle Arbeit« bestellte. Sie sollte aus unbearbeiteten, kleinen Goldnuggets des Lemmenjoki-Flusses in Lappland gefertigt werden. Weckström gefiel die blass schimmernde Farbe und die unregelmäßige Oberfläche der Goldstücke so gut, dass er sie auch in der fertigen Arbeit erhalten wollte. Er verzichtete auf die übliche Hochglanzpolitur und bewahrte den ureigenen, von Wasser und Sand geformten Charakter des Goldes; das erste Lapin-Korut-Schmuckstück war entstanden. Das Lappengold stand später auch Pate beim Markennamen Lapponia.

Die erste Anzeige von Lapin-Korut erschien 1966 in einer Tageszeitung Helsinkis mit dem Slogan: »Kihloiksi Lapin kihlat, lahjoiksi Lapin korut.« Dieser Werbespruch, »Verlobt mit Lappengold, beschenkt mit Lappland-Schmuck«, zeigt, dass man zu Beginn die traditionellen Gefühle des Schmuckschenkens, die finnische Landschaft und damit auch die nationale Identität ansprach. Mehrere glückliche Umstände führten dazu, dass das Lappengold mit den romantischen Namen wie Inselkönig, Kardinal, Opus oder Blühende Mauer zu einem Welterfolg wurde. 1971 schenkte ein Londoner Juwelier der damaligen Miss World, der Argentinierin Lucia Petterle, einen Goldanhänger Weckströms. Zehn Millionen Zuschauer sahen die Misswahl im Fernsehen. 1972 schnellten die Verkaufszahlen nach einer Dick Cavett-Fernsehshow in den USA in die Höhe. Offenbar hatte sich der Kameramann in den neuen Lapponia-Ring von Yoko Ono, die mit John Lennon zu Gast war, verliebt und zeigte ihn mehrmals in Nahaufnahme. Yoko Ono hatte das Schmuckstück Versteinerter See aus Silber mit Acryl ein Jahr zuvor in Göteborg gekauft. Er gehörte zu der Kollektion Space Silver. Die ersten Stücke waren 1969 vorgestellt worden, rechtzeitig zur Landung von Apollo 11 auf dem Mond. Weckström hatte einen Schmuck für den modernen Ikarus entwickelt. Mit der Raumfahrt verband sich die Sehnsucht nach außerirdischen Welten, nach Weite und Befreiung von der Erdenschwere.

Bis zur Kollektion Space Silver waren die Schmuckserien von Lapponia nur in Gold ausgeführt mit Farbedelsteinen wie Turmalin, Rauchquarz und Bergkristall oder Spektrolith, manchmal auch mit Diamanten und Zuchtperlen. Die »Reise« in galaktische Sphären stützte sich nun auf Silber, das von Weckström mit harten rauen Oberflächen gestaltet wurde. Dies verwies auf die metallische Struktur ferner Planeten und nicht mehr auf den romantischen Schimmer des Mondlichts. In der Kollektion Space Silver tauchten oft auch kleine Menschenfiguren auf. Eroberer oder Verlorene? Ergänzt wurde das Silber durch Acryl mit teils psychedelisch wirkenden farbigen Bläschen im Innern. Acryl war der moderne Kunststoff, der in den 1960er Jahren von Künstlern, Designern und Schmuckgestaltern wie dem Österreicher Fritz Maierhofer und dem Deutschen Claus Bury eingesetzt worden war.

Neben Björn Weckström gewann Pekka Anttila 1971 den Dänen Poul Havgaard, 1936 geboren, als zweiten Designer für Lapponia. Dieser hatte als Schmied begonnen und arbeitete einige Jahre als Keramiker, bevor er den Schmuck als sein Thema entdeckte. Für Havgaard war die Natur sinnlich und weiblich weich. Zu den zwischen 1967 und 1971 gestalteten Gürtelschließen für Pierre Cardin schreibt Kaj Kalin: »Gürtel, im Geist des ›Body Sculpture-Trends‹ geschmiedet, Verzierungen von Taschen und Broschen, waren von Haavgard kreierte Werke, mit denen man in der Öffentlichkeit sein eigenes Ich erotisch entblößen konnte.« Das 3-D Silver, so wurde die erste Kollektion von Poul Havgaard 1971 genannt, ergänzte die Arbeiten Björn Weckströms. Es war Schmuck im Sinne von Anschmiegen.

1975 begann die Zusammenarbeit mit dem Ungarn Zoltan Popovits. Er hatte seine Kindheit in Amerika verbracht und war als Kunststudent nach Helsinki gekommen. Seine erste Arbeit für Lapponia war die Gestaltung eines Schachspiels, bei dem jede Figur eine Skulptur ist. Sein Schmuck ist von den Vorstellungen der Indianer beeinflusst, deren Rituale er als Jugendlicher kennenlernte. Wie seine Skulpturen sprechen seine Schmuckserien das Unterbewusste an. Es sind individuelle Formen, inspiriert von den Erschei-

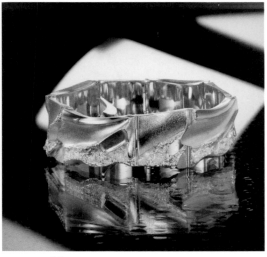

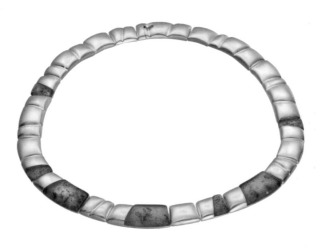

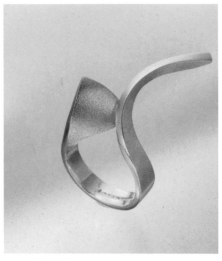

1988   1995   2005

nungen der Natur. Sie weisen immer über das Sichtbare unserer Welt hinaus. Für den Elsässer Designer Christophe Burger, geboren 1950, ist Schmuck ein Mittel der Kommunikation. Mit ihm kamen 1990 etwas strengere, manchmal auch kühne, geometrische Formen ins Programm. Seine Stücke in Gelb- und Weißgold sind ergänzt mit Diamanten und farbigen Edelsteinen. Auch zwei deutsche Gestalter arbeiten bis heute mit Lapponia zusammen. Nicht als Designer, sondern als kreative Edelsteinschleifer: Dieter Lorenz aus Idar-Oberstein und Bernd Munsteiner aus Stipshausen. Ihre frei geschliffenen Edelsteine werden seit 1972 von Lapponia verwendet.

In den 1990er Jahren begann eine wirtschaftlich schwierige Phase für Lapponia. Ein Grund dafür mag der frühe Tod des Firmengründers Pekka Anttila im Jahr 1985 gewesen sein. Auch hatte sich in den 1980er und 1990er Jahren das Schmuck-Design gewandelt. Im Jahre 2005 wurde Lapponia von der finnischen Traditionsfirma Kalevala Koru übernommen. Die Kalevala-Koru-Gruppe ist heute mit den Marken Lapponia Jewelry und Kalevala Jewelry in Finnland Marktführer und der bedeutendste Schmuckproduzent in Skandinavien. Mit mehr als 250 Mitarbeitern wird ein jährlicher Umsatz von etwa 24 Millionen Euro erzielt.

Dr. Laura Lares, die Anfang 2007 die Verantwortung für die Marken Lapponia und Kalevala übernahm, erklärt zum gegenwärtigen Schmuckkonzept von Lapponia: »Das Designkonzept verbindet heute die kreativen Wurzeln der Lapponia-Gründungsjahre mit innovativen internationalen Einflüssen.« Seit 2008 steht die Neuinterpretation des Themas *Ikaros* von Björn Weckström auf dem Programm. Der *Black Ikaros* mit Collier und passendem Ring »fliegt mit schwarzen Flügeln auf in neue Höhen.« Das neue Schmuck-set *Reef* von Zoltan Popovits, bestehend aus Collier und Armband, schimmert wie Mondschein auf der Wasseroberfläche. Mit dem Collier *Summer Romance Duo* bringt die taiwanesische Schmuckdesignerin Chao-Hsien Kuo florale Romantik in die Kollektion. Als international orientierte Marke richtet sich der Blick von Lapponia natürlich auch verstärkt nach Asien.

E — The co-founders of Lapponia, Pekka Valdemar Anttila (1931–1985) and the jewellery designer and sculptor Björn Weckström (born in 1935), met at the goldsmithing school in Helsinki, which they both attended from 1949 until 1953. In 1961 Weckström took part in the legendary first exhibition for art jewellery at Goldsmiths' Hall in London. In the early 1960s, he developed a language of forms that is indebted to Finnish scenery and Informel. It contrasted sharply with the reductive 1950s Scandinavian design.

In fine art, Abstract Expressionism in the US and Informel in Europe had replaced Constructivism and Surrealism or at least thrust it out of the mainstream. Spontaneity was more important than perfection and regimentation to painters such as Willem de Kooning and Jackson Pollock. The Finnish art critic Kaj Kalin writes as follows on the motivation underlying

the change: »Weckström's Lapponia aesthetic, which is based on Informel, clashes with the form models admired by the Modernists. We encounter a world that is full of fragments, full of the suspension of spatial arrangements and imperfections and always will be. We are moving in a space in which the possibility of seeking fragility and delicacy, the fragmentary and unfinished, is infinite.«

More obviously than was the case with central European goldsmiths, Weckström's expressive forms of jewellery were the result of a feeling for the grandeur of nature. His sources of information were gushing waterfalls, the »ornamental markings« on tree bark, the folds and breaks in rocks. He also translated the textures of snow and ice with great empathy into gold and silver. Finally, Nordic mythology and romanticisation of nature also flowed into his jewellery. Part of the Lapponia foundation legend is the story that Mrs Aho, a client of Björn Weckström, ordered an »interesting and ambitious work« in 1961. It was to be made with small unworked nuggets of gold from the River Lemmenjoki in Lapland Province. Weckström liked the pale shimmering colour and the irregular surface of the gold nuggets so much that he wanted to keep them that way in the finished work. He eschewed the usual high gloss polish and kept the primal character of the gold, formed as it was by water and sand; the first *Lapin-Korut* piece of jewellery had seen the light of day. Lap gold also gave its name to the Lapponia label.

The first advertisement for *Lapin-Korut* appeared in a Helsinki daily in 1966, featuring the slogan: »Kihloiksi Lapin kihlat, lahjoiksi Lapin korut.« This advertising slogan, which translates as »Affianced with Lap gold, dowered with Lapland jewellery,« shows that from the outset the feelings traditionally associated with giving jewellery, with the Finnish scenery and, therefore, the national identity, were being addressed.

Several fortunate circumstances led to the Lap gold creations with such romantic names as *Island King*, *Cardinal*, *Opus* and *Blooming Wall* becoming an international hit. In 1971, a London jeweller presented the then Miss World, Lucia Petterle from Argentina, with a Weckström gold pendant. Ten million television viewers watched the Miss World contest. In 1972 Lapponia sales soared after a Dick Cavett telecast in the US. A cameraman had evidently lost his heart to the new Lapponia ring worn by Yoko Ono, who was a guest with John Lennon on the show, and showed it several times in close-up. Yoko Ono had bought the piece of jewellery called *Petrified Lake*, made of silver and acrylic, the year before in Göteborg. It belonged to the Lapponia *Space Silver* collection. The first pieces had been launched in 1969 just in time for the Apollo 11 moon landing. Weckström had developed jewellery for a modern Icarus. After all, yearnings for extra-terrestrial worlds, for space and liberation from gravity were associated with space travel. Until the *Space Silver* collection came on the market, Lapponia jewellery collections had only been executed in gold set with coloured semiprecious stones

2005   2006   2008

such as tourmalines, smoky quartz and rock crystal or spectrolith and some-times also with diamonds and pearls. The »journey« to galactic spheres was now based on silver, which Weckström had configured with harsh, rough surfaces. This quality alluded to the metallic structure of distant planets rather than the romantic sheen of moonlight. Small human figures also often appeared in *Space Silver*. Were they conquerors or lost souls? The silver was complemented by acrylic, some of which featured bubbles in psychedelic colours as inclusions. Acrylic was the modern plastic that was used in the 1960s by numerous artists, designers and jewellery designers, including Fritz Maierhofer in Austria and Claus Bury in Germany.

In addition to Björn Weckström, Pekka Anttila hired in 1971 Poul Havgaard (born in 1936), a Danish jewellery designer, as the second Lapponia designer. Havgaard had started out as a smith and worked for some years as a ceramicist before he discovered jewellery as his medium of choice. As Havgaard saw it, nature was sensuous and softly feminine. Kaj Kalin de-scribes the belt buckles Havgaard designed for Pierre Cardin between 1967 and 1971 as: »Belts, forged in the spirit of ›body sculpture‹ trends, deco-ration for handbags and brooches were works created by Haavgard with which one might erotically expose one's ego in public.« *3-D Silver*, thus the name Poul Havgaard gave to his first collection in 1971, complemented Björn Weckström's work. It was jewellery in the sense that it snuggled up to the wearer's body.

In 1975 Lapponia began to work with Zoltan Popovits. Born in Hun-gary, he had spent his childhood in the US and had gone to Helsinki as an art student. The first thing he designed for Lapponia was a chess set, with each piece a sculpture. His jewellery is influenced by ideas he learnt about from the Indians, the Native Americans, whose rituals he became familiar with as an adolescent. Like his sculpture, his jewellery collections appeal to the subconscious. These are distinctive forms, inspired by natural phenom-ena and invariably transcending the visual plane of our world. For the Alsa-tian designer Christophe Burger (born in 1950), jewellery is a means of com-munication. When he joined the Lapponia team in 1990, rather more astrin-gent, sometimes quite bold, geometric forms were added to the range. His pieces in yellow and white gold are set with diamonds and coloured precious stones. Two German designers also continue to collaborate with Lapponia, not as designers, but as creative gem-cutters: Dieter Lorenz from Idar-Ober-stein and Bernd Munsteiner from Stipshausen. Lapponia has used their free-style cuts since 1972.

The 1990s marked a difficult phase for Lapponia in financial terms. One reason for the downturn may be the untimely death of Pekka Anttila, the founder, in 1985. Moreover, designer jewellery had changed in the 1980s and 1990s. Lapponia was taken over by the venerable Finnish firm Kalevala Koru in 2005. Today the Kalevala-Koru Group is, with the Lapponia Jewelry

and Kalevala Jewelry labels, the market leader in Finland and the most im-portant jewellery producer in Scandinavia. Employing a workforce of more than 250, Kalevala-Koru achieves yearly sales amounting to about 24 million euro. Dr. Laura Lares, who assumed the responsibility for the Lapponia and Kalevala labels early in 2007, explains the current Lapponia jewellery concept as follows: »Today the design concept links the creative roots of the Lapponia founder years with innovative cosmopolitan influences.« Since 2008, a re-interpretation of Björn Weckström's *Icarus* theme has figured prominently in the range. *Black Ikaros* with a necklace and matching ring, »flies on black wings to new heights«. The new Reef set by Zoltan Popovits, consisting of a necklace and bracelet, gleams like moonlight on the surface of a lake. The *Summer Romance Duo* necklace by the Taiwanese designer Chao-Hsien Kuo adds floral romanticism to the collection. As an internationally oriented label, Lapponia is also looking increasingly to Asia.

1988	Armband *Narda*, Design Björn Weckström, Gold, Platin — Bracelet *Narda*, design Björn Weckström, gold, platinum
1995	Halsschmuck *Midsummer*, Design Poul Havgaard, Silber, Bernstein — Necklace *Midsummer*, design Poul Havgaard, silver, amber
2005	Ring *Vier Jahreszeiten-Herbst*, Design Pekka Hirvonen, Gold — Ring *Four seasons-fall*, design Pekka Hirvonen, gold
2005	Ring *Cintia*, Design Zoltan Popovits, Silber — Ring *Cintia*, design Zoltan Popovits, silver
2006 –2007	Ringe *Anô Homme*, *Anô Femme* und *Anô Precious*, Design Christophe Burger, Gold, Diamanten — Rings *Anô Homme*, *Anô Femme* and *Anô Precious*, design Christophe Burger, gold, diamonds
2008	Halsschmuck *Summer Romance Duo*, Design Chao-Hsien Kuo, Silber, Gold — Necklace *Summer Romance Duo*, design Chao-Hsien Kuo, silver, gold

Björn Weckström
geboren 1935 in Helsinki. Gemeinsam mit dem Firmengründer Pekka Valdemar Anttila 1949–1953 Goldschmiedeschule Helsinki.

Björn Weckström
Born in 1935 in Helsinki. Together with the company founder Pekka Valdemar Anttila goldsmithing school Helsinki 1949–1953.

1966

1984

Bernd Munsteiner

Das Edelsteinschleifen lernte Bernd Munsteiner, geboren im Hunsrückort Mörschied, von seinem Vater. An der Kunst- und Werkschule Pforzheim erhielt der 19-jährige 1962 im ersten Semester den Auftrag, eine Werkstatt für den Edelsteinschliff einzurichten. Die kreative Aufbruchsstimmung war geprägt durch die Professoren Schollmayer, Reiling und Ullrich. Sie ermutigten Munsteiner, den althergebrachten Schliffen Neues entgegenzusetzen. Die meisten Edelsteinschliffe waren in der Renaissance im 15. und 16. Jahrhundert entwickelt worden. Die Edelsteinindustrie hatte sich bislang mit kleinen Änderungen begnügt. So wurden die Altschliff-Diamanten um 1910 durch den Brillantschliff, auch Vollschliff genannt, abgelöst.

Die Orientierung an der Bildenden Kunst war typisch für die Schmuckgestalter an den Fachakademien der 1960er bis 1980er Jahre. Wie der Finne Björn Weckström ließen sich auch in Deutschland Ende der 1960er Jahre Goldschmiede vom Abstrakten Expressionismus, in Europa Informel genannt, inspirieren. Zu ihnen zählte Klaus Ullrich, der wie Reinhold Reiling und die Mitstudierenden Robert Smit aus Amsterdam sowie Adolf Drobny aus Linz Steine mit den neuen Schliffen sofort in seinem Schmuck einsetzte.

Jahrhunderte lang waren Gemmen und Kameen nach antiken Vorbildern entstanden. Bernd Munsteiner öffnete mit seinen Achatreliefs erstmals den Blick für die Form- und Farbenvielfalt dieses in seiner Heimat traditionell verwendeten Steins. Ein weiteres Thema waren seine *Reflektierenden Perspektiven*. Mit ihren ungewohnten Einschnitten waren sie eine Provokation für die traditionelle Edelsteinindustrie. Bernd Munsteiner machte oft Kunststoffmodelle, die später in Stein geschliffen wurden. Auf ähnliche Weise arbeitete in den 1960er Jahren auch Friedrich Becker. Der Düsseldorfer Konstruktivist ließ jedoch geometrisch gestaltete Steine, Würfel und Pyramiden, nicht selten Synthesen, nach seinen Angaben in Idar-Oberstein schleifen. Doch auch Munsteiner ergänzte das Repertoire klarer Formen im Schmuck. 1965 meldete er die Schliffe *Context Cut* und *Spirit Sun* zum Patent an.

Nach Ende seiner Ausbildung reiste Munsteiner 1967 nach Frankfurt, um die innovativen Schliffe der Diamantfirma Keller & Co. anzubieten. Die Schwester des Inhabers sei sehr interessiert gewesen, erzählt Bernd Munsteiner über diese Begegnung. »Der Keller hat mich erst mal drei Stunden sitzen lassen, wie das damals so üblich war.« Aus Kostengründen hatte Munsteiner keinen weißen Diamanten, sondern einen gelben vorgelegt. Der Diamanthändler habe nicht einmal beachtet, dass der Stein eine vollkommen neue Form hatte. Er sah nur die Einschlüsse und dass der Diamant nicht weiß, sondern gelb war. Damit war das Thema für ihn erledigt. Zu den Kunden des aufstrebenden Ateliers in Stipshausen in den 1970er Jahren zählten Wolf-Peter Schwarz, Ulm, Michael Zobel, Konstanz, Dieter Pieper, Lüdenscheid, Klaus Wurzbacher, Berlin, und der schon erwähnte Adolf Drobny aus Linz. Im seriellen Schmuckdesign wurden die Munsteiner-Schliffe erstmals 1969 von der Pforzheimer Schmuckmarke art-design eingesetzt.

Munsteiner erinnert sich: »Ich habe ihnen meine Modelle vorgestellt und sie haben sich überlegt, was sie daraus machen könnten. Die sind richtig schwer eingestiegen.« 1973 schrieb der Edelsteingestalter an Björn Weckström in Helsinki, um ihm seine Schliffe anzubieten. Munsteiners Zusammenarbeit mit Lapponia entwickelte sich ebenso erfolgreich wie mit der Silberschmiede Hans Hansen, Kopenhagen, deren Schmuck auch in Deutschland gut ankam. 1975 konnte der Edelsteingestalter die dänische Firma Georg Jensen und insbesondere Torun Bülow-Hübe für seine neuen Schliffe begeistern. Nach den Skandinaviern, die Schmuckserien mit seinen Edelsteinen an ein größeres Publikum absetzten, kamen 1974 japanische, anschließend auch deutsche Firmen wie cédé in Pforzheim hinzu. In den 1980er Jahren wurden die künstlerisch geschliffenen Unikate von Bernd Munsteiner weltweit bekannt. Selbst große Juweliere wie Hans Stern in Rio de Janeiro zählten zu seinen Kunden. Viele seiner Arbeiten werden bis heute von Sammlern gekauft. Doch auch mit seinen strengen Designentwürfen hat Bernd Munsteiner Schmuckgeschichte geschrieben. 1989 wurden die beiden Schliffe *Context Cut* und *Spirit Sun* von Dr. Ullrich Freiesleben gekauft. Sie werden heute in dessen Diamantmanufaktur bei Münster geschliffen und von renommierten Goldschmiedeateliers in Unikaten und Kleinserien verwendet.

Seit 1997 wird das Edelstein-Atelier von Tom Munsteiner geführt, der ebenfalls neue Schliffe entwickelt. Zum Kreis der kreativen Edelsteingestalter zählt heute auch der Idar-Obersteiner Dieter Lorenz. Doch hat Bernd Munsteiner vor allem im kleinen Stipshausen im Hunsrück seine Nachfolger und Mitstreiter gefunden. Thomas und Jörg Stoffel, dessen Frau Claudia Adam sowie sein Sohn Tom Munsteiner haben seit den1990er Jahren eigenständige Beiträge im modernen Edelsteinschliff geleistet. Der Pionier des kreativen Schliffs, der »Picasso der Edelsteine«, wie er auch schon genannt wurde, ist längst nicht mehr allein auf weiter Flur.

E — Bernd Munsteiner, who was born in Mörschied in the Hunsrück, learned gem-cutting from his father. In his first term at the Pforzheim Kunst- und Werkschule in 1962, when he was only nineteen years old, Bernd Munsteiner was given the assignment to set up a gem-cutting workshop. The mood of setting out for new horizons prevailing at the school was shaped by Professors Schollmayer, Reiling and Ullrich, who encouraged Munsteiner to confront the traditional cuts with something new. Most gemstone cuts had been developed during the 15th and 16th centuries in the Renaissance and the gemstone industry had since then remained satisfied with only minor changes. The old rose cut, for instance, was replaced around 1910 by the round brilliant cut, which was a vast improvement on the old European cut (double-cut brilliant).

Tracking developments in the fine arts was typical of jewellery designers at specialist academies between the 1960s and 1980s. Like Björn

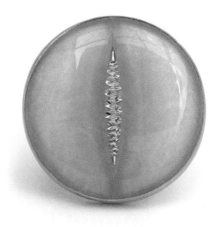

1989   1993   2001

Weckström of Finland, goldsmiths in Germany in the late 1960s were inspired by Abstract Expressionism, usually known as Informel in Europe. Among them were Klaus Ullrich, who like Reinhold Reiling and Robert Smit from Amsterdam, a fellow student, as well as Adolf Drobny from Linz, immediately started using stones with the new cuts in their jewellery.

For centuries, gemstones and cameos were cut as they had been in Greco-Roman antiquity. With his agate reliefs, Bernd Munsteiner opened up the prospects for form and colour diversity of this stone traditionally used in his native region. He was also preoccupied with the critical angle for internal-reflections of gemstones. The unusual cuts he used made his stones provocative as far as the traditional gemstone industry was concerned. Bernd Munsteiner often made plastic models for the cuts he would later make in stones. Friedrich Becker, a Düsseldorf Constructivist, also worked along similar lines in the 1960s. Becker, however, had geometrically designed stones, cubes and pyramids, often synthetics, cut in Idar-Oberstein to his specifications. Munsteiner, too, enlarged the canon of clear forms in jewellery. In 1965 he applied for a patent on two cuts: *Context Cut* and *Spirit Sun*.

After finishing his formal education and training, Munsteiner went to Frankfurt in 1967 to offer his innovative cuts to the diamond dealers Keller & Co. The proprietor's sister was very interested in this encounter as Bernd Munsteiner tells it. »Keller just let me sit there cooling my heels for three hours as was the usual practice in those days.« For reasons of economy, Munsteiner had presented him with a yellow rather than a white diamond. The diamond dealer did not even notice that the stone had a completely different, new form. All he saw were the inclusions and the fact that the diamond was yellow rather than white. That represented sufficient grounds for dismissing the subject altogether.

The 1970s clientele of the aspiring studio in Stipshausen included Wolf-Peter Schwarz (Ulm), Michael Zobel (Konstanz), Dieter Pieper (Lüdenscheid), Klaus Wurzbacher (Berlin) and Adolf Drobny from Linz, mentioned above. The Munsteiner cuts were first used in mass-produced designer jewellery by the Pforzheim jewellery label art-design in 1969. As Munsteiner recalls: »I presented them with my new models and they thought about what they might be able to do with them. They really went into it in a big way.« In 1973 Munsteiner wrote to Björn Weckström in Helsinki to offer him his new cuts. Munsteiner's collaboration with Lapponia developed into as much a success as the work he did with the Copenhagen silversmith Hans Hansen, whose jewellery was also popular in Germany. In 1975 Munsteiner succeeded in making the renowned Danish firm of Georg Jensen and Torun Bülow-Hübe in particular enthusiastic about his new cuts. The Scandinavian jewellery lines with Munsteiner's gemstones sold well and they were followed by Japanese firms in 1974 and ultimately German ones, including cédé in Pforzheim. By the 1980s Bernd Munsteiner's art-cut one-offs had become famous worldwide. His clientele included even such large jewellery stores as Hans Stern in Rio de Janeiro. Many of his works are still being bought by collectors. However, Bernd Munsteiner also made history with his austere jewellery designs. In 1989 the two Munsteiner cuts, *Context Cut* and *Spirit Sun,* were bought by Dr. Ullrich Freiesleben. Today these cuts are carried out in his diamond-cutting factory near Münster and used by upmarket goldsmithing studios in one-off pieces and jewellery in limited editions.

Since 1997 the gemstone studio in Stipshausen has been run by Tom Munsteiner, who has also been developing creative new cuts. Dieter Lorenz in Idar-Oberstein is another creative gemstone designer. Bernd Munsteiner's following and immediate successors, on the other hand, are located mainly in the small town of Stipshausen in the Hunsrück. Thomas and Jörg Stoffel, whose wife, Claudia Adam, and son, Tom Munsteiner, have been making their own independent contributions to modern gem-cutting since the 1990s. For quite some time now, the pioneer of the creative cut, the »Picasso of gemstones,« as Bernd Munsteiner has been dubbed, has not been the only creative gem-cutter far and wide in the Hunsrück.

1966	Brosche *Carneolrelief*, Gold — Brooch *Carnelian relief*, gold
1984	*Inside Selecting*, Citrin, 923,16 ct — *Inside Selecting*, citrine, 923,16 ct
1989	Bild/Brosche *Erotik*, Sarderonyxrelief, Gold, Platin, Brillant — Picture/brooch *Eroticism*, sarderonyx relief, gold, platinum, diamond
1993	Brosche *Erotik*, Aquamarin, Platin — Brooch *Eroticism*, aquamarine, platinum
2001	Ring *Reflektierende Perspektiven*, Design Jörg Munsteiner, Aquamarin, Turmalin, Platin — Ring *Reflecting Perspectives*, design Jörg Munsteiner, aquamarine, tourmaline, platinum

Bernd Munsteiner
Geboren 1943 in Mörschied. 1962–1966 Kunst- und Werkschule Pforzheim. Ateliergründung 1965, seit 1973 in Stipshausen.

Bernd Munsteiner
Born in Mörschied in 1943. 1962–1966 Kunst- und Werkschule Pforzheim. Founded studio in 1965, in Stipshausen since 1973.

1967

1976

1976

1976

Charlotte · Ehinger-Schwarz 1876

Dass Wolf-Peter Schwarz 1959 bei seinem Großvater Otto Ehinger, 1880–1967, eine Goldschmiedelehre begann, war nicht ganz freiwillig. Viel lieber gab er sich seiner Leidenschaft des Zeichnens und Malens hin. Seine frühen Arbeiten sind signiert mit dem Künstlernamen Wolf Erchanger oder kurz Werch. Von seinen Eltern vor die Alternative gestellt, entweder zur Bundeswehr oder beim Opa in die Lehre zu gehen, entschied sich Wolf-Peter Schwarz für die Ausbildung bei dem 79-jährigen Großvater. Dieser hatte 1898–1901 die Königliche Zeichenakademie in Hanau besucht, wo er als Bester ausgezeichnet worden war. Nach der Zulassung an der Kunstakademie in Paris musste er 1904 in die elterliche Firma in Ulm eintreten.

»Mein Opa war noch mit 80 Jahren ein hervorragender Handwerker«, erzählt Wolf-Peter Schwarz. Otto Ehinger II, dessen gleichnamiger Vater 1876 die »Otto Ehinger – Kunstgewerbliche Werkstätte« gegründet hatte, war Silberschmied, Goldschmied, Ziseleur und Graveur. Mit diesen Fertigkeiten, erworben zur Zeit des Jugendstils, produzierte er bis zu seinem Tod 1967 hauptsächlich historischen Ulmer Schmuck, auf den bereits Otto Ehinger I. seit 1876 spezialisiert war. Wolf-Peter Schwarz wurde schnell in die Produktion der Schmuckstücke aus Gold mit Donauperlen, Gagat oder Onyx eingelernt. Bald musste er die Barockschnörkel biegen, das Blattwerk montieren und die Steine fassen. Als Ausgleich habe er während der ganzen Lehrzeit zuhause »möglichst blutige Bilder« gemalt.

Nach der Gesellenprüfung und dem Tod von Otto Ehinger II. reiste Wolf-Peter Schwarz nach Schweden. Seine spätere Frau Ann-Charlotte organisierte ihm in Stockholm Arbeit in einer Werkstatt, in der feine Juwelen entstanden. Weil Wolf-Peter Schwarz zunächst kein Schwedisch verstand, wurde er Spezialist für verlorenen Ohrschmuck. »Man hat mir den linken hingelegt und ich habe den rechten machen dürfen oder umgekehrt.« In Stockholm lernte Schwarz zu Beginn der 1960er Jahre den modernen schwedischen und dänischen Schmuck kennen. »Im Kunstverein hat damals Sigurd Persson ausgestellt«, erinnert er sich. Persönlich traf er den Edelsteinschleifer Carlsson, der moderne Schliffe ausprobierte. Die Silberkollektionen von Georg Jensen habe dessen Designerin Torun Bülow-Hübe in den 1950er Jahren »Antistatus-Smycke« genannt, erzählt er. »Es war zum ersten Mal eine Bewegung da, die den Schmuck nicht als Statussymbol betrachtet hat.«

Schwarz malte und zeichnete auch in Schweden und interessierte sich für jede Art von Kunst. Die kreative Auseinandersetzung mit Schmuck begann jedoch erst, als er von Schweden zurückkehrte, um 1968 in Schwäbisch Gmünd seine Meisterprüfung zu machen. Hier wurde Pierre Schlevogt, der an der Fachhochschule lehrte und auch für den Meisterkurs zuständig war, sein Lieblingslehrer. Erste futuristische Ringe entstanden. In der Meisterklasse sei es verpönt gewesen, handwerklich konservativ zu arbeiten, bekennt Wolf-Peter Schwarz. 1969 übernahm der Goldschmiedemeister zusammen mit seiner Frau Ann-Charlotte das Geschäft der Familie. Sein kreatives

1967   *Fächerring*, Edelstahl — *Fan ring,* stainless steel

1976   Ring, Gold, Diamanten — Ring, gold, diamonds

1976   Brosche *Eismond*, Design Ann-Charlotte Schwarz, Gold, Diamanten — Brooch *Ice moon*, design Ann-Charlotte Schwarz, gold, diamonds

1976   *Orden*, Silber, Gold, Feueremail — *Medal,* silver, gold, enamel

1977   Brosche *Traumregen*, Platin, Chalcedon, Diamanttropfen — Brooch *Dream rain*, platinum, chalcedony, diamond drops

1984   Collier *Knitter*, Platin, Gold — Necklace *Knitter*, platinum, gold

1976   Langes Collier mit Zuchtperlen — Long necklace with cultured pearls

1976   1977   1984

Angebot und die ausgefallenen Schaufenster-Dekorationen wurden bald weit über Ulm hinaus bekannt. In Zusammenarbeit mit einem befreundeten Goldschmied aus Schwäbisch Gmünd entstand 1970 eine erste moderne Schmuckkollektion in Silber mit Bergkristall. Sie sei natürlich stark von den Skandinaviern beeinflusst gewesen, berichtet Schwarz. Es war zudem »demokratischer« Schmuck. Ein Ring mit großen Bergkristallen kostete etwa 38 Mark. Schleifen ließ Schwarz die preiswerten Edelsteine in Idar-Oberstein. In Ulm wurden die Fassungen gemacht und montiert. »Bergkristallzeit« wird diese Phase heute bei Ehinger-Schwarz genannt.

Das Angebot aus der eigenen Werkstatt wurde ergänzt durch den modernen Silberschmuck von Firmen wie Georg Jensen, Hans Hansen und Alton. Ehinger-Schwarz avancierte bald auch zu einem der wichtigsten Juweliere für Lapponia in Deutschland. Hinzu kamen die von namhaften Designern gestalteten Kollektionen *relo* und *art-design*. Mit diesem Angebot war Ehinger-Schwarz in den 1970er Jahren einer der ersten Juweliere des modernen Schmuck-Designs in Deutschland. Das eigene Goldschmiedeatelier erwirtschaftete etwa 30 Prozent des Umsatzes.

Mit zahlreichen Preisen bei Wettbewerben wie der Goldenen Lupe des Deutschen Edelsteintages oder Diamanten heute stellte Wolf-Peter Schwarz seine außergewöhnliche Kreativität regelmäßig unter Beweis. Sein Formenrepertoire reichte von prächtig dekorativem Halsschmuck in Gold mit Farbedelsteinen und Perlen bis hin zu äußerst reduzierten Stücken mit großflächigen, geometrisch geschliffenen Edelsteinen. Mit einem Collier aus weich fließenden, sich nach unten verjüngenden Silberschnörkeln und 178 kleinen weißen Perlen siegte der Ulmer Goldschmied beim Deutschen Schmuck- und Edelsteinpreis Idar-Oberstein. Neben dem 1. gewann er gleichzeitig auch den 3. Preis. Auch Stücke seiner künstlerisch talentierten Frau Ann-Charlotte Schwarz wurden ausgezeichnet, so derr Ansteckschmuck *Eismond* in Weißgold mit Brillanten und Bergkristallen in bizarren Wolkenformen. 1976 wurden die kreativen Schmuckstücke von Wolf-Peter Schwarz in einer umfassenden Ausstellung durch das Ulmer Museum gewürdigt.

Ab 1979 begann der Aufbau eines Galeriekonzeptes in Deutschland. Parallel zur Eröffnung von eigenen Geschäften in Augsburg und München wurde eine Schmuckkollektion entwickelt, die über Juweliere in Deutschland und international vertrieben wurde. Ehinger-Schwarz beteiligte sich in den 1980er Jahren auch an Marketingkonzepten des Diamantproduzenten De Beers und des World Gold Councils. Als die Platin Gilde 1976 gegründet wurde, war es für einen kreativen Gestalter wie Wolf-Peter Schwarz eine Verpflichtung, mit dabei zu sein. Zu einem Meilenstein für die Präsenz von modernem Schmuck auf der internationalen Uhren- und Schmuckmesse in Basel wurde die erste Designer-Kooperation mit Bernd Munsteiner und Günter Krauss. Später kam der Schweizer Kurt Neukomm dazu. Auslöser für diese Aktion war die Firma

Rosenthal, die ihr Ladenbaukonzept in Verbindung mit innovativem Schmuck demonstrieren wollte; dies wurde auch von der Messe gefördert. Die zweite für die Verbreitung von modernem Schmuck wichtige Kooperation begann Mitte der 1980er Jahre zusammen mit Niessing, Pur und Fillner. Die Standgemeinschaft präsentierte sich zuerst in Basel, später auch auf der Inhorgenta in München und schließlich auf der Selection in Essen 1998. »Das war ein ganz spannender Schritt«, wertet Wolf-Peter Schwarz diese Initiative. Bereits in Basel ging es für ihn um die Frage: »Wohin gehörst Du? Gehörst Du zu den Unikatlern à la Zobel oder gehörst du zu den Manufakturen?« Die Entscheidung fiel nicht schwer. Ehinger-Schwarz hatte längst den Grundstein für ein international wachsendes Schmuckunternehmen gelegt.

Dennoch kam es in den 1990er Jahren zu einem bemerkenswerten Experiment mit dem Schmuckkünstler Manfred Bischoff. Dieser hatte in München bei Professor Hermann Jünger studiert. Schwarz war begeistert von seinen expressiven Stücken, die in der internationalen Schmuckkunstszene höchste Anerkennung fanden. Die Edition von Ehinger-Schwarz mit Arbeiten von Manfred Bischoff fiel vollkommen aus dem Rahmen dessen, was ein Juwelier in der Nachkriegsära bis dahin jemals gewagt hatte. Die Entwürfe wurden in einer Werkstatt in Hongkong in kleinen Auflagen von einem chinesischen Goldschmied gefertigt. Dieser Goldschmied wurde »nicht versteckt«, sondern auch in dem begleitenden Katalog genannt. Doch musste Wolf-Peter Schwarz zu seinem Bedauern feststellen, »dass wir in der Vermittlung dieses Schmucks an Grenzen gestoßen sind.« Nur wenige Kunden hätten sich »für komplexe künstlerische Äußerungen« im Schmuck interessiert. Die Zusammenarbeit mit Manfred Bischoff war nicht der einzige Versuch, Gegenwartskunst und Schmuck zu vereinen. Zu Beginn der 1980er Jahre entstand ein Ausstellungsraum für moderne Malerei innerhalb der neuen Schmuckgalerie am Marktplatz 20. Im Geschäft des Ulmer Juweliers am Münsterplatz findet sich noch heute im Untergeschoß ein Original von Anselm Kiefer aus dieser Zeit.

Zu Beginn der 1990er Jahre stellte Wolf-Peter Schwarz auf einer Reise nach Skandinavien entsetzt fest, »dass dort die ganze Schmuckwelt zerbröselte.« Der sichtbare Niedergang veranlasste ihn, nach einem neuen Schmuckkonzept zu suchen. Eine Kundin habe ihn damals auch aufgefordert, etwas Preiswertes für ihre Tochter zu machen. Es sollte nickelfrei sein, denn die Kundin war Hautärztin. »Der Einzige ist André Ribeiro«, meint Schwarz, »der mit seinem Kautschukthema hier ein neues Konzept hatte.« Ein weiterer Impuls sei von De Beers gekommen. »Die wollten ihre Diamanten auch an Leute mit Jeans und Trainingsanzügen verkaufen«, erzählt er. So wurde Wolf-Peter Schwarz neben den bekannten Goldschmieden Günter Krauss und Georg Hornemann eingeladen, »einen Brilli für alle Gelegenheiten« zu entwerfen. Der Ulmer Gestalter befestigte Brillanten auf Acrylscheiben mit Dichtungsringen. De Beers war begeistert, aber meinte: »Wir sind noch nicht

1994

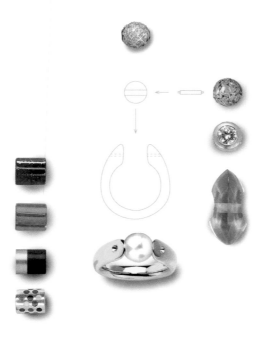

1997

1985	*Halskrause*, Gold, Biwa-Zuchtperlen — *Neck ruff*, gold, Biwa cultured pearls
1989	*Lichtuhr*, 24-Stunden Zifferblatt, Edelstahl — *Light watch*, 24 hours face, stainless steel
1994	*Charlotte Classic L*, Gold, Ebenholz, Filz, Edelsteine — *Charlotte Classic L*, gold, ebony, felt, precious stones
1994	Ring Idee *Charlotte Classic* — Ring idea *Charlotte Classic*
1997	Ring Idee *tipit* — Ring idea *tipit*
1999	Ring Idee *Charlotte 21* — Ring idea *Charlotte 21*

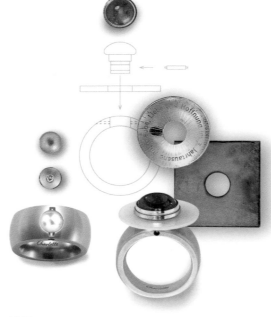

1999

1985   1989   1994

so weit.« Schwarz arbeitete an dem Thema weiter, ersetzte den Einkaräter durch einen Aquamarin und verspiegelte ihn auf der Rückseite mit Feinsilber. Die Dichtungsringe, den Filz und die Moosgummischeiben besorgte er sich. Die variierbaren Schmuckstücke erhielten den Namen seiner Frau. Es war die Geburtsstunde von *Charlotte* als Schmucksystem.

Die ersten Stücke verkauften sich im Weihnachtsgeschäft 1994 nur zögerlich. »Doch ist der Umsatz im Januar nicht wie üblich eingebrochen«, stellte der Juwelier fest: »Da haben wir wirklich Bauklötze gestaunt. Die Leute wollten immer mehr von *Charlotte* haben.« Bald kamen Jugendliche von der Schule, um die »Moosis« zu kaufen. 1995 wurde das Geschäft in der Neuen Straße in einen Mono-*Charlotte*-Store umgewandelt. Der Höhepunkt von »*Charlotte* in der Moosgummiwelt« fand als Schmuckbaukasten 1996 bei Ravensburger Spiele statt. An die 200 000 *Charlotte*-Kinder-Spielkästen wurden »spielend« verkauft.

Heute sei das Wechseln nicht mehr so wichtig wie das Addieren, beschreibt der Erfinder den Status Quo. Mit dem Slogan »*Charlotte* wird erwachsen« entfernt sich die Marke seit einigen Jahren auch von ihrer Kunststoffära. »Wir wollten uns komplett von den modischen Entwicklungen, die da gekommen sind, distanzieren. Da sind wir geflohen«, sagt Wolf-Peter Schwarz. Inzwischen werden für *Charlotte*-Schmuckstücke ausnahmslos echte Edelsteine verwendet.

Mit 120 Mitarbeitern zählt Charlotte · Ehinger-Schwarz inzwischen zu den großen Schmuckunternehmen in Deutschland. Besonders schön für Ann-Charlotte und Wolf-Peter Schwarz ist, dass es auch in der fünften Generation weitergeht. Caroline Schwarz, 1966 in Stockholm geboren, möchte zunächst dazu beitragen, das Profil der Marke zu schärfen. Zu den *Charlotte*-Läden in zahlreichen deutschen Großstädten sollen weitere in Metropolen wie New York, Rom, Paris, Lissabon, Tokio und natürlich Stockholm hinzukommen, erklärt Caroline Schwarz ihre Vision. Ihr Vater glaubt, dass mit dem Prinzip des Hinzufügens, des Addierens, *Charlotte* noch stärker »mit Werten« verbunden werden kann. Dies sei auch der humanen Idee zuträglich, die zu Beginn des modernen Schmucks in Skandinavien und in Deutschland so wichtig war. »Human bedeutet«, sagt Schwarz, »dass die Kultur auch dem kleinen Mann möglich sein muss.« Nur dann werde sich die Gesellschaft weiterentwickeln.

E — Wolf-Peter Schwarz did not volunteer to begin a goldsmithing apprenticeship in 1959 under his grandfather, Otto Ehinger (1880–1967). He much preferred indulging his passion for drawing and painting. His early works are signed with his nom d'artiste Wolf Erchanger, also abbreviated to Werch. Faced by his parents with the alternative of either doing his national service or serving an apprenticeship under his grandfather, then seventy-nine years old, Wolf-Peter Schwarz opted for the latter. Otto Ehinger had attended the Königliche Zeichenakademie in Hanau (1898–1901), where

he had distinguished himself as the best in his year. After his admission at an art academy in Paris, he had to join the family firm in Ulm in 1904.

»Even at the age of eighty, my granddad was an outstanding craftsman,« recollects Wolf-Peter Schwarz. Otto Ehinger II, whose father of the same name had founded »Otto Ehinger – Kunstgewerbliche Werkstätte« in 1876, was a silversmith, goldsmith, chaser and engraver. With those skills, acquired in the Jugendstil/Art Nouveau era, he produced mainly historical Ulm jewellery, which had also been the speciality of Otto Ehinger I until his death in 1967. Wolf-Peter Schwarz soon learned how to produce pieces of jewellery set with Danube freshwater pearls, agate or onyx. It was not long before he was entrusted with bending the Baroque scrolls, mounting the foliate decoration and setting the stones. To compensate for this task that was so distasteful to him, he says he painted »pictures that were as blood-drenched as possible« throughout his apprenticeship period.

After acquiring his journeyman's certificate and following the death of Otto Ehinger II, Wolf-Peter Schwarz went to Sweden. Ann-Charlotte, who would later become his wife, organised work for him in a workshop that made fine jewels. Because Wolf-Peter Schwarz understood no Swedish at first, he became a specialist in lost earrings. »People would lay down the left earring in front of me and I was allowed to make a right earring to match or the other way round.« In early 1960s Stockholm, Schwarz became familiar with modern Swedish and Danish jewellery. »Sigurd Persson showed work at the art association then,« he recalls. A personal acquaintance of his was Carlsson, a gem-cutter who was trying out modern cuts. The 1950s Georg Jensen silver collections were christened »anti-status jewellery« by their designer, Torun Bülow-Hübe, he says. »For the first time there was a movement that didn't see jewellery as a status symbol.«

Schwarz continued to paint and draw in Sweden and was interested in all kinds of art. His investigation of jewellery as a creative art did not begin, however, until his return to Germany from Sweden to take his master craftsman's certificate in Schwäbisch Gmünd in 1968. There his favourite teacher was Pierre Schlevogt, who taught at the Fachhochschule and was in charge of the master class. Schwarz produced his first Futurist rings. Working with conservative styles was frowned on in the master class, admits Wolf-Peter Schwarz. In 1969, now a master goldsmith, he and his wife, Ann-Charlotte, took over the family business.

His creative range in jewellery and startling shop window displays were soon famous far beyond Ulm. In collaboration with a goldsmith from Schwäbisch Gmünd, who was a friend of his, he launched his first modern jewellery collection in silver with rock crystal in 1970. Of course it revealed a strong Scandinavian influence, reports Schwarz. It was, he adds, also »democratic« jewellery. A ring with large rock crystals cost only about DM 38. Schwarz had the reasonably priced semiprecious stones cut in

1999

2002

2003

Idar-Oberstein. The settings were made in Ulm and the stones were mounted there. Today at Ehinger-Schwarz this phase is called their »rock-crystal period«.

The line from the proprietary workshop was supplemented by modern silver jewellery made by firms such as Georg Jensen, Hans Hansen and Alton. Ehinger-Schwarz also soon became one of the most important jewellery outlets for Lapponia in Germany. In addition, there were the *relo* and *art-design* collections, which were created by distinguished designers. With this diverse range, Ehinger-Schwarz became one of the first jewellers in Germany to specialise in modern designer jewellery in the 1970s. The proprietary goldsmithing studio was responsible for about 30 per cent of turnover. Wolf-Peter Schwarz regularly furnished ample proof of his extraordinary creativity by winning numerous awards at competitions, including the Goldene Lupe [Golden Magnifying glass] from the Deutscher Edelsteintag and Diamanten heute [Diamonds Today]. His repertory of forms ranged from magnificently decorated neck jewellery in gold with coloured precious stones and pearls to extremely reductive pieces featuring large precious stones in geometric flat cuts.

The Ulm goldsmith won the Deutscher Schmuck- und Edelsteinpreis Idar-Oberstein with a softly fluid necklace featuring silver scrolls that tapered downwards and 178 small white pearls. Apart from 1st prize, he also won 3rd prize at that event. Pieces by his wife, Ann-Charlotte, who was also artistically talented, won awards as well: for example, *Eismond* [Ice moon], a pin in white gold with diamonds and rock crystals in bizarre cloud shapes. In 1976 the creative pieces made by Wolf-Peter Schwarz were honoured with a comprehensive retrospective at the Ulm Museum.

In 1979 the firm began building up a gallery concept in Germany. In parallel with the inauguration of proprietary outlets in Augsburg and Munich, a jewellery collection was developed that was marketed by jewellers in Germany and abroad. Ehinger-Schwarz took part in the marketing concepts of diamond consortium De Beers and the World Gold Council in the 1980s. When Platin Gilde was founded in 1976, being involved in it represented a relevant commitment to a creative designer like Wolf-Peter Schwarz.

The first designer collaboration with Bernd Munsteiner and Günter Krauss was a benchmark for the presence of modern jewellery at the World Watch and Jewellery Show in Basel. Later Kurt Neukomm, a Swiss designer, joined in. The trade fair operation was sparked off by Rosenthal, who wanted to demonstrate their architectural shop concept in connection with innovative jewellery displays; this was also promoted by the Swiss trade fair. The second collaboration that was important for the spread of modern jewellery began in the mid-1980s with Niessing, Pur and Fillner. Ehinger-Schwarz shared a stand with them in Basel, followed by another collective appearance at the Inhorgenta in Munich and finally at the 1998 Selection in Essen.

»That was a really exciting step,« is Wolf-Peter Schwarz's verdict on those joint undertakings. Even in Basel he was already mulling over the question: »Where do you belong? Do you belong to the one-off-makers à la Zobel or do you belong to the manufactories?« The decision was not difficult after all. Ehinger-Schwarz had long since laid the cornerstone of a jewellery business with international growth prospects.

Still scope was found in the 1990s for a remarkable experiment with the artist in jewellery Manfred Bischoff. He had studied in Munich under Professor Hermann Jünger. Schwarz was very taken with Manfred Bischoff's expressive pieces, which were rapturously acclaimed in the international jewellery scene. The Ehinger-Schwarz edition of work by Manfred Bischoff was unlike anything a jeweller had attempted up to then in post-war Germany. The designs were executed in limited editions by a Chinese goldsmith working out of a Hong Kong workshop. The goldsmith was »not hidden away« but was named in the accompanying catalogue. To his regret, however, Wolf-Peter Schwarz was faced with the fact »that we reached our limits in trying to get that jewellery across.« Very few clients were interested »in complex artistic statements« in jewellery. The collaboration with Manfred Bischoff was not his only attempt at uniting contemporary art and jewellery. In the early 1980s, an exhibition room for modern painting was created within the new jewellery gallery at 20 Marktplatz. Even today an original Anselm Kiefer from those days hangs in the basement of the Ulm jeweller's Münsterplatz branch.

In the early 1990s, Wolf-Peter Schwarz was horrified to find on a trip to Scandinavia »that the entire world of jewellery was disintegrating there.« The evident decline led him to seek a new jewellery concept. A client had asked him at that time to make something reasonably priced for her daughter. It had to be unalloyed with nickel because the client was a dermatologist. »The only one to have a new concept here,« thought Schwarz, »is André Ribeiro with his hard rubber theme.« Another idea came from De Beers. »They wanted to be able to sell their diamonds to people wearing jeans and training gear,« as Schwarz tells it. Wolf-Peter Schwarz was invited along with the well-known goldsmiths Günter Krauss and Georg Hornemann to design »bling for all occasions.« The Ulm designer fastened diamonds to acrylic discs with washers. De Beers was enthusiastic but felt: »We aren't that far yet.« Schwarz continued to work up the theme, replacing the one-carat diamond with an aquamarine and backing it with fine silver. He procured washers, felt and polyurethane foam. These variable pieces were named after his wife and that was the birth of *Charlotte* modular jewellery.

The first pieces did not fly off the shelf at Christmas 1994. »But sales didn't slow down in January the way they usually do,« the jeweller realised. »You could have knocked us down with a feather. People kept wanting more *Charlotte*.« Soon teenagers were coming in after school to buy »Moosis«. In

2003   2006   2006

1995 the shop in Neuer Strasse was converted into a Mono-*Charlotte* Store. The craze for »*Charlotte* in the world of foam rubber« culminated in a modular jewellery offering at the 1996 Ravensburg Games. Some 200 000 *Charlotte* children's toy chests were sold »with the greatest of ease«.

Today change is no longer as important as adding is how the inventor describes the status quo. With the slogan »*Charlotte* grows up« the label has distanced itself for some years from its plastic days. »We wanted to distance ourselves completely from the fashion trends that emerged then. We just ran away from them,« says Wolf-Peter Schwarz. In the meantime, only genuine precious stones are used for *Charlotte* pieces.

Employing a workforce of 120, Charlotte · Ehinger-Schwarz is by now one of Germany's biggest jewellery businesses. What is particularly gratifying for Ann-Charlotte and Wolf-Peter Schwarz is that the business is now in its 5th generation. Caroline Schwarz, born in Stockholm in 1966, wants to make her own contribution to honing the profile of the label. The *Charlotte* shops in numerous large German cities are to be joined by more in metropolises such as New York, Rome, Paris, Lisbon, Tokyo and, of course, Stockholm, envisages Caroline Schwarz. Her father believes that with the principle of contributing, of adding, *Charlotte* can be linked more closely »with values«. This approach promotes the humane idea that was so important to the beginnings of modern jewellery in Scandinavia and Germany. »Humane means,« says Schwarz, »that culture must also be accessible to the man in the street.« Only if it is, can society continue to develop.

1999	*ACS Ring*, Scheiben mit Brillanten — *ACS ring,* discs with diamonds
2002	*Ring mit Krönchen*, *Charlotte 21*, Edelstahl, Süßwasser-Zuchtperlen, Gold — *Ring with crowns*, *Charlotte 21*, stainless steel, freshwater cultured pearls, gold
2003	Ringe *tipit*, Edelstahl, Silber, Saphire, Peridot — Rings *tipit*, stainless steel, silver, sapphires, peridot
2003	*tipit* Kette, Edelstahl, Silber, Saphire, Peridot, Rosenquarz, Süsswasser-Zuchtperlen — *tipit* necklace, stainless steel, silver, sapphires, peridot, rose quartz, freshwater cultured pearls
2006	Ringe *Charlotte 21*, Türkis, Tsavoriten, Smaragde, Silber, Gold, Palladium — Rings *Charlotte 21*, turquoise, tsavorits, emeralds, silver, gold, palladium
2006	*Charlotte 21* Ringe, Gold, Edelstahl, Silber, Turmalin, Hyazinthe, Saphire, Süsswasser-Zuchtperle — *Charlotte 21* rings, gold, stainless steel, silver, tourmaline, hyazinths, sapphires, freshwater cultured pearl

Wolf-Peter Schwarz
Geboren 1942 in Ulm. 1968 Meisterprüfung in Schwäbisch-Gmünd. 1969 Geschäftsübernahme der 1876 von seinem Urgroßvater Otto Ehinger gegründeten Firma.

Wolf-Peter Schwarz
Born in Ulm in 1942. Master craftsman's certificate in Schwäbisch Gmünd in 1968. Took over firm founded by great-grandfather Otto Ehinger (est. 1876) in 1969.

c. 1974

c. 1972   Armreif, Design Sigurd Persson, Gold, Diamanten — Bangle, design
          Sigurd Persson, gold, diamonds

c. 1972   Armreif, Design Sigurd Persson, Gold, weißer Achat, Onyx — Bangle,
          design Sigurd Persson, gold, white agate, onyx

c. 1973   Ring, Design Sigurd Persson, Gold — Ring, design Sigurd Persson, gold

c. 1974   Halsschmuck, Design Günter Krauss, Gold, Diamanten — Necklace,
          design Günter Krauss, gold, diamonds

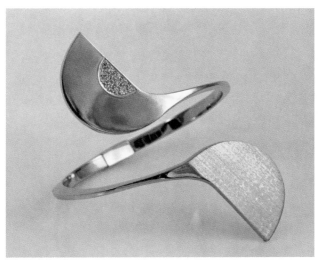

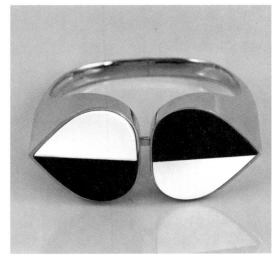

c. 1972   c. 1972   c. 1973

art-design

Die 1970er Jahre markieren den Beginn einer neuen Ära im modernen Schmuckdesign in Deutschland. Der von Künstlern und Designern gestaltete Schmuck, etwa von Georg Jensen und Lapponia, kam auch hierzulande gut an. In Deutschland blieben moderne Bestrebungen weitgehend auf akademisch gebildete Goldschmiede und einige kunsthandwerklich orientierte Werkstätten beschränkt. Doch hatte die aufstrebende Industrienation mit dem Bauhaus und der HfG Ulm wie kein anderes Land Designgeschichte geschrieben. Es war nur eine Frage der Zeit, wann sich ambitionierte Designkonzepte auch in größeren Manufakturen niederschlagen würden. Den Anfang machte die Höfflin+Lüth GmbH mit dem Markenkonzept art-design. Das Pforzheimer Unternehmen startete im Jahre 1970 furios und endete zehn Jahre später überraschend wie ein Krimi.

In der ersten Imagebroschüre von 1970, die von Hella Krauss, damals noch Hella Rummenhöller, gestaltet wurde, heißt es: »art-design ist eine Kollektion von Schmuckstücken, die fünf Designer aus Europa gestaltet haben.« Die Designer waren die Goldschmiede und Künstler Reinhold Reiling und Günter Krauss, Pforzheim, der Schwede Sigurd Persson und der Schweizer Hans Stalder. Später kam noch Carl Elsener aus der Schweiz hinzu. Krauss war 1943 geboren und Reiling-Schüler. Stalder, Jahrgang 1934, war in der Schweiz als Bildhauer bekannt. Der Pforzheimer Carl-Heinrich Lüth, geboren 1936, war seit 1969 Mitgesellschafter des Ateliers Höfflin+Lüth. Er war vornehmlich für die Produktion der Schmuckstücke verantwortlich.

Als Vorbild in der Moderne vor dem Zweiten Weltkrieg könnte man den Künstlerfabrikanten Fahrner in Pforzheim bezeichnen. Doch handelte es sich bei art-design um hochwertigen Schmuck aus Gelb- und Weißgold mit kostbaren Diamanten und Farbedelsteinen. Fahrner hingegen produzierte hauptsächlich Großserien, zumeist aus preiswerten Ersatzmaterialien. Die Vorkriegskünstler hielten sich an den Formenkanon, der durch den Jugendstil und das Art Déco vorgegeben war. art-design hingegen war geprägt von den Handschriften individueller Goldschmiede. Sie zählten in den 1970er Jahren zu den namhaftesten Persönlichkeiten ihres Metiers und standen, wie Persson und Reiling, für die Moderne im Schmuck der Nachkriegszeit. Neu war auch die Zusammenarbeit im Team, die einer modernen Schmuckmarke Profil geben sollte. So heißt es in einer Firmenschrift: »Diese fünf Gestalter haben zusammen eine Gruppe gebildet, um eine Kollektion zu schaffen, die einmalig ist. Eine Kollektion, die fünf Handschriften zeigt, aber aus einem Team entstanden ist.«

Jeder Gestalter wurde in den verschiedenen Werbebroschüren, die alle Hella Krauss konzipierte, in seiner künstlerischen Eigenart vorgestellt. In einem Beispiel heißt es: »Sigurd Persson möchte Dinge für den täglichen Gebrauch entwerfen, die schon beim Anschauen Freude machen, sei die Funktion auch noch so nüchtern.« Der Verweis auf das Gebrauchsdesign wird ergänzt durch persönliche Vorlieben und Weltanschauungen. Sigurd Perssons

Naturnähe in der bildhauerischen Tätigkeit wird so analysiert: »Es scheint, als gehe er dabei zum Ursprünglichen zurück, um Schutz zu suchen vor der Welt, die für ihn fremd und beängstigend kühl und fern geworden ist.« Professor Reiling wird in seinem Haus aus Holz, Glas und Stein gezeigt, ein schönes Beispiel für naturnahes Bauen in den 1970er Jahren.

Über die Gestaltungsmethode von Reiling ist zu lesen: »Es ist alles sauber durchdacht, alle Entwürfe sind von einer großen Reife gezeichnet. Oft gibt es auch hier das abenteuerliche Moment der Veränderung vom Entwurf zum endgültigen Schmuckstück. Er nimmt diese Veränderungen sehr ernst, entwickelt sich daran weiter. Manchmal erlaubt er sich, lustige, witzige Dinge ganz schnell und ohne Plan zu entwerfen. Er spielt dabei mit heiteren Elementen und kann ganz entspannt und locker sein.« Bei Günter Krauss wird die »erstaunliche Begabung, Dinge zu beobachten« hervorgehoben: »Er sieht Details aus Formen heraus, entdeckt an Gegenständen Gestaltungsmomente, die fast nicht sichtbar sind.« Und auch die Begeisterung des überragenden Pforzheimer Gestalters für Chansons sowie für Kochen und Essen kommen zur Sprache.

Die Schmuckserien von art-design übertreffen in ihrer künstlerischen Extravaganz bei weitem den damals »gängigen« Industrieschmuck. Sie offenbaren den Gestaltungswillen der Künstler ebenso wie den Zeitgeist der 1970er Jahre. Ein Armreif in Gold mit Brillantpavée öffnet sich und mündet in zwei gegenüberliegende Halbkreisflächen. Er ist typisch für den experimentellen, skandinavisch geprägten Stil von Sigurd Persson. Von Reiling sind Arbeiten in Gelb- und Weißgold mit Rutilquarz, aber auch mit reichlich Diamanten zu sehen. Ein Ring und Armreif aus Weißgold weisen als Schmuckelemente elegante Kurven auf, ausgefasst mit Brillanten. Günter Krauss verwendet für seine Entwürfe schon zu dieser Zeit originell geschliffene Farbsteine, in einem Fall die Achatreliefs von Bernd Munsteiner.

Allen Arbeiten gemeinsam sind konstruktivistische Anklänge, die jedoch durch polierte Goldoberflächen und den Einsatz von Diamanten und Edelsteinen einen deutlichen Juwelencharakter erhalten. Einige Stücke von Hans Stalder und Carl-Heinz Lüth sind auch vom Art Déco inspiriert. In jedem Fall offenbart die art-design-Kollektion die in den 1970er Jahren weit verbreitete Lust auf glänzendes Gold, auf Dekor und auf ausgefallene Formen. art-design war das erste Abenteuer in den Siebzigern, einen neuen Weg im deutschen Serienschmuck zu suchen: zwischen anspruchsvoller moderner Goldschmiedekunst und den bewährten Juwelen, die Juweliere verkaufen konnten und wollten. Der Geschäftsführer von art-design Höfflin nahm dabei ganz gezielt die Juweliere mit ins Boot. In einem Werbetext heißt es: »Gemeinsam mit führenden, fortschrittlichen Juwelieren haben wir uns mit diesen fünf Designern zusammengetan und präsentieren die fertigen Entwürfe.« Bereits zum Start wurde also auf Exklusivität im Vertrieb gesetzt. Hella, die spätere Ehefrau von Günter Krauss, gestaltete und produzierte Werbe-

c. 1973

c. 1973

1974

anzeigen, Displays für das Schaufenster, Präsentationselemente, alles war aufeinander abgestimmt. Es gab zudem PR in den Frauenzeitschriften »Burda International«, »Petra«, »Für Sie«, »Lady«, »Chic« und »Madame«. Der Wille einer kleinen Branchenelite, Schmuck ein neues Image und mehr öffentliche Aufmerksamkeit zu verleihen, war immer erkennbar.

Eine Werbeanzeige von 1973 beinhaltet die Botschaft des modernen Schmucks auch für die Trägerin: »Sie unterstreichen damit ihr Empfinden für guten Geschmack.« Diese Grundaussage, die weniger das Prestige, sondern den persönlichen Stil anspricht, hat sich seitdem kaum verändert. Zudem arbeiteten die art-design-Kampagnen aber auch mit der Idee von Schmuck als Geschenk: »Jedes einzelne Schmuckstück ist ein Geschenk der Liebe.« Originell ist der Hinweis, dass Stücke von art-design deshalb unvergänglich seien, »weil das Lebendige, das Frische im Design liegt.« Vielleicht eine Spitze gegen den De Beers-Slogan »Ein Diamant ist unvergänglich.«

1975 wurde in einer Imagebroschüre, gebunden in Wildleder, die Frühjahrs- und Herbstkampagne vorgestellt. Die Partnerschaft zwischen Hersteller und Fachgeschäft sei die wichtigste Voraussetzung für den Erfolg, ist dort zu lesen. Die Fotografien und Texte von Hella Krauss eröffnen einen Blick auf das Frauenbild der 1970er Jahre. Die Frau tritt sportlich auf und natürlich, mit wehendem Haar oder einem bunten Tuch auf dem Kopf, der Teint gebräunt und den Blick verträumt in die Ferne gerichtet. Ein abweichendes Motiv zeigt eine charmant lächelnde, dynamische Frau, die einen kostbaren, grünen »Apfel« mit »Diamantkernen« von Günter Krauss an einem goldenen Halsreif trägt. Der Werbetext dazu lautet: »Für mich ist Gold ein Stück Sonne. Strahlend, warm und echt.« Es beweist, dass sich art-design auch an den Kampagnen der Gold Corporation des südafrikanischen Bergbaukonzerns der Familie Oppenheimer beteiligt hat. Die verschiedenen Frauentypen wurden auch für eine Meinungsumfrage mit Gewinnspiel eingesetzt.

Viele namhafte Juweliere nahmen den Schmuck von art-design auf und lernten dadurch Ideen und Ideale der Goldschmiedekünstler kennen. Doch der Firmenchef der kreativen Marke Höfflin hatte in seinem ungebremsten Elan noch weitere Pläne. Einer trug den Namen *Creation Avantgarde*. Dies war eine Schmucklinie, die von dem Düsseldorfer Goldschmied Georg Hornemann gestaltet wurde. »*Creation Avantgarde* vermittelt Prestige, unterstreicht Charme und zärtliche Stimmung. Die Formen sprechen eine breite Käuferschicht an, besonders Menschen, die dem ganz Modernen zögernd gegenüberstehen, aber doch etwas Neues, Besonderes möchten.« Die Kollektion *Creation Avantgarde* von 1975 umfasste 100 Stücke. Sie war deutlich verspielter als die Stücke von art-design. Korallen und Farbedelsteine, der reiche Besatz mit Diamanten oder Saphiren sowie organische und florale Formen kennzeichneten die Arbeiten von Georg Hornemann. *Creation Avantgarde* sollte jedes halbe Jahr mit »vielfältigen neuen Entwürfen« ergänzt werden, heißt es in einer Broschüre.

c. 1973   c. 1973   c. 1973

Eine weitere Kollektion lief unter dem Namen relo-design. Der Name geht auf die Gründer Rainer Lutz und Renate Lay zurück. Sie etablierten 1969 in Renens bei Lausanne eine Schweizer Niederlassung. Manfred Fillner war Leiter der Echtschmuck-Abteilung in dem Unternehmen, das 1972 an Höfflin+Lüth verkauft wurde. Die Pforzheimer gründeten in Luzern die relo-design ag als Schweizer Unternehmen. Geschäftsführer wurden Manfred und seine Frau Ruth Fillner.

relo-design war im unteren Preisbereich angesiedelt. Der Schmuck in Sterling-Silber, hauptsächlich gestaltet von Carl Elsener, weist Bezüge zum skandinavischen Schmuckdesign auf. Doch auch poppige Motive, etwa ein stilisierter Mund oder Anhänger in Form von Früchten oder Glöckchen, sind zu finden. Ein wichtiges Segment waren silberne Spangenuhren. Carl Elsener gewann damit verschiedene Designpreise. Einige Silberuhren hat auch Hans Stalder entworfen. Eine Kundenbroschüre der Goldkollektion von relo-design zeigt Schmuck mit der typischen Handschrift von Günter Krauss. Originell geschliffene Farbsteine in organischen Formen mit Diamanten wecken Emotionen, die auch im Werbetext angesprochen werden: »Bewusst Gefühle zeigen mit Schmucktragen verbindet Wohlfühlen und Sichersein.«

Ende der 1970er Jahre endete das Pforzheimer Unternehmen so spektakulär, wie es begonnen hatte. Der Geschäftsführer Höfflin wollte zuviel auf einmal. Die Expansion nach Übersee überforderte die kleine Firma, die in finanzielle Schwierigkeiten geriet. Höfflin verschwand ins Ausland. Damit war dieses Kapitel des modernen Schmuckdesigns beendet. Doch die Initiative, mit den besten Designern seiner Zeit anspruchsvolle Schmuckserien zu machen, wirkt in anderen Konstellationen weiter. Aus relo-design entstand in der Schweiz die Firma Fillner&Elsener. Sie wurde später von Ruth und Manfred Fillner allein weitergeführt. Eines der schönsten Schmuckgeschäfte in Luzern für modernen Schmuck ist nicht zuletzt ein Ergebnis des Abenteuers, das Höfflin+Lüth 1969 gestartet hatte. Die Reste von art-design wurden von Eckhard Beier, Pforzheim, aufgelöst, der in Zusammenarbeit mit anderen Designern seine eigene Firma cédé aufbaute. Günter und Hella Krauss etablierten in Stuttgart ein Goldschmiedegeschäft von überragender Qualität. Ähnliches gelang Georg Hornemann mit seinem Atelier in Düsseldorf. Krauss und Hornemann zählen heute zu den besten und kreativsten Juwelieren der Welt.

E — The 1970s marked the onset of a new era in modern German jewellery design. Jewellery designed by artists and designers, for instance, from Georg Jensen and Lapponia, was highly successful in Germany as well. However, modern endeavours were largely limited to academically trained goldsmiths and a few crafts-oriented workshops. Nevertheless, as an aspiring industrial power, Germany has made history in design with the Bauhaus and the HfG Ulm as no other country has done. It was only a question of time before larger manufacturing businesses would also be based on ambitious design concepts. A beginning was made by Höfflin+Lüth GmbH with the art-design label concept. The Pforzheim business hit the ground running in 1970s, only to finish ten years later with an ending as startling as a detective story.

In the first image brochure of 1970, which was designed by Hella Krauss, then still Hella Rummenhöller, it says: »art-design is a collection of pieces of jewellery created by five European designers.« The designers were the goldsmiths and artists Reinhold Reiling and Günter Krauss of Pforzheim; a Swede, Sigurd Persson, and Hans Stalder, a Swiss. Later they would be joined by Carl Elsener, another Swiss. Born in 1943, Krauss was a pupil of Reiling. Stalder, born in 1934, was well-known in Switzerland as a sculptor. The man from Pforzheim Carl-Heinrich Lüth (born in 1936), had been a partner in the Höfflin+Lüth studio since 1969. He was mainly responsible for the production side of jewellery-making.

The Pforzheim artist-industrialist Fahrner might be regarded as the role model in modern jewellery before the Second World War. However, art-design made top quality jewellery of yellow and white gold with costly diamonds and coloured precious stones while Fahrner, by contrast, manufactured mainly on a mass-production basis, usually with inexpensive synthetic materials and base metals. Pre-war artists adhered to the canon of forms prescribed by Jugendstil and Art Déco. By contrast, art-design was shaped by the signatures of individual goldsmiths. In the 1970s they were among the most distinguished exponents of their profession and, like Persson and Reiling, stood for Modernism in post-war jewellery. Something else that was new was collaborating on teams to give a modern jewellery label a higher profile. A firm brochure points out: »These five designers have formed a group to create a collection that is unique. A collection that bears five signatures yet is the result of teamwork.«

Every designer was presented with his distinctive qualities as an artist in the various advertising brochures, all conceived by Hella Krauss. In one brochure, for instance, it says: »Sigurd Persson would like to design things for everyday use that are simply a delight to look at, no matter how utilitarian their function may be.« The allusion to utilitarian design is supplemented by the designer's personal preferences and world-view. The following analysis of Sigurd Persson's closeness to nature in his sculpture is given: »It would seem that he goes back to the primal to seek refuge from the world, which for him has become alien and frighteningly cold and distant.« Professor Reiling is shown in his house, which is made of wood, glass and stone, a stellar example of ecologically friendly architecture back in the 1970s.

On Reiling's design method the brochure states: »Everything is clearly thought out, all designs are distinguished by great maturity. Often here, too, there is an adventurous aspect of change between the design and the

c. 1974

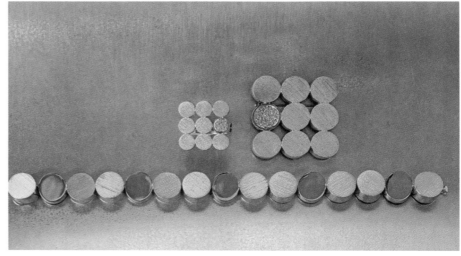

1974

finished piece of jewellery. He takes these changes very seriously while continuing to develop. Sometimes he allows himself the fun of designing amusing, witty things very quickly and without a plan. He is playing with cheerful elements and can be very relaxed and casual while doing this.« Günter Krauss's »astonishing talent for observing things« is emphasised. »He sees details from the forms themselves, discovers in objects aspects of design that are almost invisible.« And even the outstanding Pforzheim designer's foible for chansons as well as cooking and eating are touched on.

So aesthetically extravagant were the art-design jewellery collections that they far surpassed the »usual« industrially manufactured jewellery of the day. They reveal both the artists' urge to design and the 1970s Zeitgeist. A gold bangle set with pavé diamonds opens to end in two opposing semicircular surfaces. This piece is typical of the experimental, Scandinavian-inspired style made famous by Sigurd Persson. There are pieces by Reiling in yellow and white gold with rutile quartz and others lavishly set with diamonds. A ring and bangle of white gold boasts elegant curves paved with diamonds as a decorative element. Günter Krauss was even then using originally cut coloured stones, in one case Bernd Munsteiner's relief agates, for his designs.

What all these works have in common are Constructivist overtones although they noticeably retain the character of jewels with polished gold surfaces and the use of diamonds and precious stones. Some pieces by Hans Stalder and Carl-Heinz Lüth are also inspired by Art Déco. In all cases, the 1970s art-design collection echoes the widespread lust for shining gold, decoration and quirky forms. It all goes to show that art-design represented the first big adventure in the 1970s, seeking a new way in mass-produced German jewellery, one somewhere between ambitious modern art goldsmithing and the tried and tested jewels that jewellers knew sold well, the kind they felt comfortable selling. Höfflin, managing director at art-design, deliberately aimed at including exclusive jewellers. One advertising text runs: »With these five designers we have joined forces with leading, progressive jewellers and are presenting the finished designs.« From the outset, therefore, the business capitalised on targeting an upscale market. Hella, later Günter Krauss's wife, designed and produced advertising material, shop window displays, promotional elements for presentations, all of which were part of the package. There was also advertising in leading women's magazines such as »Burda International«, »Petra«, »Für Sie«, »Lady«, »Chic« und »Madame«. The drive shown by a small élite in the jewellery trade to give jewellery a new image and attract the public's attention to it more was always manifest.

An advertisement placed in 1973 contains the message conveyed by modern jewellery aimed at the wearer as well: »With it, you underscore your feeling for good taste.« This basic statement, which addresses personal style-consciousness rather than status, has scarcely changed at all since then. In addition, art-design advertising campaigns also work with the idea of jewellery as a gift: »Every single piece of jewellery is the gift of love.« An original touch is the remark that pieces from art-design are eternal »because what is lively and fresh lies in the design.« This may be a poke at the De Beers slogan »A diamond is forever.«

In 1975 the spring and autumn campaigns were presented in an image brochure bound in suede. It contains the message that success is chiefly based on the partnership between makers and specialist retailers. Hella Krauss's photos and texts convey a picture of what women were like in the 1970s. Ladies looked sporty and natural, with hair flying or wearing colourful headscarves; deeply tanned, a woman is gazing dreamily into the distance. An alternative motif is a dynamic woman sporting a beguiling smile and a costly green »apple« with »diamond seeds« on a gold torc, a work by Günter Krauss. The advertising text runs: »To me, gold is a piece of the sun. Radiant, warm and real.« This proves that art-design also shared in the campaigns launched by Anglo American plc, the transnational mining consortium founded by Sir Ernest Oppenheimer in South Africa. The various types of woman depicted in the advertising were also deployed in an opinion poll with a lottery.

Many reputable jewellers took up art-design jewellery and in doing so learned about the ideas and ideals of the art goldsmiths themselves. However, Höfflin, managing director of the creative label, had even more far-reaching plans and was unstoppable. One of those plans was called *Creation Avantgarde*. It was a line in jewellery designed by the Düsseldorf goldsmith Georg Hornemann. »*Creation Avantgarde* conveys status, enhances charm and conveys tenderness. The forms appeal to a broad target market, especially to people who are hesitant about what is ultra-modern but nonetheless would like something new and special.« The 1975 *Creation Avantgarde* collection encompasses 100 pieces. It was considerably more playful than the art-design pieces. Georg Hornemann's work featured coral and coloured precious stones, sumptuous diamond or sapphire trimming as well as organic, even floral, forms. A brochure promises that »many new designs« are to be added to *Creation Avantgarde* every six months.

Another collection was marketed under the name relo-design. The name derives from its founders, Rainer Lutz and Renate Lay. They established a Swiss branch at Renens near Lausanne in 1969. Manfred Fillner was head of the genuine jewellery department in the business that was sold to Höfflin+Lüth in 1972. The Pforzheimers founded relo-design ag as a Swiss business in Lucerne. The managing directors were Manfred Fillner and his wife, Ruth Fillner. relo-design addressed the bottom market segment. Jewellery in sterling silver, most of it designed by Carl Elsener, shows links with Scandinavian jewellery design. However Pop motifs, such as a stylised moon

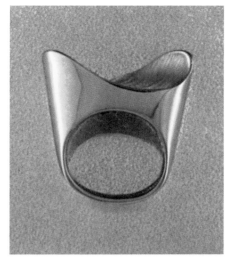

1974   1974

or pendants in fruit or bell shapes were also included. Silver bangle watches constituted an important part of the relo-design range. Carl Elsener won several design prizes for them. Hans Stalder also designed some silver watches. A brochure presenting the relo-design gold collection to retail customers features jewellery with the typical Günter Krauss signature. Coloured stones in original cuts in organic forms with diamonds arouse emotions that are also addressed in the advertising text: »Consciously showing your feelings by wearing jewellery links feeling good about yourself and self-assurance.«

In the late 1970s the Pforzheim business ended as spectacularly as it had begun. Höfflin, the manager, wanted too much at once. Overseas expansion was too much for the little firm and it suffered from financial difficulties. Höfflin disappeared abroad. Thus this particular chapter in the history of modern jewellery design ended. However, the initiative taken in hiring the best designers of the day to make ambitious jewellery collections has lived on in different combinations. In Switzerland, Fillner&Elsener grew out of relo-design. It was later managed by Ruth and Manfred Fillner alone. One of the finest jewellery shops in Lucerne is not least the result of an adventure begun by Höfflin+Lüth in 1969. What was left of art-design was dissolved by Eckhard Beier of Pforzheim, who joined forces with other designers to build up a firm of his own: cédé. Günter and Hella Krauss established a business in Stuttgart selling handmade gold jewellery of outstanding quality. Georg Hornemann has succeeded in doing much the same with his studio in Düsseldorf. Today Krauss and Hornemann are among the world's best and most creative jewellers.

c. 1974	Armreif und Ring, Design Günter Krauss, Gold, Diamanten, Achatrelief, Design Bernd Munsteiner — Bangle and ring, design Günter Krauss, gold, diamonds, agate relief, design Bernd Munsteiner
1974	Kette, Brosche und Ohrschmuck, Design Günter Krauss, Gold, Diamanten — Chain, brooch and earrings, design Günter Krauss, gold, diamonds
1974	Brosche, Design Hans Stalder, Gold, Email, Diamanten — Brooch, design Hans Stalder, gold, enamel, diamonds
1974	Ring, Design Hans Stalder, Gold — Ring, design Hans Stalder, gold

1999

1999

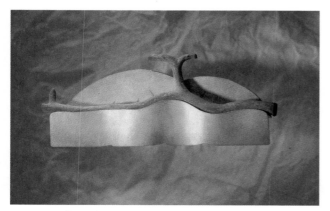

1996

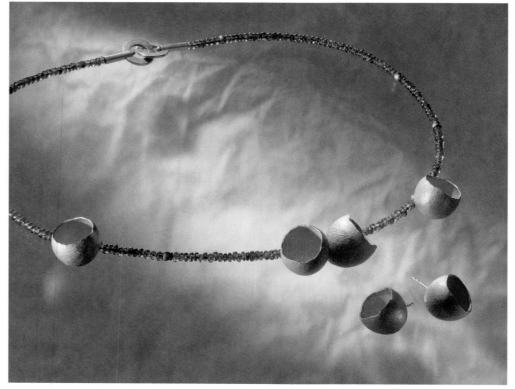

1997

1999	Halsreif *Fast Nichts*, Gold — Necklace *Virtually Nothing*, gold
1999	Armreif *Nur Blech*, Gold — Bracelet *Just Sheet metal,* gold
2000	Armreif *6er Spirale*, Gold — Bracelet *6er Spiral,* gold
2002	Hals- und Armreif *Nest*, Gold — Necklace and bracelet *Nest,* gold
1996	Brosche *Waal*, Gold, Koralle — Brooch *Waal*, gold, coral
1997	Hals- und Ohrschmuck *Spatzeneier*, Gold, Smaragd, Saphir — Necklace and earrings *Sparrow eggs*, gold, emerald, sapphire

2000   2002

Ulla + Martin Kaufmann

Dass moderner Schmuck eine Rückkehr zu den Wurzeln des Schöpferischen darstellen kann, in dem Handwerk, Kunst und Produktdesign eins werden, beweisen Ulla und Martin Kaufmann. Ihre jüngsten Gold- und Silberschmiedearbeiten sind so vielschichtig und aktuell wie die Kunst bedeutender Bildhauer der Gegenwart.

Seit ihrer Ausbildung von 1958 bis 1962 wirken Ulla und Martin Kaufmann erfolgreich in der Gold- und Silberschmiedekunst ebenso wie im Produktdesign. Nach ihrer Lehre und Meisterprüfung gingen sie gemeinsam einige Jahre nach Norwegen und Frankreich. Seit 1970 sind sie in ihrem eigenen Atelier tätig, einem ehemaligen Bauernhof in Hildesheim. Ihre frühen Arbeiten im Schmuck zeigen abstrahierte, blütenartige Formen mit kraftvoll, graphisch inszenierten Farbedelsteinen. Ergänzend entstanden Becher und Dosen. Auf einen starken Stilwechsel Mitte der 1980er Jahre verweist der Hamburger Kurator Rüdiger Joppien. Der Stilwechsel sei zeitgleich mit der Jahresausstellung im Museum für Kunst und Gewerbe und einem Entwicklungsauftrag aus der Industrie erfolgt. Die Besteckserie *Palladio* von 1986 für Wilkens, Bremen, zeigt eine Formenstrenge, wie sie für die klassische Moderne und das deutsche Design nach 1945 typisch ist. Als herausragende Produktdesigner präsentieren sich Ulla und Martin Kaufmann ebenso 1997 mit dem Besteck *Passione* für Wilkens. Zwischen 2000 und 2004 gestalteten sie Küchengeräte für Zwilling, vom Wiegemesser bis hin zur Knoblauchpresse.

Alle Designprodukte ebenso wie die Gold- und Silberschmiedearbeiten sind gemeinsame Entwicklungen. »Unsere Wurzeln liegen in uns«, sagen sie. »In der Gestaltung der Stücke sind wir immer wieder frei und offen für spannende Gedanken, die uns zu neuen Ideen, mitunter zu noch mehr Konzentration auf die Arbeit führen.« Bis in die 1990er Jahre diente nicht selten die Natur als Vorbild. Zum Beispiel im Hals- und Ohrschmuck *Spatzeneier* oder bei der Brosche *Waal*. Auch geometrisch strenge Stücke wie der Halsschmuck *Eiswürfel* entstanden.

Für den Schmuck des letzten Jahrzehnts ist einerseits ihre große Faszination für das Material Gold wesentlich. Gold symbolisiert von alters her die Sonne und Leben. Andererseits wurde das Gestalterpaar stark berührt von den Arbeiten der Bildhauer Richard Serra, Donald Judd und Eduardo Chillida sowie deren Auseinandersetzung mit dem Thema Raum. Dadurch haben sie zu ihrer eigenen Sprache und auch gleichzeitig zu dem wesentlichsten Sinn des Begriffs Schmuck, des sich Schmückens, gefunden. »Unser gedanklicher Ausgangspunkt wurde das Band. Aus ihm hat sich vieles entwickelt«, erklären sie.

Am Körper getragen, zeigen die durch das intensive Schmieden flexibel und anschmiegsam gewordenen Hals- und Armreife eine hohe Sinnlichkeit, gepaart mit strenger Reduktion. Räume, Spiegelungen und Zwischenräume entstehen. Auch das Spiel mit den Gegenpolen weich und hart,

anschmiegsam und sperrig, gerade und gewölbt, reduziert und üppig, still und laut, kraftvoll und leise ist dabei wichtig. Indem sich die Bänder überschneiden und Flächen winklig gegeneinander stehen, ergeben sich Spiegelungen. Diese lassen die Farbe des Goldes für das Auge noch lebendiger werden. »Stark reduzierte Reife werden so üppig und atmen ihre eigene Prächtigkeit am Körper«, sagen Ulla und Martin Kaufmann. »Getragen führen sie ihr eignes Leben, ausgelöst durch Bewegung. Sie verlieren ihre optische Starrheit und fangen an, mit sich selbst und dem Körper zu spielen.«

Lang ist die Liste höchster Preise und Designauszeichnungen für Schmuck, Objekte der Silberschmiedekunst und Industrie-Design. 1972 wurden sie mit dem Förderpreis des Landes Niedersachsen geehrt. 1974 mit ihrem ersten Staatspreis des Landes Hessen, dem weitere folgten: von Niedersachsen, Bayern und 2006 wieder von Hessen. Auch renommierte Designauszeichnungen wie design plus, red dot oder den iF design award gewannen die Gestalter mehrfach, zuletzt 2005. Zwei Jahre zuvor würdigte das Grassimuseum Leipzig das vielgestaltige Werk. Doch haben sich Ulla und Martin Kaufmann von Beginn an auch dem Markt gestellt. Neben Galerie- und Museumsausstellungen sind sie seit 1970 regelmäßig auf Messen präsent und verkaufen ihre Arbeiten an Schmuckgalerien und Goldschmiedegeschäfte. Die ersten geschmiedeten Hals- und Armreife mit schlichten Titeln wie *Nur Blech*, *Fast nichts*, *Kragen*, *Sich öffnend* oder *Gespiegelt* entstanden in den 1990er Jahren.

Jedem neuen Entwurf geht ein Modell voraus. Dann wird für den Reif ein passendes Band aus Gold gewalzt. »Mit dem Hammer machen wir die Form«, sagt Martin Kaufmann und erklärt, dass durch das Walzen die Goldmoleküle nur in eine Richtung gezogen würden. Erst durch das Schmieden wird 18-karätiges Gold hart und elastisch. Am Ende des Schmiedeprozesses weist das Gold die ideale Stärke von 0,35 bis 0,4 mm auf. Bevor ein neues Modell in Kleinserie gehen darf, zeigen sich Ulla und Martin Kaufmann als Perfektionisten. »Auch wenn etwas scheinbar nicht zu verbessern ist, muss man es doch versuchen.«

Die Kunsthistorikerin Maria Hoyer schrieb dazu im Jahre 2004: »*Fast nichts* nannten Ulla und Martin Kaufmann ihren mehrfach preisgekrönten Halsreif. Ein geschmiedetes Band aus matt glänzendem Gold, sonst nichts. Kein Verschluss, keine überflüssige Zier. Absolute Reduktion. Wie ein elastisch federnder Span legt sich der schlanke Reif betörend schlicht und schmeichelnd um den Hals der Trägerin, so als würde er sich mit ihr verbinden, ein Stück ihrer Identität sein.« Die feine Struktur des Goldes, die wohltuend für das Auge des Betrachters mit dem Licht spielt, erweckt die Magie des glänzenden Edelmetalls zu neuem Leben. In besonders eindrucksvoller Weise verbinden sich in diesen Stücken die Kunst eines traditionsreichen Handwerks und die Idee der Moderne. »Unser Schmuck verlangt ein Bekenntnis«, sagt Ulla Kaufmann und erzählt die Geschichte, wie der

2002   2004

Hamburger Fotograf Hans Hansen vor einiger Zeit ihren Schmuck fotografierte. »Eine reifere Frau und nicht das übliche junge Modell hat den Halsreif umgelegt. Plötzlich wurde es totenstill im Raum.« Mit dem Schmuck von Ulla und Martin Kaufmann kann man sich nicht mehr verstecken. Er verändert den Menschen, indem er seinen Charakter eindrucksvoll hervorhebt.

E — Ulla and Martin Kaufmann are living proof that modern jewellery can represent a return to the roots of creativity, where the applied and decorative arts, fine art and product design become one. Their most recent works in gold and silver are as diverse and cutting-edge as the work of leading contemporary sculptors.

After training between 1958 and 1962, Ulla and Martin Kaufmann worked successfully as goldsmiths and silversmiths and in product design. On serving apprenticeships and taking their master's certificates, they went to Norway and France to stay for several years. Since 1970 they have worked from their own studio, an old farmhouse in Hildesheim. Their early pieces boasted abstract floral forms set with vibrant coloured precious stones in a linear décor. They also produced beakers and jars. The Hamburg curator Rüdiger Joppien points out that the Kaufmanns' work underwent a radical change in style in the mid-1980s. This shift coincided, as he shows, with the annual exhibition at the Museum für Kunst und Gewerbe, followed by a commission to develop jewellery on an industrial basis. The *Palladio* line in cutlery they designed in 1986 for Wilkens in Bremen reveals the formal astringency typical of the classic Moderns and German design after 1945. Years afterward, in 1997, Ulla and Martin Kaufmann showed themselves to be outstanding product designers when they again designed cutlery for Wilkens, this time the *Passione* model. Between 2000 and 2004 they designed kitchen gadgets for Zwilling, ranging from a parsley chopper with a curved blade to a garlic press.

All Kaufmann designer products, like the Kaufmanns' work in gold and silver, are joint productions. »Our roots lie in ourselves,« they say. »In designing our pieces we are constantly liberating ourselves from preconceptions and remain receptive to stimulating thoughts that lead us to new ideas, occasionally also to more concentration on our work.« Until well into the 1990s nature was often their model, for instance, for the neck and ear jewellery *Spatzeneier* [Sparrows' eggs] or *Waal* [Whale], a brooch. They have also produced stringently geometric pieces such as the *Eiswürfel* [Ice cubes] necklace.

Their enduring fascination for gold as a material is crucial to the jewellery they have produced in the past decade. Gold has symbolised the sun and life since time immemorial. On the other hand, the work of sculptors Richard Serra, Donald Judd and Eduardo Chillida and their investigation of space have also had a major impact on the Kaufmanns as designers. Through

it, they have arrived both at their idiom and the quintessence of jewellery as adornment. »The starting-point in our thinking has been the strip. Much has developed from it,« they explain.

When worn, their torcs and bangles are springy and supple, revealing a sensuousness coupled with stringent reduction. Spaces, reflections and interstices are created. Also important is the play on dichotomies such as soft and hard, supple and bulky, straight and curved, astringent and opulent, still and shrill, forceful and reticent. Overlapping strips and surfaces positioned at right angles to each other create reflections, which make the colour of the gold look even more vibrant. »Bangles that are reduced to the utmost become so opulent and exhale their own magnificence on the body,« say Ulla and Martin Kaufmann. »When worn, they lead lives of their own. They lose their stiff look and begin to play with themselves and the wearer's body.«

The roll of top prizes and design awards they have received for jewellery, art objects in silver and industrial design is long. In 1972 they were honoured with the Förderpreis des Landes Niedersachsen [State of Lower Saxony Promotional Award]. In 1974 they were awarded their first Staatspreis des Landes Hessen [State of Hesse Award], followed by others: from Lower Saxony, Bavaria and in 2006 again from Hesse. The Kaufmanns have also won several prestigious design awards such as design plus, red dot and the iF design award, most recently in 2005. Two years previously, the Grassi Museum in Leipzig devoted a retrospective to their diverse œuvre. Nevertheless, Ulla and Martin Kaufmann have from the outset also kept an eye on the market. Apart from exhibitions at galleries and museums, they have been present at trade fairs on a regular basis and sell their work to jewellery galleries and shops specialising in gold jewellery. Their first hammered torcs and bangles bearing such simple titles as *Nur Blech* [Just Sheet metal], *Fast Nichts* [Virtually Nothing], *Kragen* [Collar], *Sich öffnend* [Opening] and *Gespiegelt* [Mirrored] were made in the 1990s.

A model precedes each new design. Then a suitable strip of gold is beaten into a torc or bangle. »We form it with the hammer,« says Martin Kaufmann and goes on to explain that beating the gold pulls the molecules of the metal in a single direction. Gold does not become durable and supple until it has been beaten. At the end of the beating process, the gold has an ideal thickness of 0.35 to 0.4mm. Before a new model may go into production as a limited edition, Ulla and Martin Kaufmann demonstrate what perfectionists they really are. »Even if something looks as if it couldn't be improved on, it should be attempted anyway.«

The art historian Maria Hoyer wrote about that in 2004: »*Fast Nichts* [Virtually Nothing] is the name Ulla and Martin Kaufmann have given to their torc, which has won several awards. A band of matt, gleaming, beaten gold, nothing else. No clasp, no superfluous decoration. Absolute reduction. Like a springy metal shaving, the slender torc drapes seductively simple and flat-

2005

2007

tering about the wearer's neck as if it were bonding with her to be a part of her identity.« The fine texturing of the gold, which plays with light, a treat to the eye of the beholder, breathes new life into the magic of the gleaming noble metal. In these pieces the art of traditional craftsmanship is linked in a particularly impressive way with the Modernist ideal. »Our jewellery exacts a pledge of commitment,« says Ulla Kaufmann and tells a story about the Hamburg photographer Hans Hansen taking pictures of her jewellery some time ago. »A mature woman and not your usual young model put the torc on. Suddenly it was deathly still in the room.« It is impossible to hide one's light under a bushel with Ulla and Martin Kaufmann's jewellery. It changes the wearer by stunningly highlighting her personality.

2002	Halsreif *Gespiegelt*, Gold — Necklace *Mirrored,* gold
2004	Armreif *Marrit*, Gold — Bangle *Marrit,* gold
2005	Ohrringe *In dem Kreis*, Gold — Earrings *In the Circle,* gold
2007	Armreif *Welle*, Gold — Bracelet *Wave*, gold

Ulla und Martin Kaufmann
Beide geboren 1941 in Hildesheim,
1958–1962 Lehre und Meisterprüfung.
Atelier in Hildesheim seit 1970.

Ulla and Martin Kaufmann
Both born in Hildesheim in 1941, 1958–1962
apprenticeship and master craftsman's
certificates. Studio in Hildesheim since 1970.

Ulla + Martin Kaufmann

1966

1985

1966 Ringe *Triset*, Gold, Diamanten — Rings *Triset*, gold, diamonds

1985 Anhänger, Brosche und Ohrschmuck *Pferdeschweif*, Platin, Gold, Diamanten — Pendant, brooch and earrings *Horsetail*, platinum, gold, diamonds

1983 Armreife und Ringe, Kautschuk, Titan, Gold, Diamanten — Bracelets and rings, caoutchouc, titanium, gold, diamonds

1985 *Gold in Fashion*, Gold, Diamanten — *Gold in Fashion*, gold, diamonds

1983

1985

Meister

Die Trauring- und Schmuckmanufaktur Meister wurde 1897 von Emmanuel Peter in Zürich gegründet. 1965 kam der 1944 geborene Theo Meister in das Unternehmen. Zwei Jahre zuvor hatte sein Vater Heinrich Meister, 1917–2006, mit dem Partner Elmer die Firma erworben. Heinrich Meister war ein begnadeter Stahlgraveur; seine Wappenringe waren sehr erfolgreich. Die Einführung des *Trisets* ab 1966 und des anschließenden *Twinsets* belebten das schon bestehende Trauringgeschäft. Bei Designwettbewerben von De Beers für Diamant- und Verlobungsringe erhielt das Unternehmen 1967 und 1968 zwei erste Preise und sechs Auszeichnungen. »Manche unserer Designs, wie die Anhänger, auch *Shorties* genannt, oder die *Akzentringe* beim *Memoire,* haben sich in späteren Jahren als echte Trends etabliert«, berichtet Theo Meister. Memoireringe, rundum mit Diamanten besetzt, erinnern an wichtige Ereignisse im Leben eine Paares. Durch die anspruchsvoll gestalteten und verarbeiteten Trauringe konnten zahlreiche Juweliere in Deutschland und Österreich als Kunden gewonnen werden. Um für diese Länder einen besseren Lieferservice zu garantieren, wurde 1964 in Singen ein zweiter Standort eröffnet. Seit 1982 werden in einem neu erbauten Produktionsgebäude in Radolfzell am Bodensee alle Trauringe und Schmuckkollektionen für den deutschen Markt und die EU-Länder gefertigt.

1974 verschwand der Name Elmer aus der Firmenbezeichnung. Theo und Lydia Meister übernahmen die Leitung. In ganz besonderer Weise war Meister 1976 an der Wiedereinführung von Platin als Schmuckmetall beteiligt. Denn das erste Stück für die 1976 gegründete Platin Gilde in Deutschland wurde bei Meister gefertigt. An den weiteren modernen Schmuckentwicklungen war maßgeblich Silvio Daldini beteiligt, der 1983 Leiter der Designabteilung wurde. Ein viel beachteter Wurf gelang 1985 mit dem *Pferdeschweifhaar*-Collier, das durch entsprechend gestaltete Broschen, Ohrschmuck und Ringe zu einer kompletten Schmucklinie ausgebaut wurde. Das Collier besteht aus einer elliptischen Hülse in verschiedenen Platin- und Goldvarianten. In einer asymmetrisch fließenden Öffnung ist ein Brillantsolitär eingespannt. Die technisch ausgeklügelte Form wirkt harmonisch und luxuriös. Die kräftige Strähne aus schwarzen, teils blau gefärbten Pferdehaaren als Trägersystem stellt einen Bezug zu archaischen Schmuckvorstellungen her.

Unter der Leitung von Theo und Lydia Meister konnte 1995 der Schweizer Betrieb mit seinen rund 80 Mitarbeitern von Zürich nach Wollerau in eine moderne Manufaktur umziehen. Die transparente Raumkonzeption macht die Verbindung von Entwicklung, Gestaltung, Technik und Handwerk sichtbar: »Damit alle teilhaben können am Entstehungsprozess der Schmuckstücke«, erklärt Theo Meister. In der funktionellen Architektur finden sich zudem symbolische Gestaltungselemente. Sie kamen auch in den Trauring-Linien zum Ausdruck, die von der griechischen Vier-Elemente-Lehre, das heißt, von den Themen Feuer, Wasser, Erde und Luft inspiriert waren. Nach der Firmenchefin wurde die Schmuckkollektion *Lydia M.* genannt, während

Theo M. den Männeraccessoires seinen Namen verlieh. Im Zeichen der Internationalisierung und eines weiteren Generationswechsels wird heute wieder der Markenname Meister geführt.

Nach dem Erfolg mit dem *Pferdeschweifhaar*-Collier hat das Unternehmen kontinuierlich in innovative Produktionsverfahren und Designentwicklungen investiert. Meister wollte nicht nur Synonym für hervorragende Qualität und exzellenten Service sein, sondern auch für innovatives Design. Dafür arbeitet das Unternehmen seit den 1990er Jahren verstärkt auch mit freischaffenden Künstlern, Schmuckdesignern und Absolventen von Designhochschulen zusammen. Die Schmucklinie *Harmony* entstand 1996 in Zusammenarbeit mit Arnd Kai Klosowski, einem Schüler von Hermann Jünger. Die Verbindung von Kreismotiv und Zylinder entsprach ganz der Harmonievorstellung von Lydia Meister.

Unter dem Motto »Accessoires für Individualisten« entwickelt Meister seit 1983 auch technisch anspruchsvolle Schmuckstücke für Männer. Der Armreif des Designers Silvio Daldini in Titan und Kautschuk, mit einem Verschluss in Gold, gilt inzwischen als Klassiker. Ausgehend von der griechischen Münzform entstanden in der Serie *Kompass*, *Sonnenuhr*, *Morsescheibe* und weitere markante Männeraccessoires. Der *Kompass* wurde 1997 mit dem red dot des Designzentrums Nordrhein-Westfalen und im Jahr 2000 mit dem IF Designaward ausgezeichnet. Auch andere Produkte dieser Serie und der Schmucklinien erhielten immer wieder Designpreise. Ebenso technisch versiert zeigte sich Meister in seiner *Girello*-Linie von 2002. Sie wurde ein wesentlicher Bestandteil der Meister-Schmucklinie. In den *Girello*-Ringen drehen sich Brillanten auf einer zweiten Ringschiene auf einem Feinkugellager. Das Konzept wurde auch auf den Männerschmuck übertragen.

Seit 2000 ist Marcus Siessegger, geboren 1966, im Designteam bei Meister tätig. Er studierte von 1993 bis 1997 Schmuckdesign bei den Professoren Schlevogt und Hess in Schwäbisch Gmünd. Der Ring *Alles im Lot* aus Titan und Gold mit einem Diamanten verbindet eine winzige Wasserwaage mit einem Winkelmesser. 2004 stellte Meister zweiteilige Ringe aus Titan mit Getriebe- oder Kupplungsverzahnung vor.

2004 begann die Zusammenarbeit mit Sabine Brandenburg-Frank und Egon Frank. Dabei entstanden prächtige Ringe und Anhänger in organisch fließenden Formen mit innovativ geschliffenen Farbedelsteinen. Die beiden Schmuckdesigner sind auch an der Entwicklung neuer Trauringe beteiligt. Die Trauringkollektion ist seit 1996 in fünf Gruppen eingeteilt. Mit den *Classics*, *Phantastics*, *Individuals*, *Symbolics* und *Futures* möchte Meister den vielschichtigen Bedürfnissen der Brautpaare des 21. Jahrhunderts entsprechen.

Fabian Meister, geboren 1977, ist heute Mitglied der Geschäftsleitung. Vor seinem Eintritt in das Unternehmen der Eltern hat er u.a. eine Ausbildung am Gemmological Institute of America (GIA) erfolgreich abgeschlossen. Fabian Meisters größter Wunsch ist es, seine Begeisterung für kreatives

1996

1996

Design und kompromisslose Qualität mit seinen Mitarbeitern ständig weiter zu entwickeln und mit den Kunden zu teilen. Er will daran mitwirken, »Tendenzen vorauszuahnen und aufzunehmen, um die Erwartungen an die Marke Meister bei den Schmuckträgerinnen und Schmuckträgern zu übertreffen.«

E — Meister was founded in Zurich in 1897 by Emmanuel Peter as a wedding ring and jewellery manufacturer. In 1965 Theo Meister (born in 1944) joined the business. Two years before, his father, Heinrich Meister (1917–2006), had acquired the firm as a partnership with Elmer. Heinrich Meister was a gifted steel engraver; his signet rings with coats of arms were very successful. The launch of trisets in 1966, followed by twinsets revived the existing wedding ring business. The firm was awarded two first prizes and six distinctions at the 1967 and 1968 design competitions held by De Beers for diamond and engagement rings. »Some of our designs, such as the pendants, also known as *shorties*, or the *accent rings* in the *eternity ring* line have become established in later years as genuine trend-setters,« reports Theo Meister. Eternity rings, set all round with diamonds, commemorate important events in the lives of a couple. With ambitiously designed and superbly worked wedding rings, Meister gained numerous retail jewellers in Germany and Austria as clients. A factory was opened in Singen in 1964 to guarantee better delivery service to those countries. Since 1982, all wedding rings and jewellery collections for the German market and other EU countries have been made at a new factory building in Radolfzell on Lake Constance.

In 1974 the name Elmer disappeared from the company name. Theo and Lydia Meister became co-directors. In 1976 Meister played a special role in the relaunch of platinum as a metal for jewellery because the first piece made for Platin Gilde (est. 1976) in Germany was manufactured by Meister. Silvio Daldini, who became head of the design division in 1983, also exerted a paramount influence on further developments in modern jewellery. An acclaimed launch was the *Pferdeschweifhaar*-Collier [Horsetail hair necklace], which was expanded into a complete line in jewellery through the addition of matching brooches, ear jewellery and rings. The necklace consists of an ellipsoid capsule in several platinum and gold variants. A diamond solitaire is held by tension in an asymmetrically fluid aperture. This technically sophisticated form looks at once harmonious and luxurious. Strong strands of black with some blue dyed horsehairs as the support system represent a reference to archaic ideas of jewellery.

Under the management of Theo and Lydia Meister, the Swiss company was able to move with some 80 employees in 1995 from Zurich to a modern factory in Wollerau. A transparent spatial conception visualises the linkage of development, design, technology and craftsmanship: »So that everyone can share in the process of creating the pieces of jewellery,« explains Theo Meister. Moreover, there are symbolic elements of design in this functional

architecture. They were also expressed in the line in wedding rings inspired by the Greek four-elements doctrine, that is, the elements of fire, water, earth and air. The *Lydia M.* jewellery collection is named after the female head of the firm while her husband gave his name to the *Theo M.* line in men's accessories. In line with globalisation and yet another change in generation, the Meister name is again registered as the company trademark.

Following up on the success of the *Horsetail hair necklace*, the firm has continued to invest in innovative production methods and designer-driven development. Meister did not wish to be perceived as merely synonymous with outstanding quality and excellent service but also wanted to be associated with innovative design. Consequently, the firm policy has since the 1990s again been to collaborate more with freelance artists, jewellery designers and graduates of design institutes. The *Harmony* line was created in 1996 in collaboration with Arnd Kai Klosowski, a pupil of Hermann Jünger. The linkage of the circle motif and the cylinder was a perfect match with Lydia Meister's idea of harmony.

Under the heading »accessories for individualists,« Meister has also been developing technically advanced jewellery for men since 1983. The bangle designed by Silvio Daldini in titanium and hard rubber with a gold clasp is now universally acclaimed as a classic. Starting with the form of ancient Greek coins, the line has included *Compass*, *Sundial*, *Morse Disc* and other memorable accessories for men. In 1997 *Compass* was awarded the red dot by the North Rhine-Westphalian Design Centre and in 2000 received the IF Design Award. Other products from this range and the lines in jewellery have continued to win design prizes. The 2002 *Girello* line again reveals how comfortable Meister feels with modern technology. It has become a crucial component of the Meister jewellery range. *Girello* spinning rings feature diamonds on a second ring shank revolving on a fine ball-bearings race. Jewellery for men is also based on this concept.

Marcus Siessegger (born in 1966) has been working with the Meister design team since 2000. He studied jewellery design with Professors Schlevogt and Hess in Schwäbisch Gmünd from 1993 until 1997. *Alles im Lot* [All there], a ring in titanium and gold with a diamond, links a minute spirit level with a protractor. In 2004 Meister launched two-piece titanium rings with gear or coupling sprockets.

In 2004 collaboration began with Sabine Brandenburg-Frank and Egon Frank. It has produced magnificent rings and pendants in organically fluid forms with innovatively cut coloured precious stones. The two jewellery designers also share in developing new lines in wedding rings. Since 1996, the wedding ring collection has been divided into five groups: *Classics*, *Phantastics*, *Individuals*, *Symbolics* and *Futures*. With this varied range, Meister wants to match the diverse needs and tastes of young marrieds in the 21st century.

2004   2006   2006

Fabian Meister (born in 1977) is now on the management team. Before joining his parents' firm, his education included graduating from the Gemmological Institute of America (GIA). Fabian Meister's greatest wish is to continue to develop his enthusiasm for creative design and uncompromising quality with his staff and share them with his clientele. He wants to be a part of »anticipating and taking up trends so that the Meister label always surpasses the expectations of the men and women wearing our jewellery.«

1996	Collier und Ohrschmuck *Harmony*, Gold, Brillanten — Necklace and Earrings *Harmony*, gold, diamonds
1996	*Kompass*, Titan, Gold — *Compass*, titanium, gold
2004	Ring *Fingerprint*, Gold,individuelle Lasergravur — Ring *Fingerprint*, gold, individual laser gravure
2006	Trauringe, Platin, Diamanten — Wedding rings, platinum, diamonds
2006	Ringe, Gold, Platin, Goldberyll, fliederfarbener Amethyst, Diamanten — Rings, gold, platinum, gold beryl, lilac coloured amethyst, diamonds

Theo Meister
Geboren 1944, Eidgen. Handelsdiplom.
Firmeneintritt 1965, Firmenleitung 1974
mit Lydia Meister.

Theo Meister
Born in 1944, Swiss federal trade diploma.
Entered firm in 1965, director of firm with
Lydia Meister in 1974.

Lydia Meister
Geboren 1945, Eidgen. Handelsdiplom.
Firmeneintritt 1974, Firmenleitung 1974
mit Theo Meister.

Lydia Meister
Born in 1945, Swiss federal trade diploma.
Entered firm in 1974, co-director of firm
with Theo Meister in 1974.

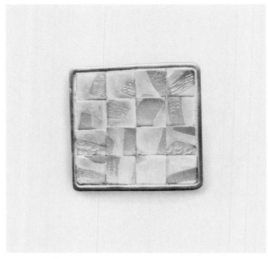

1985

1986

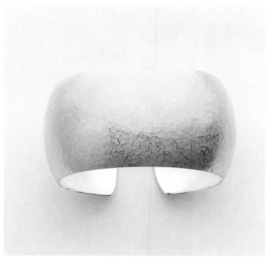

1985

1990

1985	Brosche, Silber, Gold — Bracelet, silver, gold
1986	Brosche, Gold, geschwärztes Silber — Brooch, gold, blackened silver
1989	Ohrhänger, Grünachat, Silber, Gold — Earrings, green agate, silver, gold
2005	Armreif, Gold, Onyx — Bracelet, gold, onyx
2006	Armband, Silber, Gold — Bracelet, silver, gold
1985	Armreif, Silber, Gold — Bangle, silver, gold
1990	Halsschmuck, Silber, Gold — Necklace, silver, gold

1989   2005   2006

Monika Killinger

Bei jedem ihrer Schmuckstücke achtet Monika Killinger darauf, dass Oberfläche und Form eine Einheit bilden. Ihren Arm- und Halsschmuck aus gewölbten geometrischen Formen akzentuiert die Goldschmiedemeisterin farblich mit sattem Feingold und weißem Silber. Ursprünglich fertigte sie nur Einzelstücke. Daraus entwickelte sie allmählich handwerklich anspruchsvolle Serien. Die ersten Anregungen dazu kamen von Professor Hermann Jünger. In Stralsund geboren, erlernte Monika Killinger 1958 in nur zwei Jahren das Goldschmiedehandwerk in einem renommierten Stralsunder Betrieb. 1966 machte sie ihre Meisterprüfung. Die Materialknappheit und geistige Enge der DDR ließen ihr aber nur wenig Spielraum für eine eigene kreative Entwicklung. Mit viel Glück gelang ihr 1968 die Flucht in den Westen.

Monika Killinger ließ sich in Hamburg nieder, wo sie in den 1970er Jahren eine der ersten Galerien für modernen Schmuck in Deutschland eröffnete. Zuvor arbeitete sie in verschiedenen Werkstätten und machte 1973 eine Weiterbildung an der Staatlichen Zeichenakademie Hanau. In ihrer Schmuckgalerie – zuerst noch unter ihrem Geburtsnamen Monika Kober – stellte sie bedeutende Schmuckgestalter wie Jens-Rüdiger Lorenzen und Hermann Jünger aus. Der Gründung ihrer Schmuckgalerie folgte 1979 die Mitgliedschaft in der Arbeitsgemeinschaft Kunsthandwerk, kurz ADK. In diesem Rahmen präsentierte Monika Killinger ihren Schmuck in zahlreichen Ausstellungen im In- und Ausland. Seit 1984 ist sie auf den bedeutenden deutschen Schmuckmessen und in Galerien in Österreich, Schweiz, England und Holland vertreten. 1996 verlegte Monika Killinger ihre Werkstatt und Galerie für Schmuck nach Bad Oldesloe.

Nach ihren ersten Silberarbeiten mit getupften Feingoldapplikationen entwickelte Monika Killinger zunehmend ruhigere Schmucklinien. Innerhalb von drei Jahrzehnten ist eine Kollektion von Ringen, Arm- und Halsschmuck von beachtlichem Umfang entstanden. Nach wie vor überwiegt die Zweifarbigkeit aus Silber, dem eine Schicht Feingold aufgeschweißt wird. Das Spektrum reicht von großflächig montierten Armbändern bis hin zu zarten Wickelarmreifen, von Ketten mit quadratischen bis hin zu ovalen Gliedern und Ringen mit Farbedelsteinen. Sie zählt zweifellos zu den frühen modernen Klassikern im seriellen Schmuck der Nachkriegszeit, auch wenn ihre Arbeitsweise von traditionellen kunsthandwerklichen Techniken geprägt ist. Im kontrastreichen Licht- und Schattenspiel ihrer Schmuckstücke, das durch die Struktur und Wölbung der Flächen entsteht, spiegeln sich deutlich die Ursprünge archaischer Schmuckformen.

E — Monika Killinger ensures that surface and form create an aesthetic whole in each piece of her jewellery. The master goldsmith adds trenchant touches of colour in rich fine gold and white silver to her arm and neck jewellery featuring domed geometric forms. She started out making one-offs only before gradually developing collections that reveal sophisticated craftsmanship. She was first inspired to do this by Professor Hermann Jünger. Born in Stralsund, Monika Killinger learned goldsmithing in just two years at a renowned Stralsund workshop, starting in 1958. She received her master craftsman's certificate in 1966. However, material shortages and the intellectual constraints imposed on her in the GDR left her little scope for creative development. She was fortunate in being able to flee to the West in 1968.

Monika Killinger settled in Hamburg, where she opened one of the first galleries for modern jewellery in Germany in the 1970s. Before opening the gallery, she had worked in various workshops and done further training at the Staatliche Zeichenakademie in Hanau in 1973. At her jewellery gallery – which she at first ran under her maiden name, Monika Kober – she exhibited work by such important jewellery-makers as Jens-Rüdiger Lorenzen and Hermann Jünger. She followed up the foundation of the gallery by joining the Arbeitsgemeinschaft Kunsthandwerk (ADK) in 1979. Under the auspices of this organisation, Monika Killinger showed her jewellery at numerous exhibitions in Germany and abroad. Since 1984, she has been represented at important German jewellery trade fairs as well as galleries in Austria, Switzerland, Britain and the Netherlands. Monika Killinger moved her workshop and jewellery gallery to Bad Oldesloe in 1996.

After her first work in silver with applied dots of fine gold, Monika Killinger began to develop quieter lines in jewellery. Within three decades, she has produced a remarkably large collection of rings, bracelets and necklaces. Two-tone jewellery made of silver with a layer of fine gold welded on to it, still predominates. The spectrum ranges from bracelets mounted to large feature surfaces to delicate wrap-a-round bangles, from chains with square to oval links and rings set with coloured precious stones. Monika Killinger is uncontestedly one of the early modern classics in post-war jewellery lines even though her approach has been noticeably shaped by the traditional crafts techniques. Highlighting as it does the rich contrast resulting from the play of light and shade induced by the texture and curve of surfaces, her jewellery clearly reflects its origins in archaic forms of adornment.

Monika Killinger
Geboren 1941 in Stralsund, 1966 Meisterprüfung. 1968 Flucht. 1975–1988 Schmuckgalerie in Hamburg, 1996 Bad Oldesloe.

Monika Killinger
Born in Stralsund in 1941, master craftsman's certificate in 1966. 1968 fled to West. 1975–1988 jewellery gallery in Hamburg, Bad Oldesloe in 1996.

1969   1971   1973

Barbara Schulte-Hengesbach

Zwei Ringe von 1969 und 1971 zeigen, wie gefühlvoll Barbara Schulte-Hengesbach schon damals die Moderne interpretiert hat. Sie weisen deutliche Bezüge zur Bildhauerei, aber auch zum Design der 1960er Jahre auf. Den Ringschienen erwachsen plastische, skulpturale Erhöhungen, die teils von konkaven Linsenformen »gekrönt« werden.

Das Organische dieser frühen Stücke ist inzwischen längst verschwunden. Heute sind alle Schmucklinien von Barbara Schulte-Hengesbach geometrisch klar, doch gleichzeitig emotional. Sie beinhalten oft dekorative, spielerische Elemente, ohne verspielt zu wirken. Die Düsseldorferin liebt solche scheinbaren Widersprüche, der auch in folgendem Satz, der für ihre Arbeit steht, zum Ausdruck kommt: »Die klassische Moderne – kühl – erwärmt durch ein Spiel mit Formen ohne Strenge.« 1971 absolviert Barbara Schulte-Hengesbach ihre Meisterprüfung an der Zeichenakademie in Hanau. Anschließend studierte sie an der Fachhochschule Düsseldorf. Hier erweckte Professor Friedrich Becker das Interesse der talentierten Studentin für sein großes Thema, die Kinetik. Die Bewegung, von den italienischen Futuristen in die Kunst des 20. Jahrhunderts eingebracht, interessierte Barbara Schulte-Hengesbach auch nach ihrem Diplom von 1974. Jedoch darauf bedacht, eigene Wege zu finden, ließ sie ihre Arbeit am kinetischen Schmuck drei Jahrzehnte lang ruhen. Erst 2005 stellte sie wieder neue kinetische Ringe vor. Dazwischen erforschte sie andere Themen im Schmuck. Zum Beispiel in den 1970er Jahren dreidimensionale, perspektivische Effekte, wie drei Broschen aus Edelstahl und Acryl zeigen. Ein wichtiges Thema war auch die Verwendung von Zuchtperlen im Kontext mit modernen, geometrischen Formen ab 1990. »Jedes Thema hat immer mit dem anderen zu tun«, sagt die Schmuck-Designerin rückblickend.

1975 eröffnete Barbara Schulte-Hengesbach ihr eigenes Atelier, machte Jahresausstellungen für ihre Kunden und nahm erfolgreich Kontakt zu Schmuckgalerien auf. Mehrere erste Preise bei Wettbewerben, darunter der Staatspreis des Landes Nordrhein-Westfalen, unterstrichen ihre Bedeutung. 1986 zeigte sie ihre Kollektion erstmals auf den Messen in Frankfurt und München. Ein Jahr später eröffnete sie die Schmuckgalerie Pavé in Düsseldorf, in der neben eigenen Stücken auch Arbeiten von anderen modernen Schmuckgestaltern gezeigt wurden. Mit dem Umzug in die Neubrückstraße 4, nahe der Kunsthalle in Düsseldorf, erhielt die Stadt einen Schmuckraum, der heute zu den wichtigsten Foren des modernen Schmuck-Designs in Deutschland zählt.

E — Two rings she made in 1969 and 1971 show how sensitively Barbara Schulte-Hengesbach interpreted Modernism even then. They show clear links to both the sculpture and the design of the 1960s. Three-dimensional, sculptural protuberances »surmounted« sometimes by concave lentoid forms grow out of the ring shanks.

The organic quality of those early pieces has long since given way to geometry. Today all lines in jewellery created by Barbara Schulte-Hengesbach are stringently geometric yet at the same time appeal to the emotions. They often include playfully decorative elements without looking coquettish. The Düsseldorf jewellery designer loves such apparent contradictions and this is expressed in the following sentence, which sums up her approach to her work: »Classic Modernism – cool – warmed up by a play on forms devoid of harshness.« In 1971 Barbara Schulte-Hengesbach received her master craftsman's certificate at the Zeichenakademie in Hanau, followed by studies at Fachhochschule Düsseldorf. There Professor Friedrich Becker awakened an interest in his own theme, Kinetics, in the talented student. Movement, introduced to art in the 20th century by the Italian Futurists, continued to interest Barbara Schulte-Hengesbach even after she took her diploma in 1974. However, in her striving to go her own way, she left her work on Kinetic jewellery in abeyance for three decades. It was not until 2005 that she relaunched Kinetic rings.

During the intervening years, she explored other themes in jewellery, for instance in the 1970s three-dimensional effects created by perspective, as exemplified by three brooches in stainless steel and acrylic. Another important theme was the use of pearls in the context of modern geometric forms beginning in 1990. »Each theme always has something to do with the others,« says the jewellery designer in retrospect.

In 1975 Barbara Schulte-Hengesbach opened a studio of her own, mounted annual exhibitions for her clientele and made successful contacts with jewellery galleries. Several first prizes at competitions, including the North Rhine-Westphalian State Prize, demonstrate her importance. In 1986 she showed her collection for the first time at trade fairs in Frankfurt and Munich. A year later she opened Pavé, a jewellery gallery in Düsseldorf, where she showed both her own pieces and work by other modern jewellery designers. When she moved the gallery to 4 Neubrückstraße, near the Düsseldorf Kunsthalle, the city was given a jewellery space that is now among the leading forums for modern jewellery design in Germany.

Barbara Schulte-Hengesbach
Geboren 1946 in Gladbeck. 1971 Meisterprüfung.
FH Düsseldorf von 1971–1974.
Ateliergründung 1975. Seit 1987 Galerietätigkeit
in Düsseldorf.

Barbara Schulte-Hengesbach
Born in Gladbeck in 1946. Master craftsman's
certificate in 1971. Fachhochschule Düsseldorf
1971–1974. Founded studio in 1975. Has worked
in Düsseldorf gallery since 1987.

1974

1995

2000

2003

2004

2008

1969	Ring, Gold, Mondstein — Ring, gold, moonstone
1971	Ring, Weißgold — Ring, white gold
1973	Broschen, Edelstahl, Acrylglas — Brooches, stainless steel, acrylic glass
1974	Kinetischer Ring, Gold — Kinetic ring, gold
1995	Ring *Königin*, Gold, Zuchtperle — Ring *Queen*, gold, cultured pearl
2000	Kinetischer Ring *Sternschnuppe*, Gold, Brillant — Kinetic ring *Shooting star*, gold, diamond
2003	Kinetischer Ring *Froschkönig*, Gold, Brillanten — Kinetic ring *Frog prince*, gold, diamonds
2004	*Kissenring*, Gold, Moro-Koralle — *Cushion ring*, gold, Moro coral
2008	Ring *Rose*, Gold, Mabeperle — Ring *Rose*, gold, mabe pearl

1983

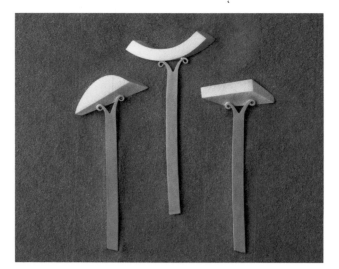

1992

1997

Claude Chavent

Die Schmuckstücke von Claude Chavent spielen mit unserer Sinneswahrnehmung. Selbst in strenger Geometrie rufen sie Illusionen hervor, versprechen Räumlichkeit und Tiefe, wo nur Fläche fühlbar ist. Schmuckstücke, die den Wahrheitsgehalt der sichtbaren Welt ins Wanken bringen. Und der Betrachter kann sich fragen, ob ein Schmuckstück nicht doch jenseits des Dekorativen ein Objekt der Bildenden Kunst sein kann?

Claude Chavent widmete sich zuerst der Chemie, bevor er eine Lehre bei einem Goldschmied in Lyon absolvierte. 1972 eröffnete er ein Studio in Lyon und ließ sich 1976 gemeinsam mit seiner langjährigen Lebensgefährtin Françoise Chavent in einem kleinen Dorf in der Nähe von Montpellier in Südfrankreich nieder. Seit 2007 führt Claude Chavent, der auch als Bildhauer arbeitet und für die maßgebenden Schmuckentwicklungen verantwortlich ist, das Atelier alleine weiter. Über seine Arbeiten, sehr häufig Broschen in den Materialien Gold, Platin, Silber, aber auch Eisen, sagt Claude Chavent: »Es ist mein Bestreben, Formen, die leicht, konzentriert und wenn möglich mehrdeutig bleiben, Volumen und Bewegung zu geben. Um dies zu erreichen, benutze ich Perspektive und Trompe-l'œil.« Die Perspektive und das Scheinbild, Themen der Malerei seit der Renaissance, erreicht der Gestalter zum Teil durch unterschiedliche Materialkombinationen. Hauptsächlich entstehen die räumlichen Tiefenwirkungen der Schmuckstücke allein durch strukturierte Metalloberflächen, die mit der Metallbürste erzeugt werden. Konturen werden kaum verstärkt. Manchmal ist das Volumen auch durch die Arbeit des Hammers angedeutet. Oft sind die Stücke völlig plan. Die Illusion wird dann allein durch die Brechung des Lichtes geschaffen, ergänzt zum Teil durch Zweifarbigkeit. »Mein Ideal ist es, immer weiter zu vereinfachen, die Spanne zwischen Idee und Objekt immer mehr zu verringern«, sagt Claude Chavent. »Reflektierte Ergriffenheit« wird als Ziel formuliert.

Der Ring Pont (Brücke) von 1983 ist eine der letzten völlig figurativen Arbeiten. Bei der Brosche Livre de Poche (Taschenbuch), aus Eisen mit Feingold, ist der Übergang zur geometrischen Abstraktion deutlich, ebenso in den Broschen Pilliers (Säulen) und Fenêtre (Fenster). Bei allen Serien, die in den 1980er und 1990er Jahren entstanden, wird die poetische Vielschichtigkeit sichtbar, die weit über das Ästhetische hinausreicht. Es geht nicht nur um optische Täuschungen. »Ein Buch ist Inhalt, ist Objekt voller Bilder. Ein Schmuckstück ist ein Bild-Objekt. Ein Buch ist ein Objekt, um glauben zu machen«, erklärte Chavent dazu in einem Beitrag des »Schmuck Magazins« im Jahre 2000. Schmuck, »um glauben zu machen«, entstand auch in völliger geometrischer Reduktion, zum Beispiel bei den Broschen Cube und Autour du Cube. Die Würfel-Broschen und ihre »Seitenwände« erscheinen in frappierender Räumlichkeit, sind aber absolut plan. Dabei wird sichtbar, wie schwierig es ist, zwischen Figürlichkeit und Abstraktion zu unterscheiden. »Die figürlichen Stücke spielen mit Themen, die von sich aus in Richtung der Geometrie weisen«, stellt der Gestalter fest.

1998   1998   2000

Die Arbeiten von Chavent wurden in zahlreichen Galerien, in wichtigen Schmuckausstellungen und Museen gezeigt, zum Teil in Einzelausstellungen. Sie sind in der Sammlung des Museums »FRAC Nord – Pas de Calais« sowie im Musée Des Arts Décoratifs, Paris, vertreten. Frédéric Bodet, Kurator am Musée Des Art Décoratifs, Paris, schreibt dazu: »Die Glanzleistung Chavents besteht darin, derart tiefgreifende Betrachtungen aus dem Kern eines so minimalen Eingriffs hervorzurufen...« Er vergleicht sie mit minimalistischer Architektur und verweist auf ihre »geometrische Strenge, ihre materielle und formelle Kargheit.« Sie sei, betont Bodet, »ebenso Ausdruck der inneren Verbindung mit unserer Intimität wie Ausdruck kollektiver Bande, die sich an den Kreis unserer Beziehungen richten.« Der Kurator spricht bei den Arbeiten von Chavent von Schmuckkunst. »Alles beruht auf der anfänglichen und definitiven, auf einer soliden, konstruktiven Logik basierenden Wahl, welche der eigentliche Ausdruck ihrer Konzentration ist.« Wäre dies nicht eine mögliche Definition der Schmuckkunst, meint Bodet: »der eigentliche Ausdruck von Konzentration?« Die Stücke von Chavent werden in Kleinserien gefertigt.

E — These are pieces that play with the way our sensory perceptions work. Even in stringent geometry they produce illusions, suggest space and depth where only surfaces are palpably present. Pieces of jewellery, which cause the truth content of the visible world to waver. And viewers can wonder whether a piece of jewellery might after all be a fine art object that transcends the merely decorative.

Claude Chavent started out by devoting himself to chemistry before serving an apprenticeship to a goldsmith. In 1972 he opened a studio in Lyon and settled down in 1976 with his wife Françoise Chavent in a small village near Montpellier in the south of France. Since 2007 the jewellery designer, who also works in sculpture and who is responsible for all jewellery developments has continued to run the studio on his own. Claude Chavent has this to say about his works, many of which are brooches made of gold, platinum, silver and even iron: »I strive to give volume and movement to forms that are light, concentrated and, whenever possible, remain polysemic. To achieve this, I make use of perspective and trompe-l'œil.« He creates perspective and illusion, themes in painting since the Renaissance, partly by combining several different materials. The effect of spatial depth is usually created in his pieces of jewellery solely through the texturing of metal surface with metal brushes. Contours are scarcely reinforced at all. Sometimes volume is also suggested by hammering. Pieces are often entirely flat. Illusion is in such cases created solely by the refraction of light, in part complemented by dichroism. »My ideal is to keep on simplifying, thus continuing to reduce the discrepancy between idea and object,« he says. »Contemplative ecstasy« is his stated aim.

Pont (Bridge), a ring he made in 1983, is one of his last entirely figurative works. Livre de Poche (Paperback), a brooch made of steel with fine gold, clearly reveals the transition to geometric abstraction and this is also the case with the brooches called Piliers (Pillars) and Fenêtre (Window). In all series made in the 1980s and 1990s, a poetic polysemy is apparent that goes far beyond aesthetics. It is not just a question of optical illusions. »A book is content, is an object full of pictures. A piece of jewellery is a picture-object. A book is an object that makes believe,« Claude Chavent explained in an essay published in Schmuck Magazin in 2000. »Make believe« jewellery has also been created in entirely reductive geometry, for instance the brooches Cube and Autour du Cube (Around the Cube). The Cube brooches and his »side walls« look stunningly spatial but are absolutely flat. This shows how difficult it is to distinguish between figuration and abstraction. »The figurative pieces play on themes that point towards geometry of their own accord,« he confirms.

Works by Chavent have been exhibited at numerous galleries, in important jewellery exhibitions and at museums, in part at solo shows. They are represented in the collections of the FRAC Nord – Pas de Calais Museum and the Musée des Arts Décoratifs in Paris. Frédéric Bodet, curator at the Musée des Art Décoratifs, Paris, writes about them: »The brilliant achievement of the Chavents consists in eliciting such profound observations from the core of such a minimal intervention...«. Comparing them to Minimalist architecture, he points out their »geometric stringency,« their »material and formal economy«. They are, as Bodet emphasises, »as much the expression of an inner bond with intimacy as the expression of collective ties that are directed at our circle of relationships.« The curator calls the Chavent works art jewellery. »Everything rests on the initial and the definitive, on a choice based on solid constructive logic, which is the actual expression of their concentration.« Might this not be a possible definition of art jewellery, as Bodet sees it: »the actual expression of concentration?« The Chavent pieces are made in small series.

Claude Chavent
Geboren 1947 in Lyon, 1971 Goldschmiedeausbildung nach einem Chemiestudium. Ateliergründung 1972 in Lyon.

Claude Chavent
Born in Lyon in 1947. Trained as a goldsmith 1971 after studying chemistry. Founded studio in Lyon in 1972.

1974

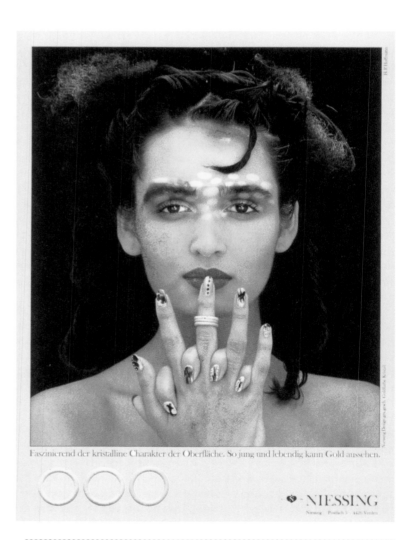

1974   Ringe *Setario*, Design Ursula Exner, Gold, Email, Diamanten — Rings *Setario*, design Ursula Exner, gold, enamel, diamonds

1977   Halsschmuck *S-Scheiben*, Design Ursula Exner, Gold, Platin — Necklace *S-Disks*, design Ursula Exner, gold, platinum

1979   *Spannring rund*, Design Walter Wittek, Platin, Brillant — *Tension ring round*, design Walter Wittek, platinum, diamond

1979   Ring *Gestaucht*, Design Walter Wittek, Gold, Brillant — Ring *Pressed*, design Walter Wittek, gold, diamond

Werbemotive, Anfang der 1980er Jahre — Motives for advertising, start of the 1980s

1977   1979   1979

Niessing

Wie konnte eine traditionsreiche Trauringfabrik aus Vreden im Münsterland in den 1970er Jahren zum Motor des zeitgenössischen Schmuckdesigns werden? Warum fanden gerade hier, fernab von den deutschen Schmuckzentren, die Ideale der Moderne ihren fruchtbarsten Nährboden? Der Beginn des modernen Schmuckdesigns bei Niessing ist ganz wesentlich Ursula Exner mit ihrem ausgeprägten Kultur- und Kunstverständnis zu verdanken. Unter der Leitung ihres Mannes, des Diplomkaufmanns Fritz Exner, geboren 1907 in Schlesien, war Niessing nach dem Zweiten Weltkrieg zum Marktführer bei Trauringen in Europa aufgestiegen. Mitte der 1970er Jahre traf Niessing die Entscheidung, das Trauringprogramm durch moderne Schmuckringe zu ergänzen. Dabei wirkte die kreative und emanzipierte Ursula Exner als treibende Kraft. Ohne sie hätte das moderne deutsche Schmuck-Design kaum seine international einmalige Sonderstellung erreicht. Ihr Sohn Jochen Exner, geboren 1951, führt seit 1982 als Geschäftsführer den begonnenen Weg konsequent weiter.

Ursula Exner wurde 1924 als Tochter von Bernhardine und Franz Niessing in Vreden geboren. Wie ihre jüngere Schwester Hannelore lernte sie nach dem Besuch des Gymnasiums das Goldschmiedehandwerk. Sie besuchte die Zeichenakademie in Hanau und war anschließend in der Werkstatt von Elisabeth Treskow, 1898–1992, tätig. Treskow wurde in den 1930er Jahren durch die Wiederentdeckung der Granulationstechnik bekannt. 1948 leitete sie die Gold- und Silberschmiedeklasse an den Kölner Werkkunstschulen. Ursula Exner lernte bei Elisabeth Treskow nicht nur traditionelle Goldschmiedetechniken, sondern auch deren Meisterschülerin Ruth Koblassa kennen. Diese kam Ende der 1950er Jahre als Leiterin der Goldschmiedewerkstatt in die Trauringfabrik nach Vreden. Bereits in den Trauringkollektionen Ende der 1960er Jahre tauchten dank der Kreativität Ruth Koblassas sehr innovative Formen auf. »Bereits da wurde, soweit dies bei einem Trauring möglich war, künstlerisch anspruchsvoll gestaltet«, weiß Jochen Exner.

Ursula Exner hatte in den 1950er Jahren Malunterricht bei Otto Andreas Schreiber. Jochen Exner erinnert sich an die »faszinierenden Farbbilder« der Mutter, die ihn und seinen jüngeren Bruder Hans in der Kindheit »regelmäßig in staunende Aufregung« versetzten. Wichtig für die gestalterische Entwicklung von Ursula Exner im Schmuck war der Architekt Maximilian von Hausen, 1919–1995. Jochen Exner rückblickend: »Meine Mutter begann unter dem Einfluss dieses humanistisch gebildeten Gestalters ein verlässliches Regelwerk aufzubauen. Die Frage nach den knappsten Mitteln, mit denen es etwas auszudrücken galt, wurde wichtig.« Max von Hausen schärfte auch das Bewusstsein für logische Konstruktionen. »Eine unlogische Form löst ein Unwohlsein aus. Sie kann nicht positiv wahrgenommen werden«, war sein Credo. Der Architekt ermahnte die Designer bei Niessing oft, sie sollten nicht so viel »kleben«, womit das Anlöten von Schmuckelementen gemeint war. Max von Hausen brachte in den 1970er Jahren oft Texte von Joseph

Beuys mit, der seinen Studenten an der Kunstakademie in Düsseldorf durch Experimente ursprüngliche Sinneseindrücke vermittelte. »Wir erkannten dadurch«, erzählt Jochen Exner, »dass die Kunst jener Zeit sehr ernsthafte Absichten verfolgte; unabhängig davon, ob sie uns persönlich gefiel oder nicht.« Zudem gab es regelmäßige Begegnungen mit bedeutenden Künstlern. Für einen Tabernakel von Joseph Beuys in einer Kirche in Münster, die Max von Hausen renovierte, spendete Ursula Exner das Gold. Der Künstler ließ eine goldene »Antenne« in den Himmel ragen, die »Antenne zu Gott«. Dabei wurde auch mit Beuys darüber diskutiert, wie Gold künstlerisch verarbeitet werden könnte.

Bereits vor 1974 pflegte Niessing Kontakte zur Werkkunstschule Köln. Zusammen mit der Grafikprofessorin Marianne Kohlscheen-Richter entstand in den 1960er Jahren eine Werbung für Niessing-Trauringe. Erste Trauring-Entwürfe von akademisch ausgebildeten Goldschmieden wie dem Düsseldorfer Peter Hassenpflug ergänzten die hausinternen Entwürfe. Ursula Exner besuchte auch regelmäßig die Ausstellungen der Galerie Orvèfre in Düsseldorf. Diese war 1969 von Hassenpflug als eine der weltweit ersten modernen Schmuckgalerien gegründet worden. Anfang der 1970er Jahre engagierte die Firmenchefin Professor Friedrich Becker für Trauringentwürfe. Die Zusammenarbeit mit dem bedeutenden Düsseldorfer Goldschmied gestaltete sich jedoch schwierig. »Da gab es auf beiden Seiten den Ehrgeiz, eine Hauptidee festzulegen«, erklärt Jochen Exner. Obwohl einige Trauring-Serien von Friedrich Becker für Niessing realisiert wurden, endete die Zusammenarbeit schließlich im Streit.

1981 brachte Niessing, nach langen technischen Versuchen, den von Walter Wittek im Jahr 1979 entworfenen *Spannring* auf den Markt. Hierzu erklärte Becker in einem Gutachten, der *Spannring* sei nicht eigentümlich und nicht würdig, Musterschutz zu bekommen. Diese Aussage verstärkte die Distanz zwischen dem Künstler und der Manufaktur in Vreden, obwohl gerade Niessing die von Becker mitbegründete Moderne im deutschen Schmuck entschieden vertrat. Kurz vor dem Tod Friedrich Beckers 1997 wurde der Zwist zwischen ihm und Jochen Exner beigelegt.

Die erste moderne Schmucklinie bei Niessing war 1974 die Ringserie *Setario*, abgeleitet aus den Wörtern Set und Variation. *Setario* markiert den Beginn des modernen seriellen Schmucks aus der Manufaktur in Vreden, weil Trauringe per definitionem der Branche nicht zum Schmuck zählen. Die Entwicklung lag in den Händen von Ursula Exner. Durch den Pillenknick waren die Geburtenzahlen in Deutschland seit 1965 stark rückläufig. Weniger Eheschließungen und geringere Trauringverkäufe waren damit vorprogrammiert. Die Entwicklung von modernem Schmuck sollte dem entgegenwirken. Jochen Exner war 1974 noch Student der Betriebswirtschaft. Zum Einstieg in das serielle Schmuck-Design erklärt er: »Wir haben uns zuerst die Frage gestellt, was wir am besten können. Das waren natürlich Ringe.«

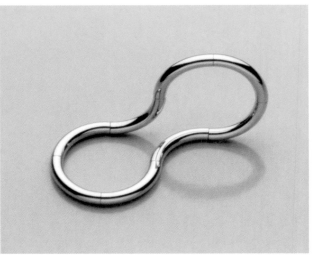

1980

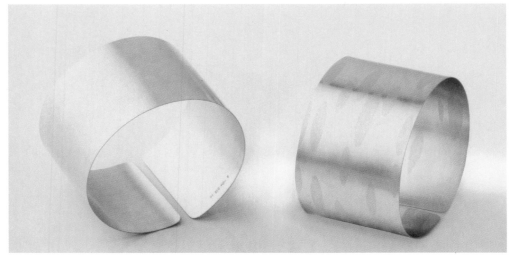

1983

Anfang der 1970er Jahre war Emailschmuck noch sehr aktuell. Mit Hilfe der befreundeten Firma Otto Klein und deren Inhaber Jens Uwe Zimmermann aus Hanau wurde in Vreden ein Knowhow im Emaillieren erarbeitet und eine Farbpalette festgelegt. Drei Ringformen in verschiedenen Materialien und Farben entstanden. An der Hand können sie kombiniert und in mehreren Varianten getragen werden. Dahinter stand der Gedanke, der Kundin für ihr Geld möglichst viel zu bieten. Der Set-Gedanke war bereits durch die Ergänzung eines Traurings mit einem Diamant-Vorsteckring bekannt. Bei Setario ließen sich jedoch alle drei Ringe gleichwertig und mit verschiedenen ästhetischen Wirkungen kombinieren. Der Erfolg der innovativen Ringserie führte dazu, dass sich Niessing auch zukünftig sehr intensiv mit dem Systemgedanken im Schmuck beschäftigte.

Bereits 1974 beauftragte Ursula Exner den Düsseldorfer Grafik- und Fotodesigner H.P. Hoffmann mit der Werbung. Niessing hatte zu dieser Zeit etwa 3000 Trauringkunden und einen Marktanteil von 25 Prozent in Deutschland. Trotzdem war der Name mit seiner gut 100-jährigen Geschichte bei den Schmuckkäufern weitgehend unbekannt. Doch verlangte nicht der Einstieg in die Produktion von modernem Schmuck eine Publikumswerbung? Fritz Exner, der bis zu seinem Tod 1982 Geschäftsführer war, entschied sich dagegen, aus Sorge vor negativen Reaktionen der Fachhändler. Juweliere betrachteten damals eine Markenorientierung im Schmuck als Affront. So tauchte der Name Niessing zunächst nur in gemeinsamen Werbekampagnen mit dem Diamantproduzenten De Beers und ab 1977 mit der Platin Gilde auf. Der erste Prospekt, den H.P. Hoffmann 1974 gestaltete, galt der neuen Ringserie *Setario*. Er wurde über Juweliere an die Endkunden weitergegeben. Für Trauringe entwickelte die Agentur eine Anzeigenkampagne, die in Fachzeitschriften geschaltet wurde. Entsprechend der Punzierung der Firma, dem von einem Pfeil durchbohrten Herzen, hieß der Slogan: »Wir haben ein Herz für Anspruchsvolle.« Um die besondere Qualität in Form und Verarbeitung der Ringe zu zeigen, wurden diese stark vergrößert abgebildet. Der Werbefachmann dazu rückblickend: »Der Schlüssel für die Kommunikation lag im Sehen und Verstehen.« Auch er selbst habe den Einstieg in das moderne Schmuck-Design gefunden, indem er die Ringe von Niessing als plastische Form betrachtet habe. Wenn Hoffmann über Ursula Exner spricht, kommt er ins Schwärmen: »Sie ist mit einem grünen Porsche 911 vorgefahren und brachte darin eine Kiste Äpfel aus ihrem Garten mit. Lange bevor es die »Vogue« in Deutschland gab, hatte sie die internationale Ausgabe auf ihrem Tisch liegen. Sie war sehr weltoffen, temperamentvoll, aber auch eine gute Unternehmerin. Sie traf Entscheidungen und hat dann die Leute aber auch machen lassen.«

Auf die Ringserie *Setario* folgten 1975 die *Konturenringe*. Ursula Exner hatte sie zusammen mit dem Designer Norbert Mürrle entwickelt. Sie weisen eine kantige, quadratische Grundform auf. Durch die unterschiedlichen

1984   1984   1986

Konturen an der Oberseite können die Ringe variantenreich getragen werden. Dies entsprach der modernen Idee, dass die aktive, zunehmend selbstbewusste Frau der 1970er Jahre wie schon bei *Setario* ihren Schmuckauftritt selbst mitgestaltet.

1976 startet in Deutschland eine Initiative, das seit dem Art Déco »vergessene« Schmuckmetall Platin wieder ins Bewusstsein der Schmuckkäufer zu rücken. Zu diesem Zwecke gründete der Bergbaukonzern Rustenburg Platinum Mines die Platin Gilde. Sie begann ihre Werbetätigkeit genau zu dem Zeitpunkt, als Niessing seine ersten modernen Schmuckserien herausbrachte. »Durch die Einführung von Platin haben wir uns schnell getraut, Halsschmuck zu machen«, bekennt Jochen Exner. Die Platin Gilde habe viel für die Wahrnehmung von modernem Schmuckdesign in Deutschland getan. Die Manufaktur in Vreden hatte bereits Erfahrung in der Verarbeitung des zähen Edelmetalls, das besondere technische Fähigkeiten verlangt. Seit langem wurden Trauringe in kleinen Stückzahlen in Platin gefertigt. »Niessing begann mit grundsätzlichen Überlegungen«, weiß auch Hoffmann. Lange bevor es um das Design ging, hat man in Vreden nach dem richtigen »Stoff« geforscht. Die zündende Idee kam Ursula Exner, als sie die Tüten von Jakobskaffee genau betrachtete. Diese waren auf der einen Seite gold-, auf der anderen Seite silberfarben beschichtet. »Sie hat sie zerschnippelt und damit immer rumgespielt«, erzählt Hoffmann. Die Spielereien führten schließlich zur Verbindung von dünnen Feingold- mit Platinblechen.

Jochen Exner meint rückblickend: »Platin hatte damals auch den Ruf, zäh und kühl zu sein. Aber wer möchte schon etwas Zähes, Kühles auf der Haut tragen? Wir haben nach einem Weg gesucht, die negativen Eigenschaften von Platin zu vermeiden und seine Vorteile zu nutzen.« Ziel war es, das Edelmetall geschmeidig und emotional zu machen. Experimente, Platin in flüssiges Gold zu tauchen, schlugen fehl. 1977 gelang es Niessing, Platin und Feingold ohne Lot praktisch unlösbar zu verbinden. Die technische Grundlage für *Niessing-S* war gefunden. Die prägnanten Stücke trugen maßgeblich dazu bei, die Wahrnehmung von Schmuck in den 1980er Jahren grundlegend zu verändern. H.P. Hoffmann erinnert sich noch genau an den Tag, als Ursula Exner in seiner Agentur erschien und sagte: »Jetzt haben wir den Stoff! Jetzt können wir anfangen zu gestalten.«

Das Farbspiel zwischen Weiß und Gelb der Platin-Feingold-Bleche reizte auch andere Firmen, in dieser Richtung zu arbeiten, und wurde schnell zu einem Trend. Niessing entwickelte kontinuierlich seine markentypische Formensprache. Gleichzeitig wurde damit ein Paradigmenwechsel im Schmuck Ende des 20. Jahrhunderts eingeleitet. *Niessing-S* war Ausdruck einer unprätentiösen, modernen Lebenseinstellung. Frauen setzten diesen Schmuck weniger als Statussymbol, sondern vielmehr als Ausdrucksmittel ihres Geschmacks ein. Ursula Exner machte sich einen Spaß daraus, die innovativen Schmuckstücke persönlich in Szene zu setzen. Mit ihrer ersten elastischen Armspange in Platin lief sie über die Messe, wickelte diese so eng wie möglich zusammen, umfasste sie mit der Hand und ließ sie vor einem überraschten Betrachter auseinander schnellen. Dass Schmuck als kreatives Ausdrucksmittel des Menschen Tragespuren zeigt, war für die künstlerisch gebildete Niessing-Chefin selbstverständlich. Das Demonstrationsobjekt mit feinen Rillen und Knickungen wurde später neben einer fabrikneuen Armspange für ein Werbemotiv fotografiert. So wurde der Öffentlichkeit demonstriert, dass die Moderne im Schmuck auch eine Rückkehr zu den Wurzeln des Schmucktragens darstellt, zeigt sich doch das Wesen von Schmuck und seine Verbindung zum Körper nicht zuletzt in den Gebrauchsspuren. Eine Reise zu den Ursprüngen des Schmucks ganz anderer Art führte H.P. Hoffmann nach Afrika, wo er 1984 *Niessing-S* an Samburu-Frauen in ihrer Stammestracht fotografierte.

Gegen Ende der 1970er Jahre hat Niessing seine Zurückhaltung in der Kommunikation mit den Endkunden aufgegeben. Die neu entwickelten Schmuckserien waren so ungewöhnlich, dass sie in der Öffentlichkeit bekannt gemacht werden mussten. Deshalb beauftragte Ursula Exner 1979 H.P. Hoffmann, zusammen mit Jochen Exner eine langfristig orientierte Werbekonzeption zu entwickeln. Obwohl es zu diesem Zeitpunkt erst wenige Innovationen gab, war die Vision und Zielsetzung klar: In der Manufaktur Niessing sollten vor allem Ringe, aber auch Hals-, Arm- und Ohrschmuck von den besten Gestaltern entworfen und gefertigt werden. Der Originalität in der Gestaltung musste die Qualität der Materialien entsprechen: mindestens 18-karätiges Gold, Platin 950 und hochwertige Diamanten. Zielperson war die selbstbewusste Frau, die aus Überzeugung und nicht aus Prestigegründen ihren Schmuck auswählt.

Die erste Anzeige schaltete H.P. Hoffmann Ende 1979 in der gerade auf den Markt gekommenen deutschen »Vogue«. In der Fotografie setzte er »geformtes Licht« als Erkennungsmerkmal ein. Während sich die Darstellung der Frau mit der Zeit veränderte, blieb die Gestaltung mit Licht 20 Jahre erhalten. Die zum Teil sehr plakative Kampagne reizte zur Auseinandersetzung und erreichte eine hohe Bekanntheit. 1999 endete die Konzeption mit der letzten Fotoserie von Frauen verschiedener Nationalitäten. Der Gedanke »One World – one Woman« wurde zum Teil in doppelseitigen Anzeigen in »Vogue« und »Elle« geschaltet. Das anschließende Werbekonzept verzichtete auf die Model-Fotografie und zeigte nur noch Produkt- und Detailfotos.

Während die markante Werbung in den 1980er Jahren zu kontinuierlichen Umsatzsteigerungen führte, intensivierte Niessing auch die Zusammenarbeit mit Gestaltern. Seit 1976 wurden Entwürfe folgender freier Schmuckdesigner und Künstler realisiert: Jürgen Bräuer, Andi Gut, Sara Harris, Herman Hermsen, Karin Hoffmann, Angela Hübel, Katja John, Ike Jünger, Günter Krauss, Hans Ufer, Hans-Hermann Lingenbrinck, W. Maertens, Wilhelm Mattar, Hermann Obermüller, Annelies Plantheydt, Rudi Sand,

1987

1989

1984

1984

1991

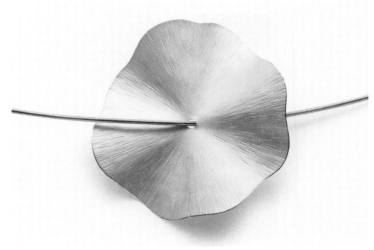

1993

Sabine Scheuble, Sylvia Schlatter, Barbara Schmidt, Piet Stockmans, Jan W. van der Zwaan, Hubert Verstraeten, Lore von Volkmann-Niessing, Günther Wermekes, Walter Wittek und Jens Uwe Zimmermann. Hinzu kamen die Entwicklungen von zahlreichen fest angestellten Designern.

1980 entstand die Ringserie *Mutatio* von Hermann Obermüller. Die Doppelringe aus acht Kreissegmenten sind flexibel, so dass verschiedene »Bilder« entstehen können. Es ist der erste kinetische Schmuck in der Manufaktur in Vreden. Die Zusammenarbeit mit dem Goldschmied und Bildhauer Walter Wittek führte 1979 zu dem bis heute bedeutendsten Klassiker des modernen Schmuckdesigns, dem *Spannring*. Hier bildet die Ringschiene selbst die Fassung. Der Stein wird nur durch die Spannkraft des Metalls gehalten und kann so seine Form und Brillanz scheinbar frei schwebend entfalten. Das revolutionäre Design vereint höchstmögliche Reduktion und Funktionalität. Auch eine Forderung der Moderne, die Verbindung von logischer Form und Schönheit, wird erfüllt. Der österreichische Architekt und Theoretiker der Moderne, Adolf Loos, hatte den Diamanten 1898 als das ideale Schmuckstück für die moderne Zeit bezeichnete, weil er »auf möglichst kleinem raume einen möglichst großen wert repräsentiert.« Vielen Schmuckkünstlern und -designern war der Diamant seit dem Jugendstil dennoch Ausdruck von Prestige und Reichtum. Mit der intelligenten, konstruktiven Form des *Spannrings* wurden diese Argumente entkräftet. Denn nichts wirkt im *Spannring* prätentiös, dekorativ und aufgesetzt. Niessing hat die modernste Alternative für die klassisch anmutende Krappenfassung gefunden.

Von der akademischen Schmuckszene wurde Niessing in den 1980er Jahren mit einer Mischung aus Respekt und Argwohn beobachtet. Einmal besuchte Professor Hermann Jünger mit seinen Studenten die Manufaktur in Vreden. Jochen Exner erinnert sich: »Wir saßen in einer lauen Sommernacht zusammen. Meine Mutter war dabei, auch Max von Hausen.« Auf beiden Seiten ist man »sehr vorsichtig und ehrfurchtsvoll« miteinander umgegangen. Es gab auch eine gewisse Skepsis. So fragte Jünger: »Ist das, was Ihr macht, Kunst?« Dies sei natürlich eine Fangfrage gewesen, meint Exner: »Wir erklärten, dass es uns um bestimmte Ideen gehe im Schmuck, die wir mit den Möglichkeiten einer Manufaktur möglichst gut umsetzen wollten.«

Die erste Begegnung mit der Münchner Goldschmiedeklasse blieb nicht ohne Folgen. 1982 kam Matthias Mönnich, ein Schüler von Hermann Jünger, als Designer zu Niessing. Er entwickelte 1984 *Iris*, eine Schmuckserie mit fließendem Verlauf von Feingold zu Silber. Verschiedenfarbige Legierungen erschienen später auch in weiteren Schmuckthemen von Niessing und sind bis heute wichtig. 1987 wurde Peter Eiber, der bei Jünger studiert hatte, Leiter der Designabteilung. Sein Thema *Hohl mit Fuge* bedeutete ein künstlerisches Konzept im seriellen Schmuckdesign, wie es in dieser Deutlichkeit noch nie gewagt worden war. Der Innenraum eines Ringes war durch einen entlang der Schiene verlaufenden

Riss geöffnet. Dadurch wurde das Ringinnere zu einem Element der Gestaltung. Bereits zuvor, zwischen 1980 und 1984, hatte Niessing in der Zusammenarbeit mit Walter Wittek und Norbert Mürrle die sichtbare Verformung von Gold und Platin als Gestaltungselement genutzt. In unzähligen Versuchen wurde Metall verformt, gestaucht, gedehnt und gepresst. Und die neuen Methoden der Verarbeitung, die das Schmuckdesign sichtbar veränderten, wurden auch in Kollektionsnamen kommuniziert. Begriffe wie »gestaucht« oder »hohl durchbrochen« hätten sich zuerst brutal angehört und waren nur »Arbeitstitel«, erzählt der Werbespezialist Hoffmann. Doch entsprachen sie, ehrlicher als jede werbliche »Verkleidung«, dem Wesen der Schmucklinien.

1986 starb Ursula Exner. Jochen Exner, seit 1982 verantwortlicher Geschäftsleiter, führte auch danach die Designkonzepte weiter. Hätte der Weg, den seine Mutter 1974 eingeschlagen hatte, unter kommerziellen Aspekten nicht auch ein anderer sein können? Jochen Exner, der von sich sagt, dass er mehr die kaufmännische Ader seines Vaters geerbt habe, antwortet: »Dass wir modernen Schmuck machen wollten, war völlig klar, weil uns dies am Herzen lag. Das Moderne, das Zeitgenössische, entstand, weil wir erkannten, wir können nur das.« Exner betrachtet es als Glück, dass er selbst keine gestalterischen Ambitionen habe. Wenn der Chef selber der Designer sei, könne sich das sehr hinderlich auf eine kontinuierliche Entwicklung auswirken: »Ich habe mich zeitlebens aus der Gestaltung herausgehalten. Ich habe nur unsere Gestalter gefördert und versucht zu kommunizieren, wie wir arbeiten und was wir machen.«

Die *Niessing-Schnur* wurde ab 1986 zu einem weiteren Meilenstein im modernen Schmuckdesign. Ihr Schöpfer war Anton Hilbing, damals Leiter der Goldschmiedewerkstatt. Die dünne, biegsame Schnur aus Gold oder Platin war das ideale Trägersystem für die zahlreichen Schmuckanhänger des Hauses. Zum Beispiel für die Linie *Terrazzo* von Christine Kube. Ende der 1980er Jahre tauchten verstärkt volumige, räumliche Körper im Niessing-Schmuck auf. Die von Dorothea Schippel 1989 konzipierte Schmucklinie *hohl durchbrochen* – sie lässt an Emmentaler Käse denken – erhielt einen Staatspreis des Landes Nordrhein-Westfalen für Design und Innovation. In der Begründung der Jury wird ein Grundproblem zwischen Produktdesign und Schmuck deutlich: »Normalerweise könnte eher eine spartanische Sicherheitsnadel einen Preis für gutes Industrie-Design gewinnen als jedes noch so raffiniert gearbeitete Schmuckstück.« Weil alle Schmuckteile von *hohl durchbrochen* kombinierbar sind, stellten die Juroren jedoch fest: »Darin ist diese Schmuckserie endlich doch dem industriellen Produktsystem-Design verwandt.« Schließlich überzeugte das Konzept wie viele andere Schmucksysteme von Niessing auch mit seinem demokratischen Charakter. Er wurde in der Juryaussage »Individuelle Verschiedenheit bei prinzipieller Gleichheit« auf den Punkt gebracht.

1993   1994   1998

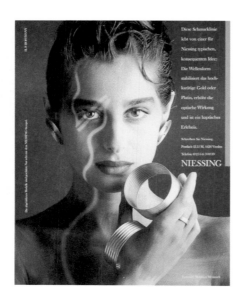

1990 beschäftigte die Manufaktur in Vreden 180 Mitarbeiter. Seit 1980 war der Umsatz verdreifacht worden und betrug 32 Millionen Mark. Niessing hatte mit seinem Designschmuck das Trauringsegment im eigenen Haus überflügelt und ein Jahrzehnt vor der Jahrtausendwende eine Basis für modernes Design im Schmuckmarkt geschaffen. Nachfolgend einige der mit zahlreichen Preisen ausgezeichneten Schmuckinnovationen: Mit der *Kreiskette* von Sabine Böning führte Niessing die Freihandzeichnung als ursprüngliches und reduziertes Gestaltungsprinzip ein. 1993 stellte die Manufaktur mit der *Radius 9* ihre erste Uhr vor, Design Günter Wermekes. Der *Porzellanschmuck* des Holländers Piet Stockmans für Niessing 1994 war bei vielen Juwelieren heftig umstritten. Nach den Entwürfen von Timo Küchler entstanden 1995 die *Faltigkeiten*. Dünne Bleche aus Edelmetall erhalten die Wirkung von gefaltetem Papier. 1995 integriert Niessing Hörgeräte in Ohrschmuck. 1997 wurde dem Handel das erste Trauringsystem präsentiert. Anhand von Ringen in unterschiedlichen Profilen, Breiten, Legierungen und Oberflächen können sich Paare ihre Wunschringe individuell zusammenstellen. Das Konzept stammte von Timo Küchler ebenso wie der *Flechtschmuck* von 1998. Hier ergeben hauchdünne, geflochtene Gold- oder Platinstreifen eine moderne Schmuckform. Sie basiert auf einer alten Handwerkstechnik und wirkt unprätentiös und edel zugleich. Zu einem großen Erfolg wurde *Abakus*, eine Ringserie aus Edelstahl mit farbigen, beweglichen Kügelchen von Timo Küchler. Niessing zeigte damit zur Jahrtausendwende, dass man auch mit ganz kleinen Akzentuierungen große Wirkungen für sich persönlich schaffen kann. Preise und Auszeichnungen wie für *FormEs* von Christopher Born oder *Papyr* erhielt Niessing inzwischen regelmäßig.

Der eigenständige, wiedererkennbare Stil von Niessing ist das Ergebnis der kontinuierlichen Designentwicklung, die bis heute im eigenen Hause betrieben wird. Im Niessing-Designteam waren bisher tätig: Christofer Born, Simon-Peter Eiber, Christine Kube, Susanna Loew, Matthias Mönnich, Norbert Mürrle, Marion Röthig, Dorothea Schippel, Petra Weingärtner und Susanne Winckler. Chefdesigner ist seit 1992 Timo Küchler, der in Stuttgart sein eigenes Designbüro führt. In Vreden sind gegenwärtig Antje Bott und Iris Weyer gestalterisch tätig.

Unter der Leitung von Timo Küchler entstand Ende der 1990er Jahre ein für die Schmuckbranche völlig neues Ladenkonzept mit dem Ziel, dem Publikum in einem schlüssigen Gesamtkonzept die Inhalte und Formen von Niessing zu vermitteln. 1999 wurde das erste eigene Geschäft im Stilwerk Berlin eröffnet. Einzelne Schmuckthemen werden in gläsernen Containern gezeigt und durch Installationen mit erklärenden Texten und Detailbildern hervorgehoben. So können die Kunden in einer Ausstellungsatmosphäre die Ideen, Materialien und Herstellungsprozesse der modernen Schmucklinien kennenlernen. Weitere Läden und Shop-in-Shop-Konzepte bei Juwelieren folgten in deutschen und internationalen Metropolen.

1993   Uhr *Radius 9*, Design Günter Wermekes, Platin — Watch *Radius 9*, design Günter Wermekes, platinum

1994   Spannring *Narciss*, Design Simon Peter Eiber, Gold, Brillant — Tension ring *Narcissus*, design Simon Peter Eiber, gold, diamond

1998   Armreife *Flechtschmuck*, Design Timo Küchler, Gold — Bangles *Braided jewellery*, design Timo Küchler, gold

1999   Anhänger *Plissee*, Design Susanna Loew, Gold — Pendant *Plissé*, design Susanna Loew, gold

1999   Ring *Signum*, Design Christofer Born, Gold — Ring *Signum*, design Christofer Born, gold

Werbemotive, Anfang der 1990er Jahre — Motives for advertising, start of the 1990s

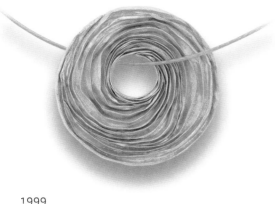

1999

1999

Der Schock, der die gesamte Schmuckbranche nach dem 11. September 2001 traf, wirkte sich jedoch auch gravierend auf die Geschäftsentwicklung von Niessing aus. Bereits in den 1990er Jahren war die Zahl der Schmuck- und Uhrenfachgeschäfte rückläufig. Die Konsumflaute nach der Jahrtausendwende traf den Facheinzelhandel in Deutschland besonders stark. Als die Angst mit der neuen Währung und noch viele andere Zukunftssorgen aufkamen, als man von der neuen Bescheidenheit sprach, sei eine Unordnung entstanden, so Jochen Exner: »Man wusste nicht mehr so recht, was gut war.« Niessing geriet in eine prekäre wirtschaftliche Lage, die erst durch die Hilfe eines Finanzpartners wieder ins Lot gebracht wurde. Die durch den neuen Reichtum in der arabischen Welt, in Asien und Russland zu beobachtende Rückkehr zum Luxus klassischer Prägung ist kein Grund für Niessing, von seinem 1974 eingeschlagenen Weg abzuweichen. Die Manufaktur möchte weiterhin die Triebfeder für zeitgemäßen Schmuck sein, der mit der Alltagskultur, mit dem Design, der Architektur und der Mode der Gegenwart etwas zu tun hat. »Wir möchten gern mit unseren Kunden kompetent und qualifiziert über gute Schmuckideen sprechen. Alles, was wir in Zukunft tun, soll sich diesem Gedanken unterordnen«, sagt Jochen Exner.

E — How could a wedding ring manufacturer in Vreden in the Münsterland become a powerhouse driving contemporary designer jewellery in the 1970s? Why did the Modernist ideals find the most fertile soil here, so far from all the German jewellery centres? Ursula Exner, with her profound understanding of cultural matters and art, can be credited with establishing modern designer jewellery at Niessing. Under the supervision of her husband Fritz Exner, a businessman born in Silesia in 1907, Niessing had advanced after the Second World War to the European market leader in wedding rings. In the mid-1970s Niessing decided to supplement their wedding ring line with other rings of modern design. Ursula Exner, who was both creative and emancipated, was the driving force behind this development. Without Ursula Exner, modern German designer jewellery would hardly have attained the unique status it enjoys worldwide. Her son, Jochen Exner (born in 1951), who has managed the company since 1982, has consistently continued on the path taken by Niessing.

The daughter of Bernhardine and Franz Niessing, Ursula Exner was born in Vreden in 1924. Like her younger sister, Hannelore, she trained as a goldsmith after attending higher secondary school. Ursula Exner attended the Zeichenakademie in Hanau before working in the workshop of Elisabeth Treskow (1898–1992). Treskow became famous in the 1930s for her rediscovery of the granulation technique. In 1948 she became head of the goldsmithing and silversmithing class at the Werkkunstschule in Cologne. Ursula Exner not only learned the traditional goldsmithing techniques from Elisabeth Treskow; through Treskow she also met Ruth Koblassa, a member of Treskow's master class. Ruth Koblassa went to the Vreden wedding ring factory in the late 1950s to manage the goldsmithing workshop. By the late 1960s, highly innovative forms were emerging in the wedding ring collections thanks to Ruth Koblassa's remarkable creative powers. »Even then, aesthetically ambitious designing took place, to the extent that this could be done with a wedding ring,« recalls Jochen Exner.

In the 1950s, Ursula Exner had taken drawing lessons from Otto Andreas Schreiber. Jochen Exner remembers his mother's »fascinating colour pictures,« which »would regularly astonish and excite« both him and his younger brother, Hans, when they were children. Maximilian von Hausen (1919–1995), an architect, was important for Ursula Exner's development as a designer. Jochen Exner in retrospect: »Under the influence of that humanistically educated designer, my mother began to build up a reliable system of aesthetic rules governing her work. The question of expressing what one had to say with the most economical means became important.« Max von Hausen also honed her awareness of logical construction. »An illogical form makes one queasy. It cannot be perceived as positive,« was his creed. The architect would often admonish the designers at Niessing not to »glue« so much, meaning soldering decorative elements on to pieces of jewellery.

During the 1970s, Max von Hausen often brought in texts by Joseph Beuys, who conveyed original sensory impressions to his students at the Düsseldorf Art Academy through experiments. »Thus we realised,« as Jochen Exner tells it, »that the art of that time was pursuing very serious aims; regardless of whether we liked it or not.« Moreover, there were regular encounters with leading artists. Ursula Exner donated the gold for a tabernacle by Joseph Beuys in a Münster church that Max von Hausen was renovating. Beuys made a gold »antenna« soar heavenwards from it as an »aerial to God«. Discussions also went on with Beuys about how gold might be worked as art.

Even before 1974 Niessing was in contact with the Cologne Werkkunstschule. Collaboration with the graphic arts professor Marianne Kohlscheen-Richter in the 1960s produced advertising for Niessing wedding rings. The first wedding rings designed by academically trained goldsmiths, including Peter Hassenpflug of Düsseldorf, were added to the Niessing range. Ursula Exner was also a regular visitor to exhibitions mounted by Galerie Orfèvre in Düsseldorf. Founded by Peter Hassenpflug in 1969, it was one of the world's first galleries specialising in modern jewellery. In the early 1970s, Ursula Exner commissioned wedding ring designs from Professor Friedrich Becker. Collaboration with that august Düsseldorf goldsmith turned out to be fraught with difficulties, however. »On both sides there was an ambition to establish a main idea,« explains Jochen Exner. Although a few wedding ring lines by Friedrich Becker for Niessing were realised, the collaboration ultimately ended in irreconcilable differences of opinion.

2000

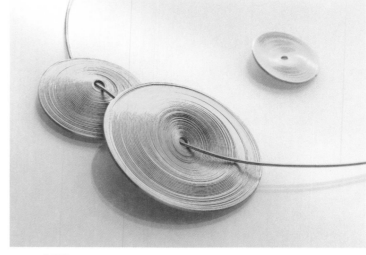

2000

In 1981 Niessing launched the *Tension ring* after protracted technical experimentation. It had been designed in 1979 by Walter Wittek. Professor Becker stated in a specialist report that the *Tension ring* was not original and, therefore, not copyright-worthy. This appraisal put even more distance between the artist and the factory in Vreden although Niessing in particular emphatically advocated the Modernism in German jewellery of which Becker was a co-founder. The quarrel between Becker and Jochen Exner was finally resolved shortly before Friedrich Becker died in 1997.

The first modern line in jewellery at Niessing was the 1974 *Setario* line in rings; the name derived from the terms »set« and »variation«. *Setario* marked the onset of modern jewellery mass production at the Vreden factory because, by definition among jewellers, wedding rings did not count as jewellery. The development was in Ursula Exner's hands. The Pill led to the baby bust in Germany from 1965. As a result, there were fewer marriages and, therefore, wedding ring sales slumped. Developing modern jewellery was a strategy adopted to counteract this downwards market trend. In 1974 Jochen Exner was still studying business organisation at university. He has this to say about getting into mass-produced designer jewellery: »The first thing we asked ourselves was what we could do best. Rings, of course.«

In the early 1970s, enamel jewellery was still very fashionable. Aided by the friendly firm of Otto Klein and its owner, Jens Uwe Zimmermann from Hanau, Niessing came up with the know-how to working with enamelling and established a range of colours. Three ring forms in different materials and colours were created. They could be worn together in various combinations and in several variants. The idea behind this was to give the clientele as much as possible for its money. The set idea was already a given since wedding rings were by then being worn with diamond engagement or eternity rings. With *Setario*, however, all three rings could be combined with equal status to create various aesthetic effects. The success of this innovative line in rings led Niessing to continue to explore the system idea very intensively.

In 1974 Ursula Exner commissioned the Düsseldorf commercial graphics and photo designer H.P. Hoffmann to do the Niessing advertising. By that time, Niessing had a retail clientele for wedding rings that numbered about three thousand and represented a 25% share of the German market. Nevertheless, the name of this firm, which looked back on at least a century of dealing with jewellery, was still for the most part unknown to the public at large. However, launching lines in modern jewellery required advertising to attract the public, didn't it? Fritz Exner, who remained acting manager of the firm until his death in 1982, opted to eschew advertising because he feared negative reactions from specialist retailers. Jewellers tended to regard pandering to market trends in jewellery as demeaning. So the name of Niessing appeared at first only in joint advertising campaigns with the diamond cartel De Beers and, from 1977, with Platin Gilde.

The first brochure designed by H.P. Hoffmann in 1974 was devoted to the new *Setario* line in rings. It was marketed by retail jewellers. The Hoffmann agency developed an advertising campaign for wedding rings that ran in specialist journals. To match the Niessing logo, a heart pierced by an arrow, the slogan ran: »We have a heart for the discerning.« It was shown greatly enlarged to indicate the quality of those rings in form and workmanship. The advertising specialist in retrospect: »The key to communication was in seeing and understanding.« He, for his part, had become involved with modern designer jewellery by viewing Niessing rings as sculptural form. When talking about Ursula Exner, Hoffmann waxes lyrical: »She drove up in a green Porsche 911 and brought us a crate of apples from her own orchard. Long before »Vogue« magazine was at newsagents in Germany, she had the international edition on her desk. She was a real cosmopolitan, very vivacious, but also an astute businesswoman. She made the decisions but then she would leave people alone to get on with it.«

The *Setario* ring line was followed in 1975 by *Contour* rings. Ursula Exner had developed them jointly with the designer Norbert Mürrle. They are basically angular and square in shape. Because the contours on the upper edge vary, these rings can be combined in all sorts of ways. This was in line with the modern idea that the active, increasingly self-assured 1970s woman co-designed her appearance in jewellery as had been the case with *Setario*.

In 1976 a trend was initiated in Germany that aimed at making the jewellery-purchasing public once again aware of platinum, which had been »overlooked« as a metal for jewellery since Art Déco. To that end, the mining concern Rustenberg Platinum Mines founded Platin Gilde International [the Platinum Guild]. It began operations just as Niessing were launching their first mass-produced lines in modern jewellery. »It was the introduction of platinum that so soon gave us the confidence to make neck jewellery,« confesses Jochen Exner. The Platinum Guild, he says, contributed a great deal to the way modern designer jewellery came to be perceived in Germany.

The factory in Vreden had already had experience in working that heavy yet ductile noble metal, which requires specialist technical skills. Small numbers of wedding rings had been made in platinum for quite some time by then. »Niessing started out with basic considerations,« adds Hoffmann. Long before the design was on the boards, the people in Vreden had been looking for the right »stuff«. Ursula Exner was the one to come up with a bright idea. She had been looking closely at Jacobs Coffee bags, which had a gold-coloured coating on one side and a silvery coating on the other. »She cut them up into pieces and then kept playing around with them,« recounts Hoffmann. That playful brainstorming ultimately led to bonding thin sheets of fine gold with sheet platinum. Jochen Exner thinks in restrospect: »At that time platinum also had the reputation of being heavy and cool. But who would want to wear something heavy and cool on their skin? We tried to

Niessing

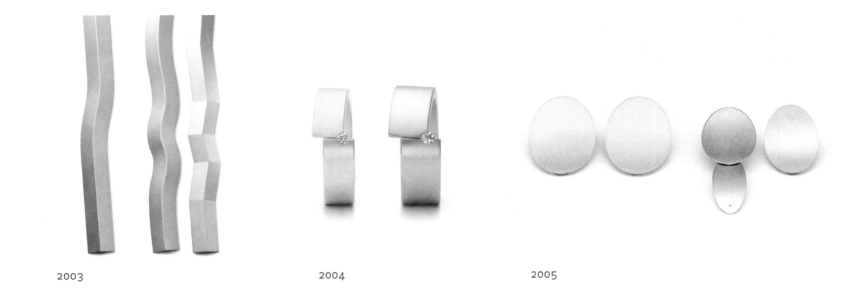

2003   2004   2005

find a way to avoid the negative properties of platinum and take advantage of its good sides.« The aim was to make the noble metal supple and emotionally appealing. Experiments in dipping platinum in molten gold were unsuccessful. In 1977, however, Niessing succeeded in bonding platinum and fine gold without soldering them so that the layers were virtually indissoluble. The technical basis for *Niessing S* had been discovered. Those memorable pieces played a paramount role in fundamentally changing perceptions of jewellery in the 1980s. H.P. Hoffmann remembers the very day when Ursula Exner appeared in his agency and said: »Now we've got the stuff! Now we can start to design.«

The attractive interplay of the colours white and yellow made possible by the bonded sheets of platinum and fine gold also induced other firms to work along similar lines and soon became trendy. Niessing continued to consistently develop the formal idiom which was their hallmark. At the same time a paradigm shift took place in jewellery at the close of the 20th century. *Niessing S* expressed an unpretentious, modern attitude to life. Women used this jewellery as an expression of their personal taste rather than as a status symbol.

Ursula Exner really enjoyed showcasing those innovative pieces of jewellery on her own person. Wearing her first springy Niessing bangle in platinum, she would stalk through a trade fair, compressing it as tightly as she could and holding it in her hand so she could astonish people by making it spring apart. For the head of Niessing, trained as she was in the applied arts as well as fine art, it went without saying that jewellery, as a means of creative expression, reveals traces left by the person who has worn it. The demonstration object with its fine grooves and nicks from wear was later photographed next to a brand-new bangle as an advertising motif. Thus the public was shown that Modernism in jewellery also represented a return to the origins of wearing jewellery. The quintessence of jewellery and its association with the human body are, after all, demonstrated in the marks left by use. A trip of an entirely different kind to the origins of jewellery took H.P. Hoffmann to Africa, where he photographed Samburu women wearing their tribal costume with *Niessing S* jewellery in 1984.

By the late 1970s, Niessing had abandoned their reticence in communicating with their retail clientele. The newly developed lines in Niessing jewellery were so unusual that the public had to be made aware of them so in 1979 Ursula Exner commissioned H.P. Hoffmann to collaborate with Jochen Exner on designing a long-term advertising strategy. Although at that time not much was available in the way of innovation, the vision and the aim were clear: rings in the first instance as well as neck, arm and ear jewellery were to be created by top designers and made at the Niessing factory. Originality in design was to be matched by the quality of the materials: at least 18 carat gold, 950 platinum and fine diamonds. The target market

was the self-assured woman, who was guided in choosing her jewellery by conviction rather than by considerations of prestige. H.P. Hoffmann had his first advertisement printed late in 1979 in the German »Vogue«, which had just been launched. He used »shaped light« as the distinguishing feature of his photography. Although the way women were represented changed with time, designing with light remained constant over twenty years. This advertising campaign, which was in part very poster-like, compelled people to think about what they were seeing and thus became very well known. The strategy came to a close in 1999 in a final series of photos of women of different nationalities. The »One World – one Woman« idea even ran to double-page advertisements in »Vogue« and »Elle«. A subsequent advertising strategy eschewed photographs featuring models and only showed the product and detail close-ups.

While catchy advertising led to steady sales growth in the 1980s, Niessing continued to intensify their collaboration with designers. Since 1976 designs by the following freelance jewellery designers and artists have been realised: Jürgen Bräuer, Andi Gut, Sara Harris, Herman Hermsen, Karin Hoffmann, Angela Hübel, Katja John, Ike Jünger, Günter Krauss, Hans Ufer, Hans-Hermann Lingenbrinck, W. Maertens, Wilhelm Mattar, Hermann Obermüller, Annelies Plantheydt, Rudi Sand, Sabine Scheuble, Sylvia Schlatter, Barbara Schmidt, Piet Stockmans, Jan W. van der Zwaan, Hubert Verstraeten, Lore von Volkmann-Niessing, Günther Wermekes, Walter Wittek and Jens Uwe Zimmermann. In addition, numerous designers were employed at Niessing on a permanent basis to develop new models.

Mutatio, a line in rings designed by Hermann Obermüller, was launched in 1980. These are double rings composed of eight circle segments that are so flexible that different »pictures« can be created. This was the first Kinetic jewellery made at the Vreden factory. Collaboration with the goldsmith and sculptor Walter Wittek produced in 1979 what has remained the most important classic of modern designer jewellery: the *Tension ring*. Here the ring shank itself forms the setting for the stone. The stone is clamped in place solely by the tensile strength of the metal so that its form and brilliancy are free to unfold in what appears to be a permanently hovering state. This radical design unites the utmost in reduction with versatility of function. Another requirement of Modernism fulfilled by this design is the logical linkage of form and beauty. In 1898, the Austrian architect Adolf Loos, a pioneering theorist of Modernism, had designated the diamond as the ideal gem for modern times because it »represented the greatest possible value in the smallest possible space.« Since Jugendstil/Art Nouveau, however, the diamond had meant prestige and affluence to many artists in jewellery and jewellery designers. Those arguments were refuted by the intelligent, Constructivist form of the *Tension ring*. Nothing about the *Tension ring* is ostentatious, ornamental or superfluous. In it, Niessing came up with the most

2006

2007

modern alternative to the classic pronged setting. In the 1980s Niessing was regarded by the academic jewellery scene with a blend of respect and suspicion. Once Professor Hermann Jünger and his students visited the Vreden factory. Jochen Exner recalls: »We sat together that warm summer night. My mother was there and so was Max von Hausen.« Each side treated the other »very cautiously and respectfully«. There was also a certain amount of scepticism. Jünger, for instance, asked: »Is what you're doing art?« That question was of course a trap, as Exner sees it: »We explained that we were concerned with specific ideas in jewellery, which we wanted to bring across as well as possible with the possibilities provided by manufacture.«

That first encounter with the Munich goldsmithing class was not without consequences. In 1982, Matthias Mönnich, a pupil of Hermann Jünger, went to Niessing as a designer. In 1984, he developed *Iris*, a set of jewellery notable for a fluid transition from fine gold to silver. Alloys in various colours would later resurface in other Niessing jewellery themes and have remained important to the present day. In 1987 Peter Eiber, who had studied under Jünger, became head of the design division. His *Hollow with Seam* theme represented an artistic concept in mass-produced designer jewellery more obviously than had ever been ventured on before. The inside surface of a ring was opened by a crack running along the shank. This feature made the inside of the ring an element of the overall design.

Even before that, between 1980 and 1984, Niessing had used the visible working of gold and platinum as a design element in collaboration with Walter Wittek and Norbert Mürrle. In countless trials, the metal was deformed, sprained, stretched and pressed. And the new methods of working the metal, which obviously changed jewellery design, were also translated into the names given to collections. Terms such as »sprained« or »hollow pierced« might have sounded brutal at first and were in fact merely »working titles,« according to Hoffmann, the advertising specialist. Nevertheless, they conveyed the essence of those lines in jewellery more honestly than any »euphemisms« selected for advertising purposes might have done.

Ursula Exner died in 1986. Jochen Exner, executive director since 1982, continued to feature the design concepts after her death. Might the path taken by his mother in 1974 not have been a different one, as viewed from the commercial angle? Jochen Exner, who maintains that he has inherited more of his father's nose for business, answers: »That we wanted to make modern jewellery was entirely obvious because that was our main concern. The modern, contemporary side arose because we realised that was the only thing we could do.« Exner views it as fortunate that he has had no personal aspirations to a career in design. As he sees it, if the boss himself is a designer, that could really hamper steady development: »All my working life I have kept out of design. I have simply been supportive of our designers and tried to communicate how we work and what we are doing.«

The *Niessing Cord* became another milestone of modern jewellery design from 1986. It was created by Anton Hilbing, who was at that time head of the goldsmithing workshop. A thin, flexible cord of gold or platinum, it was the ideal support for the many pendants designed and made by the firm, for instance, for the *Terrazzo* line by Christine Kube. In the late 1980s, voluminous bodies enclosing space increasingly surfaced in Niessing jewellery. The *hollow pierced* line designed by Dorothea Schippel in 1989 – it is reminiscent of Emmenthal cheese – won a state award for design and innovation from the state of North Rhine-Westphalia. The recommendation of the jury illustrates a basic discrepancy between product design and jewellery: »Normally a spartan safety pin would tend to win a prize for good industrial design rather than a piece of jewellery, as sophisticated as it might be in workmanship.« However, because each part of this *hollow pierced* jewellery can be combined with all others, the members of the jury affirmed: »In this respect, this line in jewellery is, after all, ultimately related to industrial product system design.« In the end, the concept, like so many other Niessing jewellery systems, was also convincing because of its democratic character. As the jury aptly summed it up, it represented »individual diversity but identity in principle«.

In 1990 the factory in Vreden employed a workforce of 180. Turnover had trebled since 1980 and by then amounted to thirty-two million marks. With its designer jewellery, Niessing had overtaken their own wedding ring division to lay the foundation for modern design on the jewellery market a decade before the turn of the century. There follow some of their numerous award-winning innovations in jewellery: with Sabine Böning's *Circle* Necklace, Niessing introduced freehand drawing as an original and reductive design principle. In 1993 Niessing launched their first watch, the *Radius 9*, designed by Günter Wermekes. The *porcelain jewellery* by Piet Stockmans, a Dutch designer, for Niessing in 1994 was highly controversial with many jewellery stores. In 1995 Timo Küchler's *Faltigkeiten* were launched: as the name indicates, thin sheets of precious metal were made to look like folded paper. In 1995 Niessing integrated hearing aids with ear jewellery. In 1997 the first wedding ring system was launched on the market. Couples could have the rings they wanted individually designed from a selection of profiles, widths, alloys and textures. This concept came from Timo Küchler and so did the 1998 *Braided jewellery*. Here whisper-thin woven bands of gold or platinum made for a modern form of jewellery. Based on an old crafts technique, it looks unpretentious yet costly. *Abacus*, a line in rings made of stainless steel with movable coloured balls, again by Timo Küchler, was a great success. With it, Niessing demonstrated at the turn of the century that great effects can be created with small, personal touches. By now Niessing was being awarded prizes and distinctions on a regular basis, for *FormEs* by Christopher Born and *Papyr*, to take just two examples.

Niessing

2008

The individual, distinctive Niessing style is the result of continuous development in design, which to the present day takes place on the premises. The following have worked on the Niessing design team: Christofer Born, Simon-Peter Eiber, Christine Kube, Susanna Loew, Matthias Mönnich, Norbert Mürrle, Marion Röthig, Dorothea Schippel, Petra Weingärtner and Susanne Winckler. Timo Küchler, who runs a design practice of his own in Stuttgart, has been head designer at Niessing since 1992. Antje Bott and Iris Weyer are currently employed as designers in Vreden.

Under Timo Küchler, a retailing concept that was entirely new to the jewellery business was designed in the late 1990s with the aim of conveying to the public the Niessing content and form in a coherent overall package. The year 1999 saw the first proprietary shop opened as Stilwerk in Berlin. Individual jewellery themes are displayed in glass containers and showcased by installations with explanatory texts and detail photos. Thus clients can familiarise themselves with the ideas, materials and manufacturing processes involved in the production of modern jewellery lines in an exhibition ambience. Other shops and shops-in-shops at jewellers have followed in German cities and abroad.

The shock given to the entire jewellery industry by 9/11 has, however, also made a negative impact on sales at Niessing. By the 1990s, the number of jewellery shops and specialist dealers in watches and clocks was already in decline. Stagnating sales after the turn of the century hit specialist dealers in Germany particularly hard. When fears about the new currency, accompanied by a host of other worries about the future, arose and there was much talk of the new moderation, priorities became confused, according to Jochen Exner: »No one really knew any longer what was good.« Niessing went through a period of turbulence, which was finally overcome with the aid of a financial partner. The return to luxury of the classic sort observed in the new affluence in the Arab countries, in Asia and Russia does not represent a reason to Niessing for departing from the path entered on in 1974. The firm hopes to continue to be a driving force in contemporary jewellery, which has something to do with lifestyle culture, design, architecture and contemporary fashion. »We would like to be able to talk competently about good ideas in jewellery from a qualified angle. Everything we plan to do in future is to be subordinated to this idea,« says Jochen Exner.

2000	Ringe *Abakus*, Design Timo Küchler, Stahl, Stahl- und Goldkugeln — Rings *Abacus*, design Timo Küchler, steel, steel- and gold spheres
2000	Anhänger *FormEs*, Design Christofer Born, Gold — Pendants *Shape it*, design Christofer Born, gold
2003	Anstecknadeln *Faltigkeiten*, Design Timo Küchler, Stahl — Needles *Foldings*, design Timo Küchler, steel
2004	Ringe *Tectus*, Design Timo Küchler, Gold, Platin, Brillant — Rings *Tectus*, design Timo Küchler, gold, platinum, diamond
2005	Ohrschmuck *Dos*, Design Salvador Mallol, Gold, Platin — Ear jewellery *Dos*, design Salvador Mallol, gold, platinum
2006	Kugeln *Kogolong*, Werksdesign, Gold, synthetischer Padparadscha, Onyx — Spheres *Kogolong*, in-house design, gold, synthetic padparaja, onyx
2007	Ringe *Circulus*, Design Bettina Geistlich, Gold, Platin, Brillant — Rings *Circulus*, design Bettina Geistlich, gold, platinum, diamond
2008	Ringe *Gravitas*, Design Iris Weyer, Gold, Platin — Rings *Gravitas*, design Iris Weyer, gold, platinum

Jochen Exner
Geboren 1951 in Vreden. Diplombetriebswirt. Seit 1982 Geschäftsführer der 1873 gegründeten Trauringfirma. Moderne Schmuckserien ab 1974.

Jochen Exner
Born in Vreden in 1951. Diploma in business management. Since 1982 managing director of wedding ring firm (est. 1873). Modern jewellery collections since 1974.

1976

1977

1972

1975

1976   *Goldkugel*, *Vollpavéekugel* und *Riefenkugel*, Gold, Brillanten — *Gold ball*,
        Pavé ball and *Grooves ball*, gold, diamonds

1977   *Broschenschloss*, Gold, Zuchtperlen, Rubine, Brillanten — *Brooch clasp*, gold,
        cultured pearls, rubies, diamonds

1982   Anhänger *Das Tor*, Gold, Zuchtperlen, Brillanten, Perlenkette
        — Pendant *The gateway*, gold, cultured pearls, diamonds, pearl necklet

1993   Kugelschließen *Galaxie*, *Dimension*, *Spaltkugel*, Gold, Platin, Brillanten, Acryl
        — Spherical clasps *Galaxy*, *Dimension*, *Notch ball*, gold, platinum,
        diamonds, acrylic

1997   *Broschenschloss Portal*, Platin, Gold, Turmalin, Diamant — *Brooch clasp Portal*,
        platinum, gold, tourmaline, diamond

1972   Perlclip, Gold, Brillanten, Opal — Pearl clip, gold, diamonds, opal

1975   *Brillantkugeln*, Gold, Perlenketten — *Diamond balls*, gold, pearl necklaces

1982   1993   1997

Jörg Heinz

Jörg Heinz hatte an der Kunst- und Werkschule in Pforzheim bei Professor Reinhold Reiling studiert. Sein Weg als Schmuckdesigner und Unternehmer basiert auf einer einzigartigen Erfindung: die moderne auswechselbare Schmuckschließe. Sie wird heute fast in jedem Juweliergeschäft und in jeder Goldschmiede angeboten.

Um sein Studium von 1961 bis 1964 zu finanzieren, arbeitete Jörg Heinz nebenbei als Goldschmied. Anschließend zog es den jungen Gestalter nach Dänemark. Während seines vierjährigen Auslandsaufenthalts lernte er den modernen Designschmuck Skandinaviens und seine Frau Irene kennen. 1968 kehrte er in seine Geburtsstadt Pforzheim zurück und gründete seine Firma im Elternhaus in der Ringstraße 4. Zunächst entwickelte Jörg Heinz hauptsächlich Perlenschmuck. Die Unikate und kleinen Serien verkaufte er mit viel Mühe an Juweliere. Die Konkurrenz in der damals boomenden Pforzheimer Schmuckindustrie war mächtig. Innovative Schmuckideen waren Ende der 1960er Jahre noch kaum gefragt. Gesegnet mit einem Talent zum Gestalten wie zu technischen Erfindungen entwickelte Jörg Heinz Anfang der 1970er Jahre Perlkettenclips und -broschen, die eine 80 cm lange Perlenkette »rafften« und mit dekorativen »Endteilen« versehen waren. Dafür wurde ein Mechanismus entwickelt, der es gestattete, die Kette auch zu schließen und mehrere Ketten zu verbinden. Daraus wurde die heutige Schließe weiterentwickelt. Der Verschluss eines Halsschmucks war bis ins 20. Jahrhundert eine von den Schmuckgestaltern wenig geliebte und vernachlässigte Notwendigkeit. Auch für die Schmuckträgerin stellte das Öffnen eines Collierverschlusses im Nacken oft ein Problem dar.

Nach den ersten Erfolgen mit seiner Endteilschließe stellte sich Jörg Heinz die Frage, ob sich dieses Funktionselement nicht auch zum Mittelteil eines Halsschmucks ausbauen ließ. »Die Idee war schnell da«, berichtet der Firmengründer, »aber die Perfektionierung der Mechanik für eine preiswerte Serienfertigung dauerte seine Zeit.« Weniger problematisch war es, entsprechende Formen für seine »schmückenden Schlösser« zu finden. 1975 stellte er die komplett auswechselbare Schmuckschließe auf der Uhren- und Schmuckmesse in Basel dem internationalen Publikum vor. Im gleichen Jahr ließ er seine Erfindung schützen. Die Zeit, in der »Schlösser« nur ein Schattendasein führen durften, verborgen unter Nackenhaaren, war vorbei. Doch war der Mechanismus nicht mit den üblichen Goldschmiedetechniken zu realisieren. In den ersten Jahren ließ Jörg Heinz die notwendigen Präzisionsteile von Zulieferern aus der Feinmechanik fertigen, bevor er die erforderlichen Maschinen und Techniken in der eigenen Firma installierte.

Die Schmuckschließe von Jörg Heinz erfüllt die Forderung des amerikanischen Architekten Louis Sullivan, dass die Form der Funktion zu folgen hat, auf ganz schmuckspezifische Weise. Denn die perfekte Funktion der Schließe ist mit der Grundfunktion des Schmückens unlösbar verbunden. Sie ist von jeder Schmuckträgerin vor dem Körper durch eine einfache Druck- und Drehbewegung auf beiden Seiten zu öffnen und zu schließen. Gleichzeitig hält die präzise Mechanik das attraktive Mittelteil sicher fest. Somit konnte die moderne Schließe fortan die Position eines eigenständigen Schmuckstücks einnehmen. Und zwar da, wo sie die Blicke unwiderstehlich anzieht. Die Erfindung im Jahr 1975 war aber mehr als nur eine technische und gestalterische Innovation. Als auswechselbares, attraktives Schmuckstück stellten seine »schönen Schlösser« eines der ersten variierbaren Systeme im modernen Schmuckdesign dar.

Eine Kette, ob aus Perlen, Gold, Platin, Edelsteinen, Korallen oder Edelstahl, lässt sich durch die auswechselbaren Schließen seitdem spielend leicht verwandeln. Damit erlaubte Jörg Heinz der Schmuckträgerin eine neue gestalterische Freiheit. Sie kann ihren Halsschmuck jeder Mode und jeder Gelegenheit anpassen: dem schlichten oder schmuckbewussten Alltag, dem gediegenen Businesslook, dem festlichen Abend. Mit scheinbar unerschöpflicher Kreativität schuf der Firmengründer seit 1974 eine große Formenvielfalt – für jeden Frauentyp und für jedes Schmuckbedürfnis. Sein wichtigstes Motto sei die Reduktion auf das Wesentliche gewesen, sagt Jörg Heinz, aber er habe auch gerne organische Formen gestaltet. Neben der klassischen Kugel in Gold mit und ohne Diamanten entstanden viele ausgefallene Kreationen mit Perlen und Edelsteinen. Sogar Gemmen wurden in den ersten Jahren oft als »Blickfang« eingesetzt. In jedem Fall entsprach die Erfindung dem gewachsenen Selbstbewusstsein moderner Frauen seit den 1970er Jahren. Mit den variablen Schmuckschließen von Jörg Heinz wurden sie zu Mitgestalterinnen ihres individuellen Auftritts.

Über vier Jahrzehnte hat die Manufaktur Jörg Heinz ihr technologisches und handwerkliches Können verfeinert. Mit dem Bau einer neuen Manufaktur in Neulingen bei Pforzheim im Januar 2007 entstand endlich der Raum, das kontinuierlich gewachsene Knowhow logistisch optimal zu nutzen. Aber auch schon im alten Pforzheimer Betrieb wurden die Schmuckschließen von Jörg Heinz weitgehend autonom produziert. CNC-gesteuerte Fräsmaschinen, Drehautomaten und Laser kommen seit langem zum Einsatz, um höchste Präzision zu erreichen.

An vielen Entwicklungen war der Firmengründer selbst maßgeblich beteiligt. Weil die Kugel eine zentrale Funktion als Blickfang und Hort der feinmechanisch anspruchsvollen Schließe einnimmt, entwickelte Jörg Heinz schon 1990 eine Technik, mit der Laserschweißen und Gravieren dreidimensional über acht Achsen möglich wurde. »Wir haben nie Maschinen gekauft um Großserien herzustellen, sondern hauptsächlich, um Dinge zu realisieren, die sonst nicht machbar waren. Die Schönheit der äußeren Formen und Oberflächen findet jedoch erst durch die Hand erfahrener Goldschmiede ihre Vollendung. So bilden Gestaltungsqualität und traditionelle Handwerkskunst auch im 21. Jahrhundert in der neuen Manufaktur die Grundlage des Schaffens.

2000   2002   2003

Der Umzug im Januar 2007 bedeutete für die 30 qualifizierten Mitarbeiter moderne Arbeitsplätze nach den neuesten Erkenntnissen. Er basiert auf dem Glauben in die eigene Kompetenz und an den Standort Deutschland. Die Zuversicht von Jörg Heinz beruht nicht zuletzt auf dem Nachwuchs in der eigenen Familie. Der Firmengründer wird inzwischen von seinen Söhnen Martin und Lars Heinz sowie seiner Tochter Andrea Mössner unterstützt. Martin Heinz ist als Mitgeschäftsführer für das Marketing verantwortlich. Lars Heinz kann als frisch gekrönter Landes- und Bundessieger der Industrie- und Handelskammer auf eine überaus erfolgreiche Goldschmiedelehre zurückblicken. Andrea Mössner ist für den Einkauf und die Auswahl von Edelsteinen verantwortlich. Zusammen mit einem langjährigen, hoch qualifizierten Mitarbeiterteam fühlt sich das Familienunternehmen den Herausforderungen in der globalisierten Welt gewachsen.

E — Jörg Heinz studied at the Kunst- und Werkschule in Pforzheim under Professor Reinhold Reiling. His career as a jewellery designer and entrepreneur is based on a unique invention: the modern interchangeable clasp for jewellery. Today it is sold in almost all jewellery stores and at every goldsmithing studio.

To finance his studies from 1961 to 1964, Jörg Heinz worked on the side as a goldsmith. Then the young designer was drawn to Denmark. During his four-year stay there, Heinz learned about modern Scandinavian designer jewellery and met his wife Irene. In 1968 he returned to his native city of Pforzheim and founded a firm at 4 Ringstraße in his parents' house. At first Jörg Heinz concentrated chiefly on developing pearl jewellery. He worked hard at marketing his one-off pieces and limited editions to jewellers. The competition from the Pforzheim jewellery industry, which at the time was booming, was stiff. Innovative ideas in jewellery were not much in demand in the late 1960s. Blessed with both a talent for design and for technical inventiveness, Jörg Heinz came up with a pearl necklace clip and brooch in the 1970s that »gathered« an 80cm long pearl necklace and was fitted out with decorated »end pieces«. A mechanism was developed that made it possible to clasp the necklace and link several necklaces. From it the present-day clasp evolved. Until the 20th century, necklace clasps were viewed by designers as a not much loved, indeed all too often neglected, necessity. For the woman wearing a close-fitting necklace, opening its clasp at the back of the neck often posed a problem.

After the first successes with his end-piece clasp, Jörg Heinz began to wonder whether this functional element might not also be expanded into the centre-piece of a necklace. »The idea was soon there,« reports the founder of the firm, »but it took a while to perfect the mechanism for affordable mass production.« It was not so difficult to invent suitable forms for his »ornamental clasps«. In 1975 Heinz presented his completely interchangeable jewellery clasp at the Basel Watch and Jewellery Fair to an international public. That same year he had his invention patented. The days when clasps were »half hidden from the eye« beneath the wearer's hair at the back of her neck were over. However, the mechanism could not be made with the usual goldsmithing techniques. In the early years, Jörg Heinz had the precision parts he needed supplied by instrument-makers before he was able to install the necessary machines and technical equipment on his own firm's premises. Jörg Heinz's jewellery clasp meets the requirement proclaimed by the American architect Louis Sullivan that form must follow function in a way that is entirely specific to jewellery. For the perfect functioning of this clasp is indissolubly linked with the basic function of adornment. Any woman wearing a piece of jewellery fitted with it can open and close it from the front with a simple movement of exerting pressure and turning. At the same time the precise mechanism securely holds the attractive centre-piece. Hence the modern clasp was in a position to represent a piece of jewellery in its own right from then on. And right where it was irresistibly eye-catching. This invention made in 1975 was, however, much more than a mere technical innovation or a design first. As an interchangeable, attractive piece of jewellery, the Heinz »beautiful clasp« represented one of the earliest modular systems in modern jewellery design.

A necklace, be it of pearls, gold, platinum, precious stones, coral or stainless steel, can be transformed by a sleight of hand with these interchangeable clasps. Thus Jörg Heinz has empowered the woman wearing his jewellery with a new freedom to take design into her own hands. She can suit her neck jewellery to every fashion and to all occasions: everyday wear, whether casual or fashionable, the sleek business look, gala evenings. Drawing on a sheer inexhaustible fund of creativity, Jörg Heinz has produced a wide variety of forms since 1974 – for every type of woman and for all jewellery needs. His overarching motto has been reducing to essentials, says Jörg Heinz, but he has also enjoyed designing organic forms. Apart from the classic modular ball clasp in gold, with or without diamonds, he has produced numerous unconventional creations set with pearls and precious stones. Even cameos or carved gems were often used in the early years as »eye-catchers«. In each case, the invention was suited to the enhanced self-confidence modern women have enjoyed since the 1970s. Jörg Heinz's variable clasps empowered them to the status of co-designers of the way they wanted to look.

Over four decades, the Jörg Heinz factory has refined its technology and crafts skills. The building of a new factory in Neulingen near Pforzheim in January 2007 finally provided the space for optimising the know-how that had accrued continuously over such a long time. But Jörg Heinz's clasps were made even in the old Pforzheim factory under largely autonomous production conditions. CNC-guided milling machines, automatic lathes and laser have long been used to achieve the utmost in precision.

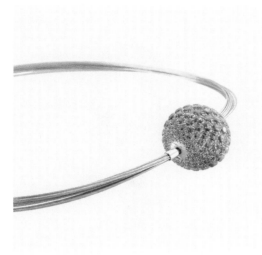

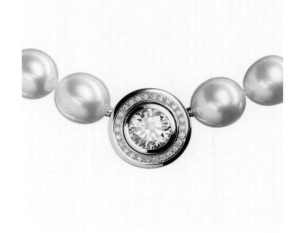

2006   2006   2008

The founder of the firm himself had a paramount share in many developments in production. Because the ball assumes a pivotal function as an eye-catcher and as the seat of the clasp, which is such a precision-engineered object in its own right, Jörg Heinz had developed a technique for laser fusing and three-dimensional engraving over eight axes by 1990. »We have never invested in machinery for mass-production purposes but rather to realise things that could not otherwise have been made. The beauty of the external form and surfaces, however, attains perfection only in the hands of experienced goldsmiths.« Thus quality in design and traditional craftsmanship has remained the basis of production in the new factory in the 21st century as well.

The move in January 2007 meant a modern, state-of-the-art workplace for the firm's thirty highly qualified employees and was based on an unshakeable belief in the firm's competence and in Germany as a good place to do business. Jörg Heinz's confidence reposes not least in the coming generation in his own family. In the meantime, he is supported by sons Martin and Lars Heinz as well as his daughter, Andrea Mössner. As co-managing director, Martin Heinz is responsible for marketing. Lars Heinz, a new Chamber of Industry and Commerce laureate at state and federal level, looks back on a highly successful goldsmithing apprenticeship. Andrea Mössner is in charge of selecting and buying precious stones. In company with a highly qualified team of long-term employees, this family business feels more than up to meeting the challenges of globalisation.

2000	*Brillant-Käfig,* Gold, Brillant, Südsee-Zuchtperlenkette — *Diamond cage,* gold, diamond, South Sea cultured pearl necklet
2002	*Sandwich-Schließe,* Gold, Edeltopas, Brillanten — *Sandwich clasp,* gold, topaz, diamonds
2003	Rahmenschließen *Doppel-Quadrat,* Ring und *Gitterschließe,* Gold, Diamanten, Zuchtperlen — Frame clasps *Double square,* ring and *Lattice clasp,* gold, diamonds, cultured pearls
2006	*Citrin-Farbsteinpavée-Kugel,* Gold — *Citrine gemstone pavé ball,* gold
2006	*Perlennetz,* Gold, Brillanten, Südsee-Zuchtperlen — *Pearl mesh,* gold, diamonds, South Sea cultured pearls
2008	*Brillant-Solitär,* Gold, Brillanten, Südsee-Zuchtperlenkette — *Diamond solitaire,* gold, diamonds, South Sea cultured pearl necklet

Jörg Heinz
Geboren 1942 in Pforzheim, 1961–1964 Studium an der Kunst- und Werkschule Pforzheim. Firmengründung 1968. Seit Januar 2007 in Neulingen.

Jörg Heinz
Born in Pforzheim in 1942, 1961–1964 studied at the Kunst- und Werkschule Pforzheim. Founded company 1968. In Neulingen since January 2007.

1978   1996   2002

Gebrüder Schaffrath

Unter der Leitung von Alexander Leuz setzt die Diamantschleiferei Gebrüder Schaffrath seit 1998 auf modernes Schmuck-Design. Ziel ist es, mit innovativem Design eine moderne Diamantschmuck-Marke zu etablieren. Wichtigstes Thema war bislang das so genannte Liberté©-Prinzip. Bei dem Gestaltungskonzept erhält der Diamant möglichst viel Bewegungsspielraum, um seine volle Brillanz spielerisch zu entfalten.

Mit sechs Diamantschleifern gründeten die Brüder Adam und Alois Schaffrath 1923 in Hanau ihr Unternehmen. Perfekt geschliffene Diamanten erlebten damals eine wachsende Nachfrage. Die Gebrüder Schaffrath überstanden die Weltwirtschaftskrise von 1929 und beschäftigten 1936 bereits 60 Mitarbeiter. Während des Zweiten Weltkriegs ruhte der Betrieb. Das Gebäude der Diamantschleiferei wurde durch Bomben schwer beschädigt. Den Neuanfang ab 1946 begünstigte das internationale Renommee, das sich die Firma in Deutschland, in Amerika und Belgien bereits vor dem Krieg erworben hatte. In den Jahren des Wirtschaftswunders arbeiteten zeitweise bis zu 400 Diamantschleifer in den Werkstätten in Hanau und Idar-Oberstein.

1960 konnte Gebrüder Schaffrath erstmals rohe Diamanten direkt bei der Zentralen Verkaufsorganisation von De Beers in London einkaufen. Die Einladung zu den so genannten Sights des Diamant-Monopolisten kam zu dieser Zeit einem Ritterschlag im Diamantgeschäft gleich. 1969 entstand die erste eigene Diamantschmuck-Kollektion. Mit der Ringserie 40085 wurde 1978 eine vollkommen reduzierte Form entwickelt. Die polierte Ringschiene korrespondiert mit dem schlichten Rund der Zargenfassung. Der Brillant im Zentrum erscheint optisch größer. Die Ringe werden als Klassiker bis heute unverändert gefertigt und erreichen eine große Bedeutung als so genannte Vorsteckringe, die ergänzend zum Trauring getragen werden. In der Serie La Luna, bestehend aus Ringen, Armreifen, Ohrschmuck und Colliers, ragt der Diamant scheinbar frei schwebend zur Hälfte ungefasst in den Raum. Beide Entwürfe sind Teil der Classics-Kollektion.

1998 übernahm Alexander Leuz die Designleitung des Familienunternehmens, das heute von ihm in der vierten Generation geführt wird. Schon 1997 arbeitete er an dem Konzept, Diamanten beweglich im Schmuck einzusetzen. »Diamanten benötigen Licht und Bewegung, erst dann kann das Feuer des Diamanten entfacht werden«, sagt Leuz. In der Kreation Diva ist ein gefasster Diamant beweglich gelagert, zeigt frei schwingend immer nach oben und kann dadurch mehr Licht einfangen. Die Kollektion Arcana von 2002 bedeutete die erste Umsetzung des frei beweglichen, ungefassten Diamanten bei Gebrüder Schaffrath. Ein schmaler Platinbügel überspannt den Edelstein. Die Verpackung, in der alle Liberté©-Ringe präsentiert werden, ist Teil des Marketingkonzepts. Durch das Öffnen des Deckels, Liberté©-Tresor genannt, wird der Ring zum Vibrieren gebracht und gleichzeitig von einer im Deckel integrierten Leuchte angestrahlt. Der Diamant nimmt die Vibrationen auf und versprüht sein Lichtspektrum in den Farben des Regenbogens. In der Lumina-Kollektion wird der Diamant nur durch die konkav geformten Enden der geöffneten Ringschiene gehalten. Der frei gelagerte Stein reagiert auf jede Bewegung und verführt zum Hinsehen. Sein Spielraum ist jedoch so präzise bemessen, dass er sicher in dem Schmuckstück gehalten wird. Zum 80-jährigen Bestehen im Jahre 2003 entwickelte die Manufaktur einen eigenen Schliff mit 80 gegenüber den üblichen 56 Facetten, die ein normaler Brillantschliff aufweist. Mit dem Jubiläumsschliff wurden 80 Lumina-Ringe bestückt.

Die Ringserie Vendetta von 2005 wurde speziell für den kleinen Finger entworfen. Sie ist eine Hommage an Shakespeares »Romeo und Julia«. Die Ringschiene in Weißgold ist seitlich ausgeschnitten und trägt hier an dieser im getragenen Zustand verdeckten »Schnittstelle« den eingravierten Kollektionsnamen. Die Innenseite des Rings bedeckt ein Inlay aus rotem Korund. »Die Leidenschaft der dramatischen Liebesgeschichte wird durch das kraftvolle Rot versinnbildlicht«, erklärt Alexander Leuz. Außen ist Vendetta mit Diamanten im Brillant- oder Prinzessschliff besetzt, die auch seitlich über die Ringschiene hinausragen. Die zweite Variante der Kleinen-Finger-Ringe trägt den Namen Lollipop. Die leuchtenden Inlays umfassen ein breites Farbspektrum von Gelb, Rosa, Hellblau über Grün bis Violett und Braun. In den entsprechenden Farben reihen sich facettierte, außen rund geschliffene Steine wie Amethyst, Quarz und verschiedenfarbige Korunde auf der Ringschiene. Das Jahr 2008 wird von Gebrüder Schaffrath in besonderer Weise gewürdigt. Die Acht, in der Physik das Symbol für Unendlichkeit und in Asien für Glück, erscheint stilisiert in der Ringform Unity. Neben Zuchtperlen werden auch Farbedelsteine verwendet. »Jeder Edelstein soll direkt mit der Haut der Trägerin in Berührung kommen«, sagt Alexander Leuz, der alle Gestaltungskonzepte leitet. Der Firmenchef möchte »Berührungspunkte zwischen Mensch und Material« schaffen und haptische Erlebnisse vermitteln. Die Trägerin soll die Energie, die kostbaren Perlen und Farbedelsteinen inne wohnt, erspüren und sich damit wohl fühlen. Auf dem Weg zur Schmuckmarke hat sich das Gestaltungsspektrum erweitert. Die Sonderstellung des »Königs der Edelsteine« wird jedoch bewahrt in der Traditionsfirma, die in 23 Ländern rund um den Globus vertreten ist.

E — With Alexander Leuz as manager, Gebrüder Schaffrath, diamond cutters, have featured modern designer jewellery since 1998. Their aim has been to establish a modern diamond jewellery label with innovative design. The most important theme to date has been what is known as the Liberté© principle. This design concept gives the diamond as much scope as possible to develop the full play of its brilliancy.

The brothers Adam and Alois Schaffrath founded their business with six diamond-cutters in Hanau in 1923. At that time, the demand for per-

2003   2005   2005

fectly cut diamonds was growing. The Schaffrath brothers survived the 1929 worldwide economic crisis and by 1936 were employing a workforce of sixty. The business was inactive during the Second World War and the diamond-cutting building sustained severe bomb damage. A fresh start in 1946 was promoted by the international renown which the firm had acquired in Germany, America and Belgium before the war. During the Economic Miracle years, up to four hundred diamond-cutters might be employed at any given time in the Hanau and Idar-Oberstein workshops.

In 1960 Gebrüder Schaffrath was able for the first time to buy uncut diamonds directly from the De Beers central sales organisation in London. Being invited to the viewings of the diamond cartel was at that time the equivalent in the diamond industry of being raised to the peerage. The first Gebrüder Schaffrath diamond jewellery collection was launched in 1969. The 1978 *40085* line in rings represented the development of a form stringently reduced to essentials. The polished ring shank matches the simple circle of the bezel setting to make the diamond solitaire at the centre look bigger. Classic rings of this kind are still being made today unchanged and have attained high status as engagement rings, which are worn together with a wedding ring. In the *La Luna* line, consisting of rings, bangles, ear jewellery and necklaces, the crown of the diamond stands above the setting so that it appears to be unset. Both designs form part of the *Classics* collection.

In 1998 Alexander Leuz became head of the design department in the family business, of which he is today the 4th-generation owner. By 1997 he was working on the concept of setting movable diamonds in jewellery. »Diamonds need light and movement to be able to develop their fire,« says Leuz. Diva is a creation with a movable diamond set so that it can be tilted up and, therefore, catch more light. The 2002 *Arcana* collection represented the first use of the freely movable, unset diamond at Gebrüder Schaffrath. A narrow bow of platinum arcs above the stone. The packaging in which all *Liberté©* rings are presented is part of the marketing strategy. Opening the lid of what is called the *Liberté©* vault makes the ring vibrate while a light integrated in the lid shines on it. Picking up the vibrations, the diamond scatters the full spectrum of its light in the colours of the rainbow. In the *Lumina* collection, the diamond is held only by the concave shaped ends of the open ring shank. Thus freely set, the stone reacts to any movement and is eye-catching. Its free play, however, is so precisely calculated that it is held securely in the piece of jewellery. To mark the company's eightieth anniversary in 2003, a proprietary cut was developed featuring eighty facets instead of the fifty-six usual in the standard brilliant cut. Eighty *Lumina* rings were set with this anniversary cut.

The 2005 *Vendetta* line was developed specially to be worn on the little finger. It is a tribute to Shakespeare's Romeo and Juliet. The ring shank in white gold is cut out at the sides and the collection name is engraved on this »interface,« which is out of sight when the ring is worn. The inside of the ring is covered with red corundum (ruby) inlay. »The passion revealed in this dramatic love-story is symbolised by the vibrant red,« explains Alexander Leuz. On the outside, Vendetta is set with brilliant or princess-cut diamonds, which also extend laterally beyond the ring shank. The second variant on the little-finger ring is called Lollipop. Glowing inlays encompass a broad colour range from yellow, pink, light blue through green to purple and brown. Faceted, round cut stones such as amethyst, rose quartz and corundum in various colours are arrayed on the ring shank in colours to match the inlay. The year 2008 is being specially celebrated at Gebrüder Schaffrath. The eight, the symbol for eternity in physics and for good fortune in Asia, appears in stylised form in the ring model called *Unity*. Both pearls and coloured precious stones are used. »Each precious stone is supposed to come into direct contact with the wearer's skin,« says Alexander Leuz, who is supervising all design concepts in his capacity as head of the company. Leuz wants to create »points of contact between the human being and the material« and communicate tactile experiences. Women wearing this jewellery are supposed to sense the forces latent in the costly pearls and coloured precious stones and feel comfortable with them. On Schaffrath's way to becoming a famous label in jewellery, they have enlarged their design spectrum. The exceptional position of »The King of Precious Stones« will, however, be kept at the venerable firm, which is represented in twenty-three countries round the world.

1978	*Classics Kollektion* Ring, Gold, Diamant — *Classics collection* ring, gold, diamond
1996	Ring *La Luna*, Gold, Diamant — Ring *La Luna*, gold, diamond
2002	Ring *Liberté©Arcana*, Platin, Diamant — Ring *Liberté© Arcana*, platinum, diamond
2003	Ring *Liberté©Lumina*, Platin, Diamant — Ring *Liberté© Lumina*, platinum, diamond
2005	Ring *Vendetta*, Gold, Diamant *Princess*-Cut — Ring *Vendetta*, gold, *princess*-cut diamond
2005	Ring *Lollipop*, Gold, Edelsteine — Ring *Lollipop*, gold, precious stones

Alexander Leuz
Geboren 1968 in Hanau. 1998 Designleitung der 1923 gegründeten Firma Gebrüder Schaffrath. Inzwischen Geschäftsführung. Modernes Schmuckdesign seit 1978.

Alexander Leuz
Born in Hanau in 1968. 1998 Design director at Gebrüder Schaffrath (est. 1923). Now managing director. Modern designer jewellery since 1978.

1983   1988

2001

1983   *Perlschmuck Set*, Design Yngvar Rolfsen, Biwa-Zuchtperlen Dragon-shape,
        Gold, Brillanten — *Pearl jewellery set,* design Yngvar Rolfsen, Biwa cultured
        pearls, dragon-shape, gold, diamonds

1988   Collier mit Brosch-Anhänger, Design Rolf Guigas, Akoya-Zuchtperlen, Gold
        — Necklace with brooch pendant, design Rolf Guigas, Akoya cultured pearls,
        gold

1995   *Fantasieketten*, Design Tove Gellner, Süßwasser-Zuchtperlen, Gold, Turmaline
        — *Fantasy necklaces*, design Tove Gellner, freshwater cultured pearls,
        gold, tourmalines

1996   Armreif, Design Michael Zobel, Südsee-Zuchtperle, Gold — Bangle, design
        Michael Zobel, South Sea cultured pearl, gold

1997   Ohrschmuck, Design Edith Bischoff, Akoya-Zuchtperle, Gold, Platin
        — Earring, design Edith Bischoff, Akoya cultured pearl, gold, platinum

2001   *Y-Collier*, Design Gellner, Ring, Design Angela Hübel, Tahiti-Zuchtperlen,
        Gold, Diamanten — *Y Collar,* design Gellner, ring, design Angela Hübel,
        Tahitian cultured pearls, gold, diamonds

Gellner

Bis Ende der 1980er Jahre galten Perlen unter den meisten modernen Schmuckmachern als antiquiert. Ab 1994 intensivierte Gellner seine Designaktivitäten und überraschte die Öffentlichkeit mit unkonventioneller Werbung. Unter der Leitung von Jörg Gellner entwickelte sich der zuvor überwiegend auf Perlenhandel spezialisierte Familienbetrieb so zur international orientierten Manufakturmarke.

Heinz Gellner, geboren 1940, baute die Firma mit dem starken Rückhalt seiner Frau kontinuierlich auf. Tove Gellner war 1962 aus Norwegen als Volontärin in eine Manufaktur für Accessoires nach Mühlacker gekommen, um Deutsch zu lernen. Im Jahr der Firmengründung 1967 erblickten ihre Töchter, die Zwillingsschwestern Eveline und Birgit, das Licht der Welt. 1968 wurde Jörg Gellner geboren. Bereits 1973 konnte Heinz Gellner einen Mitbewerber übernehmen und den Kundenkreis erweitern. 1974 stellte sich der Perlenspezialist erstmals auf der Fachmesse Inhorgenta vor. Die internationale Uhren- und Schmuckmesse in Basel folgte 1976. Bis Ende der 1980er Jahre war der Perlenmarkt durch Akoya-Zuchtperlen sehr klassisch geprägt. Mit den Süßwasser-Zuchtperlen, die in den 1970er Jahren verstärkt auf den Markt kamen, fand eine erste »Verjüngungskur« statt. In vielen Farben schillernd, vielgestaltig und deutlich preiswerter als die hellen Akoya-Zuchtperlen, verlangten sie ein neues Design. Handwerklich talentiert und mit modischem Gespür ausgestattet, begann Tove Gellner, Fantasieketten zu gestalten. Der Mix aus Süßwasser-Zuchtperlen, Edelstein- und Goldzwischenteilen sprach junge und jung gebliebene Frauen an.

In den 1980er Jahren war das Unternehmen auf 35 Mitarbeiter angewachsen. An der Entwicklung erster kreativer Schmuckserien und Unikate wirkten der vielseitige Künstler Rolf Guigas und der Goldschmied Roland Steinbrink mit. Die Kollektionen mit Akoya- und Biwa-Zuchtperlen waren kombiniert mit Gold, Farbedelsteinen und Diamanten. Der befreundete Yngvar Rolfsen fertigte in seinem Goldschmiedeatelier Gellner-Unikate mit Biwa-Dragon-Zuchtperlen. Die ausgefallenen, teils bizarren Naturformen der Süßwasser-Zuchtperlen aus dem japanischen Biwa-See wurden in organisch fließende Goldelemente eingebettet, meist verziert mit Diamanten. Das Design beschränkte sich darauf, den Naturformen zu folgen und sie zu verstärken. Die Unikate mit Biwa-Dragon-Zuchtperlen haben heute nur noch historischen Wert. Dagegen erwiesen sich die *Fantasieketten* von Tove Gellner über lange Zeit als wichtiges Thema. In einer Broschüre von 1990 heißt es: »Ihre Form ist Zufall, ihr Wesen geheimnisvoll, ihre Wirkung bezaubernd. So liegt es an der Kunst des Menschen, die Eigenschaften der Perle im Schmuck zum Ausdruck zu bringen.« Gezeigt werden mehrere Ketten mit Goldzwischenteilen, zum Teil in Perlenform gegossen. Zu dieser Zeit erhielt die Firmenchefin Hilfe im Design von ihrer Tochter Birgit Gellner-Pavlow. Sie hatte von 1986 bis 1988 die Goldschmiedeschule Pforzheim besucht und nach der Gehilfenprüfung in den USA eine Ausbildung als Gemmologin absolviert.

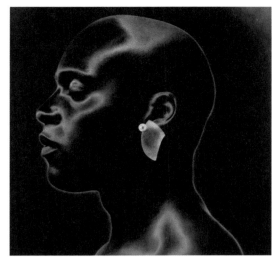

1995   1996   1997

Eveline Gellner unterstützte ihren Vater in der Organisation und bei kaufmännischen Aufgaben. Jörg Gellner sammelte noch während seines Studiums Erfahrungen im Außendienst. Mit Claus Krafzik, der 1990 in die Firma kam und bald darauf Prokura erhielt, reiste er unmittelbar nach dem Mauerfall in die neuen Bundesländer, um den Kundenstamm im Osten Deutschlands zu erweitern. Die Kooperation mit der Platin Gilde führte seit Ende der 1980er Jahre zur Entwicklung von modernem Platinschmuck mit Perlen. Zuständig dafür war der Goldschmied Albrecht Münzmay, der bis heute als freier Designer für das Unternehmen tätig ist. 1992 stellte Gellner eine Klappschließe vor, die auf dem Markt sehr gut ankam, bald aber auch Nachahmer fand. 1995 hat Heinz Gellner aus gesundheitlichen Gründen die Firmenleitung seinem Sohn Jörg übergeben.

Die 1990er Jahre waren für die Schmuckbranche in ganz Europa eine Zeit des Umbruchs. Die Öffnung des Ostens, die Globalisierung und der Wertewandel erforderten neue Konzepte. Besonders im deutschsprachigen Raum fand modernes Schmuckdesign zunehmend Beachtung. Jörg Gellner intensivierte die kontinuierliche Partnerschaft mit namhaften externen Schmuckdesignern. Bereits 1996 zeigte sich der Wandel zu einer reduzierten, modernen Formensprache. Neben hauseigenen Entwürfen von Esther Stutzmann wurden Schmucklinien der Designer Michael Zobel und Edith Bischoff vorgestellt. Michael Zobel, ein Schüler von Reinhold Reiling und Klaus Ullrich, zählte mit seinem Goldschmiedegeschäft in Konstanz zu den Kunden von Gellner. »Dies hat die Zusammenarbeit beflügelt«, berichtet Jörg Gellner. Nach gut zehn Jahren sind die expressiven Stücke noch immer aktuell und besonders in den USA gefragt.

Der *Perlspannring* von Norbert Mürrle, 1995 in die Kollektion aufgenommen, stellte eine Neuerung grundsätzlicher Art dar. Während die Perle als Kette direkt auf der Haut getragen wird, war dies früher bei Ringen selten der Fall. Typisch war die Befestigung der Naturschöpfung auf einer winzigen Metallschale. »Dies hatte auch mit der japanischen Akoyaperle zu tun, deren Schichten für eine robuste Beanspruchung zu dünn sind«, erklärt Jörg Gellner. Der Hautkontakt wurde seit dem *Perlspannring* bei Gellner bewusst in der Ringgestaltung umgesetzt. Die in den 1990er Jahren aufgekommenen Tahiti- und Südsee-Zuchtperlen sind dafür ideal geeignet. Der *Perlspannring* wurde gleichzeitig und ohne gegenseitiges Wissen sowohl von Norbert Mürrle für Gellner wie auch von schmuckwerk entwickelt. Beide Hersteller waren damit sehr erfolgreich.

1997 präsentierte sich Gellner mit einem veränderten, zeitgemäßen Marketingauftritt der Öffentlichkeit. Die Fach- und Publikumswerbung zeigte ein männliches Model mit dunkler Hautfarbe als Träger von Perlenschmuck. 1998 wurden Entwürfe der Designerinnen Doris Zühlke und Gabriele Wilms realisiert. Im gleichen Jahr lud Gellner Studenten der Fachhochschule Düsseldorf zu einem Design-Wettbewerb ein. Viele der jungen Designer wollten aus Respekt vor dem Naturmaterial die Perlen nicht durchbohren. Sie durften sich zum Beispiel in den *Klangkinegraphen* von Kirsten Grünebaum frei bewegen. Stefanie von Scheven hatte die Naturschöpfungen in einen *Perlenschwung* gefasst. Ähnlich sensibel ging auch Claudia Wieczorek in den drei Ringen *Craze* mit den Perlen um. Die Umsetzungen dieser drei Entwürfe wurden 1998 auf der Inhorgenta vorgestellt.

1999 konnte Gellner auf der Messe Selection im Designzentrum Essen auftreten. Die kreative Schau führender Schmuckdesigner und -manufakturen bestärkte das Gellnerteam in seiner Designoffensive. Neu war in diesem Jahr die Zusammenarbeit mit dem Gestalter Peter Birkenmeier und Sabine Brandenburg-Frank. Avantgardistische Entwürfe brachte der im Jahr 2000 durchgeführte Wettbewerb mit der Pforzheimer Hochschule für Gestaltung hervor. Den ersten Preis gewann dabei Natascha Rachel Reichel für *Lose Perlen im Seidenstrumpf*. Die Stücke waren allerdings wie schon die vorhergegangenen Wettbewerbsarbeiten aus Düsseldorf wenig erfolgreich. »Vielleicht weil sie für die Branche doch noch zu ungewohnt und neu waren«, meint Jörg Gellner.

Ganz anders war dies bei Schmucklinien von freien Gestaltern, die bereits Erfahrung im Markt hatten. Im Jahr 2000 wurden Entwürfe der freien Schmuckdesigner Viola Schwalm und Sabine Hauss sowie Marion Röthig aus dem Hause Gellner auf den Markt gebracht. 2001 stellte Gellner sein *Y-Collier* mit Perlen vor. Das bislang auffälligste Designkonzept für Perlenschmuck stammt von der Düsseldorfer Schmuckdesignerin Monika Seitter. Ihre Kombination von Tahitiperlen mit farbigem Kunststoff für die Serie *Hot* wirkte ebenso provozierend wie anziehend. Der ungewohnte Materialmix und die starke Farbigkeit war ein Bruch mit der Tradition im Perlschmuck. Die bunten Kunststoffschienen von Monika Seitter brachten zudem die Erkenntnis, wie wichtig das Thema Farbe und der Bezug zur Mode im neuen Jahrhundert geworden waren. Ein Jahr später engagierte Gellner den chinesischen Designer Dickson Yewn für eine freie Mitarbeit. Sein Design ist deutlich floraler als das eher geradlinige deutsche Design. Für Gellner ist es ein Brückenschlag zwischen zwei Kulturen. »Dickson Yewn geht mehr in Richtung Art Déco, ein Thema, das in Asien immer noch sehr beliebt ist«, erklärt Jörg Gellner. Demgegenüber komme das strengere deutsche Design gerade gut in den USA an, dort, wo Birgit Gellner-Pavlow und ihr Mann Randy Pavlow inzwischen erfolgreich den Markt bearbeiten. 2005 zeigte Gellner mit den *Roh-Diamanten-Colliers*, dass man auch mit dem härtesten der Edelsteine originell umzugehen weiß. Das erfolgreiche Konzept mit renommierten externen Schmuckdesignern führte 2006 schließlich zur Zusammenarbeit mit Angela Hübel und 2007 mit Egon Frank.

Sichtbares Zeichen des Erfolgs in Wiernsheim ist der Erweiterungsbau, der zum 40-jährigen Firmenjubiläum 2007 eingeweiht werden konnte. Gellner präsentiert sich in den neu gestalteten Räumen als moderne

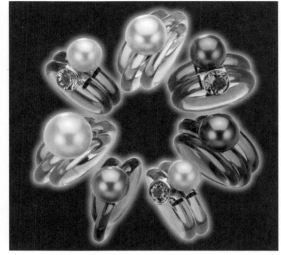

1998   1999   2004

Schmuckmanufaktur. Allein in Deutschland führen etwa 200 Partner die Kollektionen der Perlenmarke. Zum gegenwärtigen Trend sagen Jörg Gellner und seine Schwester: »Schmuck ist mehr denn je Ausdruck von Emotion. Die Frauen demonstrieren mit ihrem Schmuck ihr Lebensgefühl und ihre Persönlichkeit.« Dies sei vor zehn Jahren noch nicht so ausgeprägt gewesen. Auch das Bedürfnis nach weicheren und organischen Formen sei gewachsen.

E — Until the late 1980s, pearls were regarded as old-fashioned by most modern jewellery-makers. From 1994 Gellner intensified operations in design and caught the public unawares with unconventional advertising. Under Jörg Gellner's management, the family firm, which before his time had dealt mainly with pearls, grew into an internationally oriented designer label.

Heinz Gellner (born in 1940) steadily built up the firm with his wife as his mainstay in the business. Tove Gellner had come from Norway to Mühlacker in 1962 as an intern at an accessory factory for the purpose of learning German. The year the Gellners founded their firm, 1967, also saw the birth of their twin daughters, Eveline and Birgit. In 1968 Jörg Gellner was born. By 1973 Heinz Gellner was in a position to take over a competitor and thus enlarge his clientele. In 1974 the specialist in pearls showed work for the first time at the Inhorgenta specialist jewellery trade fair in Munich. In 1976 Gellner was represented at the World Watch and Jewellery Show in Basel. By the late 1980s, tastes on the pearl market tended towards the classic because it was dominated by Akoya (bead-nucleated cultured pearls) pearls. When Freshwater cultured pearls started to flood the market in the 1970s, however, pearls underwent their first »rejuvenation cure«. Shimmering in many colours, available in all shapes and considerably cheaper than the light-coloured Akoya cultured pearls, freshwater pearls called for new designs. A talented craftswoman with a fashion sense, Tove Gellner began to design *Fantasy necklaces*. Her blends of freshwater cultured pearls with precious stones and gold spacers appealed to young women and women who were still young at heart.

By the 1980s, Gellner had grown into a business employing a workforce of thirty-five. Rolf Guigas and Roland Steinbrink, a goldsmith, collaborated on developing the first creative jewellery collections and one-offs for Gellner. The collections featured Akoya and Biwa cultured pearls combined with gold, coloured precious stones and diamonds. Yngvar Rolfsen, a friend of the family, created one-off pieces for Gellner with Biwa Dragon cultured pearls in his goldsmithing studio. These unusual freshwater cultured pearls from Lake Biwa in Japan are by nature often in bizarre forms (stick pearls) and Rolfsen embedded them in organically fluid gold components that were usually decorated with diamonds. This was design that entailed sticking to the natural forms and simply enhancing them. The Rolfsen one-off pieces

with Biwa Dragon pearls are, however, only of historical importance today. By contrast, Tove Gellner's *Fantasy necklaces* have proven their durability as an important motif. In a 1990 brochure it says: »Their form is coincidental, their essence enigmatic, the effect they create enchanting. Thus it lies in the hand of man to bring out with art the expressive properties of the pearl.« Several necklaces with gold spacers, some of them cast in the shape of pearls, were shown in the brochure. At that time, Tove Gellner was being helped in design by her daughter, Birgit Gellner-Pavlow, who had attended the Goldschmiedeschule Pforzheim from 1986 to 1988 and, after taking her journeyman's certificate, had studied in gemmology in the US.

Eveline Gellner supported her father on the organisation side and shared in his entrepreneurial duties. While still a student, Jörg Gellner had gathered experience by working abroad. Once the Wall fell, he travelled with Claus Krafzik, who had joined the firm in 1990 and soon afterwards been made head clerk with powers of attorney, to the new German state to expand the Gellner clientele to include eastern Germany. Collaboration with the Platinum Guild in the late 1980s led to the development of modern platinum jewellery set with pearls. Albrecht Münzmay, a goldsmith who is still working as a freelance designer for Gellner, was responsible for creating it. In 1992 Gellner launched an interchangeable lever catch that was a hit on the market but was soon imitated. In 1995 Heinz Gellner stepped down as head of the firm for health reasons and his son Jörg replaced him.

The 1990s were a revolutionary era in jewellery throughout Europe. The opening up of the East, globalisation and changes in values called for new concepts. In the German-speaking countries in particular modern designer jewellery was increasingly appreciated. Jörg Gellner deepened partnerships with distinguished jewellery designers outside the firm. By 1996 the change had resulted in a reductive, modern language of forms. Alongside proprietary designs by Esther Stutzmann, lines were developed and launched with the designers Michael Zobel and Edith Bischoff. Michael Zobel, who had studied with Reinhold Reiling and Klaus Ullrich and ran a goldsmithing business in Konstanz, was a Gellner client. »This lent wings to collaboration,« reports Jörg Gellner. After ten years or more, those expressive pieces are still hot items and particularly in demand in the US.

The *Pearl tension ring* designed by Norbert Mürrle, which was added to the Gellner collection in 1995, represented a fundamental innovation. Its salient feature was fastening the pearl to a minute cup of metal. »This had to do with the Japanese Akoya cultured pearl, whose layers of nacre are too thin for robust handling,« explains Jörg Gellner. Contact to the wearer's skin has been deliberately incorporated in ring design at Gellner since the *Pearl tension ring*. The Tahitian and South Sea pearls that came on the market in the 1990s are ideally suited to this treatment. The *Pearl tension ring* was developed synchronously by Norbert Mürrle for Gellner and by schmuckwerk

2007

2007

although neither firm was aware of what the other was doing. Both makers were very successful with it. In 1997 Gellner relaunched itself publicly with an updated marketing image. The advertising for both retailers and the public at large featured a male model with dark skin wearing pearl jewellery. In 1998 designs by designers Doris Zühlke and Gabriele Wilms were realised. That same year Gellner invited students from the Fachhochschule Düsseldorf to submit entries for a design competition. Many of the fledgling designers were too much in awe of cultured pearls as a natural substance to want to drill holes in them. So pearls were allowed to move freely in Kirsten Grünebaum's *Klangkinegraphen* [Sound Kinegraphs]. Stefanie von Scheven had set the natural creations in a *Perlenschwung* [Swing of Pearls]. Claudia Wieczorek accorded cultured pearls similarly sensitive treatment in three rings called *Craze*. These three designs were executed and presented at the 1998 Inhorgenta trade fair in Munich.

In 1999 Gellner showed work at Selection, a trade fair at the Essen Design Centre. This creative show featuring leading jewellery designers and firms confirmed that the Gellner team were on the right path with their design strategy. What was new that year at Gellner was collaboration with the designers Peter Birkenmeier and Sabine Brandenburg-Frank. A competition mounted with the Pforzheim Hochschule für Gestaltung in 2000 produced avant-garde designs. Natascha Rachel Reichel won first prize at it for *Lose Perlen im Seidenstrumpf* [Loose Pearls in a Silk Stocking]. The pieces were, however, as unsuccessful as they had been at past competitions in Düsseldorf. »Perhaps because they were still too unusual and new for the trade,« suggests Jörg Gellner.

Things looked entirely different with the Gellner lines created by freelance designers who had already had some market experience. The year 2000 saw the market launch of jewellery by freelance jewellery designers Viola Schwalm and Sabine Hauss as well as Marion Röthig, who was employed on a permanent basis at Gellner. In 2001 Gellner launched the *Y Collar* with cultured pearls. The most striking design concept to date for pearl jewellery was submitted by the Düsseldorf jewellery designer Monika Seitter. Her combination of Tahitian pearls with coloured plastic for the *Hot* collection is as provocative as it is appealing. The unusual mix of materials and the vibrant colours represented a break in tradition for pearl jewellery. Monika Seitter's colourful plastic strips also made the public aware of how important colour and fashion-consciousness had become in the new millennium. A year later, Gellner employed the Chinese designer Dickson Yewn on a freelance basis. His designs are far more floral in character than German design, which tends to be angular and linear. For Gellner, collaboration with this designer means bridging a gulf between two cultures. »Dickson Yewn leans more towards Art Déco, a theme that is still highly popular in Asia,« explains Jörg Gellner. By contrast, the stringently austere German design has made a

hit in the US, where Birgit Gellner-Pavlow and her husband, Randy Pavlow, have by now successfully softened up the market. In 2005 Gellner showed with their *Rough Diamond Necklaces* that they were capable of dealing with the hardest of precious stones in a highly original manner. The successful concept of working with renowned designers from outside led in 2006 to collaboration with Angela Hübel and, in 2007, with Egon Frank.

A sure sign of success in Wiernsheim is the annexe inaugurated in 2007 on the occasion of the firm's 40th anniversary. In these new rooms, Gellner reveals itself as a modern jewellery factory. In Germany alone some 200 partner retails carry the collections made by the designer label pearl jewellery specialists. On present trends, Jörg Gellner and his sister have this to say: »More than ever, jewellery expresses emotions. With their jewellery, women express how they feel about life and their own personalities.« They add that this was not so noticeably the case just ten years ago. But the need for softer and more organic forms has grown.

1998	*Perlspannringe*, Design Norbert Mürrle, Südsee-, Tahiti-, Akoya- und Süßwasser-Zuchtperlen, Gold — *Pearl tension rings*, design Norbert Mürrle, South Sea, Tahitian, Akoya and freshwater cultured pearls, gold
1999	*Draht-Collier*, Design Tove Gellner, Süsswasser-Zuchtperle — *Wire necklace*, design Tove Gellner, freshwater cultured pearl
2004	Ringe *Schmucklabor*, Design Monika Seitter, Südsee- und Tahitizuchtperlen, Gold, Farbsteine, Kunststoff — Rings *Jewellery laboratory*, design Monika Seitter, South Sea and Tahitian cultured pearls, gold, coloured stones, plastic
2007	Perlschmuck Set, Design Angela Hübel, Tahiti-Zuchtperlen, Gold, Brillanten — Pearl jewellery set, design Angela Hübel, Tahitian cultured pearls, gold, diamonds
2007	Ring und Anhänger, Design Dickson Yewn, Südsee-Zuchtperlen, Gold, Brillanten — Ring and pendant, design Dickson Yewn, South Sea cultured pearls, gold, diamonds

Jörg Gellner
Firmengründung 1967 durch Heinz Gellner in Wiernsheim. Jörg Gellner geboren 1968. Seit 1995 Firmenleitung.

Jörg Gellner
Firm founded by Heinz Gellner in Wiernsheim in 1967. Jörg Gellner born in Wiernsheim in 1968. Since 1995 head of firm.

Der Reiz des »Echten«, in jedem Sinne, besteht darin,
dass es mehr ist als seine unmittelbare Erscheinung, die
es mit dem Falsifikat teilt.

Georg Simmel, 1908

The attraction of »authenticity« consists in every sense
in the circumstance that it is more than its immediate
appearance, which it shares with what is fake.

Georg Simmel, 1908

1978

1986

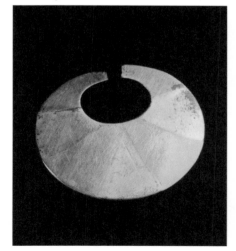

1978   Platinanzeige mit Halsschmuck von Meister, Platin — Advertisement for
         platinum with necklace by Meister, platinum

1986   Brosche, Wettbewerb Perspektiven, Simon Peter Eiber, Platin, Gold
         — Brooch, Competition Perspektiven, Simon Peter Eiber, platinum, gold

         Etwa 2000 Jahre altes, indianisches Nasenornament aus Chimu, Peru,
         Platin, Gold — About 2000-year-old indian nose ornament from Chimu, Peru,
         platinum, gold

Die Bedeutung von Platin für das moderne Schmuck-Design — The importance of platinum to modern designer jewellery

Platin Gilde International

Seit der modernen Schmuckentwicklung Ende des 19. Jahrhunderts bemühten sich Künstler und Designer, »demokratische«, preiswerte Materialien einzusetzen. Kostbares galt vielen als anrüchig. Diese Ideologisierung der Schmuckmaterialien gehört heute der Vergangenheit an. Das Material, ob ganz billig oder sehr teuer, soll der Gestaltungsidee entsprechen und »ehrlich« eingesetzt werden, vor allem nicht in Billig-Legierungen. Nicht unwesentlich dabei war die Wiedereinführung von Platin im Jahr 1976. Sie wurde in den 1980er Jahren zum »Katalysator« für moderne Designideen – ganz besonders im deutschen Sprachraum.

Bis Ende des 19. Jahrhunderts spielte Platin in der Schmuckgeschichte kaum eine Rolle. Doch wurde das natürlich weiße Metall schon um 1000 v. Chr. von den Inkas und später auch in Ägypten in kleinen Mengen im Schmuck und in Gefäßen verarbeitet. Für die spanischen Konquistadoren war platina, das »kleine, weniger wertvolle Silber«, lange Zeit ein Problem. Bis etwa 1740 behinderte es den Goldabbau in Südamerika. Grund war der hohe Schmelzpunkt von 1772° Celsius.

Um 1900 waren die Techniken zur Reingewinnung so weit entwickelt, dass französische Juweliere das weiße Edelmetall in der Belle Epoque einsetzten. So fertigte Cartier 1895 erste Platinkreationen mit großem Erfolg. Zuvor war Platin hauptsächlich für wissenschaftliche und technische Zwecke verwendet worden. Die große Bedeutung von Platin im Schmuck des Art Déco war zum einen auf die kühle Eleganz der Farbe zurückzuführen. Sie harmonierte mit den Diamanten und Perlen, ergab effektvolle Kontraste zu Farbsteinen, Korallen oder Onyx und ermöglichte dekorative und surrealistische Wirkungen. Nicht zuletzt war die hohe Festigkeit und Dehnbarkeit ideal für die Fassungen der prächtigen Juwelen.

Nach dem Zweiten Weltkrieg geriet Platinschmuck weitgehend in Vergessenheit. 1975 bildete der Bergbaukonzern Rustenburg Platinum Mines in Johannesburg eine Arbeitsgruppe, um es wieder in den Schmuckmarkt einzuführen. 1976 wurde die Platin Gilde International in Deutschland gegründet. Führende Schmuckhersteller und Juweliere beteiligten sich an der Initiative. Die erste Werbekampagne mit dem Slogan »Zu wissen, es ist Platin...« startete 1978. Die Bemühung, mit modernen Formen in Platin ein anspruchsvolles Publikum anzusprechen, war von Beginn an sichtbar.

Im Februar 1979 übernahm Dieter von Loe die Leitung der Platin Gilde International. Er diskutierte zunächst intensiv mit namhaften Herstellern, wie das vergessene Schmuckmetall zu gestalten war und im Markt positioniert werden konnte. Im Gespräch mit Ursula Exner von Niessing im März 1979 sei ein Funke übergesprungen, berichtet von Loe: »Eine erste schemenhafte Idee vom Wesen, vom Image des Platins entstand.« Einiges war bereits vorgegeben: Platin war weitgehend unbekannt und viel seltener als Gold. Es konnte damit als Inbegriff des Besonderen gelten. Platin war kaum mit feudalen Traditionen und archaischen Mythen verbunden, sondern mit modernen technischen und wissenschaftlichen Erkenntnissen. Platin hatte in der experimentierfreudigen Zeit der 1920er Jahre seine erste Blütezeit erlebt, einer für die moderne Kunst und die Emanzipation der Frau bedeutenden Epoche. All das sprach für eine zeitgemäße Formensprache. Anspruchsvoll in der Verarbeitung und mit hohem spezifischem Gewicht von 21,45 g/cm3 wird Platin mit einem Feingehalt von 950/000 nahezu rein verarbeitet. Daraus resultiert ein vergleichsweise hoher Preis. Um ihn zu rechtfertigen, waren die Schmuck-Manufakturen und Goldschmiedeateliers aufgefordert, überzeugende Design-Konzepte zu entwickeln. Schließlich war Platin auch mit seiner unprätentiösen, neutralen Farbe wie geschaffen für das Schmuck-Design der Moderne. Nicht zuletzt sollte er sich formal von traditionellem Schmuck in Weißgold unterscheiden. Dieter von Loe: »Es gab nur einen Stil für Platin-Schmuck: den zeitgenössischen Designstil.«

Bald entstanden die ersten Platin-Studios. Ihre für die damalige Zeit moderne Innenarchitektur unterschied sich deutlich von den traditionellen Juweliergeschäften. Regelmäßig erschienen modern fotografierte und gestaltete Platin-Editionen. 1986 wurde der Gestaltungswettbewerb Perspektiven für Platinschmuck ausgeschrieben. In der Jury waren Giampaolo Babetto, Padua, Hermann Jünger, München, und Björn Weckström, Helsinki. Im Begleittext dazu schreibt Bazon Brock über den neuen Qualitätsanspruch im Schmuck: »Dabei kommt es in erster Linie nicht mehr auf ›die Kostbarkeit‹ des Schmucks an, sondern auf die gestalterische und konzeptuelle Aussagekraft der Objekte.«

Nicht zuletzt angesichts des gestiegenen Preises hat sich heute »die Spreu vom Weizen« unter den Herstellern von Platin-Schmuck getrennt. Firmen ohne eigenständige Designentwicklung und Positionierung im Topsegment haben das Thema wieder aufgegeben. Aufgrund seiner hohen Exklusivität ist Platin inzwischen auch im tradierten Luxusschmuck vertreten. Jedoch hat die Verwendung von Platin bei führenden Manufakturen und Ateliers im deutschsprachigen Raum das Profil geschärft. Nicht wenige Entwicklungen aus dem kostbarsten aller Schmuckmetalle zählen inzwischen zu den Klassikern des modernen Schmuck-Designs.

E — Since jewellery took a turn towards modernism in the late 19th century, artists and designers have striven to use »democratic,« affordable materials. Precious ones were regarded by many as unprincipled. Today the ideological bias in the choice of materials for jewellery belongs to the past. The material, be it very cheap or very expensive, is supposed to correspond to the design conception and, therefore, be used in »unadulterated« form and in particular not in cheap alloys. The reintroduction of platinum in 1976 contributed substantially to this development. During the 1980s it was the »catalyst« for modern ideas in design – and particularly in the German-speaking countries.

»Moderne, zeitgenössische Gestaltung gewann im
Schmuck durch das Auftreten von Platin die Bekanntheit
und die Bedeutung, die sie verdiente.«

Dieter von Loe, 1997

»Modern contemporary design gained in jewellery
the recognition and significance it deserved through the
emergence of platinum.«

Dieter von Loe, 1997

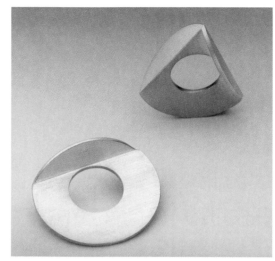

1986

Platinum played hardly any role at all in jewellery until the late 19th century. Nevertheless, this naturally white metal was worked in small quantities as early as 1000 BC by the Incas and later also in Egypt in the making of both jewellery and vessels. For the Spanish Conquistadores, platina, »the lesser, less valuable silver« long posed a serious problem. Until about 1740 platinum hampered the goldmining industry in South America. The reason was the high melting-point of platinum: 1772° C.

By 1900 techniques for refining platinum had advanced to such a degree that French jewellers could take advantage of the white noble metal in the Belle Époque. Cartier's launch of their first platinum creations in 1895 was highly successful. Before that, platinum had been used mainly for scientific and technical purposes. The enormous importance of platinum in Art Déco jewellery was due, on the one hand, to the cool elegance of its colour. It harmonised with white diamonds and pearls while providing stunning contrasts with coloured stones such as coral and onyx so that decorative, even surreal, effects could be achieved with it. On the other hand, its resistance to oxidation and to most chemical reagents as well as its ductility made platinum ideal for use in secure settings to hold magnificent precious stones.

After the Second World War platinum fell into disuse in jewellery-making. In 1975 Rustenburg Platinum Mines, a mining consortium in Johannesburg formed a study group to reintroduce the metal to the jewellery market. In 1976 Platin Gilde International was founded in Germany. Leading jewellery-makers and jewellers took part in the drive. The first German advertising campaign was launched in 1978 featuring a slogan that translates as »It's platinum, you know … «. From the outset it was obvious that platinum worked in modern forms had to be made palatable to a discerning upscale target market.

In February 1979 Dieter von Loe became head of Platin Gilde International. He started out conducting intensive discussions with reputable jewellery-makers on how the forgotten jewellery metal might be used in design and positioned on the market. In a conversation with Ursula Exner at Niessing in March 1979, a spark was lit, as Loe explains it: »A first, sketchy idea of the essence, the image, of platinum emerged.« There were, of course, some givens to be reckoned with: platinum was largely unknown and much rarer than gold, hence it could be marketed as the epitome of discerning chic. Platinum was scarcely, if at all, associated with feudal tradition and archaic mystique but instead connoted modern technology and scientific know-how. Platinum was in its heyday in the 1920s when experimentation was the order of the day in an era so important to modern art and the emancipation of women. All those factors argued for a contemporary formal idiom. Difficult to work and with a high specific gravity of 21.45 g/cm3, platinum is used in an almost pure state, as an alloy with a fineness of 950/000. As a result, platinum is relatively costly. To justify the expense of using

platinum, jewellery manufactories and goldsmithing studios were asked to develop convincing design concepts. After all, platinum, with its unfussy, neutral colour, was ideal for modern jewellery design. Finally, it was to be used in jewellery that differed formally from the traditional offerings in white gold. Dieter von Loe: »There was just one style for platinum jewellery: the contemporary designer style.« It was not long before the first platinum studios saw the light of day. The interior design of these vehicles for the noble metal contrasted sharply with conventional jewellery retail outlets. Editions in platinum featuring leading-edge design and advertised with modern photography were regularly launched. In 1986, Perspektiven, a design competition just for platinum jewellery, was inaugurated. The jury represented a roll of distinguished names in modern jewellery: Giampaolo Babetto, Padua, Hermann Jünger, Munich, and Björn Weckström, Helsinki. Lifestyle pundit and fashion arbiter Bazon Brock was succinct on the new demand for quality in jewellery: »The ›expensiveness‹ of jewellery no longer matters in the first instance; what does matter is the effectiveness of the design and the conceptual statement made by such objects.«

Finally, the rise in commodity prices has »separated the wheat from the chaff« among designers of platinum jewellery. Companies without proprietary design development departments and a secure position in the top market segment have opted out of platinum. Due to its high exclusivity ratings, platinum is in the meantime represented in traditional luxury jewellery. Nevertheless, the use of platinum by leading jewellery manufactories and studios in the German-speaking countries has sharpened its profile to cutting-edge. Quite a few developments in this most expensive of all jewellery metals have become modern designer-jewellery classics.

1986	Ringe, Wettbewerb Perspektiven, Ingrid Wriedt, Platin, Gold — Rings, competition Perspektiven, Ingrid Wriedt, platinum, gold
1988	Armschmuck von Ehinger-Schwarz, Platin, Gold, Diamanten — Bangle by Ehinger-Schwarz, platinum, gold, diamonds
1991	Armschmuck, Niessing, Platin, Gold — Bangle, Niessing, platinum, gold
2005	Platinarmreif *Spirale*, Design Sabine Brandenburg-Frank für IsabelleFa — Platinum bangle *Spiral*, design Sabine Brandenburg-Frank for IsabelleFa
1988	Halschmuck, Bunz Collection, Platin, Gold, Diamanten — Necklaces, Bunz Collection, platinum, gold, diamonds

1988

1991

2005

1988

1980

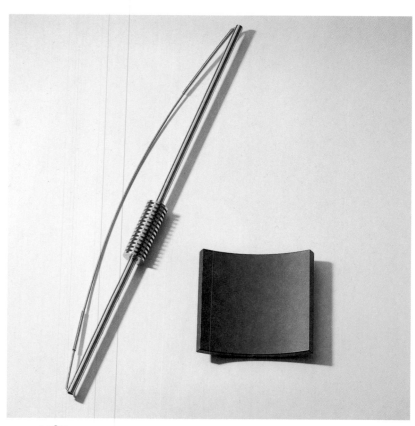

1985

1980   Broschen, brünierter Stahl, Edelstahl — Brooches, bronzed steel,
        stainless steel

1986   Broschen, Stahl, Silber, Aluminium — Brooches, steel, silver, aluminium

1990   Ketten cn/dh, Gold, Edelstahl, Titan, Silber— Chains cn/dh, gold,
        stainless steel, titanium, silver

1985   Bogennadel und Brosche, Stahl, Aluminium eloxiert — Curved pin and brooch,
        steel, anodized aluminium

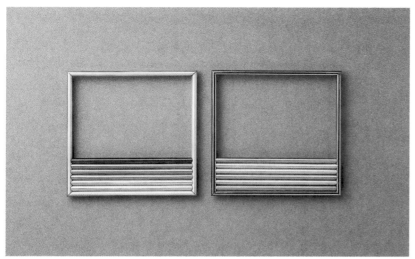

1986

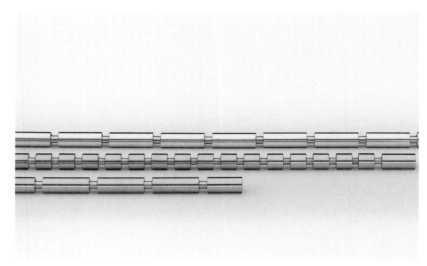

1990

Carl Dau

Es gibt Geschichten im Schmuckdesign der Moderne, die ohne eine große Liebe nie entstanden wären. Wie diejenige von Carl Dau. In Hessen und Hamburg aufgewachsen, hatte er zunächst den Beruf des Seemanns ergriffen. Damit konnte er jedoch einer Germanistikstudentin aus gutem Hause, für die er sich brennend interessierte, keine Perspektive bieten. So entschloss sich der Seefahrer im Alter von 23 Jahren, nochmals neu anzufangen. Es sollte etwas mit Gestaltung sein, und so entschied sich Dau für eine Lehre als Goldschmied. Der zweite Berufsstart war mehrfach von Erfolg gekrönt. Die Studentin wurde seine Frau Sabine und Carl Dau beeinflusste nachhaltig das moderne Schmuckdesign der 1980er Jahre.

Bereits die Lehre ab 1966 in der Werkstatt Scriba in Gießen war ein Glücksfall. Sein Meister war nur zehn Jahre älter als er und hatte an der Werkkunstschule in Offenbach die Prinzipien moderner Gestaltung verinnerlicht. Mehr als durch dessen Schmuck wurde der technisch versierte Lehrling aber durch das Kirchensilber, das Scriba fertigte, für klare Formen sensibilisiert. An der Zeichenakademie in Hanau, 1970–1972, begann sich Dau vom »handwerklichen Prozess als Selbstzweck« zu befreien. In dieser Zeit lernte er auch die Arbeiten von Schmuckgestaltern wie Friedrich Becker, Reinhold Reiling oder Emmy van Leersum kennen, die im Deutschen Goldschmiedehaus Hanau gezeigt wurden. Um die Stücke in die Hand nehmen zu können, meldete sich Carl Dau während seiner Schulzeit oft freiwillig, um bei den Ausstellungen zu helfen. »Es war für mich zu Beginn der 70er Jahre das große Augenöffnen«, berichtet der Schmuckdesigner.

Nach seiner Meisterprüfung in Hanau studierte Carl Dau von 1972 bis 1975 an der Hochschule der Bildenden Künste in Berlin, anschließend zwei weitere Jahre Industrial Design bei Professor Nick Roericht. Dieser hatte seine Designausbildung an der Ulmer Hochschule für Gestaltung absolviert und wurde vor allem durch seine Stapeltassen bekannt. In einigen frühen Arbeiten des Berliners ist noch ein gewisser Einfluss von Reinhold Reiling sichtbar. Aber bereits im Gründungsjahr seiner Firma 1980 zeigt sich deutlich der eigene Stil. Von Beginn an entstanden in der ersten Werkstatt in Berlin-Zehlendorf Stücke aus industriell vorgefertigten Teilen und nicht wie üblich im traditionell handwerklichen Prozess des Gießens, Schmiedens, Lötens und Polierens. Dau übertrug seine Kenntnisse im modernen Produktdesign konsequent auf das traditionsbehaftete Medium Schmuck. Es ging ihm nicht wie vielen anderen bedeutenden Goldschmieden jener Jahre um die Kunst des Machens, sondern um die Freude an der Gestaltung und um das perfekte Ergebnis.

Carl Dau leistete auch Pionierarbeit, was die Akzeptanz von modernem Serienschmuck anbelangte. Anfang der 1980er Jahre hatte die Serie für anspruchsvolle Schmuckmacher noch einen schlechten Klang, erinnert er sich. »So was macht man nur zum Gelderwerb«, hieß es. Wer unter den Schmuckgestaltern etwas auf sich hielt, fertigte Unikate. Serien entstanden in dieser Zeit für den täglichen Broterwerb oft anonym. Doch Handwerkskunst war nie das Thema von Carl Dau, obwohl diese zu Beginn der 1980er Jahre noch einen großen Zuspruch hatte, zum Beispiel auf der Frankfurter Frühjahrsmesse, auf der er erstmals seine minimalistische Broschen, Ketten und Ringe vorstellte.

Alle Stücke von Dau basieren auf dem »Reiz klarer Formen, auf der Schönheit logischer Konzepte und Konstruktionen sowie ihrer raffinierten Details.« Dass die Schmuckstücke von Carl Dau so klar blieben, ist elementar in seinem Wesen begründet. »Mir war die Klarheit in den Dingen wichtig. Jede Einzelform muss deutlich identifizierbar sein und sich von anderen Formen abheben.« Von dieser Gestaltungsposition lässt sich eine deutliche Linie herstellen zum Schmuck der holländischen Schmuckgestalterin Emmy van Leersum und zu den Avantgardisten der 1920er Jahre in Frankreich und Deutschland.

Bis Anfang 1980 gestaltete Carl Dau auch minimalistische Wandobjekte. In verkleinerter Form entstanden 1983 Broschen, mit denen er noch im gleichen Jahr in Berlin seinen ersten Staatspreis für Schmuck gewann. 1986 folgte der Hessische Staatspreis und 1987 der von Baden-Württemberg. Die Broschen von 1983 leben vom minimalen Reiz, der sich durch die Aufreihung mehrerer Röhrchen in unterschiedlichen Materialien ergibt. Der schlichte Kontrast der Metalle reichte Carl Dau auch bei vielen anderen Arbeiten, um Wirkungen von intensiver meditativer Kraft zu erzielen. »Bei vielen Entwürfen war ich so schnell von einer spannungsvollen Form begeistert, dass ich einfach aufhören musste«, erzählt Dau. Deshalb sind seine Schmuckstücke meist leicht zu verstehen. Doch bei näherer Betrachtung wird nicht selten eine konstruktive Raffinesse sichtbar. »Komplexe Gedanken manifestieren sich in scheinbar einfachen Lösungen«, ist Dau überzeugt. Nicht zuletzt darin unterscheidet sich sein Schmuck von billigen Nachahmungen, die Ende der 1990er Jahre den Markt überschwemmten. Die Konzentration auf reduzierte Schlichtheit brachte dem Berliner den Ruf des herausragenden Minimalisten im Schmuck der Gegenwart ein. Der Umzug 1996 in ein modernes Firmengebäude, in dem zehn Mitarbeiter seitdem die modernen Schmucklinien fertigen, gibt dieser Philosophie den passenden architektonischen Rahmen.

Nach der Jahrtausendwende wurden die Schmuckserien des Berliners deutlich farbiger und emotionaler. Er wolle damit seinen Kunden mehr Anlass zu spontaner Freude und zum Träumen geben: »Mein Schmuck wird weicher«, brachte er die Entwicklung auf einen Punkt. Der neue Stil offenbarte sich erstmals 2004 durch farbig lackierte Kugelketten und Ringe und fand ein Jahr später seine Fortsetzung in der Serie *monochrom*. Quadratische oder runde geometrische Körper aus warmem Gold umschließen verschiedenfarbige Flächen, deren Reflektionen sich sanft im goldenen Innenraum spiegeln. Es sind Schmuckobjekte voller Leuchtkraft und Lebendigkeit, die deutliche Bezüge zu den Kunstobjekten des amerikanischen Minimalisten

1998

2000

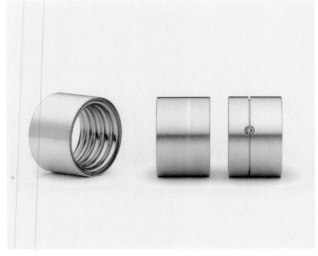

2002

Donald Judd aufweisen. Untrennbar bleibt jedoch minimalistischer Schmuck aus Edelstahl mit dem Namen Carl Dau verbunden. 1980 gab es nur Schmuckkünstler wie Friedrich Becker oder Peter Skubic, die Edelstahl einsetzten. Dau verwendet das industrielle Material, weil ihn von Beginn an hauptsächlich die Idee und Aussage sowie die Form des Schmuckstücks interessiert hat und kaum dessen Materialwert. Er setzt Edelstahl so selbstverständlich ein, wie es in Stühlen von Mart Stam und Charles Eames, in hochwertigen Bestecken und Kugelschreibern Verwendung findet. Edelstahl ist für Dau auch deshalb ein bevorzugtes Thema, weil ihm industrielle Techniken wie Drehen und Fräsen für seinen seriellen Schmuck sehr gelegen kommen.

Schmuck von Carl Dau stellt bis heute für puristisch orientierte Frauen ebenso wie für designorientierte Männer ein zeitgemäßes Ausdrucksmittel mit Klassikerqualitäten dar. 2007 zog sich Carl Dau im Alter von 65 Jahren als Inhaber in die Position des Designers zurück. Dabei zeigte sich, dass seine Formensprache und sein Image so interessant erschienen, um daraus eine Designmarke weiterzuentwickeln.

E — There are some events in modern designer jewellery design that would not have happened were it not for a love story. Like Carl Dau's story. He grew up in Hesse and Hamburg and at first worked as a merchant seaman. As such, however, he could not offer any prospects to a student of German literature from a good family. So the mariner decided to start over again at the age of twenty-three. It was to be something to do with design and so Dau opted to train as a goldsmith. His second career was crowned with success in several respects. The student became his wife Sabine and Carl Dau went on to exert a lasting influence on 1980s jewellery design.

He was lucky even in the choice of the Scriba workshop for his apprenticeship, starting in 1966. His master, who was only ten years older than Dau, had absorbed the principles of modern design at the Werkkunstschule in Offenbach. The technically adept apprentice, however, was initially more receptive to the liturgical silver with its crisp forms that Scriba made than he was to Scriba jewellery. At the Zeichenakademie in Hanau (1970–1972), Dau began to emancipate himself from the »crafts process as an end in itself«. During that period he also became familiar with the work of such stellar jewellery designers as Friedrich Becker, Reinhold Reiling and Emmy van Leersum, which was shown at the Deutsches Goldschmiedehaus Hanau. In order to be able to pick up the pieces and examine them closely, Carl Dau often volunteered while still a student to help out with exhibitions. »The early '70s were a real eye-opener for me,« reports the jewellery designer.

After taking his master craftsman's certificate in Hanau, Carl Dau studied at the Hochschule der Bildenden Künste in Berlin from 1972 until 1975, followed by two more years spent studying Industrial Design under Professor Nick Roericht. Roericht had graduated in Design at the Ulm Hochschule

für Gestaltung and was known for his stackable tableware. Furthermore, the influence of Reinhold Reiling was also apparent to some extent in Dau's early work. But by the time Dau founded his own firm in 1980, his own distinctive style was clearly manifest. From the outset, his pieces were produced from industrially made pre-fabricated elements rather than by traditional crafts processes such as casting, beating, soldering and polishing in his first workshop in Berlin-Zehlendorf. Dau consistently transferred his knowledge of modern product design to the traditional medium of jewellery. Unlike so many other leading goldsmiths in those years, he was concerned less with the art of making than he was with design and achieving perfect results.

As far as general acceptance of modern mass-produced jewellery is concerned, Carl Dau was a ground-breaking pioneer. In the early 1980s, mass production still had negative overtones for ambitious jewellery-makers. »That's only done to make money,« was what the people said. Any jewellery designer worth his salt made only one-off pieces. Mass-production of jewellery done to earn a living was often kept strictly anonymous. Craftsmanship, however, was never Carl Dau's chief concern although it was still much in demand in the early 1980s. At the spring Frankfurt trade fair, he launched his first Minimalist brooches, chains and rings.

All pieces Dau makes are based on the »attraction of clear forms, on the beauty of logical concepts and construction as well as sophisticated details«. That Carl Dau's jewellery has remained so stringently clear is grounded at an elemental level in his personality. »Clarity in things was important to me. Every individual form must be clearly identifiable and distinguishable from other forms.« From this stance on design, a line can be drawn to the pieces created by the Dutch jewellery designer Emmy van Leersum and the 1920s avant-garde in both France and Germany.

Until the early 1980s, Carl Dau also designed Minimalist wall objects. On a much smaller scale were the brooches he designed in 1983, with which he won his first State Prize for jewellery that same year. It was followed in 1986 by the Hessian State Prize and in 1987 by the Baden-Württemberg State Prize. The 1983 Dau brooches are informed by a Minimalist quality that makes the paratactic arrangement of small tubes in a variety of materials alluring. The simple contrasts provided by metals alone has been all Carl Dau has needed to achieve intensely meditative effects in many other works. »With many designs, I was so quickly enraptured with exciting forms that I simply had to stop there,« as Dau tells it. That is why his pieces are usually easy to understand. However, closer scrutiny often reveals sophisticated construction. »Complex thinking is manifested in seemingly simple solutions,« is Dau's conviction. And therein lies the difference between his jewellery and the cheap imitations that flooded the market in the late 1990s. Concentrating on reduction and simplicity earned the Berlin designer the reputation of being the leading Minimalist in contemporary jewellery. The

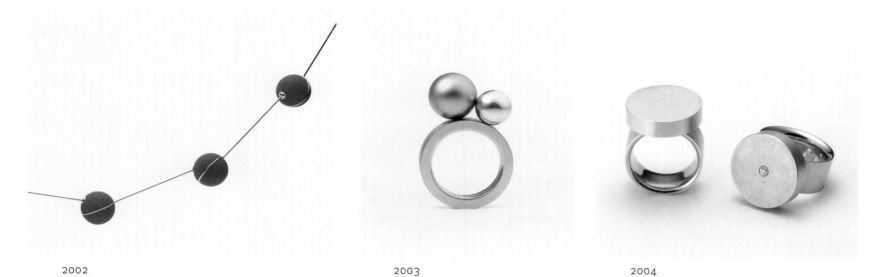

2002   2003   2004

move in 1996 to a modern company building, in which a workforce of ten have been making the modern lines in jewellery since, has provided his philosophy with the suitable architectural setting. Since the turn of the millennium, the Berlin designer's lines in jewellery have become noticeably more colourful and emotional in appeal. With this new approach he wanted to give his clientele more scope for spontaneous enjoyment and dreaming: »My jewellery is getting more gentle,« is how he has summed up this development. The new style featuring ball chains and rings in coloured lacquer was launched in 2004. The follow-up a year later was the monochrom line. Square or round geometric shapes of warm gold encompass surfaces in various colours, softly reflected in a gold inner space. These are vibrant jewellery objects that glow with life, revealing obvious affinities with the large-scale art objects by the late American Minimalist Donald Judd. Minimalist jewellery made of stainless steel, however, is what remains indissolubly linked with the name Carl Dau. The only artists in jewellery working in stainless steel in 1980 were the likes of Friedrich Becker and Peter Skubic. Dau uses the industrial material because it was the idea behind a piece of jewellery and the statement it made as well as form that interested him from the outset rather than material value. He takes the use of stainless steel as much for granted as Mart Stam and Charles Eames did in making their chairs or manufacturers of high quality cutlery or ballpoint pens have always done. Stainless steel is Dau's material of choice because industrial techniques such as turning and milling are eminently suited to his mass-produced jewellery.

To this day, jewellery by Carl Dau represents to men and women who are purists about design a contemporary mode of expression with classic qualities. In 2007 Carl Dau stepped down at the age of sixty-five as head of the business to devote himself to design. The result has been that his language of forms and his image have remained so interesting that a designer label has continued to evolve from them.

1998	Armschmuck, Gold, Edelstahl — Bracelet, gold, stainless steel
2000	Armreif, Edelstahl, Gold — Bangle, stainless steel, gold
2002	Ringe, Edelstahl, Gold, Brillant — Rings, stainless steel, gold, diamond
2002	Halsschmuck, Edelstahl, Leichtmetall Dural, Mattlack — Necklace, stainless steel, light alloy duralumin, matt lacquer
2003	Ringe, Edelstahl, Gold — Rings, stainless steel, gold
2004	Ringe, Edelstahl, Gold, Brillant — Rings, stainless steel, gold, diamond

Carl Dau
Geboren 1952 in Hamburg, 1972–1977 Hochschule der Bildenden Künste Berlin. Ateliergründung 1980 in Berlin.

Carl Dau
Born in Hamburg in 1952, 1972–1977 Hochschule der Bildenden Künste Berlin. Founded studio in Berlin in 1980.

1972   1988   1997

Fillner

In der Hertensteinstrasse 28 in Luzern ist ein auffallendes Angebot wichtiger Schmuck-Designer und Manufakturen der Moderne vertreten. Dies ist das Verdienst von Ruth und Manfred Fillner sowie ihrer Tochter Cornelia Burri-Fillner. Das Schweizer Familienunternehmen hat aber auch mit seiner eigenen Schmuckfertigung einige bemerkenswerte Beiträge zur modernen Schmuckkultur geleistet.

Manfred Fillner wurde 1940 in Danzig geboren. Nach einer Goldschmiedelehre in Schwäbisch Gmünd begann er 1961 seine Tätigkeit in Schweizer Schmuckfirmen, machte eine Ausbildung als Diamantgutachter. Er lernte seine Frau Ruth kennen, die ihn zum Bleiben veranlasste. Ab 1968 leitete Manfred Fillner die Produktion der relo-design-Kollektion in Renens bei Lausanne. Nach der Übernahme durch Höfflin & Lüth wurde 1972 die relo-design ag in Luzern gegründet. Manfred und Ruth Fillner wurden Geschäftsführer. Der Goldschmied und Designer Carl Elsener aus Urdorf bei Zürich war hauptsächlich für die Gestaltung von relo-design zuständig. Er gewann mehrere Diamonds International Awards und zahlreiche andere Schmuckwettbewerbe. Manfred und Ruth Fillner sind sich einig, dass er zu den kreativsten Schmuck- und Uhrendesignern seiner Zeit gehört.

1980 übernahm das Ehepaar die Schmuckfirma mit Elsener als Partner. Zum ersten großen Erfolg von Fillner & Elsener wurde der von Carl Elsener entwickelte Ohrschmuck mit neuartigem Klicksystem, das 1984 patentiert wurde. Durch ein Scharnier können Ohrringe sehr eng anliegend getragen werden, und zwar ohne dass die Befestigungsstifte zu sehen sind. Das Klicksystem ist inzwischen Allgemeingut geworden und aus dem Schmuck von heute nicht mehr wegzudenken. 1987 schied Carl Elsener als Teilhaber aus. Es war die Geburtsstunde von Fillner Swiss Design. In der anspruchsvollen Atelierproduktion in Stans bei Luzern arbeiteten bald auch die Tochter Cornelia Burri-Fillner und ihr Mann Urs Burri als Goldschmied und Atelierchef mit. Von Beginn an entstanden im Dialog mit externen Designern innovative Schmuckserien. Manfred Fillner konnte seine exzellenten Kenntnisse in der Produktentwicklung und seine Erfahrung mit Juwelieren, die er regelmäßig besuchte, einbringen. Auch der Ohrschmuck mit dem Klicksystem wurde durch zahlreiche Varianten ergänzt.

Ende der 1980er Jahre gestaltete der Designer Urs Meier einen Armreif sowie eine Anstecknadel für Fillner. Feine, tiefe Einschnitte gaben ihm Form und Flexibilität. Zeitgleich entstanden die hohl gedrückte Spitzspange und ähnlich konzipierte Ringe. Die volumige Außenseite in mattiertem Platin ist durch einen Falz mit der inneren polierten Goldschiene verbunden. Das Konzept wurde auch umgekehrt realisiert, mit mattem Gold außen und poliertem inneren Platinreif. Jeder Armreif erfordert in der Umsetzung eine extrem hohe technische Perfektion. Die Spitzspange zählt heute zu den Klassikern des modernen Schmuckdesigns. 1989 wurde der Armreif zur »Eintrittskarte« für die Messekooperation von Fillner mit Niessing, Pur und Ehinger-Schwarz. Die Standgemeinschaft war mehr als ein Jahrzehnt auf den Messen in Basel, München, Frankfurt, Essen und Leipzig vertreten. Sie war dabei der Treffpunkt des modernen deutschen Schmuck-Designs, das durch Fillner einen Schweizer Akzent bekam. In der Ausstellung Schmuck Europa 90 – Beispiele zeitgenössischer Schmuckgestaltung zeigte Fillner auf der Frankfurter Messe 1990 die Seidenschnüre der Textilgestalterin Erika Wienholdt. Sie wurden in dem Atelier der Künstlerin in Aachen handbemalt und bei Fillner zu Halsschmuck weiter verarbeitet. Mit den farbenprächtigen Stücken gelang der Schweizer Firma ein überwältigender Erfolg. 1994 bewegte Fillner mit seinem Männerschmuck, Design Martin Ammann, das starke Geschlecht zum Schmucktragen. Die Armbänder mit wellenförmigen und geraden Platingliedern sind seitlich durch Goldschrauben verbunden. Der Schraubenlook erscheint auch in Ringen und Anstecknadeln.

1995 eröffnete das Familienunternehmen in Luzern ein modernes Schmuckgeschäft in dem 300 Jahre alten Haus Pfyffer-von-Whyer in der Hertensteinstrasse 28. Hier werden seitdem die Kollektionen führender Manufakturen und Schmuck-Designer der Gegenwart in modernem Ambiente präsentiert. 1999 erfüllte sich Fillner einen weiteren Lebenstraum. Beide Familien zogen in ihr Dreigenerationenhaus im Stanser Rosenweg. Denn Cornelia Burri-Fillner und ihr Mann Urs haben mit ihren Kindern Vanessa und Kevin für weiteren Nachwuchs gesorgt. Da auch noch das Goldschmiedeatelier mit Verwaltung Platz fand, konnte der Traum vom Leben und Arbeiten unter einem Dach verwirklicht werden. Zusammen mit dem Schmuckgestalter Malte Meinck aus Bad Kissingen entwickelte Fillner ab 1999 die Schmuckserie Harlekin. In geometrisch strengen Ringformen und Anhängern sorgt ein wie Opal schillernder Kunststoff für erfrischende Lebendigkeit. Das jüngste Schmuckprojekt, das Fillner seit 2003 verfolgt, trägt den Namen Flower Leaves. Die Ringserie entstand ebenfalls im Dialog zwischen Fillner und Meinck. Zum Teil werden für die gefühlvoll geformten Stücke in Gold und Platin mit verschiedenen Farbedelsteinen Schliffe von Tom Munsteiner verwendet. »Wir haben uns nie als Avantgarde verstanden«, sagt Manfred Fillner. »Wir wollten immer die Klassik mit der Moderne verbinden.« Gerade damit hat das Familienunternehmen für die moderne Schmuckkultur viel erreicht.

E — At 28 Hertensteinstrasse, Lucerne, a stunning array of pieces by important modern jewellery designers and manufactories is displayed. Ruth and Manfred Fillner and their daughter, Cornelia Burri-Fillner, can be credited with this achievement. The Swiss family business has also contributed substantially with the jewellery it makes itself to the modern jewellery culture.

Born in Danzig in 1940, Manfred Fillner served a goldsmith's apprenticeship in Schwäbisch Gmünd before beginning in 1961 to work for Swiss jewellery firms. He also trained as a diamond appraiser. He met his wife, Ruth,

1994   1999   2002

who persuaded him to stay in Switzerland. From 1968 Manfred Fillner was production manager of the relo-design collection in Renens near Lausanne. After relo-design was taken over by Höfflin & Lüth, it was relaunched in 1972 in Lucerne as relo-design ag. Manfred and Ruth Fillner were managing directors. Carl Elsener, a goldsmith and designer from Urdorf near Zurich, was responsible mainly for design at relo-design. He won several Diamonds International Awards as well as numerous other jewellery competitions. Manfred and Ruth Fillner agree that Elsener was one of the most creative jewellery and watch designers of his day.

In 1980 the Fillners took over the jewellery firm with Elsener as a partner. The first great success celebrated by Fillner & Elsener was the novel Click system, developed by Carl Elsener and patented in 1984. A hinge makes it possible to wear ear-hugging earrings without pins or studs showing. By now the Click system is in universal use and today's jewellery is unthinkable without it.

In 1987 Carl Elsener gave up his partnership in the firm. This step led to the birth of Fillner Swiss Design. The Fillners' daughter, Cornelia Burri-Fillner, works in the upscale studio production at Stans near Lucerne and her husband, Urs Burri, a goldsmith, is head of the studio. From the outset, Fillner Swiss Design embarked on a dialogue with outside designers of innovative jewellery collections. Manfred Fillner was able to make good use of his excellent knowledge of product development and his personal experience of jewellers, whom he visited regularly. Numerous variants were added to the range of ear jewellery featuring the Click system.

In the late 1980s, the designer Urs Meier created a bangle and a pin for Fillner. Fine, deep incisions lent the pieces shape and flexibility. At the same time the hollow compressed *Spitzspange* bangle and rings conceived on similar lines were launched. The voluminous exterior of matt platinum is linked by a slide with the polished gold track inside. The concept has been realised in reverse, with matt gold outside and an inner band of polished platinum. Making each of these bangles exacts a high degree of technical skill. The *Spitzspange* is today regarded as a classic of modern jewellery design. In 1989 the bangle was the »ticket for admission« to trade fair collaboration between Fillner and Niessing, Pur and Ehinger-Schwarz. The collective stand was represented for more than a decade at the trade fairs in Basel, Munich, Frankfurt, Essen and Leipzig. It became a meeting place for modern German jewellery design, which, through Fillner, also had a Swiss touch. At Schmuck Europa 90 – Beispiele zeitgenössischer Schmuckgestaltung, an exhibition at the Frankfurt Fair in 1990, Fillner featured silk cords by the textile designer Erika Wienholdt. They were hand-painted in the artist's Aachen studio and made at Fillner into neck jewellery. The Swiss firm was overwhelmingly successful with the colourful pieces. In 1994 Fillner overcame male reluctance to wear jewellery with pieces designed by Martin Ammann.

Bracelets with wavy and straight platinum links are fastened at the side with gold screws. The screw look was also used in rings and tie pins.

In 1995 the family business in Lucerne opened a modern jewellery shop at 28 Hertensteinstrasse in Pfyffer-von-Whyer, a 300-year-old building. Since then, collections by leading manufactories and contemporary jewellery designers have been presented in a modern ambience. In 1999 Fillner fulfilled another long-cherished dream. The two families moved into a house for three generations in Rosenweg, Stans. Cornelia Burri-Fillner and her husband, Urs, have ensured that the family goes on through their children, Vanessa and Kevin. The dream of living and working under one roof has also come true with a complete goldsmithing studio and administrative rooms in the building occupied by the family. From 1999, Fillner has collaborated with the jewellery designer Malte Meinck from Bad Kissingen on developing the *Harlequin* collection. Set in stringently geometric ring forms and pendants, plastic as iridescent as opals is a refreshing and lively concept. The most recent jewellery project, which Fillner has been pursuing since 2003, is called *Flower Leaves*. This exciting ring collection also grew out of a dialogue between Fillner and Meinck. Some of these superbly shaped and utterly wearable pieces in gold and platinum are set with coloured precious stones and rutile quartz inventively cut by Tom Munsteiner. »We have never viewed ourselves as avant-garde,« says Manfred Fillner. »We always wanted to link the classic with the modern.« In doing just that, this family business has achieved a great deal for the modern culture of jewellery.

1972	Ring, Weißgold, Diamanten — Ring, white gold, diamonds
1988	Armreif *Spitzspange*, Gold — Bangle *Spitzspange*, gold
1997	Ohrschmuck mit Klicksystem und Ring, Platin, Gold, Brillanten — Earrings with click system and ring, platinum, gold, diamonds
1994	*Skulpturenringe*, Gold, Diamanten — *Sculpture rings*, gold, diamonds
1999	Ringe *Harlekin*, Design Malte Meinck, Gold, künstlicher Opal — Rings *Harlequin*, design Malte Meinck, gold, synthetic opal
2002	Ringe *Flower Leaves*, Gold, Weißgold, Edelsteine — Rings *Flower Leaves*, gold, white gold, precious stones

Manfred Fillner
Geboren 1940 in Danzig. Ateliergründung 1980 in Stans, Schweiz. Seit 1995 zusätzlich Schmuckgalerie in Luzern zusammen mit Ruth und Cornelia Burri-Fillner.

Manfred Fillner
Born in Danzig in 1940. Founded studio in Stans, Switzerland, in 1980. Additional jewellery gallery in Lucerne with Ruth and Cornelia Burri-Fillner since 1995.

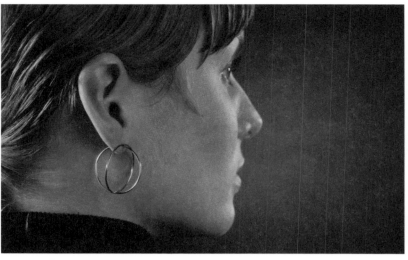

1982

1983

1989

Herman Hermsen

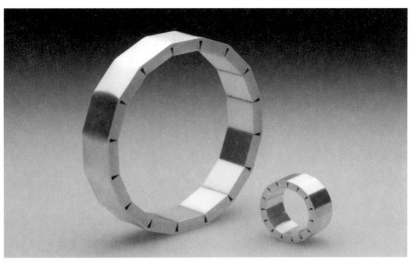

1992

1995

Herman Hermsen

Herman Hermsen studierte von 1974 bis 1979 an der Akademie voor Beeldende Kunsten in Arnheim. Anschließend war er als Assistent von Emmy van Leersum, 1930–1984, tätig. Bei der Wegbereiterin der modernen Schmuckkunstbewegung eignete sich der in Nijmegen geborene Designer autodidaktisch die handwerklichen Grundlagen der Schmuckfertigung an. Die Serie und das künstlerische Unikat betrachtet Herman Hermsen als gleichberechtigt. Seit seinem Start als Designer war es seine wichtigste Herausforderung, »nach neuen technischen Lösungen, einer zeitgemäßen Interpretation traditioneller Werte und Techniken, verbunden mit expressivem, innovativem Design, zu suchen.«

Herman Hermsen erhielt höchste Preise für Produkt-Design, so für die Lampe *Charis* von ClassiCon, wie für serielles Schmuck-Design, dem er sich seit seiner Professur 1992 an der Fachhochschule Düsseldorf verstärkt widmete. »Ich möchte betonen«, sagte der Holländer in seiner Biografie von 2006, »dass meine Auffassungen im Hinblick auf Gestaltung dabei die gleichen geblieben sind.« Ausgehend von Entwicklungen der 1970er Jahre gründen alle Entwürfe »auf einer Neuinterpretation des jeweiligen Produkts.« Er suche dabei nach einer konzentrierten, treffenden und zugleich auch verspielten Bildsprache, um die Essenz des entwickelten Konzepts auszudrücken. Ideal ist ihm dies bei den Trauringen *Mäander* für Niessing gelungen. Die Ringe stellen mit ihrer durch eine Mäanderform verbundenen, gleichzeitig aber auch geteilten Ringschiene eine der wenigen echten Designinnovationen bei Trauringen dar. Technisch raffiniert beinhalten sie eine Symbolik für die starke Verbindung und das freie Spiel, das Ehen erlauben sollten. Die Trauringe wurden mit dem red dot des Designzentrums Essen 1998 ausgezeichnet.

Noch in der Studienzeit entstand die *Nasenklammer*, ein rechtwinklig geknickter Edelstahlspiegel, in dem sich die Augen als »Kopfschmuck« spiegeln. Sie steht als Beispiel für die Schmuckavantgarde der 1970er Jahre, die mit ihren Arbeiten die Bedeutungen und Wirkungen von Schmuck hinterfragten. Die Kunsthistorikerin Barbara Maas schreibt zu den frühen minimalistischen Arbeiten: »Zahlreiche Schmuckobjekte Herman Hermsens kommen hintersinnigen, provokanten Kommentaren von teilweise schmuck- und gesellschaftskritischer Relevanz gleich. Vor allem die frühen minimalistischen Arbeiten der 1980er Jahre aus farbig lackiertem Stahldraht, Aluminium und Kunststoff, die in ihrer Linearität Parallelen zur zeitgenössischen Skulptur aufweisen und u.a. an die Raumplastiken aus Metallstäben eines Norbert Kricke erinnern, sind gängige Schmuckvorstellungen negierende oder persiflierende Formexperimente, die sich wenig an der Tragbarkeit oder gar am Aspekt des Schmückens orientieren.« Dies gilt keineswegs für den Ohrschmuck *U* in Gold von 1981; er ist ein Musterbeispiel von modernem, minimalistischem Schmuck, bei dem Funktion und Form eine vollkommene Einheit bilden.

1982	Ohrschmuck *Double circle*, Gold — Earring *Double circle*, gold
1983	Ohrclip *Lellebel*, rotes PVC — Earclip *Lellebel*, red PVC
1992	Ring und Armschmuck *Sawcuts*, Silber — Ring and bracelet *Sawcuts*, silver
1995	Ringe *Mäander*, Gold (für Niessing) — Rings *Meander*, gold (for Niessing)
1989	Brosche *Brilliant*, Edelstahl — Brooch *Brilliant*, stainless steel

Herman Hermsen

1998

1998

Mit einer raffiniert simplen Erotik überzeugt der *Lellebel* Ohrclip von 1985 aus rotem PVC. Das Ohrläppchen erscheint in den roten Kunststofflippen als lustvoll oder frech herausgestreckte Zunge. Herman Hermsen erweist sich nicht nur in diesem Fall als Meister neuartiger, integrierter Verschlusslösungen bzw. Aufhängungen. Bei dem Ohrring *Gold + Pearls* von 1989 ist ein dünner Golddraht zu einem Kreis gebogen. Die überstehenden, parallel auslaufenden Enden sind mit kleinen Perlenkugeln verschlossen. Bei der entsprechenden Kette nehmen die kleinen Perlen den Beginn und das Ende der runden Kettenglieder auf. Auch ein Ring mit loser Perle, die nur getragen fixiert wird, demonstriert, wie elegant Herman Hermsen mit einer intelligenten, funktionellen Konstruktion traditionelles Dekor ersetzt. Mit seinem Spannring für auswechselbare Edelsteinkugeln von 1989 greift er ein Thema auf, das Friedrich Becker, einer seiner Vorgänger an der FH in Düsseldorf, zwischen 1952 und 1962 in verschiedenen Varianten verfolgt hat.

Einen Leckerbissen für Freunde konstruktivistischer Schmuckästhetik bieten die Ringe *Sawcuts* von 1992. Präzise Sägeschnitte ergeben die Knickstellen für die Biegung und gleichzeitig ein feines, zeitgemäßes Dekor. Mit konstruktiver Raffinesse überzeugt auch die Serie *From the Surface*. Aus einer rechteckigen Brosche und dem runden Ohrschmuck sind »Nadel« und »Ohrstecker« ausgeschnitten und erfüllen rechtwinklig zurückgebogen ihre Doppelfunktion. Bei der *Booklest Chain* von 1997 lassen sich verschiedene Abbildungen von Edelsteinen wie bei einem Kalender umblättern. In der Serie *Upon Reflection* befasst sich Herman Hermsen zwischen 2001 und 2002 mit Spiegelungen. Halbe oder viertel Edelsteine werden in Metallspiegeln komplettiert oder ihr Licht scheint in die Haut der Trägerin einzudringen. Der Schmuck von Herman Hermsen ist heute weniger provozierend als in seiner Studienzeit, aber nicht weniger geistreich. Als Professor an der FH Düsseldorf ist er zudem ein wichtiger Protagonist des modernen Schmuck-Designs.

E — Herman Hermsen studied between 1974 and 1979 at the Akademie voor Beeldende Kunsten in Arnhem. After finishing his studies, he worked as an assistant to a pioneer of modern art jewellery, Emmy van Leersum (1930–1984), and taught himself the technical fundamentals of jewellery-making. Herman Hermsen views mass production jewellery and one-off art jewellery pieces as being on an equal footing. From the outset of his work as a designer, he has regarded »seeking new technical solutions, a contemporary interpretation of traditional values and techniques, linked with expressive, innovative design« as the most important challenges facing a designer.

Herman Hermsen has been awarded top prizes for product design, for instance for *Charis*, a lamp produced by ClassiCon, as well as for mass-produced designer jewellery, which he concentrated on after being appointed professor at Fachhochschule Düsseldorf in 1992. »I should like to emphasise,« the Dutch designer has written in his 2006 autobiography, »that my views with regard to design have remained as they have always been.« Starting with developments in the 1970s, all his designs are based »on a new interpretation of each product«. He seeks a concentrated, apt yet also playful pictorial idiom to express the essence of the concept as developed. He has achieved this to perfection in the wedding rings for Niessing called *Meander*. As the name implies, although the shanks of these rings are separate, they are interlinked through a meander form to represent one of the few real innovations in wedding ring design. Technically sophisticated, they are informed by the dual symbolism of the strong tie yet scope for individual freedom that a marriage should ideally allow. These wedding rings were awarded the Essen Design Centre red dot in 1998.

While Hermsen was still a student, he created *Nasenklammer*, a nose clip made of stainless steel bent at right angles in which the wearer's eyes are reflected as »head jewellery«. This creation exemplifies 1970s avant-garde jewellery, when such works questioned the significance and effects of jewellery as such. Barbara Maas, an art historian, writes on early Minimalist works by Hermsen: »Numerous jewellery objects by Herman Hermsen are the equivalent of quirky, provocative commentaries on the social relevance of jewellery. Particularly his early 1980s Minimalist works of steel wire lacquered in colour, aluminium and plastic, which reveal parallels with contemporary sculpture in the handling of line and in part are reminiscent of Norbert Kricke's spatial sculpture composed of metal rods, are experiments in form that negate conventional notions of what jewellery is or represent a persiflage of it and reveal little orientation towards wearability or even the aspect of adornment.« That is not in the least true of *U*, which is gold ear jewellery dating from 1981; this is a prime example of modern Minimalist jewellery, in which form and function form a perfect whole.

Lellebel is a 1985 ear clip that is compellingly sophisticated in its unabashed eroticism. These red PVC plastic lips make the ear lobe on which they are worn look like a tongue that is being put out lasciviously or simply impertinently. This is not the only case in which Herman Hermsen reveals himself a master of novel yet integrated solutions to the problem of fastening or hanging. *Gold + Pearls*, a 1989 Hermsen earring, is a thin gold wire bent into a circle. The ends running parallel to it and overlapping are finished with small pearl balls. In the matching necklace, similar little pearls mark the beginning and end of the round chain links. A ring with a loose pearl, which is only fixed in place when the ring is worn, demonstrates how elegantly Herman Hermsen succeeds in replacing traditional decoration with intelligent functional construction. In his 1989 tension ring set with exchangeable balls of precious stone, he took up a theme pursued and varied between 1952 and 1962 by Friedrich Becker, a predecessor of his at the Düsseldorf Fachhochschule.

2002   2005   2008

The 1992 *Sawcuts* rings are a treat for aficionados of the Constructivist aesthetic in jewellery. Precise saw cuts create both the bends for the shape and exquisitely contemporary decoration. The *From the Surface* series is another compelling example of Constructivist sophistication. A »pin« and »stud earring« cut out of a rectangular brooch and round ear jewellery have been bent back at right angles to fulfil their dual function. In *Booklet Chain* (1997), various representations of precious stones can be browsed through as if one were leafing through a calendar. In the *Upon Reflection* series, Herman Hermsen investigated reflections between 2001 and 2002. Precious stones cut in half or quartered are completed by being reflected in metal mirrors or the light from them seems to penetrate the wearer's skin. Herman Hermsen's jewellery may seem less of provocation today than it did in his student days but it is none the less witty for that. Moreover, in his capacity as a professor at the Düsseldorf Fachhochschule, he is an active exponent of modern jewellery design.

1998	*S-Ringe*, Gold, Edelsteine — *S rings*, gold, precious stones
1998	Ohrschmuck, *Aus der Fläche*, Gold — Earrings, *From the Surface*, gold
2002	Ring, *Upon Reflection*, Gold, Silber, Citrin — Ring *Upon Reflection*, gold, silver, citrine
2005	Ring *Excentric*, Silber, synthetischer Stein — Ring *Excentric*, silver, synthetic stone
2008	Brosche mit vielen Zirkonias — Brooch with numerous zirconia

Herman Hermsen
Geboren 1953 in Nijmegen.
1974–1979 Akademie voor Beeldende Kunsten
Arnhem. Atelier seit 1979.
Ab 1992 Professor Fachhochschule Düsseldorf.

Herman Hermsen
Born in Nijmegen in 1953. 1974–1979 Akademie
voor Beeldende Kunsten Arnhem.
Studio since 1979. Professor at Fachhochschule
Düsseldorf since 1992.

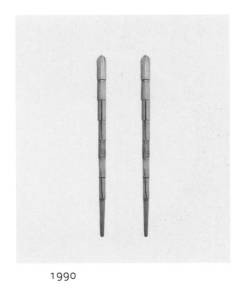

1990   2003   2004

Antonio Bernardo

Antonio Bernardos' Schmuckstücke reichen von spielerischer Leichtigkeit bis hin zu architektonischer Strenge. Sein Konstruktivismus erscheint wie eine intelligente Weiterentwicklung von frühen modernen Stücken, die im Umfeld des Bauhauses nach 1920 entstanden sind. Aber auch naturalistische und historische Themen weiß er zeitgemäß zu interpretieren. Der Brasilianer liefert den Beweis, dass modernes Schmuck-Design auch außerhalb Europas zu höchster Reife gelangt.

Präzisionswerkzeuge für die Uhren- und Schmuckfertigung lernte Antonio Bernardo schon in seiner Kindheit kennen. Sein deutschstämmiger Vater Rudolf Herrmann betrieb damit ein Geschäft in Rio de Janeiro. Zunächst schien für ihn eine technische Laufbahn in der Uhrenindustrie vorbestimmt zu sein. Nach einer Ingenieursausbildung reiste Bernardo im Alter von 20 Jahren in die Schweiz, um verschiedene Schweizer Uhrenfirmen und -institute kennenzulernen. Anschließend studierte er ein Jahr am CFH, dem Centre International de Formation de l'Industrie Horlogère Suisse in Biel.

Zurück in Rio orientierte sich Bernardo zu Beginn der 1970er Jahre beruflich noch einmal neu. Aus einer Laune heraus entwarf er in dieser Zeit des Suchens einen Silberring. Weil er nicht wusste, wie dieser zu fertigen war, überließ er die Ausführung einem Goldschmied. »Danach hörte er nie mehr auf, Schmuck zu machen«, schreibt die brasilianische Journalistin Evelise Grunow. Die folgenden acht Jahre arbeitete Bernardo bei seinen Schmuckentwicklungen mit dem Hersteller seines ersten Rings zusammen. Daneben eignete er sich selbst Kenntnisse der Schmuckfertigung an und richtete sich eine eigene Werkstatt ein. Er habe nie aufgehört zu lernen, Techniken auszuprobieren und immer wieder die Frage zu stellen, was gutes Schmuckdesign sei, erklärt er.

1975 gewann Antonio Bernardo seinen ersten nationalen Trauring-Wettbewerb, veranstaltet von dem Diamantproduzenten De Beers. Zu seinen ersten Schmucklinien zählten *Raio, Kioto, Espeto Cone* und *Espeto Gaivota*. Arbeiten aus kleinen, zusammengefügten Elementen wie der Ohrschmuck *Cobra Pastilha Longo* entstanden um 1980. Ihre fließende oder schwebende Beweglichkeit wird später zu einem wichtigen Thema des Designers.

Zunehmende Verkaufserfolge führten 1981 zur Gründung des ersten Schmuckgeschäftes und der Handelsmarke Antonio Bernardo. Mit dem Aufbau einer Schmuck-Designmarke leistete der vielseitige Gestalter, Konstrukteur und Unternehmer Pionierarbeit in Brasilien. Heute gibt es neun eigene Stores in brasilianischen Großstädten. Die moderne Designer-Marke beteiligt sich an internationalen Messen und ist in über 40 Geschäften in den USA, Europa und Asien zu finden. Dabei vergaß Bernardo jedoch nie, die Prinzipien der Moderne überzeugend, künstlerisch inspiriert und mit zeitgemäßer Frische in seinen Konzepten umzusetzen. Ausgezeichnet wurde das kreative und technisch perfekt umgesetzte Schmuck-Design durch zahlreiche internationale Preise, zuletzt den renommierten iF Product Design Award 2007.

Viele Schmucklinien von Antonio Bernardo überzeugen mit einer minimalistischen Schlichtheit. Immer wird dabei ein ernsthaftes, geistreiches Konzept sichtbar. Der Armreif *Turn* von 2004 beispielsweise verbindet strenge Geometrie mit einer wiederkehrenden, fließenden Bewegung. Exakt gewickeltes Goldblech formt den Reif, erlaubt Einblick in den Innenraum und macht ihn zu einem Gestaltungselement. Das Volumen der klassischen Kreisform erhält eine weitere Dimension. Mit noch geringerem Materialeinsatz kommen die Schmuckformen wie etwa die *Impulso* Ohrringe, der Hals- und Ohrschmuck *Duplo Sentido* und der Ring *Ciclos* aus. Elegante Bögen und Konstruktionen formen Schleifen und schaffen Räume aus dünnem Rohr oder Draht. Von großer Kunst unterscheidet sich insbesondere dieser skulpturale Minimalismus nur durch seine Dimension, den funktionalen Körperbezug, die bevorzugte Verwendung von Gold und die Serienfertigung. Dies gilt ebenso für den beweglichen Ohrschmuck *Vivo*, die Ringe *Expand, Moebius* und *Intimo*.

Mit dem Ring *Barroco com Safira* stellt Antonio Bernardo in lässiger Souveränität Bezüge zur Geschichte her. Wohl selten wurde die barocke Dekorationssucht so überzeugend in eine klare Form überführt. Im Ring *Gênesis* strömen Spermien mit brillantem Erbgut einem Diamanten entgegen. Das Dekor erschließt sich in der organischen Ringform erst bei näherer Betrachtung. Organisch lebendige Natur ist auch in dem Ohrschmuck *Green Ray* das Thema.

Auch im *Puzzlering* wird das intellektuelle und technische Repertoire des Designers sichtbar. Ein Schmuckstück, das in einer fröhlichen Runde zum unterhaltsamen Spiel dienen kann. Das Puzzle als Ornament in einer klaren, reduzierten Form wird zum Zeitdokument einer Gesellschaft, die glaubt, im Spiel etwas von ihrer verloren gegangenen Freiheit zurückzugewinnen.

E — Antonio Bernardo's pieces cover the gamut from playful lightness to tectonic stringency. His constructivist approach looks like an intelligent further development of early Modernist pieces created in the Bauhaus manner after 1920. However, he is also adept at interpreting naturalistic and historic motifs and themes in a contemporary way. The Brazilian designer provides the proof that modern jewellery design is capable of attaining the pinnacle of maturity outside Europe as well.

Antonio Bernardo became familiar in childhood with precision tools for making watches and jewellery. His father, Rudolf Herrmann, who was of German descent, ran a business selling them in Rio de Janeiro. Antonio Bernardo seemed at first predestined for a technical career in the watch-making industry. After training as an engineer, Bernardo went to Switzerland at the age of twenty to acquaint himself with various Swiss watch-making firms and horological institutes. Afterwards he studied for a year at the Centre International de Formation de l'Industrie Horlogère Suisse (CFH) in Biel. On his return to Rio, Bernardo once again re-oriented himself profes-

| 2005 | 2005 | 2006 |

sionally in the early 1970s. On a whim, he designed a silver ring during this period of trial and error. Because he did not know how to make a ring, he had a goldsmith execute his design. »After that, he never stopped making jewellery,« writes the Brazilian journalist Evelise Grunow. For eight years Bernardo collaborated on his jewellery designs with the maker of his first ring. On the side, he taught himself the fundamentals of jewellery-making and set up a workshop of his own. As he puts it, he has never ceased to learn, to try out techniques and to keep on asking what good jewellery design is.

In 1975 Antonio Bernardo won his first national wedding ring competition, hosted by the diamond-trading cartel De Beers. Bernardo's early lines in jewellery include *Raio, Kioto, Espeto Cone* and *Espeto Gaivota*. Works composed of small elements pieced together such as the ear jewellery *Cobra Pastilha Longo* date from around 1980. The fluid or floating mobility that distinguishes them would become a major hallmark of this designer.

Growing commercial success led in 1981 to the founding of the first Antonio Bernardo jewellery store and trade name. In building up a designer jewellery label, the versatile and prolific designer, engineer and entrepreneur broke ground in Brazil. Today the chain has nine branch stores in large Brazilian cities. The modern designer label participates in trade fairs worldwide and is sold in over forty stores across the US, Europe and Asia. However, Bernardo has never forgotten the importance of convincingly translating Modernist principles and aesthetic inspiration with contemporary flair in his concepts. His creative designer jewellery that is notable for consummate craftsmanship has been awarded numerous international prizes, most recently the prestigious iF Product Design Award in 2007.

Many Antonio Bernardo lines in jewellery are tellingly Minimalist in their simplicity. A serious yet witty concept is always realised. *Turn*, a bangle that dates from 2004, for instance, unites stringent geometry with recurrent, fluid movement. The bangle is formed of meticulously worked sheet gold that permits a glimpse of the inside space, turning it into a design element. Thus the volume of the classic circle form is given a further dimension. Jewellery shapes such as the *Impulso* earrings, the *Duplo Sentido* neck and ear jewellery and *Ciclos*, a ring, make do with using even less material. Elegant arcs and constructs form loops and create spaces of thin tubing or wire. This sculptural Minimalism differs from sculpture as such only in scale, the functional relationship to the body, the use of gold by preference and mass production. The same holds for the mobile ear jewellery *Vivo* and the rings *Expand, Moebius* and *Intimo*.

In *Barroco com Safira*, a ring, Antonio Bernardo links up with art history with casual assurance. Rarely has the Baroque addiction to the ornamental been translated so cogently into clear form. In the ring *Gênesis*, sperms flow with dazzling genetic material towards a diamond. The decoration scheme is only revealed in the organic ring form on closer scrutiny. Living organic

nature is also the theme informing the ear jewellery *Green Ray*. A *puzzle* ring also showcases the designer's intellectual and technical repertory. This is a piece of jewellery that can be used as an entertaining game in convivial company. The puzzle as ornament in a clear, reduced form becomes a document of a contemporary society which believes it can regain in play something of the freedom it has lost.

1990	Ohrschmuck *Cobra Pastilha*, Gold — Earrings *Cobra Pastilha*, gold
2003	Ring *Expand*, Gold — Ring *Expand*, gold
2004	Armreif *Turn*, Gold — Bangle *Turn*, gold
2005	Ring *Orbe*, Gold, schwarzer Achat — Ring *Orbe*, gold, black agate
2005	Ring *Gênesis*, Gold, Diamanten — Ring *Gênesis*, gold, diamonds
2006	Ring *Barroco*, Gold, Saphir, Brillanten — Ring *Barroco*, gold, sapphire, diamonds

Antonio Bernardo
Geboren 1947, Firmengründung in Rio de Janeiro 1981.

Antonio Bernardo
Born in 1947, founded his firm in Rio de Janeiro in 1981.

Antonio Bernardo

1984   1984   1985

André Ribeiro

Das matte Schwarz von Kautschuk bildet den extremen Kontrast zur strahlenden Brillanz echter Diamanten. In äußerster formaler Klarheit hat André Ribeiro Mitte der 1980er Jahre zwei sehr konträre Materialien zusammengeführt. Es wurde eine Begegnung des Wertbeständigen, des Ewigen, mit dem Vergänglichen, dem Wertlosen. Es war eine der auffälligsten Erfindungen im modernen Schmuck-Design.

Der Vater von André Ribeiro war Uhrmacher und führte ein kleines Fachgeschäft in der Nähe von Bordeaux. Miniaturwelten, wie das Innenleben alter Uhren, die er als Kind gerne zerlegte, haben ihn seitdem fasziniert, erzählt Ribeiro. Als Jugendlicher kaufte er sich einen kleinen Emailofen und stellte erste Schmuckstücke her. Sie bestanden aus einzelnen Kupferteilen, die er nach dem Emaillieren zusammenbaute. In der Familie und im Freundeskreis fanden die Stücke rege Abnahme. Angeregt durch einen Onkel, ein Landschaftsmaler in Wien, begann sich André Ribeiro im Alter von 17 Jahren »weitaus stärker« mit Zeichnen und Malen zu beschäftigen.

Nach dem Wehrdienst, den der Abiturient in einer französischen Garnison in Pforzheim ableistete, studierte er zunächst Touristik. Mit 21 Jahren brach er dieses Studium ab. In der anschließenden Zeit der Neuorientierung überzeugte ihn ein befreundeter Maler aus Pforzheim, sich an der damaligen Kunst- und Werkschule zu bewerben. »Entscheidend war für mich«, sagt Ribeiro, »dass die Pforzheimer Schule eine Ausbildung gemäß der Tradition des Bauhauses anbot, die das Handwerkliche mit dem Künstlerischen verband.« Während des Studiums bei Professor Reinhold Reiling von 1976–1981 konnte Ribeiro auch die Malerei, seine zweite Vorliebe, vertiefen. 1980 gewann er bei einem Wettbewerb der Intergold den ersten Preis in der Kategorie Gold mit unedlen Materialien sowie eine Auszeichnung in der Kategorie Gold. Im Wettbewerb der ASUAG, einer Gruppe Schweizer Uhrenhersteller, erhielt er im Jahr 1981 den dritten Preis für eine Taschenuhr, die auch als Tischuhr aufzustellen war. Der red dot 1998 des Designzentrums in Essen war seinem wichtigsten Thema vorbehalten: dem Kautschukschmuck mit Diamanten.

Nach dem Diplom gründete André Ribeiro 1982 sein Atelier in Schömberg bei Pforzheim und arbeitete zunächst als freier Schmuck-Designer für die Schmuckindustrie. Weil diese Arbeit nicht zufrieden stellend war, begann er, mit industriell gefertigten Formteilen zu experimentieren. »Dabei hat mich die Idee des Objet trouvé von Marcel Duchamps inspiriert«, berichtet Ribeiro. Wichtig seien auch die Impulse aus der künstlerisch orientierten Schmuckszene der 1970er Jahre gewesen. Wie die Schmuckgestalter vor allem in Holland habe er das Phänomen des Schmückens in erster Linie unter dem Aspekt der Gestaltung gesehen. Auf die Frage, warum er das Material Kautschuk gewählt habe, antwortet er: »Ich glaube, eher umgekehrt; das Material hat mich gewählt!«

Mitte der 1980er Jahre verfolgte Ribeiro in seiner Schmuckentwicklung mehrere Konzepte: Das erste war spielerisch-narrativ. Dabei kamen Silicontierchen zum Einsatz, wie man sie damals als Kinderspielzeug vorfand. Die Stücke wurden u.a. in Avantgarde-Schmuckgalerien wie V&V in Wien 1986 gezeigt. Neben großzügigen, geometrischen Schmuckgarnituren gestaltet er auch Stücke »nahe am traditionellen Schmuckverständnis.« Zum Ausgangspunkt für sein entscheidendes Konzept wurde ein Dichtungsring, wie er im Sanitärbereich verwendet wird. »Schwarz war seit jeher meine Lieblingsfarbe«, erklärt der Designer, »nur die Gussnaht und die glänzende Farbe des Dichtungsrings haben mich gestört.« Das Mattschleifen löste das Problem. »Aber es fehlte etwas, um den Bogen zwischen Ready-Made und gezieltem Erschaffen zu spannen«, erzählt Ribeiro. Zuerst steckte er dünne Silberdrahtstücke durch die Ringe oder klebte ausgestanzte weiße Kautschukelemente wie Intarsien in die Oberfläche. Schließlich stellte er sich die Frage, ob man nicht auch traditionelle Schmucksteine einsetzen könnte. Im Diamanten, dem härtesten Edelstein, der das Licht am stärksten reflektiert, fand er die ideale Ergänzung für den mattierten Kautschukring. Die Spannung des Kautschuks erlaubte eine materialgerechte, dynamische Verbindung zwischen dem in Gold gefassten Diamanten und dem weichen Trägermaterial.

Der neue Materialmix, der zunächst auf viel Unverständnis in der Schmuckbranche stieß, entsprach ganz dem philosophischen Interesse des Designers: »Die Fragestellung über den Wert des Wertlosen und den Unwert des Wertvollen spiegelt eine Grundeinstellung in meinem Leben wider«, sagt er. Die Frage, wie das Publikum ein Produkt als Schmuck akzeptieren würde, das allen konventionellen Erwartungen widerspricht, wurde bald beantwortet. Auf den Fachmessen erntete Ribeiro entweder entschiedene Ablehnung oder begeisterte Zustimmung. Die besondere kulturelle Bedeutung und Idee dieser Schmucklinie wurde 1997 vom OLG Karlsruhe urheberrechtlich geschützt. Dies war bis dahin im Schmuck-Design kaum denkbar. Durch Ankäufe des Cooper-Hewitt Museums in New York, 1989, des Musée des Art Décoratifs in Paris, 2003, und des Schmuckmuseums Pforzheim, 2004, ist der Kautschukschmuck von André Ribeiro in wichtigen öffentlichen Sammlungen vertreten.

E — The matt black of hard rubber forms an extreme contrast to the dazzling brilliance of genuine diamonds. With the utmost formal clarity, André Ribeiro has, since the mid-1980s, been linking two materials that are as different as they can be. It has been an encounter between what has lasting value and endures eternally and something perishable that is of no intrinsic value. This was one of the most striking inventions in modern designer jewellery.

A watchmaker, André Ribeiro's father ran a small specialist shop near Bordeaux. Worlds in miniature such as the works of antique watches, which André Ribeiro enjoyed taking apart when he was a child, have continued to

1996

1987–2006

fascinate him since then as he tells it. In his teens, he bought a little enamelling kiln and made his first pieces of jewellery. They were composed of individual pieces of copper, which he assembled after they had been enamelled. The pieces were much in demand in his family and among his friends. Encouraged by an uncle, who was a landscape painter in Vienna, André Ribeiro began at the age of seventeen to get »much more heavily involved« with drawing and painting.

After leaving school with university entrance qualification, Ribeiro did his national service at a French garrison in Pforzheim before embarking on tourism studies. At twenty-one he dropped out of the course. While he was subsequently re-orienting himself, a painter from Pforzheim, who was a friend of his, persuaded Ribeiro to apply for admission to what was then the Kunst- und Werkschule in Pforzheim. »What was crucial for me was,« says Ribeiro, »that the Pforzheim school offered training along Bauhaus lines, which linked crafts with fine art.« While studying under Professor Reinhold Reiling (1976–1981), Ribeiro was also able to go more deeply into painting, his second love. In 1980 he won first prize at an Intergold competition in the Gold with Base Materials category and a distinction in the category Gold. At a competition mounted in 1981 by ASUAG, a Swiss watch-making group, Ribeiro was awarded third prize for a pocket watch that could also be set up as a table clock. The 1998 red dot from the Essen Design Centre would be reserved for his paramount theme: hard-rubber jewellery with diamonds.

After taking his diploma, André Ribeiro founded a studio in Schömberg near Pforzheim in 1982, where he at first freelanced as a jewellery designer in the jewellery industry. Finding this work unsatisfactory, Ribeiro began experimenting with industrially manufactured form elements. »What inspired me was Marcel Duchamp's idea of the objet trouvé,« reports Ribeiro. Other important influences came from the art-oriented 1970s jewellery scene. Like Dutch jewellery designers in particular, Ribeiro says he saw the phenomenon of adorning oneself primarily from the design angle. Asked why he chose hard rubber as his material, he answers: »I think it's the other way round; the material chose me!«

In the mid-1980s Ribeiro pursued several concepts in developing his jewellery: the first was at once playful and narrative. He took to using little silicone animals of the kind made at the time as children's toys. Those Ribeiro pieces were shown at avant-garde jewellery galleries, including V&V in Vienna, in 1986. Alongside sets of generously proportioned geometric jewellery, he also designed pieces that were »close to traditional ideas of jewellery«. The starting point for his key concept was a rubber washer of the kind used in plumbing. »Black had always been my favourite colour,« explains the designer. »The seam lines from casting were the only thing that bothered me.« Polishing on the matting wheel solved the problem. »But something was missing, the link between the ready-made and deliberate creation,« as

Ribeiro tells it. At first he stuck pieces of thin silver wire through the rings or glued white cut-out rubber elements like intarsia to surfaces. Finally he began to wonder whether it might not be possible to use traditional gemstones as well. In the diamond, the hardest precious stone, the stone that reflects light most strongly, he found the ideal complement to his matt-polished rubber ring. The tensile strength of the rubber created a dynamic link between the diamond set in gold and the soft support material, that did justice to both materials.

The new materials mix, which at first caused a lot of head-shaking in the jewellery industry, was a perfect match with the designer's personal philosophy: »The question of the value of what is intrinsically worthless and the worthlessness of the valuable reflects a stance that is basic to my life,« says Ribeiro. The question of whether the public would accept as jewellery a product that belied all conventional expectations was soon answered. At trade fairs Ribeiro was either vociferously rejected or loudly acclaimed. The idea behind this line in jewellery was copyrighted by the OLG Karlsruhe in 1997 as being of particular cultural importance. A legal measure of that kind had previously been unheard of in connection with jewellery design. Purchases of André Ribeiro's hard rubber jewellery by the Cooper-Hewitt Museum in New York (1989), the Musée des Art Décoratifs in Paris (2003) and the Schmuckmuseum Pforzheim (2004) have ensured that it is represented in major public collections.

1984	Ansteckschmuck, Dekomaterial, Silicon, Stahlseil — Brooch, decoration material, silicone, cable rope
1984	Armreif, Kautschuk, vergoldete Kordelenden auf Kautschuk gelagert — Bangle, hard rubber, gold plated cord ends mounted on hard rubber
1985	Halsreif, Kanaldichtungsring, Kautschuk, Messing — Necklace, watertight ring, hard rubber, brass
1996	Armreif, Elastomer-Kautschuk, Brillanten, Gold — Bangle, elastomer hard rubber, diamonds, gold
1987 –2006	Ohrschmuck, Elastomer-Kautschuk, Brillanten, Gold — Earrings, elastomer hard rubber, diamonds, gold

André Ribeiro
Geboren 1953 in Bordeaux, 1976–1981 FHG Pforzheim. 1982 Ateliergründung in Schömberg bei Pforzheim.

André Ribeiro
Born in Bordeaux in 1953, 1976–1981 Fachhochschule für Gestaltung Pforzheim. Founded studio in Schömberg near Pforzheim in 1982.

André Ribeiro

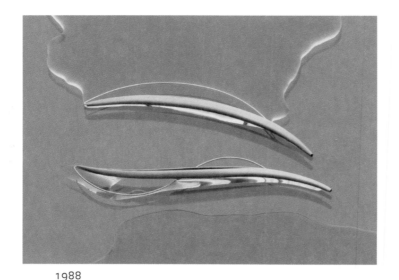

1988

1999

Sabine Brandenburg-Frank

Mit reduzierten Formen nahm Sabine Brandenburg-Frank Anfang der 1980er Jahre eine deutliche Gegenposition zum konventionellen Juwelenschmuck ein. Dass sie nach ihrem Designdiplom noch Germanistik studierte und promovierte, zeigt den intellektuellen Anspruch auch in ihrem Schmuck.

Sabine Brandenburg-Frank stammt, wie ihr Partner Egon Frank, aus Pforzheim. Nach dessen Studium zwischen 1972 und 1976 bei Professor Reinhold Reiling unterrichtete Frank selbst zwei Jahre lang an der Fachhochschule. Hier lernte er seine spätere Frau kennen. Sie wechselte nach zwei Semestern in Pforzheim und einer Goldschmiedelehre an die FH Düsseldorf zu Friedrich Becker. Im Studium bei Becker, dem Meister der Kinetik, ging es nicht nur um die Entwicklung moderner Schmuckformen. Wie an anderen Akademien setzten sich die Professoren mit ihren Studenten künstlerisch und theoretisch mit dem Phänomen Schmuck auseinander. »Wir haben uns zum Beispiel auf die Schriften von Baudrillard gestürzt«, erzählt sie. Der französische Philosoph hatte in den 1960er und 1970er Jahren die symbolische Funktion von Gebrauchsgegenständen als »reine Zeichen« untersucht. Zum Wunsch ihrer Generation, Schmuck philosophisch zu erklären, meint die Designerin: »Wir wollten nicht einfach Konsumgegenstände herstellen. Es ging darum zu verstehen, warum sich der Mensch schmückt oder warum Schmuck wertvoll sein sollte. Und wir wollten wissen, was in diesem Zusammenspiel von Körper und Gegenstand passiert?« Auch fand sie die Erweiterung des Schmuckbegriffs durch künstlerisch orientierte Goldschmiede wichtig. Den archaischen Arbeiten von Peter Skubic oder Daniel Kruger fühlt sie sich bis heute verbunden. Sabine Brandenburg-Frank lebte während des Studiums mit ihrem Mann in Düsseldorf-Oberkassel. So gab es oft zufällige Begegnungen mit Friedrich Becker. Immer habe er Schmuckstücke aus der Tasche geholt und vorgeführt. Das sei wahnsinnig interessant gewesen, erzählt Egon Frank. »Er hat uns beide sehr beeinflusst.« Gemeinsam mit vier weiteren Studentinnen bildete Sabine Brandenburg-Frank 1984 die Ateliergemeinschaft Schema F. Ein Grund war, dass an der Fachhochschule nicht genügend Arbeitsplätze für die Studenten zur Verfügung standen. Aus Schema F entstand eine Schmuckgalerie in Düsseldorf-Bilk, in der die Schmuckstücke der Studentinnen verkauft wurden. Mitglieder waren außer Brandenburg-Frank Margot Schenk-Wrobel, Francis-Paula Maas, Christina Burhop und Monika Glöss.

1983 hatte Egon Frank sein Schmuckatelier gegründet. Hier konnte Sabine Brandenburg-Frank nach dem Diplom ihr gestalterisches Talent entwickeln. Typisch waren zu Beginn klare, doch organisch anmutende Schmuckserien mit mattierten Oberflächen. Später wurden archaische Formen wie der Kreis, die Spirale und die geschwungene Linie wichtiger. Das griechische Wort Kosmos bedeutet sowohl Schmuck und Auszeichnung wie Ordnung, Weltordnung und gestirnter Himmel. »Das Spiel mit dieser Symbolik«, sagt Brandenburg-Frank, »macht für mich den Reiz von Schmuckstücken aus.«

1996 wurde ihr Reif Möbius-Bänder in die Sammlung des Schmuckmuseums in Pforzheim aufgenommen. 1999 erhielt der Armreif Faltung mit seiner raffinierten Verschlussmechanik den red dot für höchste Designqualität. Weitere Auszeichnungen folgten, zum Beispiel für den Armreif Leporello. 1989 übersiedelte die auf acht Mitarbeiter angewachsene Firma Egon Frank in neue Geschäftsräume nach Meerbusch bei Düsseldorf. 1992 kam ein modernes Schmuckgeschäft in Mönchengladbach hinzu. »Irgendwann stellten wir fest, dass wir kaum mehr Zeit fanden, neue Ideen zu entwickeln«, sagt Sabine Brandenburg-Frank. »Deshalb beschlossen wir, unser Leben grundlegend zu verändern und uns auf unsere Wurzeln zu besinnen.« Im Jahr 2003 verließen die beiden Schmuckgestalter das Rheinland und zogen nach Staufen im Markgräflerland. Hier entwickeln sie seitdem Serien für Meister in der Schweiz sowie Gellner und IsabelleFa in Deutschland. Die Brandenburg-Frank Kollektion wird seit 2005 als eigenständige Linie in der Manufaktur IsabelleFa gefertigt.

Im Jahr 2004 kam das Ehepaar Frank auf Isabelle Mössner zu und fragte, ob sie nicht die ganze Kollektion übernehmen wolle. Die Chefin von IsabelleFa überlegte nicht lange: »Ich hatte Sabines Ohrschmuck bereits 15 Jahre lang passend zu meinen Halsreifen getragen. Dann gab es noch diese unglaublichen Möbius- und Faltarmreife und viele andere Sachen. Das hat perfekt zu uns gepasst.« Mitentscheidend war auch, dass Hans-Georg Mössner und seine Goldschmiede begeistert waren, die handwerklich anspruchsvollen Stücke in ihrer Manufaktur in Eisingen zu fertigen. Die Zusammenarbeit zwischen Sabine Brandenburg-Frank als freie Designerin für IsabelleFa führte zu weiteren Entwicklungen. Seit 2005 tauchen in den klaren, reduzierten Formen verstärkt Diamanten auf. Damit wurden die Stücke für internationale Juweliere interessant. Zum Beispiel auf der Messe in Las Vegas, wo IsabelleFa mit der Kollektion von Sabine Brandenburg-Frank viel Zuspruch von amerikanischen Juwelieren erhielt. »Aber auch traditionellere Häuser fanden es spannend, einige moderne Stücke aufzunehmen. Der internationale Markt ist immer offener für diese moderne Formensprache«, sagt Isabelle Mössner.

E — With her reductive approach to form, Sabine Brandenburg-Frank unmistakably occupied a position that opposed conventional 1980s notions of what jewels were supposed to be. That she studied German literature and even took a doctorate in it after taking her diploma in design explains the intellectual ambitions informing her jewellery.

Like her partner, Egon Frank, Sabine Brandenburg-Frank is a native of Pforzheim. After studying with Professor Reinhold Reiling between 1972 and 1976, Egon Frank taught for two years at the Fachhochschule, where he met the woman who would become his wife. After two semesters in Pforzheim and an apprenticeship in goldsmithing at the Fachhochschule Düsseldorf,

2001

2006

she switched to Friedrich Becker. Studying with Becker, the master of Kinetics, involved much more than merely developing modern jewellery forms. As at other academies, professors and their students explored the phenomenon that is jewellery from both the aesthetic and the theoretical angles. »We immersed ourselves in the writings of Baudrillard, for instance,« recounts Sabine Brandenburg-Frank. In the 1960s and 1970s, the French philosopher had investigated the symbolic function of utilitarian objects as »pure signs«. The designer has this to say about the desire of her generation to explain jewellery in philosophical terms: »We didn't want to make mere consumer objects. What was at stake was understanding why human beings adorn themselves or why jewellery should be valuable. And we wanted to know what happened in this interplay of body and object.« She also found the extension of the jewellery concept through artistically oriented goldsmiths important. She still feels ties with the archaic works of Peter Skubic and Daniel Kruger. While still a student, Sabine Brandenburg-Frank lived with her husband in Düsseldorf-Oberkassel, where there were numerous fortuitous encounters with Friedrich Becker. He would invariably pull pieces of jewellery out of his pockets and present it to view. That was sheer madness, as Egon Frank tells it. »It strongly influenced both of us.« Sabine Brandenburg-Frank joined forces with four other women students in 1984 to found a collective studio, which they called *Schema F*. One of the reasons they started their own studio was that there were not enough places for students to work at the Fachhochschule. *Schema F* grew into a jewellery gallery in Düsseldorf-Bilk, where pieces made by the students were sold. The members of the collective were, apart from Brandenburg-Frank, Margot Schenk-Wrobel, Francis-Paula Maas, Christina Burhop and Monika Glöss.

In 1983 Egon Frank founded a jewellery studio. There Sabine Brandenburg-Frank could develop her talent as a designer after she had taken her diploma. Typical of her early work were clear yet organic-looking jewellery collections featuring matt surfaces. Later archaic forms such as the circle, the spiral and the wavy line had priority. The Greek word cosmos means both adornment and concepts such as order, the world order and the starry firmament. »Playing with that symbolism,« says Brandenburg-Frank, »is what makes pieces of jewellery so intriguing to me.«

In 1996 her bangle *Möbius-Bänder* [Mobius strips] was acquired for the collection of the Pforzheim Jewellery Museum. In 1999 *Faltung* [Folding], a bangle notable for its sophisticated clasp mechanism, was awarded the red dot for top design quality. Further awards followed, for instance, for the bangle called *Leporello*. By 1989 the firm of Egon Frank was employing a workforce of eight and moved to new business quarters in Meerbusch near Düsseldorf. In 1992 a modern jewellery shop in Mönchengladbach was added. »At some point, we realised that we hardly had any time anymore to develop new ideas,« says Sabine Brandenburg-Frank. »That's why we decided to change our lives radically and return to our roots.« In 2003 the two jewellery designers left the Rhineland and moved to Staufen in the Markgräflerland. There they have been developing collections for Meister in Switzerland and Gellner and IsabelleFa in Germany ever since. The Brandenburg-Frank Collection has been featured since 2005 as an independent line by the IsabelleFa factory.

In 2004 the Franks approached Isabelle Mössner and asked her whether she would like to take over the entire collection. The head of IsabelleFa didn't spend much time thinking about it: »I had been wearing Sabine's ear jewellery for fifteen years to go with my torcs. Then there were those incredible *Mobius* and *Folding* bangles and so many other things. That suited us perfectly.« Another decisive factor was that Hans-Georg Mössner and his goldsmiths enthusiastically welcomed the opportunity of making these sophisticated hand-crafted pieces at their Eisingen factory. The collaboration between Sabine Brandenburg-Frank as a freelance designer and IsabelleFa has led to further developments. Since 2005 diamonds have increasingly appeared in her clear, reductive forms. That has made the pieces interesting for jewellers abroad, for instance at the Las Vegas Fair, where IsabelleFa was acclaimed by American jewellers for the collection designed by Sabine Brandenburg-Frank. »But traditional jewellers have also found it exciting to include some modern pieces. The global market is becoming increasingly receptive to this modern language of forms,« says Isabelle Mössner.

1988	Nadeln, Platin — Pins, platinum
1999	Armreif *Faltung*, Gold — Bangle *Folding*, gold
2001	Armreif und Ring *Bänder*, Platin, Diamanten — Bangle and ring *Ribbons*, platinum, diamonds
2006	Armreif *Lotus*, Gold, Platin, Diamanten — Bangle *Lotus*, gold, platinum, diamonds

Sabine Brandenburg-Frank
Geboren 1957 in Pforzheim. FH Pforzheim und Düsseldorf. Ateliergründung mit Egon Frank 1983. Seit 2003 als freie Schmuckdesignerin tätig.

Sabine Brandenburg-Frank
Born in Pforzheim in 1957. Fachhochschule Pforzheim and Düsseldorf, founded studio with Egon Frank in 1983. Freelance jewellery designer since 2003.

Sabine Brandenburg-Frank

1993   1994

Erich Zimmermann

Die internationale Schmuckmesse Couture in Las Vegas im Juni 2007 hatte für Erich Zimmermann eine besondere Bedeutung. Für sein goldenes *Kokon-Collier* erhielt er bei dem Town&Country Couture Design Award den ersten Preis in der Kategorie Gold. 2008 gewann die von der Natur inspirierte Schmucklinie auch den Jewelers Choice Award der Messe JCK in Las Vegas. Das erste *Kokon-Collier* war 1990 entstanden und bereits 1993 durch den Wettbewerb Design-Plus ausgezeichnet worden. 2001 wurde es in die Sammlung des Kunstgewerbe-Museums Dresden aufgenommen.

Mit 16 Jahren entschied sich Erich Zimmermann, Goldschmied zu werden. Noch in der Schulzeit absolvierte er ein Praktikum bei dem Augsburger Kirchengoldschmied Walter Dochtermann. Auf das Abitur 1979 und eine eineinhalbjährige Reisezeit folgte eine verkürzte Lehre bei dem Gold- und Silberschmiedemeister Caspar Hartle in München. »Das wichtigste, was er mir mitgegeben hat, war das Gefühl für das Metall«, erklärt Zimmermann, der nach der Gesellenprüfung sofort eine freischaffende Tätigkeit in seiner Geburtsstadt Augsburg begann. 1991 absolvierte er die Meisterprüfung für Silberschmiede und 1994 diejenige für Goldschmiede. Die Aufnahme 1988 in den Berufsverband Bildender Künstler und 1991 in den Bayerischen Kunstgewerbeverein verdeutlichte sein Ziel, neben handwerklicher Perfektion auch dem Künstlerischen Raum zu geben. Dies wurde 1995 mit der Anerkennung als freischaffender Künstler durch die Akademie der bildenden Künste in München bestätigt.

Die Gold- und Silberschmiedearbeiten von Erich Zimmermann wurden auf zahlreichen internationalen Ausstellungen gezeigt. Sie erhielten aber auch deutsche Designpreise. Zum Beispiel den red dot in Essen für hohe Designqualität. Einen Höhepunkt seines Schaffens stellte 2001 die Einzelausstellung im Kunstgewerbemuseum Dresden dar. Seit 1994 leitete er Silberschmiede-Seminare an der Fachhochschule Trier, an der Hallam-University in Sheffield und lehrte 1997 und 1998 an der Fachhochschule Trier zwei Semester, stellvertretend für die Professorin Ingeborg Bornhofen.

Im Rückblick empfindet Erich Zimmermann die Silberschmiedeausbildung als die Basis seines Schaffens. Das mit dem Schmiedehammer »erspürte« Gefühl für den Charakter der Edelmetalle wird besonders deutlich in der Schmuckserie *Kokon*. Die plastisch geformten Glieder für die preisgekrönten Colliers ergeben sich beim Schmieden von Gold aus der Fläche. Sie bilden auch die Grundelemente für Armschmuck und volumige Ohrhänger. Wird die Form nicht verlötet und bleibt seitlich offen, gleicht sie einer Schote. Alle neuen Formen, für die eine mehrjährige Entwicklungszeit notwendig ist, erarbeitet der Gestalter autodidaktisch. »Bis eine neue Idee realisiert ist, werden alle Konsequenzen durchdacht und durchgearbeitet«, sagt Erich Zimmermann, der kurzlebige Trends ablehnt. Er möchte Stücke schaffen, die auch nach Jahrzehnten noch so attraktiv sind wie am ersten Tag. Als Gegenpol zur Linie *Kokon* können die *Prinzessinnen-Ringe* gesehen werden.

Sie sind 1997 als Persiflage auf den klassischen Tiffany-Ring entstanden. Denn in Amerika gilt die Größe des Edelsteins als Gradmesser für das Einkommen und den Status der Verlobten. In großzügig moderne Fassungen setzt Erich Zimmermann prächtige Farbedelsteine. Um die schönsten Steine für die Ringe auszusuchen, reist der Gestalter auch selbst in die Ursprungsländer oder er schleift die Steine direkt in der eigenen Werkstatt.

Die klassisch anmutenden *Kleopatra-Colliers* bilden die Brücke zwischen den *Kokons* und den *Prinzessinnen-Ringen*. 1994 entstand seine erste Kette aus Gold mit Lapislazuli. Die perfekte Verbindung, dauerhaft und vollkommen flexibel, von Edelsteinen und Edelmetall wurde durch den Einsatz eines Edelstahlseils möglich. Im Wechsel von Stein mit Gold entsteht ein geschmeidiger Halsschmuck, der die Schmuckkultur der Pharaonen ins Bewusstsein ruft und gleichzeitig modern und zeitgemäß wirkt.

Seit 2004 befasst sich der Augsburger Gestalter in seiner *Piraten*-Kollektion mit einem existentiellen Thema. Der Totenkopf im Kontrast zu prächtigen Edelsteinen. Die Nähe von Pracht und Tod war im Barock und Rokoko ein wichtiges Thema und wurde jüngst auch durch den englischen Künstler Damien Hirst thematisiert. Mit einem prächtigen Diamanten im grauen Schädel eines Totenkopfs konfrontiert Erich Zimmermann das Symbol des Unvergänglichen mit jenem des Vergänglichen. Er knüpft mit dem Vanitas-Motiv eine Verbindung zwischen Mittelalter und Moderne. »Auch das Spielen mit unserer Vergänglichkeit oder die oft als peinlich empfundene Erinnerung daran« macht ihm Spaß.

E — The June 2007 Couture international jewellery show in Las Vegas became a benchmark occasion for Erich Zimmermann. His *Cocoon necklace* was awarded first prize in the gold class for the Town & Country Couture Design Award. In 2008 his nature-inspired line in jewellery also won the Jewelers' Choice Award at JCK Las Vegas. The first *Cocoon necklace* saw the light of day in 1990 and by 1993 it had been awarded a distinction at the Design Plus competition. In 2001 it was acquired by the Kunstgewerbemuseum in Dresden for its permanent collection.

At the age of sixteen, Erich Zimmermann resolved to become a goldsmith. After finishing school, he did an internship with the Augsburg liturgical goldsmith Walter Dochtermann. Following his examinations qualifying him for university admission in 1979 and a year and a half of travel, Erich Zimmermann did a shortened apprenticeship with the master goldsmith and silversmith Caspar Hartle in Munich. »The most important thing he imparted to me was a feeling for the metal,« explains Zimmermann, who began to freelance in his native Augsburg once he had taken his journeyman's certificate. In 1991 he received his master's certificate in silversmithing and in 1994 the master's certificate in goldsmithing. The invitation to join the Berufsverband Bildender Künstler in 1988 and the Bayerischer Kunst-

1997   1998   2007

gewerbeverein in 1991 strengthened his resolve to add scope for the aesthetic side of goldsmithing alongside consummate worksmanship. That this was the right approach was confirmed by his being granted freelance practitioner of fine arts status by the Munich Fine Art Academy in 1995.

Erich Zimmermann's work in gold and silver has been exhibited at numerous international shows. It has also been awarded German designer prizes, such as the red dot in Essen for design quality. A solo show at the Kunstgewerbemuseum Dresden in 2001 represents a high point of Zimmermann's career. From 1994 he was head of the silversmithing seminars at Fachhochschule Trier and at Sheffield Hallam University (SHU) and taught two semesters at Fachhochschule Trier in 1997 and 1998 for Professor Ingeborg Bornhofen. In retrospect, Erich Zimmermann views his training as a silversmith as the foundation of his career. The feeling he has for »tracking down« the character of noble metals with the hammer is particularly noticeable in the *Cocoon* series. The sculpturally formed links of the award-winning necklace were created by working with sheet gold. They are also the basic elements of arm jewellery and voluminous drop earrings. When the form is left unsoldered so that it remains open at the side, it resembles a pod. The designer is self-taught and works up all new forms over a development period of several years. »All consequences have been thought out and worked through by the time a new idea is realised,« says Erich Zimmermann, who rejects fleeting trends. He wants to create pieces that are just as attractive decades later as they are on their first day.

His *Princess rings* can be viewed as the exact opposite of the *Cocoon* line. Zimmermann created them in 1997 as persiflage of the classic Tiffany ring. In America, after all, the size of the precious stone in an engagement ring is the standard by which the wealth and status of a bride and bridegroom are measured. Erich Zimmermann sets magnificent precious stones in generous modern settings. The designer travels to the countries of origins of his stones to select the finest for these rings or he cuts the stones himself in his own workshop.

The classic *Cleopatra necklaces* are the bridge between the *Cocoons* and the *Princess rings*. In 1994 Zimmermann made his first necklace of gold set with lapis lazuli. The ideal linkage of precious stones and precious metal has been realised in a form that is at once durable and entirely flexible through the use of stainless steel cord. Alternating stones and gold create supple neck jewellery, which is reminiscent of the Pharaonic jewellery culture yet looks modern and contemporary.

Since 2004 the Augsburg designer has been dealing with an existential theme in his *Pirate* collection, which features a skull contrasting with magnificent precious stones. The closeness of magnificence and death were an important theme in the Baroque and Rococo periods and has recently been showcased by the English artist Damien Hirst. With a magnificent diamond

set in a grey skull, Erich Zimmermann symbolically confronts eternity and memento mori. In using the Vanitas motif, he links the Middle Ages with the present. He also enjoys »playing with our transience or being reminded of it, which is often considered distressing«.

1993	*Kokon-Ohrhänger,* Gold, Platin — *Cocoon earrings*, gold, platinum
1994	*Kleopatra-Kette,* Gold, Onyx — *Cleopatra necklace*, gold, onyx
1997	*Prinzessinnen-Ring*, Roségold, Amethyst — *Princess ring*, rose gold, amethyst
1998	*Prinzessinnen-Ring*, Roségold, Peridot — *Princess ring*, rose gold, peridot
2007	*Piraten-Anhänger*, Roségold, Amethyst, Koralle — *Pirate Pendant*, rose gold, amethyst, coral

Erich Zimmermann
Geboren 1958 in Augsburg. 1991 Meisterprüfung für Silberschmiede, 1994 für Goldschmiede. Ateliergründung 1983 in Augsburg.

Erich Zimmermann
Born in Augsburg in 1958. 1991 Master craftsman's certificate in silversmithing, 1994 in goldsmithing. Founded studio in Augsburg in 1983.

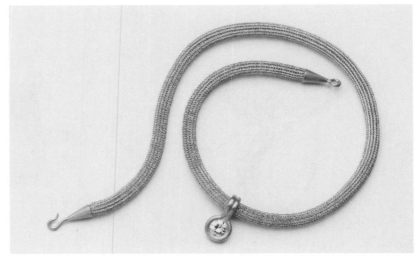

1983

1980

PUR

Im Sommer 1983 besuchte Hans-Hermann Lingenbrinck das Britische Museum in London. Ein ägyptischer Halsschmuck erweckte seine besondere Aufmerksamkeit. Das Schmuckstück, gefunden in einem Pharaonengrab, bestand aus feinen Platinfäden, die durch eine Stricktechnik verflochten waren. Inspiriert von dem archaischen Vorbild fertigte er kurze Zeit später Strickketten aus 0,2 mm dünn gezogenem Platindraht. »Das war für uns eine erste Vorstufe von Produktentwicklung«, berichtet der Schmuckgestalter und Inhaber von Pur, Atelier für Schmuckgestaltung.

Die Idee der *Strickketten* wurde in den 1980er Jahren von vielen Goldschmieden aufgegriffen. Für Pur waren sie lediglich der Einstieg in ein modernes Kettendesign und in die Gestaltung mit Platin 950. Kurze Zeit später entwickelte Lingenbrinck in Zusammenarbeit mit der Schmuckdesignerin Cornelia Bürgers die *Scheibenkette K02*, die 1985 auf der Inhorgenta in München vorgestellt wurde. Kreisrunde, sanft gebürstete Goldscheibchen werden von feinen Ringen aus Platin spielerisch durchdrungen und sicher verbunden. Die Kette erfüllte vollkommen die Forderungen der Moderne in der Produktgestaltung. Sie verbindet Funktionalität, sparsamen Materialeinsatz, Langlebigkeit und gute Form. Die *Scheibenkette* lässt auch eine konstruktive Verwandtschaft zu einigen frühen Ketten des Bauhausmeisters Naum Slutzky aus den 1930er Jahren erkennen. Dem erfolgreichen Konzept folgten bis heute rund 180 weitere *Elementketten*. Zum zweiten Standbein der Atelierproduktion wurde die Ringserie *Swivel* mit beweglichen, auswechselbaren Schmuckelementen.

Geboren wurde Hans-Hermann Lingenbrinck 1951 in Viersen, Nordrhein-Westfalen. Nach seiner Lehre als Goldschmied von 1966 bis 1969 und einigen Berufsjahren studierte er von 1973 bis 1978 an der Fachhochschule Düsseldorf bei Friedrich Becker. Bei ihm lernte Lingenbrinck, den Einsatz von Drehbänken und Fräsen für die Schmuckfertigung, um höchste technische Präzision zu erreichen. Wie groß der Einfluss Friedrich Beckers war, zeigt ein Brief, den der Schüler zum Tod seines Lehrers schrieb. Darin heißt es: »Die ersten Semester dieser Begegnung waren für mich wie der Blick auf ein Spektrum neuer Farbtöne. (...) Der Lehrer Friedrich Becker hat mich infiziert. Er hat mich, wenn auch erst viel später, als ich meine Firma gegründet hatte, zu einem Qualitäts- und Entwicklungsbesessenen gemacht.« Dass Lingenbrinck nicht zum Unikat-Künstler wurde, sondern konsequent Schmuck-Design in kleinen Serien produzierte, hat Becker sehr begrüßt.

Hans-Hermann Lingenbrinck reiste nach dem Studium nach Haiti. Nicht zum Urlaub, sondern um dort drei Jahre für eine Industriefirma Schmuck zu produzieren. Die Arbeit in dem Entwicklungsland, ohne jede Infrastruktur, während der Duvalier-Diktatur bedeutete tägliches Improvisieren. Für Lingenbrinck waren es elementare Erfahrungen, die er später beim Aufbau der eigenen Firma nutzen konnte. Bereits vor und während seiner Tätigkeit als Produktionsleiter auf der Karibikinsel beteiligte er sich an Ausstellun-

1983   *Strickkette*, Platin, Wolfram, Gold — *Rope necklace*, platinum, wolfram, gold

1988   Kette, Gold, Platin, Wolfram — Chain, gold, platinum, wolfram

2000   Kette *K97B*, Gold, Platin, Wolfram — Chain *K97B*, gold, platinum, wolfram

1980   *Doppelwandiges Gefäß*, Silber, Gold, Kupfer — *Double-walled Vessel*, silver, gold, copper

1988

2000

gen: im Goldschmiedehaus Hanau, in der Kestner-Gesellschaft in Hannover und im Stadtmuseum Düsseldorf. Sein neuer Schmuck und sein modernes Gerät in Silber wurden an Goethe-Instituten in Japan, Neuseeland und Australien sowie bei Industriedesign-Ausstellungen des Landes Nordrhein-Westfalen in Moskau, Shanghai und Singapur gezeigt. Das Schmuckmuseum in Pforzheim und das Museum Ludwig in Köln kauften seine Stücke für ihre Sammlungen.

Dass Schmuck von Pur in den 1980er Jahren zügig den Weg in die Juweliergeschäfte fand, lag aber nicht allein an der kreativen und technischen Kompetenz der Firma. Die Wiedereinführung von Platin auf dem deutschen Schmuckmarkt beflügelte generell Schmuckgestalter, die für ihre neue Formensprache ein exklusives, nicht vorbelastetes Edelmetall suchten. Lingenbrinck: »Durch seine fantastischen Materialeigenschaften hat Platin den Schmuckgestaltern eine Basis geliefert, ganz neue Ideen zu verwirklichen.« Als die Degussa eine neue Platinlegierung entwickelte, die zugleich hart und elastisch sein musste, war sein kleines Atelier an der praktischen Umsetzung beteiligt. Es entstanden Clips als Männerschmuck aus Platin 950. »Das war deshalb ein Meilenstein für den modernen Schmuck, weil wir eine Materialeigenschaft des Stahls auf Platin übertragen haben.« 1985 experimentiert Pur mit der Verschmelzung von Platin- und Goldelementen für eine Ringserie. Platin 950 entsprach in den 1980er Jahren einerseits dem Anspruch an konstruktive Klarheit in der Gestaltung. Andererseits habe man, erklärt Lingenbrinck, auch die Berührungsängste zu anderen Metallen verloren. Jedenfalls wurde Serienfertigung in Platin im Stil der klassischen Moderne ein sichtbares Segment im Schmuckmarkt.

Die Entscheidung von Pur, mit der Manufaktur Niessing sowie den Goldschmiedeateliers Ehinger-Schwarz und Fillner eine Standgemeinschaft auf Fachmessen zu etablieren, war Ende der 1980er Jahre ein deutliches Signal für Juweliere, dass eine neue Epoche im deutschen Schmuck angebrochen war. Die Standgemeinschaft mit ihren modernen Schmuckkonzepten wirkte aber auch für Absolventen der Fachakademien wie eine Initialzündung. Lingenbrinck: »Unsere Aktivitäten waren für viele Marktteilnehmer ein Orientierungspunkt. Man erkannte, wie die Moderne interpretiert werden kann.«

Bei zahlreichen Produktentwicklungen arbeitete Lingenbrinck in dieser Zeit mit der Designerin Andrea Zarp zusammen. Sie hatte ebenfalls in Düsseldorf bei Becker studiert. Die Ketten von Pur basieren auf einer originellen, konstruktiven Grundidee, einer klaren formalen Aussage und kompromissloser Materialauswahl. Maßgeblich war das Atelier daran beteiligt, den Begriff »Schmuckkette« in den 1980 Jahren neu zu definieren. Luxuriöse Schwere und Hochglanzpolitur gibt es bei Pur nicht. Stattdessen entstehen im Zusammenspiel von Präzisionsmaschinen und Handarbeit Ketten von schwebender Leichtigkeit. Die filigranen, mattierten Ring- oder

Navette-Glieder können flach oder plastisch geformt sein. Getragen wirken die Pur-Ketten kraftvoll präsent und gleichzeitig spielerisch leicht. Manche Modelle lassen sich durch einfaches Drehen so variieren, dass beim Tragen ein oder zwei zusätzliche Formen, Lingenbrinck sagt dazu auch »Bilder«, entstehen. Die Konstruktion bleibt als Element der Gestaltung sichtbar. Die Ketten von Pur, gefertigt in Platin und 18-karätigem Gold, verbinden Volumen mit Leichtigkeit und Klarheit mit Poesie – eine bis dahin im Serienschmuck selten gekannte Symbiose. Nach 2000 werden auch dezent Farbsteine eingesetzt und vor allem für sein Ringthema *Swivel* Edelstahl. Ende der 1990er Jahre wurde Pur mit einem red dot für höchste Designqualität vom Designzentrum NRW ausgezeichnet.

Das Atelier in Nettetal war früher eine evangelische Kirche. Mit 13 Mitarbeitern entwickelt sich Pur seit 1983 zu einem jener Unternehmen, das die Produktionsform des 19. Jahrhunderts in der Moderne neu entdeckte und auf ganz persönliche Art mit Leben erfüllt. »Wir entwickeln Designkonzeptionen und auch die Werkzeuge und Vorrichtungen für die Maschinen, um unsere eigenen Produkte herzustellen«, erklärt Lingenbrinck. Das Ziel sei es immer, eine perfekte Lösung für eine Idee zu finden. »Ohne den Designaspekt ist keine Entwicklung möglich«, sagt der Atelierchef und ist überzeugt, dass Erfindungsreichtum und Imagination in der Serienproduktion nicht leiden. »Die Produktion in Schmuckserien gibt uns die Chance für Entwicklungen, die für Einzelstücke nicht möglich wären.«

Pur ist auch ein Musterbeispiel für die Wiederbelebung der Manufakturidee. Es unterscheidet sich einerseits von der industriellen Produktion, die im arbeitsteiligen Prozess Schmuck als »seelenlose« Ware hervorbringt. Andererseits wird aber auch deutlich anders entwickelt und produziert als in herkömmlichen Goldschmiedewerkstätten. Durch den Einsatz modernster CNC-Technologie sind präzise, wiederholbare Ergebnisse möglich. »Wir machen Produktentwicklung«, hat Lingenbrinck immer wieder betont. Hinzu kommt das persönliche Vergnügen des Firmeninhabers, Ergebnisse in 1000stel Millimeter präzise zu messen. Der Technikeinsatz sei auch nötig, »um international wettbewerbsfähig zu bleiben«, sagt der Firmengründer. Besonders motiviert ihn, dass sein jüngster Sohn Max, der gerade seine Lehre im Atelier Pur macht, dieses Qualitätsdenken inzwischen mit ihm teilt.

»Swivel« ist der englischen Sprache entlehnt und bezeichnet einen Ring mit einem Gelenk, das sich frei in einer Ringschiene drehen kann. Einen drehbaren Hocker nennen die Angelsachsen swivel chair. Der *Swivel* von Pur, der als Warenzeichen registriert ist, steht für eine innovative Ringserie. Charakteristisch ist der bewegliche Kopf, eingespannt in eine Ringschiene aus Edelstahl oder 18-karätigem Gold. Die sanfte »Nachgiebigkeit« des schmückenden Ringkopfes verändere das Tragegefühl und den Umgang mit dem Schmuckstück. Wichtig ist auch, dass sich jeder *Swivel* flexibel mit einem zweiten oder dritten *Swivel* kombinieren lässt. Das Ringkonzept erlaubt un-

2000   2000–2005   2005

endliche Variationsmöglichkeiten. Wie die Schmuckketten von Pur lösten die *Swivel*-Ringe einen Innovationsschub aus. Lingenbrinck: »*Swivel* als Serienprodukt hat bei vielen unserer jährlich neu entstehenden Ringideen eine innovative Formensprache geradezu erzwungen.« Sogar neue Schliffe werden regelmäßig für *Swivel* erdacht. Sie ergeben verblüffende Kombinationen von Farbe und Lichtbrechung. Das Interesse der Frauen an der Wandelbarkeit von *Swivel*-Ringen motivierte das Entwurfsteam zu zahlreichen kreativen Ringserien. Der Chef von Pur liebt diese Entwicklung, denn das Leben selbst sei Veränderung und dies gelte mehr denn je für unsere Zeit, sagt er. »Unsere Kunden müssen mit unseren Produkten unterscheidbar sein und wir möchten erkennbar bleiben.«

E — In summer 1983, Hans-Hermann Lingenbrinck visited the British Museum in London. He was particularly fascinated by an Egyptian collar. The jewellery, found in a pharaonic tomb, consisted of fine strings of platinum that were interwoven by means of a rope-making technique. Inspired by this archaic model, he made *Strickketten* [Rope necklaces] of platinum wire 0.2 mm thick. »For us, that was a first preliminary to product development,« reports the owner of Pur, studio for jewellery design.

The idea for the Rope necklaces was taken up in the 1980s by many goldsmiths. For Pur they represented the threshold to modern necklace design and designing with 950 platinum. Soon afterwards Lingenbrinck collaborated with the jewellery designer Cornelia Bürgers on developing *Scheibenkette K02* [Disc chain *K02*], which was launched at the 1985 Munich Inhorgenta. Perfect discs, with a softly brushed surface are playfully penetrated with fine rings of platinum and firmly linked. This necklace perfectly met the Modernist requirements as it linked practicality, economical use of material, durability and good form. The *Disc chain* also reveals affinities in construction with early necklaces by the Bauhaus master Naum Slutzky from the 1930s. Some 180 other *Elementketten* [Modular necklaces] have followed up that successful concept. The *Swivel* ring collection, featuring movable, exchangeable decorative elements, has become the second pillar of Lingenbrinck studio production.

Born in Viersen, North Rhine-Westphalia, in 1951, Hans-Hermann Lingenbrinck served a goldsmith's apprenticeship (1966–1969), worked several years in the profession and then studied under Friedrich Becker at the Fachhochschule Düsseldorf (1973–1978). He taught Lingenbrinck how to use lathes and milling machinery in jewellery-making to achieve the highest possible degree of technical precision. How great Friedrich Becker's influence was is shown in a letter written by Lingenbrinck on the death of his teacher. It says: »The first semesters of that encounter were for me like a glimpse of a spectrum of new colour tones [...] As a teacher, Friedrich Becker infected me [with enthusiasm]. He was the one who made me into a person obsessed with quality and development, albeit much later, after I had founded my firm.« Becker highly approved Lingenbrinck's consistency in becoming a jewellery designer working with small editions rather than a maker of one-off pieces.

After finishing his studies, Hans-Hermann Lingenbrinck went to Haiti. Not on holiday but to produce jewellery there for an industrial manufacturer for three years. Working in a developing country devoid of infrastructure under the Duvalier dictatorship meant improvising on a day-to-day basis. For Lingenbrinck those were fundamental experiences which he put to good use later when he was building up his own firm.

Even before and during his stint as production director on the Caribbean island, he showed work at exhibitions in Germany and abroad: at the Goldschmiedehaus Hanau, the Kestner-Gesellschaft in Hannover and the Stadtmuseum Düsseldorf. His new jewellery and his modern tableware in silver were shown at Goethe Institutes in Japan, New Zealand and Australia as well as industrial design trade fairs organised by the state of North Rhine-Westphalia in Moscow, Shanghai and Singapore. The Pforzheim Jewellery Museum and the Museum Ludwig in Cologne have bought his pieces for their collections.

That jewellery from Pur had no problems in making its way to jewellers in the 1980s was not just due to the firm's reputation for creativity and technical competence. The reintroduction of platinum to the German jewellery market generally encouraged jewellery designers seeking an exclusive noble metal unencumbered with negative associations for their new formal idiom. Lingenbrinck: »Due to its fantastic material properties, platinum provided jewellery designers with a basis for realising entirely new ideas.« When Degussa developed a new platinum alloy that had to be both tough and elastic, Lingenbrinck's little studio shared in putting it to practical use, making tie clips as men's jewellery in 950 platinum. »That was a benchmark in modern jewellery because we transferred a material property of steel to platinum.« In 1985 Pur experimented with fusing elements of platinum and gold for a ring collection. In the 1980s, 950 platinum met the demand for clarity of construction in design. On the other hand, as Lingenbrinck explains, the awe in which other metals had been held also dissipated. In any case, industrial use of platinum for jewellery in classic modern style came to occupy a considerable segment of the jewellery market.

The decision taken by Pur to join forces with the Niessing factory as well as the Ehinger-Schwarz and Fillner goldsmithing studios on establishing a collective stand at trade fairs clearly signalised to jewellers in the late 1980s that a new era in German jewellery had dawned. However, the collective stand with its modern jewellery concepts also electrified graduates of specialist academies. Lingenbrinck: »Our activities were an orientation point for many on the market. People realised how Modernism can be interpreted.«

2000–2006   2000–2007

At that time Lingenbrinck collaborated on numerous product-development projects with the designer Andrea Zarp, who had also studied with Becker in Düsseldorf. The necklaces launched by Pur are based on an original Constructivist fundamental idea, a clear formal statement and an uncompromising choice of materials. The studio had a paramount share in redefining the term »necklace as jewellery« in the 1980s. Pur does not do heavy luxury and mirror polish. Instead, necklaces so light they seem to float were created through the interplay of precision machinery and hand craftsmanship. The delicate, matt-finished ring or navette elements can be either flat or sculptural in form. When worn, Pur necklaces make their presence felt yet feel playfully light. Some models can be varied just by being turned to generate one or two additional forms – Lingenbrinck also calls them »images«. Construction remains visible as an element of design. The Pur necklaces, made in platinum and 18-carat gold, link volume with lightness and clarity with poetry – up to then a rare synthesis indeed in manufactured jewellery. Since 2000 coloured stones have also been reticently used and, especially for the Swivel ring theme, stainless steel as well. In the late 1990s Pur was awarded a red dot by the NRW Design Centre for top quality in design.

The studio in Nettetal was once a Lutheran church. Since 1983 Pur has, with a workforce of thirteen, grown into one of those businesses that have rediscovered 19th-century production methods for modern design and re-activated them in an entirely personal way. »We develop design concepts as well as tools and attachments for the machinery in order to make our own products,« explains Lingenbrinck. The aim is always to find the perfect solution for an idea. »Without the design aspect, development is impossible,« says the head of the studio, convinced that inventiveness and imagination do not suffer from production by industrial methods. »Producing lines in jewellery with machinery gives us an opportunity for developments that would not be possible with one-off pieces.«

Pur is also a prime example of the revival of a new manufacturing idea. On the one hand, it differs from industrial mass production, which results in jewellery as »soulless« consumer ware made by the conventional division of labour. On the other hand, however, development and production at Pur differ markedly from the methods normally used in goldsmithing workshops. Through the use of state-of-the-art CNC technology, results have become reproducible. »We are doing product development,« Lingenbrinck has emphasised repeatedly. Then there is his personal delight in measuring results with a precision down to a 1000th of a millimetre. The use of technology is also necessary »for us to stay competitive on a global scale,« says the firm's founder. He finds it particularly motivating that his youngest son, Max, who is serving an apprenticeship at the Pur studio, in the meantime shares his thinking on quality.

Swivel is the name for a ring with a joint that can revolve freely in a ring shank. In English, a bar stool or office chair (swivel-chair) with a revolving seat is said to »swivel«. The Pur Swivel, which is a registered trademark, stands for an innovative ring collection. Its salient characteristic is its movable bezel, set into a stainless steel or 18-carat gold shank. The gentle »compliance« of the decorative bezel makes for wearability that feels different and a different way of dealing with this piece of jewellery: another important aspect is that any single Swivel can be flexibly combined with a second or third Swivel. This is a ring concept that allows for endless variation.

Like the Pur necklaces, the Swivel rings have sparked off a spate of innovation. Lingenbrinck: »Swivel as a serially manufactured product has really forced an innovative formal language in many of our new ideas for rings each year.« New gemstone cuts are even regularly invented for Swivel. They produce stunning combinations of colour and light refraction. The interest shown by women in the variability of Swivel rings has motivated the designer team to come up with numerous creative ring collections. The head of Pur is delighted with this development because, after all, life itself means change and this is truer than ever in our time, he maintains. »Our clientele must be distinguishable through our products and we would like to remain recognisable.«

2000   Swivel Ringe, Edelstahl, Gold, Diamanten, Farbsteine — Swivel rings,
–2007   stainless steel, gold, diamonds, coloured stones

Hans-Hermann Lingenbrinck
Geboren 1951 in Viersen. 1973–1978
Fachhochschule Düsseldorf.
1983 Firmengründung in Nettetal.

Hans-Hermann Lingenbrinck
Born in Viersen in 1951. 1973–1978
Fachhochschule Düsseldorf. Founded firm in
Nettetal in 1983.

1991

1993

1990

1992

1994

1996

2001

2002

Georg Spreng

Kartoffeln aus Platin, Eistüten aus 18-karätigem Gold »gefüllt« mit Edelsteinen und Perlen. Mit gewagten, originellen Formen und einem kräftigen Schuss Farbe belebt Georg Spreng seit Anfang der 1990er Jahre die Schmuckwelt. Inzwischen zählt er mit seinen modernen Schmuckserien zu den Klassikern des Genres. Die »Farbigkeit« wurde nach der Jahrtausendwende, als die Schmuckträgerinnen mehr Emotion im Schmuck forderten, zu einem zentralen Thema des Designers.

»Meine Lust auf Farbe begann schon sehr früh«, erzählt Georg Spreng: »Ich konnte mich nie für Blue Jeans erwärmen. Deshalb habe ich mir schon während meines Studiums farbige Stoffe gekauft und mir eigene Hosen geschneidert. Das Uniforme war mir ein Graus.« Studiert hat Georg Spreng Industriedesign an der Werkkunstschule in Schwäbisch Gmünd. Sein Vater war Meister an der Goldschmiedeschule. In diese Fußstapfen wollte er eigentlich nie treten.

Georg Spreng studierte an der Fachhochschule für Gestaltung in Schwäbisch Gmünd von 1967 bis 1971. Nach einer erfolgreichen Tätigkeit zwischen 1971 und 1982 als freier Produktdesigner und Mitbegründer der Gruppe frogdesign träumte er 1983 von einem längeren Aufenthalt in der Südsee. Auf einer vierwöchigen Urlaubsreise in Kanada verliebte er sich jedoch mit seiner vierköpfigen Familie »in ein drei Quadratkilometer großes Stückchen Land.« Zurück in Deutschland folgte der spontane Entschluss, nach Kanada auszuwandern. Als »Standbein« in Europa diente ein kleines Bauernhäuschen in den Vogesen. Von dort aus konnte Spreng weiterhin freie Designaufträge abwickeln. Doch was war der Grund für den Ortswechsel? Georg Spreng hatte alles erreicht im Produktdesign. Seine Arbeiten waren vielfach ausgezeichnet und befanden sich in Designsammlungen, zum Beispiel im Museum of Modern Art in New York. Er hatte kein Interesse, »noch einen weiteren Computer oder noch einen Zahnarztstuhl« zu entwerfen. »Ich wollte mich zurückbesinnen und etwas anderes ausprobieren: Malen, Gartenbau, Architektur«, erzählt er.

Das erste Schmuckstück von Georg Spreng entstand in Kanada fast spielerisch, »aus reinem Spaß.« Im Wald lag ein gefällter Baum, aus dem Baum wurde ein Brett herausgesägt, aus dem Brett gestaltete der Designer einen imposanten Halsreif. Er wurde ausgesägt, geraspelt und mit Schmirgelpapier ganz glatt geschliffen. Diesen Schmuck habe er für sich hergestellt, ohne viel zu überlegen, erzählt er. Zur Freude am Machen kam dann noch das Aha-Erlebnis beim Anlegen des Halsreifs hinzu: »Ich spürte, dass mit mir etwas passierte. Man ist nicht mehr ganz der Gleiche, wenn man ein besonderes Schmuckstück trägt, ob das nun ein Reif aus Holz oder aus Gold ist.« Die Zeit in Kanada, die Farbwahrnehmung in der Natur, der Indian Summer und das Licht in dieser Weite trugen dazu bei, dass die erwachte Schmucklust weitere Früchte trieb. Um für alle Fälle vorzusorgen, hatte die Familie zwei kleine Barren Gold mitgenommen und unter der Hütte versteckt. Irgendwann

grub Georg Spreng das Gold aus und fing an zu schmieden. Er benutzte die Werkzeuge, die er vorfand, einen Hammer und eine Axt als Amboss. Entstanden ist wiederum ein breiter Halsreif. »Das Gold mit seiner Farbe und seiner Geschmeidigkeit, das reizt einen natürlich«, berichtet Georg Spreng über seine zweite elementare Schmuckschöpfung. Zunächst glaubte er, Schmuck könne man nur für sich selbst machen – oder höchstens für jemand, den man sehr gut kennt. Als erfolgreicher Designer reizte es ihn jedoch zu hören, was andere zu seiner Arbeit sagten. »Es hat mir irgendwann nicht ausgereicht, Schmuck nur für mich zu machen. Ich wollte testen, wo ich stehe und wie das im Markt ankommt.«

1991 hatte Georg Spreng auf der Sonderschau der Münchner Inhorgenta die Gelegenheit dazu. Den Messestand nutzte er als Bühne für eine ganzheitliche Inszenierung. Zu seinen ungewöhnlichen Stücken hatte er auch die passende Kleidung entworfen und nähen lassen. Besonders die *Eistütenringe*, groß dimensionierte Kegel aus 18-karätigem Gold mit prächtigen Farbedelsteinen, Diamanten und Perlen, erregten Interesse. Zu seinem ersten Auftritt als Schmuckgestalter bemerkt der Designer: »Ich bin als Paradiesvogel aufgefallen. Die Presse kam, und ein Günter Krauss hat sofort einen *Eistütenring* gekauft. Das war natürlich ein Wahnsinn.«

Von dem Erfolg ermutigt, entschied Georg Spreng zusammen mit seiner Frau, auf dem anfänglichen Hobby sein zukünftiges Berufsleben aufzubauen. Kreationen wie die *Vulkanbroschen*, die *Schmucktörtchen* und die *Augenringe* entstanden. Doch nach den ersten Erfolgen habe das Geschäft erst mal gestoppt, bekennt Spreng: »Oft hat es fünf Jahre gedauert, bis Juweliere mit uns geredet haben und zehn Jahre, bis sie das erste Mal kauften.« Auch zeigte sich, dass Kanada zu weit weg war, um die Schmuckkunden in Europa zu bedienen. Auf die Rückkehr 1997, in Schwäbisch Gmünder Gefilde, folgten die nachhaltigsten Schmuckentwicklungen von Georg Spreng.

Die Ringserie *Blub* besteht aus prächtigen Farbsteinringen in runden, geometrischen Fassungen. Die einzelnen Ringe lassen sich sehr effektvoll miteinander kombinieren. Kaum weniger variantenreich arbeitete Spreng mit der Navetteform und den quadratischen Ringen *Caro*. Die Kombinationsmöglichkeit wird auch mit doppelten Ringschienen erreicht, die ineinander zu stecken sind. 2007 interpretierte Spreng das Thema der Farbsteinklassiker Saphir, Rubin und Smaragd innerhalb der *Blub*-Serie neu. Um die Kostbarkeit dieser Steine zu unterstreichen, stehen sie im Dialog mit deutlich großformatigeren Edelsteinen wie Amethyst oder Turmalin. 2008 stellte Georg Spreng die erfolgreiche Ringserie *Blub* mit Edelsteinen im Cabochonschliff vor.

Im Frühjahr folgte der Umzug in eine moderne Manufaktur in Wißgoldingen. Das Haus, das den vorläufigen Höhepunkt in der Entwicklung des vielseitigen Gestalters dokumentiert, steht an einem Ort, der vielen Schmuckfreunden noch ein Begriff ist. Jo Stotz und ihre Tochter hatten

2002

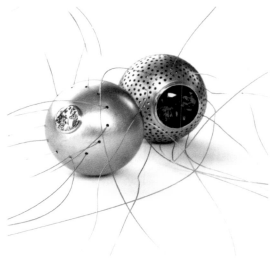

2003

2004

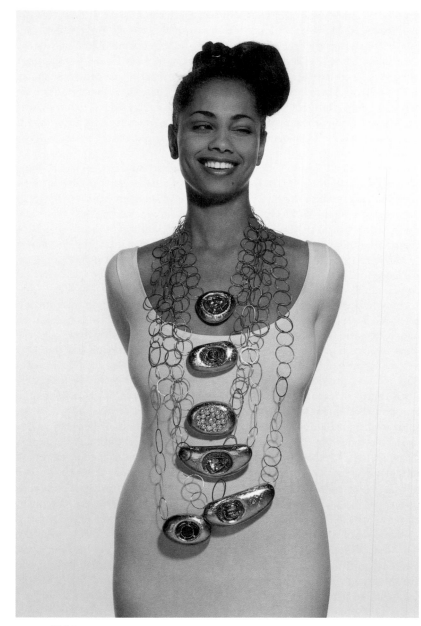

2004

hier bis in die 1990er Jahre ihre Schmucktreffen auf dem Haldenhof veranstaltet. Jetzt gibt es wieder einen Grund, in Sachen Schmuck nach Wißgoldingen zu blicken.

E — Potatoes made of platinum, cornets of 18-carat gold »filled« with precious stones and pearls. With his boldly original forms and a strong dose of colour, Georg Spreng has enlivened the jewellery scene since the early 1990s. By now his modern lines in jewellery are genre classics. Now that the women wearing jewellery are demanding that it makes more of an emotional impact, »colour« has become a pivotal theme with the designer since the turn of the millennium.

»My lust for colour set in very early,« as Georg Spreng tells it: »I never could develop any enthusiasm for jeans. That's why I bought coloured cloth even while I was a student and made my own trousers. Anything uniform gave me the creeps.« Georg Spreng studied industrial design at the Werkkunstschule in Schwäbisch Gmünd. His father was a master craftsman employed at the Goldsmithing School. Georg Spreng never wanted to follow in his father's footsteps.

He was a student at the Fachhochschule für Gestaltung in Schwäbisch Gmünd from 1967–1971. After a successful stint as a freelance product designer and co-founder of the group known as frogdesign between 1971 and 1982, he began in 1983 to dream of a long stay in the South Seas. However, on a four-week holiday in Canada, he and his wife and two children fell in love »with a piece of property covering three square kilometres«. Back in Germany Spreng spontaneously decided to emigrate to Canada. He kept a small farmstead in the Vosges as his »fall-back option« in Europe. From there Spreng could continue to handle freelance design commissions. But what was the reason for the move? Georg Spreng had made it in product design. He had received numerous awards for his work and many of his pieces were in top design collections, notably the Museum of Modern Art in New York. But he had no interest in designing »yet another computer or dentist's chair«. As he puts it, »I wanted to take stock and try out something different: painting, garden design, architecture.«

Georg Spreng created his first piece of jewellery in Canada by playing at it, »just for the fun of it«. A felled tree was lying in a wood. A plank was sawn from it and from the plank the designer created an impressive torc. It was sawn out, filed and polished very smooth with sandpaper. As he tells it, he made that piece of jewellery just for himself without giving too much thought to it. Added to his delight in making something was an »aha« experience when he put the torc on: »I sensed that something was happening to me. You're no longer the same person when you're wearing a distinctive piece of jewellery, no matter whether it's a torc made of wood or of gold.« His time in Canada, absorbing the colours of nature, the Indian Summer and

2005   2006   2007

the light over such broad expanses of land contributed to ensuring that the desire awakened in him to make jewellery continued to bear fruit.

As a nest egg for emergencies, the Spreng family had taken two little bars of gold with them and hidden them in their cabin. At some point, Georg Spreng dug up the gold and started to work it. He used any tools he had at hand, a hammer and an axe as his anvil. He came up again with a broad torc. »Gold, with its colour and its suppleness, that naturally has its attractions,« comments Georg Spreng on his second elemental jewellery creation. At first he thought it would be possible to work just for himself – or at most for someone he knew very well. As a designer who has arrived, however, he does like hearing what others have to say about his work. »At some point making jewellery just for myself wasn't enough for me. I wanted to check out where I stand and how that works out on the market.«

In 1991 Georg Spreng had his chance to do that at the special show at the Munich Inhorgenta. He used his trade fair stand as a stage for a holistic presentation. He had also designed clothes and had them made to showcase his unusual pieces. The *Ice-cream cone rings*, large cones in 18-carat gold set with magnificent coloured precious stones, diamonds and pearls were the biggest attraction at his stand. As Georg Spreng describes his début as a jewellery designer: »I stood out like a bird of paradise. The press came and a Günter Krauss bought an *Ice-cream cone ring* straight off. That was of course sheer madness.«

Encouraged by that success, Georg Spreng decided to join forces with his wife and build up a professional future from what had initially been just a hobby. Creations such as *Vulkanbroschen* [Volcano brooches], *Schmucktörtchen* [Cake jewellery] and *Augenringe* [Eye rings] were the result of that decision. However, after initial success, business stagnated for a while, admits Spreng: »It often took five years before jewellers would even talk with us and ten years before they bought something for the first time.« It also became apparent that Canada was too far away for keeping up with clients in Europe. Georg Spreng's return in 1997 to his old stamping ground in Schwäbisch Gmünd was followed by his most resounding successes.

The *Blub* line in rings features magnificent coloured stones in round geometric settings. Several rings can be worn at once to create very effective combinations. Spreng has worked with variations just as innovatively with the navette form and square rings he calls *Caro*. The possibility of combining rings is also provided by sets with double shanks that interlock. In 2007 Spreng re-interpreted the classic coloured-stone theme based on sapphires, rubies and emeralds within the *Blub* line. To underscore the preciousness of those stones, he has made them engage in a dialogue with considerably larger semiprecious stones such as amethysts and tourmalines. In 2008 Georg Spreng added a further twist to the successful *Blub* line by featuring cabochon precious stones.

That spring, Spreng moved to a modern factory in Wißgoldingen. The building, which marks the high point up to now in the career of this versatile and prolific designer, stands in a place that for jewellery aficionados is still a name to be reckoned with. Jo Stotz and her daughter used to hold their jewellery forums here at the Haldenhof on into the 1990s. Now there's just one more good reason for looking to Wißgoldingen where jewellery is concerned.

2002	*Blub* Halsspirale, Gold, Citrin — *Blub* spiral necklace, gold, citrine
2003	Halsschmuck *Pingpong*, Platin, Diamant, Tansanit s — Necklaces *Ping-pong*, platinum, diamond, tansanite
2004	*Caro* Ringe, Platin, Rubellith, Turmalin, Aquamarin — *Caro* rings, platinum, rubellith, tourmaline, aquamarine
2005	*La Gondola* Halsschmuck, Gold, Diamanten, Edelsteine — *La Gondola* necklace, gold, diamonds, precious stones
2006	Ringe *Orbit*, Gold, Zuchtperle, Diamant, Goldberyll — Rings *Orbit*, gold, cultured pearl, diamond, gold beryl
2007	Halsschmuck *Drops*, Platin, Diamant, Leder — Necklace *Drops*, platinum, diamond, leather
2004	Model: Ketten *Baked Potatoes*, Platin, Farbedelsteine — Model: Necklaces *Baked Potatoes*, platinum, coloured precious stones

Georg Spreng
Geboren 1949 in Schwäbisch-Gmünd.
1967–1971 FH Schwäbisch Gmünd.
1971–1982 frogdesign. Schmuckatelier seit 1983, heute in Wißgoldingen.

Georg Spreng
Born in Schwäbisch Gmünd in 1949.
1967–1971 FH Schwäbisch Gmünd. 1971–1982, Product designer at frogdesign. Jewellery studio since 1983, now in Wißgoldingen.

1996

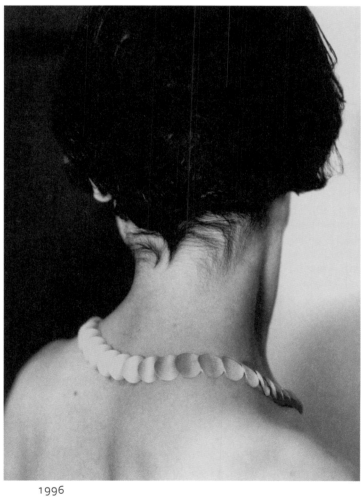

1996

1997

1996	Brosche *Schneegitter,* Silber — Brooch *Snow grid,* silver
1997	Brosche *Paraboloid*, Silber — Brooch *Paraboloid*, silver
1998	Brosche *Oval hinter Jalousie*, Gold — Brooch *Oval behind Louvre*, gold
1996	*Scheibenkette*, Gold — *Disc necklace*, gold
1997	*Scheibenarmband*, Gold — *Disc bracelet*, gold

1997

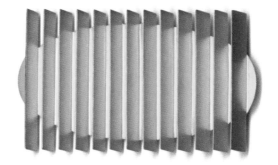

1998

Christiane Iken

Dreidimensionale, luftige Miniaturkonstrukte spielen im Schmuck von Christiane Iken mit Licht und Schatten. »Mich interessiert der Rhythmus, den der Wechsel erzeugt«, sagt sie, »die Wiederholung von Strukturen und Typologien, die Spannung zwischen positiv und negativ, zwischen Masse und Transparenz.«

Christiane Iken aus dem niedersächsischen Wildeshausen lernte ihr Handwerk von 1971 bis 1974 in der Werkstatt von Waltraut Müller in Bremen. Die Goldschmiedemeisterin stand dem Werkbund nahe. Bereits hier habe sie ihr Gefühl entwickelt, anspruchsvolle Formen und präzise handwerkliche Ausführung in Einklang zu bringen, erklärt Christiane Iken. Von 1978 bis 1983 besuchte sie die Fachhochschule für Gestaltung Pforzheim. Die Studienprojekte bei Professor Reinhold Reiling schärften ihr Gefühl für das Detail und die Gesamtkomposition, für Form und Ausdruck. Ein Jahr vor dem Diplom 1983 machte sie die Meisterprüfung im Goldschmiedehandwerk.

Die Ausstellung Dieci Orafi Padovani des Schmuckmuseums Pforzheim bewegte Christiane Iken, nach dem Studium ein Jahr nach Padua zu gehen, wo sie im Atelier von Diego Piazza arbeitete. Danach verfolgte sie in ihrer Werkstatt auf Fehmarn ihre konstruktivistische Formensprache und fertigte reduzierte künstlerische Schmuckunikate und Kleinserien. Immer wieder zog es sie dazwischen in fremde Länder, um zu arbeiten und die Sprache zu erlernen. So war sie in Italien, dann bei den Massai in Tansania und schließlich in Nepal. Dabei gab die Schmuck-Designerin auch ihr Wissen weiter. In Silberschmiedewerkstätten in Katmandu lehrte sie zwei Jahre lang die Theorie und Praxis der Schmuckherstellung im Rahmen eines UNO-Entwicklungshilfeprojekts. 1990 zog Christiane Iken mit ihrer Werkstatt nach Karlsruhe um. Ihre herausragende Gestaltungstätigkeit wurde 1999 mit dem red dot für hohe Designqualität des Designzentrums Nordrhein-Westfalen gewürdigt. Sie erhielt die Auszeichnung best of selection, den Innovationspreis der Messe München und den 33. Deutschen Schmuck- und Edelsteinpreis Idar-Oberstein. 1997 eröffnete Christiane Iken die Schmuckgalerie »der goldene schnitt« in Karlsruhe. Sorgsam achtet sie hier seit über zehn Jahren darauf, dass die Auswahl wichtiger Schmuckgestalter der Gegenwart das Spektrum ihrer eigenen Arbeiten auf gleichem Niveau ergänzt. Daneben entwickelt sie ihre eigenen Schmucklinien weiter. Mit ihren Kleinserien, hauptsächlich Halsschmuck, Broschen und Armbänder, zählt Christiane Iken inzwischen schon zu den Klassikern unter den modernen, künstlerisch orientierten Goldschmieden.

E — Christiane Iken creates airy three-dimensional miniature structures that play with light and shade in her jewellery. »I'm interested in the rhythm created by alternation,« she says, »the repetition of structures and typologies, the tensions between positive and negative, between mass and transparency«.

A native of Wildeshausen in Lower Saxony, Christiane Iken learned her craft between 1971 and 1974 at Waltraut Müller's Bremen workshop. As a master goldsmith, Waltraut Müller had affinities with the Werkbund. While working with Müller, as Christiane Iken explains it, she developed a feeling for uniting ambitious forms with precise workmanship. From 1978 until 1983 she attended the Fachhochschule für Gestaltung in Pforzheim. Study projects under the supervision of Professor Reinhold Reiling honed her eye for the relationship between details and overall composition, for form and expression. A year before she took her diploma in 1983, Christiane Iken did her master's certificate in goldsmithing.

Dieci Orafi Padovani [Ten Paduan Goldsmiths], an exhibition mounted by the Schmuckmuseum Pforzheim, inspired Christiane Iken to go to Padua a year after completing her studies. In Padua she worked in Diego Piazza's studio. She subsequently pursued a Constructivist language of forms in her Fehmarn workshop, making reductivist art jewellery one-offs and limited editions. She continued to travel abroad to work and learn the formal idiom of various countries. Her travels took her to Italy, then to the Maasai in Tanzania and finally to Nepal. Iken also willingly taught all she knew about jewellery design. For two years she taught the theory and practice of jewellery-making in silversmithing workshops in Kathmandu under the auspices of a UN development aid project. In 1990 Christiane Iken moved her workshop to Karlsruhe. She was awarded the red dot for design quality in recognition of her outstanding work in jewellery design by the North Rhine-Westphalia Design Centre. She has also received the best of selection prize for innovation awarded by the Munich Messe and the 33rd German Jewellery and Precious Stone Prize from Idar-Oberstein. In 1997 Christiane Iken opened the jewellery gallery »der goldene schnitt« [the golden ratio] in Karlsruhe. For over ten years now, she has fastidiously supplemented the range of her own work with a selection of jewellery of matching quality by leading contemporary designers while continuing to develop her own lines in jewellery. With her limited editions, chiefly neck jewellery, brooches and bracelets, Christiane Iken has become a classic modern goldsmith working in art jewellery.

Christiane Iken
Geboren 1955 in Wildeshausen. 1978–1983
Fachhochschule für Gestaltung Pforzheim.
Selbständig seit 1984.

Christiane Iken
Born in Wildeshausen in 1955. 1978–1983,
Fachhochschule für Gestaltung Pforzheim.
Self-employed since 1984.

1991   1993

1987

1993   1996

Henrich & Denzel

Henrich & Denzel gehört zu den Schmuckherstellern, die sich nach der Wiedereinführung von Platin in Deutschland kontinuierlich dem natürlich weißen Edelmetall widmeten. Nach der Gründung 1984 gelang es der Manufaktur mit Sitz in Radolfzell, sich in kurzer Zeit eine Spitzenposition in der modernen deutschen Schmuckkultur zu sichern. Charakteristisch für HD-Schmuck ist die Verbindung von herausragender Verarbeitungsqualität mit anspruchsvollem, langlebigem Design. Das erklärte Ziel der Firmengründer war es, »Schmuckklassiker zu schaffen, die über Jahrzehnte Bestand haben, ähnlich wie Stühle von Vitra, Möbel von Cassina oder Leuchten von Artemide.«

Kostbare Materie und kunstfertiges Handwerk lernte Günter Henrich schon in seiner Kindheit kennen. Geboren 1941 in Idar-Oberstein, wuchs er in der Gravieranstalt seines Großvaters auf. Wilhelm Dröschel, 1872–1955, zählte zu den besten Edelsteingraveuren seiner Zeit. Nach einer kaufmännischen Lehre in einer Diamantschleiferei sammelte Henrich erste Berufserfahrungen in der Gold- und Silberscheideanstalt Oberstein, Franz Reischauer. Neben handwerklichen Techniken kamen in der Scheideanstalt kostenintensive Produktionsverfahren wie Drehen, Fräsen, Stanzen und Prägen zum Einsatz. Günter Henrich war begeistert von der Präzision in der Fertigung und den organisatorischen Abläufen nach der Refa-Methode. Schon damals überlegte er, wie diese auch in der Schmuckindustrie eingesetzt werden könnten. Zwischen 1964 und 1983 war Günter Henrich Geschäftsführer der deutschen Niederlassung der Schweizer Schmuckmanufaktur Meister, zuerst in Singen und dann in Radolfzell.

1984 gründete Günter Henrich zusammen mit Roland Denzel als Juniorpartner die Schmuckmanufaktur Henrich & Denzel. Nicht nur handwerklich ein Perfektionist, entwickelt der Goldschmied Roland Denzel Maschinen und Steuerungen, die präzise Vorprodukte für den Goldschmied liefern. Hinzu kam die Erfahrung des Kaufmanns, Edelsteinkenners und Produktionsmanagers Günter Henrich. Gemeinsam war den Partnern die Begeisterung für Platin. »Es war die technische Herausforderung in der Bearbeitung des zähen Edelmetalls wie auch die Möglichkeit, eine neue Formensprache zu entwickeln, die uns faszinierten«, sagt Günter Henrich.

Die frühe Entscheidung für eine klare, reduzierte Formensprache in der Tradition der Moderne wurde in den 1990er Jahren zu einem Baustein des Erfolgs. Wichtig war für Henrich & Denzel die »Tradition des Bauhauses mit ihrer gradlinigen, klaren Formensprache, mit ihrer Reduktion auf das Wesentliche, mit ihrer überragenden Qualität von Proportion, Detail und Material.« Sie sollte, so heißt es in den Leitlinien, »stets nach den Erkenntnissen zeitgemäßer, moderner Gestaltung weiterentwickelt werden.« So überzeugte HD-Schmuck durch seine kantige Schönheit ebenso wie durch schlichte, weich fließende Formen. In den ersten Jahren arbeitete die Manufaktur Henrich & Denzel mit namhaften, freien Designern zusammen.

Günter Wermekes, ein Schüler von Friedrich Becker, entwickelte 1993 eine Armreif-Serie, welche in der Branche und der Presse große Beachtung fand. Mit dem Eintritt des Schmuckdesigners Jean-Paul Callau 1997, der von der Fachhochschule Idar-Oberstein an den Bodensee kam, wurde die eigene Gestaltungskompetenz gestärkt. Er ergänzte das bisherige Entwicklungsteam, bestehend aus dem Goldschmiedemeister Reinhold Denzel und dem Techniker Roland Denzel, in idealer Weise.

Die im Deutschen Werkbund und am Bauhaus formulierte Materialgerechtigkeit war auch für die moderne Schmuckentwicklung seit 1945 wichtig. Henrich & Denzel bezog in dieser Hinsicht eine klare Position: »Wir verarbeiten nur die besten, echten Materialien, welche die Natur liefert.« Wichtig ist in der Manufaktur auch der Grundsatz der Materialehrlichkeit. Als weißes Metall wird ausschließlich Platin 950 verwendet. Gelbe Schmuckstücke sind immer aus Gold 750 oder einer höheren Legierung gefertigt. Auch kommen nur echte, natürliche Farbsteine zum Einsatz. Sämtliche Diamanten werden nach den international anerkannten Richtlinien des International Diamond Council, IDC, graduiert. Schließlich wird streng darauf geachtet, dass keine Diamanten verarbeitet werden, die mit UN-Sanktionen belegt sind.

Ein Beispiel für die Symbiose aus innovativem Design, intelligenter Fertigungsqualität und bester Materialwahl ist der *Janus*-Armreif, der 1996 entstand. Durch die patentierte Drehbewegung lässt sich die Hälfte des Reifs aus Platin mit Diamanten um 360° drehen, so dass er zwei Gesichter zeigen kann. Geschlossen erscheint er in geometrisch reduzierter Schlichtheit. Geöffnet entfaltet er mit einer Diamantpavée-Fläche eine zweite, prächtigere Seite. Der *Janus*-Armreif gewann 1997 den Titel als innovativstes modernes Schmuckstück in Deutschland. Von herausragenden Erfolgen im Markt waren auch die Schmucklinie *Spiegelkerben*, 1993, der *Vegas-Ring*, 1999, sowie die Linie *Cascadem*, 2005, gekrönt. Mit einem Schmuckstück aus Platin, mit Diamanten, das einer aufklappbaren Blüte gleicht, demonstrierte Henrich & Denzel 2005 ihr technisches und gestalterisches Können. Die Qualität der Manufaktur wurde auch durch hohe Preise bei den japanischen Wettbewerben Platinum Design of the Year 1995 und 1996 belohnt. »Vor allem waren die Messeauftritte in München, Basel und Las Vegas sowie die Life-Shows der Platin Gilde in den Jahren 1990 bis 1993, mit ihrem sensationellen Medienecho, für unseren Erfolg wichtig«, erklärt Günter Henrich.

1993, neun Jahre nach der Gründung, konnte ein neues Firmengebäude errichtet werden. 1998 kam der so genannte Innovationsturm hinzu, in dem die Designabteilung untergebracht wurde. Mit der Verbindung von Platin und Diamanten konnte sich Henrich & Denzel seit Ende der 1990er Jahre auch bei Trauringen im obersten Marktsegment positionieren. »Manche unserer Entwicklungen sind inzwischen Allgemeingut geworden«, sagt der Firmengründer. 2006 ging mit dem Erreichen des 65. Lebensjahres die Ära von Günter Henrich zu Ende. Seine Tochter Carolin und ihr Mann Christoph

1999   2001   2001

Teufel, beide Diplom-Betriebswirte, übernahmen gemeinsam mit dem lang-jährigen Mitarbeiter und Mitglied der bisherigen Geschäftsleitung Herbert Kleinbruckner die Geschäftsführung.

»Dass HD-Schmuck heute zu den erfolgreichsten deutschen Schmuck-manufakturen zählt, ist das Verdienst einer Mannschaft«, sagt Günter Henrich, »die sich mit Leidenschaft, Charakter und auch mit Stolz für die herausgehobene Stellung im Markt eingesetzt hat.« Ebenso ist der Firmen-gründer den Partnern der ersten Stunde dankbar: Klaus Kaufhold, der 1980 das erste Platinstudio in Deutschland eröffnete, Dieter Hahn, Inhaber der ältesten Diamantschleiferei Deutschlands mit Sitz in Idar-Oberstein, der Allgemeinen Gold- und Silberscheideanstalt Pforzheim, vormals Degussa und nicht zuletzt der Platin Gilde International.

E — Henrich & Denzel are among the jewellery-makers who have de-voted themselves consistently to platinum after the naturally white noble metal was reintroduced in Germany. Within a short time after the factory, based in Radolfzell, was founded in 1984, it had secured a leading position in the modern German jewellery culture. Characteristic of HD jewellery is the unbeatable combination of outstanding workmanship and ambitious, timeless design. The stated aim of the firm's founder was »to create classic jewellery that would be stylish for decades, like chairs by Vitra, furniture by Cassina or lighting from Artemide.«

Günter Henrich became familiar with precious materials and fine artisanship in childhood. Born in Idar-Oberstein in 1941, he grew up in his grandfather's engraving workshop. Wilhelm Dröschel (1872–1955) was one of the best gemstone engravers of his day. After serving a business-orient-ed apprenticeship at a diamond-cutting firm, Günter Henrich had his first taste of the profession at the Gold- und Silberscheideanstalt Oberstein, Franz Reischauer. Apart from craftsmanly skills, the Scheideanstalt em-ployed cost-intensive production methods such as turning, milling, drill-pressing and stamping. Günter Henrich was enthusiastic about the precision in manufacturing and the organisation of production by the REFA method. Even then he thought about how it might be used in the jewellery indus-try. Between 1964 and 1983 Günter Henrich was managing director of the German branch of the Swiss jewellery factory Meister, at first in Singen and then in Radolfzell.

In 1984 Günter Henrich joined forces with the goldsmith Roland Denzel as his junior partner to found Henrich & Denzel, manufactory of jew-ellery. Not content with being a perfectionist in his craft, Roland Denzel also developed machinery and numerical operating systems that provided pre-cisely cut blanks for the goldsmith. His skills were supplemented by those of the businessman Günter Heinrich, who knew a great deal about precious stones and production management. Both partners were enthusiastic about

platinum. »It was the technical challenge of working that tough noble metal as well as the possibility of developing a new language of forms that fasci-nated us,« says Günter Henrich in retrospect.

The early decision taken in favour of a clear, economical formal lan-guage in the Modernist tradition became a building block to success in the 1990s. What was important to Henrich & Denzel was the »Bauhaus tradition with its formal language of straight lines, clarity, its reduction to essentials, its outstanding quality in proportion, detailing and choice and processing of materials.« It was, as it says in the guidelines, »always to be developed further in accordance with the state of knowledge of contemporary mod-ern design.« Hence HD jewellery was convincing both because of its angular beauty as well as simple, softly fluid forms. In the early years, the Henrich & Denzel factory worked with distinguished freelance designers. Günter Wer-mekes, a pupil of Friedrich Becker, developed a line in bangles in 1993 that was highly acclaimed in the jewellery trade and in the press. The firm's com-petence was enhanced by the jewellery designer Jean-Paul Callau, who came to Lake Constance from the Fachhochschule Idar-Oberstein and joined the firm in 1997. He ideally supplemented the development team, which had be-fore his arrival, consisted of the master goldsmith Reinhold Denzel and the technician Roland Denzel.

Respect for materials as formulated by the Deutscher Werkbund and the Bauhaus has also been an important guideline for the development of modern jewellery since 1945. Henrich & Denzel took up an unequivocal stance in this respect: »We work only the best, genuine, materials as provid-ed by nature.« Another important principle at the factory is material purity. The only white metal used is 950 platinum. Yellow jewellery is always made of 750 gold or an alloy with an even higher gold content. Similarly, only gen-uine natural coloured stones are used. All diamonds are graded according to the internationally recognised guidelines laid down by the International Diamond Council (IDC). Finally, Henrich & Denzel are careful not to work any diamonds that might be subject to UN sanctions.

An example of the synthesis of innovative design, intelligent work-manship quality and optimal choice of material is the 1996 Janus bangle. A patented revolving motion turns half the bangle made of platinum set with diamonds by 360° so that it can show two faces. When closed, it appears in all its geometric reductive simplicity. It opens to disclose a second, more magnificent side with a pavé diamond surface. In 1997, the Janus bangle earned the accolade of most innovative piece of modern jewellery in Germa-ny. Other outstanding market successes were the 1993 Spiegelkerben line, the Vegas ring (1999), and the 2005 Cascadem line. Henrich & Denzel demon-strated their technical and design know-how in 2005 with piece of platinum jewellery set with diamonds that resembles a flower that can be opened out. The quality standard attained by the factory has also been rewarded with

2005

2005

important prizes at the Japanese competition Platinum Design of the Year in 1995 and 1996. »Above all, our appearances at trade shows in Munich, Basel and Las Vegas as well as the live shows put on by Platin Gilde in the years 1990–1993, with the sensational media response to them, have been important to our success,« explains Günter Henrich.

In 1993, nine years after the firm was founded, a new factory was built. In 1998 a so-called Innovation Tower was added to house the design division. With the combination of platinum and diamonds, Henrich & Denzel have also maintained their position in the top segment of that market since the late 1990s. »Some of our developments have by now become public property,« says the founder of the firm. In 2006 Günter Heinrich retired at sixty-five, bringing an era to a close. His daughter, Carolin, and her husband, Christoph Teufel, both of whom have degrees in business studies, have taken over the management of the firm together with Herbert Kleinbruckner, who has been with it for many years and was already part of the management team.

»That HD jewellery today is one of the most successful German jewellery manufactories is primarily due to a team,« says Günter Henrich, »which has put itself on the line for our high market ranking with passion, character and also pride.« The founder of the firm is equally grateful to his partners of the first hour: Klaus Kaufhold, who opened Germany's first platinum studio in 1980, Dieter Hahn, proprietor of Germany's oldest diamond-cutting business, based in Idar-Oberstein, what was once the Allgemeine Gold- und Silberscheideanstalt Pforzheim and is now Degussa, and not least Platin Gilde International.

1991	Armreif, Platin, Gold, Turmaline — Bangle, platinum, gold, tourmaline
1993	Armreif, Design Günter Wermekes, Platin, Diamanten — Bangle, design Günter Wermekes platinum, diamonds
1993	Armreif und Ring *Spiegelkerbe*, Platin, Gold, Diamant — Bangle and ring *Mirror notch*, platinum, gold, diamond
1996	*Janus*-Armreif, Platin, Gold, Diamanten — *Janus* bangle, platinum, gold, diamonds
1987	Prospekt PGI: Armreif, Platin, Gold, Diamanten. Halsreif Siegfried Becker, Platin, Gold, Diamanten — Brochure PGI: Bangle, platinum, gold, diamonds. Necklace Siegfried Becker, platinum, gold, diamonds
1999	*Vegas* Ring, Platin, Diamanten — *Vegas* ring, platinum, diamonds
2001	*Tulpensolitaires*, Platin, Diamanten — *Tulip solitaires*, platinum, diamonds
2001	Trauringpaar, Platin, Diamant — Wedding rings, platinum, diamond
2005	Halsschmuck *Aufklappbare Blüte*, Platin, Diamanten — Necklace *Opening Bloom*, platinum, diamonds
2005	*Cascadem*-Armreif, Platin, Diamanten — *Cascadem* bangle, platinum, diamonds

Roland Denzel
Geboren 1951 in Singen (Hohentwiel),
Firmengründung 1984 in Radolfzell am Bodensee.

Roland Denzel
Born in Singen (Hohentwiel) in 1951,
founded firm in Radolfzell on Lake Constance
in 1984.

Günter Henrich
Geboren 1941 in Idar-Oberstein, Firmengründung
1984 in Radolfzell am Bodensee.

Günter Henrich
Born in Idar-Oberstein in 1941, founded firm in
Radolfzell on Lake Constance in 1984.

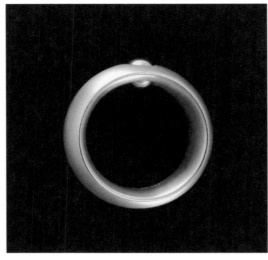

1995

1996

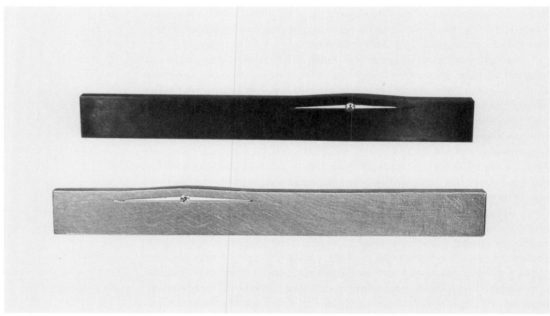

1994

1995	Ring *Roll´s*, Platin, Gold — Ring *Roll´s*, platinum, gold
1996	Ring *Kugelrund*, Platin, Brillanten — Ring *Globated*, platinum, diamonds
2001	*Ovaler Ring*, Gold, Tahiti-Zuchtperle — *Oval ring*, gold, Tahitian cultured pearl
2004	Ring *Chillida*, Gold — Ring *Chillida*, gold
1994	Broschen, Gold, brüniertes Eisen, Brillant — Brooches, gold, bronzed iron, diamond

2001   2004

Langes & Ufer

Langes & Ufer verstehen sich in erster Linie als Goldschmiede. Ihre reduzierten, klaren Formen sind nicht selten spielerisch ergänzt mit konstruktiven, teils humorvollen Elementen. So in den originellen Ringen von 1998, in denen kleine Diamanten die runde Ringschiene aufzuspalten scheinen. Oder wird da ein Fabelwesen angedeutet, das in seinem geöffneten Maul den harten Edelstein hält? Zur selben Zeit entstanden geometrisch strenge Broschen und eine würfelförmige Ohrschmuckserie. In beiden Fällen drückt sich ein Brillant durch die Kanten der streng geometrischen Körper, erzeugt Spannung und »durchbricht« die handwerkliche und formale Ernsthaftigkeit. Langes & Ufer lieben das Hintersinnige. »Jedes Thema«, betonen die Gestalter, »hat seinen Reiz und seine eigenen Gesetze, Einzelstücke ebenso wie Serien.«

Christina Langes stammt aus Trier. Auf das Abitur folgten die Goldschmiedelehre von 1978 bis 1980, ein Praktikum bei Bernd Munsteiner und zwei Gesellenjahre im Atelier von Ehinger-Schwarz in München. Nach der Meisterprüfung 1987 fand sie in der Ateliergemeinschaft mit Hans Ufer in München ihren ruhenden Gegenpol. Er kommt aus dem thüringischen Küllstedt. Nach der Goldschmiedeausbildung an der Zeichenakademie Hanau von 1969 bis 1972 und einigen Gesellenjahren besuchte Hans Ufer 1981 erneut die Zeichenakademie, die er 1983 als Staatlich geprüfter Gestalter und Techniker mit der Meisterprüfung abschloss. Durch den Ehrenpreis der Danner Stiftung wurde 1990 die schöpferische Leistung Christina Langes' gewürdigt. 1996 erhielt der Roll's Ring von Hans Ufer für Niessing den Grand Prix im Platinum Design of the Year in Japan. Eine Goldkugel liegt frei beweglich in der Ringschiene. Unten berührt sie sanft den Finger.

Seit ihrer Ateliergründung 1987 zeigen Langes & Ufer »vielgleisig« ihren Schmuck: in Einzel- und Gruppenausstellungen, in namhaften Galerien wie Isabella Hund, München, Barbara Schulte-Hengesbach, Düsseldorf, Hélène Porée, Paris, Nuria Ruiz, Barcelona oder Galerie Jungblut, Luxemburg. Der Ausstellung 1993 mit der Gruppe Aspects im Goldschmiedehaus Hanau folgten zahlreiche gemeinsame und später auch eigenständige Messebeteiligungen. Bis 2006 präsentierten die Goldschmiede regelmäßig ihre Neuheiten in Werkstattausstellungen in der Perusastraße in München. Seit der Eröffnung der Goldschmiede Langes & Ufer im Theatinerhof 2006 gibt es einen neuen Treffpunkt für die Freunde und Kunden moderner Schmuckgestaltung in München.

E — Langes & Ufer see themselves primarily as goldsmiths. Their reductive, clear forms are often playfully complemented by Constructivist elements, some of which are comical. This is true of their quirky 1998 rings, in which little diamonds seem to be splitting open the ring shank. Or is a mythic being evoked, which seems to be holding the hardest of precious stones in its open mouth?

Along with the above pieces, stringently geometric brooches and a collection of cube-shaped ear jewellery made their appearance. In both cases, a diamond presses through the edges of the severe geometric piece to create tension, »breaking into« the craftsmanly and formal seriousness. Langes & Ufer love recondite meanings. »Every theme,« the designers point out, »has something appealing about it and obeys laws of its own, one-offs as well as collections.«

Christina Langes is a native of Trier. After passing her university-entrance qualification exams, she served a goldsmith's apprenticeship (1978–1980), did an internship in Bernd Munsteiner's gem studio and spent two journeyman's years at the Ehinger-Schwarz studio in Munich. After taking her master craftsman's certificate in 1987, she found a calming opposite number in Hans Ufer, with whom she runs a joint Munich studio. A native of Küllstedt in Thuringia, he trained as a goldsmith at the Zeichenakademie Hanau (1969–1972) and spent several journeyman's years before returning to the Hanau Zeichenakademie, from which he graduated in 1983 as a state examined designer and technician with a master's certificate. A 1990 Danner Stiftung honourable mention honoured Christina Lange's creative achievement. In 1996 Hans Ufer was awarded the Grand Prix at Platinum Design of the Year in Japan for his Roll's ring for Niessing: a ball of gold moves freely in the ring shank. At the bottom it gently touches the wearer's finger.

Since they founded their studio in 1987, Langes & Ufer have shown their jewellery »on many tracks«: at solo and group shows, and at distinguished galleries, including Isabella Hund, Munich, Barbara Schulte-Hengesbach, Düsseldorf, Hélène Porée, Paris, Nuria Ruiz, Barcelona and Galerie Jungblut, Luxemburg. The 1993 exhibition with the Aspects group at the Goldschmiedehaus Hanau was followed by numerous joint appearances and later also separate presentations at trade fairs. Until 2006, the goldsmiths regularly showed their new creations at workshop exhibitions in Perusastraße, Munich. Since the goldsmiths Langes & Ufer opened in the Theatinerhof passage in 2006, there has been a new meeting place for friends and buyers of modern designer jewellery in Munich.

Christina Langes
Geboren 1958 in Trier, Meisterprüfung.
Hans Ufer
Geboren 1953 in Küllstedt, Zeichenakademie Hanau. Ateliergründung 1987.

Christina Langes
Born in Trier in 1958, master craftsman's certificate.
Hans Ufer
Born in Küllstedt in 1953, Zeichenakademie Hanau. Founded studio in 1987.

1999   2002   2003

Petra Giers

Ihre »Schmuckstücke im Auftrag der Freude« beinhalten traditionelle Symbole und individuelle Gravuren in Lagenachat, Hämatit, Bergkristall, Onyx oder Granat. Petra Giers hat wie eine Schatzsucherin die Arbeiten des Edelsteingraveurs Erwin Pauly aus Idar-Oberstein entdeckt und sie in ihren klaren Ringformen in ein zeitgemäßes Licht gesetzt. Medaillons und Anhänger mit eingravierten Liebesbotschaften sind ein weiteres Thema. »Es ist die Bedeutung des Schmuckstücks, die ihm seinen besonderen Wert verleiht«, sagt sie.

In Saarbrücken geboren, erweckten Bergkristalle, Amethyste und Rauchquarze, die Petra Giers beim Spazierengehen mit ihren Eltern im Norden des Saarlands fand, früh ihr Interesse an Edelsteinen. Von 1979 bis 1981 besuchte sie die Goldschmiedeschule in Pforzheim. Lehr- und Wanderjahre auf Ibiza und Sardinien folgten. Nach der Gesellenprüfung 1985 in Schwäbisch Gmünd studierte sie zwei Jahre im Bereich Theater und Film an der Schule von Frieder Nögge in Stuttgart. Von 1987 bis 1994 entwickelte Petra Giers ihren Schmuck in einer gemeinsamen Werkstatt mit der befreundeten Schmuckdesignerin Corinna Heller in Schwäbisch Gmünd. 1995 machte sie ihre Meisterprüfung mit Auszeichnung und gründete ihr eigenes Atelier in Schwäbisch Gmünd.

Petra Giers empfand den konventionellen Industrieschmuck in den 1980er Jahren als nicht authentisch und reformbedürftig: »Es glitzerte und schrie an der Oberfläche, schwieg jedoch im Innern«, bemerkt sie rückblickend. Ein großer Goldring, der wenig wiegt, ist für sie bis heute suspekt. Hingegen war sie fasziniert vom Schmuck der Naturvölker und schätzte Pioniere, die wie Georg Spreng die Sehgewohnheiten durch gewagte Schmuckkonzepte stark erweitert und neue Wege begehbar gemacht haben. Für die These von Joseph Beuys, »Kunst ist Leben«, sieht sie besonders im Schmuck viel Spielraum. 1986 entwickelte sie gemeinsam mit ihrem Mann und Künstler Walter Giers das Projekt *Elektronischer Schmuck*. Dabei zwitscherte und zirpte es aus kleinen Lautsprechern, Lichtspiele funkelten im Kabelgewirr. Die Gestalter erhielten dafür Preise vom Haus der Kunst in München und vom Museum of Contemporary Art in New York und wurden zu zahlreichen Radio- und Fernsehshows eingeladen.

Der völlig eigenständige Weg von Petra Giers begann mit einem stacheligen Silberring im Jahre 1986. »Der hat richtig weh getan«, beschreibt sie den provokanten Anfang ihres Schmucks. Heute sind ihre Ringe eher Handschmeichler. Die klaren, zumeist sanften Formen beinhalten als weitere Dimension eine deutliche Symbolik. Intensiv erforscht sie dafür die Mythologie und Zeichen vergangener Epochen. Besonders Drachen, die in vielen Kulturen und Religionen mit spirituellen Bedeutungen belegt sind, beschäftigen die Schmuckdesignerin. Drachen erscheinen nicht nur in Siegelringen und Gravuren, sondern auch in plastischen naturalistischen Formen auf ihren Ringen. Aber sie setzt auch moderne Symbole ein, wie etwa eine Pistole

2004   2006

in einem Siegelring. Petra Giers möchte damit aber nicht das schwache Geschlecht aufrüsten, sondern lediglich humorvoll den Kontrast zwischen sinnlicher Form und Motiv betonen. Dass Siegelringe einst Insignien der Macht waren und elitäres Bewusstsein demonstrierten, stört sie nicht im Geringsten. Viele ihrer Kunden, Frauen wie Männer, betrachteten die Siegel auch als Bild, als kleines tragbares Kunstwerk. Die Designerin: »Es gibt viele Familien, die ein Wappen haben, ihre Tradition genießen und auch zeigen. Sie identifizieren sich mit ihren Wurzeln.« Petra Giers leistet mit ihrem Schmuck einen Beitrag, dass dies kein Widerspruch zur Moderne sein muss.

E — Her »pieces of jewellery on behalf of joy« feature traditional symbols and individual engravings in banded agate, haematite, rock crystal, onyx and garnet. Like a treasure hunter, Petra Giers has discovered the work of the gemstone engraver Erwin Pauly in Idar-Oberstein and has shone a contemporary light on them in clear ring forms. Medallions and pendants with engraved love messages are another theme of hers. »It's the meaning of a piece of jewellery that makes it especially valuable,« she says.

Born in Saarbrücken, Petra Giers became interested in gemstones as a child on walks with her parents in the northern Saarland, where they discovered rock crystal, amethyst and smoky quartz. From 1979 until 1981 she attended the Goldschmiedeschule in Pforzheim, followed by an apprenticeship and journeyman's years on Ibiza and in Sardinia. After taking her journeyman's certificate in Schwäbisch Gmünd in 1985, she studied theatre and film for two years at Frieder Nögge's school in Stuttgart. From 1987 until 1994, Petra Giers developed her jewellery in the workshop she shared with a friend, the jewellery designer Corinna Heller, in Schwäbisch Gmünd. In 1995 Petra Giers took her master craftsman's certificate and founded a studio of her own in Schwäbisch Gmünd.

Petra Giers found the conventional industrial jewellery of the 1980s inauthentic and in dire need of reform: »It glittered and shouted on the surface but had nothing to say inside,« she remarks in retrospect. A big gold ring that doesn't weigh much is still an object of suspicion to her. What fascinated her was ethnic tribal jewellery and she appreciated the work of such pioneering designers as Georg Spreng, who have greatly expanded perceptual habits with bold jewellery concepts and have smoothed the way to new departures for others to go new ways. She sees plenty of scope in jewellery-making for the Joseph Beuys thesis »Art is life«.

In 1986 she and her husband, the artist Walter Giers, developed the Electronic Jewellery project. Twitters and chirps emanated from small loudspeakers; light and sound displays sparkled amid a welter of electric wiring. The designers were awarded prizes for it, from the Haus der Kunst in Munich and the Museum of Contemporary Art in New York and were invited to appear as guests on a number of radio and television talk shows.

Petra Giers started going entirely her own way with a spiky silver ring she made in 1986. »That one really hurt« is how she describes the provocative début of her piece. Now she makes rings that tend to hug the hand smoothly. On another plane, clear, usually gentle forms have an unmistakably symbolic content. To create it, she thoroughly researched the mythology and sign systems of past eras. As a jewellery designer, she is especially preoccupied with dragons, which in many cultures and religions are loaded with spiritual connotations. Dragons appear not only on signet rings and in engravings but also as naturalistic sculptural forms on her rings. But she also uses modern symbols, such as a pistol on a signet ring. However, Petra Giers is not seeking to arm the weaker sex with it; she merely wants to emphasise with a touch of tongue-in-cheek the contrast between sensuous form and the motif as such. It doesn't bother her in the least that signet rings were once the trappings of power and, therefore, demonstrated élitism. Many of her clients, both women and men, also view signets as a picture, as a small, portable work of art. The designer: »There are many families that have a coat of arms and both enjoy and demonstrate their traditions. They identify with their roots.« With her jewellery, Petra Giers is contributing to ensuring that this stance and being modern need not be a contradiction in terms.

1999	Ringe *Kleiner Drache*, Silber, Gold — Rings *Little Dragon*, silver, gold
2002	Herrensiegelring *Der große Fritz*, Palladiumweißgold, handgravierter Hämatit — Mens' signet ring *The great Fritz*, palladium white gold, haematite engraved by hand
2003	Kleiner Siegelring *Phoenix*, Handgravur, facettierter Granat, Gold — Small signet ring *Phoenix*, engraving by hand, faceted garnet, gold
2004	*Zigarrenbanderolenring*, Aquamarin, Gravur: wild at heart — *Cigar banderole ring*, aquamarine, engraving: wild at heart
2006	Ring *Rose*, Siegelring, Gold, handgravierter Hämatit — Ring *Rose*, signet ring, gold, haematite engraved by hand

Petra Giers
Geboren 1962 in Saarbrücken.
1979–1981 Goldschmiedeschule Pforzheim.
Meisterprüfung 1995. Seitdem Atelier
in Schwäbisch Gmünd.

Petra Giers
Born in Saarbrücken in 1962. 1979–1981
Goldschmiedeschule Pforzheim. Master
craftsman's certificate in 1995. Since then studio
in Schwäbisch Gmünd.

1997

1997

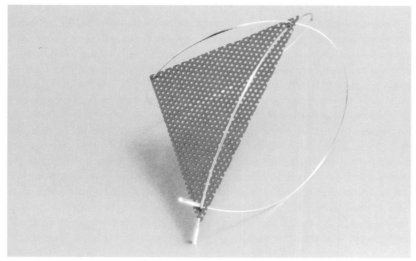

1984

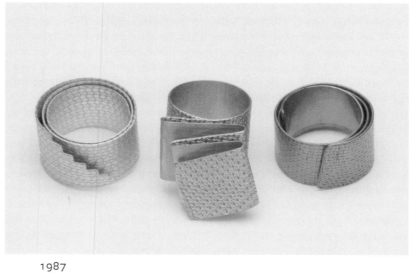

1987

1997	Ring, Gold, Heliodor — Ring, gold, heliodor
1997	Ohrschmuck *Zahnräder*, Gold, Diamanten — Earrings *Gear wheel*, gold, diamonds
1998	Ringe, Gold, Diamant, Granat — Rings, gold, diamonds, garnet
1999	Ring, Silber, Zuchtperlen — Ring, silver, cultured pearls
2001	Ring *Turmalinschlitz*, Gold, Turmalin — Ring *Tourmaline slot*, gold, tourmaline
1984	Armreif, Stahldraht, Aluminium eloxiert — Bracelet, steel wire, anodized aluminium
1987	Ringe, Aluminium eloxiert — Rings, anodized aluminium

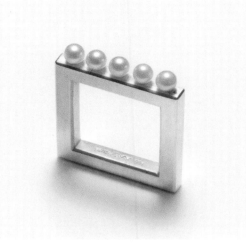

1998   1999   2001

Isabella Hund

Mit ausgeprägtem Sinn für Qualität zeigt Isabella Hund in ihrer Münchener Galerie beste Arbeiten der Gegenwart. Einzelausstellungen bedeutender Goldschmiede-Künstler, wie Francesco Pavan und Giovanni Corvaja, stehen regelmäßig auf dem Programm; dazu rund 40 Künstler und Schmuck-Designer der Galerie, von Klassikern wie Kaufmann und Dau bis hin zur jungen Avantgarde. Ihre eigene Schmuckgestaltung hat die Diplomdesignerin zugunsten ihrer Galerietätigkeit weitgehend aufgegeben.

Isabella Hund studierte von 1976 bis 1982 an der Fachhochschule für Gestaltung in Pforzheim bei Reinhold Reiling und Klaus Ullrich. Während sich die Schmuck-Professoren in dieser Zeit reduzierten, minimalistischen Formen zuwandten, erprobten die Studenten begeistert neue, expressive Ausdrucksmöglichkeiten. In radikalen, nicht selten sperrigen Schmuckobjekten drückte sich vor allem der Wunsch aus, Schmuck als körperbezogene Kunst zu emanzipieren. Isabella Hund verwendete dafür in ihren konstruktivistischen Stücken Aluminium, Edelstahl, Silber, Gold, Hämatit, Kunststoff, Gummi und Papier. Der Künstler und Philosoph Armin Saub bemerkte zu dieser Schaffensphase: »Der Wert dieser Schmuckgegenstände liegt in ihrem Esprit, ihrer frei strömenden Materialversunkenheit, Verfremdungsakrobatik, Nachdenklichkeit und ihrem lebensbejahenden Lachen...«

Nach ihrem Diplom 1982 arbeitete Isabella Hund ein Jahr als freischaffende Schmuck-Designerin in London und Ulm bevor sie 1983 mit dem Fulbright Stipendium in die USA kam. Dem Post Graduate-Studium bei Arline Fisch und Helen Shirk an der San Diego State University schloss sich ein Lehrauftrag für Kunst und Design an. Zurück in Deutschland folgte 1986 eine freie Tätigkeit für Modefirmen. Die Gründung einer Schmuckgalerie in München 1987 war der erste Schritt zur Erfüllung eines lange gehegten Traums. Als Schmuck-Designerin mit einem feinen Gespür für Mode, Design und dem Talent, Menschen zu begeistern, konnte Isabella Hund die Inhalte des Neuen Schmucks perfekt kommunizieren. Damit war jedoch auch ein Erkenntnisprozess verbunden. Er zeigte sich in ihrem eigenen Schmuck in der Rückkehr zu Edelmetallen, Perlen und Edelsteinen in reduzierten Formen. Seit dem Umzug in das Stadtzentrum Münchens 1997 präsentiert Isabella Hund den gereiften Schmuck der Moderne in einer minimalistischen Innenarchitektur. Das reduzierte Ambiente steht im Einklang mit dem vielschichtigen Wesen des modernen Schmucks ebenso wie mit dem der Galeristin.

E — With a fine nose for quality, Isabella Hund shows the best contemporary work in her Munich gallery. Solo shows of the work of leading artist-goldsmiths such as Francesco Pavan and Giovanni Corvaja are regular events; in addition, she shows some forty artists and jewellery designers at the gallery, ranging from classics such as Kaufmann and Dau to the young avant-garde. The holder of a diploma in design, Isabella Hund has largely given up designing jewellery to devote herself to her gallery.

Isabella Hund studied at the Fachhochschule für Gestaltung in Pforzheim under Reinhold Reiling and Klaus Ullrich from 1976 to 1982. Whereas the jewellery professors were turning to reductivist, Minimalist forms at that time, the students were enthusiastic about creating novel, expressive forms. Radical, often bulky jewellery objects expressed a desire to liberate jewellery to the status of body-related art. For her Constructivist pieces, Isabella Hund used aluminium, stainless steel, silver, gold, haematite, plastic, rubber and paper. Armin Saub, both artist and philosopher, had this to say about that period of her work: »The value of these jewellery objects lies in their wit, their free-flowing absorption with material, the acrobatics of defamiliarisation, their pensiveness and their life-affirming laughter...«

After taking her diploma in 1982, Isabella Hund freelanced as a jewellery designer in London and Ulm for a year before going to the US with a Fulbright Scholarship. Her post-graduate studies under Arline Fisch and Helen Shirk at San Diego State University were followed by an appointment to teach art and design. On returning to Germany, Isabella Hund freelanced for fashion houses in 1986. Founding her jewellery gallery in Munich in 1987 represented a first step towards fulfilling a long cherished dream. As a jewellery designer with a fine feeling for fashion and design and a gift for arousing enthusiasm in others, Isabella Hund was the ideal person to communicate the content of the New Jewellery. This realisation was accompanied by a process of self-knowledge. This is shown in her own jewellery, in which she has returned to noble metals, pearls and precious stones in relation to reduced forms. Since moving her gallery to downtown Munich in 1997, Isabella Hund has been presenting mature Modernist jewellery in a setting notable for its Minimalist décor. This reductivist ambience is attuned to the polysemic essence of modern jewellery and to the gallerist's protean versatility.

Isabella Hund
Geboren 1955 in Karlsruhe.
1976–1982 Fachhochschule Pforzheim.
Seit 1987 Schmuckgalerie in München.

Isabella Hund
Born in Karlsruhe in 1955.
1976–1982 Fachhochschule Pforzheim.
Jewellery gallery in Munich since 1987.

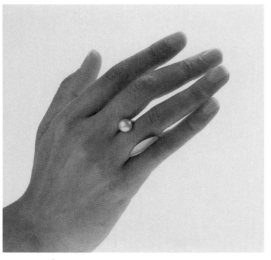

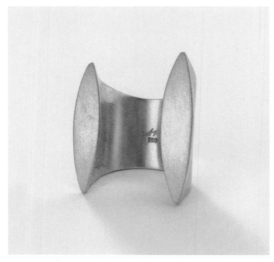

1989   1989   1990

Angela Hübel

Der Ring als Skulptur, minimalistisch, vielgestaltig und überraschend, mit Perlen, mit raffiniert geschliffenen Edelsteinen oder mit symbolischen Anklängen. Damit hat Angela Hübel in knapp zwei Jahrzehnten einen herausragenden Beitrag zum modernen Schmuckdesign geleistet. Charakteristisch ist die intensive Auseinandersetzung mit Formen, die durch Verzicht auf Überflüssiges ihr Wesen am besten entfalten können.

Nach ihrem Abitur in Tutzing bei München absolvierte die aus Bochum stammende Angela Hübel zunächst eine Lehre als Handbuchbinderin. Angeregt durch einen künstlerischen Freundeskreis begann sie 1983 an der Akademie der Bildenden Künste in München zu studieren. In der Malerklasse von Daniel Spörri erkannte sie, dass für ihr Naturell die Malerei »ein zu weites Feld« war. Sie wechselte in die Schmuckklasse von Professor Hermann Jünger und konzentrierte sich auf das Thema Ringe, einmal mehr von der Überzeugung geleitet: »Man muss sich konzentrieren, um zu einem guten Ergebnis zu kommen.«

Hermann Jünger war es wichtig, dass man Themen bis zum Ende durcharbeitet. »In dieser Hinsicht war er sehr streng«, erzählt Angela Hübel. Typisch für ihn waren Sätze wie: »Da geht doch noch ein bisschen was! Da muss doch noch was kommen!« Im Unterschied zu ihrem Professor, der mit seinen künstlerischen Unikaten weltweit bekannt wurde, widmete sich Angela Hübel ausschließlich gutem Serienschmuck. »Ich fand immer, dass ein guter Entwurf zu schade sei, um ihn nur einmal anzufertigen«, begründet sie diese Zielsetzung. Angela Hübel strebte zudem die klare Form an nach dem Motto: »So viel wie nötig, so wenig wie möglich.«

Sofort nach ihrem Studium an der Akademie eröffnete Angela Hübel 1989 eine Werkstatt in München. Sie zeigte ihre Schmuckserien auf Messen und inserierte in Fachzeitschriften. Dass die Münchner Messe Anfang der 1990er Jahre die Bestrebungen der jungen, modernen Schmuck-Designer unterstützte, half ihr beim Start. Weil sie sich anfangs kein Gelbgold leisten konnte, fertigte sie ihre Stücke auch in Silber, bevor sie sich ihr Lieblingsmaterial, sattes gelbes Gold, leisten konnte. Der bereits legendäre *Zwischenfingerring* von Angela Hübel stammt noch aus ihrer Akademiezeit. Beim »Herumspielen« mit Kugelteilen sei ein erster runder *Zwischenfingerring* entstanden, erzählt die Designerin. Daraus wurden weitere Modelle abgeleitet. Skulptural geöffnete »Ringe«, etwa in Navetteformen, Bögen oder Kugeln auslaufend, wurden typisch für ihre Kollektion.

Im Lauf der Jahre hat sich Angela Hübel »eine Art Bibliothek im Kopf« erarbeitet, ein »Regal voll mit Formen.« Regelmäßig werden diese Regale umgeräumt und neu sortiert. Immer wieder schaut die Designerin auch frühere Skizzenbücher durch. »Dann sehe ich plötzlich etwas Altes, zu dem mir eine neue Möglichkeit einfällt. Durch den unermüdlichen Prozess der Schmuckgestaltung hat Angela Hübel immer wieder neue Entwürfe »auf Lager.« Klassiker wie die *Zwischenfingerringe*, der *Diagonalring* und der

1989	*Zwischenfingerring*, Gold, Zuchtperle — *Between fingers ring*, gold, cultured pearl
1989	*Zwischenfingerring*, Gold — *Between fingers ring*, gold
1990	Trauringe *Diagonal*, Gold — Wedding rings *Diagonal*, gold
2001	Ring *Quartett*, Gold — Ring *Quartette*, gold
2002	Ring *Brillant-Atoll*, Gold, Brillanten — Ring *Diamond atoll*, gold, diamonds

2001   2002

Wellenring bleiben immer im Angebot. Auch mit Entwürfen für namhafte Schmuckmanufakturen wie Niessing und Gellner bewies Angela Hübel ihre Klasse im Schmuckdesign der Gegenwart. Ihre preisgekrönten Arbeiten wurden in folgende öffentliche Sammlungen aufgenommen: Stadtmuseum München, Kunstgewerbemuseen in Hamburg und Berlin, Kölner Museum für Angewandte Kunst sowie Pinakothek der Moderne in München.

Vor allem Menschen, die sich mit Formen beschäftigen, die Sinn für Ästhetik haben, sind es, die den Schmuck von Angela Hübel schätzen. Wie Gabriele Lueg, die Leiterin der Designabteilung im Museum für Angewandte Kunst in Köln, die im Jahre 2000 in einem Brief schrieb: »Formal und plastisch verblüffend, ausgereift, sinnlich verführend – Angela Hübels Ringe sind tragbare Skulpturen, angenehm spürbare Vervollkommnungen der Hand. Wie bei jedem guten Kunstwerk spricht aus ihnen mentale und emotionale Intelligenz. Dieser Schmuck ist für mich bereichernd und täglich ein schöner Begleiter.«

E — The ring as sculpture, minimalistic, polymorphic and surprising, set with gemstones in sophisticated cuts or loaded with symbolic connotations. In the space of just two decades, Angela Hübel has made an outstanding contribution to modern designer jewellery with just that. Characteristic of her work is an intensive exploration of forms that can best evolve their essence without superfluous trim.

After passing her school-leaving examinations qualifying her for university admission in Munich, Angela Hübel, who was born in Bochum, first served a book-binder's apprenticeship. Inspired by a circle of friends who were artists, she began to study at the Munich Fine Arts Academy in 1983. In Daniel Spörri's painting class, she realised that painting was »a field that was too broad« for her talents so she switched to the jewellery class taught by Professor Hermann Jünger. There she concentrated on rings, seeing confirmation yet again of the thought »You have to concentrate to achieve good results«.

Hermann Jünger attached importance to pushing a theme as far as it would go. »In that respect he was very strict,« reports Angela Hübel. Typical of Jünger were sentences such as: »A bit more would go there! Something else has to follow!« Unlike her professor, who became famous worldwide for his art jewellery one-offs, Angela Hübel devoted herself exclusively to good mass-produced jewellery. »I always thought that it's a shame to execute a good design only once,« is her justification for the objective she had in mind. Moreover, Angela Hübel strove for clarity of form on the motto: »As much as necessary, as little as possible«.

Immediately on finishing her studies at the Academy, Angela Hübel opened a workshop in Munich in 1989. She showed her lines in jewellery at trade fairs and advertised in specialist journals. She was helped at the start of her career by the Munich Trade Fair supporting the efforts of young, modern jewellery designers in the early 1990s. Because yellow gold was too expensive for her at first, she made her pieces in silver until she could afford her favourite material, richly gleaming yellow gold. Already the stuff of legend, Angela Hübel's *Between fingers ring* dates from her Academy period. While »playing around« with ball-bearing parts, she came up with her first round *Between fingers ring*. More models derived from it. Sculpturally open »rings,« ending in navette, arc and spherical forms became typical highlights of her collections.

Over the years, Angela Hübel has worked up »a sort of mental library,« a »shelf full of forms«. Such shelves are regularly cleared and resorted. The designer keeps on looking through earlier sketchbooks. »Then I'll suddenly catch sight of something old for which a new possibility occurs to me.« Through an unremitting process of designing, Angela Hübel keeps a fresh supply of new designs »in stock«. Hübel classics such as the *Between finger rings*, her *Diagonal* ring and *Wave* ring are always in stock. Angela Hübel has also confirmed her standing in contemporary designer jewellery with designs for renowned manufactories, including Niessing and Gellner. Her award-winning works have been acquired by the following public collections: the Stadtmuseum Munich, the Kunstgewerbe Museums in Hamburg and Berlin, the Cologne Museum für Angewandte Kunst and the Pinakothek der Moderne in Munich.

People who are concerned with form, who have a feeling for aesthetics are the ones who really appreciate Angela Hübel's jewellery. Like Gabriele Lueg, head curator of the design division at the Museum für Angewandte Kunst in Cologne, who wrote in a letter in 2000: »Formally and sculpturally astonishing, mature, sensuously seductive – Angela Hübel's rings are wearable sculpture, perfecting the hand in a way that is pleasant to the touch. As with any good work of art, they attest to mental and emotional intelligence. This jewellery is enriching for me and a beautiful companion on a daily basis.«

Angela Hübel
Geboren 1956 in Bochum.
1983–1989 Akademie der Bildenden Künste München. Atelier seit 1989 in München.

Angela Hübel
Born in Bochum in 1956.
1983–1989 Akademie der Bildenden Künste Munich. Studio in Munich since 1989.

1995

1997

1998

Corinna Heller

Vier sanft geformte Krappen fassen prächtige Farbedelsteine und Diamanten. Ringe aus Gold oder Platin, genannt *Einsteiner*. Kostbarer, edler Schmuck war lange kein Thema unter den modernen Schmuckkünstlern und Gestaltern. Corinna Heller bekennt sich klar dazu; aber ebenso zu den Idealen der Moderne, die in ihrem Schmuck auf ganz persönliche Weise lebendig sind.

Die *Einsteiner* sind typisch für das Design der 1961 in Stuttgart geborenen Schmuckgestalterin. Mit ihrem Bekenntnis zum Kostbaren meint Corinna Heller keineswegs nur das Karatgewicht der Edelsteine und edlen Metalle. Kostbarkeit ist für sie die umfassende Qualität ihres Schmucks. Das Kostbare soll sich bei der Trägerin als intensives Gefühl artikulieren, als eine Symbiose aus Gestaltungsidee und Materialwahl, aus sorgfältiger Verarbeitung und formaler Klarheit, die trotz weicher Linien und einer ausgeprägten Symbolik in ihrem Schmuck nie verloren geht.

Nach dem Abitur studierte Corinna Heller an der Fachhochschule Schwäbisch Gmünd bei den Professoren Pierre Schlevogt und Frank Hess. Die intellektuelle Annäherung an das Thema und das Wesen von Schmuck, empfand die Studentin wesentlich. »Wir sind über die kreative Freiheit präzise zum Wesentlichen gelangt«, berichtet sie über ihre Erfahrung. Ihr pragmatisches Gefühl für anspruchsvolles Design und Mode sagte ihr aber bald, dass die Schmuckgestaltung an der Hochschule nicht der gesellschaftlichen Realität entsprach. Sie war sich jedoch sicher, einen Weg zu finden, das Kreative mit dem Tragbaren zu vereinen. Ein Praktikum in einer Goldschmiedewerkstatt in Mailand zeigte ihr, wie wichtig fundiertes Handwerk im kreativen Prozess ist. Nach Abschluss des Studiums gründete Corinna Heller 1989 ihr Atelier in Schwäbisch Gmünd. Wie viele ihrer Generation begann sie mit experimentellem Schmuck. Aus neuen Materialien und Farbkombinationen entstanden große, farbige Unikate. Mit Nebentätigkeiten in einer Stuttgarter Designmanufaktur besserte sie zu Beginn ihr Einkommen auf. Auf einer Fachmesse 1995 in Frankfurt zeigt Corinna Heller erstmals Schmuck in großzügigen, voluminösen Formen. Große Steine kombiniert mit Kupfer und Kunststoff. Alles preiswerte Materialien, mehr konnte sie sich anfänglich nicht leisten.

Bis heute verwendet die Schmuckdesignerin neben sehr hochwertigen Materialien auch synthetische Steine und Silber, damit ihr Schmuck auch für kleinere Budgets erschwinglich bleibt. »Preiswerter Serienschmuck und exklusive Einzelstücke sind für mich kein Gegensatz«, sagt Corinna Heller, »Schmuck darf auch provozierende Elemente beinhalten, so wie etwa die Mode von Vivienne Westwood.« Ihr gefällt deren Idee des Gesamtkunstwerks, die Ironie und der Witz. Diesen sieht sie auch im zeitgenössischen seriellen Schmuck. Er solle außergewöhnlich und nicht gefällig sein, erklärt sie. Das Niveau der Topdesigner in der Mode müssten Schmuckgestalter unbedingt anstreben. Im Gegensatz zur Mode, so die Designerin, hat Schmuck

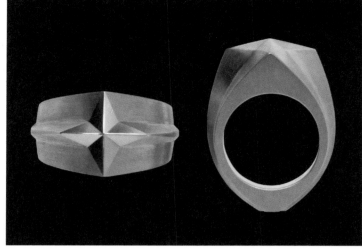

2003   2006   2007

die Chance, als Skulptur, als Kunstwerk zu wirken, selbst wenn er nicht getragen wird. Corinna Heller beginnt jede Arbeit mit Skizzen. Dabei lässt sie sich von Menschen und Städten, von Architektur und Malerei, von Design und Mode inspirieren. Das Herzsymbol nimmt in ihrem »modernen Juwelenschmuck«, so die Definition der Designerin, einen großen Raum ein, obwohl sie gar nicht so ein großer Herzfan sei. Ihre Anhänger *Herz im Kreuz* mit Farbsteinen und 18-karätigem Gold, Platin oder Silber gibt es in einer Vielfalt mit Brillanten, Saphiren, Rubinen und anderen Edelsteinen. Längst betreibt die Schmuckdesignerin ein erfolgreiches Atelier in Schwäbisch Gmünd. Die ausdruckstarke Symbolik, die gefühlvolle Sinnlichkeit und die expressive, emotionale Eleganz kennzeichnen dabei ihr gesamtes Schaffen.

E — Four gently formed prongs hold magnificent colour stones and diamonds. Rings of gold and platinum, called *Einsteiner* [Solitaires]. Costly, elegant jewellery was taboo for a long time among modern artists in jewellery and designers. Corinna Heller, however, clearly professes her allegiance to it but also to the ideals of Modernism, which inform her jewellery in a distinctively personal way.

Solitaires are typical of the jewellery created by this designer, who was born in Stuttgart in 1961. With her undisguised preference for precious jewellery, Corinna Heller does not mean just the weight in carats of precious stones and noble metals. The overall quality of her jewellery is what makes it precious according to Corinna Heller. The precious side is to be articulated for the wearer as an intense feeling, as a symbiosis of design idea and choice of material, of meticulous craftsmanship and clarity of form, which, despite the soft lines and pronounced symbolism, is never lost in Corinna Heller's jewellery. After passing her school-leaving examinations qualifying for university admission, Corinna Heller studied at the Fachhochschule Schwäbisch Gmünd with Professors Pierre Schlevogt and Frank Hess. As a student, she found it crucial to approach the subject and the essence of jewellery from the intellectual angle. »We went beyond creative freedom to arrive precisely at the quintessential,« she reports on that experience. A pragmatic feeling for ambitious design and fashion soon told her, however, that jewellery design at the Fachhochschule had nothing to do with social reality. Nevertheless, she felt sure she would find a way of uniting creativity with wearability. An internship at a goldsmithing workshop in Milan showed her how important well-grounded craftsmanship is to the creative process.

After finishing her studies, Corinna Heller founded her studio in Schwäbisch Gmünd in 1989. Like so many others of her generation, she started out with experimental jewellery. Large, coloured one-offs emerged from new materials and colour combinations. At the outset of her career, she earned extra income by working on the side with a Stuttgart designer factory. Corinna Heller first showed jewellery, featuring spacious, voluminous

forms, at a 1995 trade fair in Frankfurt. Big stones combined with copper and plastic. All inexpensive materials because at first she couldn't afford more.

Even today the jewellery designer continues to use synthetic stones and silver alongside extremely costly materials to keep her jewellery affordable even for more limited budgets. »Affordable mass-produced jewellery and exclusive one-off pieces do not represent a contradiction in terms to me,« states Corinna Heller. »Jewellery can also have provocative elements, like Vivienne Westwood's clothes.« What she likes about them is the idea of the total work of art, the irony and wit informing them. She also finds this in contemporary mass-produced jewellery. It should, she feels, be exceptional and not just pander to popularity, she explains. Jewellery designs absolutely have to strive for the quality level attained by top fashion designers. Unlike fashion, adds Corinna Heller, jewellery has the chance of being effective as sculpture, as an art work, even when it is not being worn.

Corinna Heller starts each work with sketches. She draws inspiration for them from people and cities, architecture and painting, design and fashion. The heart symbol plays a big role in her »modern gemstone jewellery« as the designer defines it. Her *Heart in the Cross* pendant set with coloured stones and made in 18-carat gold, platinum or silver is available featuring a wide variety of precious stones, including diamonds, sapphires and rubies. The jewellery designer has run a successful studio in Schwäbisch Gmünd for a long time now. Expressive symbolism, tender sensuousness and eloquently emotional elegance are the hallmarks of all her work.

Corinna Heller
Geboren 1961 in Stuttgart. 1982–1986
Fachhochschule Schwäbisch-Gmünd.
Ateliergründung 1989 in Schwäbisch Gmünd.

Corinna Heller
Born in Stuttgart in 1961. 1982–1986
Fachhochschule Schwäbisch-Gmünd. Founded
studio in Schwäbisch Gmünd in 1989.

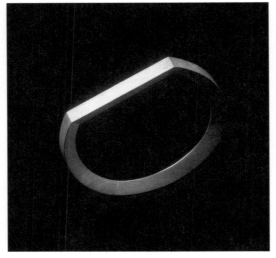

1990   1992

Batho Gündra

Die Arbeiten des Schmuckdesigners und Goldschmiedelehrers Batho Gündra sind reduziert und funktional. Bei den Anhängern und Ringen stehen modern geschliffene Edelsteine im Fokus. Die Einheit von Form und Funktion kennzeichnen seine puristischen Ketten.

An der Zeichenakademie Hanau, 1978–1982, hatte Batho Gündra »zur richtigen Zeit die passenden Lehrer.« Ihre Herangehensweise und Systematik bildeten eine gute Grundlage für sein Studium von 1982 bis 1989 an der Fachhochschule Düsseldorf. Durch das Ausscheiden von Professor Friedrich Becker 1981 lernte er verschiedene Schmuckauffassungen kennen. In dieser Zeit unterrichteten in Düsseldorf Franz-Josef Bette, Ilse Dawo, Johanna Dahm und Giampaolo Babetto. Besonders die zwei Jahre bei dem Goldschmiedekünstler aus der Schule von Padua empfand er als Glücksfall, »weil er mich meinen eigenen Weg finden ließ.« Batho Gündra schätzte zudem die klare Trennung zwischen Unikat und Serie und das kulturelle Umfeld in Düsseldorf. Von 1986 bis 1989 war er Assistent bei Professorin Sigrid Delius im Bereich Email. Bei einem Studienaufenthalt 1987 im Veneto hinterließen die Villen Palladios und die Architektur von Carlo Scarpa prägende Eindrücke. »Die Detailgenauigkeit und Ausarbeitung, das minutiöse Durcharbeiten eines ganzen Gebäudes bei Scarpa, haben meine Arbeit als Schmuckgestalter beeinflusst.« Bei einem Besuch verschiedener Schulen in England 1989 erlebte Batho Gündra eine wesentlich freiere Annäherung an das Thema Schmuck als in Hanau und Düsseldorf. »Die unterschiedlichsten Materialien wurden ausprobiert und eingesetzt, handwerkliche Aspekte außer Acht gelassen.« Es war ein Schmuckverständnis, das in seiner späteren Tätigkeit als Lehrer Bedeutung erlangte.

Nach seinem Diplom als Schmuckdesigner gründete Batho Gündra 1989 in Worms eine Werkstatt. 1992 begann seine Lehrtätigkeit an der Goldschmiedeschule Pforzheim. Dazu erklärt er: »Ich versuche den Schülern die Fähigkeit zu vermitteln, ihr eigenes Formenvokabular zu finden, weiter zu entwickeln, aber auch kritisch zu hinterfragen.« Seit 1981 beteiligte sich Batho Gündra regelmäßig an Ausstellungen. 1984 erhielt er den Förderpreis des Kunsthandwerks Rheinlandpfalz, 1988 zwei Auszeichnungen der Firma SKS im Wettbewerb Rund um den Tisch. 1993 war er Stipendiat beim Gestaltungspreis des Handwerks in Rheinhessen. Seit 1999 ist er Präsidiumsmitglied der Gesellschaft für Goldschmiedekunst.

Batho Gündra fertigt sowohl Unikate wie Schmuckserien. Bei seinen Farbstein-Anhängern ist der Ausgangspunkt immer der Edelstein. Die Gestaltung habe das Ziel, Stein und Schliff zu betonen und deren Wirkung zu steigern. Bis auf wenige Ausnahmen verwendet er die Schliffe *Context Cut* und *Spirit Sun*, »da sie meiner Formensprache am besten entsprechen«, erklärt er. Damit sich die Konzentration vollkommen auf den Stein richtet, verwendet er die reduziert geschliffenen Edelsteine nie als Akzente oder fügt weitere Elemente hinzu. Alles soll ganz selbstverständlich aussehen.

Bei der Entwicklung seiner Ketten hält Gündra zunächst die Idee zeichnerisch fest. Anhand von Prototypen werden die Proportionen und Bewegungen untersucht. »Funktion und Gestaltung müssen eine Einheit bilden«, betont er. Die Prototypen sind notwendig, um die Bewegung im Gesamten und den Eindruck der Kette beim Tragen zu kontrollieren. Der Schmuckgestalter stellt bei jedem neuen Entwurf die gleichen Fragen: »Ist die Bewegung ausreichend? Welche Länge braucht die Kette im Verhältnis zur Gliedergröße? Welche Wirkung will ich erzielen? Soll die Kette zweidimensional wirken oder raumgreifend sein? Welche Herstellungsmöglichkeiten kann ich einsetzen? Wie viel Handarbeit und wie viel Maschinenarbeit sind notwendig? Muss ich neues Werkzeug bauen? Wie viel Zeit braucht die Kette in der Herstellung?« Auch bei seinen seriell hergestellten Stücken ist es Batho Gündra wichtig, die handwerkliche Aura zu bewahren.

Bei der *Tönnchenkette* aus Gold mit Niello können sich die Glieder frei drehen. Jedes Tönnchen hat eine Gold- und eine Nielloseite, die abwechselnd zum Vorschein kommen; das heißt, es gibt keine Vorder- oder Rückseite. Wird die Kette beim Tragen bewegt, ändert sich das Bild ständig und die Reihung wird variiert. Die reduzierte Form erhält damit eine spielerische Wirkung. Ein weiteres Anliegen des Gestalters bei der *Tönnchenkette* war es, kein Seil zu verwenden, »da die Kette sonst nicht so ›fließt‹, wie ich es mir vorstelle.« Die Kette kann wahlweise mit Steinen, etwa Lapislazuli, mit Korallen oder auch mit jedem anderen Stein, der in dieser geometrischen Form zu schleifen ist, gefertigt werden.

E — The work of the jewellery designer and goldsmithing instructor Batho Gündra is reductive and functional. Precious stones in modern cuts are the focal point of pendants and rings. His purist necklaces are distinguished by a unity of form and function.

At the Zeichenakademie Hanau (1978–1982), Batho Gündra had »the right teachers at the right time.« Their systematic approaches to their subjects formed a sound foundation for his studies at the Fachhochschule Düsseldorf from 1982 to 1989. When Professor Friedrich Becker left in 1981, Gündra was made familiar with a wide variety of ideas of what jewellery was meant to be. At that time, Franz-Josef Bette, Ilse Dawo, Johanna Dahm and Giampaolo Babetto were teaching in Düsseldorf. Gündra viewed the two years he spent being taught by the artisan goldsmith of the Padua School as a particular stroke of luck »because he [Babetto] allowed me to find my own way.« Batho Gündra also appreciated the clear distinction drawn between one-offs and mass production and the cultural environment in Düsseldorf. He was an assistant to Professor Sigrid Delius in the enamelling department from 1986 to 1989. While spending some time for study purposes in the Veneto, Gündra was left with indelible impressions made by the villas of Palladio and Carlo Scarpa's modern buildings. »Scarpa's precision of

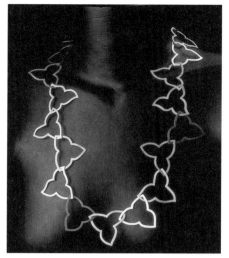

1994   1994   1997

detail and execution, the meticulous attention he paid to all aspects of an entire building has influenced my work as a jewellery designer.« On a visit to various schools in England in 1989, Batho Gündra experienced a much more liberated approach to jewellery than anything he had known in Hanau and Düsseldorf. »All sorts of materials were tried out and used, the craftsmanly aspects were disregarded.« That was an idea of jewellery that would later become important when he taught.

After taking his diploma in jewellery design, Batho Gündra founded a workshop in Worms in 1989. He began teaching at the Goldschmiedeschule Pforzheim in 1992. He describes his approach to teaching as follows: »I try to impart to my pupils an ability to discover their own formal lexis, to develop it further but also to question it critically.« Since 1981 Batho Gündra has participated regularly in group shows. In 1984 he was awarded the Förderpreis des Kunsthandwerks Rheinlandpfalz [Rhineland-Palatinate Promotional Prize in the Applied Arts] and, in 1988, two distinctions by the firm of SKS in the Rund um den Tisch [Round Table] competition. In 1993 he held a bursary for the Design Prize awarded by the Rhine-Hessian Crafts Guild. Since 1999 he has been a member of the board of directors of Gesellschaft für Goldschmiedekunst.

Batho Gündra makes both one-off pieces and mass-produced jewellery. The starting point for his pendants with coloured stones is always a precious stone. The design, as he sees it, always has the aim of emphasising the stone and its cut and to enhance the effect they make. With few exceptions, he uses the Context Cut and Spirit Sun »because they suit my formal language best,« he explains. To ensure that the focal point is the stone, he never uses precious stones with these reductive cuts as accentuating touches nor does he add other elements. Everything is supposed to look entirely unembellished. To develop his necklaces, Gündra first captures his idea in sketches. Proportions and movement are explored with prototypes. »Function and design must form an aesthetic whole,« he emphasises. The prototypes are necessary for monitoring movement throughout and the impression the necklace will make when worn. With each new design, Gündra asks the same questions: »Is there enough movement? How long does a chain have to be in relation to link size? What effect am I aiming for? Is the necklace intended to look two-dimensional or is it supposed to intervene in space? What methods can I use to make it? How much should be done by hand and how much by machine? Do I need to construct new tools? How much time will it take to make this necklace?« It is important to Batho Gündra to retain the artisanal aura.

The links of his Tönnchenkette [Little barrel necklace] made of gold with niello revolve freely. Each little barrel has a gold and a niello side that can be displayed alternately. That means there is no front or back side. If the necklace is moved while it is being worn, the way it looks changes constantly

and the paratactic arrangement is varied. A playful look is thus achieved with reductive form. Another concern of the designers was to avoid using cord with the Little barrel necklace »because otherwise the necklace isn't as ›fluid‹ as I want it to be.« The necklace can be made up as desired with stones, such as lapis lazuli, with coral or any other stone that can be cut in this basic geometric form.

1990	Armreif, Gold — Bangle, gold
1992	Kette, Gold — Necklace, gold
1994	Anhänger *Sputnik*, Gold, Rhodolith, Aquamarin im *Spirit Sun* Schliff — Pendant *Sputnik*, gold, rhodolith, aquamarine *Spirit Sun* cut
1994	Halsschmuck, Gold, Edelstahl — Necklace, gold, stainless steel
1997	*Tönnchenkette*, Gold, Niello — *Little barrel necklace*, gold, niello

Batho Gündra
Geboren 1957 in Worms. 1989 Diplom Fachhochschule Düsseldorf.
Seit 1989 Atelier in Worms.

Batho Gündra
Born in 1957 in Worms. 1989 diploma at Fachhochschule Düsseldorf.
Since 1989 Atelier in Worms.

1990

1992

2006

Sabine Hauss

1990   Kugelohrschmuck, Silber, Hämatit — Ball earrings, silver, haematite

2006   *3x Ringcreole*, Gold, Diamanten — Earrings *3x Ring creole*, gold, diamonds

2006   Ohrschmuck *Lacknoten* groß, Verschlusselemente, Silber, japanischer Lack
— Earrings *Lacquer notes* big, closing elements, silver, japanese lacquer

1992   Scheibencreolen, Verschlusshalbkugeln, japanischer Lack — Disc creoles,
closing hemispheres, japanese lacquer

2006   Ohrschmuck *Lacknoten* groß, Verschlusshalbkugeln, Silber, japanischer Lack
— Earrings *Lacquer notes* big, closing hemispheres, silver, japanese lacquer

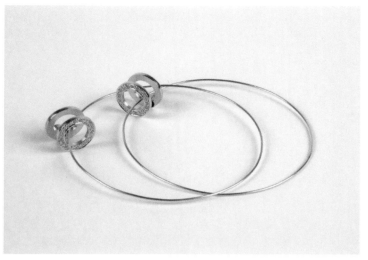

2006

2006

Sabine Hauss

Urushi nennen die Japaner ihre berühmte Lacktechnik. Sabine Hauss setzt sie seit 1989 in ihrer Schmuckgestaltung ein. Gleichzeitig entwickelte sie sich mit einer klaren Formensprache zur Spezialistin für Ohrschmuck. Durch frei variierbare Grundelemente wird die Trägerin zur Mitgestalterin.

Von 1981 bis 1986 studierte Sabine Hauss in ihrer Geburtsstadt Pforzheim an der Fachhochschule bei den Professoren Stark, Reiling und Lorenzen Schmuck- und Gerätedesign. Von 1988 bis 1989 besuchte sie als Stipendiatin des DAAD die Escuela Massana in Barcelona. In der Klasse des katalanischen Goldschmiedekünstlers Ramón Puig Cuyàs, die sie bis 1990 besuchte, lernte sie die japanische Lacktechnik kennen. Nach dem Studium gründete sie ihr Atelier in Pforzheim. In verschiedenen Kursen an der Fachhochschule für Schmuckdesign Contacto Directo in Lissabon und am Centro de Joalharia do Porto gab Sabine Hauss ihr profundes Wissen in der Lacktechnik an Schmuckstudenten weiter. Zwischen 1998 und 2002 war sie als freie Designerin für Gellner tätig.

Charakteristisch für den Ohrschmuck von Sabine Hauss sind geometrische, reduzierte Formen. Das Steckprinzip basiert auf den drei Elementen Kugel oder Halbkugel und Verbindungsstift. So lässt sich der Ohrschmuck beliebig variieren und erweitern. Alle Teile passen zueinander und können auf die individuellen Bedürfnisse und die Kleidung der Trägerin abgestimmt werden. Ergänzt werden die Grundelemente durch Kreisstecker, Kreolen oder Scheiben. Doppelhaken lassen die Kugeln wie Kirschen am Ohr hängen. Je nach Kombination wirkt der Ohrschmuck formal streng oder dekorativ und verspielt. Durch die Materialien Gold, Silber, Edelstahl, Tahitiperlen, Diamanten und Farbedelsteine in Kombination mit Japanlack ergibt sich eine breite Farbpalette.

Urushi wird aus dem Harz des ostasiatischen Lackbaums gewonnen und kann sehr hell oder dunkel wie Bernstein sein. Durch Farbpigmente erhält er seine Leuchtkraft und ist zudem strapazierfähig und elastisch. Dem Schmuck von Sabine Hauss verleiht *Urushi* eine Farbtiefe von magischer Intensität. Sie entsteht durch zahlreiche übereinander aufgebrachte Lackschichten. Neben dem Ohrschmuck fertigt die Schmuck-Designerin auch Ketten und Ringe. Der Schmuck von Sabine Hauss ist in zahlreichen Schmuckgeschäften und Galerien auch international vertreten.

E — *Urushi* is a celebrated Japanese lacquering technique. Sabine Hauss has been using it in her designer jewellery since 1989. At the same time, she has turned into a specialist in ear jewellery known for clarity of form. The wearer becomes a co-designer by selecting from a range of freely variable basic elements.

From 1981 until 1986 Sabine Hauss studied jewellery and tableware design at the Fachhochschule in her native Pforzheim with Professors Stark, Reiling and Lorenzen. From 1988–1989 she had a DAAD study bursary to attend the Escuela Massana in Barcelona. In the class taught by Professor Ramón Puig Cuyàs, the Catalan goldsmith, which she attended until 1990, she became acquainted with the Japanese lacquering technique. After finishing her studies, she founded a studio in Pforzheim. Sabine Hauss has passed on her profound knowledge of the lacquer technique to students of jewellery-making in Portugal at the Contacto Directo Lisboa school for jewellery design and the Centro de Joalharia do Porto. Between 1998 and 2002 she freelanced as a designer for Gellner.

Geometric reductive forms are the hallmark of Sabine Hauss's ear jewellery. The stud principle is based on a connector system featuring three elements: the ball, the hemisphere and the linking pin. Hence ear jewellery can be varied and expanded as the wearer pleases. All parts match and can be attuned to the wearer's individual needs and her clothing. The basic components can be supplemented with round-headed studs, turned into creole earrings and discs. Balls are made to dangle from the ear like cherries from double hooks. The use of materials such as gold, silver, stainless steel, South Sea pearls, diamonds and coloured precious stones in combination with Japanese lacquer provides a broad colour range.

Urushi is made from the resinous sap of the East Asian lacquer tree and may be either very light-coloured or dark like amber. The addition of coloured pigments make it lustrous and it is extremely durable and elastic. Sabine Hauss's jewellery gives *urushi* a depth of colour that is magical in its intensity, an effect created by applying coat after coat of lacquer. Apart from ear jewellery, the designer also makes necklaces and rings. Sabine Hauss's jewellery is sold at numerous jewellery shops and galleries around the world.

Sabine Hauss
Geboren 1961 in Pforzheim.
1981–1986 Fachhochschule Pforzheim.
Ateliergründung 1990 in Pforzheim.

Sabine Hauss
Born in Pforzheim in 1961.
1981–1986 Fachhochschule Pforzheim.
Founded studio in Pforzheim in 1990.

Sabine Hauss

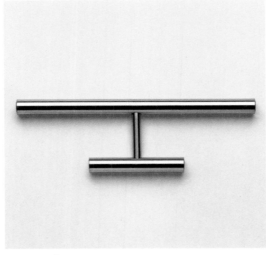

1985   1992

Günter Wermekes

»Minimalismus bedeutet, Dinge immer weiter einzugrenzen auf ihr eigentliches Wesen und dieses dadurch sichtbar und erlebbar zu machen«, sagt Günter Wermekes. Seit 1990 dokumentiert er eindrücklich, wie Minimalismus im Schmuckdesign aussehen kann: reduzierte geometrische Grundformen, Verzicht auf jegliches Dekor, präzise Proportionen. Dadurch intensiviert der Designer die Wirkung der Materialien Edelstahl und Diamanten, ihre Symbolik und die körperhafte, räumliche Präsenz der Stücke.

Günter Wermekes wurde in Kierspe im Sauerland geboren. Wesentlich für seine Entwicklung war die Lehrzeit bei Friedrich Becker in Düsseldorf, die er nach dem Abitur 1975 als Lehrling begann und 1990 als Werkstattleiter beendete. Bei dem großen Wegbereiter des modernen Schmucks in Deutschland lernte Wermekes, Edelstahl und Diamanten mit Hilfe moderner Techniken zu verarbeiten. »Eine Technikverliebtheit entstand dabei jedoch nie«, erklärt er, Technik bleibe für ihn das Hilfsmittel, um eine perfekte Form zu erzeugen. Und für jede Form gibt es nach Wermekes auch ein ideales Material. Ganz wie es die Klassiker der Moderne gefordert hatten, von denen er besonders Mies van der Rohe schätzt.

Nach der Gründung seines Ateliers brachte er als erster Designer 1990 eine komplette Schmuckkollektion aus Edelstahl mit Diamanten auf den Markt. Die Kombination des bevorzugten Werkstoffs der Moderne mit dem härtesten und in der Regel auch teuersten aller Edelsteine war für viele Juweliere in den 1990er Jahren noch ein Sakrileg. Für Günter Wermekes war es eine sehr durchdachte Entscheidung. »Der Diamant passt aus verschiedenen Gründen zum Edelstahl«, sagt er: »Der Diamant verkörpert mit seiner Jahrmillionen alten Entstehungsgeschichte die Vergangenheit der Erde. Edelstahl, der Stoff der Konstrukteure und Architekten, steht für die vom Menschen geschaffene Kultur der Gegenwart.«

Neben Schmuck hat Wermekes auch innovative Uhren, zum Beispiel die Radius 9 für Niessing, Türklinken, Pokale sowie freie Objekte und Skulpturen bis hin zu urbanen Räumen gestaltet. Er erhielt Auszeichnungen wie den Designpreis NRW, das Platinum Design of the Year 1994, den red dot für hohe Designqualität des Designzentrums NRW. Seine Arbeiten sind in öffentlichen und privaten Sammlungen im In- und Ausland zu finden. 2006 wurde sein Werk mit einer Einzelausstellung in Colorado und der Erwähnung als einer der 13 wichtigsten europäischen Designer im »New York Times Magazine« gewürdigt.

Obwohl sich Günter Wermekes klar als Designer definiert, gibt es durchaus künstlerische Konzepte in seinen Schmuckserien. Zum Beispiel in dem Ring, der aus zwei separaten Edelstahlschienen und einem von Hand geschmiedeten Goldring bestehen. An der Hand getragen bleibt der Goldring mit seiner lebendigen Struktur unsichtbar unter der strengen Form des Edelstahls verborgen. Der Träger kann damit etwas ganz für sich behalten. Er besitzt ein Schmuckobjekt, das für sich steht, geheimnisvoll, vieldeutig

und überraschend. Nur selten ist es einem Schmuckgestalter gelungen, auf so schlichte Weise archaische Goldschmiedekunst mit modernem Design zu vereinen. Zur Diskussion, ob im Schmuck nicht nur Unikate wegen ihrer Einzigartigkeit »von Wert« sind, sagt Wermekes: »Mein Schmuck ist nicht das Resultat einer kreativen Laune oder einer plötzlichen Inspiration, sondern er repräsentiert eine Haltung. Erst die Serie macht deutlich, wie sehr jedes Schmuckstück neu und anders wirkt durch den Menschen, der es trägt. Mein Schmuck wird getragen von Menschen, die diese Haltung teilen und die sie verbindet. Das könnte ein Unikat niemals leisten.«

Mit der Serie Einkaräter gibt Günter Wermekes eine Antwort auf die Frage: Wie viel Design muss sein? »Ein wertvoller Stein. Eine Fassung. Eine Ringschiene. Mehr braucht es nicht für diesen Solitär. Die Fassung orientiert sich an der Form des Steines. Als Gehäuse dient ein zylindrisches Rohr, das den Stein aufnimmt. Durch die runde Öffnung kann die höchstmögliche Menge an Licht in den Brillanten einfallen. So kann er das Licht zu fast 100 Prozent reflektieren. Gleichzeitig bietet diese geschlossene Fassung den größtmöglichen Schutz. Von der Unterseite her wird der Brillant durch ein kleineres Rohr gehalten. Beide Rohre werden durch eine Einfräsung in die Ringschiene eingepasst und mit einem einzigen Stift fest miteinander verankert. Das ist alles.« Der Designer lässt sich bei dem ruhigen, unspektakulären Entwurf leiten von der Technik, vom Handwerk, vom Material. All dies soll am Ende jedoch wieder im Hintergrund stehen. Sein Ziel ist immer ein Schmuckstück, »das versucht, zu wirken mit der Lautstärke der Stille.«

E — »Minimalism means continuing to delimit things to their essence and making this visible and experiential,« says Günter Wermekes. Since 1990 he has been impressively documenting how Minimalism can look in designer jewellery: reductive basic geometric forms, eschewal of decoration, precision in proportion. Thus the designer intensifies the effects created with stainless steel and diamonds as his materials, enhancing the symbolism and the physical spatial presence of the pieces.

Günter Wermekes was born in Kierspe in the Sauerland. Crucial to the development of his career was the apprenticeship he served in Düsseldorf with the ground-breaking pioneer of modern jewellery in Germany Friedrich Becker. Wermekes began in 1975 as a fledgling apprentice after finishing his school-leaving examinations qualifying for university entrance and was head of the workshop by the time he left in 1990. From Becker he learned how to work stainless steel and diamonds by applying cutting-edge techniques. »Nevertheless, there was never any question of being enamoured of technology,« explains Wermekes. As he sees it, technique and technology remain aids to producing perfect form. And, according to Wermekes, there is always an ideal material for each form, as called for by the classic Modernists, of whom he particularly admires Mies van der Rohe.

1999   2000   2007

After founding a studio, Wermekes was the first designer (in 1990) ever to launch an entire collection in stainless steel and diamonds on the market. In the 1990s many jewellers still regarded the combination of the Modernist material of choice with the hardest and usually most expensive of all precious stones as a sacrilege. For Günter Wermekes it represented a completely deliberate choice. »Diamonds suit stainless steel for several reasons,« he says. »With the millions of years it takes to form, a diamond embodies the earth's history. Stainless steel, the material of builders and architects, stands for present-day culture, which is man-made.«

Apart from jewellery, Wermekes has also designed innovative watches, including the *Radius 9* wristwatch für Niessing, door handles, trophies and free objects and works of sculpture on up to urban spaces. He has received awards, such as the NRW Design Prize, the Platinum Design Award of the Year 1994 and the NRW Design Centre red dot for high-quality design. Work by Wermekes is owned by both public and private collections in Germany and abroad. In 2006 his achievement was honoured with a solo show in Colorado and mentioned in the »New York Times Magazine« section as one of the thirteen most important European designers.

Although Günter Wermekes defines himself unequivocally as a designer, fine arts concepts definitely inform his lines in jewellery. For instance, the ring consisting of two separate bands of stainless steel concealing a hand-beaten gold ring. When the piece is worn on the finger, the gold ring with its vivid texture remains invisible within the astringent stainless steel form. Wearers can thus keep something entirely to themselves. They own a jewellery object that stands alone, enigmatic, polysemic and astonishing. Rarely indeed has a jewellery designer succeeded in uniting the archaic art of goldsmithing and modern design with such compelling simplicity. On the discussion about whether one-offs are the only pieces of jewellery »of value« because they are unique, Wermekes has this to say: »My jewellery is not the result of a creative mood or a sudden burst of inspiration but rather represents a stance. The series makes clear how every piece of jewellery is new and looks different because of the person wearing it. My jewellery is worn by people who share this attitude and are linked by it. That is something a one-off could never achieve.«

The *Einkaräter* [One Carat] edition is Günter Wermekes' answer to the question of how much design must there be.« A valuable stone. A setting. A ring shank. That's all that's needed for this solitaire. The setting is oriented to the form of the stone. The casing is a cylindrical tube that holds the stone. Through the round opening the greatest possible amount of light can shine on the diamond. So it can reflect almost 100 per cent of the light. At the same time, this closed setting provides the greatest possible security. The diamond is held by a smaller tube from the underside. The two tubes are fitted into the ring shank by being milled into it and firmly anchored to

one another by means of a single pin. That's all there is to it.« The designer lets himself be guided in this quiet, unspectacular design by technology, by craftsmanship, by the material. All this, however, is ultimately meant to recede into the background again. His objective is always a piece of jewellery »that strives to make its impact with the volume of its silence.«

1985	*Zwischenfingerring*, Edelstahl — *Between fingers ring*, stainless steel
1992	Ringe, Edelstahl, Brillanten — Rings, stainless steel, diamonds
1999	Ringe *Das Goldset*, Edelstahl, Feingold — Rings *The Gold set*, stainless steel, fine gold
2000	Ringe, Edelstahl, Brillanten — Rings, stainless steel, diamonds
2007	Ring, Edelstahl, rostender Stahl, Brillant — Ring, stainless steel, oxidised steel, diamond

Günter Wermekes
Geboren 1955 in Kierspe.
1975–1990 als Lehrling und
Werkstattleiter bei Friedrich Becker.
Atelier in Kierspe seit 1990.

Günter Wermekes
Born in Kierspe in 1955. 1975–1990 apprentice and studio foreman under Friedrich Becker.
Studio in Kierspe since 1990.

»Der moderne mensch verwendet die ornamente früherer und
fremder kulturen nach seinem gutdünken. Seine eigene erfindung
konzentriert er auf andere dinge.«

Adolf Loos, in »Ornament und Verbrechen«, 1908

»modern man uses the adornments of earlier, alien cultures as he
sees fit. he concentrates his own inventiveness on other things.«

Adolf Loos, in »Ornament and Crime«, 1908

2002   1992   2002

2002   Kinetischer Ring *Headlight*, Design Des4, Platin, *Spirit Sun* Diamant,
        Bugatti Collection — Kinetic ring *Headlight*, design Des4, platinum,
        Spirit Sun diamond, Bugatti Collection

1992   Spannring, Design Niessing, Platin, *Context* Cut Diamant — Tension ring,
        design Niessing, platinum, *Context* Cut diamond

2002   Kinetischer Ring *Torque*, Design Des4, Platin, *Spirit Sun* Diamant,
        Bugatti Collection — Kinetic ring *Torque*, design Des4, platinum, *Spirit Sun*
        diamond, Bugatti Collection

Diamantmanufaktur in der Tradition der Moderne — A Diamond Manufactory in the Modernist Tradition

Freiesleben

Dr. Ulrich Freiesleben, geboren 1949, begann 1975 mit dem Diamanthandel. 1988 gründete er als bisher einziger deutscher Händler ein Büro an der weltgrößten Diamantbörse in Antwerpen. 1991 entschied sich Freiesleben, die modernen Diamantschliffe *Context Cut* und *Spirit Sun*, entwickelt von Bernd Munsteiner, weltweit auf den Markt zu bringen. Seit 1998 führt er gemeinsam mit seiner Frau Gabriele in Münster eine moderne Diamantmanufaktur.

REINHOLD LUDWIG Zu Beginn der 1990er Jahre hatten Sie 15 Jahre Erfahrung als Diamantgroßhändler. Warum kamen Sie plötzlich auf die Idee, »ein neues Sinnverständnis für den Diamanten aufzuzeigen«, wie Sie in Ihrer Firmenphilosophie schreiben?

ULRICH FREIESLEBEN Der Brillantschliff, wie viele andere Edelsteinschliffe, entspricht dem Geist des Barock. Mit der Moderne haben sich die Formen in Kunst, Architektur und Design entscheidend verändert. Anfang der 1980er Jahre lernte ich auf einer Messe die Schliffe des Edelsteinkünstlers Bernd Munsteiner und das moderne Schmuck-Design deutscher Hersteller kennen. Ich erkannte die Chance, mit den Munsteiner-Schliffen ein neues Bewusstsein für den Diamanten schaffen zu können. Der *Context Cut* kommt den schönsten Naturformen der Diamantkristalle nahe. Wie auch der *Spirit Sun* bringt er in der Formensprache der Moderne das Wesen des Diamanten zum Ausdruck: seine Klarheit, seine Transparenz, sein Licht, seine Härte und seine Reinheit.

REINHOLD LUDWIG Sie haben Ihre neuen Schliffe mit dem Wertewandel in den 1990er Jahren in Verbindung gebracht. Wie sah dieser Wertewandel im Allgemeinen und speziell für die Schmuckbranche aus?

ULRICH FREIESLEBEN In den 1990er Jahren verstärkte sich der Trend zum Individualismus. Bestimmte Käufergruppen begannen, sich vom gedankenlosen Massenkonsum abzugrenzen. Dabei spielten Billigimporte und das wachsende Umweltbewusstsein eine Rolle. Hinzu kam eine höhere Sensibilität für ethische Werte in der Produktion von Gütern. Der Manufakturgedanke erlebte in Europa eine Renaissance. So genannte Connaisseurs interessierten sich für qualitativ hochwertige Produkte mit einer besonderen Geschichte. Sie musste mit den neuen Werten harmonieren, also auch ökologische, ethische und gestalterische Fragen beantworten. Bei Schmuck äußerte sich dies vor allem in einer klaren, prägnanten Formensprache in der Tradition der Moderne. In der Verbindung von Form und Funktion erscheint mit unseren Schliffen auch der Diamant in einem neuen Licht.

REINHOLD LUDWIG Welche Erfahrungen haben Sie seitdem gemacht? Wer waren Ihre Kunden bei den Schmuckdesignern?

ULRICH FREIESLEBEN Unsere neuen Diamantschliffe wurden von Anfang an von erstklassigen Schmuck-Designern und Goldschmieden eingesetzt. Sie haben sofort verstanden, dass modern gestalteter Schmuck, meistens hochwertige Unikate, mit den reduzierten Schliffen harmonierte. Die Gestalter wurden dadurch auch inspiriert, neue Formen zu entwickeln. Heute werden die *Context-* und *Spirit*-Schliffe in mehr als 20 Ländern in modernem Schmuck verwendet.

REINHOLD LUDWIG Auf die Euphorie des Jahrtausendwechsels fand die Katastrophe des 11. Septembers mit den bekannten politischen Folgen statt. Dies bedeutete nicht zuletzt auch eine Zäsur für die Schmuckhersteller und Juweliere.

ULRICH FREIESLEBEN Die Schmuckbranche war vor allem durch die Verunsicherung in Wirtschaft und Politik betroffen: durch Krisenherde, mangelnde Altersvorsorge, hohe Arbeitslosenzahlen oder steigende Energiepreise. Die Käufer haben die Anschaffung langlebiger Wirtschaftsgüter verschoben oder gänzlich darauf verzichtet. Die Juweliere und Schmuckgeschäfte mussten neue Konzepte entwickeln, zu denen nicht alle in der Lage waren. Aber manche haben die Probleme als Chance verstanden, sich mit der neuen Schmuckkultur zu profilieren.

REINHOLD LUDWIG In China, Russland und einigen arabischen Ländern erlebt der Luxus im alten Stil seit Jahren einen Boom. Was bedeutet dies für moderne Schmuckgestalter oder für eine Diamantmanufaktur, die sich einer neuen Formensprache in der Tradition der Moderne widmet?

ULRICH FREIESLEBEN In diesen Ländern war Opulenz schon immer Ausdruck eines positiven Lebensgefühls. Die Paläste, Tempel und Moscheen zeugen davon. Verständlicherweise greifen die neuen Reichen dort erst einmal zu den protzerischen Produkten, den Klunkern, genauso wie es vor 100 Jahren auch in Amerika und Europa der Fall war. Aber bereits jetzt differenzieren sich die Märkte und verlangen auch nach dem stilleren Luxus. Wir haben bereits in China erste positive Erfahrungen in diese Richtung gemacht.

REINHOLD LUDWIG Wie sehen Sie die Zukunft des Schmucks im 21. Jahrhundert, wo es doch so wichtige Dinge gibt, wie die Menschen zu ernähren oder die Klimakatastrophe zu bewältigen?

ULRICH FREIESLEBEN Am Schmuck und den Diamanten wird es nicht liegen, ob die Herausforderungen der Zukunft unseres Planeten bewältigt werden oder nicht. Aber wir müssen noch mehr darauf achten, dass Schmuck den Sinn für gute Gestaltung und für die Schönheit der Natur zum Ausdruck bringt. Modernes Schmuck-Design in der Tradition der Moderne verfolgt genau diesen Ansatz. Ein Diamant vermittelt uns, dass es noch Dimensionen gibt, die weit über die Geschichte der Menschheit und ihrer Probleme hinausreichen. Das macht seine Faszination für uns Menschen aus, die im besten Fall 100 Jahre ein Gastspiel auf dieser Erde geben dürfen.

»›Schmuck‹ ist kein Sammelbegriff für ›schöne Dinge‹, aber
vielleicht ein Sammelbegriff für magische Objekte.«

Thomas H. Macho, 1987

»›Jewellery‹ is not a generic term for ›beautiful things‹ but
perhaps it is a generic term for magical objects.«

Thomas H. Macho, 1987

E — Dr. Ulrich Freiesleben, born in 1949, began trading in diamonds in 1975. In 1988 he founded a branch office at the world's largest diamond exchange in Antwerp, hitherto the only German diamond dealer to do so. The year 1991 saw Dr. Freiesleben opt for launching the modern diamond cuts *Context Cut* and *Spirit Sun*, developed by Bernd Munsteiner, on the market worldwide. Since 1998, Dr. Freiesleben and his wife, Gabriele, have operated a modern diamond business in Münster.

REINHOLD LUDWIG By the early 1990s you had had fifteen years of experience as a diamond wholesaler. What made you suddenly come up with the idea of 'demonstrating a new definition of what diamonds can mean', as you write in your firm's philosophy statement?

ULRICH FREIESLEBEN The brilliant cut, like so many other precious-stone cuts, matches the Baroque spirit. With the advent of Modernism, forms have decisively changed in art, architecture and design. In the very early 1980s, I became acquainted at a trade fair with the cuts by the artist in precious stones Bernd Munsteiner as well as modern designer jewellery by German makers. I recognised a chance to be able to create a new awareness of diamonds with the Munsteiner cuts. The *Context Cut* approximates the most beautiful natural diamond crystal forms. Like *Spirit Sun*, it, too expresses the essence of the diamond in the Modernist language of forms: its clarity, its transparency, its light, its hardness and its purity.

REINHOLD LUDWIG You have linked your new cuts with the 1990s change in values. What did that change in values look like in general and for the jewellery trade in particular?

ULRICH FREIESLEBEN In the 1990s, there was a growing trend towards individualism. Certain target markets began to put distance between themselves and mass consumption. Cheap imports and growing environmental awareness played a role in this. Moreover, there was a sensitivity to ethical values in manufacturing goods. The manufactory idea underwent a renaissance in Europe. So-called connoisseurs were interested in high-quality products with a special history. It had to be in harmony with the new values, that is, address issues related to ecology, ethics and design. In jewellery this was expressed mainly in a clear, succinct language of forms in the Modernist tradition. In connection with form and function, diamonds, too, appeared in a new light in our cuts.

REINHOLD LUDWIG What has been your experience since then? Which jewellery designers represented your clientele?

ULRICH FREIESLEBEN Our new diamond cuts were used from the outset by top jewellery designers and goldsmiths. They grasped immediately that jewellery in modern designs, usually upscale one-off pieces,

matched the reductivist cuts. Designers were also inspired by those cuts to develop new forms. Today the *Context* and *Spirit* cuts are being used in modern jewellery in more than twenty countries.

REINHOLD LUDWIG The turn of the millennium euphoria gave way to the 9/11 disaster with its well-known political consequences. That meant not least a discontinuity for jewellery-makers and jewellers.

ULRICH FREIESLEBEN The jewellery trade was especially hard hit by the economic and political uncertainty: by flashpoints, inadequate pensions provision, high unemployment rates and rising energy costs. Potential buyers postponed acquiring durable goods or did without them altogether. Jewellers and jewellery shops had to develop new concepts but not all of them were in a position to do so. However, some of them saw the problems as an opportunity to establish reputations for themselves with the new jewellery culture.

REINHOLD LUDWIG In China, Russia and some Arab countries, old-style luxury has been booming for years. What does this mean for modern jewellery designers or for a diamond business which is devoted to a new language of forms in the Modernist tradition?

ULRICH FREIESLEBEN In those countries, opulence has always been an expression of a positive feeling about life. The palaces, temples and mosques bear witness to that. Understandably, the nouveau-riche first tended to snap up the ostentatious products, clunky bling, just as was the case a hundred years ago in America and Europe. But by now those markets have become more sophisticated and are also demanding more reticent luxury. We have already had our first positive experience in China in that direction.

REINHOLD LUDWIG How do you see the prospects for jewellery in the 21st century, where there are such important things as ensuring that people have enough to eat or dealing with the climate catastrophe?

ULRICH FREIESLEBEN It won't be the fault of jewellery and diamonds if the challenges posed by the future of our planet are met or not. But we do have to take heed that jewellery expresses a feeling for good design and the beauty of nature. Modern designer jewellery in the Modernist tradition is pursuing this very approach. A diamond tells us that there are still planes that extend far beyond the history of humanity and its problems. That is what makes it so fascinating for us human beings, who are permitted to give a guest performance of a hundred years at most on this earth.

1996

1999

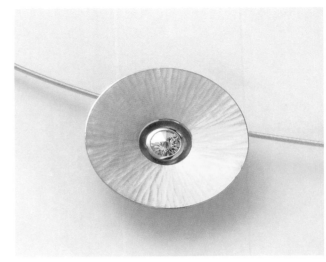

2000

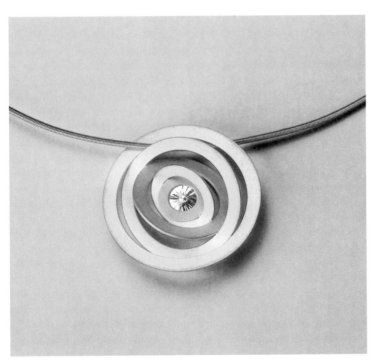

1999

1997

1996

1996   Brosche, Design Michael Zobel, Gold, *Spirit Sun* Diamant, Brillanten
— Brooch, design Michael Zobel, gold, *Spirit Sun* diamond, diamonds

1999   Ring, Design Michael Zobel, Gold, *Context* Cut Diamant, Brillanten
— Ring, design Michael Zobel, gold, *Context* Cut diamond, diamonds

2000   Anhänger, Design Lothar Kuhn, Gold, *Spirit Sun* Diamant — Pendant, design
Lothar Kuhn, gold, *Spirit Sun* diamond

1999   Anhänger, Design Batho Gündra, Gold, *Spirit Sun* Diamant — Pendant,
design Batho Gündra, gold, *Spirit Sun* diamond

1997   Ring, Design Kurt Neukomm, Gold, *Context* Cut Diamant — Ring, design
Kurt Neukomm, gold, *Context* Cut diamond

1996   Anhänger, Design Michael Good, Gold, *Spirit Sun* Diamant — Pendant,
design Michael Good, gold, *Spirit Sun* diamond

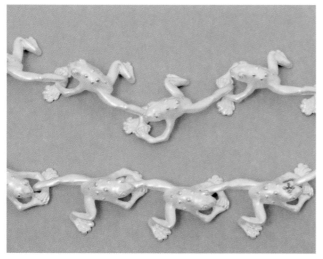

1996   1997   2004

Gitta Pielcke

Die Formenvielfalt der Natur liefert Gitta Pielcke unerschöpfliche Inspiration für ihre figurativen Arbeiten. Um damit unbeschwerte Lebensfreude zum Ausdruck zu bringen, müssen sie mit einer Prise Humor und Ironie gewürzt sein. Denn ihre Schmuckserien sollen Spaß machen!

Gitta Pielcke wurde 1964 in Hamburg geboren. Nach dem Abitur und einer anschließenden Ausbildung als Restauratorin in Florenz besuchte sie von 1987 bis 1991 die Zeichenakademie Hanau. Im Goldschmiedeberuf sah sie die Chance, ihr handwerkliches Talent kreativ zu entfalten. Der Minimalismus im Schmuck Ende 1980 entsprach nicht ihrem Lebensgefühl. So suchte sie während der Ausbildung nach einem neuen Weg. Die Gestalterin registrierte zudem, dass viele Frauen positiv auf figürliche, poesievolle Formen reagierten. Ihre ersten figürlichen Arbeiten sägte Pielcke aus Blech oder bog Figuren aus Draht. Die *Turnerkette* von 1991 bestand aus unterschiedlichen menschlichen Figuren, die in der Reihung eine graphisch abstrakte Wirkung erzielen.

Nach dem Examen 1991 in Hanau zog Pielcke für drei Jahre in das kreative Berlin. 1994 entstand ihre *Geckokette*, die ebenso wie die *Froschkette* von 1996 zu ihrem Markenzeichen wurde. Die Modelle werden wie kleine Skulpturen aus einem harten Wachsblock geschnitzt. Bei dieser Serie soll das natürliche Vorbild möglichst exakt wiedergegeben werden, jedoch in einer Bewegung, die eine elegante, humorvolle Reihung ermöglicht und einen Verschluss überflüssig macht. Die Kette kann an jedem Element geöffnet und beliebig verlängert und verkürzt werden. Bei den Ringen achtet die Gestalterin darauf, dass die einzelnen Miniskulpturen nicht genau gleich aussehen, sondern dass es bei näherer Betrachtung »etwas zu entdecken« gibt. Bei der Ringserie *nature* von 1998 wendet Pielcke eine andere Technik an. Einzelne Elemente wie Blütenformen, Knospen oder originelle Köpfchen werden aus weichem Wachs geknetet und so zusammengefügt, dass sie möglichst eine Ringschiene überflüssig machen. Die Beschäftigung mit der Natur führte im Jahr 2000 zu den *Blumenketten*, in denen echte, gepresste und getrocknete Blüten in durchsichtigem Kunststoff eingeschlossen sind. Eine dieser Arbeiten wurde durch das Grassimuseum Leipzig 2001 angekauft. 2004 ergänzte sie ihre Serie *nature* durch Edelsteine und bewegliche Blütenkelche im *Valentinring*. Seit 1995 arbeitet Gitta Pielcke mit ihrem Mann, Erich Zimmermann, im gemeinsamen Atelier in Augsburg zusammen.

E — The diversity of forms in nature provides Gitta Pielcke with an inexhaustible source of inspiration for her figurative works. In order to express carefree joie de vivre, they must be leavened with a pinch of humour and even irony. Her jewellery collections are meant to be fun!

Gitta Pielcke was born in Hamburg in 1964. After her high school diploma she trained as a restorer in Florence before attending the Zeichenakademie Hanau (1987–1991). She saw goldsmithing as her chance to develop

her creative talents but the prevailing Minimalism of late 1980s jewellery did not match her feelings about life so she opted for finding a new way after finishing her training. Moreover, the designer noticed that many women react positively to figurative, poetic forms. Pielcke sawed her first figurative works from sheet metal or bent figures from wire. Her 1991 *Turnerkette* [Gymnasts necklace] consisted of a variety of human figures with which she achieved a linear abstract effect through paratactic arrangement.

After graduating in 1991, Pielcke went to Berlin for three years to soak up the creative ambience. In 1994, she launched her *Geckokette* [Gecko necklace], which, along with her 1996 *Froschkette* [Frog necklace], has become her trademark. She carved the models for the animal figures like miniature pieces of sculpture from a block of hard wax. In this collection, the natural model is supposed to be reproduced as accurately as possible yet caught in a movement that makes elegant but comical parataxis possible and renders a clasp unnecessary. The necklace can be opened at each element and lengthened or shortened as the wearer pleases. In her rings, the designer is careful to ensure that the individual mini-sculptures do not all look alike but, when subjected to closer scrutiny, provide »something to discover.«

In designing the 1998 *nature* ring collection, Pielcke used a different technique. Individual elements such as floral forms, buds or quirky little heads were kneaded of soft wax and fitted together so that a ring shank is in many cases unnecessary. Nature study led in 2000 to *Blumenketten* [Flower necklaces], in which real pressed and dried blossoms are enclosed in transparent plastic. One of these pieces was bought by the Grassi Museum Leipzig in 2001. Gitta Pielcke added the *Valentinring* [Valentine ring] to her nature collection in 2004: it is made variously with individual gemstones and movable flower calyces. Since 1995, Gitta Pielcke has been working with her husband, Erich Zimmermann, from their studio in Augsburg.

1996	*Froschkette*, Silber, Gold — *Frogs necklace*, silver, gold
1997	Ringe *Froschkönig*, Silber, Gold, Platin, Brillant — Rings *Frog prince*, silver, gold, platinum, diamond
2004	*Valentinring*, Gold, Brillanten — *Valentine ring*, gold, diamonds

Gitta Pielcke
Geboren 1964 in Hamburg.
1987–1991 Zeichenakademie Hanau.
Atelier seit 1991, heute in Augsburg.

Gitta Pielcke
Born in Hamburg in 1964.
1987–1991 Zeichenakademie Hanau.
Studio since 1991, now in Augsburg.

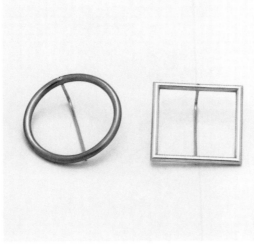

1993

1995

2001

Monika Glöss

Ihre Formen sind geometrisch und streng. Als spielerische Elemente wirken Kontraste zwischen verschiedenen Metallen sowie raffinierte, teils bewegliche Konstruktionen. Doch setzt Monika Glöss in jüngster Zeit auch die knalligen Farben von Acryl ein.

Nach ihrer Goldschmiedeausbildung arbeitete Glöss in verschiedenen Werkstätten. Von 1982 bis 1986 studierte sie in Düsseldorf Schmuck-Design. Es war eine Zeit des Umbruchs an der Fachhochschule. 1982 beendete Friedrich Becker seine Lehrtätigkeit und Professor Sigrid Delius war mit der Neuorganisation des Studiengangs befasst. Monika Glöss entwickelte ihre strenge Formensprache und setzte sich mit Kunst- und Designtheorien auseinander. Besonders interessierte sie sich für die klassische Moderne der 1920er Jahre. In ihr Diplom 1986 flossen Reflektionen zu gesellschaftlichen Themen ein. Dabei wurde sie betreut von Dr. Dieter Fuder, Professor für Designtheorie, und dem Goldschmied und Designer Franz Bette.

Seit 1993 lebt Monika Glöss als selbstständige Schmuck-Designerin in Berlin. Ihr Hauptthema war bis 1993 serieller Schmuck aus Aluminium eloxiert, kombiniert mit Edelstahl. Seither fertigt sie vorwiegend kleine Serien aus Silber, Gold und Platin, zum Teil auch mit Farbedelsteinen. In ihrer Werkstatt entstehen auch Unikate, wie die Skulptur für den Unternehmerinnenpreis 2004 des Berliner Senats. Ihre Kollektion umfasst Ringe, Ohrschmuck, Halsschmuck und Broschen. Bereits 1992 entdeckte Monika Glöss die Edelstahlschnur für die Schmuckherstellung und nutzte sie für variable Halsschmuckserien. Diese wurden 1993 bei den Wettbewerben Design Plus der Messe Frankfurt, der Form 1994–1998 sowie Best of Selection 2000 in Essen ausgezeichnet. Bei den kreisförmigen und quadratischen Ohrsteckern von 1994 und 1995 ist die Mechanik integriertes Element der Gestaltung. Ihre Spiral- und Doppelringe wurden mehrfach in der Auswahl Form des Bundes der Kunsthandwerker gezeigt. Die Doppelringe von 2001 aus Silber bestehen aus zwei beweglich übereinander liegenden Ringschienen. Ein Quadrat-, Kreis- oder Linienkubus aus Gold auf dem inneren Ring durchdringt die entsprechende Öffnung des äußeren. Dadurch sind die beiden Ringe lose miteinander verbunden. Das Dekorative ist bei Monika Glöss immer an den konstruktiven Aufbau des Schmucks gebunden. »Meine Schmuckformen sprechen für sich, so wie zum Beispiel das Quadrat für sich spricht«, erklärt sie.

E — Her forms are geometric and utterly austere. The playful element is confined to contrasts between different metals as well as sophisticated constructions, some of which move. However, Monika Glöss has also been using acrylic in lurid colours recently.

After training as a goldsmith, Glöss worked in several workshops before studying jewellery design in Düsseldorf (1982–1986). That was a time of change at the Fachhochschule. Friedrich Becker retired from teaching in 1982 and Professor Sigrid Delius was in charge of reorganising the curriculum. Monika Glöss developed here austere formal idiom and investigated theories of art and design. She was particularly taken with 1920s classic Modernism. Social themes were incorporated in her 1986 diploma project, which was supervised by Dr. Dieter Fuder, professor for the theory of design, and Franz Bette, goldsmith and designer.

Since 1993 Monika Glöss has lived in Berlin as a self-employed jewellery designer. Until 1993, her main theme was serial jewellery of anodized aluminium combined with stainless steel. Since then she has made mainly small collections in silver, gold and platinum and some pieces are set with coloured precious stones. She also makes one-off pieces in her workshop, such as the sculpture for the Unternehmerinnenpreis 2004 [2004 Business-woman of the Year Prize] awarded by the Berlin Senate. Monika Glöss's collection comprises rings, ear jewellery, neck jewellery and brooches.

Back in 1992, Monika Glöss discovered stainless steel cable for jewellery-making and has used it for variable neck jewellery collections. They were singled out for distinction at the 1993 Design Plus competition at the Frankfurt trade fair, at Form (1994–1998) and as Best of Selection in Essen in 2000. The mechanical aspect is an integral design element in her circular and square stud earrings from 1994 and 1995. Her Spiral and Double rings have been shown several times in the Bund der Kunsthandwerker Form selection. Her 2001 silver Double rings consist of two movable, overlapping ring shanks. A square, circle or linear gold tenon on the inner ring fits into the matching aperture of the outer ring, thus loosely linking the two rings. In Monika Glöss's work, the decorative aspect is always tied in with the construction of a piece. »My jewellery forms speak for themselves, just as the square, for instance, speaks for itself,« she explains.

1993	Variabler Halsschmuck, Gold, Edelstahlseil — Variable necklace, gold, stainless steel cable
1995	Ohrschmuck, Gold — Earrings, gold
2001	Doppelringe, Gold, Silber — Double rings, gold, silver

Monika Glöss
Geboren 1955 in Essen,
1982–1986 Fachhochschule Düsseldorf.
Seit 1993 Atelier in Berlin.

Monika Glöss
Born in Essen in 1955,
1982–1986 Fachhochschule Düsseldorf.
Studio in Berlin since 1993.

Monika Glöss

1987   1987

1989

1988   1993   1997

IsabelleFa

Moitié-Moitié sagt man im Französischen zu halb und halb. Ein schlichter Name für eine handgearbeitete Kette aus hochkarätigem Gold und feinstem Platin. Die einzelnen Glieder in Navetteform sind an den Enden ohne sichtbare Naht perfekt zusammengefügt. Der spannungsvolle Wechsel von zwei edlen Metallfarben, von seidenmatten Außen- und polierten Innengliedern, unterstreicht das Duett aus Form und Farbe. Mit Entwürfen dieser Art zeigt IsabelleFa mit Sitz in Eisingen seit Mitte der 1990er Jahre, wie sich traditionelles Qualitätsdenken mit modernen Gestaltungsideen in Einklang bringen lässt.

Moitié-Moitié gilt inzwischen als Klassiker in der Kollektion. Langlebige Formen sind immer das Ziel der Gestaltung bei IsabelleFa. Ebenso die Perfektion in jedem Detail. Sie entspringt einem handwerklichen Selbstverständnis, das seit der Renaissance bedeutende Gold- und Silberschmiedewerkstätten ausgezeichnet hat. Bei handgefertigten Ketten sind höchste Präzision und ein perfektes Finish aber noch aus einem anderen Grund entscheidend. »Sie garantieren«, sagt Isabelle Mössner, die zusammen mit ihrem Mann Hans-Georg die Manufaktur leitet, »dass eine Kette reibungslos gleitet und angenehm am Körper aufliegt.« Nur die perfekte Politur an der Innenseite der Glieder gewährleistet, dass diese Meisterwerke über Generationen erhalten bleiben. Dies gilt für die klassischen Gliederketten ebenso wie für ihre modernen Interpretationen. Dass die Symbiose aus Tradition und Moderne Wirklichkeit werden konnte, ist wesentlich Isabelle Mössner zu verdanken.

Der Name IsabelleFa entstand 1992 als exklusive Produktlinie des Hauses Mössner. Der Firmengründer Emil Mössner war Kettengoldschmied und Silberschmied. Er setzte bereits 1955 auf handwerkliche Atelierfertigung. Dies bedeutete kurz nach dem Zweiten Weltkrieg eine vollkommen andere Herstellungstechnik als in der Pforzheimer Schmuckindustrie üblich. Denn diese war industriell ausgerichtet, seit Markgraf Karl Friedrich von Baden 1767 dem Franzosen Jean François Autran die Gründung einer Taschenuhrenfabrik in Pforzheim erlaubt hatte. Kettenmaschinen wurden bereits in der ersten Hälfte des 19. Jahrhunderts für die Massenproduktion eingesetzt. Ateliers hingegen, in denen Gold- und Silberschmiede Einzelstücke und Kleinserien herstellen, kommen aus der Tradition des künstlerischen Handwerks. Vorbilder lieferte die Arts-and-Crafts-Bewegung Ende des 19. Jahrhunderts. Um sich von fernöstlichen Billigimporten zu unterscheiden, kehrten zahlreiche europäische Firmen Ende des 20. Jahrhunderts zur Manufakturfertigung zurück. Dies führte nicht nur in der Uhrenindustrie seit den 1980er zu einem Paradigmenwechsel, sondern auch in deutschen Schmuckmanufakturen.

1981 kam Isabelle Fagnoul aus Belgien, geboren 1963, nach Pforzheim, um an der Goldschmiedeschule ihre Ausbildung zu absolvieren. Hier lernte sie Hans-Georg Mössner kennen, der gerade die Meisterprüfung im Goldschmiedehandwerk ablegte. Ihre Anschlusslehre und Gesellenjahre absolvierte die junge Belgierin von 1983 bis 1988 in der Werkstatt von Juwelier Jacobi. 1985 zeigte er einige besonders große Stücke von Mössner in einer Ausstellung, die seine Kunden spontan begeisterten. Ebenso kamen die außergewöhnlichen Arbeiten bei führenden Juwelieren in der Schweiz gut an. So entwickelte sich eine Premium-Kollektion bei Mössner für ausgewählte Juweliere. Mit der Heirat von Isabelle Fagnoul und Hans-Georg Mössner erhielt das Familienunternehmen eine überzeugende Botschafterin mit einem ausgeprägten Gespür für die Tradition der Moderne; 1988 begann sie ihre Tätigkeit in der Firma. »Jugendstil und Art Déco waren in Belgien sehr wichtig«, erklärt sie. Belgien habe seit Henry van de Velde zahlreiche moderne Architekten und Gestalter hervorgebracht. Für die gelernte Goldschmiedin sind moderne Formen ebenso wichtig wie handwerkliche Qualität.

Die Zusammenarbeit mit der Platin Gilde führte 1990 zu einer Intensivierung moderner Formen. »Platin hat für uns eine entscheidende Rolle gespielt«, sagt Isabelle Mössner. In der Manufaktur in Eisingen entstanden vollkommen reduzierte Hals- und Armreife, wie sie nur ein Hersteller der Spitzenklasse realisieren kann. »Je einfacher die Form, desto schwieriger ist sie herzustellen«, sagt Isabelle Mössner. »Man darf sich nicht den geringsten Fehler leisten.« Noch schwieriger sei es, mit Materialien wie Platin oder Roségold zu arbeiten. Der einfachere Weg, einen hohen Silberanteil zu verwenden, damit sich die Glieder und Reife leichter biegen lassen, kam jedoch nie in Frage. »Wir haben uns mit sehr anspruchsvollen Materialien auseinandergesetzt und uns für diese Formensprache entschieden.«

Im Jahr 1994 erhielt die Kollektion außergewöhnlicher Ketten und Platinschmuckstücke den Namen IsabelleFa. Damit wurde auch die gestalterische Leistung der Firmenchefin gewürdigt. Charakteristisch für die Modelle sind neben der Verwendung von Platin die selbst entwickelte Roségoldlegierung. Sie wird in der Manufaktur geschmolzen und komplett bis zum fertigen Produkt verarbeitet. Neben dem dezenten Roséschimmer und den klaren Formen sind es vor allem die Volumina, die bei IsabelleFa überzeugen. »Eine perfekte Kettenform kann nicht gezeichnet werden. Das muss ausprobiert werden«, sagt Isabelle Mössner. Manche Stücke mussten langsam wachsen. Der erste große Halsreif war zunächst 12 Millimeter breit. Dann entstanden Stücke in Platin und Roségold von 14, 16 und 18 Millimeter. Inzwischen gibt es Arbeiten mit rechteckigem und ovalem Profil von 24 Millimeter Breite. Die heutige überragende Qualität hat die Manufaktur nicht zuletzt ihren Mitarbeitern zu verdanken, von denen Isabelle Mössner überzeugt sagt: »Sie sind unglaublich. Es sind wirklich die Besten.«

Die Qualität zeigt sich auch in den integrierten, nahezu unsichtbaren Verschlüssen. Zum Beispiel bei dem weich fließenden Collier und Armband *Grace*. Ein Diamant zeigt, welches das Glied mit der Öffnung ist. Perfekte Verbindungen dieser Art erlauben, dass eine Kette problemlos mit

1998

1998

einem Armband verlängert werden kann. Eine Kette mit schlichten runden Gliedern in rechteckigem Querschnitt wurde beim Platinum Design of the Year 1996 in Japan ausgezeichnet. Ihr androgyner Charakter macht die *Platinpreiskette*, wie sie intern genannt wird, auch bei Männern beliebt. Mit Arbeiten dieser Art hat IsabelleFa in der Fertigung handgearbeiteter Ketten seit 1994 klare Akzente gesetzt. Dass Navetteketten inzwischen IsabelleFa-Ketten genannt werden, zeigt, wie sehr die Manufaktur in diesem Sektor tonangebend ist. Eine Platinkette in Navetteform von 120 cm Länge mit einer großen weißen Südseeperle heißt *La Mer*. »Sie strahlt eine Schönheit aus«, sagt Isabelle Mössner, »die mich an Botticellis Venus erinnert.«

E — *Moitié-moitié* means »half-and-half« or »fifty-fifty« in French. A simple name for a hand-crafted necklace of almost pure gold and the finest platinum. The individual links in navette shape are seamlessly fitted together at the ends. The exciting alternation of two noble metal colours, of silky matt finished exterior and polished inside underscores the duet of form and colour. With designs like this, Eisingen-based IsabelleFa has demonstrated since the mid-1990s how traditional thinking on quality can be reconciled with modern design ideas.

Moitié-Moitié is by now regarded as the classic in the collection. Forms with a long fashion life have always been the aim of design at Isabelle-Fa. So has perfection in all details. The call for these qualities comes from an ideal of craftsmanship that has distinguished important goldsmithing and silversmithing workshops since the Renaissance. With hand-crafted necklaces, utmost precision and perfect finish are crucial for another reason. »They guarantee,« says Isabelle Mössner, who runs the factory with her husband, Hans-Georg, »that a necklace glides without friction and rests comfortably on the wearer's body.« Only a perfect polish on the inside of links ensures that these masterpieces last for generations. This is just as true of classic articulated necklaces as it is of modern interpretations of them. To Isabelle Mössner much of the credit is due for realising a synthesis of traditional and modern.

The IsabelleFa label was created in 1992 for an exclusive line marketed by Mössner. The founder of the firm, Emil Mössner, was a chain goldsmith and silversmith. As early as 1955 he insisted on studio crafting. So soon after the Second World War that meant a production technique that was entirely different to the norm in the Pforzheim jewellery industry, which had been industrial in nature since Karl Friedrich, Margrave of Baden, issued a patent for founding a pocket-watch factory in Pforzheim to a Frenchman, Jean François Autran, in 1767. Chain-making machines were already in use in mass production by the first half of the 19th century. Studios, on the other hand, in which goldsmiths and silversmiths made one-offs and limited editions, come from the crafts tradition. This practice was modelled after

the late 19th-century Arts and Crafts movement. To set themselves apart from cheap Far Eastern import wares, many European firms returned to industrial manufacture in the late 20th century. This trend has led to a paradigm shift since the 1980s, not just in watch-making but also in the German jewellery industry.

In 1981 Isabelle Fagnoul (born in 1963) went from Belgium to Pforzheim to train at the Goldschmiedeschule. There she met Hans-Georg Mössner, who had just taken his master's certificate in goldsmithing. The young Belgian continued with her apprenticeship and did her journeyman's training at the workshop of Juwelier Jacoby (1983–1988). In 1985 Jacoby showed some particularly large pieces by Mössner at an exhibition which aroused spontaneous enthusiasm in his clientele. These extraordinary pieces also made a hit with leading jewellers in Switzerland. Thus a premium collection by Mössner for select jewellers developed. The marriage of Isabelle Fagnoul and Hans-Georg Mössner gave the family business a convincing ambassadress with a keen sense of tradition in Modernism; in 1988 Isabelle Mössner began to work for the firm. »Jugendstil and Art Déco were very important in Belgium,« she explains. Since the days of Henry van de Velde, Belgium has produced a great many modern architects and designers. For her, as a trained goldsmith, modern forms and fine craftsmanship are on an equal footing.

Collaboration with Platin Gilde in 1990 led to an intensified exploration of modern forms. »Platinum has played a crucial role for us,« says Isabelle Mössner. From the Eisingen factory, hoop necklaces and bangles emerged that were reduced to the simplest of forms as only a top-quality maker can realise such pieces. »The simpler the form, the harder it is to make,« says Isabelle Mössner. »You can't allow yourself to make the slightest mistake.« It is even more difficult, she says to work materials such as platinum or rose (pink) gold. However, the simpler method of using a higher silver content to make links and hoop necklaces easier to bend was never seriously considered. »We investigated very difficult materials and decided on this particular language of forms.«

In 1994, the collection of extraordinary necklaces and platinum jewellery was given the IsabelleFa label, which also represents a tribute to the head of the firm's achievement as a designer. Characteristic of these models are, apart from the use of platinum, a proprietary rose gold alloy. It is melted in the factory and worked there from start to finished product. Apart from the reticent pink gleam and clarity of form, volumes are what make the IsabelleFa collection so stunning. »The perfect necklace form cannot be drawn. It has to be tried out,« says Isabelle Mössner. Some pieces have to grow slowly. The first hoop necklace was 12mm wide. It was followed by pieces in platinum and rose gold that were 14, 16 and 18mm wide. By now there are pieces that are rectangular or oval in profile and 24mm wide. The

2003

2004

exceptional quality achieved today is due not least to the factory employees, of whom Isabelle Mössner says with conviction: »They're incredible.
They are really the best.«

Quality is also shown in integrated clasps that are virtually invisible,
for instance, on the softly fluid *Grace* necklace and bracelet set. Only a diamond marks the link that opens. Perfect linkage of this kind makes it possible
that a necklace can easily be lengthened by attaching the matching bracelet.
A necklace with simple round links that are rectangular in section was designated Platinum Design of the Year in Japan in 1996. Its androgynous character makes the »Platinum-Prize chain,« as it's called in the firm, popular with
men as well. With works of this kind, IsabelleFa has made a decisive mark as a
maker of hand-crafted necklaces since 1994. That navette necklaces are now
generically known as »IsabelleFa necklaces« indicates that the business is the
trend-setter in this sector. A navette necklace in platinum and 120 cm long
with a large, white South Sea pearl is called *La Mer*. »It radiates a beauty,«
says Isabelle Mössner, »that reminds me of Botticelli's Venus.«

1987	Kette und Armband *Navette*, kombinierbar, Platin — Necklace and bracelet *Navette*, can be combined, platinum
1987	Kette *Navette La Mer*, Platin — Necklace *Navette La Mer*, platinum
1988	Kette *Cascade*, Gold seidenmatt — Necklace *Cascade*, gold matt de luxe
1993	Kette und Armband, Platin — Necklace and bracelet, platinum
1997	Kette *Navette Moitié-Moitié*, Platin, Gold — Necklace *Navette Moitié-Moitié*, platinum, gold
1989	Halsreif, Gold — Necklace, gold
1998	Kette *La Lune et le Soleil*, Platin, Gold, Diamant — Necklace *La Lune et le Soleil*, platinum, gold, diamond
1998	Ringe, Platin, Diamanten — Rings, platinum, diamonds
2003	Halsreif, Armreif, Ring, Ohrschmuck, Gold, Diamanten — Necklace, bangle, ring, earrings, gold, diamonds
2004	Panzerarmband, 6 Ösen, Gold, Brillant — Bracelet, 6 bails, gold, diamond

Isabelle und Hans-Georg Mössner
Firmengründung durch Emil Mössner 1955,
Markengründung IsabelleFa 1992 durch Isabelle
und Hans-Georg Mössner.

Isabelle and Hans-Georg Mössner
Firm founded by Emil Mössner in 1955, brand
IsabelleFa launched by Isabelle and Hans-Georg
Mössner in 1992.

1992

2007

1992   Ringe *Froschkönig*, Silber, Silber feingoldplattiert, Süßwasser-Zuchtperle
       — Rings *Frog prince*, silver, silver fine gold plated, freshwater cultured pearl

1994   Anhänger *Eiserne Jungfrau*, Silber, Topaskegel — Pendant *Iron Maiden*,
       silver, topaz cone

1996   Ring und Collier *Dragonheart*, Silber feingoldplattiert, Süßwasser-Zuchtperle
       — Ring and necklace *Dragonheart*, silver fine gold plated, freshwater
       cultured pearl

2001   Anhänger und Ring *Giftfroschkönig*, Silber, Silber feingoldplattiert,
       Süßwasser-Zuchtperle, Brandlack — Pendant and ring *Poison frog prince*,
       silver, silver fine gold plated, freshwater cultured pearl

2007   Schmuckset *Liebeszauber*, Silber feingoldplattiert, Süßwasser-Zuchtperle,
       Achatgemme — Jewellery set *Love charme*, silver fine gold plated, freshwater
       cultured pearl, agate cameo

1994   1996   2001

Drachenfels Design

Franziska von Drachenfels macht märchenhaften Schmuck. Frosch-könige, traumhafte Elfen und andere Fabelwesen, vergangene und gegen-wärtige Mythen und Symbole sind ihre Themen. Mit ihren Schmuckserien, zumeist aus Silber feingoldplattiert, etablierte sie in wenigen Jahren eines der erfolgreichsten neuen Schmuckateliers in Deutschland. Mitten in der Goldstadt Pforzheim, gegen jeden Trend und entgegen der allgemeinen Ent-wicklung in der Traditionsindustrie.

Franziska von Drachenfels stammt aus einer Pforzheimer Familie, in der sich alles um Schmuck drehte. Vater und Großvater waren Modellgold-schmiede, Tante Valasek hatte eine Juwelengoldschmiede. »Ich habe als Kind den Geruch des Bunzenbrenners eingeatmet«, erzählt von Drachenfels. Aber genau deshalb und »weil in Pforzheim in den 1980er Jahren jeder dachte, er weiß alles über Schmuck«, wollte sie diesen Beruf nicht ergreifen; obwohl die Freude am Gestalten weit zurückreicht. In der Juwelengoldschmiede Valasek, die sie als Kind oft besuchte, gab es immer lose Perlen und Edelsteine. Wenn Franziska kam, wurden sie aus der Schachtel gekippt, um »Blümchen« zu legen. Bis es der Tante zu bunt wurde und sie das kreative Spiel verbot.

Schließlich ging Franziska von Drachenfels 1987, nach der Fachhoch-schulreife, dann doch auf die Goldschmiedeschule. Sie wählte den bewähr-ten Beruf, weil sie schwanger wurde und für ihre kleine Tochter sorgen muss-te. Das Berufskolleg »Formgebung für Schmuck und Gerät« ergänzte die allein erziehende Mutter mit einer Ausbildung zur Juwelengoldschmiedin bei ihrer Tante. 1992, direkt nach der Gesellenprüfung, machte sie sich selb-ständig. Wie ihr Vater begann sie für die Pforzheimer Industrie Schmuck-entwürfe und Modelle zu machen. Zwei Jahre lang arbeitete von Drachen-fels parallel dazu als Grafikerin. Das Auskommen als Designerin in Pforzheim war bescheiden und die Zusammenarbeit mit der Industrie eine einzige Katastrophe. »Ich dachte, ich werde wahnsinnig in den Auseinandersetzungen mit diesen – ich sage es ganz böse – Pforzheimer Industrietypen, die mir da gegenübersaßen.« Franziska von Drachenfels hatte das Gefühl, sie würde nur zurechtgestutzt. Lob gab es nie. So versuchte sie wie viele andere junge Schmuckgestalterinnen in den 1990er Jahren ihr Glück mit einer eigenen Schmuckkollektion.

Die große Bewährungsprobe kam 1993 auf der Messe Inhorgenta. Ihr erstes großes Thema hieß *Froschkönig*, das sie auch heute noch pflegt. »Ich hatte einfach das Gefühl, ich will einen Teil meiner Gedanken und Interessen, meiner Traumwelt, im Schmuck verwirklichen.« Doch die Stücke mit der Sym-bolik aus der Märchenwelt widersprachen der reduzierten Formensprache der Designer ebenso wie den gängigen Juwelen der Schmuckindustrie. Entsprechend waren die ersten Reaktionen. Juweliere kamen an den Stand, nur um zu sagen, dass ihr Schmuck »das Allerletzte« sei. »Damit muss man erst mal klarkommen«, sagt die Unternehmerin heute: »Man macht die Kol-lektion, organisiert die Messe, dekoriert die Fenster für den ersten großen Auftritt. Und dann hat man das Gefühl, jetzt könnte man auch nackt daste-hen.« Sie wurde von den Schmuckkünstlern angegriffen, von den Designern und von der Industrie. Niemand habe sie verstanden, erzählt sie. Es sei ein Spießrutenlauf gewesen. 6000 DM kostete das Messeabenteuer. Am Mittag des letzten Tages hatte sie einen einzigen Ring für 220 Mark verkauft.

Kurz vor dem Messeschluss kam eine bekannte Schmuckhändlerin aus Zürich an den Stand. »Sie hat sich alles angeschaut und bestellte«, erinnert sich Franziska von Drachenfels. Der Auftrag war so groß, dass sie gar nicht wusste, ob sie ihn bewältigen konnte. Die Schmuckdesignerin konnte es nach der vorausgegangenen Enttäuschung kaum fassen, dass eine Kundin ihr Geld investierte und ihren Schmuck so interessant fand. Dieser Auftrag habe sie wirtschaftlich noch nicht gerettet, aber das Selbstwertgefühl wieder her-gestellt. Franziska von Drachenfels wusste jetzt, dass sie nur die Menschen finden musste, die ähnlich wie sie empfinden. Es war die Initialzündung für den Start des Unternehmens Drachenfels Design. Um den Auftrag aus der Schweiz ausführen zu können, sprach sie ihre Freundin Stefanie Spöhr an, die damals noch Schmuckdesign an der HfG in Pforzheim studierte. Sie heißt in-zwischen Stefanie Harer und ist ihre Geschäftspartnerin. Auch andere Freun-de wurden aktiviert. Inzwischen ist das Unternehmen Drachenfels-Design auf 25 fest angestellte und eine beträchtliche Zahl von freien Mitarbeitern gewachsen. Und in der Modellgoldschmiede arbeitet ihr Vater mit.

Seit der denkwürdigen Messe entstanden kontinuierlich ideenreiche Kollektionen. Das Thema *Froschkönig* wurde um Serien wie *Flammeninferno*, *Dragonheart* und *Dragonfly*, *Giftpfeilfrösche*, *Jeanne D'Arc*, *Liebeszauber*, *Chandaliery* oder *Löwenmäulchen* bereichert. Die Namen der Schmucklinien offenbaren nicht selten ein ironisches Augenzwinkern. Die ersten Dinge sei-en ganz »aus dem Bauch« heraus gekommen, aus dem Gefühl, sagt Franziska von Drachenfels. »Mein Gedanke war damals, was bin ich und was will ich.«

Der Erfolg, den Drachenfels in den letzten 15 Jahren hat, ist wie jener des Romanhelden »Harry Potter« ein deutlicher Hinweis, dass die Sehn-sucht nach Märchen und Magie, nach dem Irrationalen, lebendig ist. Wie im Jugendstil übernimmt Schmuck die Funktion, die Frau neu zu definieren als Persönlichkeit, die sich zu ihren Gefühlen, zu ihrer Sexualität und Sinnlich-keit öffentlich bekennt. »Eine Frau, die unseren Schmuck trägt, muss natür-lich selbstbewusst sein. Sie muss auch mit Konfrontationen klarkommen«, sagt Franziska von Drachenfels. »Je größer das Stück ist, desto mehr muss sie damit rechnen, dass es Rivalität hervorruft. Sie trifft damit eine Aussage, sie tritt ins Rampenlicht.« Sie gebe damit etwas von sich preis. »Eine Frau, die ein *Inferno-Herz* trägt, gibt indirekt zu, dass sie das emotionale Infer-no kennt.« Und wer das Inferno kenne, habe auch schon Chaos hinter sich, Sexualität, Streit. »Sie signalisiert unmittelbar: Pass auf, sei vorsichtig! Ganz einfach bin ich nicht!« Ist es der Schmuck für die »Femme fatale« unserer Zeit? Es sei ein Spiel mit allem, sagt Franziska von Drachenfels. Sie hat Themen kre-

2005   2006   2007

iert, die sich mit der »Femme fatale« beschäftigen. Doch gibt es auch liebliche Themen, »für das Gefühl, sich ein bisschen auszuruhen von der harten Realität.« Drachenfels-Design will nicht in einer Richtung fokussiert sein, schon deshalb, weil die Frauen vielschichtige Wesen sind. »Die Femme fatale kann genau so leben in der Frau, die ein Ruhebedürfnis hat oder das Gefühl von Sicherheit braucht.« Es gebe nie nur eine Facette in einer Persönlichkeit. Die Gestalterin bietet eine Menge Stoff, um verschiedene Aspekte auszuleben. Sie kennt sogar gute Niessing-Kundinnen, die ihr *Infernoherz* tragen, einen *Frosch* oder ein *Piuskreuz.* »Manche Frauen lieben es einfach zu spielen. Sie möchten sich jeden Tag neu erfinden«, meint Franziska von Drachenfels. Mit ihrem Schmuck können sie Prinzessin sein, Drache oder Hexe. »Wichtig finde ich, dass es die Frau selber in der Hand hat, was sie da inszeniert.«

Ein Gestaltungsthema war für die Schmuckgestalterin eine ganz wichtige und bewusste Entscheidung. Mit der Serie *Eiserne Jungfrau* wollte sie gegen ihren eigenen Käfig angehen. »Es ist uns nicht um eiserne Jungfrauen und Folterinstrumente gegangen, wie man uns vorgeworfen hat«, erklärt sie. »Ich hatte einfach nur das Gefühl, jetzt muss ich diese Käfige loswerden, die mich seit meiner Arbeit für die Pforzheimer Schmuckindustrie umklammert hatten.«

E — Franziska von Drachenfels makes fairy-tale jewellery. Frog princes, dreamy elves and other mythical beings, past and present mythologies and symbols are her subject matter. With her edition jewellery, most of it silver fine gold plated, she has become established within just a few years as one of the most successful new jewellery studios in Germany. At the very heart of the golden city of Pforzheim, bucking all trends and going counter to the general development in this traditional industry.

Franziska von Drachenfels is from a Pforzheim family in which everything revolves around jewellery. Her father and grandfather were model goldsmiths. Her aunt Valasek had a goldsmithing workshop that made jewellery set with gemstones. »As a child, I breathed in the fumes of the Bunsen burner,« von Drachenfels recounts. But for that very reason and »because in Pforzheim in the 1980s everyone thought he knew everything there was to know about jewellery,« she did not want to take up this profession, even though her delight in design goes far back. There were always loose pearls and unset precious stones lying about in the Valasek jewellery workshop. Whenever Franziska went there to visit, they were tipped out of the box to make »flowers«. Until it became a bit too much for her aunt and she forbade this creative game.

Finally, after taking her exams qualifying for polytechnic entrance, Franziska von Drachenfels did go to the goldsmithing school after all, in 1987. She chose this familiar profession because she had had a little girl and had to support her as a single mother. She supplemented the Berufskolleg »Formgebung für Schmuck und Gerät« [Professional College for Jewellery and Tableware Design] by training as a jewellery-maker and goldsmith with her aunt. In 1992, as soon as she had her journeyman's certificate, she became self-employed. Like her father, she began to design jewellery and make models for the Pforzheim jewellery industry. For two years, von Drachenfels worked on the side as a graphic artist. Being a designer in Pforzheim meant modest earnings and collaboration with the jewellery industry was disastrous. »I thought I'd go mad having to deal with those – I'll put it very unkindly – Pforzheim salesmen types sitting across from me.« Franziska von Drachenfels had the feeling her wings were being clipped. She never received any praise. So, like many another young jewellery designers in the 1990s, she decided to try her luck with a jewellery collection of her own.

The big test came in 1993 at the Munich Inhorgenta. Her first big theme was the *Frog prince*, which she still cherishes. »I simply had the feeling I wanted to realise some of my thoughts and interests, my dream world, in jewellery.« However, her pieces with their fairy-tale symbolism clashed with other designers' reductivist formal idiom as well as the conventional jewellery produced by the jewellery industry. The initial reactions to her work were as expected. Jewellers came up to her stand just to pronounce that her jewellery was »dire«. »You first have to learn to come to terms with that,« says the enterprising artist today. »You make the collection, organise the trade fair, decorate the windows for that first big appearance. And then you have the feeling you might as well just be standing there naked.« She was attacked by artists in jewellery, by designers and the jewellery industry. No one understood her, she says. It was an ordeal. The trade fair venture cost DM 6000. By noon on the last day she had sold just one ring for 220 Marks. Just as the trade fair was about to close, a well-known jewellery dealer from Zurich came up to the stand. »She looked at everything and placed an order,« recalls Franziska von Drachenfels. The order was so large that she wasn't even sure whether she would be able to handle it. After all the disappointments, the young jewellery designer could hardly believe that a client was investing good money in her jewellery because she found it so interesting. This order was not yet enough to pull her out of the red but her self-confidence was restored. Franziska von Drachenfels realised now that all she had to do was find people who felt the way she did. That was the spark that ignited the fire under Drachenfels Design as a business.

To be able to fill the order from Switzerland, she enlisted the help of a friend, Stefanie Spöhr, who was then still a student of jewellery design at the HfG in Pforzheim. Now her name is Stefanie Harer and she is Franziska von Drachenfels' business partner. To return to the story: other friends were contacted and put to work. Now Drachenfels Design employs a permanent workforce of twenty-five as well as quite a number of freelancers. And her father collaborates on making the models.

2008

Imaginative collections have continued to emerge on a regular basis since that memorable trade fair. The Frog Prince theme has been supplemented by such editions as *Flammeninferno* [Flame inferno], *Dragonheart* and *Dragonfly*, *Giftpfeilfrösche* [Poison dart frogs], *Jeanne d'Arc*, *Liebeszauber* [Love charme], *Chandaliery* [Chandeliery] and *Löwenmäulchen* [Snapdragon]. The names of these lines in jewellery often reveal a tongue-in-cheek irony. The earliest things were simply »from the gut,« intuitive, says Franziska von Drachenfels. »My feeling then was what am I and what do I want.«

The success that Drachenfels has had in the past fifteen years is, like that of novel hero Harry Potter, a clear indication that yearnings for fairy-tales and magic, for the irrational, are alive and well. As in Jugendstil/Art Nouveau, Drachenfels jewellery assumes the function of redefining a woman as a personality who is open about her feelings, her sexuality and her sensuality. »A woman who wears our jewellery must, of course, be self-assured. She also has to be able to handle confrontations,« says Franziska von Drachenfels. »The bigger the piece, the more she has to be prepared for rivalry. With it she's making a statement, she's stepping into the limelight.« She is revealing something of herself to do so. »A woman wearing an *Inferno heart* is admitting indirectly that she has known an emotional inferno.« And anyone who has known an inferno also has chaos behind her, sexuality, strife. »She is signalising directly: look out, be careful! I'm not all that simple!«

Is this jewellery for the »femme fatale« of our time? It's a game with everything at stake, says Franziska von Drachenfels. She has created motifs related to the »femme fatale« theme. However, there are also gentle themes »for the feeling of being able to take a brief rest from harsh reality.« Drachenfels Design does not want to focus in a single direction, if only because women are such multilayered beings. »A femme fatale can be just as alive in a woman who has a need for respite or a feeling of security.« There is never just a single facet to a personality. The designer provides a great deal of material for expressing various aspects of one's personality. She even knows faithful Niessing clients who wear her *Inferno heart*, a *Frog* or a *Pius cross*. »Some women simply love to play. They like reinventing themselves every day,« believes Franziska von Drachenfels. Wearing her jewellery, a woman can be a princess or a dragon or a witch. »What I feel matters is that a woman is taking matters into her own hands when she is putting on something.«

One design motif has entailed a very important and deliberate decision on the jewellery designer's part. With the *Eiserne Jungfrau* [Iron maiden] line she wanted to break down the bars of her own cage. »We weren't concerned with iron maidens and other instruments of torture as we were accused of being,« she explains. »I simply had the feeling I had to get rid of this cage which has imprisoned me since my work for the Pforzheim jewellery industry.«

Franziska von Drachenfels
Geboren 1967 in Pforzheim. 1987 Berufskolleg »Formgebung für Schmuck und Gerät«. Ateliergründung 1992 in Pforzheim.

Franziska von Drachenfels
Born in Pforzheim in 1967. 1987 Berufskolleg »Jewellery and Tableware Design«. Founded studio in Pforzheim in 1992.

1994

1995

1997

Rudi Sand

Die Schmuckstücke von Rudi Sand entstehen ausnahmslos aus hochkarätigem Gold oder Platin. Bearbeitet im weitgehend handwerklichen Prozess
des Verformens und Schmiedens erscheint die kostbare Materie schließlich
in weichen, natürlich wirkenden Falten. »Eine gute Bewegung soll die Form
ergeben, wie fließender oder geschlungener Stoff«, sagt der Designer.

Geboren wurde Rudi Sand in Calw. Sein ursprünglicher Berufswunsch
war es, Kinderspielzeug zu entwerfen. Nach dem Abitur 1982 machte er zunächst eine Schreinerlehre in Baden-Baden. Dann folgte an der Fachhochschule für Design in Schwäbisch Gmünd das Studium Produkt-Design. Nach
dem Vordiplom wechselte er zum Schmuck-Design. Hier war an der früheren Gewerbeschule schon sein Urgroßvater zum Ziseleur ausgebildet worden. Rudi Sand erinnert sich an eines seiner Reliefs, auf dem Neptun aus den
Wellen steigt. Es hing über dem Sofa der Großeltern: »Es gab dadurch schon
einen Bezug zum Gestalten mit Metall.«

In dem damals noch eigenständigen Studiengang in Schwäbisch
Gmünd ging es bei den Professoren Pierre Schlevogt und Frank Hess immer
um ganzheitliche Schmuckprojekte und -themen. Eine einzelne, originelle
Idee zu haben, war zu wenig. »Erst musste ein Thema formuliert werden.
War es zu schwach, wurde es wieder fallen gelassen«, erzählt der Schmuck-
Designer. »Die Professoren sahen Schmuck im gesellschaftlichen Kontext«,
berichtet er. Eines der provokanten Statements von Hess war: »Schmuck
kommt vor.« Dies habe eine bescheidene Zurückhaltung gefordert. Von
Schlevogt merkte er sich den Satz: »Schauen Sie sich die Leute an, die den
Schmuck tragen sollen, ebenso die Situationen und Anlässe.« In seiner
Diplomarbeit befasste sich Rudi Sand mit Wellen. Dafür studierte er ihre
physikalischen und geologischen Erscheinungsformen und machte eine
Fotoserie von Streifenmustern im Wasser, die er in Schmuck übersetzte.

Nach dem Diplom ging er 1992 nach Amsterdam. Dem einjährigen
Gaststudium an der Gerrit Rietveld Academie folgte die Gründung des eigenen Ateliers. Kontinuierlich stellte er seitdem seine handgefertigten
Schmuckserien auf Messen aus, wie der Ambiente in Frankfurt, der Selection
in Essen (von 1998 bis 2000) und ab 1994 in München auf der Inhorgenta.
Seit 2000 ist Rudi Sand in Berlin ansässig. Aus dem »Wellenstudium« entstand sein großes Thema *Faltenwurf*, das ihn seit 15 Jahren beschäftigt.

Viele große Bildhauer und Maler haben seit der Antike das dreidimensionale, bewegte Faltenspiel der Bekleidung in ihren Arbeiten thematisiert. Rudi Sand sieht seine Schmuckstücke allerdings nicht als Skulpturen.
Er möchte vielmehr einen Bezug zur Haute Couture herstellen, weil dort
ebenfalls ganz bewusst handwerklich gearbeitet wird. Er erklärt: »Die Hand-
werklichkeit ist meine Leidenschaft, aber die wird am Ende nicht sichtbar.
Bei meinen Ringen und Armreifen sieht man keinen Hammerschlag, obwohl
viel geschmiedet wird. Das wird hinterher alles wieder rausgefeilt. Für mich
ist die Erscheinung am Ende maßgebend. Es muss eine fließende Bewegung

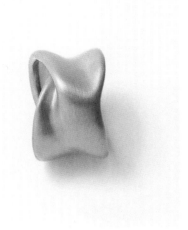

1999

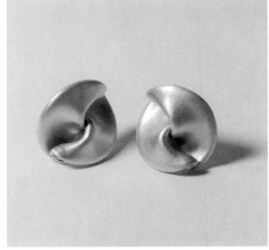

2006

2008

sein.« »Der Faltenwurf ist aber kein kompliziertes Thema«, sagt Rudi Sand. Es sei eher nahe liegend. »Da braucht man nur mal den Stoff zu betrachten, der sich in der Armbeuge eines Pullovers oder eines Hemdes staucht.« Das Thema hat also mit Kleidung zu tun. Und Kleidung sei der erste Eindruck, den man wahrnehme, wenn man jemandem begegne. Deshalb ist seiner Meinung nach die Kleidung auch das Übergeordnete. Der Schmuck hingegen sei nur Akzent. Rudi Sand: »Erst bei näherem Betrachten wird der Akzent zum Übergeordneten, zum Zauber.«

E — Rudi Sand's pieces are all of almost pure gold or platinum. The costly material is worked mainly by hand, bent and beaten, to appear ultimately in soft, natural-looking folds. »The form should result in good movement, like that of flowing or wrapped material,« says the designer.

Born in Calw, Rudi Sand originally wanted to design children's toys. After passing school-leaving exams qualifying for university entrance in 1982, Sand first served a carpenter and joiner's apprenticeship in Baden-Baden, followed by product-design studies at the Fachhochschule für Design in Schwäbisch Gmünd. After completing the foundation course, he switched to jewellery design. His great-grandfather had trained as a chaser at the same institution, which used to be a school for the applied arts. Rudi Sand recalls one of his reliefs, depicting Neptune rising from the waves that hung above his grandparents' sofa: »That created a link to working with metal.«

In what at that time was still a separate course of studies in Schwäbisch Gmünd, Professors Pierre Schlevogt and Frank Hess were always concerned with holistic approaches to jewellery projects and themes. Just having a single, original idea wasn't enough. »First a subject had to be formulated. If it wasn't feasible, it was dropped,« recounts the jewellery designer. »The professors also viewed jewellery in its social context,« he reports. One of the most provocative statements made by Hess was: »Jewellery occurs.« That was a call for modesty and reticence. He noted the following dictum pronounced by Schlevogt: »Take a look at the people who are supposed to wear the jewellery as well as the situations and occasions [for wearing it].« In his diploma project, Rudi Sand investigated waves, studying their physical and geological properties and types and taking a series of photos depicting striped patterns in water, which he transferred to jewellery.

After taking his diploma, he went to Amsterdam in 1992. Following a one-year stint auditing courses at the Gerrit Rietveld Academie, he founded a studio of his own. Since then he has regularly shown his hand-crafted jewellery collections at trade fairs, such as Ambiente in Frankfurt, Selection in Essen (from 1998 to 2000) and from 1994 at the Munich Inhorgenta. His big theme, *Faltenwurf* [Fall of folds], which he has been exploring for fifteen years, derives from his »wave studies«. Since Greco-Roman antiquity, many great sculptors and painters have focused in their work on the three-

dimensional, lively play of apparel folds. Rudi Sand, however, does not view his pieces of jewellery as sculpture. On the contrary, he wants to link up with haute couture because there, too, hand-crafting is a deliberately chosen work process. He explains: »Craftsmanship is my passion but at the end is invisible. You don't see any hammering in my rings and bangles although a lot of smithing has gone on. Afterwards that's all filed away. What counts for me is the final appearance. There has to be a fluid movement.«

»The fall of folds is not, however, a complicated matter,« says Rudi Sand. On the contrary, it suggests itself. »All you have to do is take a look at the material that bunches in the crook of a sweater or shirt sleeve.« The subject is, therefore, also related to clothes. And clothes make the first impression perceived on an encounter. Consequently, in Rudi Sand's opinion, that is why clothing is also supreme. Jewellery, on the other hand, is just a finishing touch. Rudi Sand: »Only on closer scrutiny does that touch become supremacy, enchantment.«

1994	Ringe *Diamantrosette*, Gold, Diamant — Rings *Diamond rosette*, gold, diamond
1995	Ringe *Guillochierte Welle*, Gold — Rings *Guilloche Wave*, gold
1999	Ring *Faltenwurf*, Gold — Ring *Fall of folds*, gold
2006	Ohrschmuck *Faltenwurf*, Platin — Earrings *Fall of folds*, platinum
2008	Ringe *Bänder*, Gold — Rings *Ribbons*, gold
1997	Ohrschmuck *Faltenwurf*, Gold — Earrings *Fall of folds*, gold

Rudi Sand
Geboren 1963 in Calw. Fachhochschule Schwäbisch Gmünd und Gerrit Rietveld Academie Amsterdam. Atelier seit 1993, heute in Berlin.

Rudi Sand
Born in Calw in 1963. Fachhochschule Schwäbisch Gmünd and Gerrit Rietveld Academie Amsterdam. Studio in 1993, now in Berlin.

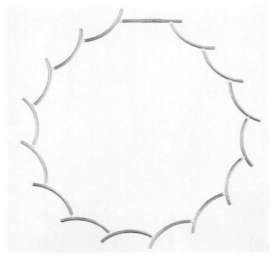

1994   1996

Eva Maisch

Fliegen oder Ameisen auf Schmuckstücken müssen kein Zufall sein. Bei Eva Maisch resultieren sie aus der Faszination für Insekten und der Verbindung von Goldschmiedekunst mit Porzellanmalerei. Bekannt wurde die Schmuckgestalterin und Galeristin 1999 mit der Serie *Ein Punkt tritt an die Seite*. Seit 2004 werden in ihrem Würzburger Atelier mit Galerie auch andere Schmuckdesigner ausgestellt. Mit Veranstaltungen wie Faltungen oder Architektur-Schmuck-Fotografie stellt Eva Maisch regelmäßig Bezüge her zwischen modernem Schmuck und anderen Bereichen.

Zunächst studierte Eva Maisch Reha- und Behindertensport. 1988 besuchte sie die Internationale Sommerakademie der Bildenden Künste in Salzburg. In der Schmuckklasse von Johanna Dahm, später Professorin an der HfG Pforzheim, entdeckte sie ihre wahre Berufung. Zwischen 1989 und 1992 erlernte sie in verschiedenen Werkstätten die handwerklichen und künstlerischen Grundlagen der Schmuckfertigung. Wichtige Stationen waren Conrad Klein, München, die Würzburger Alpha-Galerie und Workshops bei Alexandra Bahlmann und Felix Flury. Dabei entstand eine permanente und anregende Auseinandersetzung mit den Strömungen des zeitgenössischen Schmucks. Doch auch der Blick auf den Schmuck fremder Kulturen interessierte Eva Maisch. Nach ersten Erfolgen mit Ausstellungen in Schmuckgalerien widmete sie sich voll und ganz dem zeitgenössischen Schmuck. »Die Abgrenzung vom konventionellen Schmuck der Juweliere war in dieser Zeit für anspruchsvolle Gestalter wichtig«, erläutert die Gestalterin. Zu Beginn wäre sie nie auf die Idee gekommen, ihren Schmuck einem Juwelier vorzustellen. »Inzwischen ist jedoch eine Reihe von Juwelieren deutlich offener für die Arbeiten moderner Schmuck-Designer«, sagt sie.

Mit der *Dollarkrause* entstand 1994 eine künstlerische Arbeit, die sich mit Schmuck als Prestigeobjekt und Wertanlage auseinandersetzte. 1996 wurde sie in der Ausstellung zum Dannerpreis 1996 in der Neuen Sammlung in München gezeigt. »Mit experimentellen Stücken dieser Art kann man Öffentlichkeit herstellen, aber kaum den Lebensunterhalt verdienen«, meint ihr Mann, der seinen Beruf als Dokumentarfilmer aufgab, um seine Frau beim Aufbau ihrer Firma zu unterstützen. 1996 beschloss das Paar, das inzwischen zwei Kinder hat, alle Aktivitäten gemeinsam der Familie und dem Schmuck zu widmen. Dies machte einen Spagat notwendig zwischen Verkäuflichkeit und künstlerischem Anspruch. Inzwischen sieht Eva Maisch dies jedoch als Vorteil, weil ihr Schmuck dadurch dem Menschen näher gekommen ist.

Bereits 1994 war der *Jahresschmuck* entstanden, der zum »demokratischen« Preis von 100 Mark in Designshops und Museumsshops verkauft wurde. Eva Maisch: »Das war die Zeit, als sich alle Museen plötzlich einen Shop einrichteten.« Hinter dem Namen *Jahresschmuck* stand die Idee, jedes Jahr das Sortiment um ein neues Schmuckstück zu erweitern. Für den ersten Messeauftritt in München 1999 entstand das Konzept *Ein Punkt tritt an die Seite*. Dreh und Angelpunkt ist eine kleine Kugel. Seitlich positioniert ver-

bindet sie Glieder unterschiedlichster Form zu reduzierten, geschmeidig fließenden Kettenformen. Große Beachtung fanden die *Steinketten*. Reduziert gefasste, verschiedenfarbige Edelsteine im Cabochon-Schliff unterschiedlicher Größe sind nach dem Prinzip der Gänseblümchenkette verbunden.

Auf der »Suche nach Traditionen« entdeckte Eva Maisch Porzellan. Mit der Königlichen Porzellan Manufaktur KPM in Berlin fand sie einen Partner, der für sie ovale Porzellanscheiben produzierte, die in Ringen und Ketten verarbeitet werden können. Die Motive, die im Schmuck als »historische Zitate« verwendet werden, entdeckte die Schmuck-Designerin in den Archiven von KPM. Die für ihre Handwerkskunst berühmten Porzellanmaler der Manufaktur wurden aber neben den traditionellen Motiven auch mit Ideen der Schmuck-Designerin beauftragt. So entstand 2003 der Porzellanschmuck mit Insektenmotiven. Eva Maisch bestätigt mit diesem Projekt einmal mehr ihre interkulturelle Sichtweise. Im Jahr 2006 beteiligte sie sich mit viel Erfolg am Schmuckwettbewerb Hommage à Angela. Eine Kette zeigt die Köpfe der Vorgänger der Bundeskanzlerin, von Konrad Adenauer bis Gerhard Schröder. Dadurch angeregt entstand das jüngste Schmuckkonzept. Eva Maisch nennt es *Traumpaar – Traumfamilie*. Es ist ein Spiel mit der Illusion, das als Collier oder Anhänger den Hals schmückt. Zuerst sind abstrakte Formen erkennbar, die an Vasen oder Gefäße erinnern. Plötzlich kippt der Bildeindruck; es werden menschliche Profile sichtbar. Das Phänomen ist aus der Wahrnehmungspsychologie als Rubinsche Vase bekannt. So erhielt der dänische Psychologe Rubin, nach dem das Phänomen benannt ist, eine späte Ehrung von einer Schmuckgestalterin unserer Zeit.

E — Flies or ants on pieces of jewellery need not be fortuitous. They appear in Eva Maisch's work because she is intrigued by insects and the association of gold jewellery with porcelain painting. The jewellery-designer and gallerist became famous in 1999 with *Ein Punkt tritt an die Seite* [A dot appears at its side]. Since 2004, other jewellery-designers have exhibited at her Würzburg studio-cum-gallery. Featuring events such as *Faltungen* [Foldings] and Architecture-Jewellery-Photography, Eva Maisch creates links between modern jewellery and other media on a regular basis.

Eva Maisch started out by training in rehabilitation and sports for the disabled. In 1988 she attended the International Summer Academy of Fine Arts in Salzburg. It was in the jewellery class taught by Johanna Dahm, who would later become a professor at the HfG Pforzheim, that Eva Maisch discovered her true vocation. Between 1989 and 1992 Maisch learned the techniques and fundamentals of making jewellery at various workshops. Important stops along her way to a career in jewellery design were Conrad Klein in Munich, the Alpha Gallery in Würzburg and workshops with Alexandra Bahlmann and Felix Flury. During those years Eva Maisch became involved in a constant and stimulating investigation of trends in contemporary jewellery.

2002   2003   2007

However, she was also interested in taking a look at jewellery produced by cultures foreign to her. After her first successes with exhibitions at jewellery galleries, she devoted herself exclusively to contemporary jewellery. »At that time it was important for designers with ambitions to distance themselves from conventional jewellery-store jewellery,« explains the designer. At first she would never have dreamt of presenting her jewellery to a jewellery shop. »By now, however, quite a few jewellers have become noticeably more receptive to the work of modern jewellery-designers,« she says.

Dollarkrause [Dollar ruff] was a 1994 art work that examined jewellery as a status object and investment. In 1996 it was shown at the Neue Sammlung in Munich at the 1996 Danner Award exhibition. »With experimental pieces of that kind, one can go public but hardly earn a livelihood,« says her husband, who gave up his career as a documentary film-maker to help his wife build up her business. In 1996 the couple, by then the parents of two children, decided to devote all their energies to the family and jewellery. Taking this step necessitated a balancing act between marketability and aesthetic aims. By now Eva Maisch sees this discrepancy as an advantage because her jewellery has become more people-friendly as a result.

As early as 1994, she had launched *Jahresschmuck* [Year jewellery], which was sold at designer and museum shops at the »democratic« price of DM 100. Eva Maisch: »That was the time when all museums suddenly began to open shops.« Informing the name *Jahresschmuck* was the idea of enlarging the range annually by adding a new piece of jewellery. For her first appearance at the Munich jewellery trade fair in 1999, Maisch developed the *Ein Punkt tritt an die Seite* concept. It revolves around a small ball. Laterally positioned, it connects links of varying forms to create supple, fluid chain forms that are reductivist in the extreme. *Steinketten* [Stone necklaces] features precious stones of various colours and sizes cut as cabochons in very simple settings. They are linked according to the daisy chain principle.

»In search of tradition,« Eva Maisch discovered porcelain. In the venerable Royal Porcelain Factory (KPM) in Berlin, she found a partner who would produce oval porcelain plaques for her that could be worked into rings and chains. The jewellery-designer discovered the motifs she uses in her jewellery as »historical quotations« in the KPM archives. Eva Maisch also commissioned renowned KPM porcelain painters to execute both the traditional motifs and ideas of her own. That is how porcelain jewellery featuring insect motifs came into being in 2003. That project represented further confirmation of Eva Maisch's intercultural approach to her work. In 2006 Eva Maisch was very successful in a jewellery competition called Hommage à Angela. A Maisch necklace features portrait heads of the present Chancellor's predecessors from Konrad Adenauer to Gerhard Schröder. This work inspired her most recent jewellery concept, which Eva Maisch calls *Traumpaar – Traumfamilie* [Ideal couple – Ideal family]. Based on optical illusion, it adorns necks

as a necklace or pendant. At first sight, abstract forms reminiscent of vases or other vessels are discernible. Suddenly the visual impression reaches the tipping point: human profiles are visible. This pattern-matching phenomenon is known in the psychology of perception and in phenomenology as the Rubin face or the figure-ground vase. Thus Edgar Rubin, the Danish psychologist (d. 1951) for whom the figure-ground perception is named, has received a belated tribute from a jewellery-designer of our time.

1994	Halsschmuck *Dollarkrause*, Silber, Dollarnoten — Necklace *Dollar ruff*, silver, dollar notes
1996	Halsschmuck *Ein Punkt tritt an die Seite*, Gold, Zuchtperlen — Necklace *A dot appears at its side*, gold, cultured pearls
2002	*Steinkette*, Gold, Edelsteine — *Stone necklace*, gold, precious stones
2003	Porzellanringe *Insekten*, Gold, KPM-Porzellan — Porcelain rings *Insects*, gold, KPM porcelain
2007	Halsschmuck *Traumpaare*, Silber geschwärzt, Seidenkordel — Necklace *Ideal couples*, blackened silver, silk string

Eva Maisch
Geboren 1964 in Würzburg.
Ateliergründung 1993.
Seit 2004 Atelier mit Galerie in Würzburg.

Eva Maisch
Born in Würzburg in 1964.
Founded studio in 1993. Studio with gallery in Würzburg since 2004.

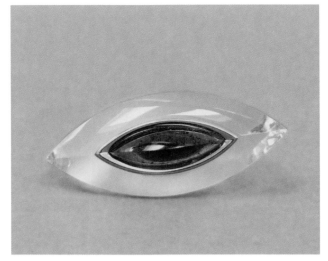

1992   1994

Stoffel Design

Er sei in Idar-Oberstein bei Stipshausen geboren und mit Steinen aufgewachsen. Mit dieser humorvollen Anspielung will Thomas Stoffel andeu-
ten, dass in der kleinen Hunsrückgemeinde Stipshausen die kreativsten
Edelsteingestalter der Region leben. Mit seinen Bergkristall- und Onyx-
ringen zeigte er in den 1990er Jahren, dass der Stein allein Schmuck und
Objekt zugleich sein kann.

1953 gründete Heinz Stoffel eine Edelsteinschleiferei mit Goldschmiede in Stipshausen. Wie in den Betrieben im Hunsrück traditionell
üblich, absolvierte Thomas Stoffel seine Lehre bei seinem Vater. 1988 besuchte er die Fachschule für Edelstein- und Schmuckgestaltung in Idar-Oberstein und beendete 1990 die zweijährige Ausbildung mit dem Abschluss
als Staatlich geprüfter Gestalter und dem Meisterbrief. Der 1. Preis im internationalen Wettbewerb Verarbeitung heimischer Mineralien zeigte schon in
der Ausbildungszeit sein Talent, die natürliche Ausdruckskraft der Edelsteine
in innovativen Formen umzusetzen.

Nach seiner Ausbildung leitete Thomas Stoffel den elterlichen Betrieb.
Gleichzeitig begann er mit kreativen Schliffen und Schmuckkonzepten, einen
vollkommen neuen Bereich in der Traditionsschleiferei aufzubauen. 1994
übernahm er die Firma und gab ihr den Namen Stoffel Design, Edelsteinschleiferei und Goldschmiede. Im gleichen Jahr wurde er Sieger des Wett-
bewerbs Deutscher Schmuck- und Edelsteinpreis Idar-Oberstein. Zahlreiche
weitere Ehrungen und Auszeichnungen bestätigten immer wieder seine Fähigkeit, Edelsteine in künstlerische Objekte oder in komplette Schmuckstücke
zu verwandeln. Mit dem Staatspreis für Kunst und Formgebung 2001, dem
Designpreis des Landes Rheinland-Pfalz 2003 sowie mehreren Nominierun-
gen für den Designpreis der Bundesrepublik Deutschland demonstrierte
Thomas Stoffel, das auch mit Edelsteinen ein innovativer Beitrag zur modernen Designentwicklung möglich ist. Seit 1995 wird der Edelsteinschmuck
von Stoffel Design regelmäßig auf internationalen Messen und Ausstellungen präsentiert. »Ich habe nicht nach einem neuen Schliff gesucht, eher hat
mich die Formgebung und der Edelstein inspiriert, etwas Neues zu schaffen«, erklärt der Edelsteingestalter. Auch in der modernen Architektur fand
Thomas Stoffel Beispiele, die ihn inspirierten. Ein persönliches Vorbild sei
ihm unter anderem der Pionier der Edelsteingestaltung Bernd Munsteiner
gewesen, »der an sich und seine Arbeit glaubt.«

Mit der Serie *Classic* begann er 1990, komplette Ringobjekte aus
Edelstein zu schleifen. Die Basis bilden Bergkristall oder Onyx mit sanften,
mattierten Oberflächen. Während die hellen Quarze durchscheinend schim-
mern, wirkt der Onyx kraftvoll und körperhaft präsent. Diese Edelsteine machen in seinem Schmuck zusätzliche geschmiedete oder gegossene Metall-
ringe überflüssig. Doch tragen die Ringobjekte in Fassungen aus Gelb- oder
Weißgold ergänzend je einen zentralen Farbstein wie Aquamarin, Amethyst,
Turmalin, Citrin oder auch eine Perle. Zwar gab es schon früher aus Stein ge-

schliffene Bandringe. Die Gestaltung des Edelsteins in einer geometrisch
ausdrucksstarken Schliffform als Ring, in dem ein zweiter Stein den Höhepunkt bildet, war 1990 jedoch neu in der Schmuckgeschichte. Das Konzept
wurde zum wichtigsten Gestaltungsthema von Stoffel Design. Jahrtausende
lang wurden Schmucksteine eingesetzt, das Auge zu erfreuen. In den Stücken von Thomas Stoffel werden sie zu fühlbaren, haptischen Objekten. An
der Hand getragen wirken die Edelsteine überraschend angenehm, leicht
und warm. 1993 entstanden nach dem gleichen Prinzip die *Navette-Ringe*.
Die Modelle *doubles uno* und *doubles duo* ergänzten in den folgenden Jahren
dieses Konzept. Hierbei sitzen jedoch ein oder zwei in Edelmetall gefasste
Farbsteine in einem »geöffneten Edelsteinring« und bilden den krönenden
Abschluss des Ringobjekts.

Weiterentwicklungen stellten die *new art* Ringe dar, die mit dem
Staatspreis des Landes Rheinland-Pfalz bedacht wurden. 2005 stellte Thomas
Stoffel seine mit dem Designpreis des Landes Rheinland-Pfalz geehrten
eggs-Ringe vor. Der farbige Schmuckstein sitzt dabei ohne Metallfassung in
dem Basisring aus Bergkristall. Bei den Modellen *Kreuz* und *Herz* bildet allein
die reduzierte symbolträchtige Form den Edelsteinring.

E — He was born in Stipshausen near Idar-Oberstein and grew up with
stones. With this playful pun (»Stein« means »stone«), Thomas Stoffel is sug-
gesting that the region's most creative gem designers live in the little town
of Stipshausen in the Hunsrück. In the 1990s Stoffel demonstrated with his
rock-crystal and onyx rings that stones can be both jewellery and object in
their own right.

In 1953 Heinz Stoffel founded a gem-cutting and goldsmithing workshop in Stipshausen. As is the usual practice in the Hunsrück where businesses of this kind are concerned, Thomas Stoffel served an apprenticeship with
his father. In 1988 he enrolled at the Fachschule für Edelstein- und Schmuckgestaltung in Idar-Oberstein and finished his two-year course of study there
as a state-examined designer with a master craftsman's certificate. The fact
that he won first prize in the international competition Verarbeitung heimischer Mineralien [Working Regional Minerals] while still a student shows
how talented he is at translating the naturally expressive properties of precious stones into innovative forms.

After finishing his education and training, Thomas Stoffel ran the family business. At the same time he embarked on building up an entirely new
field within traditional gem-cutting with creative cuts and jewellery concepts. In 1994 he took over the firm and changed the name to Stoffel Design,
Edelsteinschleiferei und Goldschmiede. That same year he won the German
Jewellery and Gemstone Prize Idar-Oberstein competition. Numerous subsequent distinctions and awards continued to confirm his talent for transmut-
ing precious stones into art objects or whole pieces of jewellery. In winning

2001

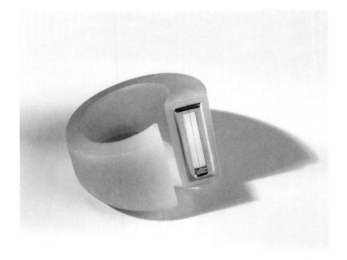

2003

2005

the 2001 State Award for Art and Design, the 2003 Design Award of the State of Rhineland-Palatinate and several nominations for the Design Award of the Federal Republic of Germany, Thomas Stoffel has furnished ample proof that an innovative contribution to the development of modern design can also be made with precious stones. Since 1995, jewellery with precious stones by Stoffel Design has been shown regularly at international trade fairs and exhibitions. »I have not been seeking a new cut; on the contrary, it was design and precious stones that inspired me to create something new,« explains the designer. Thomas Stoffel has also found inspiration in modern architecture. His personal role model, as he tells it, has been Bernd Munsteiner, the pioneering gemstone designer, »who believes in himself and his work«.

With the *Classic* line, Thomas Stoffel began to cut whole ring objects from gem stones. They were based on rock crystal or onyx with soft, matt-finished surfaces. Whereas the light quartz varieties have a translucent glow, onyx weighs in with a powerful physical presence. They are gemstones that render beaten or cast metal ring shanks superfluous. Nevertheless these ring objects do have a supplementary setting in yellow or white gold to support a central solitaire that is a coloured semiprecious stone such as aquamarine, amethyst, tourmaline or citrine or a single pearl. Bands of semiprecious stone cut into rings were known in the past. However, in 1990 designing a gemstone in a geometrically highly expressive cut as ring centred on a second stone represented an innovation in jewellery in the historical sense. The concept would become one of the paramount design themes at Stoffel Design. For thousands of years gemstones have been used to please the eye. In Thomas Stoffel's pieces, they become palpably tactile objects. When worn, the gemstones feel surprisingly pleasant, light and warm on the hand. In 1993 Stoffel Design came up with *Navette rings* based on the same principle. In subsequent years, the *doubles uno* and *doubles duo* models enlarged this concept. However, they feature one or two coloured stones set in noble metals in an »opened gemstone ring« and mark the culmination of the Stoffel Design ring object.

Further developments are represented by the *new art* rings, which received the Rhineland-Palatinate State Award. In 2005 Thomas Stoffel launched *eggs* rings, with which he had worn the Rhineland-Palatinate Design Award. A coloured gemstone sits without a metal setting in a rock crystal base ring. In the *Kreuz* [Cross] and *Herz* [Heart] models, the gemstone ring has been reduced to emblematic form pregnant with symbolism.

1992	*Classic* Ring, Onyx, Aquamarin *Spirit Sun*, Gold — *Classic* ring, onyx, aquamarine *Spirit Sun*, gold
1994	*Navette-Ring*, Bergkristall, Turmalin, Gold — *Navette ring*, rock crystal, tourmaline, gold
2001	*new art* Ring, Onyx, Citrin *Spirit Sun*, Gold — *new art* ring, onyx, citrine *Spirit Sun*, gold
2003	*doubles uno* Ring, Naturachat, Aquamarin, Gold — *doubles uno* ring, nature agate, aquamarine, gold
2005	*eggs* Ring, Naturachat, Aquamarin, Bergkristall — *eggs* ring, nature agate, aquamarine, rock crystal

Thomas Stoffel und Sohn
Geboren 1965 in Stipshausen. 1988–1990 Fachschule für Edelstein- und Schmuckgestaltung Idar-Oberstein. Meisterprüfung. 1990 Atelierleitung. 1994 Gründung von Stoffel Design in Stipshausen.

Thomas Stoffel and son
Born in Stipshausen in 1965. 1988–1990 Fachschule für Edelstein- und Schmuckgestaltung Idar-Oberstein. Master craftsman's certificate. Head of studio in 1990. Founded Stoffel Design in Stipshausen in 1994.

Stoffel Design

1991   1996

schmuckwerk

Während in vielen Traditionsfirmen der Schmuckindustrie Krisen-stimmung herrschte, gründete Markus Schmidt gemeinsam mit seiner Frau Heike die Firma schmuckwerk 1994 in Ratingen. Im historischen Ambiente der früheren Papiermühle Bagel von 1852 entstehen seitdem so origi-nelle Kollektionen wie die *Wolkenringe*, die *Rasselringe* oder *Cliff*. Immer wieder überrascht schmuckwerk mit geistreichen, die Sinne anregenden Schmuckerlebnissen.

Ein Goldschmiedepraktikum 1983 im südafrikanischen Port Elisabeth entfachte bei Markus Schmidt die Begeisterung für das Schmuckmachen. Nach der Lehre von 1984 bis 1987 wirkte er in der deutschen Produktions-stätte von Chopard an der Herstellung von Luxusuhren mit und fertigte kost-bare Geschmeide für arabische Prinzessinnen. Von 1989 bis 1991 war Markus Schmidt in einem Goldschmiedeatelier in Haan tätig. Dort wurden für eine Schmuckkollektion, nach dem Vorbild des Verhüllungskünstlers Christo, kleine »Goldinseln« mit farbiger Email umgeben. Parallel zur Tätigkeit als Juwelengoldschmied studierte Markus Schmidt Betriebswirtschaft. Ab 1991 betreute er eines der Geschäfte von Juwelier Klaus Kaufhold in Köln und war an der Entwicklung hauseigener Schmuckserien beteiligt. »Erstmals ging es bei Kaufhold darum«, erzählt der Gestalter, »etwas vollkommen Neues zu entwickeln.« Anfang 1994 richtete Markus Schmidt seine Werkstatt ein. Im März setzte er sich ans Goldschmiedebrett und baute seine erste Kol-lektion, mit der er im April Juweliere besuchte. Die Aktion war erfolgreich und konnte wiederholt werden. Markus Schmidt: »Wir konnten völlig frei, ohne Vorbelastungen und Vorgaben unsere Vision von einer Firma realisie-ren.« Bereits im ersten Jahr wurde ein Mitarbeiter eingestellt, der noch heu-te technischer Werkstattleiter ist. Jedes Jahr kamen ein bis zwei Mitarbeiter hinzu. Ausgangspunkt für die erste Schmucklinie war ein moderner Perlring, den Markus Schmidt 1991 noch bei Kaufhold entworfen hatte. Der Perl-spannring war sein Beitrag für einen japanischen Perlschmuckwettbewerb. Darauf aufbauend entstand eine Kollektion, in der Perlen zeitgemäß einge-setzt wurden. Später kam der Brillant als zentrales Schmuckthema hinzu.

Wenn Markus Schmidt neue Schmuckserien entwickelt, stellt er sich immer eine ganz spezielle Frau vor, eine ideale Trägerin. Als historische Per-sönlichkeit betrachtet er Coco Chanel. Ihre geradlinigen, eleganten Kleider und ihre langen Perlenketten beeindruckten ihn bereits in der Jugend. »Sie hat die klare Form der Moderne mit weiblicher Eleganz verbunden«, sagt er. Ihr Einfluss auf das moderne Frauenbild wirke bis heute nach. Markus Schmidt unterscheidet auch klar zwischen den Aufgaben eines Künstlers und eines Schmuck-Designers und möchte mit seinem Schmuck der Welt nichts vermitteln. Das sei die Aufgabe der Kunst, aber nicht die eines Designers, betont er. Für ihn stehen die Wünsche der Frauen im Vordergrund, die sich schmücken möchten: »Es geht darum, dass die Schmuckträgerin Spaß mit ihrem Schmuck hat und sich wohl fühlt.« In der *Wolkenkollektion* des Jahres

2000 schweben kleine Perlen wie Seifenblasen aus der Ringschiene. Die Perlen sind nicht in einer starren Fassung befestigt, sondern beweglich an kaum sichtbaren Kunststoffschnüren. So kann die Trägerin spielerisch die Anordnung der Perlen und damit die Anmutung des ganzen Schmuckstücks verändern. Die *Wolkenkollektion* entsprach nach der Strenge im modernen Schmuckdesign der 1990er Jahre dem Wunsch nach mehr Verspieltheit und Weichheit. Nach dem 11. September 2001, als das Bedürfnis der Schmuck-käufer nach gefühlvolleren Formen noch wuchs, wurde der *Wolkenschmuck* von schmuckwerk zu einem großen Erfolg.

Bei dem *Pickelring* regen kleine, aus der Ringschiene hervortretende Perlen den Tastsinn der Schmuckträgerin an. Zudem nimmt schmuckwerk verbal ein Reizthema junger Leute ironisch aufs Korn. In dem *Rasselring* er-scheinen in der geöffneten Ringschiene Perlen wie Erbsen in ihrer Schote. Der Name entstand, als ein Radioteam über den innovativen Schmuckher-steller berichtete. Der Reporter meinte, dass dieser Ring die »teuerste Baby-rassel der Welt« sei. Das zweite Thema, das schmuckwerk seit seiner Grün-dung 1994 innovativ belebt, ist der Diamantschmuck. Bei dem Memoirering *Erbstück* durchlaufen verschieden große Brillanten in runden Zargenfassun-gen locker versetzt die breite Ringschiene. In der Werbung heißt es dazu: »Wir helfen Ihnen, den alten Glanz in neuer Form zu bewahren. Gerne kön-nen Sie in unseren Ring Ihre Diamanten einsetzen lassen.« Die Grundidee der Manufaktur wird auch in diesem Konzept erkennbar. schmuckwerk will »die Frauen bewegen, sie sollen sich mit Schmuck beschäftigen und neue Din-ge erleben.« Gegenwärtig hat schmuckwerk 400 qm der alten Papiermühle in Ratingen in Beschlag genommen. Die Schmuckserien, innovativ gestaltet und perfekt verarbeitet, die man hören, fühlen und mit Diamanten aus dem Familienschatz ergänzen kann, finden sich bei namhaften Juwelieren und Galerien. 250 Fachgeschäfte in Europa und der USA werden insgesamt von der jungen Manufaktur beliefert. Dass die Stücke von schmuckwerk so er-folgreich sind, hat aber auch ganz wesentlich mit Heike Schmidt zu tun. »Ich bin der Kreative und Verrückte«, sagt Markus Schmidt, »meine Frau führt das alles wieder auf das Machbare zurück.«

E — While many venerable firms in the jewellery industry were being rocked by a crisis, Markus Schmidt and his wife, Heike, founded schmuck-werk in Ratingen in 1994. Since then such original collections as *Wolkenringe* [Cloud rings], *Rasselringe* [Rattle rings] and *Cliff* have emerged in the historic setting provided by the old (1852) Bagel paper mill. The firm continues to astonish the public with witty jewellery experiences that titillate all the senses.

Serving a goldsmithing internship in Port Elisabeth, South Africa, in 1983, enflamed Markus Schmidt with enthusiasm for making jewellery. After serving an apprenticeship (1984–1987), he worked at the German Chopard

2000

2005

2008

factory making luxury watches and opulent jewellery for Arab princesses. From 1989 until 1991 Markus Schmidt worked at a goldsmithing studio in Haan. There little »islands of gold« were surrounded in coloured enamels in a manner reminiscent of environmental installation artist Christo. While making gold jewellery set with jewels, Markus Schmidt studied business management on the side. From 1991 he ran one of the Cologne outlets of the jeweller Klaus Kaufhold and collaborated on designing the proprietary jewellery collections. »That was the first time developing something new mattered to Kaufhold,« recounts the designer. Early in 1994 Markus Schmidt set up his own workshop. In March he sat down at his workbench and built up his first collection, with which he approached jewellers in April. The campaign was successful and worth repeating. Markus Schmidt: »We were completely free to realise our vision of a firm without being burdened by anything or anyone telling us what to do.« Even in the first year, an employee was hired, who is still with schmuckwerk, now as technical workshop foreman. Each year one or two employees have been added. The point of departure for the first schmuckwerk line in jewellery was a modern pearl ring, which Markus Schmidt had designed in 1991 while still at Kaufhold. That pearl tension ring was his entry for a Japanese pearl jewellery competition. Building on it, schmuckwerk created a collection featuring pearls used in a cutting-edge way. Later diamonds were added as a pivotal jewellery theme.

When Markus Schmidt develops new editions in jewellery, he always imagines a particular woman, an ideal wearer. He regards Coco Chanel as a special historical person. Even in his youth, he was impressed by her elegant clothes with their straight lines and the long Chanel ropes of pearls. »She linked the clear Modernist form with feminine elegance,« he says. Her influence on the way the modern woman looks is still operative today. Markus Schmidt also draws a clear distinction between the tasks of an artist and those of a jewellery designer. He does not want to impart any messages to the world with his jewellery. That is the task of art rather than of a designer, he stresses. As he sees it, the wishes of women who want to adorn themselves have priority: »What matters is that the wearer of the jewellery has fun with her jewellery and feels happy with it.«

In the *Wolkenkollektion* [Cloud collection] he launched in 2000, little pearls float like soap bubbles out of the ring shank. These pearls are not rigidly fastened in a setting but are mobile because they are attached to barely visible plastic cords. The wearer can play with the arrangement of the pearls and thus change the overall appearance of the piece of jewellery. After the austerity in 1990s modern designer jewellery, the *Cloud collection* represented a response to a desire for more playfulness and softness. As jewellery purchasers' need for more emotional forms grew even more pronounced following 9/11 in 2001, the schmuckwerk *Cloud collection* became a resounding success.

Small pearls protruding smoothly from the shank of the *Pickelring* [Pickle pearl ring] titillate the wearer's sense of touch. However, on another plane, schmuckwerk is also playing word games, in German at least, to poke fun at what is nothing less than an adolescent obsession. The *Rasselring* [Rattle ring] features an open shank filled with pearls like peas in a pod. The name goes back to a radio broadcast on the innovative jewellery maker. The reporter was of the opinion that this ring was »the world's most expensive baby rattle«. The second theme that schmuckwerk has innovatively revived since it was founded in 1994 is diamond jewellery. *Erbstück* [Heirloom], a ring in the memoire line, features diamonds of varying size in round collet settings in a staggered arrangement on a broad ring shank. The advertising blurb reads: »We can help you to preserve old glories in a new form. You are welcome to bring your own diamonds to have them set in our ring.« The basic idea underlying schmuckwerk is recognisable in this concept as well. The schmuckwerk motto is »Get women to investigate jewellery and experience new things.« At present, schmuckwerk is using the 400 square metres of the old paper mill in Ratingen to capacity. Their lines in jewellery, with innovative design perfectly matched by consummate craftsmanship, pieces that can be heard, felt and even set with the purchaser's inherited diamonds, are sold at prestigious jewellers and galleries. 250 specialist shops in Europe and the US buy from the young jewellery factory. The success of the schmuckwerk pieces is also due in large measure to Heike Schmidt. »I'm the creative, crazy one,« says Markus Schmidt, »it's up to my wife to get everything back to what is practicable.«

1991	*Perlspannring*, Gold, Zuchtperle — *Pearl tension ring*, gold, cultured pearl
1996	*Rasselring*, Gold, Zuchtperlen — *Rattle ring*, gold, cultured pearls
2000	*Wolkenring*, Gold, Zuchtperlen — *Clouds ring*, gold, cultured pearls
2005	Ring *Cliff*, Platin, Diamanten — Ring *Cliff*, platinum, diamonds
2008	*Rankenring*, Gold, Brillanten — *Tendrils ring*, gold, diamonds

Markus Schmidt
Geboren 1965 in Esslingen. 1984–1987 Goldschmiedeausbildung. Firmengründung von schmuckwerk 1994 in Ratingen.

Markus Schmidt
Born in Esslingen in 1965. 1984–1987 Trained as a goldsmith. Founded schmuckwerk in Ratingen in 1994.

schmuckwerk

1993

1994

2001

Heiko Schrem

Wellen in matt glänzendem Edelstahl oder hochkarätigem Gold waren das erste Schmuckthema von Heiko Schrem, das er bis heute pflegt. Über die physische Erscheinung hinaus interessiert ihn jedoch ihre metaphysische Deutung. So ist es kein Zufall, dass auch die Spiralform, diese faszinierende Grundform in der Natur und im Kosmos, sowie Spiegelungen in seinen Schmucklinien thematisiert werden. Eine ausgereifte, moderne Formensprache im Einklang mit traditionellem Goldschmiedehandwerk bildet die Basis.

Heiko Schrem besuchte ein technisches Gymnasium in seiner Geburtsstadt Ulm und studierte nach dem Abitur zwei Jahre Produktionstechnik. Daran anschließend, 1985–1987, absolvierte er eine Goldschmiedelehre. Im Atelier des renommierten Goldschmieds und Juweliers Wolf-Peter Schwarz in Ulm lernte Schrem, Schmuck-Design als Prozess zu verstehen. Bevor er an die Fachhochschule für Gestaltung in Schwäbisch Gmünd ging, sammelte er weitere Erfahrungen in namhaften Goldschmiedeateliers. In seinem Studium entstanden teils sehr raumgreifende Körperobjekte, in denen bereits Wellenformen experimentell eingesetzt wurden. Bei Workshops mit den Schmuckkünstlern Anton Cepka und Manfred Bischoff sowie den Textilkünstlern Hamid Zenati und René Hepp vertiefte Heiko Schrem seine künstlerische Auseinandersetzung. Nach dem Diplom als Schmuckdesigner gründete er 1995 sein eigenes Unternehmen in Neu-Ulm. Aus dem Thema Welle entwickelte er seine erste Kollektion. Typisch waren weiche, jedoch immer klare Formen, hauptsächlich in Edelstahl, aber auch in Gold. Die Stücke entsprachen dem Designempfinden der 1990er Jahre und wurden zu einem beachtlichen Erfolg.

Bis heute lässt sich der Schmuck-Designer und Goldschmied gerne auf gestalterische und technische Experimente ein und arbeitete mit den unterschiedlichsten Materialien. Edelstahl sei für ihn wichtig, betont er, »weil es mit moderner Schmuckgestaltung seit dem Bauhaus elementar verbunden ist.« Inzwischen nehmen Arbeiten in Gold und Platin einen zunehmend größeren Raum ein. Heiko Schrem schätzt ihre Farbe und Materialästhetik, ihre Wertigkeit und ihren Mythos. Traditionelle handwerkliche Techniken wie das Schmieden spielen in seiner Schmuckfertigung eine wichtige Rolle. In seinem Atelier werden aber auch innovative Techniken eingesetzt. Als Unternehmer, der zielstrebig seine Position im Markt verfolgt, hat sich der Ulmer nie gesehen. Sein Alternativkonzept: »Wir machen Schmuck für Menschen und nicht für Märkte.« Sich Zeit lassen und auch mal Umwege gehen, diese Haltung war bereits in den Lehr- und Wanderjahren typisch für Schrem. Schon früh hat er damit begonnen, die Dinge genau zu beobachten und ist ihnen manchmal über Jahre hinweg auf den Grund gegangen. Besonders wichtig ist ihm die klare gestalterische Aussage in seinem Schmuck. Sie erscheint nie als Dekor, sondern vielmehr als sichtbares Konstruktionsprinzip. Seit seiner Ateliergründung stellt Heiko Schrem regelmäßig auf Fachmessen aus. So auch 1998–2000 auf der Selection in Essen. Seine Arbeiten sind bei

1993   Studienarbeit *Modulare Systeme*, Konzept *Welle*, Edelstahl, Aluminium — Assignment *Modular Systems*, concept *Wave*, stainless steel, aluminium

1994   Ring und Broschen *Welle*, Platin — Ring and brooches *Wave*, platinum

2001   Ringe *Welle Perspektiv*, Edelstahl — Rings *Wave Perspective*, stainless steel

2002   Ringe *Spira*, Edelstahl — Rings *Spira*, stainless steel

2003   Ring und Anhänger *Helios*, Edelstahl, Tahiti-Zuchtperlen — Ring and pendant *Helios*, stainless steel, Tahitian cultured pearls

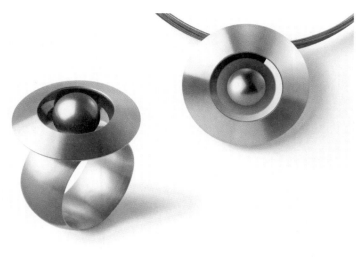

2002   2003

namhaften nationalen und internationalen Juwelieren präsent, unter anderem bei Stuart Moore in den USA. 2004 bezog er mit einem kleinen Team qualifizierter Mitarbeiter sein heutiges Atelier in Elchingen bei Ulm.

In seinen beiden wichtigsten Schmucklinien *Helios* und *Spira* verbindet Heiko Schrem funktionales, modernes Schmuck-Design bewusst mit Elementen der Juwelierstradition. Die Serien basieren auf einer durchdachten und über Jahre gereiften Gestaltungsidee, die er meisterhaft im vorwiegend handwerklichen Prozess umsetzt. Ein charakteristisches Gestaltungsmerkmal von *Spira* ist die konkave Ringschiene. Sie entsteht beim Biegen und Schmieden mit dem Hammer. Bei *Helios* spiegeln sich Edelsteine in konkaven Flächen und erzeugen Reflexionen, die der Schmuck-Designer als »Unschärfen« bezeichnet. Abgesehen von dem physikalischen Phänomen verleihen sie den Schmuckstücken eine sympathische Aura, erklärt er.

E — Waves in matt finished stainless steel or high-carat gold were the first jewellery themes approached by Heiko Schrem and he is still addressing them today. Above and beyond their physical appearance, he is, however, interested in their metaphysical meanings. Consequently, it is no coincidence that the spiral form, that fascinating form basic to nature and the universe, and reflections are what he works with in his jewellery lines. The whole is grounded in a mature, modern formal idiom that is nonetheless attuned to traditional goldsmithing.

Heiko Schrem attended a technical higher secondary school in his native Ulm. After taking the exams qualifying him for university admission, he studied production technology for two years, followed by a goldsmithing apprenticeship (1985–1987). At the Ulm studio of the renowned goldsmith and jeweller Wolf-Peter Schwarz, Schrem learned to understand designing jewellery as a process. Before attending the Fachhochschule für Gestaltung in Schwäbisch Gmünd, Schrem broadened his experience at distinguished goldsmithing studios. During his studies, Schrem produced body objects, some of which intervened considerably in space, with wave forms already experimentally in evidence. At workshops with the artists in jewellery Anton Cepka and Manfred Bischoff as well as the textile artists Hamid Zenati and René Hepp, Heiko Schrem delved deeper into aesthetics. After taking his diploma as a jewellery-designer, he founded a business of his own in Neu-Ulm, developing the wave theme for his first collection. It was distinguished by soft-edged yet invariably clear forms, chiefly in stainless steel as well as gold. Those pieces matched the 1990s feeling for design and were remarkably successful.

Even today the jewellery-designer and goldsmith enjoys experimenting with design and technique, working with a wide variety of materials. Stainless steel is important to him, he points out, »because it has been linked with modern jewellery design on an elemental plane since the Bauhaus.« By

now working in gold and platinum is increasingly on his agenda. Heiko Schrem appreciates their colours, the aesthetic of these materials, the fact that they are precious and the myths surrounding them. Traditional crafts techniques such as forging play an important role in the way he makes jewellery. Schrem has never viewed himself as an entrepreneur aiming at positioning himself on a tight market. Alternatively, his concept is: »We make jewellery for people, not for markets.« Taking time and occasionally going a roundabout way are habits typical of Schrem even during his apprenticeship and journeyman's years. Early on he began to observe things closely and has sometimes taken years to go into depth in some areas. What is particularly important to him is making an unequivocal design statement in his jewellery. Never decorative, it is informed by a visible principle of construction. Since founding his own studio, Heiko Schrem has regularly shown work at trade fairs, for instance at Selection in Essen (1998–2000). His works are marketed by reputable jewellers in Germany and abroad, including Stuart Moore in the US. In 2004 Schrem and his small team of qualified employees moved into his present studio in Elchingen near Ulm.

In his most important lines, *Helios* and *Spira*, Heiko Schrem deliberately links functional modern jewellery design with elements derived from traditional jewellery-making. The two lines are based on a carefully thought out design idea, which has matured over many years and which he translates with consummate mastery into what is primarily a crafts process. A salient design feature of *Spira* is its concave ring shank, created by being bent and hammered. In *Helios* precious stones are reflected on concave surfaces to create reflections that the jewellery-designer calls »unclearnesses«. Apart from the physical phenomenon, they lend these pieces of jewellery a pleasant aura, he explains.

Heiko Schrem
Geboren 1961 in Ulm. 1991–1994 FH
Schwäbisch Gmünd. Ateliergründung 1995,
seit 2004 in Elchingen bei Ulm.

Heiko Schrem
Born in Ulm in 1961. 1991–1994 FH Schwäbisch
Gmünd. Founded studio in 1995, in Elchingen
near Ulm since 2004.

1999   2000

Achim Gersmann

Auf den ersten Blick wirken viele Ringe von Achim Gersmann konstruktivistisch streng: reduzierte Formen aus verschiedenfarbigem Gold, gebürstete Oberflächen, manchmal mit Diamanten akzentuiert. Näher betrachtet überraschen spielerische Elemente, entstehen unerwartete Bewegungen. Dem Designer geht es um klare formale Aussagen und technische Präzision, aber ebenso um Poesie und die Lust, Schmuck zu tragen.

Achim Gersmanns Vorfahren führten seit 1872 in Dortmund ein Uhren- und Schmuckgeschäft. Nach dem Tod des Vaters 1987 wurde der junge Goldschmiedegeselle Inhaber. Dank der Mithilfe seiner Mutter konnte er die Firma weiterführen und gleichzeitig seine berufliche Ausbildung vertiefen. Diese hatte 1984 an der Zeichenakademie Hanau begonnen. Die Weiterbildung zum Diamantgutachter in Königstein 1986 und zum Gemmologen 1989 in Idar-Oberstein war nicht untypisch für einen jungen Juwelier.

»Meine Gesellenjahre von 1987 bis 1988 waren geprägt von Camillo de la Horra«, erzählt Achim Gersmann. Die Exaktheit und Präzision des aus Spanien stammenden Goldschmieds haben seine Arbeitsweise nachhaltig beeinflusst. Doch die präzise Ausführung eines traditionellen Schmuckstücks war dem kunst- und designinteressierten Goldschmied nicht genug. In Hanau begann Gersmann, das »Spannungsfeld Körper und Schmuck« neu zu verstehen. Dies hat er von 1989 bis 1994 im Bereich Edelstein- und Schmuck-Design in Idar-Oberstein vertieft. Einen Anstoß für sein Studium gab auch die Begeisterung für die Arbeiten von Giampaolo Babetto.

Nach dem Diplom brach Achim Gersmann 1995 mit der 123-jährigen Firmentradition seines Hauses in Dortmund. Das Uhren- und Schmuckgeschäft wurde geschlossen. Der Schmuckdesigner gründete ein Atelier in Bamberg und konzentrierte sich auf die Entwicklung innovativer Schmuckserien. Seit 1998 stellt er als Gründungsmitglied gemeinsam mit der Gruppe Delicatesse auf Messen aus. 1999 erhielt Achim Gersmann den red dot für hohe Designqualität. Der preisgekrönte Ring *Floater* besteht aus einem transparenten Bergkristallzylinder. Außen und innen ist der streng geschliffene Kristall mit dünnen Edelmetallschienen umgeben. Dadurch entsteht die Illusion, der äußere Reif würde schweben. Weitere Preise und Auszeichnungen folgten: Deutscher Schmuck- und Edelsteinpreis Idar-Oberstein, Design Innovationen 1999 sowie im Jahr 2000 ein zweiter red dot des Designzentrums Essen.

Bei dem Ring *Nebeleben* ließ sich Achim Gersmann durch den Roman »Der Alchimist« von Paulo Coelho anregen. Auf der Suche nach seinem Lebensweg verlässt sich ein Junge auf einen weißen und einen schwarzen Stein, immer wenn er seine innere Stimme nicht hören kann. Die ist im Ring *Nebeleben* mittels einer doppelten, beweglichen Ringschiene nachvollziehbar. Je nach Drehung erscheint das Bild des schwarzen oder weißen Steins. Die ersten Stücke der Serien *Circle* und *Square* entstanden um 2000. Zwei oder drei übereinander liegende Ringschienen sind in zwei Zapfen oder karda-

nisch gelagert. Manchmal wird dabei ein Diamant zum Dreh- und Angelpunkt. Die Ringe *Crown O*, *Crown QR* und *Crown S* spielen in geometrischer Reduktion mit dem Mythos goldener Kronen. Zur erfolgreichsten Schmuckserie von Achim Gersmann wurden die *Pusher*. Ihre ersten Varianten stellte er 2003 vor. Mehrere geöffnete Ringelemente sind durch eine Achse beweglich miteinander verbunden. An den Kopfenden sind sie mit Diamanten besetzt. Die *Pusher* stellen ungetragen ein luxuriöses Spielobjekt dar. 2008 integrierte der Designer Keramikelemente in diese Ringkonstruktion und nannte sie *Segments*.

Achim Gersmann hat seit seinem Studium bei den Professoren Ingeborg Bornhofen und Udo Ackermann eine eigenständige Formensprache erarbeitet. Sein Schaffen ist der Beweis, dass es möglich ist, die Vielfalt im modernen Schmuck zu erweitern und authentisch zu bleiben. An der Sommerakademie Salzburg kommt er regelmäßig seinem Bedürfnis nach schöpferischer Auseinandersetzung und Anregung nach: bei Schmuckgestaltern wie Giampaolo Babetto oder Caroline Broadhead, bei dem Künstler und Architekten Marcello Morandini oder im Bereich Skulptur und Installation bei Nancy Davidson.

E — At first sight, many of Achim Gersmann's rings may look forbiddingly Constructivist: reductive forms in gold of various colours, brushed surfaces, sometimes with diamond accents. On closer scrutiny, surprisingly playful elements are revealed and unexpected movements are created. This designer is concerned with clear formal statements and technical precision but also poetry and delight in wearing jewellery.

Achim Gersmann's family had run a watch and jewellery shop in Dortmund since 1872. On his father's death in 1987, the young journeyman goldsmith became the owner. His mother's help made it possible for him to continue to run the business while deepening his professional training, which had begun at the Zeichenakademie Hanau in 1984. Further qualification as a diamond appraiser in Königstein in 1986 and a gemmologist in Idar-Oberstein in 1989 were not atypical of the training a young jeweller might pursue.

»My journeyman's years (1987–1988) were formatively influenced by Camillo de la Horra,« recounts Achim Gersmann. The exacting precision for which the Spanish goldsmith is known exerted a lasting influence on Gersmann's work. However precisely executing a piece of traditional jewellery was not enough for the goldsmith, who was interested in both art and design. In Hanau Gersmann came to a fresh understanding of the »charged field of body and jewellery«. He deepened his awareness of it in the field of gemstone and jewellery design in Idar-Oberstein between 1989 and 1994. A further motivation for studying was his enthusiasm for the work of Giampaolo Babetto.

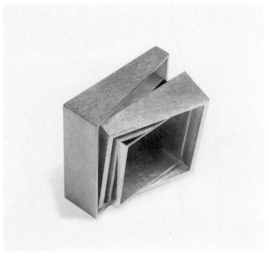

2001   2003   2004

After taking his diploma, Achim Gersmann broke in 1995 with the 123-year tradition of his family firm in Dortmund. The watch and jewellery shop was closed down and the jewellery designer founded a studio in Bamberg, where he has concentrated on developing innovative jewellery collections. Since 1998 he has exhibited work at group shows held at trade fairs by the Delicatesse group, of which he is a founder-member.

In 1999 Achim Gersmann was awarded the red dot for top-quality design. The award-winning ring, *Floater*, consists of a transparent cylinder of rock crystal sheathed on the outside and inside with thin shanks of precious metal, creating the illusion that the outer ring is floating. The red dot award was followed by other prizes and distinctions: the Deutscher Schmuck- und Edelsteinpreis Idar-Oberstein, Design Innovationen 1999 and, in 2000, a second red dot from the Essen Design Centre.

The ring called *Nebeleben* [Ring of fate] was inspired by the Paulo Coelho novel »The Alchimist«. On his quest through life, a boy relies on a white and a black stone whenever he is unable to hear his inner voice. It is represented in the ring *Nebeleben* by a double, movable ring shank. The ring can be turned to reveal the black or the white stone. The first pieces in the *Circle* and *Square* collections emerged around 2000. Two or three ring overlaid shanks are joined by two tenons or a cardan (universal) joint. Sometimes a diamond is the pivot. The *Crown O*, *Crown QR* and *Crown S* rings play on the myth of gold crowns in geometric reduction. Achim Gersmann's most successful ring design has been the *Pusher*. He launched the first edition in 2003. Several open ring elements are movably linked by a tenon running through them. They are set with diamonds at the ends. When not worn, the *Pusher* rings represent a luxurious play object. In 2008 the designer integrated ceramic elements in this ring construction and called it *Segments*.

Since studying with Professors Ingeborg Bornhofen and Udo Ackermann, Achim Gersmann has developed a distinctively individual formal idiom. His work furnishes ample proof that it is possible to push the bounds of diversity in jewellery while remaining authentic. At the Salzburg Summer Academy, he is regularly able to satisfy his need for creative exchange and inspiration: with jewellery designers such as Giampaolo Babetto and Caroline Broadhead, the artist and architect Marcello Morandini and Nancy Davidson in sculpture and installation.

1999	Ring *Floater*, Platin, Bergkristall — Ring *Floater*, platinum, rock crystal
2000	Ring *Nebeleben*, Gold, Niello, Brillant — *Ring of fate*, gold, niello, diamond
2001	Ring *Square III V*, Gold — Ring *Square III V*, gold
2003	Ring *Crown S*, Gold, Brillanten — Ring *Crown S*, gold, diamonds
2004	Ring *Pusher*, Platin, Gold, Brillanten — Ring *Pusher*, platinum, gold, diamonds

Achim Gersmann
Geboren 1962 in Dortmund.
1989–1994 Fachhochschule Trier/Idar-Oberstein.
Atelier in Bamberg seit 1995.

Achim Gersmann
Born in Dortmund in 1962.
1989–1994 Fachhochschule Trier/Idar-Oberstein.
Studio in Bamberg since 1995.

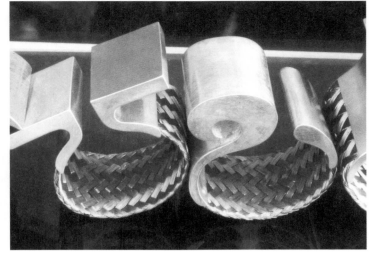

1987   1995

Ursula Gnädinger

Sie sind expressiv, raumgreifend und skulptural. Schmuckstücke, die einen Dialog mit dem Körper aufnehmen, seine Konturen verändern und eine Persönlichkeit (heraus)fordern. Arbeiten von Ursula Gnädinger. Zumeist aus Silber mit Feingold erzeugen sie bei aller formalen Klarheit Wirkungen von intensiver Kraft. »Ich gestalte im Spannungsfeld zwischen Körper, Bewegung, Form und Licht. Voluminöse prägnante Formen, die ihren eigenen Raum mit ihrem Träger erzeugen und durch Bewegung lebendig werden«, sagt Ursula Gnädinger.

Ihr Handwerk erlernte die aus Radolfzell stammende Gestalterin von 1982 bis 1986 in der Goldschmiede Bazak in Konstanz. Auf der Sonderschau der Handwerksmesse München sah sie als 16-jähriger Lehrling erstmals modernen Schmuck. »Es war ein richtiges Schlüsselerlebnis«, erzählt sie. Nach der Gesellenprüfung arbeitete Ursula Gnädinger in Schmuckateliers in Konstanz, Freiburg, Hamburg und Berlin. Abendkurse im Malen, Zeichnen und Modellieren intensivierten ihr Interesse an künstlerischer Gestaltung über das Handwerkliche hinaus. 1989 ging Ursula Gnädinger an die Hamburger Pentiment-Akademie, um im Bereich Skulptur bei Professor Detlev Birgfeld zu studieren. Als Pentiment-Preisträgerin erhielt sie 1990 ein Stipendium bei dem Bildhauer Jan Koblasa. Trotz dieser Erfolge in der Bildenden Kunst kehrte Gnädinger wieder zum Schmuck zurück. »Weil sich damals viel bewegte im modernen Schmuck und weil Schmuck wie kein anderes Medium als Zeichen einer individuellen Lebenshaltung dienen kann«, erklärt sie. Durch eine Begabtenzulassung konnte Ursula Gnädinger ab 1991 an der Hochschule für Gestaltung in Pforzheim im Bereich Schmuckdesign studieren.

Als selbständige Schmuckdesignerin in Berlin stand danach zunächst weniger die Verkäuflichkeit als vielmehr die eigene künstlerische Position auf dem Programm. Für ihren Lebensunterhalt arbeitete Ursula Gnädinger nebenher für andere Goldschmiede, z.B. für Gudrun Maass in Hamburg und Barbara Reister in Berlin. Dies war bis in die 1990er Jahre nicht ungewöhnlich unter ambitionierten Schmuckmachern, die ihr Medium neu definierten. »Wer verkäuflichen Schmuck macht, versaut sich«, hieß es damals.

Auf dem Gemeinschaftsstand der Berliner Kunsthandwerker in Frankfurt stellte Ursula Gnädinger ihre Arbeiten erstmals Galeristen und Fachhändlern vor. Regelmäßige nationale und internationale Ausstellungen und Messebeteiligungen folgten. Damit war auch die Entwicklung von Serienschmuck verbunden, den die heute in Potsdam lebende Schmuck-Designerin für den besseren Schmuck hält. 2004 erhielt sie für ihr gesamtes künstlerisches Werk den Staatspreis für das Deutsche Kunstwandwerk des Landes Hessen.

»Eine neue Schmucklinie zu gestalten, dauert oft Wochen«, sagt Ursula Gnädinger. Bis zu zehn Formen sind notwendig, bis eine Kette perfekt ist. Auf ihre bildhauerische Erfahrung mit großen Skulpturen möchte sie dabei nicht verzichten. »Ausschlaggebend war für mich das Gefühl, unter etwas zu stehen, unter vier Meter hohen Skulpturen. Das war eine wahnsinnig schöne körperliche Erfahrung.« Schwebende Volumen und kraftvolle Formen kennzeichnen bis heute ihren Schmuck. Doch liebt sie auch die Grenzen, die Schmuck ihr auferlegt, vorgegeben durch den menschlichen Körper. »Es macht Spaß, in der Gestaltung diese Grenze zu spüren und damit zu spielen«, sagt Ursula Gnädinger. Ob eine Form zu einem Menschen passt, sehe man erst, wenn sie getragen wird.

Die Kette mit der Bezeichnung K59 besteht aus räumlich konstruierten Dreiecksgliedern in Silber mit Feingold beschichtet. Im Zusammenspiel mit der Schmuckträgerin erzeugt dieser Halsschmuck eine schwer erklärbare Aura zwischen Abwehr und Anziehung. Das Kettenmodell K69, dessen rechteckige, gewölbte Glieder in Silber in den konkaven Oberflächen vergoldet sind, verbindet zurückhaltend strenge Kühle und anmutig strahlende Prächtigkeit. Wie viele andere Stücke behaupten beide Arbeiten ihre skulpturale Eigenständigkeit und sind gleichzeitig vollkommen auf den Körper bezogen. Die imposanten Armspangen und -reife, für die Ursula Gnädinger neben Silber und Gold auch Edelstahlgeflecht einsetzt, folgen den gleichen Prinzipien.

In der Gestaltung überlässt sie nichts dem Zufall. Zu jeder Form plant sie die Wirkung der Oberflächen. Das Gold, Inbegriff der Kostbarkeit, wird mit der Hand gebürstet, um ihm Struktur und Plastizität zu geben. Innen, wo Metall die Haut berührt, ist es glatt poliert. So nimmt es die Wärme des Körpers schnell an. »Dann spürt man auch das Gewicht kaum, obwohl die Stücke schwer sind«, sagt sie. Die äußere Struktur lockt einerseits durch das sanfte Leuchten. Gleichzeitig entsteht, in Verbindung mit der Form, aber auch Distanz. Damit bringt Ursula Gnädinger intuitiv die Ambivalenz zum Ausdruck, die seit Urzeiten zum Wesen des Schmucks gehört. Das Wechselspiel zwischen Anziehung und Abwehr ist in vielen ihrer skulpturalen Stücke lebendig.

E — Expressive, intervening in space, sculptural: these are pieces of jewellery that enter on a dialogue with the body, changing its contours and challenging it to reveal its personality. Works by Ursula Gnädinger. Usually made of silver with fine gold, they create intensely powerful effects despite the formal clarity distinguishing them. »I design in the charged field between body, movement, form and light. Voluminous, striking forms, which create their own space with their support and come alive through movement,« says Ursula Gnädinger.

A native of Radolfzell, the designer learned her craft at the Bazak goldsmithing workshop in Konstanz between 1982 and 1986. She first saw modern jewellery at the special show at the Munich Crafts Fair. »That really was a key experience,« she recounts. After taking her journeyman's certificate, Ursula Gnädinger worked in jewellery studios in Konstanz, Freiburg,

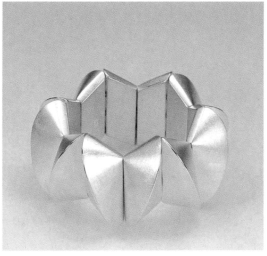

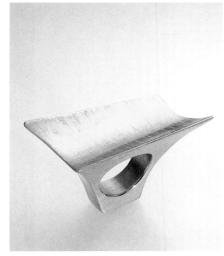

1999   2002   2002

Hamburg and Berlin. Evening courses in painting, drawing and modelling deepened her interest in art design above and beyond craftsmanship. In 1989 Ursula Gnädinger went to the Pentiment-Akademie in Hamburg to study sculpture with Professor Detlev Birgfeld. As a Pentiment prize winner, she was awarded a bursary in 1990 to study with the sculptor Jan Koblasa. Despite all these successes in fine art, however, Gnädinger returned to jewellery. »Because so much was going on in modern jewellery then and because jewellery can serve as a sign of individual lifestyle as no other medium can,« she explains. In 1991 Ursula Gnädinger was admitted on the basis of talent as a mature student to study jewellery design at the Hochschule für Gestaltung in Pforzheim.

As a self-employed jewellery designer in Berlin, Ursula Gnädinger gave priority on her agenda to establishing her own artistic stance before worrying about marketability. To earn a living, Ursula Gnädinger worked on the side for other goldsmiths, including Gudrun Maass in Hamburg and Barbara Reister in Berlin. Spreading their options in this way was not at all unusual for ambitious jewellery-makers who were redefining their medium in the 1990s. »Anyone who makes jewellery for the market is wrecking themselves,« was the buzzword then.

Ursula Gnädinger first presented her work to gallerists and specialist retailers at the collective stand manned by the Berlin craftsmen in Frankfurt. That début was followed by regular appearances at exhibitions and trade fairs in Germany and abroad. This included the development of industrially produced jewellery, which the designer, who now lives in Potsdam, regards as better jewellery. In 2004 she was awarded the Hesse State Prize for German Applied Arts for her lifetime achievement in art.

»Designing a new line in jewellery often takes weeks,« says Ursula Gnädinger. Up to ten moulds are needed to make a necklace perfect. She is glad of her experience in working with large-scale sculpture. »Paramount for me was the feeling of standing beneath something, beneath sculptures that were four metres high. That was a really beautiful physical experience.« Her jewellery is distinguished to the present day by hovering volumes and powerful forms. However, she also loves the constraints imposed on her by jewellery and the parameters of the human body. »It's fun in design to sense these constraints and play with them. Whether a form suits a person isn't apparent until you see it being worn.

The necklace designated K59 consists of spatially construed triangular links in silver gilt with fine gold. The interplay of this neck jewellery with the woman wearing it generates an indefinable aura between repulsion and attraction. The necklace model K69, featuring rectangular, curved links in silver, the concave surfaces of which are gilt, unites reticently cool astringency with gracefully radiant opulence. As in many of her pieces, both works insist on sculptural autonomy while being completely attuned to the wearer's

body. The same principles inform the grand bangles and bracelets for which Ursula Gnädinger uses stainless steel mesh alongside silver and gold.

She leaves nothing up to chance in her designs. For every form she plans the effects to be created by the texturing of its surfaces. Gold, the epitome of the precious, is brushed by hand to give it texture and plasticity. Inside, where the metal touches skin, it is polished smooth. Hence body heat quickly warms it. »Then you hardly feel the weight although these pieces are heavy,« she says. On the one hand, the external texturing with its soft gleam is appealing. On the other, however, the form creates distance. Thus Ursula Gnädinger intuitively expresses the ambivalence that has been the quintessence of jewellery since time immemorial. The interplay of attraction and repulsion animates many of her sculptural pieces.

1987	Ring, Silber, Feingold — Ring, silver, fine gold
1995	Armspangen, Silber, Feingold, Edelstahl — Bangles, silver, fine gold, stainless steel
1999	Armspange S20, Silber — Bangle S20, silver
2002	Ring R68, Silber, feingoldplattiert — Ring R68, silver, fine gold plated
2002	Kette K59, Ohrschmuck O45, Gold — Necklace K59, earrings O45, gold

Ursula Gnädinger
Geboren 1965 in Radolfzell. 1989 Pentiment-Akademie Hamburg. 1991 Hochschule für Gestaltung Pforzheim. Selbständig seit 1995. Heute Atelier in Potsdam.

Ursula Gnädinger
Born in Radolfzell in 1965. 1989 Pentiment-Akademie Hamburg. 1991 Hochschule für Gestaltung Pforzheim. Self-employed since 1995. Now has studio in Potsdam.

1997   2004

Franziska Rappold

Den modernen Schmuckketten Franziska Rappolds liegt ein außergewöhnliches »Wachsen« zu Grunde. »Die elementaren Formen ihrer Gestaltungslinien sind der Natur entliehen«, erklärt die Schmuckdesignerin ihre wichtigste Inspirationsquelle. Franziska Rappolds Schmuck beeindruckt durch die große Vielfalt volumiger Schmuckformen, die sie als *Hülse*, *Kapsel* oder *Knospe* bezeichnet.

Seit 1995 ist Franziska Rappold mit ihrer Kollektion auf dem deutschen und internationalen Schmuckmarkt präsent. 1960 in Speyer geboren, studierte sie zuerst Sonderpädagogik an der Universität Würzburg. Anschließend besuchte sie von 1983 bis 1987 die Goldschmiedeschule Pforzheim. Die Anschlusslehre absolvierte sie bei Eberhard Dechow, Goldschmiede für Unikat- und Designschmuck in Ludwigshafen. Nach einigen Gesellenjahren und freischaffender Goldschmiedetätigkeit in Speyer studierte sie von 1990 bis 1994 im Studiengang Schmuck und Gerät an der Hochschule für Gestaltung in Pforzheim.

Im Gestaltungskonzept von Franziska Rappold gibt es weder in der Form noch im Volumen strenge Grenzen. Die Grundform ihrer Schmuckkörper wird intuitiv und frei modelliert. Darüber wird im Electroforming in mehreren Arbeitsgängen eine Schicht aus Edelmetall gelegt. So wächst das Volumen nach außen, während innen ein Hohlraum entsteht, der den Frucht- und Blütenformen einen guten Tragekomfort gibt. Die »angewachsene« Oberflächenstruktur und die manuelle Nachbearbeitung der Schmuckkörper ergeben ein unverkennbares Äußeres. Franziska Rappold macht kleine Serien aus Feinsilber oder mit Feingold plattiert. Schlicht aneinandergereiht, als Geflecht oder als einzelnes Element bildet die Kombination von Schmuckkörper und Seil einen spannungsreichen Kontrast der Leichtigkeit von Volumen und Linie. Die Kollektion aus Ketten, Anhängern und Ohrschmuck interpretiert Franziska Rappold immer wieder neu und bereichert sie um neue Schmuckformen. In den *Wellen-* und *Bogenketten* fügen sich viele gleiche Einzelelemente zu variabel tragbaren Ketten zusammen; sie können auch als Armschmuck getragen werden. Auf einem transparenten Gummiband frei angeordnet, vermitteln die silbernen Einzelteile durch ihre besondere Oberflächenstruktur und Form ein organisches Ganzes.

E — Franziska Rappold's modern necklaces are based on an extraordinary »growth«. »The elementary forms of their design lines are borrowed from nature,« is how the jewellery designer explains her most important source of inspiration. Franziska Rappold's jewellery is so stunning because it encompasses so many voluminous forms, which she designates as pods, capsules or buds.

Franziska Rappold has been present on the German and international jewellery market with her collection since 1995. Born in Speyer in 1960, she first studied special education at Würzburg University before attending the Goldschmiedeschule Pforzheim (1983–1987), followed by an apprenticeship served under Eberhard Dechow, a goldsmith for one-off and designer jewellery in Ludwigshafen. After her journeyman's years and freelancing in Speyer as a goldsmith, she took the jewellery and tableware course at the Hochschule für Gestaltung in Pforzheim (1990–1994).

Franziska Rappold's concept of design is devoid of stringent boundaries in form and volume. The basic forms of her jewellery elements are modelled freehand and intuitively. Over them a skin of noble metal is deposited by electroforming in several work stages. Thus the volume grows outwards, causing a cavity to remain inside, which makes these fruit and blossom forms comfortable to wear. The »organically grown« surface structure and manual reworking of the constitutive elements result in an unmistakably distinctive appearance. Franziska Rappold makes fine silver or fine gold plated small collections. Paratactically arrayed, as a tissue or as a single element, the components form in combination with cord an exciting contrast in lightness based on volume and line. Franziska Rappold continues to re-interpret her collection of necklaces, pendants and ear jewellery by adding new forms. In her *Wellen-* und *Bogenketten* [Wave and Arc necklaces], many identical individual elements are fitted together to make necklaces that can be worn in a variety of ways: they can also be worn as arm jewellery. Distributed freely on a transparent cord, the individual silver elements convey the effect of an organic whole due to their distinctive texturing and form.

1997   *Hülsenkette*, Feinsilber, Edelstahl — *Pod necklace*, fine silver, stainless steel

2004   *Linsenkette*, Feinsilber, Edelstahl — *Nugget necklace*, fine silver, stainless steel

Franziska Rappold
Geboren 1960 in Speyer. 1990–1994
Fachhochschule für Gestaltung Pforzheim.
Seit 1995 Schmuckatelier in Freiburg.

Franziska Rappold
Born in Speyer in 1960. 1990–1994,
Fachhochschule für Gestaltung Pforzheim.
Jewellery studio in Freiburg since 1995.

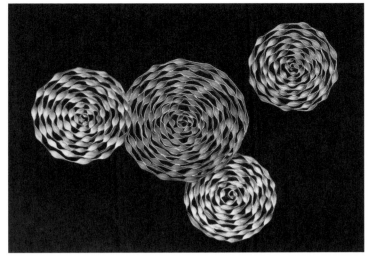

1999

2004

Kazuko Nishibayashi

Die Schmuckserien von Kazuko Nishibayashi resultieren immer aus einer Grundform, die dreierlei Eigenschaften haben muss: »Sie muss«, sagt sie, »zeitlos sein, sich variieren lassen und funktional sein.« Lange, bevor sie an die Gestaltung einer eigenen Schmuckkollektion dachte, interessierte sich die Gestalterin, die jetzt in Düsseldorf lebt, für die europäische Schmuckgeschichte. 1962 in Ibaragi in Japan geboren, begann sie ihre künstlerische Laufbahn am Women's College of Art in Tokio, wo sie von 1981 bis 1984 allgemeines Metalldesign studierte. An das Goldschmieden führte sie die japanische Schmuckgestalterin Minato Nakamura heran. Sie war es auch, die Kazuko Nishibayashi ein Schmuckstudium an der Hochschule für Gestaltung in Pforzheim empfahl. Als Gasthörerin von 1989 bis 1991 interessierte sie sich in erster Linie für die Goldschmiedetechniken.

Das vielfältige Angebot und die individuellen Lehrmethoden der Dozenten unterschieden sich sehr von den Unterrichtsmethoden japanischer Schulen, stellte Kazuko Nishibayashi fest. Diese seien viel stereotyper und programmatischer konzipiert. In Pforzheim begegnet sie der japanischen Schmuckkünstlerin Erico Nagai, die als Dozentin an der Hochschule lehrte. Im Seminar von Erico Nagai begann die Studentin, Naturphänomene in ihrem Schmuck umzusetzen. Die Natur als Ausgangspunkt ist bis heute für ihre Arbeiten wichtig. Seit 1995 gestaltet sie Schmuck in ihrer Düsseldorfer Werkstatt.

Eine weitere Inspirationsquelle entdeckte Kazuko Nishibayashi in der charakteristischen Eigenschaft von Japanpapier. Sie ersetzte das Papier durch silberne Metallstreifen. Aus Faltungen, japanisch Musubi genannt, entsteht Knotenschmuck. Die endlosen, knotenförmigen Verschlingungen sind den traditionellen japanischen Familienwappen nachempfunden. Spiralen winden sich in Wellenlinien, die variantenreich in Kreise, Sechsecke oder Quadrate münden.

Nach wie vor betrachtet die Schmuck-Designerin Minato Nakamura als Vorbild. »Ihre freie Gestaltung führt zu gefühlvollen und scheinbar zufälligen Skulpturformen«, sagt Nishibayashi. Ihre eigene Schmuckkollektion ist hingegen gekennzeichnet durch eine Balance zwischen Materialität und Dreidimensionalität. Wichtig ist ihr die Tragbarkeit der Schmuckstücke, die sie von Hand in kleinen Serien produziert. Zugleich empfindet sie sich als Handwerkerin, die einen Designentwurf durch eine gute Ausführung harmonisch gestalten möchte.

E — Jewellery editions by Kazuko Nishibayashi invariably result from a basic form that must have three qualities: »It must,« she says, »be timeless, variable and functional.« Long before she even thought of designing a jewellery collection of her own, the designer, who now lives in Düsseldorf, was interested in the history of European jewellery. Born in Ibaragi, Japan, in 1962, she began her career as an artist at the Women's College of Art in Tokyo, where she studied general metalworking design (1981–1984). She was introduced to goldsmithing by the Japanese jewellery designer Minato Nakamura, who also recommended to Kazuko Nishibayashi that she should study jewellery-making at the Hochschule für Gestaltung in Pforzheim. While auditing courses there from 1989 to 1991, she was primarily interested in goldsmithing techniques.

The wide range of course and diversity of individual teaching styles differed from the curriculum and instruction at Japanese schools, as Kazuko Nishibayashi was quick to realise. In Pforzheim she made the acquaintance of the Japanese artist in jewellery Erico Nagai, who taught at the Hochschule. In her seminar, Kazuko Nishibayashi began to translate natural phenomena in her jewellery. Today nature is still important as the starting point for her work. After taking her diploma, Kazuko Nishibayashi founded a studio in Düsseldorf.

Kazuko Nishibayashi discovered the characteristic quality of Japanese paper as another source of inspiration. She replaces the paper with strips of silver. Knot jewellery is made from folds, called »musubi« in Japanese. The endless interlacing of knots is reminiscent of the traditional Japanese family badges. Spirals twist into wavy lines to end in rich variations on circles, hexagons or squares.

Kazuko Nishibayashi still regards the jewellery designer Minato Nakamura as her role model. »Her free design leads to sensitive and seemingly arbitrary sculptural forms,« says Nishibayashi. Her own jewellery collection is, on the other hand, characterised by a balance between material substance and three-dimensionality. What is important to her is the wearability of her pieces of jewellery, which she makes by hand in limited editions. At the same time she views herself as a craftswoman who wants design and good execution to be in harmony.

1999	Ohrstecker und Brosche *Spirale*, Silber, Gold — Earrings and brooch *Spiral*, silver, gold
2004	Brosche *Kiku*, Silber — Brooch *Kiku*, silver

Kazuko Nishibayashi
Geboren 1962 in Ibaragi, Japan. Studium am Women's College of Art in Tokio und FH Pforzheim. Werkstatt seit 1995 in Düsseldorf.

Kazuko Nishibayashi
Born in Ibaragi, Japan, in 1962. Studied at Women's College of Art in Tokyo and Fachhochschule Pforzheim. Workshop in Düsseldorf since 1995.

1992   1993   1993

parsprototo

Alle Kollektionen von parsprototo basieren auf klaren, reduzierten Grundformen. Gleichzeitig sind die Stücke anschmiegsam, leicht und verzichten auf jegliche konstruktive Härte. Was nur wenigen Schmuck-Designern gelang, hat Birgitta Schulz, die Designerin, spielend geschafft. Sie entwickelte ein populäres Schmuckdesign, ohne auf die Grundprinzipien der Moderne zu verzichten.

Ihre Schmuckausbildung absolvierte die 1962 in Düsseldorf geborene Birgitta Schulz von 1990 bis 1994 in Zürich bei Antoinette Riklin. Bei der großen Schweizer Schmuckgestalterin und Künstlerin habe sie vier Jahre lang Unikate gefertigt, berichtet Schulz. Auch wurde sehr intensiv mit den anderen Schülerinnen über Sinn und Qualität der Entwürfe diskutiert. Während der Zeit bei Antoinette Riklin entstand die *Schneeflöckchen-Kette*. Sie besteht aus einem Stahlseil, auf dem in Abständen kleine weiße Südsee-Zuchtperlen fixiert sind. Der Entwurf führte später zur *Galaxie*-Kollektion, mit der parsprototo, das Label von Birgitta Schulz, bekannt wurde. Bei einem Schmucksymposium im slowakischen Kremnica, an dem auch die Schmuckkünstler Anton Cepka und Vratislav Novak teilnahmen, entstand 1995 der *Luftbesen*. Er wurde in die Sammlung der Staatsgalerie in Bratislava aufgenommen.

Mit der Gründung von parsprototo entstanden 1995 erste Schmuckserien. »pars pro toto« heißt wörtlich übersetzt »Ein Teil für das Ganze«. Das Schmuckstück werde Teil der Trägerin und bleibe auch immer ein Teil der gesamten Kollektion, so die Designerin zum Namen der Schmuckkollektion. Die Konzepte folgen alle dem gleichen Grundprinzip: Aus sich wiederholenden Einzelteilen entsteht ein unverwechselbares Ganzes. Seit 2007 produziert parsprototo in einem Bau der Jahrhundertwende in der Innenstadt von Freiburg. Alle Schmuckstücke entstehen in Handarbeit. Birgitta Schulz hat sich ganz bewusst für die Produktion in Deutschland entschieden. »Nicht nur aus Gründen der Qualitätssicherung, sondern auch, um das deutsche Handwerk zu erhalten und zu fördern«, sagt sie. Eine Galerie für Ausstellungen und Begegnungen ist Teil der Firmenräume, die nach den Vorgaben der Schmuckdesignerin restauriert wurden. Sie bieten eine optimale Umgebung für kreative Gestaltung und künstlerischen Austausch.

Charakteristisch für den hochwertigen Designschmuck von parsprototo sind runde Formen und edle, flexible Materialien, die leicht und anschmiegsam zu tragen sind. Birgitta Schulz geht von klaren, reduzierten Grundformen aus und verzichtet auf Ornamente und Verzierungen. »Meine Intention ist es«, betont sie, »seriellen Schmuck herzustellen, mit eigener Aussage und eigenem Wesen, der gleichzeitig eine feminine, romantische und poetische Aussage beinhaltet.« Alle Kollektionen von parsprototo bestehen aus Colliers, Arm- und Ohrschmuck. Bei der *Galaxie*-Kollektion »schweben« in regelmäßigen Abständen filigran und anmutig kleine Chinaperlen auf dünnen Stahlseilen. Die Perlen sind nicht wie beim klassischen Perlcollier

auf eine Schnur aufgereiht, sondern in regelmäßigen Intervallen auf einem Metallseil fixiert. Dies rückt die Schönheit der Perle auf eine moderne Art in den Vordergrund. Bei mehrreihigen Colliers entsteht das für parsprototo typische luftige und bewegliche Volumen. Doch bleibt der Halsschmuck der geometrischen Form treu, jener Idee reduzierter Klarheit, wie sie in den 1920er Jahren in Architektur, Design und im Schmuck entstanden ist. Neu war zum Ende des Jahrhunderts die poesievolle Leichtigkeit der Stücke.

Die Verbindung von Stahl- und Goldseilen mit Perlen kennzeichnet auch die Hals- und Armreife *Zero*. Die Perlen sind wiederum in regelmäßigen Abständen auf einzelne Seilreife fixiert. Aus einer Vielzahl von Reifen entsteht aus der puristischen Form ein vibrierender, dekorativer Schmuck. Die neuen Ringcolliers von parsprototo gehen von der Grundform des Kreises aus. Er beginnt und endet in der Perle. Stahl- und Goldseile geben dem Halsschmuck Stabilität und Flexibilität zugleich. Die Ringe nehmen Impulse auf, geben diese weiter, sind fest verbunden und doch frei beweglich. Die Anordnung erzeugt ein dreidimensionales Volumen. Elegant und beschwingt verändert sich die Form mit jeder Bewegung. Mit den *Ringcolliers* hat die Designerin Birgitta Schulz ihr Konzept fortgesetzt, das im Label parsprototo begründet ist. Aus den sich wiederholenden Einzelteilen entsteht ein unverwechselbares, einzigartiges Ganzes.

E — All parsprototo collections are based on clear, reductive basic forms. At the same time, their pieces are supple, light and eschew all Constructivist harshness. Designer Birgitta Schulz has succeeded where only a very few jewellery designers have; she has developed a popular design in jewellery without, however, having to eschew basic Modernist principles.

Born in Düsseldorf in 1962, Birgitta Schulz trained in Zurich with Antoinette Riklin from 1990 until 1994. Schulz reports that she made one-off pieces under the supervision of the great Swiss jewellery designer and artist for four years. There was also a lot of intense discussion with other pupils on the meaning and quality of their designs. During her time with Antoinette Riklin, Birgitta Schulz created the *Schneeflöckchen-Kette* [Snowflake chain]. It consists of steel wire, to which small white South Sea cultured pearls are attached at intervals. The design was later included in the *Galaxy* collection, with which parsprototo, the label under which Birgitta Schulz markets her work, became famous. At a jewellery symposium in Kremnica, Republic of Slovakia, where participants also included artists in jewellery Anton Cepka and Vratislav Novak, she created *Luftbesen* [Air broom] in 1995. It was acquired for the collection of the State Gallery in Bratislava.

Her first collections were launched when parsprototo was founded in 1995. Translated literally, »pars pro toto« means »part for the whole«. A piece of jewellery becomes part of its wearer and also remains part of the overall collection, is how the designer explains the name of the jewellery

1995

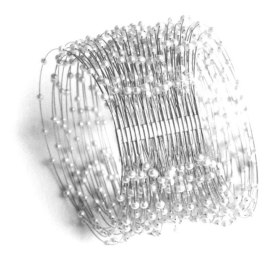

1996

label. All design concepts follow the same basic principle: a distinctive whole is created from recurring individual components. Since 2007 parsprototo has been producing jewellery in a fin de siècle building in downtown Freiburg. All pieces are made by hand. Opting to produce in Germany was a conscious decision on Birgitta Schulz's part. »Not just for reasons of quality control but also to preserve and promote German crafts,« she says. A gallery for exhibitions and meetings is part of the firm's rooms, which were restored according to the jewellery designer's plans. They provide an optimal environment for creative design and the exchange of ideas on art.

Characteristic features of the top-quality designer jewellery made by parsprototo are round forms and springy precious materials that are light and supple to wear. Birgitta Schulz starts with clear, reduced basic forms, eschewing ornament and decoration. »My intention is,« she emphasises, »to make lines in jewellery with a statement of their own and a distinctive essence which at the same time contains a feminine, romantic and poetic message.« All parsprototo collections comprise necklaces, arm and ear jewellery. In the *Galaxy* collection delicate little Chinese pearls »hover« gracefully at regular intervals on thin steel wire. Unlike the classic pearl necklace, these pearls are not strung on a string but attached to wire at regular intervals. This arrangement showcases the beauty of the pearl in a modern way. Multi-strand necklaces create the airy, mobile volume so typical of parsprototo. Still this neck jewellery has remained true to the geometric form, the idea of reductive clarity formulated in architecture, design and jewellery in the 1920s. What was new at the close of the past century, however, was the poetic lightness of these pieces.

The linkage of steel and gold cord with pearls is also the distinguishing feature of the torc and bangle collection called *Zero*. Again pearls are affixed at regular intervals to individual bands of steel. A multiplicity of bands creates vibrant, decorative jewellery from purist form. The new *Ringcolliers* [Ring necklaces] from parsprototo start with the basic form of the circle. It begins and ends with the pearl. Steel and gold wire gives this neck jewellery stability combined with flexibility. The rings take up spontaneous movement, transmit it, are firmly attached yet completely mobile. The three-dimensional arrangement creates volume. The form changes elegantly and airily with the wearer's every movement. In her *Ring necklaces*, designer Birgitta Schulz has continued the concept in which the parsprototo label is grounded: an inimitable, distinctive whole is created from reiterated individual components.

1992	*Galaxie* Collier, Edelstahl, Zuchtperlen — *Galaxy* necklace, stainless steel, cultured pearls
1993	Armband *Zero*, Edelstahl, Zuchtperlen — Bracelet *Zero*, stainless steel, cultured pearls
1993	Armband *Nest*, Edelstahl, Zuchtperlen — Bracelet *Nest*, stainless steel, cultured pearls
1995	Ohrschmuck *Luftbesen*, Silber, Edelstahl — Earrings *Air broom*, silver, stainless steel
1996	Armreif *Supergalaxie*, Edelstahl, Zuchtperlen — Bracelet *Super galaxy*, stainless steel, cultured pearls

Birgitta Schulz
Geboren 1962 in Düsseldorf. Ausbildung 1990–1994 bei Antoinette Riklin, Schweiz. 1995 Gründung von parsprototo in Freiburg.

Birgitta Schulz
Born in Düsseldorf in 1962. Trained 1990–1994 with Antoinette Riklin, Switzerland. Founded parsprototo in Freiburg in 1995.

1996

1999

2000

Jochen Pohl

Ausgangs- und Kristallisationspunkt aller Schmuckstücke von Jochen Pohl sind ausgewählte Edelsteine der Spitzenklasse. Auf ihrer Einzigartigkeit und Ausstrahlung basiert sein ganzheitlicher Gestaltungsansatz. In der Edelsteinstadt Idar-Oberstein geboren, entwickelt der Schmuck-Designer seit 1996 eindrucksvolle Ringserien. Charakteristisch sind klare, doch gefühlvoll weiche Formen, großzügige Volumina und luxuriöse, schmeichelnde Oberflächen.

Die Goldschmiedelehre in Idar-Oberstein beendete Jochen Pohl 1989 mit Auszeichnung. Anschließend lernte er bei einem Juwelier in Palma de Mallorca die romanische Schmuckauffassung kennen. 1991 folgten zwei Jahre in Idar-Oberstein bei einer Edelsteinschleiferei mit Schmuckfertigung. Hier wirkte Pohl an Neuentwicklungen mit und fertigte Prototypen. Anschließend besuchte er die Fachschule für Edelstein- und Schmuckgestaltung in seiner Heimatstadt und absolvierte 1994 erfolgreich die Meisterprüfung. Nach weiteren zwei Jahren in der Industrie vollzog er den Schritt in die Selbstständigkeit. Wesentlich war ihm dabei, zukünftig als Designer und Produzent seine eigenen hohen Qualitätsmaßstäbe zu definieren.

Von Beginn an verwendete Pohl für seine Edelsteinringe ausschließlich hochglänzend poliertes Roségold und Platin. Glänzende Metallflächen und die warme, rötliche Goldfarbe widersprachen 1996 dem vorherrschenden Paradigma im modernen deutschen Schmuck-Design mit seinen mattierten strengen Formen. Synthetische Steine waren ebenfalls kein Thema für Jochen Pohl. »Die Art und Weise, wie ich die Materialien auswähle und kombiniere, entspricht meiner Sicht der Welt«, erklärt er. Die Leidenschaft für Edelsteinraritäten nimmt darin einen herausragenden Platz ein. Die Formgebung seiner Ringe dient in erster Linie dazu, den Edelstein wirken zu lassen und der Schmuckträgerin ein ganzheitliches visuelles und haptisches Erlebnis zu vermitteln. Wie bei einer gelungenen Architektur ergeben die an dem Goldenen Schnitt orientierten Proportionen aus jeder Perspektive ein schlüssiges Bild. Jochen Pohl lehnt provokative Elemente im Schmuck ab. Vielmehr erfüllen seine Stücke das Bedürfnis vieler Frauen nach sinnlichem Luxus und authentischen Materialien.

Für seine ersten Ringe von 1996 verwendete der Designer Edelsteine in kräftigen Farben im Oval- und Prinzessschliff. Über mehrere Jahre vergrößerte er dann systematisch die Volumina, »weil erst in einer gewissen Dimension die Schönheit der Formen, der präzisen Linien und der fein polierten Flächen, sichtbar werden.« 1997 stellte Pohl Ringe mit Morganit in zartem Rosa und Beryll in sanftem Gelb vor. Die zurückhaltenden »Sorbet-Farben« unterstützten das beabsichtigte »Wachstum«. »Die sanften Farben nahmen den groß dimensionierten Ringen die Wucht«, erklärt Pohl. Mit seiner sensiblen Farbgebung setzte er in kürzester Zeit Trends im Edelsteinschmuck, die auch von großen Luxusmarken aufgenommen wurden. Doch wird die Wahl der Edelsteine nicht zuletzt auch von neuen Edelsteinfunden

2002   2003   2005

beeinflusst. Durch seinen idealen Standort in Idar-Oberstein und seine lang-jährigen persönlichen Beziehungen zu den Edelsteinhändlern seiner Heimat erfährt er sehr früh von interessanten neuen Vorkommen und wird sofort aktiv, wenn die Spitzenware in Idar-Oberstein ankommt.

2000 fertigte das aufstrebende Atelier Jochen Pohl erstmals Farbstein-ringe mit Diamantlünetten. Im gleichen Jahr stellte es auf einer Schmuckmes-se in Monte Carlo den Ring *101 C* vor. Das Oval des Edelsteins ist von einem markanten Rand umgeben. Inspiriert ist die Form von einer aufgebrochenen Kastanie, deren kräftige Schale die schimmernde Frucht schützend umgibt. Aufgesetzte, zu viel versprechende Kollektionsnamen empfindet Pohl gene-rell als einschränkend. Stattdessen erhalten all seine Ringserien Nummern, ähnlich den Referenzen von Luxusuhren. Die Emotion soll allein durch die Vollkommenheit des Schmuckstücks ausgelöst werden. Der Ring *P 51* des Jahres 2002 war der erste rechteckige Cabochonring im modernen Schmuck-Design. Die Bezeichnung *P 51* ist vom Pier 51 in Hannover abgeleitet, dessen markanter Glaskubus in ähnlicher Form in den Marschsee ragt.

Durchbrochene Formen als Gestaltungselement sind in der Architektur seit der Romanik und der Gotik in Europa bekannt. »Sie machen das Monu-mentale sichtbar«, sagt der Designer, der 2005 erstmals Ringe mit fünf run-den Öffnungen in der Schiene vorstellte. 2007 entstanden Ringe mit Riefen, die wie ein Gitternetz die Oberfläche überziehen. Die Gliederung der Form erinnert an die Nähte von Lederarbeiten, wie bei Handtaschen und Sitzmö-beln. Die jüngste Designentwicklung von Jochen Pohl ist der Neuinterpre-tation des Schmucks mit weißen Diamanten gewidmet. Für den Schöpfer grandioser Edelsteinringe ist es der Ring für die andere Hand. Das Weiß des Diamanten als Kontrast zum Farbstein.

Jochen Pohl liebt es, wenn Menschen über das normale Maß hinaus-wachsen. Computergesteuerte CNC-Maschinen findet man deshalb in sei-nem Atelier nicht. Dagegen setzt er auf versierte Handarbeit mit den klas-sischen Werkzeugen des Goldschmieds. Alle Edelsteine wählt er selbst aus und produziert ausschließlich in seinem Atelier in Idar-Oberstein. Dies habe den Vorteil, die Qualität jedes einzelnen Schmuckstücks kontrollieren zu können, erklärt der Firmenchef: »Damit hat meine Punze noch die gleiche Bedeutung wie die Signatur eines Künstlers.« An dieser Philosophie hat auch der Umzug in das neue Manufakturgebäude Anfang 2008 nichts geändert.

E — Precious stones of the highest class are the point of departure around which all pieces of jewellery by Jochen Pohl are crystallised. His holistic approach to jewellery design is based on their uniqueness and their radiance. Born in the gemstone city of Idar-Oberstein, this jewellery design-er has been developing truly impressive ring collections since 1996. Charac-teristic features of his work are crisply defined yet sensitively ductile forms, spacious volumes, flattering surface textures.

Jochen Pohl finished his goldsmithing apprenticeship in Idar-Ober-stein with distinction in 1989. Then he went to Palma de Mallorca to work for a jeweller and acquaint himself with the Mediterranean slant on jewellery. In 1991 he embarked on a two-year stint at an Idar-Oberstein gemstone-cut-ter's where jewellery was made. There Pohl contributed to developing new lines and made prototypes. After that he attended the Fachschule für Edel-stein- und Schmuckgestaltung in Idar-Oberstein and took his master crafts-man's certificate in 1994. After working in the jewellery industry for two years, Pohl became self-employed. What mattered to him was being able in the future to set his own high quality standards in design and production.

From the outset, Pohl has used only mirror-finished pink gold and platinum for his rings set with precious stones. In 1996, high-gloss metal surfaces and the warm, reddish colour of pink gold ran counter to the par-adigm then prevailing in modern German jewellery design, which featured matt texturing and astringent forms. Jochen Pohl has never had any use for synthetic stones. »The way I select materials and combine them corresponds to my world-view,« he explains. A passion for rare precious stones figures prominently in it. The design of his rings serves primarily to showcase pre-cious stones and convey to the woman wearing them a holistic visual and tac-tile experience. As with a successfully designed building, proportions based on the golden ratio result in a compellingly cogent image from every angle. Jochen Pohl eschews provocative elements in jewellery. On the contrary, his pieces meet the need felt by so many women for sensuous luxury and authentic materials.

For the first rings he made in 1996, the designer used precious stones in vibrant colours in the oval and princess cuts. Over the years, he has set about systematically increasing volumes »because not until a certain size has been attained do the beauty of forms, the precision of line and the fine finish of surfaces become apparent.« In 1997 Pohl presented rings set with delicate pink morganite and beryl in a soft yellow. These reticent »sorbet colours« reinforced the intended »growth«. »The soft colours deprive these large rings of their massiveness,« explains Pohl. His sensitive handling of col-our lost no time in setting trends in jewellery set with precious stones, which were also taken up by the great luxury labels. However, Pohl's choice of pre-cious stones is also, and not least, influenced by discoveries of new kinds of precious stones. Through living in the ideal place, Idar-Oberstein, and long years of personal links with the gemstone dealers in his native region, he is among the first to know about interesting new finds and engages actively with these top-quality gems as soon as they arrive in Idar-Oberstein.

In 2000 the ambitious Jochen Pohl studio made rings set with col-oured stones and lunette-cut diamonds for the first time. That same year the Pohl studio showed the *101 C* ring at a jewellery trade fair in Monte Carlo. The oval precious stone is surrounded by a pronounced edge. The form was

2006

2007

2008

inspired by a chestnut that has broken open to reveal the gleaming fruit protected by a powerful shell. Pohl generally finds pompous names for collections that promise too much a constraint on his style. Instead, all his ring editions are given numbers like the references on luxury watches. Emotions are to be aroused solely by the perfection of the piece of jewellery itself. The *P 51* ring (2002) was the first ring in modern designer jewellery to be set with a rectangular cabochon. The name *P 51* alludes to Pier 51 in Hannover, whose remarkable glass cube in a similar form juts out into a marshy lake.

Pierced-work or tracery forms as an element of architectural design have been known since the Romanesque and Gothic periods. »They are what visually define monumentality,« says the designer, who launched his first rings with five round apertures in the shank in 2005. He created rings with grooves that cover the surface like a grille in 2007. The articulation of the form is reminiscent of seams in leather goods such as handbags and seat furniture. Jochen Pohl's most recent development in design has been devoted to reinterpreting jewellery with white diamonds. For the creator of grand rings showcasing coloured precious stones, this is the ring for the other hand. The white of the diamonds contrasting with the coloured stones.

Jochen Pohl loves it when people are larger than life. That is why you will not find computer-aided CNC machines in his studio. On the contrary, he capitalises on consummate craftsmanship, using the classic goldsmiths' tools. He selects all his precious stones himself and produces his jewellery exclusively in his Idar-Oberstein studio. As Jochen Pohl explains it, this has the advantage that he can control the quality of every piece himself: »That means my stamp still has the same meaning as an artist's signature.« A move to a new factory building early in 2008 has not changed an iota of this philosophy.

1996	Ringe, Roségold, Farbsteine — Rings, rose gold, coloured precious stones
1999	Ring *230 L*, Platin, Morganit, Brillanten — Ring *230 L*, platinum, morganite, diamonds
2000	Ring *4000 XS*, Roségold, Mandaringranat, Brillanten — Ring *4000 XS*, rose gold, mandarin garnet, diamonds
2002	Ring *101C*, Roségold, brauner Mondstein — Ring *101C*, rose gold, brown moonstone
2003	Siegelringe *P 51*, Platin, Lagenachat — Signet rings *P51*, platinum, agate
2005	Ring *400 XS*, Roségold, Paraiba Turmalin aus Mosambique — Ring *400 XS*, rose gold, Paraiba tourmaline from Mosambique
2006	Ring *P51*, Roségold, rosa Turmalin — Ring *P51*, rose gold, rose tourmaline
2007	Ring *LLR*, Roségold, Brillanten — Ring *LLR*, rose gold, diamonds
2008	Ring *Space L*, Platin, Brillanten — Ring *Space L*, platinum, diamonds

Jochen Pohl
Geboren 1969 in Idar-Oberstein,
1992–1993 Fachschule für Edelstein- und
Schmuckgestaltung, 1994 Meisterprüfung.
Firmengründung 1996 in Idar-Oberstein.

Jochen Pohl
Born in Idar-Oberstein in 1969, 1992–1993
Fachschule für Edelstein- und Schmuckgestaltung,
Master craftsman's certificate in 1994.
Founded firm in Idar-Oberstein in 1996.

2000

2001

Gudrun Jäger

Gudrun Jäger wuchs in München auf. Ihre künstlerisch und handwerklich interessierte Mutter regte sie an, sich kreativ zu betätigen. Nach einem Goldschmiedepraktikum entschied sie sich für das Thema Schmuck. In der Lehre bei Marita Paulick in Mosbach von 1985 bis 1987 und 1988 bei Adelheid Helm in München liebte Gudrun Jäger den Umgang mit dem Material und die Präzision, die ihr das Handwerk abverlangte. Noch mehr war sie von der Idee begeistert, selbst Schmuck zu entwickeln.

Von 1988 bis 1992 studierte Gudrun Jäger an der Fachhochschule für Gestaltung in Schwäbisch Gmünd bei den Professoren Pierre Schlevogt und Frank Hess. In der »Perfektion der Natur und deren Umsetzung in eine abstrakte Form« erkannte sie ihr wesentliches Thema. Vorbilder fand sie in den Klassikern am Bauhaus, in dem dänischen Designer Arne Jacobsen, in zeitgenössischen Architekten wie Tadao Ando und Mario Botta oder den Schmuckkünstlern Otto Künzli, Gijs Bakker und Nel Linssen. Nach dem Studium arbeitete Gudrun Jäger zwischen 1992 und 1997 als Designerin in verschiedenen Unternehmen. In Ulm war sie als Design- und Marketingassistentin von Wolf-Peter Schwarz tätig. Parallel dazu entwickelte sie eigenen Schmuck, der bald in bekannten Galerien wie V&V in Wien und Hilde Leiss in Hamburg ausgestellt wurde.

Nach der Gründung des Ateliers für Gestaltung in Ulm 1997 folgte eine intensive Entwicklungsarbeit. Die Kollektion *Blätter* wurde 1999 auf der Inhorgenta in München und der Selection in Essen ausgestellt. Sie ist bis heute aktuell. Die spiralförmigen Ringe und Anhänger entstehen durch mechanische Verformung. Ein sanfter Knick, der die abstrakte Naturform verdeutlicht, erzeugt eine hohe Stabilität. Die *Blätter* können auch eine Perle oder einen Edelstein tragen. Im Jahr 2000 entstanden die ersten *Funkel-Steine*. In einem Spiegel aus poliertem Metall sitzen Diamanten und Farbedelsteine in Krappenfassungen. Dadurch entsteht ein facettenreiches Bild in der »Hohllinse«. *Aus einer Fläche* heißt eine Schmuckserie von 2001. In rechteckigen oder ovalen Formen ist die Mitte durchbrochen. Die beiden Seiten sind sanft gegeneinander verschoben. Manchmal sitzt ein Diamant wie ein funkelnder Tautropfen im Schnittpunkt. Von 2005 bis August 2008 führte Gudrun Jäger die Galerie formschön am Judenhof in Ulm.

E — Growing up in Munich, Gudrun Jäger was inspired by her mother, who was interested in art and crafts, to do something creative. After a goldsmithing internship, she opted for jewellery. Serving an apprenticeship under Marita Paulick in Mosbach (1985–1987) and in 1988 with Adelheid Helm in Munich, Gudrun Jäger loved handling the material and the precision exacted of her by the craft. She was even more enthusiastic about the idea of designing and making jewellery herself.

Gudrun Jäger studied at the Fachhochschule für Gestaltung in Schwäbisch Gmünd with Professors Pierre Schlevogt and Frank Hess from 1988 to 1992. She realised that her essential theme was the »perfection of nature and translating it into an abstract form«. Her role models were the Bauhaus classics, the Danish designer Arne Jacobsen, contemporary architects such as Tadao Ando and Mario Botta and artists in jewellery Otto Künzli, Gijs Bakker and Nel Linssen. After finishing her studies, Gudrun Jäger worked between 1992 and 1997 as a designer for various firms. In Ulm she worked for Wolf-Peter Schwarz as a design and marketing assistant. In parallel, she developed jewellery of her own, which was soon shown at distinguished galleries, including V&V in Vienna and Hilde Leiss in Hamburg.

After founding a design studio in Ulm in 1997, she concentrated on developing her work. Her *Blätter* [Leaves] collection was shown at the Munich Inhorgenta and Selection in Essen in 1999 and is still cutting-edge. Spiral-shaped rings and pendants are created by mechanical forming. A gentle bend that emphasises the origin in a natural form, creates convincing stability. The leaves may also support a pearl or a gemstone. In 2000 she launched *Funkel-Steine* [Sparkle Stones]. Diamonds and coloured precious stones are placed in collet settings on concave mirrors of polished metal. Thus a multi-faceted image is created in a »hollow-ground lens«. *Aus einer Fläche* [From a Surface] is her 2001 jewellery collection. The centre of rectangular or oval forms is pierced. The two sides are gently touching but moved out of alignment. Sometimes a diamond sits like a sparkling dewdrop at the interface. From 2005 to August 2008 Gudrun Jäger managed the gallery formschön at the Judenhof in Ulm.

2000	Ringe *Funkel-Steine*, Edelstahl, Farbedelsteine — Rings *Sparkle Stones*, stainless steel, precious stones
2001	Ohrringe *Aus einer Fläche*, Gold — Earrings *From a Surface*, gold

Gudrun Jäger
Geboren 1964 in München, 1988–1992 Studium an der Fachhochschule für Gestaltung in Schwäbisch Gmünd. Ateliergründung 1997 in Neu-Ulm, 2005–2008 Galerie formschön in Ulm.

Gudrun Jäger
Born in 1964 in Munich, studied at the Fachhochschule für Gestaltung in Schwäbisch Gmünd. Founded studio in 1997, 2005 to 2008 Galerie formschön, Ulm.

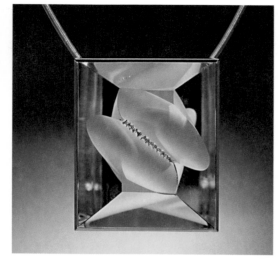

2001   2003

Atelier Tom Munsteiner

Tom Munsteiner versteht die Edelsteingestaltung als »schöpferische Reflexion über das Wesen der Kristalle.« Deshalb schleift er keine Facetten nach den vorgegebenen traditionellen Regeln. Bei der Bearbeitung der Kristalle empfindet er, dass diese »wie etwas Organisches ein Eigenleben an der Schwelle zwischen unbelebter und belebter Natur führen.« Dieses Eigenleben, die »poetische Natur der Kristalle«, will Tom Munsteiner »zum Klingen« bringen.

In Bernkastel-Kues im Hunsrück geboren, lernte er zwischen 1985 und 1989 das Edelsteinschleifen bei seinem Vater Bernd Munsteiner. So wie dieser schon das diffizile Handwerk im Atelier seines Vaters erlernt hatte; das war Tradition in der Edelsteinregion. Bernd Munsteiner hat sich bereits seit den 1960er Jahren künstlerisch mit dem Edelsteinschliff auseinandergesetzt und viele neue Schliffe kreiert. Für Tom Munsteiner war dies schon in der Ausbildung ein Thema. Es folgten vier Gesellenjahre im väterlichen Atelier und eine Ausbildung zum Gemmologen. Von 1993 bis 1995 besuchte er die Fachschule für Edelstein- und Schmuckgestaltung in Idar-Oberstein, die er als Staatlich geprüfter Schmuck- und Edelsteingestalter und Meister beendete. Ganz offenbar war Bernd Munsteiner 1997, im Alter von 54 Jahren, so von den Fähigkeiten seines jüngeren Sohnes überzeugt, dass er ihm die Atelierleitung übertrug.

Sein Talent und seinen Willen, einen eigenen Beitrag zum kreativen Edelsteinschliff zu leisten, hatte Tom Munsteiner schon zuvor bewiesen. 1991 erhielt er die erste Belobigung beim Deutschen Schmuck- und Edelsteinpreis. Ein Jahr später den Förderpreis des Landes Rheinland-Pfalz. Zahlreiche weitere internationale Preise folgten, viele davon in den USA. Als junger Atelierchef fand Tom in seiner Frau eine ambitionierte Weggefährtin. Geboren 1968 in Hermeskeil, hatte auch Jutta Munsteiner nach einer Goldschmiedelehre die Ausbildung zur Staatlich geprüften Gestalterin für Edelstein und Schmuck absolviert und die Meisterprüfung als Goldschmiedin abgelegt. Sie begnügte sich keineswegs damit, die kreativen Schliffe von Tom und Bernd Munsteiner in Schmuckstücken zu verarbeiten. Mit eigenständigen, preisgekrönten Entwürfen trug sie zum weltweiten Ansehen des Ateliers in Stipshausen bei.

Die ersten Arbeiten von Tom Munsteiner, zu Beginn der 1990er Jahre, zeigen kugelige Einschliffe. Trotz der geometrischen Ordnung der äußeren Form, entsteht der Eindruck von organischen, blasenförmigen Gebilden. Sie können als Hinweis auf das Fließende oder die kosmische Vollkommenheit der Kristalle gedeutet werden. Jedenfalls erzeugen sie ungewohnte, weiche Lichtspiele. Die Rückseiten der geometrisch geschliffenen Außenformen wie Prismen, Kreise, Navetteformen und Quadrate sind manchmal auch mit schlitzförmigen Einschnitten versehen. Zum Beispiel in dem Thema *Stairs*. Dabei geht es Tom Munsteiner um eine »innere konstruktivistische Architektur des Steins.« In der Serie *Nature* macht der Edelsteingestalter wiederum

in klaren Außenformen die Schönheit natürlicher Einschlüsse und bizarrer Hohlräume hauptsächlich in Quarzen sichtbar. Aus der individuellen Natur jedes Edelsteins, die Tom Munsteiner schätzt und sichtbar macht, entstehen vorwiegend Schmuckunikate und Objekte. Doch ist auch sein Einfluss auf den seriellen Schmuck nicht unbedeutend. Zum Beispiel verwendet Angela Hübel in ihrer Ringserie *Turmalin-Schiffchen* sowie die Schweizer Firma Fillner in ihrer Ringserie *Flower Leaves* die künstlerisch geschliffenen Edelsteine. Sehr erfolgreich ist zudem die Pforzheimer Firma cédé mit den Schliffen von Tom Munsteiner in ihrem Schmuck. Schließlich widmet sich Tom Munsteiner auch einem Thema, das schon dem Goldschmiedeklassiker und Objektkünstler Friedrich Becker ein Anliegen war. Mehrfach hatte dieser die Hässlichkeit von Pokalen beklagt und eigene Vorschläge gemacht. An dem Objekt, das Tom Munsteiner 1999 für den Innovationspreis Oberfranken gestaltet hat, hätte Becker sicher seine Freude. Mit dem DFL-Ligapokal hat der Edelsteingestalter aus Stipshausen auch einen Beitrag zur Sportgeschichte geleistet.

E — Tom Munsteiner views his designs for cutting precious stones as »creative reflection on the essence of crystals«. That is why he does not cut any facets according to the prevailing traditional rules. In working crystals, he feels that they »lead lives of their own like something organic on the threshold from inanimate to animate nature«. Tom Munsteiner wants to »make« these lives, the »poetic nature of the crystals, resound«.

Born in Bernkastel-Kues in the Hunsrück, Tom Munsteiner learned gem-cutting from his father, Bernd Munsteiner, between 1985 and 1989, just as Bernd Munsteiner had learned this exacting craft in his own father's studio. That is tradition in the gemstone region. Bernd Munsteiner had been investigating cutting gemstones as art since the 1960s and had created many new cuts. For Tom Munsteiner this skill was already part of his training. His four years in his father's studio were followed by training in gemmology. From 1993 to 1995 he attended the Fachschule für Edelstein- und Schmuckgestaltung in Idar-Oberstein, from which he graduated as a state-examined jewellery and gemstone designer and master. Bernd Munsteiner was evidently so convinced of his younger son's abilities that he made Tom Munsteiner head of the studio in 1997 although he himself was only fifty-four years old at the time.

Tom Munsteiner had already shown his talent and his drive to make a contribution of his own to creative gem-cutting. In 1991 he was awarded his first honourable mention for the German Jewellery and Gemstone Prize, followed a year later by the Förderpreis des Landes Rheinland-Pfalz [Rhineland-Palatinate State Promotional Prize]. Many more international awards followed, quite a few of them in the US. The young studio head has found an equally ambitious companion in his wife. Born in Hermeskeil in 1968, Jutta Munsteiner served a goldsmith's apprenticeship before also training as

| 2007 | 2008 | 2008 | 2008 |

a state examined designer of gemstones and jewellery and taking her master craftsman's certificate in goldsmithing. It was not enough for her simply to work the creative cuts invented by Tom and Bernd Munsteiner into jewellery, however. She has contributed to the international reputation of the studio in Stipshausen with award-winning designs of her own.

Tom Munsteiner's first pieces, done in the early 1990s, feature spherical incisions. Despite the geometric arrangement of the external form, an impression of organic, bubble-like configurations is created. They can be interpreted as an allusion to the flow of all things or to the cosmic perfection of crystals. In any case, they create an unusual, soft play of light. The reverse of the geometrically cut outer forms, such as prisms, circles, navette shapes and squares, are sometimes also provided with incisions like slits. Take, for example, the *Stairs* theme. Here Tom Munsteiner is concerned with an »inner Constructivist architecture of the stone«. In the *Nature* edition, on the other hand, the gemstone designer has used clear outer forms and mainly quartz stones to make visible the beauty of natural inclusions and grotesque cavities within. Most of the pieces of jewellery and objects created from the individual nature of each precious stone that Tom Munsteiner appreciates and reveals are one-offs. But he has also exerted a major influence on mass-produced jewellery. Angela Hübel, for instance, uses his artistically cut gemstones in her *Turmalin-Schiffchen* [Tourmaline shuttles] line and so does Fillner, a Swiss firm, for their *Flower Leaves* ring collection. The Pforzheim firm cédé is also highly successful with jewellery featuring Tom Munsteiner's creative cuts. Finally, Tom Munsteiner also devotes himself to a theme that was once of great interest to the classic goldsmith and object artist Friedrich Becker. Becker often deplored the ugliness of cups used as trophies and made suggestions of his own for improving them. He would have loved the object that Tom Munsteiner designed in 1999 for the Upper Franconian Innovation Award. The gemstone designer from Stipshausen has made a contribution to the history of competitive sports with the DFL League trophy cup he designed.

2001	Objekt *Prisma*, Aquamarin 144,80 ct — Object *Prisma*, aquamarine 144,80 ct
2003	Halsschmuck, Platin, Aquamarin — Necklace, platinum, aquamarine
2007	Turmalin *Imagination*, Paraiba 34,25 ct — Tourmaline *Imagination*, Paraiba 34,25 ct
2008	Ring, Gold, Peridot 12,10 ct — Ring, gold, peridot 12,10 ct
2008	Halsschmuck *Persönlichkeiten, Madonna*, Rauchquarz 60,66 ct, Edelstahl — Necklace *Personalities, Madonna*, smoky quartz 60,66 ct, stainless steel
2008	Halsschmuck *Persönlichkeiten, Joe Louis*, Rutilquarz 305,30 ct, Gold — Necklace *Personalities, Joe Louis*, rutile quartz 305,30 ct, gold

Jutta Munsteiner
Geboren 1968. Meisterprüfung.
Tom Munsteiner
Geboren 1969. 1993–1995 Fachschule
für Edelstein- und Schmuckgestaltung.
Atelierübernahme 1997.

Jutta Munsteiner
born in 1968. Master craftsman's certificate.
Tom Munsteiner
born in 1969. 1993–1995 Fachschule für
Edelstein- und Schmuckgestaltung.
Head of studio in 1997.

Atelier Tom Munsteiner

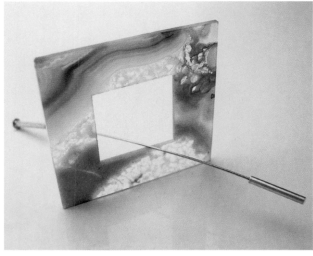

2002   2005   2006

Adam & Stoffel

Beide haben ab 1991 im Fachbereich Edelstein- und Schmuckdesign in Idar-Oberstein studiert. Claudia Adam machte zuvor ein Goldschmiedepraktikum; Jörg Stoffel eine Lehre als Juwelengoldschmied. Beide erhielten regelmäßig Preise und Auszeichnungen, die meisten beim Deutschen Schmuck- und Edelsteinpreis. Auch in der Auswahl Best of Selection des Designzentrums Nordrhein-Westfalen im Jahr 2000 waren sie mit dabei. Seit 1997 zählen sie zur kreativen Generation der Edelsteingestalter nach Bernd Munsteiner.

Künstlerisch geschliffene Edelsteine sind das zentrale Thema ihrer Schmuckgestaltung. Sie haben zusammen zwei Kinder und leben als Gestalterpaar in Stipshausen, dem Geburtsort von Jörg Stoffel. »Für mich war das Studium notwendig«, sagt Jörg Stoffel, »weil die Arbeit als Goldschmied, das Ausführen von Reparaturen und das Arbeiten nach Kundenwünschen keine Erfüllung bot.« An der Schule legte Professor Udo Ackermann Wert darauf, dass jeder Student einen eigenen Zugang zum Stein fand. Jörg Stoffels Bezug ist ebenso intellektuell wie emotional. Die Ring- und Anhängerserie *acht* mit Farbedelsteinen wie Turmalin und Aquamarin im *Spirit Sun*-Schliff entfaltet die Aura eines modernen Schmuckklassikers. Sie ist perfekt und logisch in der Form, die für alle Zeit gültig scheint. In der Serie *aeria* überrascht Jörg Stoffel mit einem optischen Effekt: Kugelförmig geschliffene Edelsteine, hauptsächlich Rutil-, Rauch- oder Lemonquarze, scheinen den Blick in ein »Schwarzes Loch«, in das »Auge eines Hurricans« zu lenken. Der verblüffende optische Eindruck entsteht durch einen speziellen Schliff auf der Rückseite der Steine.

Claudia Adam ist es gelungen, dem Edelstein eine Eigenschaft zu verleihen, die er in seiner Jahrtausende alten Geschichte noch nie besessen hat. Während sie zu Beginn schwere, skulpturale Anhänger schliff, die an flüssig fließendes Glas erinnern, entfalten ihre späteren Stücke eine ungeahnte Leichtigkeit. Beispielsweise die Serien *calla* und *dish*, die sich leicht und transparent zu öffnen scheinen. Die Strukturen und Nadeln des Rutilquarzes und Bergkristalls, die morbide oder pastellige Farbe des Achats oder der »bewegte« Schwarzweiß-Kontrast von Onyx verführen das Auge. Lichtbrechung und Schattenwurf erhalten durch die Edelsteingestalterin eine neue Aufgabe. In Verbindung mit diesen organischen Formen entsteht der Eindruck von tragbaren Skulpturen.

Claudia Adam macht streng geometrische Schliffe, so für die Broschenserie *quadrat*, oder organisch weiche für die Linie *splash*. Durch Struktur und Farbe der Steine hat jedes Stück Unikatcharakter. Mit den »dünnwandigen Sachen« fing sie schon Ende des Studiums an. Dabei wird der Stein von innen nach außen bearbeitet. Zunächst wird eine kleine Öffnung mit einem Diamantwerkzeug gebohrt, dann werde »sehr viel herausgearbeitet«, erklärt sie. Dabei entstand zunächst die Form einer Amphore. Die Entwicklung der Serie *Cava* im Jahr 1998 stellt einen Höhepunkt in ihrer Arbeit dar. Kühn

durchdringt die Ringschiene einen hohl geschliffenen Edelstein von oben und hält ihn fest. Mit schwebender Leichtigkeit überzeugt auch der Halsschmuck *swing*. Edelsteine, dünn geschliffen wie Kartoffelchips, vermitteln hier ein völlig neues Trageerlebnis.

Claudia Adam und ihr Mann Jörg Stoffel arbeiten in der Schleiferei Stoffel, die gegenwärtig von Thomas Stoffel geführt wird und zu den Traditionsbetrieben in der Edelsteinregion Idar-Oberstein zählt. Um ihre innovativen Schliffe zu realisieren, mussten sie einige zusätzliche Maschinen anschaffen. »Man muss sich auch technisch spezialisieren, um solche Sachen machen zu können«, sagen die beiden. Im Jahr 1997 hat das Paar erstmals auf der Messe in Basel ausgestellt, gefördert vom Land Rheinland-Pfalz. Dann entstand die Idee, innerhalb eines größeren Standes mehr Aufmerksamkeit zu erregen. Dies führte zur Gründung der Gruppe Delicatesse, die seit 1998 gemeinsam auf internationalen Messen auftritt und zu der auch die Schmuckgestalter Achim Gersmann und Christina C. Carstens gehören.

Jörg Stoffel befasst sich seit langem auch mit Objekten. Besondere Freude empfindet der »Philosoph« der Gruppe Delicatesse, wenn er einem Besucher *eo ipso* vorführen kann. Es ist ein flach geschliffener Stein in verschiedenen Formen und Materialien. *eo ipso* erlaubt es seinem Benutzer nur, ihn in eine Richtung rotieren zu lassen. »Falsch herum« gedreht, fängt er nach kurzer Zeit an zu wackeln, stoppt und bewegt sich wie von Zauberhand rückwärts. »Dies haben«, sagt Jörg Stoffel, »schon die Kelten gewusst.«

E — Both studied gemstone and jewellery design in Idar-Oberstein from 1991. Claudia Adam did a goldsmithing internship before studying; Jörg Stoffel served an apprenticeship in jewellery goldsmithing. Both have been regular winners of prizes and awards, notably the Deutscher Schmuck- und Edelsteinpreis. In 2000 they were also in the North Rhine-Westphalia Design Centre Best of Selection. They belong to the creative generation of gemstone designers after Bernd Munsteiner. Artistically cut gemstones are the central theme of their jewellery designs. They have two children and live as a designer duo in Stipshausen, where Jörg Stoffel was born.

»Studying was necessary for me,« says Jörg Stoffel, »because working as a goldsmith, carrying out repairs and doing what customers wanted was not satisfying.« At the school in Idar-Oberstein, Professor Udo Ackermann insisted on every student finding his or her own personal approach to stones. Jörg Stoffel's relationship with stones is both intellectual and emotional. The *eight* collection of rings and pendants set with coloured semiprecious stones such as tourmalines and aquamarines in the Bernd Munsteiner *Spirit Sun* cut radiates the aura of a modern jewellery classic. It is perfect and logical in a form that seems likely to be timeless. In the *aeria* collection, Jörg Stoffel exploits an optical illusion: spherically cut semiprecious stones, usually rutile, smoky or lemon quartz, seem to lead the gaze into a »Black Hole«

2000

2008

or »the Eye of a Hurricane«. This astonishing optical illusion is created by a special cut on the back of the stone. Claudia Adam has succeeded in lending gemstones a quality they have never had in thousands of years of history. Although she at first created heavy sculptural pendants reminiscent of fluid molten glass her later pieces are notable for an inconceivable lightness. To take two examples, her *calla* and *dish* pieces seem to open lightly and transparently. The structures and needles of rutile quartz and rock crystal, the morbid or pastel shades of agate or the »lively« black and white contrast of onyx are seductive to look at. The refraction of light and casting of shadows have been reassigned by the gemstone designer. In combination with these organic forms, they create the impression of being wearable sculpture.

Claudia Adam creates stringently geometric cuts, for instance for the *square* edition of pins, or soft organic ones for the *splash* line. Each piece is like a one-off due to the unique structures and colours of the stones used. She started on »thin-walled things« towards the end of her student days. The stone is worked from inside out. First a small aperture is drilled with a diamond-tipped tool, then »a lot is worked out,« she explains. An amphora shape emerges. The development of the *Cava* line in 1998 represents a high point of her career. The ring shank boldly pierces a hollow-cut semiprecious stone from above and holds it fast. Her neck jewellery *swing* is also so implausibly light that it seems to float. Stones cut as thin as potato crisps create an entirely new wearing experience.

Claudia Adam and her husband Jörg Stoffel both work in the Stoffel gemstone cutting workshop, currently run by Thomas Stoffel and one of the venerable businesses of its kind in the gemstone region Idar-Oberstein. To realise their innovative cuts, they had to procure additional machinery. »You have to be specialist technicians to be able to make things like that,« they both say. In 1997 the couple first showed work at the Basel trade fair, with the support of the state of Rhineland-Palatinate. Then the idea came up of attracting more attention by sharing a larger stand. That led to founding the Delicatesse group, which has exhibited collectively since 1998 at international trade fairs. The jewellery designers Achim Gersmann and Christina C. Carstens also belong to the group.

Jörg Stoffel has long been preoccupied with objects. The »philosopher« of the Delicatesse group really enjoys showing *eo ipso* to a visitor. This is a flat cut stone in various forms and materials. *eo ipso* only allows its owner to rotate it in one direction. Turned »the wrong way round,« it soon starts wobbling, stops and moves backwards as if guided by a magician's hand. »This is something,« says Jörg Stoffel »that the Celts already knew about.«

2002	Ring *calla*, Achat — Ring *calla*, agate
2005	Collier *lacrima*, Gold, Rutilquarz — Necklace *lacrima*, gold, rutile quartz
2006	Brosche *quadrat*, Achat, Edelstahl, Silber — Brooch *square*, agate, stainless steel, silver
2000	Ring *acht*, Gold, Turmalin — Ring *eight*, gold, tourmaline
2008	Ring *aeria*, Gold, Bergkristall — Ring *aeria*, gold, rock crystal

Claudia Adam
1968 geboren. 1991–1998 Fachhochschule Trier/Idar-Oberstein.
Claudia Adam
Born in 1968. 1991–1998 Fachhochschule Trier/Idar-Oberstein.

Jörg Stoffel
1964 geboren. 1991–1996 Fachhochschule Trier/Idar-Oberstein.
Jörg Stoffel
Born in 1964. 1991–1996 Fachhochschule Trier/Idar-Oberstein.

Gemeinsame Ateliergründung 1997 in Stipshausen.
Founded joint studio in Stipshausen in 1997.

1998   2002

Atelier Striffler & Krauß

Moderne, reduzierte Schmuckketten sind seit Mitte der 1980er Jahre im modernen Schmuck-Design ein wesentliches Thema. Kann man danach, im 21. Jahrhundert, noch eigenständige Akzente setzen? Dorothee Striffler hat dies in ihrer »Auseinandersetzung mit dem Einfachen und Schlichten« eindeutig bewiesen. Ihr Halsschmuck, den sie heute gemeinsam mit Stefan Krauß unter dem Namen Atelier Striffler & Krauß gestaltet, basiert auf dem Formenrepertoire der Moderne und bereichert es durch eine ganz eigene Note.

Nach ihrer Lehre von 1988 bis 1992 an der Goldschmiedeschule Pforzheim und im Schmuckatelier M. Mämecke, Heidelberg, studierte Dorothee Striffler von 1993 bis 1997 an der Fachhochschule Pforzheim bei Johanna Dahm und Rudolf Bott, unterbrochen 1996 durch einen Studienaufenthalt in Venedig bei Piergiuliano Reveane. Seit 1997 ist sie in Mannheim selbständig. Ergänzend sammelte sie als Assistentin an der HfG Pforzheim von 1998 bis 2003 und bei einem dreimonatigen Lehrauftrag 2007 an der Haute École d'Art et de Design, Genf, weitere Erfahrungen. Im Januar 2002 gründete sie ein gemeinsames Atelier in Ludwigshafen mit Stefan Krauß.

Stefan Krauß lernte von 1990 bis 1994 Goldschmied im Atelier Kurt Kubik in Heidelberg und studierte nach einer zweijährigen Gesellentätigkeit von 1996 bis 2000 ebenfalls an der HfG Pforzheim, die er wie seine Partnerin als Diplomdesigner beendete. Ziel des gemeinsamen Ateliers sei es, »die seit der ersten Messeteilnahme 1998 aufgebauten Geschäftsbeziehungen auszubauen und das gestalterische Spektrum zu erweitern«, sagt Stefan Krauß.

Dorothee Strifflers Schmuckketten wurden 2004 mit dem Staatspreis Gestaltung Kunst Handwerk Baden-Württemberg ausgezeichnet. Kurz nach ihrem Diplom war sie bereits bei namhaften internationalen Galerien wie Marzee, Nijmegen, Hélène Porée, Paris, Sofie Lachaert, Gent, Isabella Hund, München oder Voigt, Nürnberg vertreten – nicht selten mit Einzelausstellungen. »Der Reiz des Schlichten liegt im scheinbaren Widerspruch«, erklärt die Schmuckdesignerin, »dass gerade die formale Beschränkung auf einfache, elementare und lineare Formen eine erstaunliche Vielfalt in sich birgt.« Basierend auf geometrischen Grundformen wie dem Quadrat entfalten ihre Ketten in der Reihung Raum und Volumen. Das Wechselspiel von Licht und Schatten in den Innen- und Zwischenräumen intensiviert die Wirkung und lässt den Halsschmuck erfrischend lebendig erscheinen.

E — Modern, reductive necklaces have been a key theme in modern designer jewellery since the mid-1980s. Is it still possible, so long afterwards in the 21st century, to make a personal mark? In her »investigation of the simple and uncluttered« Dorothee Striffler has unequivocally proved that it is. Her neck jewellery, which these days she designs jointly with Stefan Krauß under the Striffler & Krauß label, is based on the Modernist canon of forms but enriches it with a distinctively personal touch.

After serving an apprenticeship (1988–1992) at the Goldschmiedeschule Pforzheim and the jewellery studio M. Mämecke in Heidelberg, Dorothee Striffler studied under Johanna Dahm and Rudolf Bott at Fachhochschule Pforzheim from 1993 until 1997, interrupting her academic studies to spend some time in Venice for additional training with Piergiuliano Reveane. She was self-employed in Mannheim from 1997. She also widened her experience by working as an assistant at the HfG Pforzheim from 1998 until 2003 and spending three months in 2007 teaching at the Haute École d'Art et de Design in Geneva. In January 2002 she joined forces with Stefan Krauß to found a joint workshop in Ludwigshafen.

Stefan Krauß trained as a goldsmith in Heidelberg from 1990 until 1994. After two journeyman's years (1996–2000), he, like his partner, studied at HfG Pforzheim, taking a diploma in design. The aim of their joint studio is »to strengthen the business ties that have been forged since our first trade fair appearance in 1998 and to enlarge our design range,« says Stefan Krauß.

Dorothee Striffler was awarded a Baden-Württemberg State Prize for Design, Arts, Crafts for her neck jewellery in 2004. Not long after taking her diploma, she was exhibiting work at distinguished international galleries, including Marzee, Nijmegen, Hélène Porée, Paris, Sofie Lachaert, Ghent, Isabella Hund in Munich and Voigt in Nuremberg – quite often at solo shows. »The attraction of simplicity lies in the apparent contradiction,« explains the jewellery designer, »that it is the formal limitation to simple, elemental and linear forms that can subsume such an astonishing diversity.« Based on basic geometric forms such as the square, her necklaces develop space and volume through paratactical arrangement. The interplay of light and shadow in the inner spaces and interstices enhances the effect to make this neck jewellery look refreshingly vivid.

| 1998 | *Rautenkette*, Gold — *Rhombus necklace*, gold |
| 2002 | Kette *Viele*, Gold — Necklace *Many*, gold |

Dorothee Striffler
Geboren1967. 1993–1997 HfG Pforzheim.
Stefan Krauß
Geboren 1969. 1996–2000 HfG Pforzheim.
Gemeinsames Atelier seit 2002 in Mannheim.

Dorothee Striffler
Born in 1967. 1993–1997 HfG Pforzheim.
Stefan Krauß
Born in 1969. 1996–2000 HfG Pforzheim.
Joint studio in Mannheim since 2002.

1995   1998–2004   2007

Kay Eppi Nölke

Die Schmuckstücke von Kay Eppi Nölke beinhalten ursprüngliche und gegenwärtige Erfahrungen des sich Schmückens. In seinen bekanntesten Ringserien bilden gewickeltes Gras und Wundpflaster die Vorlagen. Mit den *Gras-* und *Pflasterringen*, die seriell in Silber, Gold, Eisen oder Edelstahl gefertigt werden, bringt uns der Gestalter auf ganz individuelle, emotionale Weise das Thema Schmuck nahe.

Kay Eppi Nölke, in Bielefeld geboren, absolvierte 1980 bis 1983 eine Goldschmiedeausbildung. An der Zeichenakademie in Hanau besuchte er von 1989 bis 1991 die Klasse von Alexander Zickendraht. Nach dem Abschluss als Staatlich geprüfter Gestalter und der Meisterprüfung studierte er von 1993 bis 1998 in Pforzheim an der Hochschule für Gestaltung. Seine Diplomarbeit betreuten Jens-Rüdiger Lorenzen und der Silberschmied Rudolf Bott.

Gestalteter Schmuck, der als Unikat entsteht und auch in der Serie funktioniert, ist ein wichtiges Thema für Kay Eppi Nölke. 1995 erhielt er im Wettbewerb Kunst der Serie, veranstaltet vom Verband der Deutschen Schmuck- und Silberwarenindustrie, für seine *Pflasterringe* den ersten Preis. Eine ganz alltägliche Handlung formt dabei das Schmuckprodukt. Wie der gewickelte Ring aus Grashalmen entsteht auch der *Pflasterring* durch seinen zukünftigen Träger. Aus verschieden breiten Wundpflastern lässt sich in mehreren Lagen ein Fingerring formen. 1998 entstand eine Ringserie aus Filz mit dem Titel *Vater, Mutter, Haus und Garten*. Dazu gehörte auch eine Waschanleitung. 2007 entstand die Serie *Erinnern heißt auswählen*. In kleinen Tütchen aus Polyethylen können wertvolle und persönliche Dinge aufbewahrt werden: eine Muschel vom Strand, ein Steinchen vom bezwungenen Berg, eine Haarlocke des/der Liebsten oder auch einige Körnchen Feingold. Auch archaisch anmutende Eisengefäße mit lebendigen Oberflächen hat Kay Eppi Nölke gestaltet. Die Schalen mit dem Titel *...Aus dem Feuer nehmen...* sind gefüllt mit geschmolzenem Silber von 200 Gramm bis zu einem Kilo. In der Version als Anhänger sind die kleinen Gefäße Schmuckunikate.

Nach vielen Jahren in Pforzheim lebt und arbeitet der ehemalige Mitgründer der Gestaltergruppe Juni heute in Konstanz. Hier konzentriert er sich ganz auf seine gestalterischen Ziele mit dem Menschen als Mittelpunkt. »Mit jedem getragenen Ring«, sagt Kay Eppi Nölke, »entsteht eine neue Geschichte – Ihre Geschichte.«

E — Kay Eppi Nölke's pieces represent primal and current experiences in adornment. Twisted grass and sticking plasters were the models cast for his best-known ring collections. With the *Grass* and *Sticking plaster rings*, which are manufactured in silver, gold, low-grade steel or stainless steel, the designer brings us close to jewellery in an entirely individual way that addresses our emotions.

Born in Bielefeld, Kay Eppi Nölke trained as a goldsmith (1980–1983). At the Zeichenakademie in Hanau he attended the class taught by Alexander Zickendraht (1989–1991). After finishing as a state examined designer with a master craftsman's certificate, he studied at the Hochschule für Gestaltung in Pforzheim (1993–1998). His diploma project was supervised by Jens-Rüdiger Lorenzen and the silversmith Rudolf Bott.

Designer jewellery, made as one-off pieces and also viable as lines, is an important theme for Kay Eppi Nölke. In 1995 he convinced the jury with his *Sticking plaster rings* at the Kunst der Serie competition mounted by the German Jewellery and Silverware Industry to reward him with first prize for his »democratic jewellery«. A simple everyday act forms the jewellery product. Like the ring of twisted grasses, the *Sticking plaster ring* is shaped by its future wearer. A finger ring is formed by several layers of broad plasters. In 1998 he produced a collection of rings made of felt called *Vater, Mutter, Haus und Garten* [Father, Mother, House and Garden] with instructions for washing included. He came up with *Erinnern heißt auswählen* [To remember means to choose] in 2006: valuables and personal effects can be kept in little bags of polyethylene. They might include a shell from the beach, a stone from the mountain you conquered, a lock of your beloved's hair or a few grains of fine gold. Kai Eppi Nölke has also designed archaic-looking iron pots with lively surface texturing. Bowls called *...Aus dem Feuer nehmen...* [Take from the Fire...] are filled with between 200 g and a kilogram of melted-down silver. In the pendant version, the little vessels are one-off pieces of jewellery.

After many years in Pforzheim, Nölke, once a co-founder of the designer group called Juni, now lives in Konstanz. There he concentrates on his aims in design with the human being as his point of reference. »With each worn ring,« says Kay Eppi Nölke, »a new story is created – your story.«

1995	*Pflasterringe*, Edelstahl, Silber, Gold — *Sticking plaster rings*, stainless steel, silver, gold
1998	Anhänger ...*Aus dem Feuer nehmen...*, Eisen, Silber, Gold — Pendants ...*Take from the Fire...*, iron, silver, gold
2007	Broschen *Erinnern heißt auswählen*, Polyethylen, Foto, Karton, Edelstahl, Gold — Brooches *To remember means to choose*, polyethylene, photo, carton, stainless steel, gold

Kay Eppi Nölke
Geboren 1960 in Bielefeld.
1993–1998 Fachhochschule Pforzheim.
Atelier seit 1998, heute in Konstanz.

Kay Eppi Nölke
Born in Bielefeld in 1960.
1993–1998 Fachhochschule Pforzheim.
Studio since 1998, now in Constance.

2001   2004

Monika Seitter

Gekonnt schlägt Monika Seitter eine Brücke zwischen gediegener Goldschmiedekunst und aktueller Mode. Ihr Erfolgsrezept: ein Mix aus hochwertigen Edelsteinen, gefasst in Gold, mit farbigem Kunststoff. Seit der Jahrtausendwende bringt sie damit Farbe und Bewegung in die Auslagen von Juwelieren und in Galerien.

Monika Seitter stammt aus Pforzheim. In der Manufaktur ihrer Eltern erlebte sie die Fertigung von Medaillons zu einer Zeit, in der die Schmuckindustrie noch in voller Blüte stand. Dennoch fand sie den Goldschmiedeberuf zunächst wenig attraktiv. Nach dem Abitur arbeitete sie in einer Werbeagentur. Das Studium der Werbewirtschaft erschien konsequent. Bald merkte Monika Seitter jedoch, dass ihre Leidenschaft für Farben, Formen und für kreatives Machen dabei zu kurz kam. Kurz entschlossen entschied sie sich 1992, die Pforzheimer Goldschmiedeschule zu besuchen. Die ergänzende Praxisausbildung im Atelier Egon Frank endete 1995. Das Studium an der Fachhochschule Düsseldorf, das sie 2001 als Diplomdesignerin beendete, war entscheidend für ihren ungewöhnlichen Erfolg. »Die kreative Freiheit sowie die systematische Lehre der Produktentwicklung waren ideal«, sagt Monika Seitter, »um innovative Schmuckkonzepte zu entwickeln.« Bereits 2000 gründete die Designstudentin ihr eigenes Atelier.

Ihre Goldschmiedeausbildung befähigte Monika Seitter schon während des Studiums, handwerklich perfekte Schmuckstücke zu fertigen und sich an Wettbewerben und Ausstellungen zu beteiligen. Sie reichte Arbeiten ein zur Silbertriennale 1998, zum Deutschen Schmuck- und Edelsteinpreis 1999 oder zum Gestaltungswettbewerb Junges Handwerk NRW. Zahlreiche Ausstellungsbeteiligungen folgten. Im gleichen Jahr stellte sie ihre Kollektion innerhalb der Sonderschau Form 2001 auf der Tendence Frankfurt aus. 2002 nutzte Seitter auch das Design Podium auf der Inhorgenta in München. Im gleichen Jahr wurde ihr Ring *Sirius* mit dem red dot für hohe Designqualität ausgezeichnet. Bald erhielt sie auch erste Designaufträge von Gellner und Swarovski.

Künstlerisch und handwerklich ambitioniert, zudem noch mit einem Feeling für aktuelle Mode ausgestattet, hatte sie seit der Jahrtausendwende nach einem neuen Thema in der Schmuckgestaltung geforscht. Sie fand es mit ihrem *Schmucklabor*. Die Arbeiten sind farbenfroh und sinnlich anschmiegsam, wertvoll und zugleich unkonventionell. Für die Ringschienen oder Collierschnüre verwendet die Designerin farbig glänzenden, zumeist transparenten Kunststoff. Dadurch entsteht eine variable Farbigkeit in ihrem Schmuck. So konnte eine attraktive Preisklasse entstehen, die sich in einem neuen Segment zwischen hochkarätigen Juwelen und Modeschmuck ansiedelte. Das *Schmucklabor* und die darauf folgenden Schmucklinien wie *Haute Couture* oder *Kronjuwelen* entsprechen aber auch einer Grundidee der Schmuckavantgarde der Gegenwart, nämlich der Erweiterung des Schmuckbegriffs durch den Mix unkonventioneller mit traditionellen Materialien.

2002

2001   *Schmucklabor*-Ringe *Maui* und *Sora*, Gold, Farbedelsteine, Kunststoff — *Jewellery laboratory* rings *Maui* and *Sora*, gold, coloured precious stones, plastic

2002   *Schmucklabor* Ringe und Anhänger *XL* und *Onuris*, Silber, farbige Synthesen, Kunststoff — *Jewellery laboratory* rings and pendants *XL* and *Onuris*, silver, coloured syntheses, plastic

2004   *Haute Couture* Ringe *Fumiko*, Edelstahl, Farbedelsteine, Leder, Fell — *Haute Couture* rings *Fumiko*, stainless steel, coloured precious stones, leather, fur

2006   *Nuggets* Ringe *Nugget Rama*, Farbedelsteine *Concave* Cut, Gold — *Nuggets* rings *Nugget Rama*, coloured precious stones *Concave* Cut, gold

2008   *Marbles* Ringe *Solitairblüte*, Gold, Brillanten, mineralischer Kunststoff — *Marbles* rings *Solitaire bloom*, gold, diamonds, mineral plastic

2006

2008

»Daraus resultiert ein Spannungsverhältnis«, erklärt Monika Seitter, »das die Menschen regelrecht anzieht.« Im Atelier der Designerin wird hochkarätiges Gold und wertvolle Farbedelsteine in aufwendiger Handarbeit mit farbigem Kunststoff kombiniert. Damit wird für die Schmuckträgerin eine Brücke hergestellt zwischen Tradition und Gegenwart.

2008 hat Monika Seitter ihre Kollektion um ein neues Thema erweitert. Diesmal verbindet sie einen für die Schmuckbranche innovativen mineralischen Kunststoff mit hochwertigen Edelsteinen. In der Ringserie *Marbles* erlauben Härte und Widerstandsfähigkeit des verwendeten Materials neuartige Formen von Ringen und Armreifen. Die Leichtigkeit des Schmuck-Designs von Monika Seitter geht in eine neue Phase.

E — Monika Seitter adroitly bridges the gap between elegant goldsmithing and trendy fashion. The recipe for her success: a mix of top-quality precious stones set in gold and coloured plastic. Since the turn of the millennium, she has been bringing colour and movement to jewellers' shop windows and galleries with her work.

Monika Seitter comes from Pforzheim. At her parents' factory she experienced medallions being made at the time when the jewellery industry was still flourishing. Nevertheless, she at first found goldsmithing not all that appealing as a profession, so she worked for an advertising agency after taking her university entrance qualification exams. Studying advertising seemed the consistent thing to do next. However Monika Seitter soon realised that it gave too little scope to her passion for colours, forms and creative work. Without further ado, she decided in 1992 to attend the Pforzheim Goldschmiedeschule. She completed her supplementary on-the-job training at the Egon Frank studio in 1995. Studying at the Fachhochschule Düsseldorf, from which she graduated with a degree in design in 2001, was crucial to her exceptional success. »The creative freedom as well as the systematic teaching in product development were ideal,« says Monika Seitter, »for developing innovative jewellery concepts.« By 2000 she founded a studio of her own while still a student.

Her training as a goldsmith enabled Monika Seitter to make perfectly hand-crafted pieces of jewellery and to show them at competitions and exhibitions during her studies. She submitted works to the Silbertriennale 1998, for the Deutscher Schmuck- und Edelsteinpreis 1999 and the design competition Junges Handwerk NRW. Those entries were followed by pieces exhibited at numerous exhibitions. The year she graduated, she showed her collection at the special show Form 2001 at Tendence in Frankfurt. In 2002 Seitter also took advantage of the Design Podium at the Munich Inhorgenta. That year her ring *Sirius* was awarded the red dot for top-quality design. It was not long before she had her first design commissions from Gellner and Swarovski.

Ambitious in both art and crafts and also gifted with a feel for current fashion trends, she has been exploring a new theme in jewellery design since the turn of the millennium. She found it with *Schmucklabor* [Jewellery laboratory]. The pieces that have come out of this undertaking are colourful and sensuously supple, at once valuable and unconventional. The designer uses glossy, usually transparent, plastic in bright colours for her ring shanks and necklace cords to create colour diversity in her jewellery. Thus she has created an attractive price bracket which occupies a new niche market between high-carat jewels and costume jewellery. *Jewellery laboratory* and the lines that followed it, including *Haute Couture* and *Kronjuwelen* [Crown jewels] also tally with an idea basic to the contemporary jewellery avant-garde: enlarging the concept of jewellery by mixing unconventional with traditional materials. »A tension results from that,« explains Monika Seitter, »which really draws people.« In the designer's studio high-carat gold and valuable coloured precious stones are combined with coloured plastic in a complex hand-crafting process. With it, the wearer of this jewellery has been given a bridge between tradition and present.

In 2008 Monika Seitter has enlarged her collection to include a new theme. This time she has innovatively linked a mineral plastic compound that is new to jewellery with top-quality precious stones. For her *Marbles* line in rings, she exploits the hardness and durability of the material used to create rings and bangles in new forms. The lightness that is the distinguishing feature of jewellery designed by Monika Seitter has entered a new phase.

Monika Seitter
Geboren 1970 in Pforzheim.
1995–2001 Fachhochschule Düsseldorf.
Ateliergründung 2000 in Düsseldorf.

Monika Seitter
Born in Pforzheim in 1970.
1995–2001 Fachhochschule Düsseldorf.
Founded studio in Düsseldorf in 2000.

2001

2004

2006

Dorothea Brill, Juni

Die Gruppe Juni wurde von fünf Absolventen der Fachhochschule Pforzheim 2001 gegründet. Zu Juni gehören neben Dorothea Brill die Schmuck-Designer Claudia Geiger, Udo Jung, Patrick Malotki und Oliver Schmidt. Sie treten mit einem gemeinsamen Marketingkonzept auf, wobei jeder Gestalter seine individuelle gestalterische Handschrift pflegt. Das Corporate Design der Gruppe erhielt 2003 den red dot award.

Mit dem Blick für das Wesentliche gestaltet die Designerin Dorothea Brill, geboren 1968 in Freiburg, Schmuck in kleinen Serien. Auf die humorvolle Note verweisen Kollektionsnamen wie *meter-weise*, *Propeller* oder *Dachterrasse mit Sonne*. *meter-weise* ist ein Halsschmuck aus endlos aneinander gereihten Ösen-Schlingen, besetzt mit Brillanten. Der goldene *Propeller*-Ring suggeriert Bewegung, schwungvoll ausgedrückt durch zwei kreisförmige Blätter. Gutes Wetter verspricht dagegen die Ringserie *Dachterrasse mit Sonne*. Es sind Kunststoffringe, die mit Zwirn in vielen Farben vernäht sind. Gestalten und Experimentieren liegen bei Dorothea Brill eng beieinander. Während des gestalterischen Prozesses macht sie oft eine ganz neue Entdeckung. Jede Schmuckreihe ist eine abgeschlossene Geschichte, überraschend und im Ergebnis raffiniert.

Dorothea Brill besuchte von 1988 bis 1991 das Berufskolleg für Formgebung, Schmuck und Gerät in Schwäbisch Gmünd. Bis 1994 war sie freischaffend für namhafte Münchner Goldschmiede wie Barbara Seidenaht und Marie-Eugenie Hinrichs tätig. Die wichtigste Station aber war 1993 die Tätigkeit im Atelierhaus von Hermann Jünger. Ihr Schmuckdesignstudium an der Hochschule Pforzheim beendete sie 1999 und war anschließend als Assistentin im Fachbereich Kunst- und Designwissenschaften tätig. Gezielt sprach sie einige Kollegen bereits während des Studiums an, um die Gruppe Juni zu gründen. So begann »ein großes und nicht immer einfaches Abenteuer«, gesteht sie heute. Dorothea Brill lebt seit 2005 in Berlin und ist von dort aus für Juni in Pforzheim tätig. »Es kommt auf das sensibel ausbalancierte Verhältnis zahlreicher Komponenten an, dann springt der Funke einer Idee über«, erklärt die Schmuck-Designerin ihre Arbeitsweise. Edelmetallen gibt sie den Vorzug. Sie schätzt die freie Kunst mit ihrer zweckfreien Ausrichtung und lässt sich davon gerne inspirieren. Ihre *Dachterrassen*-Ringserie wurde 2003 in die Sammlung des Schmuckmuseums Pforzheim aufgenommen.

E — The Juni group was founded by five graduates of Fachhochschule Pforzheim in 2001. Its members are, apart from Dorothea Brill, the jewellery designers Claudia Geiger, Udo Jung, Patrick Malotki and Oliver Schmidt. They represent a collective marketing concept, with each designer featuring his or her individual signature. The group received a red dot award in 2003 for their corporate design.

As a designer, Dorothea Brill, who was born in Freiburg in 1968, creates jewellery in limited editions. Collection names such as *meter-weise*

[metre wise], *Propeller* and *Dachterrasse mit Sonne* [Roof terrace with Sun] indicate a tongue-in-cheek approach. *metre wise* is neck jewellery consisting of endless loops created by lugs in paratactic arrangement and set with diamonds. *Propeller*, a gold ring, is evocative of motion, expressed with verve by two round propeller blades. Good weather is promised by the line in rings called *Roof terrace with Sun*. These are plastic rings sewn together with thick thread in many colours. Designing and experimenting are two sides of the same coin as Dorothea Brill sees it. During the designing process, she often discovers something entirely new. Each line in jewellery is a story in itself, surprising and sophisticated.

Dorothea Brill attended the Berufskolleg Formgebung, Schmuck und Gerät in Schwäbisch Gmünd (1988–1991). Until 1994 she freelanced for reputable Munich goldsmiths, including Barbara Seidenaht and Marie-Eugenie Hinrichs. Her most important stop on the way to an independent career was, however, a stint in 1993 in Hermann Jünger's home studio. After finishing her studies at the Hochschule Pforzheim in 1999, Brill became an assistant in the Art and Design Department there. While still a student, she had approached several of her fellow students with the idea of founding the Juni group. Thus began »a great adventure that was not always easy,« she admits today. Dorothea Brill has lived since 2005 in Berlin and works from there for Juni in Pforzheim. »What counts is a well-balanced relationship between numerous components: then the spark of an idea lights a fire,« is how the jewellery designer explains her approach to her work. The noble metals are her materials of choice. She appreciates the non-utilitarian orientation of the fine arts and is only too happy to draw inspiration from them. Her *Roof terrace* line in rings was acquired by the Schmuckmuseum Pforzheim for its collection in 2003.

2001	*Nähringe Dach-Terrasse mit Sonne*, Kunststoff, Perlseide — *Sew rings, Roof terrace with Sun*, plastic, silk bead cord
2004	Halsschmuck *meter-weise*, Gold, Brillanten — Necklace *metre wise*, gold, diamonds
2006	*Propeller* Ringe, Gold, Brillant — *Propeller* rings, gold, diamond

Dorothea Brill
Geboren 1968 in Freiburg. 1994–1999 Fachhochschule Pforzheim. Mitglied der Gruppe Juni 2001.

Dorothea Brill
Born in Freiburg in 1968. 1994–1999 Fachhochschule Pforzheim. Member of the Juni group since 2001.

2000   2003

Claudia Geiger, Juni

Claudia Geiger bereichert die Kollektion der Gruppe Juni mit ihren leichten und flexiblen *Mol*-Ketten aus Zuchtperlen und Schmucksteinen. In der Wiederholung und Kombination einfacher Elemente entstehen komplexe Strukturen von hohem sinnlichem Reiz.

1968 in Freiburg im Breisgau geboren, lernte Claudia Geiger in ihrer Geburtsstadt von 1988 bis 1992 das Goldschmiedehandwerk. In den Ateliers von Uwe Berger, Radolfzell, und Beatrice Rossi, Konstanz (heute Zürich), vertiefte sie ihre Berufserfahrungen. Anschließend studierte sie Französisch an der Université de Franche-Comté in Besançon. Um auch in Frankreich arbeiten zu dürfen, legte Claudia Geiger die Goldschmiedeprüfung noch einmal in französischer Sprache ab. Im Atelier Francis Ficht und bei ihrem Studium an der École des Arts Décoratifs de Strasbourg entwickelte sie ihre eigenen Schmuckkonzepte. Bereits hier begann ihre Arbeit mit Perlen, eingewebt in runde Kokons.

Im Atelier von Michael Zobel in Konstanz setzte sich Claudia Geiger ab 1993 intensiv mit außergewöhnlichen Techniken der Metallverarbeitung im Schmuck auseinander. Während der dreijährigen Tätigkeit in dem renommierten Atelier verstärkte sich ihr Wunsch, eigenen Ideen mehr Raum zu geben. Die künstlerische Auseinandersetzung fand während ihres Schmuckstudiums in Pforzheim von 1993 bis 2000 statt. Gefördert mit dem Leonardo da Vinci-Stipendium, absolvierte die Studentin 1998 ein Praxissemester bei der Schmuckkünstlerin Sophie Hanagarth in Paris.

Claudia Geigers zentrales Thema ist seit 1998 die Schmuckgestaltung mit Perlen. Dabei hat sie ein System ersonnen, das Perlen nicht nur aneinander reiht. Vielmehr verteilt sie Zuchtperlen zusammen mit schwarzen Diamanten oder facettierten Edelsteinen unregelmäßig auf flexible, dünne Seile. Die Dehnbarkeit des Materials macht es möglich, dass das Geflecht als Halsschmuck oder als Armschmuck zu tragen ist. Ihr patentierter Schmuck ist in der langen Geschichte der Perle ein ganz neuer Aspekt. Die *Mol*-Ketten, wie Claudia Geiger sie entsprechend der Anordnung von Molekülen auf einem DNA-Strang nennt, sind mal luftig, mal dichter konzipiert. Die jüngste Halsschmuckkreation heißt *Ling*. Hier reihen sich gleiche Paillettenpaare, gefertigt aus recyclebaren Kunststoff-Folien, dicht an dicht, ergänzt durch einzelne Goldpailletten. *Ling* erinnert an flatternde Schmetterlingsflügel, die durch ein dünnes goldenes Seil miteinander verbunden sind.

E — Claudia Geiger enriches the Juni group mix with her light, flexible *Mol*-Ketten [Mole chains] made of cultured pearls and gemstones. Complex structures that are appealingly sensuous are created by the repetition and combination of simple elements.

Born in Freiburg in Breisgau in 1968, Claudia Geiger learned goldsmithing in the city of her birth between 1988 and 1992. She deepened her professional experience by interning in the studios of Uwe Berger (Radolfzell) and Beatrice Rossi (then in Constance, now in Zurich). After that she studied French at the Université de Franche-Comté in Besançon. To be able to work in France as well as Germany, Claudia Geiger resat the examinations qualifying for goldsmith status in French. At the Atelier Francis Ficht and during her studies at the École des Arts Décoratifs de Strasbourg, she developed her own ideas of what jewellery should be. Even back then she worked with pearls enmeshed in round cocoons.

From 1993 Claudia Geiger investigated in depth unusual metalworking techniques in jewellery-making at Michael Zobel's studio in Konstanz. During her three years at that renowned studio, she began to feel the need for more scope for her own ideas. Her personal exploration of aesthetics took place while she was studying jewellery-making in Pforzheim between 1993 and 2000. Supported by a Leonardo da Vinci grant, Claudia Geiger spent an internship semester in 1998 as part of her course of study with the artist in jewellery Sophie Hanagarth in Paris.

Claudia Geiger's main theme since 1998 has been designing jewellery with pearls. She has worked out a system that is not simply paratactic. Instead of stringing her pearls in a line, she clusters cultured pearls along with black diamonds or other faceted precious stones irregularly about on thin, flexible cable. The elasticity of the material makes it possible to wear these clusters as neck or arm jewellery. Her patented jewellery represents an entirely new take on the pearl, which looks back on such a long history. Some of these *Mol* chains, as Claudia Geiger calls them because they resemble the arrangement of molecules on a strand of DNA, are airy in conception while others are more densely structured. Her most recent neck jewellery creation is called *Ling*. Here identical pairs of sequins made of recyclable plastic foil are strung very close together, interspersed with gold sequins. *Ling* resembles fluttering butterfly wings linked together by a thin gold cord.

2000	Halsschmuck *Goldwirbel* und *Eisenwirbel*, Gold, Eisen — Necklaces *Gold cluster* and *Iron cluster,* gold, iron
2003	*Mol* flexibler Halsschmuck, Beryll, Edelstahldraht — *Mol* flexible necklace, beryl, stainless steel wire

Claudia Geiger
Geboren 1968 in Freiburg, 1993–2000
Fachhochschule Pforzheim. Mitglied der Gruppe
Juni 2001.

Claudia Geiger
Born in Freiburg in 1968, 1993–2000
Fachhochschule Pforzheim. Member of the Juni
group since 2001.

2003   2004   2004

Udo Jung, Juni

Udo Jung verbindet in seinem Schmuck die klassischen Goldschmiedetechniken mit einem zeitgemäßen Design. Sein hohes handwerkliches Können setzt er hauptsächlich in Ringkollektionen ein. Der Gestalter betrachtet
Schmuck als Resultat eines kulturellen Zusammenspiels, gleichwertig mit
anderen Kulturgütern, die anspruchsvolle Menschen umgeben.

Seine Ausbildung und die anschließende Goldschmiedetätigkeit absolvierte der 1961 in Essen geborene Schmuckdesigner bei Traditionsjuwe-
lieren in Düsseldorf. Udo Jung sieht diese Zeit als wichtigen Schritt für seine
weitere Entwicklung. In ausgesuchten Werkstätten für Gold- und Juwelenschmuck erlernte er das Goldschmiedehandwerk mit allen Techniken und
Feinheiten. Den Besuch der Meisterschule an der Zeichenakademie Hanau
von 1983 bis 1985 versteht er als einen Brückenschlag zwischen dem Goldschmiedehandwerk und den Grundlagen der Schmuckgestaltung. Fünf Jahre später begann er das Studium für Schmuck und Gerät an der Hochschule
Pforzheim. Bevor er gemeinsam mit seinen Kollegen die Gruppe Juni aus der
Taufe hob, arbeitete er als freier Schmuck-Designer.

Aus seinen Studienprojekten und den vielseitigen Themen der Kunst
leitete Udo Jung die Idee zu den *Drehringen* ab. Sie sind sein Kollektions-
schwerpunkt und gelten mittlerweile als Klassiker bei Juni. Es war die Auseinandersetzung mit dem Thema Zeit, die ihn zu diesem Schmuckkonzept
inspirierte. Der *Drehring* ist mehr als nur ein schmückendes Element. Er
bezeichnet den Moment des Innehaltens und kurzen Verweilens. Die zwei
Ringhälften lassen sich gegeneinander drehen, so dass ein sich verjüngen-
der oder breit laufender Ring entsteht. Die reduzierte Form wird durch quer
laufende schmale Gold- und Brillantbänder und einzelne Brillanten ergänzt.
Charakteristisches Formmerkmal ist die leicht konisch verlaufende Kontur.
Formaddition, die sich reduziert ausdrückt, das schwingt auch im *Mandarin*
Ring mit. Wiederum spielt der Designer mit zwei Elementen, die ein Ganzes
ergeben. Wie die Scheiben einer Frucht, so liegen die beiden Ringe aneinander. Die Zweifarbigkeit, Gelbgold und Weißgold oder wahlweise Edelstahl,
unterstreicht die Form. Den Drehmechanismus hat Udo Jung über Jahre hinweg entwickelt und optimiert. Der *Drehring* der Juni-Kollektion mit dieser
speziellen Finesse blieb im modernen Schmuckdesign bislang einmalig.

E — Udo Jung's jewellery unites classic goldsmithing techniques with
contemporary design. He lavishes his consummate craftsmanship mainly on
ring collections. This is a designer who views jewellery as the outcome of
cultural interaction, something that is on an equal footing with the other cultural artefacts with which discerning people surround themselves.

Born in Essen in 1961, the jewellery designer did his goldsmiths' training and the subsequent internships with traditional jewellers in Düsseldorf.
In retrospect, Udo Jung views those internships as an important step towards further development. He learned the craft of goldsmithing with all its

techniques and refinements at distinguished workshops specialising in gold
jewellery set with gems. He sees his time in the master classes at Zeichenakademie Hanau (1983–1985) as bridging the gap between craftsmanship in
goldsmithing and learning the fundamentals of jewellery design. Five years
later he began to study jewellery-making and tableware at the Hochschule
Pforzheim. Before he joined colleagues to found the Juni group, he freelanced as a jewellery designer.

Drawing on projects he had engaged in as a student and the vast the-
matic pool in the fine arts, Udo Jung came up with the idea of *Drehringe*
[Rotation rings]. They represent a focal point of his collection and by now
are regarded at Juni as classics. It was his investigation of the time theme
that inspired this jewellery concept. A *Rotation ring* is more than just an element of adornment. It signifies the aspect of pausing to reflect and brief-
ly linger. The two halves of the ring can be revolved in opposing directions
to create a tapering or flaring shank. The reduced form is complemented
by narrow perpendicular bands of gold and diamonds as well as solitaire
diamonds. A characteristic formal feature is the slightly conical contour. A
paratactic approach to form that is expressed in reduction also informs the
Mandarin Ring [Mandarin ring]. Here, on the other hand, the designer is
playing with two elements that form a whole. Two rings fit closely together
like the segments of a citrus fruit. The use of two colours, yellow and white
gold or, if desired, stainless steel, underscores the form. Udo Jung has taken
years to develop and optimise the rotation mechanism. The *Rotation ring* in
the Juni collection featuring this sophisticated touch has remained without
parallels in modern jewellery design.

2003	*Mandarin* Ring, Gold, Eisen — *Mandarin* ring, gold, iron
2004	*Drehringe*, Edelstahl PVD beschichtet, Diamanten — *Rotation rings*, stainless steel PVD coated, diamonds
2004	*Drehringe*, Gold, Edelstahl — *Rotation rings*, gold, stainless steel

Udo Jung
Geboren 1961 in Essen. Fachhochschule Pforzheim
1990–1995. Atelier seit 1996. Mitglied der Gruppe
Juni 2001.

Udo Jung
Born in Essen in 1961. Fachhochschule Pforzheim
1990–1995. Studio since 1996. Member of the
Juni group since 2001.

2002

2002

2004

Patrick Malotki, Juni

Mit dem *Tautropfenring* ist Patrick Malotki eine Persiflage auf seine amerikanische Heimat gelungen. Denn nach amerikanischer Tradition besteht ein Verlobungsring der Frau aus einem möglichst großen Edelsteinsolitär. Für seine puristischen, technisch raffinierten Ringserien wie *Gemini* oder *Ur-Sprung* konstruiert der Schmuck-Designer die Werkzeuge nach Möglichkeit selbst. Patrick Malotki ist in San Diego, Kalifornien, geboren und in Arizona aufgewachsen. Er absolvierte die Northern Arizona University, die er mit dem Bachelor of Fine Arts abschloss. Die Hochschule Pforzheim besuchte er zuerst als Gast, um dann von 1998 bis 2002 im Studiengang Schmuck und Gerät zu studieren. Studienarbeiten bei dem Pforzheimer Schmuckdesigner Norbert Mürrle gaben Patrick Malotki wichtige Impulse. Er ist von Beginn an bei Juni. Daneben ist er heute auch für andere Schmuck- und Uhrenhersteller als Designer tätig.

Eine der ersten wichtigen Arbeiten von Patrick Malotki war der *Tautropfenring*, ein klar gestalteter Kunststoffring, der einen Brillantsolitär umhüllt. Nach vielen Versuchen gelang es ihm, den Brillanten exakt in den bruchsicheren und UV-stabilen Kunststoff einzubetten. Der Edelstein wirkt dadurch überraschend größer. Der Effekt ist auf die guten optischen Eigenschaften des Kunststoffs zurückzuführen. Aus der Beobachtung von gerissenem Eisen entstand die Ringserie *Ur-Sprung*. In Edelstahl sowie in Gelb- oder Weißgold zählen die Ringe mit dem Materialbruch zu seinen begehrtesten Stücken. Inzwischen hat Malotki den *Ur-Sprung*-Ring programmatisch weiterentwickelt. Der Riss ist nicht mehr dem Zufall überlassen. Zwischen seinen spröden Kanten können Brillanten oder Goldnuggets zarte Akzente setzen. Die Trauringvariationen *Herz*, *Bogen* und *Acht* spiegeln den Gedanken der Gemeinsamkeit in einer Partnerschaft wider. Das Trauringpaar bildet eine Einheit, wenn es zusammengelegt oder gesteckt wird. Mit der Ringserie *Gemini* verfolgt Patrick Malotki ein ähnliches Konzept. Hier werden allerdings zwei Ringhälften wie die Teile eines Puzzles ineinander geschoben und ergeben dann ein Ganzes. Die zwillingsgleichen Teile bestechen durch ihre präzise Form. Durch unterschiedliche Materialkombinationen wie Edelstahl, schwarz keramisch beschichtet, mit Gold entstehen markante zeichenhafte Wirkungen mit Symbolkraft. Als Partner-Ringe können die *Gemini*-Ringe auch mit Diamanten akzentuiert werden.

E — With the *Tautropfenring* [Dewdrop ring], Patrick Malotki has succeeded in parodying his country of birth, the US. After all, American tradition calls for engagement rings for brides featuring the biggest gemstone solitaire their fiancés can afford. The jewellery designer constructs his own tools as far as possible to make such purist, technically sophisticated lines in rings as *Gemini* and *Ur-Sprung* [Crackle]. Born in San Diego, California, Patrick Malotki grew up in Arizona. After graduating from Northern Arizona University with a BA in Fine Arts, he audited courses at the Hoch-

schule Pforzheim before matriculating there to study jewellery-making and tableware from 1998 to 2002. Student projects he did with the Pforzheim jewellery designer Norbert Mürrle were important sources of inspiration for Patrick Malotki. A co-founder of Juni, he has remained with the group. Today he also works on the side as a designer for other jewellery-makers and watchmakers.

One of Patrick Malotki's most important works has been the *Tautropfenring* [Dewdrop ring], an astringently designed plastic ring surrounding a diamond solitaire. After a protracted period of trial and error, he succeeded in precisely embedding a diamond in plastic which is unbreakable and unaffected by UV radiation. Embedding the precious stone makes it look surprisingly bigger. The effect is due to the good optical properties of the plastic. The *Ur-Sprung* [Crackle] line in rings developed out of observing fissured iron. Made in stainless steel as well as yellow or white gold, these rings featuring a crack in the material are among Patrick Malotki's hottest designs. In the meantime Malotki has systematically developed the *Crackle* line. The fissure is no longer left up to chance. Diamonds or nuggets of gold clamped between its rough edges add an exquisitely delicate touch.

Herz [Heart], *Bogen* [Bow] and *Acht* [Eight] are variations on wedding bands that reflect the idea of togetherness in partnerships. The pair of wedding bands forms a whole when juxtaposed or worn. In the *Gemini* line, Patrick Malotki pursues a similar concept. Here, however, two halves of a single ring interlock like pieces of a puzzle to form a whole. The twin pieces are strikingly clear-cut in form. Memorable sign-like effects with symbolic power are created by the use of various combinations of materials, including stainless steel with a black ceramic coating combined with gold. As partnership rings, *Gemini* can also be enhanced with diamonds.

2002	Ring *Tautropfen*, Kunststoff, Brillant — *Dewdrop* ring, plastic, diamond
2002	*Herz* Trauringe, Gold — *Heart* wedding rings, gold
2004	Ring *Ur-Sprung*, Edelstahl keramisch beschichtet, Diamant — Ring *Crackle*, stainless steel ceramic coated, diamond

Patrick Malotki
Geboren 1974 in San Diego. Hochschule Pforzheim 1998–2002. Mitglied der Gruppe Juni 2001.

Patrick Malotki
Born in San Diego in 1974. Hochschule Pforzheim 1998–2002. Member of the Juni group since 2001.

Patrick Malotki, Juni

2003   2004   2005

Oliver Schmidt, Juni

Die Schmuckideen von Oliver Schmidt entstehen im gestalterischen Prozess und beim Erforschen neuer Wege. Nichts soll verdeckt, nichts verziert werden; Klarheit und Präzision sind wesentlich. »Im Verformungsprozess und beim Bewegen von Metall gibt es einen Punkt, der die Richtung vorgibt. Da muss man weitermachen.« Das ist sein Credo.

Geboren in Wasserburg am Bodensee lernte Oliver Schmidt von 1992 bis 1995 bei Maile Andreas in Konstanz das Goldschmiedehandwerk. Von 1996 bis 1998 vertiefte er in einem zweijährigen Gaststudium für Schmuck und Gerät an der Hochschule Pforzheim sein Wissen. Hier traf er den Gold- und Silberschmied Rudolf Bott, einen Schüler von Hermann Jünger, den er heute als wichtigen Wegbegleiter nennt. In gemeinsamen Projektarbeiten entstand neben Tafelsilber auch sakrales Gerät. Weitere Erfahrungen im Silberschmieden machte Schmidt bei einem Workshop mit Wilfried Moll, Hamburg. Die intensive Arbeit des Biegens und Verformens von Metall gab Oliver Schmidt viele Anregungen für seine Schmuckentwicklungen. 1999 machte er sich als Schmuck- und Gerätedesigner selbstständig. Mit der Gründung der Gruppe Juni 2001 eröffnete sich für ihn ein neuer Weg. Gemeinsam plante er mit seinen Mitstreitern die ersten Ausstellungen, die Zusammenstellung der Schmuckkollektionen, und er entwickelte seine eigenen Konzepte weiter. 2002 gewann Schmidt den Schoonhoven Silver Award. 2005 wurden seine Arbeiten im Museum of Arts and Crafts in Itami, Japan, gezeigt.

Große Resonanz fanden die *Knotenringe* von Oliver Schmidt, die er zunächst in Eisen herstellte. Ein schmales Metallband mündet in einen festgezogenen Seemannsknoten, der das Schmuckelement des Ringes bildet. Der tradierte Knoten wirkt modern, überzeugend und klar. Oliver Schmidts Umgang mit Metall ist meisterhaft. Gezielt setzt er die Techniken des Schmiedens und Walzens in der Schmuckfertigung ein. Die zart anmutenden Stücke mit ihren fließenden Konturen bergen noch die Spuren der Materialverformung. Fingerringe und Armspangen schmiedet er aus einem offenen Band. Aus den Ideen zu Ringen, Arm- und Ohrschmuck entstehen Serien. Gerne integriert er technische Details unauffällig in die Schmuckformen. Alle Stücke sind spannungsreich und gleichzeitig geschmeidig. Von der Natur inspiriert sind seine Ohr- und Armschmuckserien *Libellen*, *Blätter* oder *Schlaufen*, die an Tropfen erinnern. In seiner Werkstatt entstehen aber immer noch Gefäße und Bestecke mit den für seine Arbeitstechnik charakteristischen Metalloberflächen.

E — Oliver Schmidt's ideas for jewellery emerge from the process of designing and exploring new approaches. Nothing is to be hidden; nothing is to be decorated: clarity and precision are essential. »In every process of forming and in moving metal, there is a point which gives the direction. You have to keep going from there.« That is his artistic creed. Born in Wasserburg on Lake Constance, Oliver Schmidt trained in goldsmithing from 1992 until

1995 with Maile Andreas in Constance. Between 1996 and 1998, he deepened his knowledge and skills by auditing courses in jewellery and tableware for two years at the Hochschule Pforzheim. There he met the goldsmith and silversmith Rudolf Bott (who had studied under Hermann Jünger), whom Oliver Schmidt today calls his most important mentor. Table silver as well as liturgical vessels were created in joint projects with Bott. Schmidt had other important experiences in silversmithing at a workshop with Wilfried Moll in Hamburg. The intensive work of bending and forming metal has given Oliver Schmidt many fresh ideas for developing his jewellery. In 1999 he became self-employed as a jewellery and tableware designer. Co-founding the Juni group in 2001 opened up a new career for Schmidt. With fellow Juni members, Schmidt planned their first group shows and organised the jewellery collections while continuing to develop his own concepts. In 2002 Schmidt won a Schoonhoven Silver Award. In 2005 works of his were shown at the Museum of Arts and Crafts in Itami, Japan.

Oliver Schmidt's *Knotenringe* [Knot rings], which he first made of iron, have been widely acclaimed. A narrow metal band ends in a drawn seaman's knot. The traditional nautical knots look convincingly modern and well-defined. Oliver Schmidt handles metal with consummate mastery. He uses the techniques of forging and rolling in making his jewellery. The delicate-looking pieces with their fluid contours still reveal traces of how the material has been worked. Oliver Schmidt forges rings and bangles from flat strip metal. He develops a line in jewellery out of individual ideas for rings and arm and ear jewellery. He likes to integrate technical details unobtrusively in his jewellery forms. All his pieces are excitingly taut yet supple. The lines in ear and arm jewellery he calls *Libellen* [Dragonflies], *Blätter* [Leaves] and *Schlaufen* [Loops], which look like drops, are inspired by nature. Nevertheless, he still produces vessels and cutlery in his workshop that also feature the texturing characteristic of the techniques with which he works.

2003	*Knotenringe*, Eisen, Gold — *Knot rings*, iron, gold	
2004	Ringe *Herzapfel*, Gold — Rings *Heart apple*, gold	
2005	*Pagodenring Tiger*, Bronze — *Pagoda ring Tiger*, bronze	

Oliver Schmidt
Geboren 1970 in Wasserburg am Bodensee.
1996–1998 Gaststudium an der Fachhochschule Pforzheim. Atelier seit 1999.

Oliver Schmidt
Born in Wasserburg on Lake Constance in 1970.
1996–1998 audited courses at Fachhochschule Pforzheim. Studio since 1999.

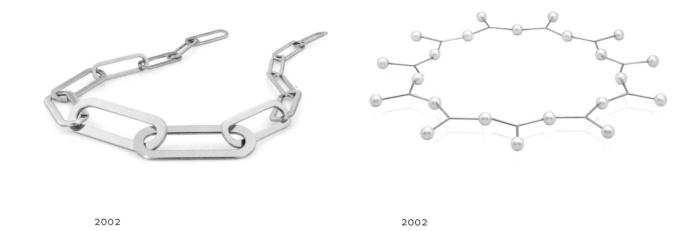

2002   2002

Biegel

In dem Konzept Bodysign realisiert Marc-Jens Biegel seit 2002 Schmuckentwürfe international renommierter Produktdesigner. Allen Arbeiten liegt eine einfache, doch geistreiche Gestaltungsidee zugrunde. Sie regt an zur gedanklichen Reflexion, zur Meditation und wird dadurch zur »precious simplicity«, zur kostbaren Einfachheit. Das Konzept zeigt, wie nahe sich heute modernes Produkt- und bestes Schmuck-Design stehen.

Während der Goldschmiedelehre von 1988 bis 1992 bei seinem Vater Werner Biegel besuchte Marc-Jens Biegel die Berufsschule an der Zeichenakademie Hanau. Von 1992 bis 1997 studierte er Produkt-Design an der HfG in Offenbach und in London. »In Offenbach lernte ich, wie das Produkt mit dem Menschen kommuniziert«, berichtet Biegel. Er konzipierte in seinem Studium u.a. Liegen, Uhren mit neuen Anzeige-Systemen sowie Ausstellungs- und Displaysysteme für Museen. Seine Diplomarbeit, ein Schmuckstück, wurde jedoch zu einem Politikum. »An deutschen Hochschulen für Produkt- oder Industriedesign erwartet man die altengerechte Küche, das behindertengerechte, öffentliche Verkehrsmittel«, erklärt er. Schmuck hingegen hafte das Vorurteil an, zu stark im Bereich des Hedonismus angesiedelt zu sein. Die Auseinandersetzung an der HfG Offenbach, die sich in der Tradition der Ulmer Schule sieht, regte ihn jedoch an zu den Fragen: »Warum wird Schmuck-Design nicht die gleiche öffentliche Wertschätzung zuteil wie Möbel-Design? Warum schmückt sich der Mensch überhaupt, und wie könnte Schmuck für unsere Zeit aussehen?«

Nach dem Studium trat Biegel 1997 in das elterliche Schmuckgeschäft ein, das 1964 in Frankfurt gegründet worden war. 2002 startete er das Projekt Bodysign mit den drei Produktdesignern Axel Kufus, Uwe Fischer und Konstantin Grcic. Als Gründungsmitglied von »Ginbande« hat Uwe Fischer das Neue Deutsche Design mitgeprägt. Die Produkte von Axel Kufus wurden in internationalen Museen wie dem Centre Pompidou gezeigt. Konstantin Grcic, München, gilt als Wegbereiter des Neokonstruktivismus und gehört seit 1991 zu den Stars der internationalen Designszene. Für das Projekt Bodysign sollte jeder eine Schmuckgarnitur, bestehend aus Ring, Hals-, Arm- und Ohrschmuck, entwerfen. Bei ihrer Recherche stellten die Industrie-Designer u.a. fest, dass heute nicht selten Begriffe wie »Facet«, »Diamond« oder »Crystal« verwendet werden, um Alltagsprodukte aufzuwerten. Ein Hinweis etwa für die Sehnsucht nach Kostbarem, die nur noch in der Illusion falscher Produktversprechen existiert?

Der Entwurf Gran Prix von Konstantin Grcic beinhaltet eine Neuinterpretation der klassischen Gliederkette. Dazu erklärt Biegel: »Bevor Grcic am Royal College in London studierte, hat er Möbelschreiner gelernt. Seine Erfahrung mit so genannten Langloch-Verbindungen setzte er in der schlichten Kette um.« Beim Tragen entsteht eine überraschende Dreidimensionalität. Von Uwe Fischer stammt das Schmuckset Molecular. Es versinnbildlicht einen DNA-Strang. Die Symbolik aus der Genforschung wirkt gleichzeitig als Funktionskonzept. Die anschmiegsame Kette liegt perfekt auf dem Körper. Der Entwurf von Axel Kufus wird in Feingold mit Hilfe traditioneller Schmiedetechnik umgesetzt. Er erzielt seine Wirkung durch die symbolträchtige Form der Schlaufe. Durch den sichtbaren Hammerschlag entsteht eine archaische Wirkung. Zu den Schmuckkollektionen der Produktdesigner bemerkte Volker Fischer, Kurator am Museum für Angewandte Kunst, Frankfurt: »Die Kollektionen offenbaren eine Schönheit, die aus der Einfachheit erwächst, eine Einfachheit, die nicht simpel ist, sondern sich den Luxus der Reflexion leistet.«

2003 realisierte Biegel die Schmuckentwürfe von Hannes Wettstein, von Shin und Tomoko Azumi aus Japan sowie den Brüdern Ronan und Erwan Bouroullec. Der Schweizer Innenarchitekt und Designer Wettstein gestaltete rechteckige Gold- oder Platin-Rahmen. Sie können puristisch getragen werden oder als Passepartout für Farbedelsteine dienen. An den Außen- und Innenkanten lassen sich auch kleine Brillanten einsetzen. Das Ehepaar Shin und Tomoko Azumi gestaltete seine Schmuckgarnitur aus dünnen Goldstreifen. Die in der japanischen Kunst bekannten Themen Welle und Faltung erscheinen in diesem Schmuck in räumlich geometrischer Klarheit. Die Schmuckgarnitur Spike des englischen Designers Tom Dixon entstand 2004. In einen Zickzackrahmen aus Gold ist eine feine, goldene Netzstruktur eingespannt. Die dadurch entstehenden parabolisch verzogenen Netze erinnern an architektonische Konstruktionen wie sie z.B. von Frei Otto bekannt sind. Im Schmuck erscheinen sie als filigrane Netze, die mit dem Licht auf der Haut spielen. Im gleichen Jahr entstand das Schmuckset des deutschen Designers Werner Aisslinger, der in jüngster Zeit durch sein mobiles Wohnsystem Loftcube von sich reden machte. Auch sein Schmuck Dome beinhaltet ein modulares System. Es besteht aus Wabenformen, verbunden durch feine Scharniere. Sie bilden beim Hals- und Armschmuck eine geometrische Reihe. In die einzelnen Wabenformen können ganz individuell Farbedelsteine eingesetzt werden.

Das Schmuckset Oyster der Designer Saskia & Stefan Diez überrascht mit einer neuartigen Perlen-Fassung. Die Perle wird im Ring oder im Ohrschmuck durch eine Faltung gehalten. Die dadurch entstehende Doppelform entspricht dem Prinzip einer zusammengeklappten Auster. Im Halsschmuck bilden die »Austern« die Glieder der Kette.

Auch bei seinen eigenen Arbeiten beschränkt sich Marc-Jens Biegel auf eine reduzierte, geometrische Formensprache. Ihm geht es allerdings darum, »die Wirkung und Schönheit der Materialien hervorzuheben.« Das Angebot aus der eigenen Goldschmiedewerkstatt bildet damit einen deutlichen Gegenpol zu den vornehmlich konstruktivistischen Schmuckideen der Produktdesigner. Seine Ringserie Bishop mit einer quadratischen Ringfassung, die sich nach unten konisch verjüngt, ist inspiriert von dem traditionellen Bischofsring. Die Kollektion Princess on the Cushion (Prinzessin auf dem

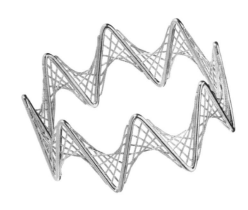

2002   2004   2004

Kissen) ist eine Neuinterpretation des klassischen Solitaire-Rings. Sicher eingebettet sitzt ein Farbedelstein in einem edlen Kissen aus Gold oder Platin. Bei der Serie *Stars* sind Farbedelsteine in eine Sternform aus Gold oder Platin eingespannt. In der Serie *Lido* erscheinen Edelsteine in schlichten, archaisch wirkenden Formen in Feingold. »Es gibt immer noch viele Menschen, die sich einfach Perlen oder Diamanten kaufen«, erklärt Biegel. Aber zum Glück wachse die Zahl derjenigen, die sich über die Schönheit der Materie hinaus für intelligente Gestaltung interessieren: »Denn daraus ergibt sich im Schmuck eine viel höhere Individualität«, sagt der Goldschmied und Designer am Goetheplatz in Frankfurt. Ein Vorteil von gutem Schmuck-Design sei auch, dass man ihm den Preis nicht auf den ersten Blick ansieht.

E — In the Bodysign concept, Marc-Jens Biegel has been realising jewellery designs submitted by internationally acclaimed product designers. A simple yet witty design idea informs all these works. Because it elicits contemplative reflection and meditation, it becomes »precious simplicity«. This concept demonstrates the closeness of modern product design to top jewellery design today.

While serving a goldsmithing apprenticeship (1988–1992) under his father, Werner Biegel, Marc-Jens Biegel attended Berufsschule [vocational school] at the Zeichenakademie Hanau. From 1992 until 1997 he studied product design at the HfG (Hochschule für Gestaltung) in Offenbach and in London. »In Offenbach I learned how a product communicates with human beings,« reports Biegel. Products he designed while still a student include daybeds, watches with novel faces and exhibition and display systems for museums. His diploma project, a piece of jewellery, raised a political-correctness issue. »At German institutes for product or industrial design, you are expected to design kitchens adapted for the elderly and public transport that accommodates the disabled,« he explains. Jewellery, on the other hand, suffers from the drawback of being perceived as too closely related to hedonism. Nonetheless, his conflict with the HfG Offenbach, which considers itself in the Ulm HfG tradition, encouraged him to consider the following questions: »Why doesn't jewellery design enjoy the same status with the public at large as furniture design does? Why do human beings adorn themselves at all and how should jewellery for our time look?«

After finishing his studies, Biegel started working in 1997 at his father's jewellery business (established in Frankfurt in 1964). In 2002 Biegel launched the Bodysign project jointly with three product designers: Axel Kufus, Uwe Fischer and Konstantin Grcic. As a founder-member of »Ginbande,« Uwe Fischer has made a significant contribution to Neues Deutsches Design. Products designed by Axel Kufus were shown at such internationally renowned museums as the Centre Pompidou. Konstantin Grcic in Munich is a pioneering Neo-Constructivist, who has been a star in the international

design firmament since 1991. For the Bodysign project, each designer was to create a set of jewellery comprising a ring as well as neck, arm and ear jewellery. While looking into the matter, the industrial designers notice that today concepts such as »facet,« »diamond« and »crystal« are often used to upgrade humdrum products. An indication of the delusive longing for luxury, which only exists nowadays in the false claims made for products?

Gran Prix, a design by Konstantin Grcic, represents a novel interpretation of the classic link chain. Biegel explains: »Before Grcic studied at the Royal College in London, he trained as a cabinet-maker. He applied his experiences with what are called slotted hole fasteners to making a simple chain.« Wearing the chain makes it look astonishingly three-dimensional. Uwe Fischer is the creator of the jewellery set called *Molecular*. It symbolises a strand of DNA. Symbolism from genetics also provides the functional concept. This supple chain nestles against the body, making it comfortable to wear.

Axel Kufus's design executed in fine gold has been worked with the traditional technique of forging. What makes it so stunning is the loop, a form pregnant with symbolic meanings. Leaving the marks made by the hammer creates an archaic effect. As Volker Fischer, curator at the Museum für Angewandte Kunst in Frankfurt, has remarked on the jewellery collections launched by these product designers: »These collections reveal a beauty that grows out of simplicity, a simplicity that has nothing simple about it but rather permits itself the luxury of reflection.«

In 2003 Biegel executed jewellery designed by Hannes Wettstein, Shin and Tomoko Azumi of Japan and the brothers Ronan and Erwan Bouroullec. Wettstein, a Swiss interior designer and designer, created rectangular frames in gold and platinum. They can be worn by purists just as they are or be used to showcase coloured precious stones. Small diamonds can also be set into the outer and inner edges. The married designers Shin and Tomoko Azumi created their set of jewellery from thin strips of gold. The wave and fold motifs so familiar from Japanese art appear in this jewellery in geometric spatial clarity. *Spike*, a set of jewellery by the English industrial designer Tom Dixon, goes back to 2004. A fine gold mesh structure is stretched over a zigzag frame of gold. The parabolic curve of the nets thus created recalls architectural constructions such as those made famous by Frei Otto. In jewellery they appear as a delicate reticulated tracery that plays with the light falling on the wearer's skin. That same year saw the launch of a set of jewellery by the German designer Werner Aisslinger, whose mobile living system Loftcube has recently been a buzzword. His *Dome* jewellery also represents a modular system. It consists of honeycomb shapes linked by fine hinges. Used in neck and arm jewellery, they are an array of geometric forms. Coloured precious stones can be set in the individual honeycomb forms as desired.

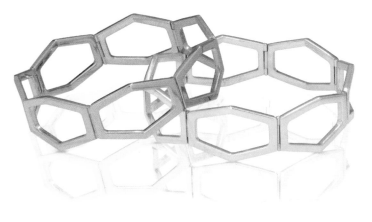

2004

2007

2007

Oyster, a set of jewellery by Saskia & Stefan Diez, astounds with a novel setting for pearls. The pearl is held in place in a ring or earring by means of a fold. The double form thus created corresponds in principle to an oyster with its shell closed. These »oysters« form the individual links of the necklace.

In his own work, Marc-Jens Biegel also limits himself to a reductive geometric canon of forms. However, he is concerned with »showcasing the impact and beauty of the materials«. The range from his own goldsmithing workshop is noticeably at the opposite extreme to the mainly Constructivist-inspired jewellery concepts created by the product designers. Biegel's *Bishop* line in rings featuring a square bezel that tapers conically towards the shaft is inspired by the traditional episcopal ring. The *Princess on the Cushion* collection is a new take on the classic solitaire ring. A coloured precious stone is securely bedded in an elegant cushion made of gold or platinum. In the *Stars* collection, coloured precious stones are set in a star shape in gold or platinum. The *Lido* collection features precious stones in simple, archaic-looking forms in fine gold. »There are still plenty of people who simply buy pearls or diamonds for themselves,« explains Biegel. Fortunately, however, the number of those who, apart from the beauty of the materials used, are interested in intelligent design is growing: »For that results in jewellery that is far more individual,« says the goldsmith and designer at Goetheplatz in Frankfurt. A further advantage of well designed jewellery is that the price paid for it is not immediately obvious.

2002	Collier *Gran Prix*, Design Konstantin Grcic, Gold — Necklace *Gran Prix*, design Konstantin Grcic, gold
2002	Collier *Molecular*, Design Prof. Uwe Fischer, Gold, Zuchtperlen — Necklace *Molecular*, design Prof. Uwe Fischer, gold, cultured pearls
2002	Ring *Loop*, Design Prof. Axel Kufus, Gold — Ring *Loop*, design Prof. Axel Kufus, gold
2004	Armband *Spike*, Design Tom Dixon, Gold — Bracelet *Spike*, design Tom Dixon, gold
2004	Ring *Bishop*, Design Marc-Jens Biegel, Gold — Ring *Bishop*, design Marc-Jens Biegel, gold
2004	Armreife *Dome*, Design Werner Aisslinger, Gold — Bangles *Dome*, design Werner Aisslinger, gold
2007	Ring *Passepartout*, Design Hannes Wettstein, Gold — Ring *Passepartout*, design Hannes Wettstein, gold
2007	Ring *Lido*, Design Marc-Jens Biegel, Gold — Ring *Lido*, design Marc-Jens Biegel, gold

Marc-Jens Biegel
Geboren 1967 in Frankfurt. 1992–1997 HfG Offenbach und London. Selbstständig seit 1998 in Frankfurt.

Marc-Jens Biegel
Born in Frankfurt in 1967. 1992–1997 Hochschule für Gestaltung Offenbach and London. Self-employed in Frankfurt since 1998.

Biegel

2003

2005

Claudia Hoppe

Manche Stücke von Claudia Hoppe erinnern auf den ersten Blick an Kinderspielzeug, manche an Klassiker des modernen Schmuckdesigns. Reduzierte, klare Formen in Gold und Silber, aber auch in farbigem Kunststoff und lackiertem Schichtholz kennzeichnen ihr Werk. Vornehmlich auf Armschmuck konzentriert, entwickelte sie in kürzester Zeit eine erstaunliche Vielfalt.

Von 1996 bis 2002 besuchte Claudia Hoppe die Fachhochschule Düsseldorf und die Escola Massana in Barcelona. Auf der Inhorgenta 2004 gewann die aus Kiel stammende Designerin den Innovationspreis, der alljährlich in der Halle C2 für herausragende Leistungen im zeitgenössischen Schmuckdesign vergeben wird. Ihre quadratisch, flächige Armspange *Kubus* wurde im gleichen Jahr in die Kollektion von Niessing aufgenommen. 2008 erhielt sie den Innovationspreis der Inhorgenta für den *Flex*-Armreif. Inzwischen ist Claudia Hoppe in namhaften internationalen Schmuckgalerien und dem Museums-Shop des Bauhauses in Berlin vertreten.

Guter Schmuck muss nicht teuer sein. Diese Forderung moderner Gestalter ergänzte Claudia Hoppe mit dem Angebot, ihn auch zu versenden oder zu schenken. Ihr *Postkartenschmuck* beinhaltet Broschen aus je zwei kreisrunden Kunststoff-Schalen. Exzentrisch gelocht, in unterschiedlichen Größen und Farben, lassen sich daraus bunte Broschen gestalten. Mit einem kleinen Gummiring werden sie auf dem Stoff eines Kleides oder T-Shirts fixiert. Eine Assoziation zu Kinderspielzeug ist unvermeidbar bei dem Armschmuck in hellem, an den geraden Flächen farbig lackiertem Schichtholz. Die Formen dafür werden mit einem Wasserstrahl präzise ausgeschnitten. Die raumgreifenden kreisrunden oder quadratischen Stücke mit ihren Farbflächen erinnern an das Spielerische im Schmuck. Dies macht Claudia Hoppe auch mit ihrem *Kombi*-Armschmuck deutlich. Er besteht aus konkav geformten Metallreifen in Silber und Gold, die beliebig ineinander gesteckt werden können. Farbige Kunststoff-Armreife lassen diese ausdrucksstarken Stücke zeitgemäß und archaisch zugleich erscheinen. Zu einem sehr zurückhaltenden Spiel mit Farbe lädt Claudia Hoppe mit ihrer Neuheit von 2008 ein. Es sind schlichte Armbänder mit einem raffinierten integrierten Verschluss. Innen mit leuchtenden Farben lackiert, projizieren sie ihre Farbigkeit dezent auf die Haut der Trägerin. Einmal mehr ist es der jungen Gestalterin gelungen, ein bekanntes Thema der Kunst und des modernen Schmuck-Designs so raffiniert neu zu interpretieren, dass die Betrachter ins Staunen kommen.

E — At first sight, some of Claudia Hoppe's pieces are reminiscent of children's toys while others look like modern designer-jewellery classics. Reductive, clear-cut forms in gold and silver as well as coloured plastic and lacquered plywood are the hallmarks of her work. Concentrating mainly on arm jewellery, she has developed an astonishing diversity within a very brief time span.

From 1996 until 2002 Claudia Hoppe, a native of Kiel, attended the Düsseldorf Fachhochschule and the Escola Massana in Barcelona. At the 2004 Inhorgenta fair, the designer won the Innovation Prize, which is awarded annually in Hall C2 for outstanding achievement in contemporary jewellery design. *Kubus*, a square, flat bangle by Claudia Hoppe, was incorporated in the Niessing Collection that same year. In 2008 she received the Inhorgenta Innovation Prize for her *Flex* bangle. Today Claudia Hoppe's work is sold at prestigious jewellery galleries worldwide and the Bauhaus Museum Shop in Berlin.

To be good, jewellery need not be expensive. Claudia Hoppe has supplemented this modern designer dictum by offering to send or even to give her jewellery away. Her *Postkartenschmuck* [Postcard jewellery] consists of brooches each made of two plastic discs. With off-centre holes and available in different sizes and colours, the discs can be used to make brightly coloured brooches. They can be attached to the material of a dress or T-shirt by means of a small rubber ring. Her arm jewellery in light-coloured plywood lacquered in colours on the straight surfaces inevitably elicits associations with children's toys. The shapes are precisely cut out with a water-jet cutter at high velocity and pressure. The circular or square pieces with coloured surfaces feature the playful side of jewellery. Claudia Hoppe also makes this clear with her *Combi* arm jewellery, consisting of concave-shaped metal bangles in silver and gold, which can be interleaved as desired. Bangles in coloured plastic make these powerfully expressive pieces look both cutting-edge and archaic. With her novelty for 2008, Claudia Hoppe invites wearers to participate in very reticent colour play. These pieces are simple bangles with a sophisticated integrated clasp. Lacquered inside in vibrant colours, they project muted tints onto the wearer's skin. Once again, this young designer has pulled off the coup of reinterpreting a theme familiar from both art and modern designer jewellery in such a sophisticated way that viewers are left stunned.

Claudia Hoppe
Geboren 1972 in Kiel. 1996–2002 Fachhochschule Düsseldorf. Atelier seit 2003 in Düsseldorf.

Claudia Hoppe
Born in Kiel in 1972. 1996–2002 Fachhochschule Düsseldorf. Studio in Düsseldorf since 2003.

2007

2003

2003   *Kombinationsarmreife*, Gold, Silber, Kunststoff — *Combination bangles*, gold, silver, plastic

2005   Armreif *Bebop*, geschichtetes Holz, Lack — Bangle *Bebop*, plywood, lacquer

2007   Armreif *Flex*, Gold — Bangle *Flex*, gold

2003   *Postkartenschmuck*, Kunststoff — *Postcard jewellery*, plastic

Rückblick—Review

CHARLES ROBERT ASHBEE
—Seite / page 12
Photo: Günter Meyer,
Schmuckmuseum Pforzheim.

OTTO BAKER
—Seite / page 12
Photo: Rüdiger Flöter,
Schmuckmuseum Pforzheim.

FRIEDRICH BECKER
—Seite / page 32, 33
oben links / above left:
aus / from: *Friedrich Becker,
Schmuck, Kinetik, Objekte,*
Arnoldsche, Stuttgart, 1997,
Seite / page 46.
Sonstige / other:
Schmuckmuseum Pforzheim.

RENÉ BOIVIN
—Seite / page 16
Photo: Günter Meyer.
Schmuckmuseum Pforzheim.

GUSTAV BRAENDLE
—Seite / page 16
Photo: Günter Meyer.
Schmuckmuseum Pforzheim.

MARIANNE BRANDT
—Seite / page 19
aus / from: Judy Rudoe, *Decorative
Arts 1850–1950. A catalogue of
the British Museum Collection,*
London 1991, Nr. 26

WILLIAM LUKAS VON CRANACH
—Seite / page 15
Photo: Günter Meyer,
Schmuckmuseum Pforzheim.

CHRISTIAN DIOR / HENKEL & GROSSE
—Seite / page 22
aus / from: Lawrence Feldmann,
The Fior Collection, London. Wer-
beaufnahme, Herbst 1956, Willy
Maywald, aus / from: *Christian
Dior,* Arnoldsche, Stuttgart, 2007,
Seite / page 159.

THEODOR FAHRNER
—Seite / page 12
Photo: Günter Meyer,
Schmuckmuseum Pforzheim.

MAX FRÖHLICH
—Seite / page 26
aus / from: *Neuer Schmuck,*
Karl Schollmayer, Verlag Ernst
Wasmuth, Tübingen,
Seite / page 19, 20.

JOSEF HOFFMANN
—Seite / page 14
Photo: Rüdiger Flöter, Schmuck-
museum Pforzheim.

PATRIZ HUBER
—Seite / page 12
Photo: Günter Meyer.
Schmuckmuseum Pforzheim.

HERMANN JÜNGER
—Seite / page 36
oben / above:
aus / from: *Neuer Schmuck,*
Karl Schollmayer, Verlag Ernst
Wasmuth, Tübingen,
Seite / page 85.
Unten / below:
aus / from: *Ornament as Art,*
Arnoldsche, Stuttgart, 2007,
Seite / page 170.

RENÉ LALIQUE
—Seite / page 14
Photo: Günter Meyer.
Schmuckmuseum Pforzheim.

EMMY VAN LEERSUM
—Seite / page 38, 39
aus / from: *Ornament as art,*
Arnoldsche, Stuttgart, 2007,
Seite / page 315.
Aus / from: *Schmuck der Moderne,*
Fritz Falk, Cornelie Holzach,
Bestandskatalog / Inventory Cata-
logue Schmuckmuseum Pforzheim,
Arnoldsche, Stuttgart, 1999,
Seite / page 67.

LIBERTY & CO.
—Seite / page 12
Photo: Rüdiger Flöter,
Schmuckmuseum Pforzheim.

WIWEN NILSON LUND
—Seite / page 16
Photo: Rüdiger Flöter,
Schmuckmuseum Pforzheim.

BRUNO MARTINAZZI
—Seite / page 24
aus / from: *Schmuck der Moderne,*
Fritz Falk, Cornelie Holzach,
Bestandskatalog / Inventory Cata-
logue Schmuckmuseum Pforzheim,
Arnoldsche, Stuttgart, 1999,
Seite / page 85.

SIGURD PERSSON
—Seite / page 28
oben / above:
Schmuckmuseum Pforzheim.
unten / below:
Photo: Hella Krauss.
Seite / page 29
aus / from: *Neuer Schmuck,*
Karl Schollmayer, Verlag Ernst
Wasmuth, Tübingen,
Seite / page 33.

MARIO PINTON
—Seite / page 24, 30
aus / from: *Contemporary Jewel-
lery – The Padua School* by Graziella
Folchini Grassetto, Arnoldsche,
Stuttgart, 2005.
—Seite / page 17
Photo: Rüdiger Flöter,
Schmuckmuseum Pforzheim.
Oben rechts / above right:
aus / from: *Neuer Schmuck,*
Karl Schollmayer, Verlag Ernst
Wasmuth, Tübingen
Abbildung / figure 81.

REINHOLD REILING
—Seite / page 24, 34
aus / from: *Schmuck der Moderne,*
Fritz Falk, Cornelie Holzach,
Bestandskatalog / Inventory Cata-
logue Schmuckmuseum Pforzheim,
Arnoldsche, Stuttgart, 1999,
Seite / page 76, 80.

NAUM SLUTZKY
—Seite / page 18
aus / from: *Naum Slutzky, Meister
am Bauhaus,* Monika Rudolph,
Arnoldsche, Stuttgart, 1989. BAB,
FA-Inv.-Nr. 7309 / 2 und 9030 / 39,
erw. 1965 bei Weinreb, London,
Nachlass von Friedl Dicker / Franz
Singer.

KLAUS ULLRICH
—Seite / page 35
aus / from: *Schmuck der Moderne,*
Fritz Falk, Cornelie Holzach,
Bestandskatalog / Inventory Cata-
logue Schmuckmuseum Pforzheim,
Arnoldsche, Stuttgart, 1999,
Seite / page 48.

MAISON VEVER
—Seite / page 14
Photo: Günter Meyer.
Schmuckmuseum Pforzheim.

THEODOR WENDE
—Seite / page 17
Photo: Günter Meyer,
Schmuckmuseum Pforzheim.

SCHMUCKMUSEUM PFORZHEIM
—Seite / page 12, 14, 16, 28, 30,
32, 33, 34, 35, 36
Photo: Rüdiger Flöter.
—Seite / page 12, 14, 15, 16, 17,
18, 32
Photo: Günther Meyer.

Entwicklung—Development

ADAM & STOFFEL
—Seite / page 106, 107, 382, 383
Photo: Adam & Stoffel.

ART-DESIGN
—Seite / page 250–255
Photo: Hella Krauss, Stuttgart.

ANTONIO BERNARDO
—Seite / page 64–67, 306, 307
Photo: Rodrigo Lopes, Hugo
Denizart, Archiv Antonio Bernardo.

BIEGEL
—Seite / page 111, 141, 393–395
Photo: Andreas Koschate, Thomas
Lemnitzer.

SABINE BRANDENBURG-FRANK
—Seite / page 78–81, 310, 311
Photo: H.P. Hoffmann.

DOROTHEA BRILL
—Seite / page 204, 205, 388
Photo: Markus Geldhauser.

**CHARLOTTE ·
EHINGER-SCHWARZ 1876**
—Seite / page 152–155, 244–249
Photo: Alexander Rapp, Firmen-
archiv.

CHAVENT
—Seite / page 118, 119, 268, 269
Photo: Chavent und Frédéric
Jaulmes (Brooch Cube, Autour du
Cube, Fenêtre à l'Arbre), Jurgen
Holzer (Ring Pont), Olivier Proust
(Brooches Piliers), Kestin Teixido
(Portrait).

CARL DAU
—Seite / page 44–47, 296–299
Photo: Matthias Hoffmann, Archiv
Carl Dau.

DRACHENFELS DESIGN
—Seite / page 208–211, 354–357
Photo: Drachenfels Design.

FILLNER
—Seite / page 102, 103, 300, 301
Photo: Beat Kehrli, Foto Perret
(Spitzspange).

FREIESLEBEN
—Seite / page 344–347
Photo: Freiesleben, imagina,
Oberelchingen (Anhänger, Design
Lothar Kuhn).

CLAUDIA GEIGER
—Seite / page 200, 389
Photo: Markus Geldhauser,
Pforzheim.

GELLNER
—Seite / page 130–134, 288–291
Photo: Gellner.

ACHIM GERSMANN
—Seite / page 185, 368, 369
Photo: Achim Gersmann.

PETRA GIERS
—Seite / page 190, 191, 330, 331
Photo: Goethe 29 / San Hung Kim.

MONIKA GLÖSS
—Seite / page 71, 349
Photo: Jü Walter, Düsseldorf,
Ringe *cube*, Fotomontage,
Christian Bauer, Düsseldorf.

URSULA GNÄDINGER
—Seite / page 122, 123, 370, 371
Photo: Friedhelm H. Putzar,
3P Design, Reutlingen.

BATHO GÜNDRA
—Seite / page 51, 338, 339
Photo: Klaus Baranenko, Worms.

SABINE HAUSS
—Seite / page 156, 157, 340, 341
Photo: Serge de Waha.

JÖRG HEINZ
—Seite / page 148–151, 282–285
Photo: Miko, Pforzheim, Olaf
Köster, Kaufbeuren, Jörg Heinz.

CORINNA HELLER
—Seite / page 100, 101, 136, 192,
193, 336, 337
Photo: Barbara von Woellwarth.

HENRICH & DENZEL
—Seite / page 162–167, 324–327
Photo: Matthias Hoffmann.
Modelfotos PGI

HERMAN HERMSEN
—Seite / page 50, 108, 302–305
Photo: Thanh-Koa Tran, Düssel-
dorf, Frank Kanters, Arnhem, Jörg
Reich photodesign, Düsseldorf,
Michiel Heffels, Nijmegen, Jens
Weine, Erfurt (Porträt).

CLAUDIA HOPPE
—Seite / page 72, 73, 396–397
Photo: Matthias Hoffmann,
Jörg Zaber (Postkartenbrosche,
Kombiarmreif), Oliver Schwalm
(Portrait).

ANGELA HÜBEL
—Seite / page 70, 96, 120, 121,
135, 334, 335
Photo: Matthias Hoffmann.

ISABELLA HUND
—Seite / page 332, 333
Photo: Thomas Koller, Gisela
Schenker.

CHRISTIANE IKEN
—Seite / page 57, 322, 323
Photo: Dirk Altenkirch. Modelfotos
Kai Loges.

ISABELLEFA
—Seite / page 168–171, 350–353
Photo: H.P. Hoffmann.

GUDRUN JÄGER
—Seite / page 140, 379
Photo: Gudrun Jäger.

GEORG JENSEN
—Seite / page 236, 237
Photo: Georg Jensen.

UDO JUNG
—Seite / page 174, 390
Photo: Markus Geldhauser
(Drehringe), Klaus Kerth
(Mandarin Ringe), Pforzheim.

ULLA + MARTIN KAUFMANN
—Seite / page 60, 61, 256–258
Photo: H.P. Hoffmann,
Ulla + Martin Kaufmann.

MONIKA KILLINGER
—Seite / page 84, 85, 264, 265
Photo: Nik Schölzel (Armreife),
Manfred Mahn.

LANGES & UFER
—Seite / page 77, 328, 329
Photo: Thomas L. Fischer,
Angela Bröhan.

LAPPONIA
—Seite / page 116, 117, 238–241
Lapponia.

EVA MAISCH
—Seite / page 186, 187, 360, 361
Photo: Eva Maisch.

PATRICK MALOTKI
—Seite / page 202, 203, 391
Photo: Markus Geldhauser.

MEISTER
—Seite / page 178, 179, 260–263
Photo: Meister, Modelfoto,
Gold in Fashion: IGC.

BERND MUNSTEINER
—Seite / page 88, 89, 242, 243
Photo: Jürgen Cullmann,
Schwollen.

ATELIER TOM MUNSTEINER
—Seite / page 90, 91, 380, 381
Photo: Jürgen Cullmann,
Schwollen.

NIESSING
—Seite / page 5, 52–55, 182–184,
270–281
Photo: H.P. Hoffmann,
Matthias Hoffmann, Niessing.

KAZUKO NISHIBAYASHI
—Seite / page 68, 69, 372
Photo: Rainer Schäle, Wuppertal.

KAI EPPI NÖLKE
—Seite / page 196, 197, 385
Photo: Kai Eppi Nölke,
Nik Schölzel, Neu-Ulm (Grasringe).

PARSPROTOTO
—Seite / page 56, 138, 139, 374,
375
Photo: Parsprototo.

GITTA PIELCKE
—Seite / page 206, 207, 348
Photo: Atelier Zimmermann,
T. Kaltenbach.

PLATIN GILDE INTERNATIONAL
—Seite / page 292–295
Photo: Platin Gilde International.

JOCHEN POHL
—Seite / page 98, 99, 376–378
Photo: Ernesto Martens, Stuttgart.
H.P. Hoffmann, Seite / page 376,
erstes Bild / first image.

PUR
—Seite / page 48, 49, 109, 158,
159, 314–317
Photo: Atelier PUR.

FRANZISKA RAPPOLD
—Seite / page 82, 83, 372
Photo: Jörg Höflinger, Stuttgart.

ANDRÉ RIBEIRO
—Seite / page 62, 63, 308, 309
Photo: H.P. Hoffmann, Jürgen
Schoner.

RUDI SAND
—Seite / page 124, 125, 358–359
Photo: Matthias Schormann,
Berlin.

GEBRÜDER SCHAFFRATH
—Seite / page 112, 176, 177, 286,
287
Photo: Gebrüder Schaffrath.

OLIVER SCHMIDT
—Seite / page 198, 199, 392
Photo: M. Glauner, M. Geldhauser.

SCHMUCKWERK
—Seite / page 142–144, 172, 173,
364, 365
Photo: Gerd Schmidt,
schmuckwerk.

HEIKO SCHREM
—Seite / page 113, 137, 175, 368,
367
Photo: Matthias Hoffmann,
imagina, Margit Fröhle.

BARBARA SCHULTE-HENGESBACH
—Seite / page 74, 75, 266, 267
Photo: Herbert Schulze, Rüdiger
Knobloch, Claudia Schmedding,
Düsseldorf.

MONIKA SEITTER
—Seite / page 110, 134, 194, 195,
386, 387
Photo: Monika Seitter.

GEORG SPRENG
—Seite / page 92–95, 188, 189,
318–321
Photo: Sabine Freudenberger und
Georg Spreng.

STOFFEL DESIGN
—Seite / page 104, 105, 362, 363
Photo: Stoffel Design.

ATELIER STRIFFLER & KRAUSS
—Seite / page 76, 384
Photo: Petra Jaschke,
Ulrich Oberst.

GÜNTER WERMEKES
—Seite / page 58, 59, 342, 343
Photo: Dirk Albrecht und
H.P. Hoffmann.

ERICH ZIMMERMANN
—Seite / page 97, 126, 127, 312,
313
Photo: Atelier Zimmermann,
T. Kaltenbach.

BRIGITTE ADOLPH
Karlsruhe
geboren / born 1975 in Fulda
—Seite / page 219
Photo: Anja Meister.

NUTRE ARAYAVANISH
London
geboren / born 1981 in Bangkok
—Seite / page 227
Photo: Suthipong J.

INES ARNDT
Eppertshausen
geboren / born 1968 in
Braunschweig
—Seite / page 226
Photo: Ines Arndt.

MIN-JI CHO
London
geboren / born 1982 in Seoul
—Seite / page 228
Photo: Min-Ji Cho.

JANINE EISENHAUER
Idar-Oberstein
geboren / born 1972 in Heidelberg
—Seite / page 218
Photo: F. Rink, Wiesbaden.

TANJA EMMERT
Idar-Oberstein
geboren / born 1971 in Stuttgart
—Seite / page 221
Shirkan, Manfred Philippbaar.
Aschenputtel und Schneewittchen,
Hiltrud und Jürgen Cullmann.

TANJA FRIEDRICHS
Duisburg
geboren / born 1971 in Duisburg
—Seite / page 222
Photo: Timo Strauch.

JO HAYES WARD
London
geboren / born 1978 in London
—Seite / page 226
Photo: Jo Hayes Ward.

KATJA HUNOLD
Lehrte
geboren / born 1977 in Düsseldorf
—Seite / page 220
Photo: Jonas Gonell.

ANNETTE JANECKE
Uelzen
geboren / born 1973 in Uelzen
—Seite / page 217
Photo: Annette Janecke.

CHRISTINA KARABABA
Düsseldorf
geboren / born 1970 in Athen
—Seite / page 232
Photo: Christina Karababa.

ANDREAS LEHMANN
Düsseldorf
geboren / born 1977 in Bochum
—Seite / page 214
Photo: Herbert Schulze,
FH Düsseldorf.

SVETLANA MILOSEVIC
Stuttgart
geboren / born 1976 in Reutlingen
—Seite / page 216
Photo: Johannes Tolk.

DENISE JULIA REYTAN
Berlin
geboren / born 1980 in Düsseldorf
—Seite / page 230, 231
Photo: Mareen Fischinger.

CLAUDIA SCHMEDDING
Düsseldorf
geboren / born 1978 in Düsseldorf
—Seite / page 215
Photo: Claudia Schmedding.

KAROLA TORKOS
London
geboren / born 1975 in Essen
—Seite / page 229
Photo: Karola Torkos.

NICOLE WALGER
Stuttgart
geboren / born 1970 in
Ludwigsburg
—Seite / page 223
Photo: Nicole Walgser.

GABY WANDSCHER
Idar-Oberstein
geboren / born 1973 in Oldenburg
—Seite / page 224
Photo: Gaby Wandscher.